The
ARTS MANAGEMENT
Reader

The
ARTS
MANAGEMENT
Reader

written and edited by
ALVIN H. REISS

foreword by
KITTY CARLISLE HART

AUDIENCE ARTS
a division of
MARCEL DEKKER, INC./NEW YORK · BASEL

Reiss, Alvin H
    The arts management reader.

    Includes index.
    1. Arts–Management. I. Arts management.
II. Title.
NX760.R45   1979   658'.91'7   79-19330
ISBN 0-8247-6850-7

The articles contained in this volume originally appeared in the newsletter
Arts Management (1962-1978), published by the Radius Group, Inc., and
The Arts Management Handbook (1st ed., 1970; 2d ed., 1974), published by
Law-Arts Publishers, Inc.

MARCEL DEKKER, INC.
270 Madison Avenue, New York, New York 10016

Current printing (last digit):
10 9 8 7 6 5 4 3 2 1

PRINTED IN THE UNITED STATES OF AMERICA

To Steven, Robert, and Michael, my sons,
who pitched in to help me whenever I needed it

Foreword

During the past quarter century, American arts institutions have shed their upper-crust cocoon and stepped into the mainstream of daily life. To reach new audiences, cultural groups have tried every conceivable marketing and promotional approach, reflecting the fervor and imagination worthy of a P. T. Barnum. Lecture-demonstrations, preconcert symposia, and performances in shopping centers—even factories—began to involve the uninvolved, those many people for whom the arts seemed to be a hard-to-learn foreign language.

At the heart of this cultural awakening has been the arts manager, the unheralded organizer whose job is to make sure that the artistic product is seen, heard, and supported. The business of the arts, while secondary to the art itself, became primary to new growth. Evidence of the success of arts administrators is all around us in the form of growing audiences for every art form, the variety of imaginative arts presentations (often in unlikely settings), and vastly increased nonprofit support from government, business, and individuals.

Through the years the new trends of arts institutions and their administrators have been chronicled by Alvin H. Reiss in his lively and informative publication, *Arts Management.* Since 1962, as the first publication of its kind, this newsletter has been reporting on the arts in straightforward language that arts managers can understand and adapt to their own needs. Mr. Reiss made news himself by developing the Advertising Council's multimedia public service campaign on behalf of the arts. He also authored the first Resolution on the Arts passed by the U.S. Conference of Mayors. Both programs have been vital to the growth and development of the arts.

The New York State Council on the Arts and Mr. Reiss have even made some history together. Not only has Mr. Reiss frequently worked with the Council as a consultant and organizer of conferences and programs, but he also created and edited the Council's own newsletter, the first state arts council publication in the nation.

The Arts Management Reader gives practical, "how-to" advice detailed in case histories. Directors of cultural institutions, social historians, and supporters of the arts will find it a helpful tool. I am happy to recommend this collection that documents the inexorable growth of the art world.

Kitty Carlisle Hart
Chairman
New York State Council on the Arts

Preface

If change was the single yardstick by which all progress was measured, then the arts in America would surely be considered one of the most progressive areas of national development. Over the past two decades, scarcely a month has passed without a major new program being initiated or an event of significance taking place in the field. During the 60s and 70s, artists and arts institutions came out of protective shells they had built up over the years to tap audiences and, at the same time, forge new alliances with such seemingly disparate forces as government, health and welfare, religion, and business.

Change, however, is meaningless without substance and fortunately, substance and quality have been an integral part of modern-day arts development. Excellence and artistic integrity have been the watchwords of artistic directors as they have moved their organizations in an upward spiral encompassing program growth, the fulfillment of artistic goals, and the reach for larger audiences. A key partner in these efforts has been the arts manager, the behind-the-scenes gadfly attending to the endless detail of organizational management and pursuit of available funds, so that the artistic effort could succeed.

The beneficiaries of this partnership have been the citizens of communities throughout the country who have witnessed the development of arts industries in their own backyards, with local theatres, dance companies, galleries, and arts centers growing up around them. Working artists have moved onto the scene and become involved and recognized forces in community development. Nancy Hanks, the former chairperson of the National Endowment for the Arts, perhaps best summarized the meaning of this ferment when she responded to a critic who decried the involvement of so many artists in CETA programs. "By the way," he asked, "What does CETA stand for, anyway?" Nancy reflected for just an instant before launching her *riposte.* "Why, don't you know? Comprehensive enjoyment of the arts."

If enjoyment has been comprehensive for many and varied audiences, then the effort to make it pleasurable has had, along with the monumental labor, at least some measure of enjoyment as well. The job of raising money—or more importantly, giving it— has never been a laughing matter, but there are times when a light touch can ease the burden a little. The light touch as well as the hard touch, the innovative as well as the routine, and the long-range as well as the immediate, have all characterized arts development in the past two decades and it is this diversity of effort and approach that *Arts Management* has attempted to chronicle over the years.

Beginning in 1962, when the first issue of *Arts Management* was published, it has tried to fill a needed niche: to serve as an objective reporter of the entire spectrum of concerns faced by the working arts administrator. The gossip and small talk of the industry, as easy as it might have been to gather and disseminate, was not as important to us or to our readers, we felt, as were the real developments in the field. We were interested in what was happening, how it was happening, and why it was happening. We set our sights on pinpointing emerging trends and rounding up news of these developments so that readers could discern new directions and relate them to their own institutions. Guesswork and surmisal was not part of our job, nor were snap judgments and criticisms based on hearsay or less-than-concrete evidence.

In the early years, when there were fewer organizations in the field, including very little of what we now know as an entire arts service industry, reporting was quite different. Printed materials on the arts were virtually nonexistent, and through phone calls, personal meetings, and laborious detail work, *AM* tracked down the news. Frequently, because of limited communications, the publication itself took the lead not only in reporting developments, but in making them happen. We helped organize and present the nation's first college course in arts management, undertook surveys when little or no information was available, and organized meetings with leaders in such areas as business, labor, and education, in order to more deeply involve these fields in the arts.

As the field grew, *Arts Management* grew along with it, although the finances of the publication were as fragile as the finances of the field it covered. We set out to make *AM* available to everyone who wanted to read it and developed in the early days several unique sponsorship arrangements. In succession, the New York State Council on the Arts, The Kennedy Center in Washington, D.C., and the New York Board of Trade each sponsored the newsletter (through somewhat different arrangements) and sent free copies to their audiences. Later, when *AM* was forced to return to its subscription policy, the $10-a-year subscription price remained the same, as it still does.

In more recent years, the reportorial job changed considerably. As the field burgeoned and new organizations came into existence, the flow of materials increased dramatically. Directories, articles, surveys, and books, along with the steady flow of press releases and organizational reports, arrived on *AM*'s doorstep with unrelenting intensity. The job of reading, digesting, and interpreting material, before the job of story selection could ever begin, became an enormous one, although it was and still is a labor of love. Also, as the sole and entire editorial staff of *AM* (yes, Virginia, I am *it*), my personal involvement with the field continued to grow. Virtually every week during the season, I was going off somewhere to speak, to attend a conference, or to run a workshop. Much of the material gathered for stories in *AM* and now included in the *Arts Management Reader*—or the consumer magazines I wrote for, resulted from these field experiences.

The arts offer fertile opportunities for editorial exploration and in the pages that follow there are many examples of where that exploration can lead. Case histories of successful audience development promotions, how-to stories on funding, publicity, and management and brief tips on myriad aspects of arts administration, all drawn from the pages of *Arts Management,* are included here within the *Reader.* Also included, to make the work more valuable as a reference source, are chronologies of developments in various areas of the arts over the years, brief reviews of significant books and studies published during the 70s, and checklists of important periodical articles during the same period. This is a book that, in addition to serving as a practical resource, may also provide insights and reflections into social development of the arts over several decades. As such, it may prove useful to the social historian and arts patron, as well as to its primary audience, professional arts administrators and students in the field.

While I hope this work becomes a deskside tool, I hardly prescribe its reading at a single sitting. Instead, I suggest dipping into it, culling from it, mulling over it, and, I fervently hope, returning to it frequently. And if arts managers enjoy this book, it is only fitting for, in a very large sense, they helped to write it. Without their imagination, energy and sheer tenacity of effort there would have been no stories to write. They have my lasting gratitude.

Alvin H. Reiss

Acknowledgments

I would like to express my sincere thanks to the many arts managers and artistic directors who, over the years, have willingly shared their successes as well as their frustrations with me. To Alvin Toffler, who since has gone on to great success in areas other than the arts, I owe a lasting debt for his insight and persuasiveness in getting me involved in the project that resulted in *AM*. Although I lost him as a partner in these activities many years ago, I will never forget his many contributions to the *AM* concept.

In the early years of the newsletter I had several editorial and proofreading assistants, and I am grateful to each of them. Over the past decade, however, the job has been mainly mine and therefore, while accepting plaudits, if any, I also must bear the responsibility for any errors or inaccuracies.

My special thanks go to my wife Ellen, who has suffered my many deadlines with me patiently and with understanding, and to my children, each of whom has served as a subscription assistant on the newsletter.

A.H.R.

Contents

Dancer/choreographer Carol Rae Kraus, a 1975 Affiliate Artist with the Arts Council of Rochester, New York, giving an "informance" for a group of young people. (Courtesy of Affiliate Artists)

The Arts Organization

TECHNIQUES OF MANAGEMENT

Metropolitan Opera Wins
Friends with New Look Program

Faced with a large and growing deficit, lagging subscription sales, and a slightly tarnished image, one of America's largest and best known cultural groups turned around nearly every phase of its operation over the past two years in one of the biggest administrative face-liftings ever undertaken by an American arts group. The turnabout is far from complete, and a record deficit still exists, but the results thus far indicate major and growing success in virtually every area of concern. Moreover, to maintain its momentum the Metropolitan Opera is now striking off in several new operational directions, including live television and the presentation of outside productions.

The wheels were set in motion for the changes to follow when the Met board abolished the position of general manager—a post with total authority—and set up a division of administrative and artistic responsibility among three key individuals, beginning late in 1974. With artistic responsibility in the hands of music director James Levine, and production director John Dexter, new executive director Anthony A. Bliss was able to concentrate on audience development, fund raising, image building, and finances.

The campaign thus far has been based on some firm Bliss credos: that a sound marketing program is essential to both fund raising and ticket sales, that an organization must spend money to make money; and that the quality of the performance on stage is the ultimate concern of everyone in the organization. Working within this overall framework, Bliss has helped engineer some remarkable changes in the two years since he joined the Met staff. The advertising budget has tripled, subscriptions have reached a new level, the board has been reorganized, a new marketing program has reached young people and other special audiences, the fund-raising campaign has tapped new markets and new program concepts, and earned income concepts have been introduced. In the process, new staff members and consultants, many with specialized skills, have been brought into the fold, morale within the organization has increased, and the Met's public image has improved considerably. As one staff member told *Arts Management* "It's become an exciting place to work."

Although money has been a continuing need at the Met—its operation budget of $30 million a year dwarfs other American performing arts budgets—fund raising has been viewed as an activity to follow and to build on accomplishments in other areas. Thus, while the artistic team was working to improve casting at both star and supporting lead level, diversify the repertoire, and upgrade the level of the conducting staff, Bliss launched into a major promotional campaign designed to attract subscribers and individual ticket buyers. Using double-page spreads in the *New York Times* and a direct mail campaign which featured full-color brochures, the company invited potential subscribers to "Strike a Blow for Civilization." From 86 percent of capacity in 1974-75, the Met reached 94.5 percent in 1975-76, a figure it is maintaining.

Advertising has had a decidedly livelier and less formal look than in the past. Newspaper ads, for example, headlining "Bravo! The Met," have been almost jocular in describing upcoming operas. One read, "Take a comedy to heart. Come see and hear *Le Nozze di Figaro.* It's a love story. It's a human comedy. It's social satire." The new Met image of a more open and less intimidating organization—a theme that ads and direct mail sustain—was helped earlier this season when "Sills and Burnett at the Met," a lighthearted CBS special filmed at the opera house, reached an audience of 23 million. The company used the video-taping, importantly, as a fund raiser, with attendees donating $25 to the Met.

The audience development program has struck out in several new directions. A first-time sampler campaign, aimed at the under-35 audience, offered orchestra seats to three different productions for $30, a substantial discount from regular prices, along with other benefits. Free, informal lunchtime concerts, featuring four Met singers and a pianist, have been presented throughout the metropolitan New York area, funded entirely by the opera company. Schoolchildren have been reached with a new 11-foot pyramid exhibit on *Aida* which includes photos. Also, the Met has continued its Student Rush program initiated several seasons ago, and now participates in the Theatre Development Fund's discount ticket program.

The current fund-raising program has its roots in reorganization of an unwieldy board of 150 directors, now subdivided into new operational categories: managing board, the key voting insiders, advisory board, and honory board. Also, new members representing special areas of interest, including labor and education, were brought onto the board.

Special programs have encouraged greater support from those already involved. A patrons campaign, newly structured to include a variety of giving levels rather than a single one and built around such new benefits as a patron's intermission lounge (the board room during the day) and program listing, hopes to up patron giving by $1 million this season. A new national $15 Associate Membership in the Metropolitan Opera Guild has its sights set on upward of $1 million more. The sale of the Met's "product line"—records, books, T-shirts—has been stepped up in the in-house gift shop and by mail order where, working with an expanded list of nearly 500,000 names, the Opera Guild has increased profits substantially.

Helped by overall promotion and ad mail campaigns, the Met's special fund-raising events, an annual bazar and a radio marathon (which was aired in stations in 11 different cities around the country) both raised much more money than the previous year. Other new income sources, including the New Production Fund, a one-time corporate fund drive with special permission from the Lincoln Center Fund, to which the Met belongs, and a rescaling of ticket prices have been instituted.

Perhaps the most dramatic and far-reaching aspect of the fund-raising campaign links the opera company with a leading stereo manufacturer, Pioneer Electronics. The corporation, which last year helped the New Jersey Symphony raise $7500 with a campaign based on the approach, "Give the New Jersey Symphony a C, not E or a G, and Pioneer will match it note for note," has initiated a similar although greatly expanded, campaign on behalf of the Met with a $400,000 goal. More than 2500 Pioneer dealers now feature point-of-purchase displays telling customers, "When you give a quarter, the Met gets a buck," since Pioneer will match all funds raised and the Arts Endowment will match the first $100,000 in gifts. The campaign has been backed up by personal solicitation letters to all Pioneer dealers by company president Bernard Mitchell and a Pioneer-paid-for advertising campaign.

Looming immediately ahead are two major new Met endeavors. In mid-April it makes its debut as a presenter by co-sponsoring of an eight-week American Ballet Theatre season at the Opera House, and later it will share sponsorship of the Stuttgart Ballet Company. To generate additional income, it will try to increase Sunday rentals at the Opera House. On March 15, to a fanfare of publicity, a live PBS telecast of *La Boheme* will be telecast from the Met, signalling a new involvement that could lead the company into cable television and perhaps into the marketing of video cassettes.

Although newness and excitement surround the Met, a record $12.4 million deficit still hangs over the organization. The immediate concern now is to raise $5 million more than last year's contribution level of $8.7 million. Anthony Bliss approaches the task with guarded optimism. "I feel that the Met should be able to meet its immediate challenge," he told *AM*. "I am fearful of the future, however, unless we can begin to see more support from government and business." *Note: In both the 1976-77 and 1977-78 seasons, the Metropolitan Opera made up its operating deficits with grants and contributions.*

January-February 1977

Management Expert
Advises Long-range Planning

H. Lawrence Wilsey

Established arts organizations are noted for their ability to stave off financial disaster and organizational collapse year after year. Newer arts organizations lead a more tenuous existence, with enthusiasm often being their basic asset. In view of the relatively insecure and unstable life of an arts organization, there are compelling reasons for imaginative, yet practical, long-range planning.

A long-range plan for any arts organization calls for basic decisions at each of seven planning levels. The following are examples of questions that should be considered and answered in order in planning:

Philosophy. What should the role of arts organizations be in meeting the cultural needs of society and the individual? What knowledge, skills, and interests need to be developed to meet the needs of society and the individual? (A simple, brief statement of philosophy sets the perspective of the organization and provides the reason for its existence.)

Objectives. What are the cultural expectations of the people of this community? To what extent should this organization strive to meet or modify them? Which are the publics that this organization should interest? Are the cultural needs of these publics being satisfied by other arts organizations? If so, should the broad objectives of this organization be extended or modified? What are the levels of audience exposure for which this organization should strive in future years? What should be its membership goals?

Programs. What should be this organization's type and range of programs in order to achieve its objectives? What should be the optimum frequency of arts events? In what locations should such events be held? What program effort should this organization direct toward school age children to assure future audiences? What effort should be directed toward groups with extensive leisure time?

Organization. What human abilities are required to execute this organization's programs? What boards, committees, professionals, and administrative positions are required to plan, conduct, and evaluate the work of this organization? What functions and responsibilities should be assigned to each board, committee, and administrative position? What working relationships and reporting responsibilities will help conduct the organization's work most effectively? How should external relationships be conducted?

Staffing. What numbers of people with what qualifications and characteristics are required to provide effective board, volunteer, and professional staff leadership for this organization? What kinds of incentives can be given to volunteer workers? What type of classification, salary, and professional development program is required?

Facilities. What numbers, kinds, quality, and location of facilities are required to serve program needs, as previously defined? Are the proper types of facilities being planned for future expansion, programs, flexibility, and economy?

Finance. What operating and capital funds will be required to support the agreed-upon arts programs and to provide necessary staff, facilities, equipment, and supplies? When will these funds be required? From what sources can they be obtained? What financial programs can be modified? What can be extended, depending upon levels of support? Is federated giving appropriate to this organization and its objectives?

The effort involved in the planning process is demanding. However, the results may far outweigh the time and mental stress involved in its development. Benefits that can realistically be achieved include:

1. Better definition of the organization's objectives, with assurance that its goals are in reasonable harmony with the community's expectations

2. More effective arts programs

3. A higher level of morale and enthusiasm by those who feel a part of the organization and its future

4. A sounder approach to financing arts programs, with financial goals keyed to achievable and desirable program levels

5. Greater assurance that the organization is contributing effectively towards meeting cultural needs of the community

July 1963

Tip on Group Structure

The way an organization is structured can have a great impact on its effectiveness. Voluntary groups like orchestra associations or theater societies can make better use of their members' energies by taking a tip from management experts. Dr. Rensis Likert, director of the Institute for Social Research, University of Michigan, suggests one technique art managers might bear in mind:

> The organization should be built into highly effective groups linked together by persons who hold overlapping memberships in at least two groups. For example, a superior of one work group is a subordinate in the work group at the next higher echelon. Organizations built on this principle can achieve higher motivation, better coordination, better communication, greater confidence and trust, higher productivity, and lower costs than those relying on a man-to-man pattern of organization.

July 1962

Skilled Leadership Key
to Good Group Meetings

Meetings of arts groups need not be a bore or chore. They can be creative and satisfying. Skilled leadership is the key.

"Discussion leadership is becoming a science," says University of Michigan psychologist Norman R. F. Maier, noted for his studies on group problem solving.

According to Professor Maier, the skillful leader uses certain principles of group behavior derived from research in various fields of psychology. What are they, and how can they serve to improve problem-solving discussions?

The starting point of a problem is richest in possible solutions. Partial success in moving toward a goal makes people reluctant to start all over again, but a fresh start is the only way to increase the variety of solution possibilities.

Encourage the group to be more problem-minded. The first prerequisite for reaching agreement on a solution is reaching agreement on what the problem is.

Avoid dead ends. Stick to "surmountable" obstacles. All too often "a particular obstacle is selected and pursued despite the fact that it cannot be remedied."

Disagreement can lead either to hard feelings or to innovations, depending on the discussion leadership. The leader "must not only prevent the suppression of disagreement, but also encourage a respect for disagreement and thereby turn it into a stimulant for new ideas."

The idea-getting process should be separated from the idea-evaluating process. The latter is the practical side of problem solving and involves the testing and the comparison of solutions in the light of what is known. Idea-getting requires a willingness to break away from past experience and search for something different or new.

Problem situations should be turned into choice situations. "The fact that one solution is found does not preclude the possibility that there may be others, yet people frequently behave as though this were the case."

"Solutions suggested by the leader are improperly evaluated and tend to be either accepted or rejected." Thus he must "refrain from introducing his views or passing judgment on the ideas expressed by participants. His job is to conduct the discussion."

Maier examines these principles in his book, *Problem Solving Discussions and Conferences* (McGraw-Hill, New York, New York, 1963).

December 1963

Making Our Symphony Orchestras More Efficient

The slightly abridged article which follows originally appeared in the February 22, 1974 issue of Science.

I am deeply indebted to the office of Management Resources for permission to share with the reader portions of a recent study, OMR-CY 54-8-095, which earned a commendation at the Secretaries level for thoroughness and originality.

Briefly, the problem that gave rise to the report was this: The symphony orchestra of one of our largest cities was found to be non-cost-effective. Since 37 different agencies contributed to its support, the government responsibility was clear, and a 38th agency was assigned to investigate. With due respect to the rights of minorities, it was decided to appoint a member of the group not previously given sufficient recognition—the totally deaf. The investigator was therefore less subject to bothersome auditory distractions, and his study is remarkable for its insight and clarity. I quote from it directly:

It took only the most casual observation to discover that, while musicians are paid in full for their time, they do not play all the time. The fault is partly in the choice of music. Using a simple computer program, it was possible to score musical programs for degree of involvement for each player. This has resulted in a Musician Participation Program that will be administered through the newly created Office of Participation Improvement, which has a skeleton staff of 148.

Closer analysis of musical scores, however, revealed that many composers considered a full orchestra unnecessary and therefore obviously wasteful. By selecting works scored for smaller groups, very large savings are possible.

There appears to be little evidence of modern technology and modern management principles. The piccolo clearly needs to be redesigned, and no attempts appear to have been made to improve violin design since the last century. However, the most immediate improvements are to be had by applying management expertise to orchestral direction. As is well known in military circles, no one can direct 100 people effectively except through subordinates. Clearly, subdirectors are required, and at least one should be appointed in each section to receive instructions from the conductor and pass them on to the performers. In this way responsibilities can be more clearly fixed and goals and tasks assigned.

I have also found that communication within the orchestra is deficient. Some portion of each performance should therefore be set aside for discussion to improve the flow in information and to allow subdirectiors, through probing questions, to see if instructions and goals are understood. Much improvement is also to be made through standardization. For example, different conductors take different lengths of time to perform the same work. In addition, there is much useless repetition.

However, the most glaring defect is in the reporting system. It is astounding to discover that no reports are written. All sorts of advance notice, programs of intent, and so forth are given, but there is little evidence on file of solid performance. Continued government support should not be provided in its absence.

The matter of training and education has also been examined. There simply are not enough positions available to justify musical education on the scale now practiced. Only four or five replacements per year are needed and training should clearly be restricted. Further, little attention is given to the balance between instruments taught and requirements. Most instruction is in piano—an instrument often omitted from concerts entirely. And when one is used, it is almost always played by an outsider who busies himself serving many different orchestras. This policy of manpower sharing should be more widely adopted, especially as regards performers needed only occasionally, such as harpists.

There is one specialty that appears to be in short supply and therefore demands a high salary, which contributes greatly to cost. This specialty is conducting. Of all performers, the conductor is the most vigorous, the only one who performs constantly. The basic reason there are few conductors is that there are no good texts. Training programs should therefore be encouraged and should teach the essentials in this field once they have been catalogued. That will take some time, however. For the present, we need innovative solutions such as the one I propose here. Time-motion and eye-movement studies confirm my observation that conductors are able to fix visually different performers at precisely defined times and then make sweeping gestures in their direction. In a prior study, I found that successful quarterbacks do the same thing, singling one player out of many after a precise number of counts and, with a precise overhand motion projecting a score object in that player's direction. Since plots of quarterback and conductor ages show little overlap, it is evident that one could quite successfully become the other. This concept, Sequential Career Commonality Utilization, is now being applied in other fields, and the Sequential Career Commonality Utilization Branch is slated to achieve bureau status soon.

Modesty forbids that I dwell too long on my final point, but I cannot omit mentioning the question most often asked me: "What accounts for your unbroken string of sucess and innovations?" My success is, I believe, due to my advantage of the broader view, of seeing how it all fits together. That's really the secret. The narrow, nonmanagement trained specialist should be on tap, but never on top.

Summer 1974

Save Time and Money by Weeding Out Old Records

Eleanor Oshry Shatzkin

Every modern business and organization recognizes the need for written records, but too few of them recognize the need for their destruction. The larger the organization, the more it needs a systematic program of record retention and disposal. Such a program can increase the efficient use of records that are retained and can also result in saving money that would otherwise be spent on filing cabinets, space, and clerical time.

To control the growth of files one must first control the creation of new records and, second, the destruction of old records. The most effective way to limit the paperwork problem is to practice "birth control" with respect to the creation of new papers. Unless new forms and reports are limited to those that satisfy a proven need and unless the number of duplicate copies of each is controlled, files will overflow an office.

Even if a report is necessary, its useful life may be limited. Certainly, if it has been issued in many copies, it need not remain in the permanent files of each of the individuals who received it.

When a new report is approved, the ultimate disposition of each copy should be determined. At this time, too, plans should be made for the consolidation of data that may be needed only in summary form after a given period of time. In this way the removal from active to inactive storage and the destruction of papers that have outlived their usefulness will be automatically controlled.

Almost every inventory of an organization's files will turn up papers that can be destroyed without further consideration. For the remaining ones, each group should set up destruction schedules based on its individual needs, taking into consideration legal requirements, the degree of risk in not having the record, and frequency of reference to the record.

October 1962

Inadvertent Humor

Every letter or document that leaves the office of an arts organization contributes to or detracts from the image of the organization. Although proofreading is tedious, the good administrator can't afford to sign his name to a letter or a proposal which he hasn't carefully read. Seems obvious? The following quotations were taken directly from material mailed by arts groups. "We would like to begin a new *pogram* in the arts," said one. A second organization requested "matching *fun* grants."

Spring–Summer 1969

Insurance Lowers Risks for Cultural Groups

All the activities, and the properties, of cultural groups add up to one word—risk— for the organizations involved. Arts groups are in constant contact with the public and employ a variety of workers, volunteer and paid, who could suffer injuries on the job.

Arts groups are frequently the custodians of priceless works of art, expensive musical instruments, costumes, and scenery. They may own a variety of equipment, from showcases to typewriters, and it is not uncommon for them to have large amounts of cash on hand, as money comes in from advance ticket sales, benefits, and so on.

Every arts manager and every cultural group should therefore be aware of the risks incurred and the kind of insurance protection needed.

One of the first things to consider is the extent of the group's liability. This varies, depending on whether or not the group is incorporated and what state it is in. There are legal questions involved, and they should be settled by a lawyer.

Once liability is determined, it is necessary to ask what kind of insurance is needed. Each group will have to decide on the basis of its activities and its budget. However, there are several kinds of insurance that should be part of a good insurance package.

The following description of the policies is meant not to be definitive, but to provide some guidelines.

Liability: Public liability is almost a must for any group that deals with the public. It can be short-term (special events) or long-term, depending on the need. When thinking of it, bear in mind that the group deals with the public not only in the concert hall or theater, but also in elevators, on the grounds, and in the parking lot. Liability also includes employees, some of whom may be covered by compensation laws. These vary considerably from state to state and should be checked.

Bonding: Anyone who is responsible for large sums of money should be bonded. If many persons handle the money, it is possible to get a blanket bond, or a position bond, which, within a fixed time limit, allows for the theft to be discovered and reported to the insurance company. This is important in situations in which an inventory (of costumes, for example) is not made frequently.

Fine arts policy: An all-risk policy covering all kinds of losses—fire, theft, breakage, water damage, and so on. It can cover property (usually paintings and sculpture) belonging to the group and property on loan, either to them or by them. It can be short-term—as little as one day—to long-term—up to three years. Payment may be a flat fee decided on in advance, or it may be a monthly fee that varies, depending on what valuables are on hand at the moment. A similar policy can insure costumes and sets.

Floaters: There are two types of floaters of interest to arts groups—the theatrical floater, designed for an acting group, both while traveling and on location, and an instrument floater, which offers protection on an individual or an orchestra basis. (Rates decline as the number of instruments insured goes up.) These floaters insure against fire, theft, accidents, etc.

Equipment, including office equipment: It should be protected against the usual hazards, both natural and manmade. The policy might include an all-risk office contents clause. In some states vehicle liability insurance is compulsory, but if any vehicles are rented, the kind of coverage the leasing agent provides should be investigated.

Where can arts groups go to get good insurance advice? Most groups include individuals who either sell insurance themselves or can recommend someone reliable. Another possibility is the agent who handles insurance and bonding for the local school district. Many of the problems are similar, so that the agent comes to the arts group with a good idea of what is needed. He is also familiar with local laws and can help guarantee that there are no gaps.

It is part of an insurance agent's job to give insurance advice without fee, although, of course, he hopes it will lead to a sale. It is also his job to plan a policy that gives maximum coverage for minimum cost.

When considering coverage, a committee should evaluate the proposals before making recommendations. Keep in mind that there are two kinds of insurance salesmen, those who work for a mutual company and can sell only the insurance of their company, and independent agents who represent many companies and choose among them.

August 1963

Check Your Security, Detectives Warn Arts

The following article was prepared by staff members of Pinkerton's, Inc.

A rash of art thefts in recent years have made international headlines. The stories about them make exciting reading, but for the arts managers whose institutions have suffered, the theft of a valuable painting is not at all entertaining. The fact is that sooner or later almost every artistic enterprise needs to take a look at its security program. This applies as forcefully to theaters, orchestras, and other performing arts groups as it does to museums, although, of course, the problems of each kind of institution may differ.

For many years Pinkerton has provided protection for theaters and music halls, museums and galleries, carnivals, fairs, conventions, exhibits, and special events of every description. From this experience has emerged a set of guidelines that arts administrators, responsible for the safety of people and property, should bear in mind.

For many institutions the box office is the most vulnerable point. The prudent theater or orchestra management makes sure that the box office staff is locked in to avert a surprise entry. The cubicle should be equipped with an audible alarm, which should have a concealed button, to alert the public and the nearest police station in the event of emergency.

The backstage areas of arts facilities should be carefully policed, and unauthorized persons kept out. A stage doorman must never leave his post to summon a performer; he should deputize someone for such an errand. Backstage help and the regular stage crew should be instructed to protect the personal property of the performers onstage. Ideal backstage planning should permit only one exit to the street and only one exit to the front. Both should be under constant surveillance. Temporary openings—for carting scenery, properties, trunks, instruments—also may require guarding against unauthorized entry.

Performers and musicians should be cautioned against leaving money and valuables backstage. The concert hall or theater, moreover, should provide lock-up storage for portable musical instruments and lockers for street clothing and personal property.

"No smoking" rules must be enforced, and reasonable and safe areas for smoking should be provided. Watch out for cleaning fluids, faulty wiring, and electrical appliances which are potential fire hazards.

Although it is best for museums and galleries to get advice from a professional security agency and follow it, there are several general rules to be followed. Uniformed guards should be stationed so as to command constant surveillance of all valuable exhibits. Electronic security devices can insure protection from loss or damage. In some cases, close public inspection must be prevented by roping off sections. All areas, including washrooms, should be patrolled to prevent concealment after hours. Building security should prevent entrance through the roof, shaftways, or windows.

When large crowds are anticipated for special exhibits, plainclothesmen should circulate among the public. Wherever possible, however, visitors should be limited to a number that can be readily watched at all times. Of course, good door, lock, and key controls are essential.

Festivals and other arts programs held in the open air should have a minimum number of entrances and exits which can be easily watched. The use of uniformed guards and close cooperation with local police will minimize thefts, arguments, disorders, and diversions.

Take security seriously. Don't let artistic temperament or a genteel atmosphere result in haphazard security or relaxed protection.

Remember that you are not only leaving yourself open to management's losses, but you must also protect the public, your public.

July 1962

Thanking the Speaker

Letters of appreciation should be sent to guest speakers immediately following their appearances at meetings of your organization. The letters are not only good ways of thanking them for their efforts, but may also help to insure their return.

January 1966

Addresses on Publications

When sending out published material, be sure to put the address of your organization within the publication. *AM* recently received an eight-page newsletter that was handsomely produced and well-written. However, nowhere within the newsletter was an address given for the sponsoring institution.

October 1963

Answering Service

If your organization uses a telephone answering service, be sure that it is equipped to give simple, routine information such as the name of your production or presentation. A well-informed answering service operator can make friends for your arts group.

June 1963

Answering Letters

Letters to a cultural organization should never go unanswered. If an executive of your organization will be away from his office for a definite period of time, a system of acknowledging his mail should be instituted. A reply should be mailed immediately to the letter writer stating that the official is away and giving the date of his return. The reply should also indicate whether the matter referred to is being discharged by another member of your organization's staff or if it must await the executive's return for further action.

November 1964

BOARD OF DIRECTORS

The Board of a Cultural Organization: Its Structure and Its Significance

Richard C. Trenbeth

Each year an increasing number of able individuals willingly take on the responsibilities of board membership in cultural groups. A few strong institutions may be the lengthened shadow of a single man, but many more are the outgrowth of countless board and committee meetings. By working collectively, boards of trustees or directors provide continuity and permanence to the organization and counterbalance the effects of a single strong opinion. No matter how interminable the regime of a durable chief executive may seem, the collective control, assistance, and wisdom of a strong board usually will long outlast the influence of any one person.

Generally speaking, an organization's board is comparable to the legislative branch of government. Board members represent many different segments of the community. Because they both influence and are influenced by the groups they represent, board members, as a rule, synthesize varying points of view into broad policy which is widely acceptable. In this sense even the most aristocratic of boards (and they seem to abound in cultural organizations) represent the spirit of democracy at work.

One of the broad functions of a board is to interpret the organization's program to the community. A well-informed board member can tell his friends and associates how the program is going to affect the community. And in so doing he is in a position to be the most effective fund raiser for the organization and its projects—as indeed he should be, for the right to control and improve plans carries with it the responsibility for seeing to it that money is available to accomplish those plans.

The ideal board should be so constituted that its members have a wide variety of special skills, talents, and contacts that can be used for the benefit of the organization. No board should expect its members with special skills to give an unlimited amount of volunteer work in the field in which they earn their living. Board service should be a refreshing avocation rather than a way of continually contributing professional services.

Some large cultural agencies may have more than one type of board. Usually, the basic unit is the controlling board of trustees or directors that have direct legal responsibility for the institution and the authority to hire the staff at all levels. Occasionally, there are functions that the controlling board cannot carry out itself; these may be assigned to specially created auxiliary boards.

Women's boards or auxiliaries are often formed to handle official entertaining or to staff projects that require constant volunteer help. Some larger art organizations also form young men's groups for specific assignments. Members of such groups get many opportunities for thorough indoctrination in the affairs of the organization. These special groups thus frequently become a kind of training group for future appointments to the controlling board. Sometimes the presidents of auxiliary boards are ex-officio members of the controlling board.

A third type can be classified as associational boards because their only responsibility is connected with the affairs of a membership group or satellite association, as in the case of opera guilds, friends of the orchestra, theater, and so on. Like auxiliary boards, these groups not only carry out specific duties but also broaden the circle of informed persons capable of interpreting the agency's program. They also broaden the base of financial support.

Why do people join boards and give freely of their time and energy? A number of studies indicate that some of the most important motivations are a sense of civic duty (sometimes related to carrying on a family tradition); persuasion by friends or business associates (occasionally on the boss's orders);

interest in the field (art, music, drama); recognition, honor, prestige; and a challenging opportunity to learn something new.

One characteristic that distinguishes cultural board members from trustees of health, education, and welfare organizations is a nearly professional knowledge of the cultural area served. Noncultural trustees rightly feel unqualified to compare their own ideas on technical subjects with the ideas of staff professionals trained in medicine, education, or social welfare. In the arts, many an informed collector of art or student of symphonic music or opera can, and often will, challenge the opinions of the staff professionals. Cultural boards also tend to be higher in prestige value, especially among women, who often look upon board membership in certain organizations as a symbol of having arrived socially.

Cultural boards range from 5 to 50 members, somewhat smaller than boards in other fields. Arts organizations often make less effort to indoctrinate new members and to keep them informed, either because the staff is overburdened or because it underestimates the importance of such orientation.

Another rather common, and regrettable, difference between cultural boards and those of most other agencies is inadequate attention to wisely constructed bylaws and other written directives, procedures, and policies. Some organizations lack even a basic statement of objectives as a basis for planning their program.

September 1963

How to Organize the Board of a Cultural Group

Richard C. Trenbeth

Although cultural boards vary considerably in size, scope of responsibility, and complexity, most of them follow a similar pattern in organization. At the top is the key man, the board chairman. In many cultural organizations he is called the president. Two or more vice-chairmen are common, and the treasurer is sometimes a volunteer and occasionally a paid officer. In large institutions the secretary almost always is a salaried staff member.

Board business is carried out in committees, the number of which depends on the complexity of the organization. Almost all have executive committees composed of the officers and top committee heads. When physical properties are important—as they are to museums and theaters—there generally is a committee to make major decisions on managing and maintaining the property. Most agencies have finance or budget committees to plan budgets and manage endowment funds.

Cultural groups often overlook the desirability of a personnel committee to keep informed about salary scales in comparable organizations—and especially on trends in college faculty and staff salaries, permitted outside sources of income, and contributory investment plans for retirement. All organizations should have a development committee to supervise planning, publications, and publicity, membership sales, and fund raising.

Functional committees may vary in accordance with the program. Museums usually have exhibitions committees, orchestral groups will frequently have a committee concerned with concert material and guest artists, and theaters generally have a committee concerned with the types of plays to be offered, guest stars, and other production problems.

Miscellaneous committees may include one on the business aspects of a museum store, another on selling advertising in programs for concerts and theatrical productions, and perhaps a library committee when that is a function of the organization. An increasing number of organizations have permanent nominating committees to keep a constantly watchful eye for potential board replacements.

The effective board, of course, is much more than an organization chart with impressive boxes connected by solid and dotted lines. It is a uniquely qualified group of people acting in delicate balance with each other and with the needs and opportunities of the community which can be fulfilled through the skills of the professional staff.

Ideally, however, there must be clearly understood channels of operation on overall policy with some shortcuts to help deal with specific problems. On broad policy matters, the chain of command must be from the chairman through the board to the chief salaried executive, and thence to the department heads. To handle specific activities, the wise chairman and executive may delegate authority to department heads to work directly with board committee chairmen or other qualified individual board members. All such arrangements, however, should be subject to frequent review and direction.

A university president propounded the "Rule of Three W's" for board membership. The three W's are Wisdom, Work, and Wealth, and the rule states that a man possessing any two of the three characteristics is a good prospect for board membership. For a cultural board, however, something more is definitely needed. And that something more is at least a quiet enthusiasm for and knowledge of the cultural discipline in which the board member's organization functions.

Most arts organizations are fortunate in having among the most interested people in the community a number of men or women with a flair for advertising, marketing, public relations, and related promotional work. Board members with these talents must assume leadership in impressing the rest of the board with the importance of the consumer. If the agency is a small one without an adequate promotional staff, such a board member can be invaluable in directing the complex job of marketing the organization's services and perhaps even assigning his own employees to help with writing and production.

In larger organizations, however, the promotionally oriented board member must not only be careful to maintain his role as an effective teammate of the professional staff, but to also guard against any inclination to require all details to be cleared through him for final decisions.

Some boards are constituted almost by formula. Some of the factors taken into consideration include the proportion of members by sex and by age, religious, ethnic, and economic status, location of residence, special capacities for board work, experience on other boards, and potential for future board leadership. There is a tendency in older, well-established cultural organizations to lean toward an aristocratic rather than a democratic board. The postwar years have clearly indicated that neither an above-average lay knowledge of the arts nor the willingness to work for an organization is limited to the economically or socially favored few. For a truly dynamic, working board there is much to be said for including in its membership at least two or three intelligent, responsible people who have not yet "arrived" in either a social or business sense, but who show considerable promise as effective board members.

No organization whose board represents a narrow perspective or a hyperconservative approach can ever hope to win wide participation or support.

October 1963

Work of Cultural Boards Needs
Periodic Review: Check These 12 Points

Richard C. Trenbeth

Books can be written on the importance of adequately orienting and indoctrinating new board members and then keeping them informed and interested. The effective executive is one who cheerfully spends his time with new board members in an effectively planned, thorough indoctrination program, followed by specific job assignments.

Although boards theoretically work only on the policy level, the business, legal, and fund-raising aspects of the organization permit assignments that go more deeply into administration. There are other areas in which board work can and should go far beyond policy level. Some board members may be most effective in speaking assignments and public relations appearances. Others may prefer behind-the-scenes work cultivating and then soliciting prospects for large gifts.

The wise board chairman steers his fellow trustees away from attempting to take over types of work and decisions that should be handled by experienced professional executives and staff.

The work of an executive and his staff directly bears upon the amount of time required of the effective board member. On some boards the staff planning, research, and documentation is so thorough that committee and board meetings are brisk and businesslike, requiring only major decisions instead of endless discussion. In such fortunate organizations, a board member may be highly effective in 3 or 4 hours of actual work each month, whereas in others good board work requires 30 or 40 hours monthly.

Periodic evaluation of the work of a board is both healthy and necessary for the continuing welfare of a relatively volatile arts organization. A series of financially disastrous concert or theatrical seasons, for example, may require a drastic change in board policies and personnel that might have been avoided through a frank assessment of continuing trends.

Who should make the evaluation? In his excellent book, *The Effective Board* (Association Press, New York, 1960), Cyril O. Houle observed that the rating should be done by anyone interested, and particularly by the chairman of the board, the executive committee, any board member (especially new members), and the salaried executive. To this list could be added a qualified public relations or management consultant hired from the outside.

The rating scale offered by Professor Houle includes the following characteristics, to be rated as excellent, good, average, poor, or very poor:

1. The board should be made up of effective individuals who supplement one another's talents.
2. It should represent the interests to be consulted in formulating policy for the institution.
3. It should be large enough to carry all necessary responsibilities, but small enough to act as a deliberative group.
4. The basic structural pattern (board, board officers, committees, executive, staff) should be clear.
5. There should be an effective working relationship among the board, executive, and staff.
6. The members of the board should understand the objectives of the agency and how they are achieved by the activities undertaken.
7. They should have a feeling of social ease and rapport with each other.
8. Each member of the board should feel involved in the board's work.
9. The board should formulate specific goals to guide its work.
10. Decisions on policy should be made only after full consideration by all parties concerned.
11. The board should maintain effective community relationships.
12. Its members should have a sense of accomplishment and progress.

In addition, the board should be willing to accept financial responsibility for its decisions. And it should approach the career problems of the agency staff with the same considerations as the board members' own companies would give to their employees of comparable rank and responsibility.

Even the most effective board is at best a fragile and fluid thing, inheriting the human characteristics of its members. But, in generating points of view that may at first be little understood, and even unpopular, boards of cultural institutions, perhaps more than any other type, can exert a deep and lasting influence on our society.

November 1963

For a Cool Head and Cold Feet
Add a Tax Lawyer to the Board

Joseph L. Wyatt, Jr.

Setting up or restructuring your board? It pays to have at least one member who is a specialist in tax and estate planning.

At the very beginning, an experienced lawyer-trustee can show a new organization how to achieve tax-exempt status quickly. I know of a group that was able to apply for immediate exemption (it normally takes at least a year) by altering its proposed board of trustees before it was actually set up.

Once a group is established, its lawyer-trustee can guide it in drafting literature for distribution among prospective donors and to other lawyers among whose clients there may be many potential benefactors. While the best of these brochures are excellent, the worst of the lot are superficial, unimaginative, and dangerously gimmicky. The lawyer on the board can avoid embarrassment to the institution—and to its patrons.

His knowledge can help an institution plan an endowment campaign that takes advantage of the latest Internal Revenue Service rulings.

For example, he can explain what is good, bad, or uncertain about recent rulings on the so-called Pomona Plan under which would-be givers transfer cash or assets to an institution and receive a contract from it to pay them income from the gift for life.

A well-trained lawyer can help in other forms of fund-raising activity as well. A fund solicitation, widely publicized on the West Coast, suffered much adverse publicity recently when it appeared that the group had failed to comply with local law requiring approval of such campaigns by a municipal bureau. Its future drives are now under a cloud.

Do not expect the lawyer-trustee to obtain tax-exempt status, draw up articles of incorporation, or draw up a handbook of sample will clauses gratis. Pay him or his firm—or some other lawyer—for such work.

Do expect him to exercise professional judgment and help widen the institution's circle of contacts in the community. He is there to consult, to guide, to prevent. The board lawyer's occupational disease is cold feet, and a pair of them is most useful to have around.

March 1962

Artists on the Board

Should a practicing professional artist be a member of a cultural board? There is no doubt that some professionals can be a definite asset, but the possibility of jealousy may offset any advantages. Some organizations get around this by electing to their boards only retired professionals—such as former actresses for a theatrical group—or older professionals whose status is so well-established that the possibility of criticism is minimized.

December 1963

Keeping the Board Posted

Clippings, reports, letters, and other materials that may interest board members often go unnoticed because board members don't receive them. Collect and put aside all items of interest until a staff member has the time to duplicate copies for the board on a copying machine. Also, maintain one copy of each item in a big looseleaf scrapbook to which board members can refer.

September 1962

Getting to Know You

By giving recognition to board and committee members, you can help to keep them interested in the organization. Every month in its newsletter, Roberson Center in Binghamton, New York highlights a different board or committee of one of its member groups. It lists every member by name and asks readers to call them if they have questions about the center or the group.

Fall 1970

Board Game

Interested in recruiting members? Why not get your board involved in a "sweep-stakes"? At its fall meeting, the National Association for Regional Ballet asked each director to personally sign up five new associate members by its April meeting. The results? Collectively the board recruited 49 new members, with 5 of the 30 reaching their assigned quotas.

March-April 1976

THE INDIVIDUAL ARTIST

Performing Groups
Find Painters-in-Residence

The historic association between visual artists and performing arts groups is still very much alive. Modern painters and sculptors continue to draw inspiration from ballet and theater performers, and, in a number of instances, also work with performing arts groups or use their art to help the groups raise funds. In Phoenix, for example, sculptor John Waddell, who created a group of striking dance sculptures for the Phoenix Civic Plaza, now is helping the Phoenix Metropolitan Dance Theater by making promotional sketches for the group.

In New York, the recent run of the Alvin Ailey Dance Theater featured two exhibits in the theater alcove, both focusing on Ailey dancers—22 batiks by Hilda Demsky, her second exhibit of Ailey works, and 15 original drawings and an etching of Alvin Ailey by Selene Fung. The exhibits were sponsored by the Friends of Alvin Ailey, which kept a percentage of the sales price as a commission.

In Hartford, Connecticut, something more unusual has happened. Instead of a "moving" performer, a symphony orchestra has provided the inspiration for an artist. For the past two-and-a-half years, in fact, artist Estelle Laschever has been unofficial "painter-in-residence" for the Hartford Symphony and has created scores of drawings and etchings featuring orchestra performers.

A former musician who studied piano for many years, Ms. Laschever became fascinated by the relationship between the musician and instrument, and she asked for permission to attend Tuesday night dress rehearsals. Her work progressed so well that about a year ago she started attending rehearsals three or four nights every week, sketching in pencil and then adapting and reworking the sketches in her studio.

Last April, a Laschever show was held at an East Hartford gallery, featuring 60 works—water colors and etchings—all on the Hartford Symphony. The show attracted many orchestra supporters, and the artist contributed a sizeable percentage of the sales to the symphony.

"I feel a kinship with the musicians," Ms. Laschever told *AM.* "I like to enter their world and see the discipline in their work. What I really react to is the player becoming the music."

November-December 1976

Group Lends Support to Artists

Performing artists are being helped through a program now reaching its fruitional stage after three years of development. Linking performers, universities and, hopefully, corporations as sponsors, the Affiliate Artists program offers young professional artists employment at universities at an annual salary of $6500. Unlike artists-in-residence programs, however, performers spend only about 56 days a year on campus, spread over four to six visits, and are free during the remaining time to perform professionally elsewhere. On campus, artists' duties are flexible and are not tied to specific classroom assignments—they perform, participate in student seminars, and sometimes lecture.

Matching artists and universities is the job of Affiliate Artists, Inc., the nonprofit organization that conceived the program and administers it. Artists interested in participating (there are now 300 on file) submit background information to the organization at 155 West Sixty-eighth Street, New York, New York 10023. Resumes are screened by an advisory committee, which then reaches its final decisions following attendance at auditions or performances. Schools expressing interest in the program are visited by an organizational representative who evaluates the school and the department to be involved. Two or three artists are then recommended to the school. The selected artist visits the school with an official of Affiliate Artists to work out the year's program. Colleges and universities pay 20 percent of the total fee for each artist and outside sponsors pay the balance.

For one artist in 1966, the program has grown to 15 in 1967 and to 26 this year. Major support thus far has come from foundations, the National Endowment for the Arts, and church organizations, but a key to future growth is business sponsorship.

November-December 1968

Services and Jobs for Artists Are on the Increase

Growing attention is being paid to the economic plight of the individual artist. In addition to Comprehensive Employment and Training Act (CETA) programs, which are providing at least 6000 new arts jobs this year, legislation to benefit the artist has been introduced in Congress, major new aid programs and concepts have been developed, the Arts Endowment has organized a task force to study their education, training, and professional development, and artists themselves are finding new ways to increase their public visibility.

Change, Inc., the foundation headed by artist Robert Rauschenberg, recently started a campaign for a $10-million bank of donated art that could be used as payment for hospitalized needy artists. Some works have been received already, and one institution, the Hospital for Joint Diseases in New York, has been treating several artists under the program. Another important health-oriented program, the Center for Occupational Hazards, (56 Pine St., N. Y., N.Y. 10005) has initiated the Art Hazards Information Center to provide advice on safety precautions and the hazards of arts and crafts materials in response to inquiries. The Foundation for the Community of Artists, which includes a page on art hazards in each issue of its *Art Workers News,* recently introduced a major new benefit program for artists. In addition to the regular Blue Cross–Blue Shield plan, the Foundation is making available to its artist-members, at a discount rate, the major health, disability, and life insurance package offered by the Support Services Alliance, Inc.

To protect visual artists in another area, against piracy of their works, the new nonprofit Visual Artists and Galleries Association has just been established. VAGA (1 World Trade Center, N.Y., N.Y. 10048) will act as a clearinghouse for licensing reproduction rights for works of art and hopes to offer the visual artist the kind of protection that ASCAP offers composers. In California, where the Resale Royalty Law requires sellers to pay artists a 5 percent royalty when the artist's work is resold at a profit and over $1000, the Artists Royalties Legal Defense Fund has been established. The group has the joint mission of defending the law against legal attack—a suit has been brought against artist Andre Balyon and the California Arts Council by dealer Howard Morseburg—and promoting the artist royalty concept nationally.

Another new service, the Artists and Craftspersons Housing and Studio Exchange Program, has been established by the Center for the Study of Public Policy and the Arts, P.O. Box 5395, Berkeley, California 94705. The Exchange program, which has a $15 registration fee, will enable artists to use other artists' studios and facilities while traveling or in residence.

On the legislative front, bills introduced in the House by Congressmen Brademas and Richmond are designed to end inequities suffered by artists. The Brademas bill would allow artists to deduct from taxes on their art income one-third of the market value of paintings they donate. The Richmond bill would reduce tax liabilities for artists' heirs by requiring estate taxes to be based on the value of materials in the work of art rather than the market value of the work. Congressman Waxman is working on an artists' resale bill patterned after the California royalty bill with one significant difference—a portion of the proceeds would be used for the purchase of works of little-known artists for public display. Congressman Pressler will reintroduce his bill to establish a Congressional Art Bank, authorizing Congress to borrow art for six-month periods for display in the halls of Congress.

Meanwhile, CETA arts programs continue to grow, although they account for only a small percentage of all CETA programs. Overall, the government is funding some 560,000 CETA jobs during the current fiscal year at a cost of $8 billion with the job figure expected to rise to 725,000 by early 1978. In the arts, about 3000 jobs were funded in 1975 and 1976 at a cost of about $25 million, according to an October 28 bulletin from the National Endowment for the Arts. During the current year Carl Stover of NEA estimates that well over 6000 new arts jobs representing over $50 million have been developed.

Although legislation authorizing CETA expires next September, Secretary of Labor Ray Marshall has predicted that the program will be continued and expanded. Moreover, the government's experience with public service employment through CETA could provide a foundation for arts jobs through other federal programs. In a recent speech before the U.S. Conference of Mayors' Arts Task Force, Assistant Secretary of Labor Ernest G. Green pointed to the job component of the Administration's Welfare Reform bill which could create 1.4 million job slots by 1981. "For welfare reform alone," said Mr. Green, "we estimate that at least 75,000 of the positions will be in the area of cultural enrichment."

Currently, Green and Carl Stover are working together in planning a major first-time national conference on CETA and the arts to be held next spring.

A booklet published by the North Carolina Arts Council, *Third Century Artists, A North Carolina Public Arts Experience,* offers an insight into the development and operation of one of the nation's largest CETA arts programs. The attractive, illustrated 113-page booklet chronicles the $1-million program, employing 150 artists in 87 counties from October 1975 through March 1977. In the same state, the North Carolina Museum of Art is circulating through next September "One-From-a-Third," an exhibit of works completed under the CETA program.

Meanwhile, examples of increased exposure for artists continue to develop. The U.S. General Services Administration is placing greater emphasis than ever before on public art—its "Living Buildings" program from November 21-25 featured arts activities in ten regional offices—and groups such as the Organization of Independent Artists have utilized exhibition provisions in the Public Buildings Cooperative Act. In San Francisco, some 700 individuals now hold licenses as street artists with double that number seeking licensing.

November-December 1977

Visiting Artists on Move in Rural Counties

Artists in virtually every discipline have become full-time resources to 37 counties —most of them rural—throughout North Carolina, thanks to the cooperative efforts of several state agencies and an interesting funding device. The project has proved so successful that it has led to the development of permanent arts programs in several communities, involved workers and children for the first time, and even led to the formation of an artist fan club in one town.

Introduced in 1971 as a joint project of the state's Arts Council and the Department of Community Colleges, the Visiting Artist Program, as it is now known, was designed originally to provide musicians-in-residence for a limited number of the state's two-year community colleges and technical institutes in those counties where cultural exposure was minimal. During their nine-month residencies at colleges or technical schools, participating musicians did not teach regular classes, but were available for concerts, lecture-demonstrations, and informal visits both at the school and throughout the county. Artists' salaries of $9000 each were split equally between the state arts council and each sponsoring college.

After several years under the original formula, the program's success prompted its sponsors to broaden it, in order to involve artists from other disciplines and to encourage the participation of new institutions and the continued involvement of schools already in the program. The new funding policy introduced in 1973, gave Full-time Equivalency credit (FTE is a funding formula used in higher education) from the Department of Community Colleges to schools which had already participated, enabling them to receive total salaries as well as travel expenses if they remained in the program. First-time institutions were given one-third of an artist's salary by the state arts council, but could receive FTE credits and full funding after a year's participation. Under the new arrangement, which added sculptors, dancers, actors, writers, printmakers, and craftsmen to the program, the number of participating schools jumped from 5 to 18 last year, and up to 37 this year.

Under the program, visiting artists have traveled throughout their counties and worked at schools, factories, churches, and civic clubs. Performers average about 200 appearances during residencies, and one artist made 420 different appearances, visiting every elementary and secondary school classroom in his county.

To find artists for the program, the council mails notices to schools and organizations throughout the country soliciting applications. Salaries are $10,000, but individual schools can supplement them if they wish. Once selected for the program, artists make their own decisions as to the kind of activities that will be most beneficial to their areas, although the state council will make suggestions in advance. "We don't want them to stay on campus for the entire nine months," said J. Alan Butler, the state arts council's community director, "and none have."

The impact of the artists has been considerable thus far, especially in those areas where arts programming has been minimal. "They've got a real missionary spirit about their work," added Butler, "and they've dispelled a lot of myths about the arts."

One harpsichordist won special admiration from the workers at a glass factory in Clinton for his musical abilities demonstrated during a lunch-hour concert and because he had built his own instrument. As a result, many of the workers later came to concerts he presented in the local school auditorium. Another artist, pianist Gary Towlen, communicated so well with youngsters that high school students in Smithfield started a fan club complete with Gary Towlen bumper stickers on their cars. When one of his concerts was inadvertently and unfortunately scheduled on the same night as a high school basketball game, he still drew a full house of 400.

With 56 community colleges and technical institutions in the state's 100 counties, the program in three years of operation already reaches two-thirds of the two-year schools and more than half the counties in the state. According to the program's sponsors, participation is expected to continue to grow in coming years.

November-December 1974

MEMBERSHIP

Recipe for Recruiting Members
Includes Good Food, Fine Art

Good food, fine art, and an ultra-soft-sell campaign for new members are the ingredients of a successful new program presented every Wednesday afternoon at the High Museum of Art in Atlanta, Georgia. Conceived and sponsored by the museum's Members Guild as a volunteer activity, the program, which began last October features a "petit gourmet" luncheon for members and their guests in the museum's members' room at noon ($2.50 a person), sandwiched between regular 11 A.M. and 1:30 P.M. museum docent tours. In addition, visitors are encouraged to arrive at 10 A.M. to attend the weekly "Great Artist" lecture.

Because the luncheons were designed to promote membership, they operated initially on an "each one reach one" principle, with every attending member bringing along a nonmember guest. Attendance for the first two luncheons was slightly less than capacity, although a number of guests became members. The museum then sent 5000 members a special lighthearted mailing featuring a "Peanuts" cartoon about museums with a message reading, "Man does not live by art alone. Join us." As a result of the mailing and a subsequent full-page picture story with luncheon recipes by the food editor of the *Atlanta Constitution,* the luncheons soon became sell-outs, with reservations a must. To permit more members to attend, the guest requirement was waived, although potential members still constitute about one-third of each week's diners.

A key to the program's success has been the volunteer effort. Guild hostesses, completely responsible for preparing and serving meals, take turns as chefs, and cook much of the food at home first because of the tiny museum kitchen. Recent luncheons have featured such entrees as shrimp and cheese casserole and chicken in wine.

Although no formal membership presentation is made, a wine sipping preceding lunch gives members the opportunity to promote membership. *Objects d'art* from the museum's shop are used as table centerpieces, and matches with the museum logo and "Are you a member?" printed on them are handed out as favors. According to publicity director Elizabeth M. Sawyer, it is conceivable that the low-keyed recruitment approach may be upgraded in the future to include special membership programs at lunch.

The launching of the noon program coincided with the museum's initiation of a fall membership drive and helped to promote it. The drive topped its goal.

January-February 1972

Turn On Brings Turnout

Want to have a good turnout at your annual meeting? Try to make it interesting as well as businesslike. The Pro Arte Symphony Orchestra in Hempstead, New York announced that its recent annual meeting would be "adhering not strictly to business." At the meeting, the business portion was limited to only 45 minutes and was preceded by a potluck buffet and followed by a piano recital.

Fall 1970

A Taste of Things to Come

In an attempt to attract new members, New York's Museum of Modern Art invited visitors to sample membership before buying it. Beginning May 5, following payment of a $2 admission fee, each museum visitor received a yellow registration card which read, "Your next visit to the Museum of Modern Art can be free as a Member for a Day." In return for filling out a registration form on the card, the visitor received a special pass and information packet good for a free one-day visit anytime prior to August 1. The pass included such regular membership benefits as 25 percent discounts on purchases, use of the members' restaurant, and access to the art lending service, but only for the one day.

By the time the two-month promotion ended, more than 1000 visitors had taken advantage of the offer. Pleased with the response, the museum staff followed up with a special mailing in an attempt to convert the one-day members into real members.

Summer 1975

Membership Program
Can Reap Unusual Benefits

Richard C. Trenbeth

Mr. Trenbeth, the Chicago Symphony's Director of Development when this article was written, initiated an orchestra membership program in 1971 which has since recruited some 5000 members and brought in well over $100,000. In this article, adapted from an internal report, he reviews the Chicago Symphony Society's first two years, 1971 to 1973.

The Chicago Symphony Society was envisioned as the most feasible way of building broad involvement with the orchestra despite limited seating for regular concerts. In 1970 we developed basic plans for a membership program based on annual dues of $20 and attractive benefits and privileges which were later to include local and overseas tours, premiums (a bonus Symphony recording among them), and discount tickets for such nonsubscription events as civic orchestra and chamber music concerts. The concept of awarding honorary life memberships to donors whose cumulative gifts amounted to $1000 or more was based on my own experience with a similar program I developed for the Art Institute of Chicago.

Our proposal received impetus when trustee John W. B. Hadley became so convinced of the long-range value of the program that he offered to underwrite any first-year loss up to $50,000. As predicted, the heavy start-up costs were more than offset by the enthusiastic dues income which produced a net gain of $27,167 in the first nine months of the society's existence, far above the normal and highly acceptable standard of breakeven or small loss for the first year.

The first invitations to membership were mailed in October 1971, just as the symphony returned from its first European tour. Substantial dues income was first received in November, and by June 30, 1972 had reached $60,220. An 18-month delay in producing a promised bonus record kept first-year expenses to a modest $33,053, resulting in a net profit of $27,167. By June 30, 1972 there were 3011 annual members paying $20 dues and 1122 honorary life members. Of the new annual members, 1622 had had no earlier affiliation with the symphony, and 489 were season ticket subscribers who had never before contributed to the symphony.

We began the society's first full fiscal year in the summer of 1972 with a sprinkling of Civic Orchestra concerts and the first tour (45 members spent a week at the Aspen Music Festival). Local tours drew hundreds of members. About 35 members participated in our first overseas tour to Spain, and 14 went to San Francisco for the symphony concert there. Growing interest in society tours indicates that they provide an attractive privilege of membership, especially during periods when concert-related discounts are delayed.

Sales of new memberships during 1972-73 continued to be strong during the fall and winter months and picked up again in the spring when the bonus record was finally produced and delivered. By June 30, 1973, there was a total membership of 4761 including 3519 annual members and 1252 honorary life members. Despite complaints on the lateness of the bonus record, an attractive program of privileges and a strong series of renewal mailings resulted in a first-year renewal of 66.6 percent, considerably higher than normal for new groups.

With production of the bonus record in May 1973, the premium costs for the year before, the current year, and much of the following year had to be absorbed in the 72-73 expense. Still, dues income of $68,480 surpassed society expense by $1900.

It has been estimated that society participation in Civic Orchestra and Symphony Chamber Music concerts averages close to 300 per concert. The Civic Orchestra reported at least $1200 in additional ticket revenues last year, and society members added about $2500 to the Chamber Music series income. Also, a great many members subscribed to a new Friday evening and Sunday afternoon series this season.

Tour participation during the current season grew significantly. Approximately 18 participated in the second Aspen Music Festival tour, 18 spent a weekend at Interlochen, 53 went to London for a Christmas week, 32 went to London and Paris earlier in December, and 48 went to Russia in March.

The influence of membership on sustaining funds during the society's first 24 months is not only measurable, but highly exciting. Through November 1, 1973, 212 new members never before affiliated with the symphony contributed $13,012 in addition to their dues. Of the 361 society members who contributed before becoming members, 125 increased their giving, 197 continued giving at the same rate, and 39 (most of whom had previously given $10 or less) decreased their sustaining fund giving, but were actually giving more through their $20 dues.

Total sustaining fund gifts from annual members in the society during the first 24 months were $52,815 in addition to dues.

The flood of letters of warm thanks from past contributors of $1000 or more who were elected to honorary life membership is only one indication of the cultivation value of this program. In the first year after their election, the 772 family units represented by the 1252 individual members increased their sustaining fund giving by a full $41,470 over the year before.

Our experience would seem to indicate that only when there is a professionally directed program of direct marketing aimed at satisfying the wants and desires of the most likely prospects will success result. Attendance at society programs, tours, and social events indicates that many of our members welcome planned programs at which they can meet others with similar interests. The highly favorable reaction to electing contributors of substantial amounts to honorary life membership demonstrates that in the long run this opportunity for recognition alone could justify the establishment of the Society.

As years go by, it is highly likely that many whose first interest in the symphony was kindled through society membership will provide far more gift support and eventually more bequests than, for example, the large number of present concert subscribers who choose not to contribute at all.

March-April 1974

Careful Timing Can Cut Down
Your Membership Work Load

The clerical work of renewing annual memberships, which may be considerable for a large organization, can be eased at the peak period if a special appeal is made to members for early renewal.

The National Geographic Society, with nearly 3.5 million members, has found its Summer Remittance Plan a great help in evening out the flow of work connected with membership records and dues payments. More than half of the *National Geographic* members now pay the coming year's dues by the middle of October.

Early in July the society sends a notice to all members explaining that renewing yearly membership in the summer preceding the dues-year has helped to cut office costs and keep membership dues low. The alternatives, it points out, would be expensive overtime for the staff, or hiring a huge and costly part-time force.

March 1964

Membership Renewals

Getting members to renew after the first year is a constant problem facing arts groups. One renewal inducement used with great success is a plastic card case offered to continuing members by the Art Institute of Chicago. The wallet-sized case has two pockets with the Art Institute's crest embossed on the outside. One pocket holds a printed membership card and the other a card listing the museum hours and the members' room hours. Each card case costs the institute only 7¢.

July 1963

Exchanging Members

By cooperating with cultural institutions in nearby cities, you might increase your reach substantially. In Florida, three museums—the Jacksonville Children's Museum, Orlando's John Young Museum and Planetarium, and Daytona Beach's Museum of Arts and Sciences—have offered a joint membership since September. Members have full privileges at each of the museums with a single membership card.

November-December 1976

Hearing Aid

Getting prospective supporters inside the doors of your institution may be the first step towards enrolling them as members. To make the barrier crossing easier, the Museum of the City of New York encloses, along with its membership recruitment letters, four tickets, each good for one free electronic Acoustiguide tour of the museum.

September-October 1974

Reader's Service

A technique used by many commercial publications to help arouse added reader interest in their advertisers is now being tried by a dance company to win added support for its activities. In issues of its new organization newsletter, the Pennsylvania Ballet briefly describes such activities as the coming season's subscription program, summer residency, membership campaign, and Association tour to Paris. In a special box marked Reader's Service, recipients are invited to check off any of six different items if they wish to receive added information on these activities.

Summer 1974

Conducting Members

The Chicago Symphony Society, which uses a variety of benefits to lure new members including free admissions, ticket discounts, open rehearsals, newsletters, tours abroad, parties, and a special bonus record, is now appealing to the Walter Mitty in potential members. A new benefit, created especially for those "who feel moved to conduct when listening to great records," is a perfectly balanced 14-inch baton imprinted with the words "Chicago Symphony Society."

November-December 1972

Annual Ball Helps Arts Group Win New and Keep Old Members

An annual social event is helping the Minneapolis Society of Fine Arts win new members and keep old ones. The society is the governing and supporting organization for the Minneapolis Institute of Arts, a museum. A key to the success of the organization's Members' Ball, held in the institute's galleries, is that tickets at half price are offered as added inducements to both new members and to the current members who recruit them.

For five years prior to the first ball, which was held in 1963, the society's various efforts to build new membership and reduce dropouts proved only moderately successful. An evaluation of these methods, however, revealed that special programs were the greatest incentive to membership and that "happy members were the best recruiters of new members."

These combined principles resulted in the current Members' Ball. In 1965, for example, the price for the entire evening, including dinner and dancing to a chamber group of 14 musicians from the Minneapolis Symphony Orchestra, was $15. However, new members, and every member who brought in a new member, were entitled to purchase two tickets for the price of one. All half-price requests had to be accompanied by membership dues for the recruits.

More than 80 percent of the tickets sold each year were purchased at the reduced rate—an indication of the popularity of the incentive plan. Although half-price tickets have been underwritten to some extent by the membership promotion budget, the effort has paid off handsomely in the form of increased income from the $15 annual membership dues and increased renewals.

Each year, attendance at the ball has risen, the event has become more self-sustaining, and the membership ranks have grown proportionately. Of the 458 new members who joined the society in 1965, 358 were recruited through the ball.

Planning for each event begins a year in advance and is carried out by a volunteer committee of approximately 14 members who work under the supervision of Miss Helen M. Lethert, the Society's Director of Membership. Miss

Lethert told *AM,* "We feel that this is a most successful recruiting event because not only does it bring in new members, but it gives them a gay and impressive first introduction to the museum."

June-July 1966

New Members

One way to show your new members that you appreciate their support is to plan a special function in their honor. The Art Gallery of Toronto, for example, has a reception in April that is open to members who have joined the organization since the preceding November.

March 1962

Display Your Publicity

Members and volunteers may miss seeing important articles about your organization when they appear in print. Often, these articles may serve to heighten members' pride in the organization. Establish a central location, such as the members' room, where articles may be posted regularly, along with other items of interest.

December 1963

Getting Action

Are these issues on which you'd like your members and volunteers to take action? Allied Arts of Seattle just initiated a new technique in its monthly newsletter. The word "ACT" now appears in the left-hand column of the newsletter next to items where "there is suggestion that you can 'ACT' as an arts supporter."

March-April 1978

Film Showings

Looking for a service to institute for your membership? Try arranging free film programs on subjects relating to your organization's interests. There are many excellent motion pictures, filmstrips, and slides on a wide range of topics, available free or for small rental fees. A number of directories are published annually which list free or low-rental films by titles and subjects.

July 1963

Naming Names

Seeking better relations with patrons and volunteers? Inform them in advance when their names appear in your group's publication or newsletter. Inexpensive mimeographed form postal cards can be used for this purpose, with the page and date of the publication in which the name appears filled in by hand.

February 1965

Matchbooks

Inexpensive items featuring an arts group's symbol, distributed free to members, may help to remind them of the organization. The Virginia Museum of Fine Arts in Richmond, Virginia distributes members' matchbooks in its members' suite.

February 1966

Member Benefit

If your group is seeking a new kind of member benefit, you might consider trips of a day's duration or less that tie in to your artistic program. The Chicago Symphony Orchestra has had an excellent response to its bus trips to music instrument factories in the Chicago area, offered to members at cost. Trips have included all-day visits, with lunch stops, to brass and woodwind factories in Wisconsin and a trip to a Chicago harp factory which attracted 200 members.

January-February 1974

Premiums Pay in Direct
Mail Membership Drive

A study of a cultural institution with one of the most successful membership programs in the country indicates that direct mail has been the single most important promotion factor, by far, in achieving recent membership growth. At the Art Institute of Chicago, the fiscal year ending this June was the most successful in the organization's 63-year history.

Overall, the institute showed a record membership of more than 28,000 by June 1963. This total was about evenly divided between annual members and life members. Total membership receipts ran to $196,000, as against $147,000 the year before.

The greatest growth was in annual memberships, with sales up 49.2 percent over the year before. As of June 30, 1962, the institute claimed 10,970 annual members. Among this group the renewal rate—a figure of critical importance in membership promotion planning—was 83.7 percent. With slightly more than 9000 of these members renewing, and with a sale of 4665 new annual memberships, the institute was able to boost annual membership to 13,814 by June 30, 1963.

While the overall renewal rate for annual members was 83.7 percent, the rate for first-year members was much lower—65.3 percent. Institute officials believe this indicates the need for added concentration on making membership a meaningful experience during the first year. Once a member renews for the first time, the chance of holding him for many more years increases sharply.

The role of direct mail in the museum's membership program is highlighted by the fact that, of the 4665 new annual memberships sold, nearly 2600 were sold through direct mail promotion. This represented a jump of 68 percent over the number brought in by direct mail the year before. In the words of an institute report, "Direct mail promotion was not only the most important single factor in membership growth, but far surpassed reasonable expectations." What accounted for the difference? According to the institute, an increase in the size of the promotional budget, a revised sales letter, better mailing lists, and an excellent premium combined to make the big difference. The choice of a premium was vital.

Selection of a more attractive membership premium increased the rate of mail return by .87 percent. This was two-and-a-half times more than the amount needed to pay for the total cost of purchasing premiums for the entire year's promotion. Ordered in the middle of the fiscal year, when supplies of a first premium were exhausted, the new premium, a remainder supply of a handsome book on Van Gogh, enabled the institute to complete the fiscal year with a strong sales record in late winter and spring, and with enough copies remaining for the first mailings this fall. A new premium, an attractive book on Degas, was ordered for use later this year. This book, however, can be reordered in any quantity, if it proves successful, thus eliminating the uncertainty created by using remainders which are soon exhausted.

The institute, which mailed out a total of 123,000 pieces during the year, finds it increasingly difficult to locate large and productive lists of prospects. It was helped last year by trustees and men's council members who provided it with various kinds of directories that yielded small but highly selective lists.

Among the lists used by the Art Institute were those of a radio station, several local department stores, and a magazine read by female office workers. Other significant lists included the names of book buyers, members of a university faculty, art teachers, social study teachers, doctors, and dentists.

The heaviest mailings were sent out in the fall, at the beginning of the institute's season. Thus 57,500 pieces were mailed in September and 20,000 in October. Additional mailings of 10,500 in December 1962, 16,400 in March 1963 and 18,700 in June 1963 completed the direct mail drive. In terms of responses, the September and March mailings were the best, with each drawing nearly 3 percent. The worst response followed the June mailing, which drew under 1 percent.

At the same time that it was scoring notable success with its direct mail campaign, the institute was finding that a membership recruitment desk, placed in the museum lobby for more than a year as an experiment, was not proving worthwhile. The desk was discontinued when it proved to be uneconomical.

January 1964

Free Gifts Win Members for Cultural Group

A free gift promotion is being used by a major Eastern arts institution to attract new members. The Brooklyn Academy of Music in Brooklyn, New York, which sponsors more than 300 cultural events each season, has conducted a free gift program for the past six years that offers personal and household items to new subscribers with their $20 membership fee. This has been an important factor in increasing membership.

In addition, members of the organization are offered a free gift for each new member they help to enroll. The entire gift purchase program is conducted at no risk to the academy because the items are brought on consignment.

The gift promotion idea was initiated by William McKelvy Martin when he joined the Academy as director in 1958 in an effort to boost lagging membership. While many factors such as an expanded cultural program have contributed to a rise in enrollment, Sarah Walder, membership coordinator and head of the gift program, told *AM* that the promotion has significantly aided the success of the membership drive. Since its inception, membership has risen at the rate of about 500 per year, except for last year when it dropped by 500 subscribers, a decline attributed to a $5 fee increase. Membership today stands at 3500.

Members are entitled to discounts on special events in addition to free admission to regularly scheduled academy programs such as lectures, films, instrumental recitals, concerts, opera, theater, folk and ballroom dancing, ballet, and modern dance recitals. There is also a full children's program.

According to Mrs. Walder, the gift program has stirred many members to a concerted effort to attract their friends to the academy. This year an initial order of 707 gifts has been placed by the organization with its supplier, Gifts for Thrifts, Inc. of Nevada, in anticipation of a large response to the promotion.

Gift items usually retail at twice the price paid for them by the academy. They are usually brand name products, and the academy saves on their wholesale cost by buying in volume. Membership gifts cost the organization about $1–$2.50. New members, as well as members enrolling one person, choose from one of eight items offered, including a weekend case, a chip and dish set, a scale planter, a tropical server, an eight-piece kitchen tool set, a French purse, a blanket, and a multiserver. If they wish, members may accept $5 instead of a gift for each new member they enroll.

For members enrolling two new subscribers, gifts cost the academy about $5 or $6 and include any of the following items: a salt and pepper set, a clock, a slicer knife, a three-piece luggage set, a set of steak knives, and an ice chest. Those bringing in three members are entitled to one of four items including an electric coffee maker, a sugar, creamer, and tray set, a pair of binoculars, and a camera.

The membership drive is held from September to May, and the academy defines a new member as anyone who joins for the first time or who has not been a member since the 1958–59 season. However, the gift offer, which is made each September, expires at the end of November.

The offer is promoted by the academy with a lobby display and in newspaper advertisements of its events series. In addition, wide use is made of posters announcing the offer in subway stations, in banks, and in churches.

October 1964

Increasing Membership

An arts center in Brooklyn, New York is trying a unique method of boosting its membership. The Brooklyn Academy of Music, which has offered free gifts to new members for several years, is instituting a "point" system this year. Members received two points for initial membership and five more for each new member they recruit. Gifts will be distributed on a point basis, with the higher the point value, the more valuable the gift. The 53 gifts range from carving sets at two points to vacuums at 25 points.

October 1966

Clarify the Picture

A number of arts groups, especially those in dance, have interrelated activities such as schools, their own foundations, parent bodies, or "friends" groups. If the relationships are not made clear to the public, there is frequently confusion. One solution used successfully by the Dayton Civic Ballet was to issue a booklet specifically commenting on interrelationships. In clear terms, it discussed the ballet company, the civic ballet company, the school of dance, and the organization's "friends" program. Data on finances and staffing was included.

September-October 1973

Humorous Cards Prod Members
to Renew Season Subscriptions

Membership renewal is a serious problem facing many cultural organizations. In Midland, Texas, the Midland Community Theatre, Inc. has helped to solve this problem with a humorous approach to its direct mail program. Each year, toward the end of its annual membership drive, it sends "painless prods" to unrenewed members, which, according to Art Cole, the group's director, "really do the job for the person who has simply forgotten to put the check in the mail, or the person who has been on the fence."

One of the more effective mailing pieces the organization uses is a group of three-by-six-inch cards clipped together in sequence. The first card in the series asks, "Perhaps you've been . . . sick?" Each succeeding card then shows an old-fashioned drawing and asks a question relating to it, such as "Busy at the office?" with a drawing of two blacksmiths at work; or, "been listening to your hi-fi?" with a drawing of a gramaphone. The next-to-last card in the series states, "Whatever it is you've no doubt been too busy to mail your 1965 Community Theatre membership check. We need it and we don't want you to miss . . .," followed by a card listing programs for the coming season.

According to Mr. Cole, the series usually evokes favorable comments and thank you notes, accompanied by membership checks. To take advantage of the surprise element, the series of cards is always mailed in unmarked envelopes.

Holiday greeting cards for St. Patrick's Day and Valentine's Day are other successful renewal devices used by the group. Each card features a humorous drawing and an appropriate membership reminder. The Valentine's card, for example, shows a cover drawing of an amorous swain with an arrow through him, and the greeting, "Happy Valentine's Day to you." Inside there is a membership message and a drawing of the same swain receiving a blood transfusion. This is followed by a postscript, "Don't spoil our beautiful friendship," and a second postscript, "We need your blood."

During the rest of the year the theater conducts an ardent campaign to woo all newcomers to the community to its membership. A small brochure, "Theatre in West Texas?," which includes an exchange coupon for free attendance at one production, is mailed to new residents. For one recent production, 23 percent of the persons using the free tickets became members immediately.

Situated in a town of about 60,000 persons, the theater attracted an audience of 30,000 persons last year, and a membership of 3000.

May 1965

Date Stickers

One way an arts group can help its members to remember important dates is to send them notices typed on gummed or pressure-sensitive labels. Members can be urged to paste the labels directly on their home calendars. The organization's message can't be missed when the date of the occasion arrives.

April 1965

Block Membership

Arts councils and cultural groups that have a close relationship to other arts organizations in their community might consider a block ticket and membership offer to stimulate subscriptions. This program enables a subscriber who is a member of two or more arts groups to send in one check to cover dues or subscriptions to the various groups in which he is interested. The Greensboro Community Arts Council in North Carolina achieved up to 33 percent increase over the previous year in response to a block ticket mailing.

May-June 1964

Graduation Gifts

Recently graduated students represent an excellent and untapped area of membership potential for your organization. Now is the time to begin planning a campaign to promote memberships as meaningful and unique June graduation gifts. To highlight the promotion, consider the possibility of establishing a special new membership category at slightly reduced rates for recent graduates.

February 1964

Point of Sale

In addition to offering outlets for sales, shops run by cultural groups can promote membership in the organization. The Art Institute of Chicago used its museum store recently to house a membership display. The group promoted membership by offering a 10 percent discount on items in the store to its members. Many inquiries resulted from the display, and about 15 percent of them resulted in new memberships.

May 1965

Rewarding Members

One way to reward members of an arts organization for their loyal support is to hold a special "Two-Fer" performance in their behalf. The Old Globe Theatre in San Diego, California allowed its members to purchase two tickets for the price of one to a "members only" performance.

November 1965

New Members

The discriminating distribution through existing members of free tickets to an event can be a key to winning new members. In Binghamton, New York, for example, the Roberson Memorial Center instituted a complimentary guest slip program. In its monthly publication, the center printed a page with four guest slips so that members could share their special interest in the arts group with their guests. It advised members to fill out the slips with the name of a friend, a neighbor, or a new resident in the community, and the event he wished to attend. They were told to mail the slips back to the organization so that it could be kept informed of the number of nonpaying guests to expect at a particular event. In addition, this system alerted the center to "roll out the red carpet" for the guests invited by the member. The complimentary tickets are for events for which there would ordinarily be a charge for nonmembers.

November 1964

VOLUNTEERS

Follow Five Rules When
Using Volunteer Forces in Fund Work

The volunteer worker is the backbone of most fund-raising drives. Organizing a volunteer force for a campaign, enrolling the volunteers, and inspiring them to do an effective job calls for advance planning and plenty of hard work. Here are five basic points to remember when gearing up for a volunteer effort.

First, it is important to develop a proper relationship between the volunteers and the staff. Staff professionals may guide and advise the volunteer leaders, but basic policies should be set by the volunteer organization, not handed down by professionals. In the words of one professional fund raiser, "In a fund-raising campaign it is deadly when the volunteers are made to feel that the professional staff is running the show. It is important to indoctrinate and help train volunteer leaders at top levels so that they actually lead the remainder of the volunteer forces." Volunteer leadership will feel little responsibility for policies formulated by others.

This means that the campaign chairman should be involved from the start in all planning for the drive. The chairman must offer personal leadership. He, not the staff, should speak to volunteer meetings, outlining the "case" on which the drive is to be built, and expressing his own enthusiasm for the cause. Volunteers should have an opportunity to participate fully in these meetings. The volunteer who never meets the volunteer leadership is not likely to make an effective solicitor.

Second, when volunteers are enrolled they should know exactly what will be expected of them during the campaign. If the volunteer is expected to organize a committee, solicit in person, or carry out other functions, this should not come as a surprise to him at the last minute.

Third, during the weeks or months of the campaign, enthusiasm may easily flag. Simply reiterating that an emergency exists is not enough to keep the volunteer force working effectively. Leadership must maintain continuity of communication with the lower echelons. This means meetings, in person, with individuals or groups. It means periodic progress reports.

Fourth, meetings to which volunteers are invited should be planned carefully in advance. A dull meeting can not only kill the volunteer's spirit, but create resentment that his time is being wasted.

Fifth, it is vital to recognize and acknowledge the work of the volunteer, not merely after the campaign, but during its progress. This, too, requires advance planning.

November 1963

Training Leaders

Ask your committee chairman to train one member as a replacement before he resigns, so the new chairman will know all sides of the committee's work when he takes over. One season as trainee obviates many errors. A busy person can often be persuaded to accept a chairmanship if assured he can count on a successor after a fixed term.

June 1962

Volunteer Effort

Volunteer recruitment is a serious business for arts organizations, but one Oregon group has had success with an informal approach. The Corvallis Arts Center organized "Art Assist" last year, a loosely structured group of volunteers who help the center. Prospective members are recruited through a questionnaire which asks them to indicate their preferences among 11 general areas of help—i.e., membership drive, spring dinner, monthly receptions—and the kind and degree of involvement they'd like to have. Questionnaires emphasize the fun and informality of belonging and offer assurance that while Arts Assist members will be called on for help now and then, "this does not commit you on a regular basis unless you prefer it to be so."

November-December 1974

How to Improve
Volunteer-Staff Relationships

The following article, which has been slightly abridged, is taken from a bulletin prepared by Barnes & Roche, Inc., consultants in development planning and programs for nonprofit institutions.

When money is raised, it usually results from the combined efforts of professional staff and committed volunteers. Yet the interrelationship of volunteers and staff often is troublesome (and troubling) to both parties. Both volunteers and staff must know how and when to exert influence and *what to expect* from colleagues across the desk.

What a volunteer should expect of staff and himself:

- To have the time he is freely giving used to its best advantage, not wasted on things others can do or on unimportant tasks
- To receive from staff options and recommendations for activity, not "what should we do about this or that?" or "how should we handle this?"
- Staff member adherence to points of view the staff believes are professionally correct, notwithstanding the attitude of volunteers. (At this same

time, a volunteer should expect a staff member to be flexible and to in-
corporate the views of volunteers into the program as appropriate)

- To view the staff member as a valued professional colleague who is neither
dictated to nor put on a pedestal
- To be "programmed" by a staff member; to have his role and activities
identified and to receive all necessary background information to carry out
his responsibilities
- To be told bad news or problems (as well as good news) and involved,
when appropriate, in developing solutions
- Polite but firm pressure from a staff member to achieve objectives and to
move forward according to an agreed-upon plan
- To give the time that he commits
- To put limits on his involvement when he cannot meet his responsibilities
- To bring to his work the same level of intellectual commitment and judg-
ment he would in his own business
- To respect the individuality and style of the institution he is currently in-
volved with, and not to assume "what worked at Uptown will work at
Downtown"

What a staff member should expect of volunteers and himself:

- Volunteer creativity in addressing the programs and issues he brings before
them and not a "rubber stamp" performance. (At the same time, he
should expect the volunteers to respect his judgment and—by and large—to
accept his recommendations)
- The expectation that volunteers will be more effective if he stays in continuing contact with them and visits regularly with them. (Most volunteers—especially those at a distance—do nothing until a staff member is
enroute to see them, is with them, or has just left)
- A recognition that volunteers (no matter how involved and committed)
need continuing education. (Every staff contact should tell volunteers
more about an institution and why things are being done a particular way)
- Neither fear nor denigration of volunteers, but rather a view of them as
valued colleagues
- Awareness that volunteers want to do the right thing (as they see it) and
that, when challenged, they will respond well
- That volunteers expect to be asked the hard questions
- Recognition that volunteers have individual strengths and characteristics
which must be identified and put to special use

- Sensitivity to the personal and business priorities of volunteers which may impinge upon their ability to serve an institution. (Awareness that the staff job, however, is to keep asking for help—with sensitivity—while being certain that the things being asked for are substantive and important)
- To remember that more good volunteers are lost because too little is asked of them than too much is asked of them
- To prepare plans and guidelines for volunteers so they can react to specifics, not generalities
- To view himself as a member of a team, and give public credit to volunteers for successful programs
- To provide not just service but leadership—providing options for activity, setting a positive and forthright atmosphere, and creating confidence in his judgment and the program that is being carried out
- To have free access to volunteers and assurance that all contacts with them are productive and professional

All human interrelationships depend upon the nature of the personalities involved. Within the framework of known expectations, these personalities can—and do—work together in harmony and enjoyment in advancing the aims of private institutions.

Summer 1978

Hundreds of Volunteer Workers
Help Make Fund Event a Success

Viewed as either a fund-raising or "fun-raising" event, the annual Cast Party Festival of Young Friends of City Center is a huge success. A pre-Christmas fixture for the past four years, the festival, a combination carnival-bazaar-entertainment organized and conducted by volunteers, has increased in scope, attendance, popularity, and profitability each year. Moreover, unlike many other charity events, it has achieved its success with an "open door" policy that keeps admission down to $3 per person. This year's event, held at the New York State Theater between 5:00 and 10:00 P.M. on December 5, drew over 3000 people and raised more than $21,000—a 50 percent increase over last year—for City Center's educational programs and member companies.

The only event in which all the center's constituents participate, the festival is a six-month planning effort that draws on the involvement of nearly 400 volunteer members of Young Friends, City Center's supportive guild of men and women 40 years old and younger. The festival engenders so much excitement that this summer and fall nearly 100 people paid membership dues of $15 and up to join Young Friends and participate in the effort.

Serious planning for the December festival began June 1 with the selection of four cochairmen and 21 committee chairmen responsible for such activities as handicrafts, tickets, artist participation, security, and finance. Chairmen were also named for festival booths of such center constituents as the New York City Opera, the Alvin Ailey and Joffrey dance companies, the New York City Ballet, and the Young People's Theater. During the summer chairmen concentrated on planning and began to solicit donations of merchandise for resale and for raffle prizes. In September, at a general meeting, chairmen explained committee work and recruited members.

Throughout October and November, committees were deeply involved in their special areas and in acquiring merchandise. The entertainment committee worked out performance plans with each City Center company, and the manpower committee organized a plan to divide the 400 volunteers into three two-hour shifts. Weekly handicraft sessions attracted groups of 20 to 40 volunteers who made hundreds of items for sale at the festival.

Meanwhile, as donated goods arrived at the Friends' office, volunteers sorted and priced them, generally at one-third less than retail. (Goods valued at $28,000 were donated for resale, and $12,00 worth of goods was donated for the raffle.) Finally, a week prior to the event a full meeting of all the committees was held.

On festival day—the only date in the entire year when the State Theater was dark and all the City Center companies were available in the city—a group of volunteers arrived early to set up and decorate the booths and display the merchandise. Since the theater was being readied for the City Ballet's *Nutcracker* opening in two days, the promenade floor became the main festival area, complete with carnival games, booths for autographs, photographs, raffles, and one booth for each of the center's constituents. The two balcony rings above had booths selling food, clothing, books, records, and costumes.

An hour prior to the 5:00 P.M. opening, the transformation was complete, and the first volunteers' shift reported to a check-in area, received identification badges, and went to their booths. The "Cast Party" theme was visible everywhere. Instead of numbers, a "Repertoire Roulette" wheel of fortune featured *Manon, Astarte, Cry,* and *Carmen.* "On Your Toes" participants tried to toss rings around ballet slippers, and "Hit the High Note" players threw balls through the mouths of cardboard opera characters. Performers from Joffrey, Ailey, and other center companies manned booths along with volunteers and signed autographs. Throughout the evening, entertainment floated down to the promenade from the second balcony. Occasionally an off-beat performance was presented—dancer John Clifford of the New York City Ballet delighted attendees by singing Gershwin songs.

Special care was taken to avoid problems. To keep money handling at a minimum, purchases were not paid for directly, but were tallied on a list which indicated item, price, and the booth at which it was bought. At special check-out desks, partygoers paid for all their purchases. At locations where money was used—games, food areas, and raffle booths—cash was collected regularly by authorized workers.

According to Young Friends chairman Mrs. Stanley Nelson, the festival brought City Center performers much closer to the public. "Some artists even baked cakes and made handicrafts," she said. "Also, planning the event helped us develop a cohesive group which is involved in all our activities."

November-December 1972

National Volunteer Center Offers Arts Aid

Arts groups interested in expanding their volunteer programs or learning more about successful volunteer projects elsewhere have a relatively new national organization ready to provide these and other services to them without charge. The National Center for Voluntary Action in Washington, D.C., which serves as a coordinating body for the field of volunteer activity, is interested in increasing its service to the arts.

"We hope the arts will regard us as a resource," David Jeffreys, the center's vice-president for organizational resources, told *AM*. "To date, our organization's main involvement has been with national and local organizations in the area of social concerns. However, we've received some intriguing examples of how the arts have used volunteers. We'd appreciate receiving more."

The examples of volunteer activity are a key resource of the center's clearinghouse, which disseminates material and information. Some 4000 case histories have been digested and catalogued, and when requests for information are received they are answered with appropriate samples. Because case histories are written by the organizations themselves, they vary in length and detail, although nearly all are brief.

Those wishing more detailed information are provided with names of people to contact and published material to read. A "Green Sheet" published by the clearinghouse includes information on organizations involved in various aspects of the human and social service fields and lists films, pamphlets, and published material relating to all aspects of volunteerism. The clearinghouse service is available free of charge to any group or individual. Requests may be made by mail, phone or personal visit to the clearinghouse.

The center also publishes a newsletter, *Voluntary Action News*, and makes speakers available at no fee. Of potential help to arts groups are the local Voluntary Action Centers which are designed to identify a community's needs and recruit and train volunteers to meet those needs.

Summer 1971

Buddy System

A core of experienced volunteer solicitors can be built by using the "buddy system." An old member takes a new one first to a friendly contributor, then to at
least one who is known to be skeptical. After seeing how the old hand deals with
both types, the beginner is better prepared to make calls on her own. The
League of Women Voters in Hutchinson, Kansas has found this team system
highly effective both in the amount of money raised and number of solicitors
taking part.

December 1962

Volunteers Can Perform
Highly Specialized Work

Cultural organizations have a better chance of finding and keeping skilled volunteers if they program in advance to utilize the talents they discover. The Brooklyn Children's Museum in Brooklyn, New York, recently faced with a critical
need for gallery guides, lecturers, teaching assistants, library assistants, and specialists in classifying and cataloguing objects, based a volunteer appeal upon a
prearranged program, and the results were outstanding. Little more than a
month after the appeal was first issued, 19 volunteers, each with a college background and a professional skill in a definite area, were at work.

In January 1963 the museum's staff issued press releases describing the
skills needed and specifically outlining the duties of volunteers. A fact sheet for
volunteers had been prepared and arrangements made for training them under
staff curators. More than 100 inquiries resulted from news stories about the
museum's needs, and 38 people turned out for the first of a series of orientation
classes. By the end of the orientation period, 19 especially capable men and
women remained. Although it was the original intention of the museum to use
volunteers only on Saturdays, the response was so favorable and the calibre of
those remaining in the program so high that the program was expanded to weekdays also.

Among the volunteers now being used by the museum are an anthropolo-
gist, a public relations executive who is cataloging the museum collection, and a
history teacher who is assisting the curator of the cultural history department at
the museum. In addition, because two capable volunteers are now available,
children once forced to admire objects through glass cases can take them out and
handle them.

Because of the program's success, the museum is now considering using
volunteer workers during the summer. In September, the entire program will be
enlarged and additional skilled volunteers will be recruited.

Mrs. Nancy Paine, coordinator of special activities for the museum, is delighted at the volunteer response and believes that careful planning was responsi-

ble for the success of the campaign. "I would urge that any organization facing a similar need for volunteers with special skills have a definite idea in advance of how they would use the people they find."

April 1963

Volunteer Support a
Key to Successful Festival

An annual arts festival, which has grown in 11 years from a backyard affair attracting 1700 visitors to an event that expects some 250,000 visitors this year, has discovered the keys to its success in flexibility, good organization, and unusual volunteer dedication.

The Atlanta Arts Festival, which will be held in Piedmont Park, Atlanta, Georgia from May 24-31 this year, is an eight-day outdoor event that includes both the visual and the performing arts. Featured performing groups this year include the Atlanta Symphony Orchestra, three Atlanta theater companies, all ballet and modern dance groups in the city, and the performing arts departments of three local colleges. Eminent professional artists will exhibit at an invited show, and amateur and professional artists alike may purchase display space for $5 for an open show.

A nonprofit voluntary organization, the festival operates on an annual budget of $25,000, compared to $327 during its first year. Receipts include about $13,000 from an annual fund-raising campaign, $4500 from individual and family memberships, a $3000 grant from the city of Atlanta, $2500 from a 20 percent commission on all sales made during the festival, and $2000 from exhibition fees and program sales. In addition, the city of Atlanta contributes the park area where the festival is held.

Organization of the festival is virtually a full-time project. A 45-member board of trustees meets monthly, except during July and August, to plan policy. An executive committee operates and directs the festival activities within the framework. Committee chairmen and the excutive committee are rotated annually. According to Mrs. Alvin M. Ferst, Jr., chairman of the board, "The festival is structured so responsibilities are clear-cut without being confining. Bylaws, standing rules and organizational charts are guides rather than a rigid framework."

The planning of each new festival begins shortly after the conclusion of the old one. In June, committee chairmen report to the board of trustees on all facets of the recently concluded festival operation, and the advisory committee evaluates the festival as a whole. During the early fall months, committee chairmen are appointed and tentative fund-raising plans are discussed. By December, festival dates are definitely set, a budget is presented and approved, and committee chairmen report to the board on progress made in such areas as art placement, scholarships, membership, fund raising, etc. The annual sustaining fund drive, held in February, has been carefully planned in advance, and by January members are recruited to act as volunteer solicitors. From March on, after the completion of the fund drive, each of the 41 committees active in the conduct of the festival moves at an accelerated pace until it opens in May.

Because the festival is a mammoth undertaking conducted without paid staff, extraordinary volunteer support is necessary for it to be successful. Thus, more than 1000 volunteers, representing every segment of the community, work on it. Artists, in addition to exhibiting, often serve on committees throughout the entire year, and businessmen, who manage the organization's budget, are frequently craftsmen and amateur artists who display at the festival. A majority of the original founders are still active in festival work, and organizational leaders estimate that well over 50 percent of all the volunteers have been associated with the festival for more than five years.

One volunteer leader who has been with the Atlanta Arts Festival for several years attributes the success of the volunteer program to the fact that full participation in it is open to anyone. "Unlike many other cultural organizations in Atlanta," she told *AM*, "we don't attract the dilettantes and debutantes. We do attract those people who have a sincere appreciation for the arts and want to bring enjoyment of the arts to other people."

April 1964

Volunteers Play
New Role in Fund Campaign

To ease the strain on volunteer solicitors who ring doorbells in its annual fundraising campaign, an arts council in Binghamton, New York is trying an unusual experiment. The Roberson Memorial Center has enrolled nearly 100 women to serve as "secretaries" or assistants during its united fund drive which runs from April 18 through April 23. The campaign goal is set at $61,650.

Each of the secretaries will be working with four or five male volunteers, business and professional men, who will be doing the actual solicitation of funds. The women will confirm appointments, make sure that their "bosses" have all the necessary campaign materials with them when they visit prospects, and prepare written reports both during the drive and after it ends.

According to Keith Martin, director of the center, the new approach will not only free solicitors from routine duties, but will ensure the best use of female volunteers. "Many women never participated in fund drives because they were reticent to ask for money," Mr. Martin told *AM*. "As secretaries, they can still become totally involved in the fund campaign without ever actually leaving the office." Mr. Martin pointed out that a number of the women have previously been volunteer workers in other phases of the council's program.

Prior to the start of the campaign, the secretaries have been attending preliminary meetings where their duties have been explained. In addition, small groups of them have been meeting informally with their future bosses to establish rapport.

April 1966

Summer Opera Plans Thoroughly, Starts Early

Year-round planning, the enlistment of a small army of volunteer workers, community fund-raising, and tight control over expenditures are all part of the system under which the Central City Opera Festival in Colorado has become a standout summer success.

The festival, in the mountain mining town an hour's drive west of Denver, is held in the old Central City Opera House, an ornate relic of the gold-mining days, now owned by the University of Denver. The opera program of two alternating productions lasts through July, and is followed by a Broadway play suitable for summer entertainment.

The festival is organized by a community association that involves some 500 people in the work of nearly 40 volunteer committees in which places are filled by invitation. Because it is now an established tradition, the festival is supported by many who have learned the ropes of committee work through the years. And local business values the festival as a strong summer tourist attraction to the Denver area.

Robert Brown, general manager of the festival association, adheres to a firm policy of pegging ticket prices to production costs. Admission price is fixed on the basis that a complete sellout covers 67 percent of the festival costs, the other 33 percent being raised by a financial drive in the greater Denver area and nearby towns. The drive is handled entirely by mail.

Brown establishes a realistic budget, allocating costs in the following proportion: artists—25 percent; orchestra—25 percent; stagehands—30 percent; administration—10 percent; and costumes—10 percent. Brown insists that he must be "ruthless about this budget" because there is very little room for maneuver on the revenue side once the total plan is made up.

The association starts early and works systematically around the calendar. Here is its schedule: September—select production for the following season; October—close books and prepare to audit; November through January—begin engaging cast, orchestra, directors, and designers; February—engage all staff members and begin financial campaign; March—start publicity campaign; April—get volunteer committees to work; May—open ticket sales; June—stars arrive and festival opens.

June 1962

Explanation for Husbands

The husband of a volunteer worker in the arts can either encourage his wife's efforts or, if he knows little about the value of his wife's work, he can object strenuously to the time she gives. An informal supper for husbands sponsored by the women's committee can serve as an occasion at which the group's work is explained and awards for achievement are given out. At one such function in Highland Park, Illinois, 200 people attended and the husbands picked up the tab.

November 1962

Political Clubs

A local political club may be a good source of volunteer aid or program support. In New York, for example, the Ansonia Democratic Club formed an arts committee which has sponsored cultural events and helped local arts groups.

October 1965

Building a Library

Finding it difficult to keep up with everything written about the arts? Afraid you might miss a relevant article in a magazine not specifically concerned with culture? Ask your members to help you. The resource file of Allied Arts of Seattle has grown substantially, thanks to organizational members who have volunteered to clip newspapers and magazines for articles on arts issues and on the environment.

January-February 1971

Volunteer Deductions

When income tax deadline time approaches it's a good idea to let your volunteers know that they're allowed to deduct out-of-pocket expenses incurred in helping you—provided, of course, that they can substantiate the expenses. For travel to and from meetings or other volunteer activities, the IRS permits deductions to cover gas, tolls, and parking fees.

January-February 1973

Retired Executives
Aid Cultural Organizations

The retired executive can perform many useful volunteer tasks for cultural organizations. However, most cultural organizations do not have a systematic way to reach these individuals and, even on finding them, have no programs that can take full advantage of their skills.

In New York an educational program started by a college last year is not only keeping retired professionals active and busy, but is also providing cultural and other nonprofit groups with the use of "students" in key volunteer capacities. At the New School for Social Research, the Institute for Retired Professionals has enrolled more than 400 retired men and women in a program of classes and cultural activities. A part of the institute, its Community Service Committee seeks outlets through which institute members, retired teachers, business executives, musicians, lawyers, artists, and others may use their skills to assist other people. The committee invites requests from organizations seeking the free voluntary services of its members.

According to Hyman Hirsch, chairman of the institute, "This kind of program is important because it taps the resources of people who are retired, but who can remain culturally alert. Retired people are looking for opportunities to do something of significance, and, if they are presented with the right kind of program, they will respond."

Mr. Hirsch told *AM* that he believes a program similar to that created at the institute can work in other cities, provided that it begins on a smaller scale.

April 1964

Key Programs of Junior League
Now Oriented to Needs of Arts

Volunteer support, administrative help, and financial assistance are the essential ingredients of a widespread program in the arts sponsored by the Association of the Junior Leagues of America, Inc. According to Mrs. L. R. Breslin, Jr., the association's arts consultant, the volunteer organization of young women now supports more activities in the arts than in any other area. Last year it invested $668,256 in support of 538 arts projects involving 8,759 league volunteers.

In Buffalo, New York, for example, the local league is now launching an audience development program for the city's new professional resident theater company, the Studio Arena Theatre. Here, as in many of its projects, a good portion of the league's financial assistance will be invested in the salary of a professional to supervise the project. An audience development expert, who will soon begin working with the theater, will be paid from the league's $8500 project allotment.

As part of the Buffalo project, league volunteers also will administer an annual college undergraduate production and two annual meetings involving community theater leaders and English teachers.

In Jackson, Mississippi, the Junior League organized the first Mississippi Arts Festival, held last year, and invested $5000 in it. Volunteers helped book major attractions, and promoted the festival concept to community service organizations, schools, businesses, and the press throughout the state. The league supported this year's recently-ended festival as well. In line with the league's philosophy of administering a project until its support is no longer essential, it will turn over the entire festival package to an independent organization of local and state cultural leaders following the 1967 festival season.

Community arts councils have been continuing beneficiaries of league activity. Since the end of World War II, the organization has played major roles in the founding and development of approximately 30 councils, including the first two in this hemisphere—in Winston-Salem, North Carolina and Vancouver, B.C., Canada.

In San Antonio, Texas, for example, the local league helped to organize a council in 1961 and worked with the fledgling group until last year, when the council was strong enough to exist without league support. League assistance included an initial survey of the community's cultural resources, the development of a master mailing list and addressing service in cooperation with local arts groups, the publication of a calendar of events in two Sunday newspapers, and a financial investment totaling $10,000. A team of six league volunteers worked on the project over a three-year period. Further developments have included: creation of a Fine Arts Commission by city ordinance, publication of a monthly arts magazine, and plans for an arts festival.

Other league arts programs over the years have included such varied activities as providing guided museum tours for the schools, undertaking public education programs, producing booklets and films, conducting historical surveys, and initiating children's concert programs. One of its major achievements was the conception and implementation of a long-range program to establish the Arkansas Arts Center in Little Rock.

How can arts organizations take advantage of Junior League services? According to Mrs. Breslin, a cultural group should write to its local Junior League outlining its specific areas of need. "Projects are undertaken," Mrs. Breslin told *AM,* "only after comprehensive research has established the validity of a need, the best means for filling it, and the community's ability to maintain and continue to develop the new or extended service after it has been brought to maturity."

May 1966

Winning Workers

A special "Volunteers Night" is one method of attracting new volunteer workers. Ask each of your present volunteers to invite one or two of their friends to attend such a session at your institution. Then, have a special program at which the work of the organization is explained by one of its leaders and each of the volunteer chairmen talks briefly about the work of her committee and answers questions from the audience. A tour of the institution or a short program of entertainment might then follow.

February 1964

Men Wanted?

Want to interest men in your organization? The Junior Women's Committee of the Art Gallery of Toronto sponsors regularly scheduled special luncheons "for men only" during the normal working week. The same institution also reaches men at Family Nights, which begin with supper served from 5:45 to 7:15 P.M. and feature continuous showings of art films, tours of the gallery, and informal family drawing sessions.

May-June 1964

Area Representatives

Do you want to attract audiences from nearby communities? You might consider appointing volunteers from these communities to serve as your on-the-spot representatives. The Milwaukee Repertory Theater recently organized a Radius Committee composed of volunteers from 19 cities within a 100-mile radius of Milwaukee, Wisconsin. Volunteers provide publicity materials to media in their communities, arrange for local presentations by the theater's staff, stimulate ticket purchases, and distribute posters and brochures to businesses and organizations.

Summer 1967

Volunteer Exchange

If a volunteer project falls at a time when it's difficult to attract a sufficient number of your own workers, it may be worthwhile to suggest a volunteer exchange with other organizations. Under this arrangement, their workers may assist your organization on one project, and your volunteers will assist them on one of theirs. Aside from developing a rapport between the organizations, volunteers might welcome the change.

October 1963

College Students Ring Bell

Need doorbell ringers for fund raising? One group seldom tapped, is the arts-oriented college student. At Brooklyn College recently, a coed organized a committee of students to engage in a fund-raising campaign for a local cultural group. Chairmen of music, art, drama, or dance departments can be helpful in supplying a list of interested students, and some may even make announcements in class or post a notice on the department bulletin board.

September 1962

Promotional Help

Youngsters can help to promote cultural events. In New York, the Nassau County Regional Arts Center increased attendance substantially at its Sunday in the Park Arts Festival this summer by having children distribute promotional materials on the event to adults attending Little League baseball games in the park.

October 1965

Rewarding Volunteers

Public recognition of the contributions made by your volunteers may give them special incentives to renew their efforts in your behalf. In Chicago, the Ravinia Festival presents "Howie" awards annually (named in honor of the group's first sustaining fund drive chairman) to the top ten fund raisers on its sustaining fund committee. Special awards have been given for those who've served on the committee for a decade.

November-December 1975

The Extra Hour

The hour saved when Daylight Savings Time ends may be put to good use by an enterprising arts organization. Tell your volunteers and members that your group would appreciate one extra hour of help from each of them so that important projects may be completed. Suggest that they donate the hour at a time when they won't miss it—after they turn their clocks back.

October 1964

Attracting Volunteers

One way to recruit volunteers to your organization is to reward them with free membership privileges. With this inducement, the Museum of the City of New York recently recruited more than 90 volunteer tour guides, information desk, and museum shop assistants. In addition to receiving full privileges of museum membership, which includes a 10 percent discount at the shop, invitations to museum events and previews, and discounts on tours and workshops, the volunteers are treated to a series of monthly evening programs featuring guest speakers, discussions, and refreshments.

December 1965

Volunteer Recognition

Volunteers for a cultural organization's fund-raising campaign should receive recognition for their efforts. One means of doing this is to send them an inexpensive gift at the end of a campaign. The Chicago Heart Association thanked its 30,000 volunteers for their direct solicitation work by sending each one a plastic bookmark. The marker was enclosed in a folder which simply said "in appreciation" and was signed by the organization's president.

June 1965

Sense of Participation

Members and volunteers in a fund-raising drive can be given an extra charge of interest by being invited to a private affair. For some years the National Symphony Orchestra in Washington, D. C. has invited sustaining fund workers to a rehearsal on the eve of the drive. "It makes them go out of the hall with a sense of participation," an orchestra spokesman says.

March 1962

ARTS ADMINISTRATION AND TRAINING

Study Cites Need for Management Training

Strong administrative leadership in the arts is lacking, cultural groups experience difficulty in finding qualified managers, professional college training programs for arts administrators are not available, and the salaries for arts administrators are not competitive with comparable positions in other nonprofit fields. Furthermore, unless training and experience needs are met very soon, the administration of arts organizations and programs will stay at a doubtful status quo—or may even regress.

These are among the key conclusions reached in a comprehensive study of future administrative needs in the arts, limited to New York State, but with implications for arts groups throughout the nation. Prepared for the New York State Council on the Arts by consultant George Alan Smith, the report is based on a questionnaire-survey of arts groups in New York (189 of 338 groups responding), supplemented by the author's personal interviews with arts and civic leaders in the state's major cities. The answers to three basic questions were posed: what job opening in arts administration now exist; what openings will become available; and what were the necessary qualifications and experience for these positions.

According to report findings, there are now 58 arts administration positions open in New York State at an average starting salary of $11,157. Within the next three to five years, an additional 151 positions will become available at an average salary of about $9000. Of the respondents who gave reasons for jobs going unfilled, 87 cited budgetary limitations as the prime factor, and 23 indicated that there was a lack of trained personnel. In answer to a separate question, 79 percent indicated that an adequate reservoir of administrative personnel for the arts does not exist.

Another section of the report, devoted to arts administration in education, revealed that within the next three to five years there will be 66 positions open a at colleges and universities, including 15 now unfilled, at an average annual salary of about $13,000. Budget limitations and a lack of recognition that administrative personnel were required were cited as prime reasons for the gap. In this area respondents also felt that there was an inadequate pool of trained administrators. Interestingly, responding arts groups indicated that they would prefer administrators without an arts background to artists with administrative potential to fill upcoming positions. Educational institutions took the opposite position.

Parallel investigations by arts consultant Smith pinpointed the national need for administrative programs. "Across the country," he said, "there are virtually no structured programs over a continuum in higher education directed to arts administration. . . . The clear and over-riding conclusion, therefore, is that a sizeable commitment is needed now to attract young people to the profession of arts administration and to prepare them for it."

Mr. Smith concluded his report with the recommendations that the New York State Council on the Arts lend financial aid to organizations needing qualified administrators but lacking the resources to hire them, that the council commission a study to define arts administration, identify criteria, and develop a pilot arts administration curriculum; and that the council provide support to universities and colleges in the state willing to offer this curriculum experimentally.

Summer 1968

Former Ford Interns
Win Key Management Posts

Since the Ford Foundation initiated its Program for Administrative Interns in 1961 to help train and develop administrators for the performing arts, it has underwritten fellowships for 71 men and women as full-time, on-the-job trainees with professional performing arts institutions. In some instances, the twelve-month fellowships were renewed for a second or even a third year, accounting for a total of 101 awarded.

Recently, the foundation increased the annual fellowship stipend to $6500. Extra allowances of $1000 for married fellows and $500 for each dependent child were also authorized. According to Mrs. Marcia Thompson, a program officer in the Ford Foundation's Division of Humanities and the Arts, "It would have been impractical to raise the stipend earlier because some of the fellows might then have earned more than the administrators they were working for. Happily, salaries in the field have since increased."

In an attempt to determine the program's success, *AM* reviewed a status report on the current [1969] activities of the 71 interns accepted into the program since it began. Thirty-nine interned with theaters, 20 with symphony orchestras, 10 with opera companies, and 2 with dance companies.

Of the 71 interns, 51 are currently employed in some capacity in the arts, including 5 who are still interning. Twenty-nine are presently working as administrators in the specific area in which they apprenticed, and 13 are administrators with other kinds of art groups. Four former interns are working in such related fields as theater criticism, production, and theater technology. One maintains a vicarious involvement with arts administration through her marriage to an orchestra manager.

The 20 former Ford Foundation interns no longer involved in the arts include four now working in the educational field as either teachers or administrators, and six currently inactive. The employment status of ten others is unknown, although several of them held positions as arts administrators following completion of their internship.

A study of the status report indicates that a little training can be a valuable asset to the job-seeker in the arts. Although 20 of the 71 withdrew from the program prior to completing internships, 17 did so to accept managerial positions with arts organizations. Currently, top positions in arts administration are held by many former interns. Ten serve either as managing directors or general managers of professional theater companies, six are orchestra managers, four are directors or coordinators of large arts centers, one is an arts council director, and one is manager of an opera company.

The intern selection process begins with the Ford Foundation soliciting nominations from arts leaders several months prior to the January 31 deadline. The number of those solicited has grown steadily each year, reaching 800 this year. Candidates are then asked to provide background information and a statement of interest for screening by a panel. Prime candidates are interviewed by foundation representatives and by those arts groups where internship may be provided.

Interestingly, between 1962 and 1967, the number of interns selected annually diminished. In 1962, for example, 22 interns were selected from 171 nominations. The figures in following years were: 1963, 99 nominations and 27 fellowships; 1964, 86 nominations and 24 fellowships; 1965, 119 nominations and 13 fellowships; 1966, 131 nominations and 8 fellowships; and in 1967, 120 nominations and 5 fellowships. Asked to explain the decline, Mrs. Thompson told *AM*, "The program has become more selective, and we're now aiming for candidates who, in time, can become principal spokesmen for the arts. Also, the nature of the field has changed with the advent of many new arts organizations, all seeking administrators, and people with a minimum of experience can and do find jobs. We're interested in candidates with a deep-rooted and long-range interest in the field who recognize the value of internship training."

Although Mrs. Thompson thinks that the program has been an effective one, and will continue indefinitely, she mentioned the difficulty in selecting the arts institutions with which the interns train. "We evaluate arts groups," she added, "with the same care with which we evaluate candidates. Too few groups, however, have both the capacity and the willingness to train interns."

January-February 1968

CHRONOLOGICAL DEVELOPMENTS IN MANAGEMENT TRAINING

In January 1971, Hyman R. Faine became the full-time director of the graduate arts administration program at UCLA (he served as a visiting regents professor in the program from January to June 1970) and assumed what is believed to be the nation's first regular professorship in the field of arts administration. Within coming weeks Norman Kaderlan, recently named supervisor of performing arts for Arlington County, Virginia will receive America's first Ph.D. in arts administration from the University of Wisconsin. Elsewhere, there are other positive developments, including the initiation of a new graduate training program for arts managers at Drexel University in Philadelphia.

Faine's appointment as adjunct professor of arts administration in the Graduate School of Business Administration marks a permanent commitment to the program by UCLA. The program has been additionally strengthened by a substantial grant given it by Lloyd E. Rigler, president of Adolph's, a business concern.

The fourteen students currently entered in the program, including three of its original enrollees, are averaging about 14 hours of class per quarter and supplement their three or four courses with three-month internships during the fall quarter of the second year or during the preceding summer. Interestingly, such courses as "Environment of the Arts World" and "Programming Policies of Arts Institutions" are attracting students from other university departments, and a number of young law students have suggested that law and arts administration be combined into a single four-year program. In addition to its courses, the program currently has ten research projects funded and underway and hopes to develop an arts executives training program featuring short courses for cultural administrators.

The graduate arts administration program at the University of Wisconsin, under the direction of Professor E. Arthur Prieve in the School of Business, is also making considerable progress. In addition to the Ph.D. to be awarded Kaderlan, at least two students should receive arts administration M.A.s by this June. Last semester, the seven enrolled students gave special attention to publications in the arts, and this semester, with several new students added, the seminar program will focus on such areas as contracts, promotion, and fund raising. Currently students are interning with such groups as the Milwaukee Repertory Theater, the Wisconsin Arts Council, and the university's own office of arts programs.

Arts administration training with a more commercial orientation is proving successful at the University of Miami. The School of Music offers an undergraduate program leading to a degree in music merchandising—a field encompassing publishing, recording, copyright, teaching, performing, musical promotion, and musical instruments. The program, in which 21 students are currently enrolled, provides internships for all students during the final semester of their senior years. According to Alfred Reed, the program's director, "every intern thus far has been hired by the firm in which he worked, and I have more calls for interns than I can possibly fill in the immediate future."

January-February 1971

Among key developments in arts management training are the introduction of new programs and the continued growth and development of existing ones. Harvard University's second annual Summer School Institute in Arts Administration, for example, held this July, again attracted capacity enrollment, including a number of students from Europe and Asia. Just published is the Institute's *Cases in Arts Administration.*

Programs to be initiated this fall include NYU's School of Education's one-year M.A. in performing arts administration and Southern Methodist University's two-year M.A. program in arts administration, a combined effort of its School of Business and Meadows School of Art.

Elsewhere, business school interest in arts administration continues. At the University of Utah, the College of Business is cooperating with the theater department in offering an M.F.A. program in management, and at Rollins College the theater arts department and Crummer School of Finance and Business Administration are offering an M.A. in performing arts management. At the University of Santa Clara, the School of Business initiated a new undergraduate course in management and the arts during the last quarter as a precursor to a possible program.

An important spur to the arts management training movement was a two-day conference at York University in Ontario, Canada, several months ago, which brought together representatives of programs at York, UCLA, Harvard, Yale, and the University of Toronto. Commenting on the meetings, D. Paul Schafer, the director of York's arts management and administration program said, in part, "It was felt that case study research was necessary at one level, but that some of the research should be directed towards broader issues such as international and continental cultural policies, shifts in arts patronage, and trends in the arts. It was felt that attempts should be made to relate the development of programs in arts management and administration to the general trends and changes that are taking place in the arts in North America today."

Summer 1971

In Toronto, Ryerson Polytechnical Institute introduced a four-year arts administration program this fall as one of the major areas in its newly-established theater department. New university courses being introduced elsewhere this semester include: performing arts management in Ohio State's theater department, arts administration at American University's business administration school, and business problems of the film and entertainment industries at the New School for Social Research in New York.

January-February 1972

New programs at the graduate level have been launched at several universities. At Golden Gate University in San Francisco, the program in Arts Administration is offering the first of its six three-credit graduate level seminars this semester within the University's Graduate School of Business Administration. At Drexel University's Institute for Urban Management in Philadelphia, the graduate arts administration program announced last fall has finally gotten under way. To be eligible for either of the above programs applicants must have an accredited undergraduate degree.

September-October 1972

The Banff Centre's new Cultural Resources Management Program in Banff, Canada becomes fully operational this March when George Moore assumes its direction. Beginning with a two-week-long executive development course in March, the program will conduct a continuing series of short courses and symposia throughout the year. Upcoming events include three-day seminars on cultural resources marketing in April, and financial matters and taxation in May. Two-week programs in commercial art gallery management and performing arts management are scheduled for June, and a six-week program in festival management will be held this summer. As the program develops, 500 to 600 people are expected to participate annually in some aspect of it.

January-February 1973

The proliferating graduate degree programs in arts administration—some 15 have been established within the past four years—have varied widely from school to school in terms of approach, curriculum, kind and lengths of internships, the use of visiting experts, and the aegis under which they've been presented. Now, in an attempt to examine those differences and assess strengths and weaknesses, the University of Utah, with support from the William H. Donner Foundation, has undertaken a full-scale study of existing graduate arts administration programs.

Between now and this June, Douglas Richards, former director of Performing Arts and Public Media at the National Endowment for the Arts, will be visiting such institutions as Yale, UCLA, Wisconsin, and York and speaking to scores of arts administrators. An ultimate study aim is the development of a new program with a model curriculum to be introduced at Utah in the fall of 1975. Although that program will not be finally structured until the study is complete, initial plans call for a primary faculty composed of the administrative heads of such Salt Lake City cultural groups as Ballet West, the Utah Symphony, and the Pioneer Memorial Theater. Also, students would receive a stipend to allow them to concentrate on their studies. Hopefully, the study will produce curricular guidelines and recommendations on key program aspects for general use.

Meanwhile, another study of existing programs with a somewhat different approach has just been completed. Leslie Wyatt, assistant to the dean of the College of Fine Arts at the University of Texas at Austin, has written a 160-page report,"A Status Study of Curricula for Fine Arts Administration in North America," which analyzes existing programs to determine their adequacy in training students for arts administration positions with institutions of higher education. Mr. Wyatt's report, which contains useful comparative data on the different programs, was his doctoral dissertation study.

New graduate degree programs continue to be developed. This summer the State University of New York at Binghamton will initiate its new two-year M.B.A. in the Arts program. Offered by the School of Management in conjunction with the departments of theater, music, art, and art history, the program will provide a sequence of integrated subjects in seven-and-a-half-week minisemesters, with the first four months of the second year devoted to an arts internship. In addition to its core M.B.A. program, workshops with invited guest lecturers and six specially designed arts courses will be offered. Another institution, Texas Tech at Lubbock, has enrolled its first Ph.D. candidate in fine arts with a concentration in arts administration.

November-December 1973

College and university interest in arts management training continues to accelerate. The recent Donner Foundation survey of arts administration training listed 11 graduate arts administration programs as fully operational by the fall of 1974 with an additional 15 in the planning or scheduled stage. The list is still growing and it is estimated that by the 1980s 200 students a year will graduate from these programs. More significant than numerical growth, however, is the fact that existing programs are taking a careful look at their efforts to date—the field is less than a decade old—in an attempt to strengthen programs and determine future directions.

Recent impetus to the movement was provided by the National Endowment for the Arts, which initiated and sponsored an arts administration educators conference in mid-October. The more than 70 participants, including representatives of 31 different colleges and universities with existing or planned arts management programs, endowment staff members, outside resource people, and arts administrators spent a day and a half discussing such key areas of concern as curriculum, research, financial support, administrative support, career opportunities, and future directions. Because the conference was a first—a much smaller meeting of then existing programs was held at Sangammon State in 1974—there was no attempt to develop a consensus on major issues. However, there were recurrent themes running throughout the conference, including the need for massive gathering and dissemination of data on new developments and employment prospects, finding ways to broaden internship opportunities, a greater emphasis on marketing as a tool, providing students with realistic appraisals of job opportunities, greater use of intensive short term training programs, and a desire by those in the field to work together more closely in the future.

The general feeling that a cautious and carefully considered approach is necessary to the development of new programs was reflected in activities at several colleges represented at the conference. Both the University of Utah and the University of Cincinnati, whose programs were scheduled to be introduced this fall, have put off their opening until September 1976. Other schools with new programs in developmental stages but no definite beginning date as yet include SUNY at Albany, the University of Maryland, Baruch College of the City University of New York, and SUNY at Buffalo. Elsewhere, Northern Arizona University has introduced a two-year B.S. program in creative arts management; Adelphi University has just started a series of community seminars and credit courses under its new director of arts management programs, *AM* editor Alvin H. Reiss; Evergreen State College is introducing a contract/internship program in arts management; and Texas Tech is considering but is not yet committed to introducing an emphasis in arts administration in its Ph.D. program in fine arts.

September-October 1975

Masters degree programs in museum studies have been introduced recently at Lone Mountain College in San Francisco and at the University of Toronto, the latter in association with the Royal Ontario Museum. Somewhat unique is the Canadian Museums Association's basic correspondence course in museology, at $30, for volunteers and inexperienced workers in established museums.

Management internship opportunities are growing. Continuing-three month summer programs include the National Arts Endowment's $1950 work-experience internship and the North Carolina Arts Council's $1500 program involving one month's work in each of three community arts councils in the state. Pilot programs include a six-month Museum Minority Training Program at New York's American Museum of Natural History and the Texas Historical Commission's one-year museum internship program designed specifically to train directors of smaller museums.

Among developments of national interest is a new program designed to train staff and board members of state arts commissions. With the aid of an $82,600 grant from the Donner Foundation, the Western States Arts Foundation is initiating a new Skills Development Institute to serve states in its region. Meanwhile, the Task Force on the Certification of Arts Administrators, headed by Raymond C. Mesler, Jr., of the Tampa-Hillsborough County Arts Council, is progressing towards its goal of presenting a proposal for the certification of arts administrators by May 1976. Largely working through the mails—a meeting attended by some 50 people was held in Ottawa in January—the group has solicited responses to key questions involving such areas as definition of an arts administrator, need for certification, current practises in the field, the meaning of professionalism, including possible code of ethics and individual rights. Upcoming considerations include possible benefits such as pensions, types of accrediation, and alternatives to accreditation for administrators.

January-February 1976

Two graduate degree programs in arts administration are about to step up their activities. In Salt Lake City, the University of Utah, thanks to a three-year, $96,500 grant from the Donner Foundation, will expand its current theater management curriculum to include all the arts beginning this September, with six students enrolled. Business courses will be supplemented by seminars taught by the managing directors of five local professional arts groups. Students will receive work-fellowships for part-time school year and full-time summer internships with three of the five arts organizations. New York University, whose graduate program in performing arts administration has been presented through its Division of Music Education in collaboration with Town Hall since 1971, will offer a greatly expanded year-and-a-half M.A. program this fall. A joint effort of the Graduate School of Business Administration and the School of Education, Health, Nursing, and Arts Professions, the program will admit some 20 students, up from 4 or 5. A year-long internship during the program's second and third semesters will supplement a continuing full course load.

Meanwhile, the National Assembly of Community Arts Agencies (NACAA) task force on certification of arts administrators presented its completed report to the assembly at the annual American Council for the Arts meeting in Seattle in July with three major recommendations: that an association of arts administrators be formed within six months of adaption of the recommendation; the the possibility of certifying arts administrators be further explored with a task force completing exploration within 12 months of actual formation of the proposed association; and that a task force closely examine the relationship of boards to arts administrators. Instead of voting on the amendments, the assembly voted to turn them over to NACAA's executive committee with instructions to consult various arts organizations around the country and come back with its recommendations within the next year. *[As of press time, no further action had been taken on certification.]*

Summer 1976

The profession of arts management is attracting increased attention as educational programs continue to develop, new groups are organized, and the job market broadens. Within the past few months alone, major stories on education in arts management have appeared in such publications as *California Living, MBA Magazine, Art Workers News,* and the *Los Angeles Times.*

Although the recently published *Survey of Arts Administration Training in the United States and Canada* (American Council for the Arts) lists 19 graduate arts administration programs, some ten other institutions are exploring the possibility of introducing new programs—Boston University and the University of Washington among them—and many more have instituted special courses or seminars. The University of Georgia has been studying the feasibility of introducing a special summer institute in arts management for the southeastern region. At Columbia University, the Graduate School of Business has joined with Museums Collaborative to introduce a continuing education program aimed at middle and executive level personnel in museums, zoos, historical societies, and botanical gardens called, "Principles of Management for Cultural Institutions." The program includes an initial week-long seminar beginning February 26, followed by individual study and research for ten weeks, and a final group seminar at the end of May.

Aware of continued development in the field, the directors of ten existing graduate programs in arts administration met at Indiana University on November 17-18 to exchange information and to formally organize a new national group. The Association of Arts Administration Educators is an alliance of ongoing college and university arts administration programs organized to encourage high academic and professional management standards, exchange information, and stimulate research. The organization will operate out of the office of its first chairman, E. Arthur Prieve of the University of Wisconsin's Center for Arts Administration.

Additional insights into the value of existing programs will be available when several of Prieve's students complete a new study. Alumni of graduate arts administration programs are being surveyed to determine how valuable they think their formal education has been to their professional careers. Universities, meanwhile, are broadening their programs by sponsoring outside seminars aimed at professionals in the field. On the international level, the results of a UNESCO research program on the training of arts administrators and cultural animators in Europe and Canada should be published by the summer of 1978.

In a move designed to make management professionals in other fields aware of career and educational development in arts management, *AM* editor Alvin H. Reiss has arranged to have management of the arts featured in a major national management meeting for the first time. The joint annual conference of the Institute of Management Sciences and the Operations Research Society of America, which will attract over 2,000 business, government, and university management professionals to New York from May 1-3, 1978, will feature sessions on management concerns in the arts, arts management education programs, and business and the arts.

In Canada, the country's first professional organization of arts administrators, the Association of Cultural Executives, has completed its initial year successfully. The group, whose admission is open to anyone who thinks he or she qualifies, with dues of $100 a year, currently has about 115 members and is concerned with the establishment of professional standards and the improvement of working conditions for its members. With a volunteer staff headed by President Peter Swann (1916 Tupper St., Montreal, Quebec, Canada H3H 1N5), the association thus far has drawn up a draft employment contract, Code of Professional Conduct, and formulated model job descriptions. Areas of concern include lobbying for the field, a job referral service, and information resources in such areas as taxes and salary guidelines.

Meanwhile, the employment referral service for arts administrators in the United States, Opportunity Resources for the Arts, has compiled some statistics on its operation. Of 270 jobs available to OR applicants through the service last year, 36.3 percent were filled, up 3 percent from the previous year. The average salary for jobs filled by OR has gone up considerably, from $10,000 in 1975-76 to $11,000 in 1976-77, to $19,733 in the first quarter of 1977-78. Currently, the organization has some 3600 applicants to file.

According to OR director Freda Mindlin, the service no longer accepts all applicants, but only registers those with arts management experience or some other marketable skill. Those not in the field may, however, receive free career guidance. Currently OR is organizing a major drive to recruit development directors and is working on a new publications list.

November-December 1977

A new, year-long graduate certificate program in arts management, one of the first to be aimed specifically at working professionals in the arts, will be introduced this fall by Adelphi University at its Urban Center in New York City. Under the direction of *AM* editor Alvin H. Reiss, the 24-credit, trimester program, offered through Adelphi's School of Business Administration, will complement the work schedules of arts administrators and crossover professionals from other fields.

The State University of New York at Albany will introduce a concentration in the management of cultural institutions within its M.B.A. program beginning this fall. At New York University, where an M.A. in performing arts administration has been offered for several years, a new M.A. program in art administration for museums was introduced this past semester, along with a new graduate interdisciplinary program in museum studies. The Parsons School of Design and Bank Street College have collaborated on a new Visual Arts focus within the master's degree program in Supervision and Administration set to begin this July.

Several universities are joining Harvard in presenting special short-term summer programs in arts management. New programs include the Banff Centre's Management Development for Arts Administrators; NYU's Summer Institute in the Economics and Financing of the Arts, offered by the graduate School of Public Administration; and the University of Georgia's Arts Administration Institute.

Other summer training programs include ACUCAA's three-week-long arts management workshops, the American Film Institute's symposium for film educators, and Pennsylvania State University's focus on crafts administration. Penn State also will conduct a financial management seminar for arts groups.

March-April 1978

A new program, designed to help train administrators and artists to work with older audiences in the arts, the Creative Arts Center for Older Adults, will be introduced at the New School for Social Research in New York this fall. Rockland Community College in Suffern, New York introduced an undergraduate program in arts management at the same time as did Wagner College in Staten Island, New York.

September-October 1978

ARTS MANAGEMENT ABROAD

The Administration of Arts Programs in Australia

Carillo Gantner

The following article, which originally appeared in AM, *No. 73, was updated by the author to reflect developments through 1978.*

There is a growing awareness in Australia that increased public support for the arts, evidenced in increasing federal and state subsidy, the creation and operation of large state cultural centers, and the growth of national, state, and regional companies, demands a new kind of trained administrator. A national survey on "Theatre Staff in Australia," commissioned by the Australian Council for the Arts, found in December 1969 that 61 full-time theater administrators were employed in this country. This figure was not definitive, both because of the frequent fluctuations of theatrical activity and because of the rapid growth of many new arts organizations. The interesting point, however, which is stressed in the survey, is that

> of this number it may be said that none received training as administrators, but that each one reached his position through work in some other branch of the theatre. This is the traditional procedure, whereby successful or promising directors, box office men, stage managers, and occassionally actors move to positions of administrative responsibility. To this procedure there may be a few exceptions, men who become theatre administrators with professional experience only in business or accountancy, but such men are rare and regarded with initial suspicion in an intensely conservative profession.

No courses in arts or theater administration existed in Australia until 1978. The major professional theater training schools, such as the National Institute of Dramatic Art in Sydney, the Victorian College of the Arts in Melbourne, and the Drama Discipline at Flinders University in Adelaide, have for some years provided introductory sessions on theater management problems, but none of these institutions yet provide a regular full-time administration programme.

Initial moves towards the training of theater administrators were made by the Australian Council for the Arts following its establishement in 1968. The council (now the Australia Council) is the federal government's policy-making and subsidy-giving body in the arts. One of its important concerns is with the training of professional personnel in all aspects of the arts, as well as funding major training institutions such as the National Institute of Dramatic Art and the Australian Ballet School. The council has made provision for the in service training of administrators with existing companies.

Trainees have been attached to organizations for varying periods of time, usually a minimum of one year. In this time they work as an understudy in most aspects of the organization's administration, as well as assume specific responsibilities within that organization. The council has funded attachment of trainee administrators with such groups as the Adelaide Festival of Arts and the Melbourne Theatre Company.

As another step towards improved management skills, the council sponsored a Theatre Administration School in March 1972, which ran concurrently with the Adelaide Festival of the Arts. This occasion, chaired by Elizabeth Sweeting, Administrator of the Oxford Playhouse in England, catered to about 40 administrative personnel from national, state, and regional performing arts companies (subsidized and commercial) around the country. This was the first occasion on which arts administration was acknowledged as a serious profession and the first time arts administrators had come together to examine problems and share skills. Papers were given by senior administrators on such topics as financial management, fund raising, law and the arts, industrial relations, public relations, and touring. Arising from this conference was a determination to improve in-service training for working administrators and to develop new professional training courses for future administrative personnel.

The process has not been as straightforward as hoped, but in 1978 the first full-time professional arts administration program opened at a College of Advanced Education in Adelaide under the direction of Elizabeth Sweeting. Ms. Sweeting was brought back to Australia by the South Australian government to develop this course and to act as a consultant to the Arts Council of South Australia (responsible for country touring). At the same time, a graduate diploma course in Arts Administration at the Victorian College of the Arts was given academic approval, but was delayed from starting by federal government restrictions in the educational budgets. The Victorian College is a logical place for such a course, as it is a multidisciplinary arts school with the resources of the soon-to-be-completed Victoria Arts Centre and the major companies it will house near at hand.

In the last few years, the Australia Council and the arts organizations, themselves have begun to look at ways in which businsess and industry can be encouraged to participate more closely in the arts. In 1977 a study group on private support for the arts, established and run by the Myer Foundation, produced a major report on this important area. One of the major recommendations was the establishment of a "broker" organization between business and the arts which would be concerned not only with stimulating business involvement in the arts financially, but also in initiating research and training programs applicable to both parties. As a result of the Myer Study Group, ARTS (Arts Reserach Training and Support) was established. In 1978, they were actively involved in arts consultancy work, in fulfilling the "marriage broker" role, and in planning a two-week residential course for senior arts managers who will be in Sydney in September this year. ARTS, with funding from Mobil and the Australia Council, has also recently launched a series of awards for business participation in the arts.

While Australia lags behind the United States in both the professional training of arts administrators and in private sector involvement in the arts, large strides are now being made. Inevitably, the current economic climate has slowed the growth of government involvement. This provides even greater incentive for Australians, who traditionally have been accustomed to turn to the government to provide their every need, to increase the whole community's appreciation of and involvement in the arts. It is vitally important that all sections of the community share the responsibility for putting the arts where they belong—at the very center of our lives.

November-December 1971

British Management Training Program a Success

An interesting approach to the training of arts administrators initiated five years ago by the Arts Council of Great Britain, is proving highly workable. Unlike many successful American and Canadian training programs, the British concept does not involve postgraduate university study. Instead, the 11-month program alternates periods of highly concentrated classroom study at a technical institute with three different periods of residency or secondment.

Until the Arts Council developed the current program, there was little formal training available in England. However, with the council's own grant disbursement program growing annually and with many recipient groups administered less than professionally, it became evident that proper management and financial administration was indeed a council concern. (The council's budget for the 1971-72 season is the equivalent of about $30 million, up from less than $1 million some 25 years earlier. It subsidizes, directly or indirectly, 1200 different organizations.) In 1967 the council funded and developed the current course at the London Polytechnic's School of Management Studies. When the program began, it barely attracted the full quota of 18 students. Now there is strong competition for a program place, and more than 100 annual applicants, most having a university background and some beginning arts experience, are carefully screened.

The program begins each September with a four-day orientation at the Polytechnic, followed by a one-month secondment at an arts institution. In October, students return to the Polytechnic for an intensive training program which lasts until Christmas. Emphasis is on finance, with Polytechnic instructors lecturing on such subjects as accounting, marketing, statistics, and economics, and such guests as Anthony Fields, the council's finance director, discussing arts accounting and box office management. In addition, experts are brought in to discuss virtually every area of arts management, including publicity, audience research, funding, and relations with local governments. Following a brief vacation, students begin their second secondment, a three-month residency devoted to some special project. They return to the Polytechnic on April 1 for three more months of advanced classroom work and conclude their training with a final secondment during July.

The program's positive results have been evident thus far. Of the 18 students accepted annually, about 16 become professional arts administrators. The council's program responsibility includes job placement, although many students find positions during the training period. This past year, for example, 13 graduates were placed with such organizations as the London Symphony, New Philharmonia, Contemporary Dance Theatre, Midland Arts Center, Festival Ballet, and Royal Shakespeare Theatre. In four instances, students returned to places of secondment. The experience of one recent graduate, a 30-year-old woman with teaching experience and a slight background but strong personal interest in the visual arts, indicates the kind of development possible. During her first secondment she served as assistant to an art gallery director. Her second secondment was spent with another gallery, wherer she organized and conducted an audience survey. She took a job with a different visual arts organization prior to her third secondment.

Several months ago, a special committee completed a detailed analysis of the progam. Its just-published report confirmed the success of the program and recommended its continuation, with some slight modifications.

January-February 1972

As theater company, Playwrights Horizons moves into its new home on what is now "42d Street Theatre Row" in New York City, it removes the sign of the previous resident. (Photo by Nathaniel Tileson. Courtesy of Playwrights Horizons)

2

Operations and Communications

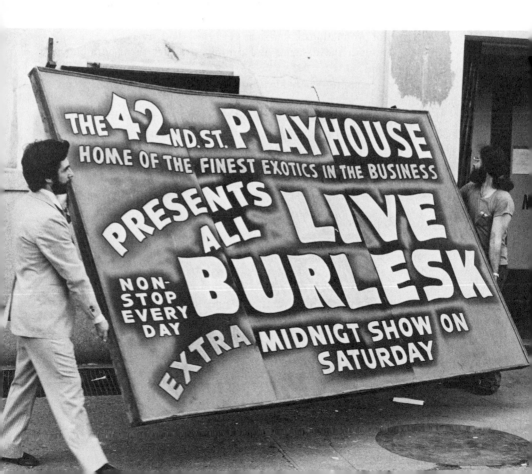

VISUALS AND PRINTED MATERIALS

Artists Lay Down
Rules for Promotional Design

A panel of artists meeting to consider the graphic quality of printed materials circulated by health and welfare groups in New York has come up with a series of guidelines broadly applicable to the problems of cultural organizations as well.

In planning brochures, pamphlets, and other literature, they agreed that the first step is to know what general style or tone will appeal to the target audience.

Illustrations and text should both be used sparingly, allowing ample white space. In general, they found that a few large illustrations are more effective than a great many small ones.

The inside of the folder or brochure should be just as carefully planned as its cover, and just as well designed.

Color—an expensive extra—should be used with economy. A little bit can go a long way. Many two-color jobs are more striking and effective than far more expensive four color productions.

Work closely with the designer and printer, and give them both enough time to do a good job.

Do not try to cram too many ideas into a single piece of literature. Keep it simple and direct.

According to J. K. Kansas, chief of press relations for Esso Research and Engineering and a member of the panel, basic decisions must not be left to the designer or printer. "The public relations man must make all decisions relevant to his materials, since he alone fully understands what he hopes to accomplish with the specific printed piece."

August 1962

Annual Reports

Annual reports can be dull and deadly documents, with many relegated to the glance and file category by their intended users. An attractive cover and interesting layout can help to encourage readership and a service aspect that insures regular use can be even more effective. It St. Paul, Minnesota, the Annual Report for 1971-72 of the Arts and Sciences Council not only has eye appeal with a silver cover and pages printed on different colored stock, but serves a practical purpose as well. Along with pictures and written reports are calendar pages which list local arts events throughout 1973, with ample space left for adding new events as they are scheduled.

Summer 1973

Popping Up

Looking for attention-getting direct mail fund appeals? You might steal a leaf from children's books and try pop-ups. A recent North Carolina School of the Arts brochure seeking funds for a concert hall renovation read, "Some colleges seek gifts for endowed chairs." Opening the cover, the reader was greeted with a auditorium chair popping up from the page above the heading, "Your $50 will purchase one endowed seat."

Summer 1973

Visual Impact

Brochures must make a visual impact on the recipient or often they'll go unread. The new brochure of Hospital Audiences, Inc. won't suffer that fate. Its covers are pieces of plain tan corrugated cardboard featuring only a button popping through the front cover, reading HAI in logotype. Inside the 8½ x 11 inch brochure are ten pages, printed on stock the same color and general appearance as the cover. Four of the pages feature very brief descriptions of the group's program, while four others feature offsets of handwritten letters sent by audience members. The only picture is on the inside back jacket. The design and printing was a gift from business—a contribution to HAI from Standard Oil of New Jersey.

September-October 1972

Breezy Report

The Province of Ontario Council for the Arts Fifth Report 1968–1969 is a bright, breezy, colorful, irreverent, and highly effective brochure printed on blue, yellow, and white stock. Its message is brief yet complete, and its language is nontraditional. In describing its innovative five-year plan for the arts, the report says in bold, black letters more than three-fourths of an inch high, "Huzzah for the program grant," followed by a statement reading, "You cannot foster the arts, or anything else for that matter, on a kind of cultural welfare. For five years we've fussed over symptoms, trying to patch them up with operating grants. Now we're after cures." The "Huzzah" sentiment is illustrated with a bright and colorful full-page drawing.

September-October 1969

Colorful Promotions

Has your group ever taken a comic approach to the serious business of promotion? In Washington, D.C., Arena Stage mailings features Jules Feiffer comic strips on the backs of subscription envelopes while in Providence, Rhode Island, Trinity Square's current subscription flier was in the form of a coloful eight-page comic book. In another variation, the Seattle Arts Festival program, Bumbershoot, handed out 1000 coloring books a day to children at a special science and art exhibit. The books, designed by a local artist, featured complete schedules, lists of contributors, sketches to color and fill-in-the-dots drawings.

September-October 1975

What's Your Line?

Arts groups are using provocative cover lines in their promotional pieces to attract audience attention. The Hartford, Connecticut Peace Train suggestively states, "No one else does this in public," while the Houston Ballet, in a brochure asking for funds, proclaimed, "We're not going to tiptoe around." Recently, the Philadelphia College of the Performing Arts announced "almost free concerts," and the Trinity Square Repertory Company in Providence announced "Gift offer inside," on the cover of an envelope that contained a letter suggesting theater tickets as good Christmas gifts. An upcoming brochure of the Long Island Symphony will declare, "We play around a lot."

November-December 1977

Effective Brochures

Eye-catching program brochures need not be expensive. At the University of California in Santa Barbara, entertaining yet low-cost brochures are helping to promote the arts and lecture series. The format utilizes graphics and pictures from very old books and magazines (there is no copyright problem) to illustrate, page by page, arts events in fanciful and frequently amusing style. The brochures themselves are printed in booklet form on news presses using paper one grade above news stock, thus accounting for considerable savings.

Summer 1972

Soft Soap Donors

Looking for instant recognition to attract donors for its annual united fund drive, the United Arts Council of Greensboro, North Carolina recently kicked off its campaign with a brochure whose cover bears a marked resemblance to an easily recognized household item—a detergent box. Printed in red and yellow on a blue base, with the words virtually leaping off the page, the cover extolls "New! Improved Greensboro Arts" (the latter word in giant red letters) as "loaded with action!" Its "active ingredients" are listed as Arts Festival, Crafts For All, More Music Theater, New Headquarters Building, Youth Symphony, and Project Listen. Once the cover has enticed the reader to open the brochure, the approach is anything but tongue in cheeek. In a direct manner, pictures and text tell potential contributors about the many new community arts activities in Greensboro, which now cost more than ever before to support. The approach may be unorthodox, but the stakes are high. The campaign goal is a record $130,000.

January-February 1972

Public Domain

Looking for interesting visuals to brighten programs and promotional pieces? One answer might be pictures in the public domain. The University of California at Santa Barbara's fall 1977 arts and lecture series brochure, for example, superimposed guest artists into the foreground of Jan Vredeman de Vries' Sixteenth century engravings of architectural fantasies. A good source for public demain pictures, all useable without fee or permission and all easily photostated to any size for reproduction, is the Hart Picture Archives series by Hart Publishing, 12 East 12 Street, New York, New York 10003). The books, each dealing with a separate theme, vary in length and price and include anywhere from 300 to 2100 pictures.

January-February 1978

Inviting Interest

Because invitations to arts openings compete with a plethora of other direct mail pieces, they must be noticeable. The Minneapolis Institute of Arts' unique Artists Exhibition Program, which directly involves state artists in the selection and creation of exhibitions, has used specially created materials from exhibiting artists for its invitations. The paper publications by the artists are enclosed within a self-mailer which announces both exhibition and opening, and the invitation itself then becomes part of the exhibition. Elsewhere, New York University's Grey Art Gallery reproduced part of a telephone message pad, with the section marked "please call" checked off as an invitation. The International Center of Photography in New York used an accordian picture foldout as an invitation, with the photo exhibition subject, a lion, looming increasingly larger in each of the panels.

March-April 1978

Reading the Writing

Not everyone uses a typewriter, and handwritten responses for tickets or meetings are frequently illegible. If you've had this problem, you might try a tactic used by a growing number of arts organizations. Try using a self-mailer with the form to be filled out located directly opposite the recipient's name on the address label. When the form is returned, you flip it over and find your original label.

March-April 1978

Paper Power

To promote an exhibit of "Masterworks on Paper," the Pace Gallery in New York City spotlighted the "paper." Instead of traditional fliers or announcements, the gallery mailed small 4 x 5 inch memo pads featuring "Don't Forget" on top and the gallery name and address on bottom. On the first two pages of each pad was a printed reminder, "Dec. 7–Jan. 4 Masterworks on paper, including Dubuffet, Picasso, Matisse. . . .

November-December 1974

Opening Thrust

Looking for a unique way to invite the press and VIPs to an important opening event? To herald its move to a new national headquarters last month, Hospital Audiences, Inc., sent out invitations in the form of 25-inch long scrolls. When unrolled to its full length, the scroll, in addition to its invitational message, listed all the invited guests—over 500—in alphabetical order.

September-October 1974

Easy Invite

Artists Space in New York uses a single but effective mail means of announcing new shows. Inside a 3¼ x 4¼ envelope, it encloses "business cards" with each including artist's name, gallery address, hours, and exhibition dates.

March-April 1976

A Good Dose

In planning their annual administration workshop, officers of the Association of College, University, and Community Arts Administrators wondered how they might call attention to their program. Someone's description of the workshop as a clinic triggered a flow of medicinal images, with the result that delegates to the December 1976 annual conference were confronted with an offbeat flier.

Wrapped in commonplace medicinal vials, with the printing visible from outside, were special messages from "ACUCAA Pharmacy" offering as Rx "Dr. Miracle's Genuine Patented, Super-Potency Workshop." The imagery was carried out in copy which promised "workshops on budget surgery . . . clinics for gaining audiences and losing deficits and R&R in an informal atmosphere." Because the vials are no longer used by pharmacists—they don't have matching arrows as required—they were obtained without cost.

November-December 1976

Old-fashioned Promotion

Looking to attract attention to an upcoming event? The Rhode Island School of Design recently sent postcard invitations, featuring a photo on the message side, to the opening of its faculty exhibition. The picture of the "faculty" was an archive-type photo of turn-of-the-century men and women attired in dress of the period.

March-April 1974

A Light Approach

The Ontario Arts Council, a government agency in Canada, is trying a popular approach to reach potential audiences throughout the province. A new accordian-fold flier, when opened, pictures a neon sign announcing the spot to go, "Arts' Place." The copy discusses the council's activities and programs and describes Arts' Place as "everywhere in Ontario. It's in your home, your school, club, library or community centre. . . ."

November-December 1973

Visual Appeal

A new package for a familiar product can often be a useful promotional aid. This year's annual report of the Ohio Arts Council, its tenth, is a large foldout brochure about the size of the old *Life* magazine page. When fully opened, it reveals a three-color poster dominated by the number ten on the reverse side. The Kentucky Arts Commission has published as its brochure this year a two-color, front-opening packet, with an inside pocket containing ten different handsomely printed sheets. Each is devoted to a separate aspect of the council's program.

Summer 1976

Charting Progress

An arts organization with an impressive record of growth can effectively dramatize it by using charts and graphs in its publications to tell the story at a glance. In a recent issue of its newsletter, the Art Gallery of Toronto showed its growth from 1935 to the present with a bar graph. Next to the graph, three columns of figures compared the growth of its programs in numbers and percentages. A quick look at the illustrations was better than words in telling the story.

March 1965

Effective Charts

A chart in your printed materials can often dramatize a point better than a thousand statistics. But it can also confuse. An effective chart must be uncluttered and simple. Use the brightest colors for the most important points, duller hues for subordinate ideas. Avoid clichés like the "fund drive thermometer."

September 1963

Local Artists

Performing arts organizations can highlight their printed materials by showcasing the work of local artists. The Oklahoma City Symphony Orchestra, for example, featured a different three-color abstract print by local artist Harrison Taylor on the cover of each of its new programs. In addition, the orchestra displayed the entire series of prints in its auditorium lobby and offered them for sale.

February 1965

The Shape of Things

Changing the look of your promotional materials may increase readers' awareness of them. This year's button for Lincoln Center's Mostly Mozart festival was just such a departure—a square button proclaiming the festival in black script on a yellow background. Brooklyn College's flier for its guest artist series was an odd-shaped 11½ x 3 inches, which unfolded into three panels.

September-October 1977

Go-Go Logo

Logos, the visual organizational symbols that appear on letterheads, programs, etc., can reap extra publicity—in advance. If your group doesn't have a logo or needs a new one, you might turn to the community for help. The Cleveland Area Arts Council held a well-publicized logo contest among local design students, with all entries exhibited in the lobby window at the Cuyahoga Savings Association. The bank also donated a cash award for the winning design, which has since been adopted as the permanent symbol of the council. In Seattle, the Arts Commission recently approved a $500 award for a design contest to find a new Commission logo.

September-October 1972

FILM AND AUDIO

Film Makes Dramatic, Versatile Promotion Aid; Arts Groups Can Get Free Help From Cinema Clubs

Can your organization use a motion picture film to display its activities? The recent rapid growth of cinema clubs in all parts of the country may provide the means.

A 19-minute color film made by a club of skilled amateurs, accompanied by original music and commentary on tape, has preserved the highlights of a 1961 community arts festival and helped in building an arts council in Williamsport, Pennsylvania.

Mrs. Barnard C. Taylor, executive director of the Greater Williamsport Arts Council, outlined for *AM* how the novel filmmaking project was carried out and how it has been used to promote the cultural development of the city. Costing only $900 to produce because almost all work was donated, the picture and tape would have cost about $9000 had it been made commercially.

"We offer it to anyone who wishes to see what we did," Mrs. Taylor said. "There will be a fee for postage and handling."

The original sponsor of the project was the Junior League of Williamsport, which contributed $500 of the originally-estimated cost. The vital filmmaking talent came from members of the Susquehanna Cinema Club, who volunteered time, equipment, and filming services, and from Hugh MacMullan, a former Hollywood director who had also previously directed a film for a Williamsport welfare agency.

MacMullan directed the scriptwriting, building it from scenes and groups participating in the festival. Much of the recording was done months after the festival ended in early May 1961. Titles were painted by Mrs. Taylor's husband, a graphic artist, commentary was delivered by a local radio announcer, John Archer, and music for the film was composed by Dr. Glen Morgan of the Lycoming College Music Department.

The film was first shown at a dinner attended by 250 people who had participated in the 1961 festival. Mrs. Taylor took this occasion to present plans for the 1962 arts festival. Since opening night, the picture has been shown to 23 organizations that had taken part in the filmed festival, and to schools. No fees were asked. Cinema Club members ran the film.

"Three groups that had not been involved the year before were introduced to the idea of the festival through the film," Mrs. Taylor told *AM*.

The picture also served the broader publicity interests of Williamsport. It was run twice on local television (reaching audiences in several counties) and was shown to both the staff of America House and a representative of the Museum of Modern Art in New York. Congressman Herman T. Schneebeli has asked that the U.S. Information Agency consider making use of it.

Mrs. Taylor told *AM:*

> The Junior League members, who underwrote it, feel very good when they see the film as a record of the events presented under their financing. The clubs enjoyed seeing friends and neighbors perform and the sections of performances they missed. Others were sorry they missed the 1961 festival after having seen the film.
>
> To other communities planning a similar venture, I would ad-

vise holding a planning session with the filmmakers to reach conclusions on the emphasis the arts group wishes for its future educational use. To show what has evolved, and how it will develop, is difficult for one who has not been knee-deep in the process, and this should be discussed until a definite approach can be decided upon.

August 1962

Theater Films

Do you have any high quality films about your organization that might be suitable for showing in movie theaters? Here are some tips. Theaters prefer color to black and white and require that all prints be 35-millimeter. As a rule, running time of each film should not exceed ten minutes. Also, the films offered to theaters should not have previously appeared on television. Finally, films, although informative, should have some entertainment value, and the material in them should not be dated. Such films are distributed to theaters by national agencies.

May-June 1964

Color Slides

Color slides taken by members of a cultural group on one tour can do double duty in illustrating a lecture and in indirectly promoting the next tour. On October 1 the Walters Art Gallery in Baltimore presented an illustrated lecture on English art, using pictures taken by members last April during a two-week charter flight tour of English galleries and private collections. The program, open to the public, was held two weeks before the deadline for joining the Walters gallery in order to take part in its charter flight art tour of Southern France next April.

October 1962

Supermarket Slides, LP
Records Potent Arts Promotional Tools

Arts groups, often with the help of local corporations, are developing unusual promotional devices for use in raising funds, reaching new audiences, and promoting programs. In St. Louis, where the Arts and Education Council's annual united fund drive has a $1-million goal this year, flags, slide showings, and phone recordings are among the devices currently being used in support of the campaign.

A staple of the council's annual promotion diet, and a very effective one, is the tape-and-slide showing prepared with the voluntary help of Batz-Hodgson-Neuwoehner, a local advertising agency, for dissemination to civic groups and other organizations. Focusing on the activities of the fund's ten beneficiary cultural and educational groups, the showing features 140 slides and a 20-minute taped narrative.

With business assistance, the sight and sound of the fund reaches thousands of people daily during March and April. Flags, imprinted with the fund logo, fly from business offices downtown and in the suburbs. The time and temperature phone service sponsored by the First National Bank of St. Louis has added a taped message during the drive, "Support the Arts and Education Fund—the time is now." At 43 locations of St. Louis's largest food chain, Schnuck's, shoppers waiting in check-out lines are treated to slide showings from special rear projection machines. Although the machines have been installed mainly to flash commercial messages at the rate of one every six seconds, some 20 slides in each carousel of 100 are devoted to public service spots, with about 5 to 10 at each store promoting the Arts and Education Fund. Another slide show, this at member banks of Mark Twain Bancshares, features six slides devoted to the drive in each of eight projectors. Slides alternate pictures of the fund's participating agencies and a title reading "Another reason to give to the Arts and Education Fund."

In Philadelphia, Franklin Concerts, Inc., an organization which helps young professional musicians begin their careers is using a long-playing record, "Stars of Tomorrow," as one of its prime promotional tools. Underwritten by Sears Roebuck last year, the demonstration stereo LP features performances by five Franklin ensembles and six artists. It has been used successfully in introducing potential concert buyers and foundations to the artists and as a gift to donors.

March-April 1972

Taped Appeal

Looking to reach big contributors? Cassettes may be your answer. The Pacifica Foundation recently gave away both cassette players and prerecorded tapes in an unusual campaign designed to reach donors in the "high gift" category ($5000 to $100,000). Pacifica, a listener-sponsored FM broadcasting service, hand-delivered to 300 patrons free players and four tapes, contributed by Lafayette Radio and Electronics, which synopsized ten years of its programming on tapes. In addition, a half-hour tape narrated by Thomas Hoving and featuring several notables discussed Pacifica and its need for capital funds to build a broadcasting center. The tape concluded with an invitation to listeners to attend a scheduled meeting.

January-February 1971

Using Cassettes

Prerecorded cassette tapes sold to subscribers can be a useful tool in educating audiences. The Indianapolis Symphony, for example, recorded listening tips and program notes for each concert in its 1970-71 subscription series and offered subscribers either 16 of these programs on eight cassettes for $49.95 (for concert series A) or eight programs on four cassettes for $29.95 (series B or C). The orchestra also offered cassette recorder-players to subscribers at an announced discount price of $39.95.

Summer 1971

Opening the Circuit

With large apartment developments beginning to experiment with the use of scheduled closed circuit TV programming for their tenants, arts groups might be able to promote themselves and their activities by getting in on the act early. In New York, the Queens Council on the Arts now pipes a regular Friday evening program on the arts, featuring live interviews, films, and tapes, into some 1300 apartments in Parker Towers from an on-site studio in the housing complex. Soon, the council will start a project designed to teach individuals and arts groups how to operate video equipment. The council envisions an extra benefit from the current experience—it will be prepared to program for cable TV when it comes to Queens.

November-December 1972

Community Arts

Available to groups interested in neighborhood and community arts programs is a 28-minute documentary on ½-inch videotape which summarizes activities at the landmark Community Arts and Community Survival Conference held in Los Angeles in 1972. Produced by the American Council for the Arts in Education, the tape shows the work of many neighborhood groups and helps to provide a definition of community arts.

September-October 1973

The Institutionalized

If your organization is interested in providing arts programs for the institution-alized you'll want to see a new film recently produced for Hospital Audiences Inc. Titled, "People Who Care," the 28-minute long, 16mm color film explores the growing HAI program for patients, prisoners, the aged, and others. Prints, at $40 each, are available for rental from HAI, 1540 Broadway, New York, New York 10036.

September-October 1975

Arts Talk

Would you like a top arts administrator in your community—vicariously? Sangamon State University has prepared a videotape series featuring leading arts administrators in informal conversations about their areas of expertise. The black-and-white tapes on ¾-inch cassettes are available for five-day periods on a free basis from the Community Arts Management Program, Capital Campus, Sangamon State University, Springfield, Illinois 62708.

November-December 1975

DIRECT MAIL

Four Methods for Building a Mailing List

Directors of arts groups are in a unique position to build mailing lists, according to one of the most experienced authorities in direct mail work.

"Because these directors are conducting ventures that will benefit the whole community, they can hope to enlist the support of sources for names that would be closed to the ordinary profit-making organization," declares Milton Smoliar of Names Unlimited, a New York list brokerage firm. Smoliar made this statement when asked by *AM* about the most efficient methods to build a mailing list. There are several basic ways.

Establishing personal contact with local sources of names, as Smoliar suggests, is advisable when a relatively small, selective list is needed. For example, when a museum or educational institution wants to reach prospective patrons, the local civic clubs, college alumni groups, and business associations may very well be willing to furnish their own lists.

Personal contacts may be supplemented by research in directories. The best are the city directories published by R. L. Polk, Social Registers, and the *Guide to American Directories for Compiling Mailing Lists.*

By collecting recent programs of events staged by local organizations, cultural and otherwise, you can obtain lists of officers, board members, and benefactors printed in the programs. The society page of the newspaper is another source of names of patrons or active volunteer workers. A good typist familiar with the city in question can search and type these names and home addresses from the phone book at a rate of 30 an hour or faster.

The telephone book itself is the best source from which to compile a so-called saturation list. When the aim is a large response, this is by far the most efficient way to start. A home typist can reproduce a list from the directory at a cost of a cent per name or less.

A third method of building a mailing list, using a commercial list compiler, is more expensive. There are list compilers in almost every sizeable town, but their fees range from $10 to $15 per 1000 names, and some specialized lists cost much more. Moreover, commercial list houses sometimes provide lists that are essentially duplications of the phone book.

List brokers—not the same as list compilers—are helpful when an arts group is planning a mailing of national dimensions, but are quite ineffective for a local project. The broker is a middleman who knows what lists are available from publishers, mail-order houses, industries, and compilers.

List brokers charge at least $15, and sometimes as much as $50, per 1000 names, and this fee generally covers rental of the list for one-time use only.

April 1962

How Experts Use
Direct Mail to Raise Money

Sidney Green

Soliciting funds by direct mail is one of the most expensive ways to bring in contributions. Moreover, for direct mail activity to yield good results it must be tried over a period of years, and with expectation of losses at first. Nevertheless, if an arts organization is committed to a long-term fund-raising effort and can meet certain preconditions, this technique can prove highly successful. Moreover, tests and experience indicate that once a prospect has contributed through a direct mail drive, he usually remains a contributor.

Institutions that have employed this-fund raising device with success enjoy a large following. They must, inasmuch as mailings to fewer than 50,000 possible patrons seldom prove very profitable. Second, these organizations have concrete, simply expressed needs, and their needs are related to broader social or cultural issues. That is, while they may be asking for money for a new music building, they are able to argue convincingly that support of the campaign would help advance the cause of music in general, or help revitalize downtown, or serve some purpose over and above the organization's own. Finally, they have money to invest and they are in a position to buy, create, or obtain through exchange the necessary mailing lists of potential donors.

Let us look at the development of a recent direct mail campaign conducted successfully by a relatively small but financially sophisticated national organization. This group mailed an appeal to 280,000 prospective givers. It drew up this extensive mailing list by renting some lists from professional list sellers and by exchanging its own lists with other groups. Thus, its overall list was a composite that included lists of subscribers to various magazines, members or contributors to parallel organizations, and names compiled from *Who's Who* and other directories. About 10,000 of the names were on the group's own list of past contributors—always the best source of fresh donations.

Individuals should be on the list only because their past record in some way indicates they are likely to respond to the appeal. There is, for example, no reason to believe that a subscriber to *Field and Stream* magazine would respond to an appeal for funds sent out by an art museum. Nevertheless, this same subscriber might be an excellent prospect for a conservation organization. The success of any organization's direct mail campaign depends most heavily on how skillfully the lists are selected and compiled.

For reasons of economy and brevity, the customary mail appeal consists of a letter—running to no more than two pages—and a postage-paid reply envelope. Sometimes these are supplemented by a printed folder describing the sponsoring organization in more detail than the letter. The appeal letter, carefull composed, should, if at all possible, be signed by an individual of national reputation. This individual need not necessarily be connected in any way with the sponsoring organization, but must, of course, be willing to permit the use of his or her name in this way.

The appeal letter may be printed by any of a number of processes, but the least expensive and therefore the most commonly used are photo offset or mutligraph. A typical printing bill for 100,000 two-page letters produced by a large printing establishment in a major city might run $1200 to $1600 for photo-offset or multigraph, with the latter method the more expensive. The same letter printed by letterpress would cost about $5000. And if the letters were individually typed by automatic machine instead of printed, the bill would zoom to an astronomical $27,500—which is, for all practical purposes, out of the question.

Other costs now come into play. Addressing and stuffing the envelopes—unless done by the group's own volunteers—costs between $10 and $20 per thousand. Postage costs can be kept to a minimum by sticking to third class.

The total cost of the 280,000 letter campaign described above was $30,000. Of this, roughly $10,000 went for supplies and printing. About $18,500 went into mailing, addressing, and similar expenses. And approximately $1500 went for the rental of lists.

This, obviously, is a big investment for a cultural institution—or for any other kind of organization. Is is worth it? The organization that carried out the above mailing of 280,000 letters thinks so. It drew contributions from 2.5 percent of those mailed to. The average contribution ran to $15.00 Thus, this campaign brought in slightly over $100,000, or nearly $3.50 for every $1.00 spent.

Another recent mailing by the same organization drew 3.4 percent returns with an average gift of $15.85, yielding over $5.50 for every dollar spent.

The unusually good responses indicate how useful direct mail can be and are a tribute to the care and professionalism displayed by the sponsoring organization. This care continues long after the last check has been received for, after each mailing, lists must be carefully analyzed and culled. Those yielding poor results must be set aside. They should not be discarded, however, but should be tested at least three times, since very often a fresh letter over another signature sent to the same prospect can do what an earlier letter failed to accomplish. Work must begin soon on the next mailing, for the direct mail campaign depends on continuity to help it succeed. Appeals should go out at about the same time each year, preferably during the last three months of the year, when potential givers are thinking about their tax situation and are often receptive to the letter that tells them their contribution is tax deductible.

November 1962

Right Word

Wording can make a difference on direct mail appeals for funds or members. The Community Gallery of the Brooklyn Museum in Brooklyn, New York seeking donations in three different categories ranging from $5 to $25 tried a different approach by renaming the categories. The lowest gift category, $5, remained Friend, a traditional membership designation, but $15 givers became Good Friends and $25 givers were identified as the Best of Friends.

Winter 1969-70

Attracting Attention

Looking for a unique way of attracting attention? The Dramatic Arts Center in Ann Arbor, Michigan mails packets of wallet-sized picture cards to promote its programs. The front of each card shows a different and unusual photograph of a live action scene. The back of each card carries specific information on tickets, programs, and the performing group.

March 1965

Direct Mail Brings in Members and Money

Promotion of membership by direct mail brings both immediate and long-range cash results, leaders of the Art Institute of Chicago were told in a special 1962 report. The report includes percentage response figures that other cultural institutions may find useful.

Richard C. Trenbeth, supervisor of development and membership, submitted the memorandum to the institute's Committee on Development in support of a plea for greater emphasis on direct mail activity. He pointed out that although figures needed for a comparison with the experiences of other leading museums are lacking, the Chicago Art Institute's rate of return and actual profit compare favorably with those of the Automobile Club of Maryland, an organization held up as a model by a leading direct mail trade publication. "At practically every point of measurement our record of selling memberships . . . is at least two or three times better," Trenbeth declared.

Last year Trenbeth's department mailed 115,352 pieces of membership solicitation material. This brought in 1809 memberships at $12.50 each. This is a return rate of 1.6 percent. The auto club, selling memberships at $17.50, drew a response of slightly under 0.5 percent.

The museum's cost per new member enrolled this way was $3.21, leaving a profit of $9.29 each. Cost is thus slightly over 25 percent. In contrast, the auto club's memberships cost the organization $14.69 each, or roughly 84 percent of the amount brought in.

The high cost of initial enrollments is compensated for by membership renewals after the first year, the report points out. First year renewals, universally the hardest to achieve, run about 65 percent for the Art Institute, Trenbeth said, compared with 60 percent for the Maryland organization. The overall renewal rate—i.e., including the first and subsequent renewals—runs 82 percent for the institute.

The report points out the following: "Our average annual member renews for four more years, adding $50 of profit to the $9.29 of the first year. If we spent even one-half of our first year income, we could offer a much more expensive and attractive premium (to new members) and enroll many more than we do now."

Long an ardent advocate of direct mail techniques in membership building, Trenbeth told *AM*, "I am convinced that major museums, theaters, and other arts groups could do far better with direct mail than they now imagine, especially where there is a strong record of renewal."

July 1962

Eye Appeal

Arts groups are turning increasingly to direct mail techniques used by business to reach potential audiences and donors. WNET/Channel 13, New York, sent its most recent fund appeals in envelopes with a drawn chain surrounding the name and address of the recipient on the front and continuing completely on the reverse side. The letter inside told readers, "Don't break the chain," explaining that this wasn't a chain letter, but "a letter about a chain—the chain that links you with 250,000 other thoughtful people." The American Museum of Natural History's new membership letter asked readers to insert a printed token in the "yes" slot to begin membership.

September-October 1976

Visual Identity

Visual symbols can be useful in calling attention to direct mail pieces, funding appeals, and press releases. Atlanta '78 reinforced awareness of the arts festival's twenty-fifth season, its silver anniversary year, by using raised letter silver logos on its envelopes, stationery, and fliers, while New York's Gilbert and Sullivan Players attached miniature plastic swords to press releases to herald its production of *The Pirates of Penzance*. For its special exhibition on embroidery, the Cooper-Hewitt Museum featured small embroidered patches picturing the museum building, on press kit covers.

Summer 1978

List Exchange

Need additional lists? Before the summer season ends offer to exchange lists with any special summer festival series in your area. Their lists will be current and may add a few names for your next fund-raising drive. On the other hand, your lists, lent to them after your drive is completed, may be helpful to them as they begin their promotion before the start of next summer's season.

August 1963

Save the Stamp

An organization with a large and loyal following that it solicits by mail can save some of the mailing cost by adopting an idea used successfully by a number or colleges. Suggest to your donors that they put their own stamp over the pre-paid marker on the return envelope.

November 1963

Hitch a Ride

Is there a dignified business firm in your community that conducts an active direct mail promotion program? It may be possible to enlist its backing for your ticket sale campaign or fund drive. In New York, Channel 13, the educational T.V. station, lined up the support of the Book-of-the-Month Club, which sent a special mailing to its subscribers in the TV station's market area urging them to contribute to the station. If the business will not do a special mailing, it may be willing to permit your organization to "piggy-back"—i.e., enclose material along with one of the company's own mailings. Make sure that the company's mailing list is appropriate, however.

March 1964

Novel Mailing Pieces Make
New Friends and Money

A striking mailing piece can spell the difference between a successful fund-raising campaign and a poor one. The Equity Library Theatre, a nonprofit showcase in New York affiliated with Actor's Equity, completely redesigned its 1963 mailing piece. The new look not only increased revenue substantially, but also aroused tremendous public interest.

An amateur rendering, the new mailer was conceived by David Lunney, the ELT tour coordinator. Aware that previous annual mimeographed letters were unsuccessful, he designed a folder that solicited money by entertaining rather than cajoling. It was produced and mailed at a cost of $300 for 1600, and the initial response alone brought in almost $2000, double the best past result.

The mailing piece, an accordion fold, printed on one side in sepia, tells the story of a fictitious ELT actress, Heliotrope Fenwick, and humorously suggests, in original sketches and text, the costs of mounting a production. It concludes, "And here is the envelope (gummed, self-addressed, and stamped) that holds the check (a large sum) that supplies the cash that pays the bills that support the theater that showcases the actor. . . ." and tells how Miss Fenwick was hired, "all because she was seen at Equity Library Theatre, the theater that you built."

According to Lunney, letters and telephone calls have come in to the fictitious Miss Fenwick, and many contributors have turned the piece over to friends, suggesting that they contribute to ELT.

February 1963

Mailing Piece

Promotional mailing pieces must capture the reader's interest if they are to be retained and referred to. Often, an unusual visual device can accomplish this. In New York, for example, a flier for a children's show mailed by the Paper Bag Players featured black brushstroke outlines of a face against an orange background. To gain reader attention, two holes were cut in place of the eyes, which did not significantly add to the cost of the piece.

November 1965

Over and Out

Don't carry a good thing too far. A prominent West Coast cultural group which used its postage meter stamp to advertise a special arts week was still using the announcement on its envelopes 11 days after the special week had ended!

January-February 1971

Stamp Schedule

An idea used by colleges to promote their football teams might be applicaable to arts groups interested in promoting upcoming productions. The University of Bridgeport, for example, used postage meters to print this year's entire ten-

game football schedule on its envelopes next to the metered stamp. Included in
the miniature advertisement, which although small was still readable, was the
date of each game, opponent, and starting time. An eight-play season or concert
series might just as easily fit on the envelope.

November-December 1972

Showing Off

Picture post cards can be effective promotional mailing pieces if you have a message with visual appeal. The Studio Museum in Harlem, New York used attractive cards with pictures of African masks, figures, and musical instruments to
invite viewers to its "Impact Africa" exhibit.

Fall 1970

Coding Responses

By coding reply forms, groups can determine which of several mailing lists used
drew the best response. One unobtrusive and inexpensive coding system, successfully employed by a number of arts groups, has a series of letters in alphabetical order printed in small type on reply forms. Before mailing to each list,
the printer removes one or more of the letters. The last remaining letter in the
series represents the list to which the mailing is directed. For example, a response
with ABCD on it indicates that it came from the D list. One reading AB, came
from the B list.

September 1965

Surveys

Planning a mail survey? Experts say that the rate of return on questionnaires is
greater if a stamped, self-addressed envelope is enclosed with the survey form.
Also, accurate typography on good quality paper, they claim, will bring higher
returns.

October 1965

ARTS FACILITIES

Planning a New Arts Building?
Pick Your Architect Carefully

The possibility that millions of dollars are in the cultural pocketbook for building
activities means that cultural groups must learn how to collaborate with architects on a scale not seen before. Many have no experience along this line.

After the functions of the building are decided, the next step is selecting precisely the right architect. Just finding a "good" architect is not enough. The right architect for an arts building must not only understand the community's tastes, traditions, and cultural patterns; he must also have a thorough knowledge of the rather special technical and mechanical requirements of theaters, museums, or concert halls.

He must be able to estimate construction costs realistically. He should know the business side of his profession—the best supply sources, the time to solicit bids, and the responsibility of contractors.

For these reasons the best bet is an architect who has had definite experience with the special needs of arts groups. The local chapter of the American Institute of Architects can often recommend someone.

When several candidates are found they should be invited to make their presentations individually to a screening committee. They will show picture of buildings they have completed, letters of commendation, and perhaps brochures explaining their services. Frequently they offer to arrange field trips to examples of their work. At these meetings the client has an opportunity not only to see the work, but to assess the individual. Since the relationship between client and architect is a close one that lasts months, it is important that they be able to work together amicably. Candidates for the account should not be asked to submit free sketches.

After the choice is made, however, the architect prepares a preliminary schematic design for discussion. This should be modified or expanded until both client and architect are satisfied. At this critical stage, both sides must be understanding and willing to make needed compromises.

Next, the architect submits preliminary drawings of both interior and exterior and should explain the reasoning behind them. He should understand the technical problems involved, local and state building codes, and inspection requirements. When he recommends building materials and equipment, clients have a right to know his reasons for his choice in terms of price, durability, and ease of maintenance. He should also provide samples of materials so the client can make a choice.

All the work is not on the side of the architect, however. A good client helps him do the best possible job. For example, the arts group should, if possible, consult the architect before selecting the site, because one with difficult terrain can add to the cost.

The architect should be told the financial limitation that may affect the project. If there are fixed limits, the client should put these in writing.

The arts group will, of course, try to negotiate the best possible fee, but it is wise to be wary of a bid which is considerably lower than the others because it may mean that the bidder does not understand the problems involved. On occasion an architect may give an arts group the best possible price because its cultural aims interest him.

Fees vary widely. The AIA chapters in each state have established a recommended schedule of fees for various categories of building, and this schedule can be a point of departure. The fee also depends on such variables as size, time limits, and the complexity of the building and its equipment.

December 1962

Audience Invests in its Theater—
1,000 Buy Building Fund Bonds

Thomas C. Fichandler

Early in its life, almost every growing cultural organization faces the big decision whether to rent, buy, or build new quarters. Although rental is sometimes the solution, often the answer lies in raising capital funds with which to buy and remodel an available building, or, even more costly, to build a new one.

Arts managers in various fields may find something of value in the unusual experience of the Arena Stage in raising $225,000 toward its building fund through a bond drive. Our success in selling bonds bearing interest at 6 percent was a key factor in financing the beautiful new theater.

When we decided in 1959 to build, there were several reasons why we decided to borrow money through a bond issue:

1.   Generally speaking, people are not used to the idea of giving money to a theater. They are accustomed to fund drives for the symphony orchestra, but not for the stage.

2.   Washington is a city without industrial fortunes rooted in the community.

3.   We needed funds quickly, because we were soon to lose our rented property. We had no established fund-raising organization, nor time to build one.

4.   Our big asset was the following Arena Stage had won through the nine years of life. This included nearly 5000 season ticket subscribers.

5.   The general economic climate of the times had led many middle-income people to become modest investors when offered the prospect of a reasonable return for their money.

Our decision, therefore, was to raise the $225,000 we needed by asking our playgoing friends to buy 6 percent sinking fund debentures at $100 face value each. Thus, they would be helping a cultural cause and at the same time getting a better return than they would from most other investments.

We announced our bond drive in the fall of 1959, issuing two mailings to our own list of more than 10,000 Arena theatergoers. We explained in detail the purpose and method of the bond offering and asked our friends to send back pledge cards for the interest-bearing loans. Between the acts of our first play of the season, the bond campaign was announced and bond literature was available at the theater for several months.

We found the bond sales campaign a relatively painless way to raise a large sum (though admittedly the repayment process will be felt somewhat). The main expense was for printing and postage. After the mailings were prepared, the bond campaign required little manpower.

While our main effort was in getting individual loans through bond sales, we did of course accept gifts to the building fund. At the same time, foundation support and business gifts were actively pursued. Various methods of recognition of both donors and loaners were spelled out in our literature, such as listing names in the theater lobby and placing individual nameplates on theater seats. In each category of recognition, bond money counted just half the value of outright gifts.

Altogether, close to 1000 individuals brought $225,000 worth of bonds. Single purchases of $100 each were most common. About 75 percent of the people participating brought in lots of either $100 or $200. The number of pledges not honored was minuscule—about 1 percent. We could tell by the end of January 1960 that our effort was going to succeed, and the bulk of the money was in hand by late April.

We now put aside 7 percent of our total loan annually for interest payments and debit retirement. We draw lots yearly to determine which bonds will be paid off; the entire list is to be liquidated in 35 years. We were happily surprised to find that some bondholders, when sent their 6 percent interest in 1961, mailed it back to us as their gift to Arena Stage.

April 1962

Donors "Shingle" Roof

Arts leaders in a small west Texas community, faced with the prospect of raising $2500 to begin converting an historic hotel into a museum, resorted to a "model sales" program to reach the goal.

When the heirs of Annie Riggs, the owner of the oldest hotel in Fort Stockton, Texas, donated the building to the local historical society, the organization found itself without funds to remodel the building. Since a new roof was necessary before additional restoration could be undertaken, the initial fund effort concentrated on the roof.

A local carpenter constructed a model of the building without a roof. The model was displayed throughout the town—in store windows, in the leading bank, and in local schools. When not circulating, the model was kept on the porch of the museum building. Small shingles were sold to townspeople for any amount they wished to donate, and the shingles were then inscribed with the name of the donor and lightly tacked onto the museum model. When the shingles completely covered the top of the model, they were removed and new shingles were sold.

The drive captured the imagination of the community. Grade school students donated small amounts so that a shingle could be bought in the name of their class. Local businesses gave larger amounts. Following the success of the initial drive, additional remodeling was undertaken.

November-December 1967

Building Bricks

Want to dramatize a building fund campaign or renovation drive and win funding support as well? Theatre London in Ontario, Canada, involved in a $5.5million renovation of the historic Grand Theater, has been selling building bricks for minimum donations of $150 each. Once purchased, bricks are engraved with any name of the donor's choice and laid so that names can be read in an interior wall of the mezzanine lobby. The lobby has been officially designated as the Donor Gallery and includes a brass plaque for donations over $1000 and another plaque listing committees involved in the renovation project. Thus far over 400 bricks have been sold for a total of about $140,000.

September-October 1978

Bed and Board

Group rates on motel rooms may be available to touring companies. The Association of American Dance Companies, for example, has initiated a group program with Holiday Inns which saves member companies 20 to 40 percent.

March-April 1977

Cinema Becomes State
Arts Center in 14 Months

An unusual set of circumstances has, in 14 months. returned a seedy movie house to a semblance of its former glory as a leading legitimate theater. In the process, the theater, acquired without cost, reopened on February, 1973 as Delaware's first performing arts center.

Built in 1871 by the Masons of Delaware as both Masonic Temple and theater, the four-story-high Grand Opera House was one of the handsomest buildings in Wilmington, with an imposing cast iron facade and one of the largest stages in the country. However, following decades of use as a legitimate theater, the house declined along with the surrounding downtown area and became a second-run movie theater. The Masons, who continued to use the building's top two floors as club and meeting rooms, were concerned with the deterioration and were interested in restoring the theater to its former state. They recognized, however, that the tax situation and financial problems would prevent them from undertaking the task.

The building's centennial anniversary year provided a group of concerned leaders, including members of the Delaware Arts Council and Greater Wilmington Development Council, with a springboard for direct action. On the one hundredth anniversary of its opening, December 22, 1971, the Delaware Governor and Grand Master of the Masons presided over a gala held at the opera house to mark the beginning of the cultural center campaign. Then the wheels began to turn. A new, nonprofit corporation was formed and immediately set up meetings with Mason officials to determine how the building could be transformed into a cultural center while allowing the Masons rent-free use of meeting facilities.

After months of discussion, a plan was worked out under which the Masons gave building title to the City of Wilmington without cost, and the city, in turn, immediately conveyed title to the newly created Grand Opera, Inc. The roundabout maneuver not only formalized city recognition, but served a more practical purpose. As building owner, the city waived the real estate transfer tax, saving Grand Opera thousands of dollars.

In a matter of months, the 1100-seat theater was readied for its new role. Foundation grants paid for cleaning and theater renovation, Dupont donated carpeting and furniture for offices, and Delaware Power and Light donated box seats and orchestra chairs while also offering the Opera House the free use of its adjacent auditorium for receptions. Immediate income was available from the rental of two street-level stores and a patronage campaign was launched concurrent with the announcement of a six-event inaugural season running from February through May. In its first 20 days the drive snared 130 grand patrons at $100 each and won 400 season subscribers. According to Lawrence J. Wilker, a University of Delaware faculty member who donated his time to serve as theater director, "It really snowballed."

As opening night neared, Wilmington business rallied to support the new center. Virtually every local store promoted the Opera House with fliers and window cards, nearby parking lots offered discounts to ticket holders, and ten area restaurants offered special "grand opera dinners" at reduced prices. The opening night Delaware Symphony concert drew an enthusiastic overflow audience.

With its initial season a reality, Grand Opera, Inc. is now turning its attention to long-range development and fund raising. A professionally booked season of 12 to 15 events is being planned for next year, and several leading state cultural groups may move into the building.

"We've got the theater painted and cleaned," said Wilker, "but it will take $3 million to restore it to what it was." With its recent designation as an architectural landmark, however, the possibility of federal funds for restoration exists. Also, theater leaders hope to turn the vacant second floor into a minimall of arts-oriented shops to produce additional income.

January-February 1973

College Combines Culture
and Athletics in New Campus

The first college "Theatron"—a $2-million cultural and physical education center on the campus of Monticello Junior College, Alton, Illinois—will open in October with a full program of cultural events for students and the community. The dedication takes place just two years after Monticello's president, Dr. Duncan Wimpress, persuaded the board of trustees that a proposed physical education building, with a stage at one end of a gymnasium should be, instead, a cultural center with physical education facilities for the college and the community.

A new physical education building had been suggested in 1961 by Mrs. Spencer T. Olin, an alumna of Monticello, and her husband, who planned to donate the funds. After accepting Dr. Wimpress's suggestion that the gift was an opportunity to serve the cultural needs of both community and campus, a committee was formed to choose an architect. The administration and the faculty then worked with him to integrate the needs of the 325 students with those of the community of about 80,000. The result was Hatheway Hall, called a "Theatron," the Roman term for a building combining facilities for games and the arts.

The building includes two gymnasiums, a pool, a 1000-seat theater, and an art gallery large enough for permanent displays and traveling exhibits.

Before invitations to bid were issued, the architect estimated costs on the basis of "quantity take off." This involves tabulating each quantity in the building—concrete, glass, steel, floor covering, and others—and then judging costs based on the quantities involved. This type of estimate, in the opinion of the college, provides a much more accurate basis than a square foot or cubic area basis.

September 1963

Advocate/Planner Helps
New Town Arts Develop

New towns, the planned communities in various stages of development around the country, have become targets for cultural programmers and planners. In Cedar/Riverside, a New Town in-Town under construction on 340 acres of urban renewal land in Minneapolis, a cultural precedent has been set. Since March 1972, Ann Payson, a former press officer for the Walker Arts Center, has been providing a vital link between Cedar Riverside Associates, the private firm developing 100 acres of the new town, and cultural groups in the area by serving as America's first arts advocate/planner.

Cedar/Riverside, located along the banks of the Mississippi in a former "skid row" section of Minneapolis, will, within 20 years, have some 30,000 occupants living in 10,000 units developed by Cedar Riverside Associates, with assistance from HUD's Community Development Corporation. One of the nation's most ambitious housing concepts, C/R will be ethnically mixed, with high and low income families sharing the same buildings.

When 400 residents moved into C/R's first completed building this spring, they found a cultural life equal to that of virtually any town in the country. For over the past five years as the developer was purchasing the land, arts groups began moving into the area, attracted by the cheap space available and by Cedar/Riverside's proximity to the nearby University of Minnesota. Currently C/R occupants include such groups as the Minnesota Dance Theater, the Minnesota Opera, Theater in the Round, the Grand Illusion Cinema, and Shakespeare in the Streets.

Ms. Payson entered the scene because Cedar Riverside Associates recognized the importance of cultural development to a new community and the need to insure the survival of arts groups already located there. At the suggestion of the state arts council, a proposal to pay the salary of an arts advocate/planner was submitted to the National Endowment for the Arts.

In taking on her new assignment, Ms. Payson had no established guidelines and no models to follow. "Nobody told me what to do," she told *AM,* "but I knew from the beginning that my primary responsibility would be to the arts groups rather than the developer." Viewing her role as one of facilitator and expeditor, as a pipeline between the developer and arts groups, and as an ombudsman to the local cultural organizations, Ms. Payson investigated such key areas as possible ordinance changes to subsidize arts spaces, city tax support, licensing matters, retention of usuable performance facilities, planning ahead for new facilities, and developing city-wide arts and education interest and involvement in Cedar/Riverside. Largely through her efforts an old firehouse was transformed into a community cultural center for rehearsal, instruction, and performances and residences by such dance companies as James Cunningham and Twyla Tharp. She also played a major role in helping to organize a Cedar/Riverside Arts Council, incorporated this April.

Ms. Payson has been able to help the developer as well by learning to understand his needs and problems. She has recognized, for example, that the construction of costly cultural facilities which might later go unused are not in the best interests of either the developer or local arts groups. Through her day to day involvement in the community, moreover, she can provide the developer with insights into both the economics and social values of various kinds of arts activities and facilities.

As a result of Ms. Payson's success, Cedar/Riverside Associates has agreed to pay half of her salary for the next year. A renewal of the Arts Endowment grant, currently pending will pay the remainder of her salary and consultant fees. Rental costs for local cultural facilities have been paid for from an Endowment Expansion Arts Program grant.

Ms. Payson is optimistic about the future. "Arts interest is extremely high here," she added. "The residents who just moved in already have formed a task force to work with the arts council."

Summer 1973

Amateur Company
Turns Professional in 40 Days

The purchase of a downtown nightclub in Buffalo, New York last August signaled the start of a new era for one of the city's oldest amateur theater groups. In an unusual display of local cooperation and support, the nightclub was transformed into a theater within 40 days, in time for the Studio Arena Theater to present its first professional performance in its new home. Assistance from the New York State Council on the Arts helped bolster the local effort.

It was the ambition of Neal Du Brock, executive director of the Studio Theater, to turn the 38-year-old community group into a top professional performing company. When a local nightclub, the Town Casino, was put up for sale, he saw it as an ideal site for a new theater. He asked his trustees for support and, although funds were not on hand, they backed the project.

In mid-September the board, headed by two local bankers, started an ambitious fund-raising drive for the new theater. Since then, more than $100,000 toward the goal of $175,000 has been raised. In addition, a campaign to sell memberships, seat dedications, and subscriptions for the fall season has been highly successful.

In the meantime, an architect and a construction company began renovating the old nightclub. Members of the company and volunteers helped ready the theater.

The State Council provided the theater with technical assistance. Milton Lyon, head of Equity's program to extend professional theater, and Marvin Kraus, general manager of Guber, Ford, and Gross, a producing company, advised the group and helped it locate and hire a front-of-house staff. In addition, the council provided the theater with support to hire Rod McManigal, an expert in audience recruitment, for three months. Commenting on council aid, Mr. Du Brock said, "The New York State Council on the Arts has virtually guaranteed our life."

On October 7, the new three-quarter-round theater with 550 seats opened with Eugene O'Neill's, *A Moon for the Misbegotten,* directed by José Quintero and starring Coleen Dewhurst and James Daly. The new production was critically acclaimed, and attendance since the opening has averaged more than 80 percent of theater capacity. In its first professional season, the comapny has presented three productions, and four more are scheduled through next spring.

Members of the old amateur group are appearing in the new company, and new actors and directors have been hired. Next year, the theater hopes to have its own resident group of Equity players.

December 1965

Let the City Build Your Cultural Facility

William A. Briggs

If grants and campaigns can't give you your tailor-made theater or concert hall, has it ever occurred to you that organizations like the Biscuit Bakers' Institute or the Ambulance Association of America might be the key to your own stage door? Last year such groups spent over a billion dollars at conventions.

Most conventions were held at civic centers in cities that are desparately seeking this foreign dollar and are willing to spend capital funds to secure it. It may be that a facility to house the arts is already high on the city's list, since entertainment is a paramount part of the pitch used in booking conventions. Tourist bureaus and chambers of commerce are also becoming aware of this need. Nevertheless, elected officials must always portray their personal furthering of the desires of their constituents, while often side-stepping the enmity of others. When the civic center issue is publicly aired, your council chamber will be SRO with groups you never dreamed of, upstaging one another to impress the authorities. Familiar and unfamiliar groups will be trying to get into the act—all with sharp axes, awaiting whetting.

Shouldn't you start right now to get acquainted with your chamber of commerce, your civic club directors, your convention manager, and your tourist bureau? Foresight could put you in the forefront when the cards are turned face-up! Cohesion could be stronger than coercion in securing facilities tailored specifically to your requirements if your groups cooperate rather than compete, and start voicing their needs and beneficial deeds in the council chamber and elsewhere now. Understanding the evolution can help!

The nebulously named civic center has finally shed its cocoon of all-purpose auditorium–arena and is nestling profitably into an equilateral triangle whose base is convention money. Sports and spectaculars comprise one leg of the triangle, and the other legs are reserved for live performing arts and conventions.

Due to the new "triangular concept," groups can now plan meetings not just in New York, Chicago or Miami, where there is more than scenery to look at after the business sessions, but in scores or cities all over North America. Businessmen can bring their families and be assured of comfortable lodging, good food, sports, and top cultural events. This is one way the convention base helps support local arts. Extra performances mean bigger box offices because you're playing to a new audience—an audience not even approached by your season subscription.

The new triangular concept was inevitable. It jelled in the minds of progressive civic leaders and talent promoters eight or ten years ago when they realized the old "civic auditorium" (usually a "multipurpose" coliseum with portable or fixed stage at one end) just didn't fulfill the new needs of local cultural groups or sports-oriented citizens, nor did it begin to satisfy the demands of the tourist or conventioneer.

The forward lookers knew the answer—bricks and mortar to create suitable settings for the talent that baits the convention. But new buildings cost taxpayers money, and few politicans would risk reelection on a platform that promised much beyond patching streets and sewers. However, pressures were bearing down on the city fathers. The downtown merchant found his cutomers straying off to new shopping centers. Local industry was losing key personnel to cities offering recreation and cultural programs in facilities properly designed for the purpose. As more and more businesses evacuated downtown for better surroundings, the once sparkling shop window lights dimmed. The city population dwindled and took with it the tax dollar. The city that wanted to live had to act, and the city fathers had to take off their blinders. Their motive was no altruistic effort toward aid for arts or sports; rather, they had to find ways to garner foreign funds for elevating the tax base and reviving the central business district.

The civic center seemed to be the answer. Federal and state grants, planning loans, and other sources of financial assistance were available if they knew where to look. They looked and found ways and acted—some with commendable cohesiveness of effort—resulting in bright new architectural beauties that quickly increased interest and activity in the arts and sports. But due to expediency and an understandable lack of experience in the design of such long-forgotten building types, some of these gems were myopically envisioned, functionally inadequate, or just plain wrong. There were few guidelines and almost no appropriate prototypes. In the rush to get the house built, little study was devoted to specific local needs, and there was no long-range programming.

Now, however, guided by the new triangular civic center concept, great strides are being made. Here's your cue! Capitalize on the strength of a concept that doesn't drain the budget. It can build the two things you need most—the right facility and the large foreign (not alien) audience. To get into the act, first get together. Then get the merchant's ear, the manufacturer's eye and the city fathers' voices, and you may soon be helping the architect design your home in the civic center. Today's civic centers can't thrive without culture! Don't worry about the audience—the chamber of commerce will have extra performances booked long before the show can be mounted.

March-April 1968

Mix Business with Pleasure

Cultural groups can provide their members and contributors with a pleasurable social experience while educating them to the organization's needs. The Montgomery County Arts Center in Maryland, which is planning to build a theater, gallery, and educational unit, recently sponsored to visit to an arts center with facilities similar to those it is planning for itself. The center chartered a bus to the Goucher College Art Center in Towson, Maryland to see how the performing, training, and exhibiting facilities at the school are operated. A champagne supper was served aboard the bus, and a quartet-in-residence at the college performed for the visitors. Those unable to take the trip were urged by the organization to visit Goucher on their own. Arrangements were made for future visitors to be shown the facilities by college officials.

September 1964

Arts Afloat: Ships Provide New Programs Vehicle

Luxury ships have been utilized for arts programs recently. In Belgium, the yacht S.S. *Goedu I* was transformed into a floating art museum to traverse the Meuse River and its waterways. Its first public exhibition fittingly is a retrospective titled "Painters of the Meuse and its Tributaries." In the Carribean, the Theatre Guild sponsored a 16-day cruise with the Holland American Lines, featuring a company of famous Broadway actors in regular performances as well as lectures and demonstrations provided by the American Academy of Dramatic Arts.

One arts group, meanwhile, is using lake cruises as a subscription benefit. Early subscribers to the 1975 summer season of the Lake George Opera Festival are being given a bonus—a free Sunday evening "Opera-On-The-Lake" cruise. The two-hour cruise, which usually costs $10, features opera company artists performing selections from operas.

March-April 1975

Custom-Designed Mobile Gallery in Use

A new museum on wheels, believed to be the first such vehicle specifically designed for this purpose, and intended as a prototype for mobile units being developed by organizations throughout the country, is now touring Illinois. In comparison to other traveling museums now in use, which are usually standard trailers converted to their new function, the new unit, called the Art Resources Traveler, has been completely custom designed and includes many unique features.

The mobile museum, which consists of a tractor and an exhibit trailer 40 feet long by 10 feet wide, was designed by Frank Carioti for the Illinois Department of Public Instruction with funds provided by the Educational Facilities Laboratories, a nonprofit organization established by the Ford Foundation to help American schools and colleges with their physical problems. The department, which owns and operates the unit, has received additional project support through the Title V program of the Elementary and Secondary Education Act.

Completed in August 1967, the Traveler is equipped with sculpture and paintings loaned by leading museums and private collectors. Manned by a driver and lecturer, it began touring the state on September 12.

Among the features of the new unit are seamless display walls designed to make it easier to mount and dismount exhibits; climate and humidity controls (said to be superior to those in most museums); built-in projection and sound systems to accommodate films, slides, tapes, or any type of audiovisual material; an incandescent lighting system programmed into prerecorded lecture systems; an air suspension system to provide maximum protection to the collection when in transit; special safety controls; distinct exterior design with smooth panel construction to assure no visual identification with other mobile units; and a built-in wall stage which serves as a lecture platform.

The unit is heavier than standard commercial trailers and it is said to be far more durable. Also, it is self-supporting, with parts and equipment replaceable and repairable at the most remote location, and with all electric and hydraulic systems operable by hand.

Prior to the Traveler's arrival in a community, posters and press releases are sent to schools and other local agencies. Teachers receive filmstrips and instruction manuals which relate to the 35- to 40-minute programmed lectures presented to students in the trailer. Programmed lectures are planned also for adult groups and for teacher training classes. The unit accommodates 20 people for lectures and about 30 for regular viewing of the collection. Although the prototype cost $100,000 to build, it is estimated that additional units could be constructed at a cost of between $70,000 and $80,000.

Meanwhile, in Rochester, New York, another unusual new mobile unit is providing local schoolchildren with a rare cultural experience—the opportunity to see movies, filmstrips, and slides of places of interest, while they are *traveling* to these facilities. The theater-on-wheels, which looks like an ordinary yellow school bus on the outside, has a sloping theater floor, seats for 40 children, a screen, projectors, tape recorders, special control panel, and six loudspeakers in the bus and five outside it. Built with funds provided under Title I of the Elementary and Secondary Education Act, the bus cost $43,910. Local officials claim that it is the only bus in the country that can show visual materials while in motion.

During its first four months in operation, which began in September, some 4000 Rochester children will have taken trips on the bus to museums, art galleries, industrial sites, and college campuses. Along the way, lecturers will prepare them for their visits with audiovisual materials and special commentary. Tape recordings of gallery talks and lectures will be made at stopover points and played back later in the bus.

September-October 1967

Student Architects Aid
in Planning New Theatre

A unique project that joined a cultural institution with a class of college architectural students resulted in excellent publicity for the arts group and provided it with valuable research material and a 143-page documented report containing many useful ideas.

The project began after the Mummers Theatre in Oklahoma City, Oklahoma, recipient of a $1.25-million grant from the Ford Foundation and $750,000 from local contributors, announced plans for the construction of a new theater building. In spite of the fact that the actual building and theater were to be designed by accomplished professionals, architect John Johansen and theater designer David Hays, the senior architecture class in design and working drawings at Oklahoma State University offered to undertake the design of a new Mummers Theater. It was understood that none of the working drawings submitted by the class would be used for construction of the new theater and that the effort would be viewed strictly as a class project. It was felt, however, that the results of the student project might contribute valuable ideas for the actual construction.

The Mummers Theater presented the basic concept of the building and the kind of theater desired to the class. Jointly, a building program was drawn up, and the class of 44 students, under the supervision of professors, was divided into an executive committee and nine working committees in the following areas: sociological conditions, site selection, physical conditions, code requirements, technical investigations, acoustics and lighting, theater equipment and stage design, and finance and project planning. The project was completely realistic, with students interviewing persons who were concerned with the new building and gathering detailed information in each of the committee areas. In addition, several technical consultants were called in, and the students worked with actual building sites under consideration in Oklahoma City.

The result of these efforts was a detailed, carefully documented, 143-page report which was complete enough to allow for the actual construction of the theater building. The report, completed early this year, was accompanied by working drawings and elevations prepared by each of the students. According to David Lunney, Ford Foundation administrative intern at the Mummers Theater, the students contributions were greatest in the areas of audience, shop, and office space.

The Mummers received excellent publicity as a result of the student project. Just last month, one of the leading banks in downtown Oklahoma City presented an exhibition featuring some of the outstanding working drawings prepared by the students. The exhibition generated community excitement and focused attention on the forthcoming new building and the theater itself.

April 1964

Arts Groups on Right Track
with Railroads and Subways

Railroad and subway stations are playing a growing role in the arts as areas for exhibits and performances and as settings for fund-raising events. Two Educational Facilities Laboratories reports on reusing railroad stations, published several years ago, spurred interest in old stations as arts and education centers, but in the past year arts groups have discovered other uses.

In Minneapolis last summer, the Minnesota Opera used the old Great Northern Railway station as the setting for a fund-raising ball, the "Minnesota Opera Train." Featuring turn-of-the-century atmosphere, the ball included a dining car dinner, performances by company members, railroad memorabilia exhibits, dancing, and a box car auction. Although 400 diners were expected, publicity was excellent and 900 turned up. The event netted $40,000 and drew many new faces. "We were better known nationally than locally before," company director Charles Fullmer told *AM*, "and the event gave us a lot of recognition." A related development brought the company reams of unexpected publicity. When the opera auction winner turned up to claim her prize—luncheon with Minnesota Governor Rudy Perpich—she was identified in newspaper accounts as one of the Twin Cities best-known former madams.

Another railroad ball in Jacksonville in November 1977 drew over 6000 donors to the city's Union Station, last used in 1974. The sponsor, Riverside Avondale Preservation, sold all its tickets on a wave of publicity and cleared over $40,000 in the process. In St. Louis, education TV Channel 9 is planning a week-long "Great TV Auction" to be held at historic Union Station from April 8-16. This December a corner of the same station was converted into the new 150 seat home of the Theater Project Company.

The train image has brought mobility to two arts groups. North Carolina's Beaufort County Arts Council, housed in a converted train depot, used its setting as theme for a new mobile arts unit last summer, "Caboose on the Loose." In Hartford, Connecticut, the Peace Train, a caboose built around the chasis of a 1964 Dodge, has presented programs in parks and neighborhoods for the past five years, including 150 concerts last summer.

The railroad depot itself will be the focus of a new exhibition opening this May. With $50,000 funding from the Humanities Endowment, the Danforth Museum in Framingham, Massachusetts will offer, "The Railroad Depot: Focus of a New England Town's Growth."

Subways, meanwhile, have become an increasingly popular arts setting. Platforms for Design, a pilot project in four New York subway stations sponsored by the Arts and Business Council and Public Arts Council proved so successful that the Urban Mass Transportation Administration recently awarded a $500,000 matching grant for the beautification of other stations. New York's Metropolitan

Transit Authority pledged to match private donations, up to $25,000 to enable Cityarts Workshop to create permanent murals in cement and mosaic for a downtown subway station. In Atlanta, art will be a key feature of the new MARTA transit system. Every station has included art purchase money in its overall budget.

Subways also are on exhibit in New York. The Cooper-Hewitt Museum has a free exhibition at a Forty-second Street subway station, "Subways," as part of its "Immovable Objects" series and Cityana Gallery is offering "A New York Subway Map Retrospective."

January-February 1978

Floating Conference

If you're planning a convention, perhaps the program for the 1966 annual conference of the American Community Theatre Association may provide you with some lively thoughts on keeping the conference moving. The ACTA meeting was billed as "the newest established floating conference," since the program took place in five different Minnesota cities. Thus, attendees had the opportunity to see eight performances and tour nine different theater buildings. Seminars on such practical topics as fund raising and audience development were held aboard buses going to and from conference sites.

August-September 1966

CHRONOLOGY OF BUILDING DEVELOPMENTS IN THE ARTS

Cultural Building Boom Biggest in History

This concludes a two-part series based on AM's *1962 survey of chambers of commerce.*

Rising public interest in the arts has created a boom of wholly unprecedented proportions in the construction of new buildings to house cultural activities, *AM's* latest survey reveals. The survey, which drew detailed replies from chamber of commerce officials in 147 cities, asked a series of questions about construction of new arts facilities. The results are dramatic evidence of the scope of the cultural upsurge.

Some form of building activity in connection with the arts was reported to be planned or under way in 69 communities, virtually half of those replying to the construction questions. The projects mentioned in the survey represent a budgeted or contemplated expenditure of at least $120 million. The survey results suggest that the total national building bill for the arts (including Lincoln Center in New York and others not covered in the survey) may run around $375 million. This means that for the first time in history the nation's cultural establishment has become an economically important market for commercially produced goods and services. This is a historic development that can have a deep impact on the long-range relationship between business and the arts in America.

Within the construction boom can be seen the increasing influence of the interdisciplinary movement in the arts. Combined facilities—art centers sheltering a number of different kinds of cultural activity—are being planned or built in 40 of the 147 cities covered in the survey, 27.2 percent.

These range in size from the ambitious plans for the National Cultural Center in Washington, estimated to cost $30 million (only Lincoln Center will be bigger) down to the estimated $10,000 for an art center in Key West, Florida. Peoria has engaged Victor Gruen Associates to design a new $700,000 center. Syracuse, New York reports plans for a center to be part of a community plaza development to be built as part of its urban renewal program.

Winter Park, Florida is planning a theater, museum, and concert auditorium in a single facility to cost between $1.5 and $2 million. Laramie, Wyoming, Trenton, New Jersey, Hartford, Connecticut, and San Leandro, California all report plans for combined arts facilities, and plans are in the talking stage in cities like Odessa, Texas, Gadsden, Alabama, and Tenafly, New Jersey, to mention a few.

A breakdown of the kinds of facilities planned shows that museums are running slightly ahead of theaters and concert halls in terms of numbers of cities now building or planning them.

Fully 34 communities, 23.2 percent of the total, reported new museums going up. Washington's Board of Trade estimates that $25 million will be spent there on new museum construction. Milwaukee is spending $5.5 million. New museums range in type from Oklahoma City's $400,000 combined arts and science museum to Tampa's children's museum and the museum of American Indian artifacts planned in Quincy, Illinois.

In 30 of the cities covered by the survey—20.4 percent of the total—new concert auditoriums are either rising or being blueprinted. A number, like the ones in Baltimore and St. Petersburg, Florida, are part of civic centers. Others, like those in Hartford, and Lakeland, Florida, are connected with colleges.

Theater construction is indicated in 28 of the reporting communities. Framingham, Massachusetts., for example, is building a permanent theater in the round. Ypsilanti, Michigan, is spending $400,000; Asheville, North Carolina, $500,000; and Salt Lake City, $1.25 million.

The survey results also indicate that a great deal of money is being spent on remodeling and enlarging existing facilities in every area of the arts. Savannah, Georgia, and Beckley, West Virginia are remodeling theaters. Tampa's concert auditorium is being remodeled at a cost of $350,000. The arts center in Tacoma, Washington is being altered and furnished. Museums in Greensboro, North Carolina, Grand Rapids, Michigan, and Colorado Springs, Colorado are being expanded.

The long-range significance of this hectic activity is hard to interpret but, inevitably, the increase in physical facilities will bring with it the need for greater than the ever numbers of trained arts managers to man the bigger, more complex arts "plant." In turn, the growth of the arts management profession is likely to have profound consequences on the content and character of the arts of the future.

June 1962

Urban Renewal
Spurs Arts Building Activity

Urban renewal programs are playing an important role in the cultural building boom, a nationwide survey just compiled by *AM* reveals. Although cultural facilities in urban renewal areas are mostly on the drawing boards today, the survey indicated that the next few years should produce new arts structures in every area of the country.

The survey, believed to be the first of its kind, drew replies from urban renewal agencies in 95 cities, ranging in size from New York, with its eight million persons, to Edinburgh, Texas, with a population of 15,000. Responses to *AM* questionnaires came from 31 states and the District of Columbia.

In the urban renewal program, federal funds are used to purchase land, which is then cleared and developed, rehabilitated, or conserved. While the government must approve the urban renewal plans of local agencies, it does not provide construction funds. In the majority of instances, private developers construct the facilities.

Of the 95 cities surveyed, 43, or nearly half, include the construction of arts facilities in their urban renewal plans. Of these cities, some have more than one urban renewal project involving the arts. In some instances, there are several arts facilities included in a single project. Of the projects reported, 14 are under construction, 26 are in the planning stage, 4 in remodeling, and 4 have been completed since 1960. In addition, four other cities in the early stage of urban renewal planning are leaning towards the inclusion of arts facilities. A preponderance of these arts facilities are theaters, with arts centers and museums receiving the next greatest emphasis.

Of the major cities surveyed, most include the arts in their urban renewal programs with the exceptions of Minneapolis, St. Louis, Los Angeles, San Antonio, Texas, and Buffalo, New York. New York has the largest project, the Lincoln Center complex, as well as the Washington Square theater. However, other metropolises, like Philadelphia, which is planning the expansion of its Academy of

Music and College of Art and the possible creation of a cultural center around existing institutions, also have ambitious programs.

Chicago's program includes cultural facilities on a new University of Illinois campus, a theater, and two cultural centers. Atlanta will have an auditorium to replace an existing city auditorium, and an exhibit hall. Washington, D. C., has its Arena Stage completed in its southwest renewal area, and Pittsburgh is building a theater and a center for the arts which will house its Symphony Orchestra. In Baltimore, one urban renewal project in the planning stage calls for additions to the Peabody Institute of Music and the Walters Art Gallery, and another calls for a new theater to replace Ford's Theater.

In San Francisco, arts facilities are planned in several urban renewal areas. Two commercial theaters, a museum and a Japanese cultural and trade center will be built there. Although a site was sought for the city's Actor's Workshop, the renewal agency said that "the project is likely not to materialize in view of the departure of the principal members of the organization to the Lincoln Center Repertory Theater."

Detroit is considering the inclusion of theaters in two of its urban renewal projects. Its agency reported, "It is entirely possible that in the future there will be a cultural center urban renewal project in the vicinity of our Institute of Arts, Main Library, and Historical Museum."

In medium-sized cities, those with 200,000 to 500,000 persons, six of ten agencies include the arts. Providence, Rhode Island, has proposed in its master plan, "Downtown Providence 1970," that a center for the performing arts of Rhode Island be included. Miami, which has recently submitted an application to the government for its first urban renewal project, has proposed a large community center to include theater facilities.

In Rochester, New York, an urban renewal program in the planning stage calls for the construction of a performing arts theater in the downtown business district within five to ten years. In Norfolk, Virginia, an adjunct to the Norfolk Art Museum is being restored, in San Jose, California, a theater is planned, and in Tulsa, Oklahoma, a theater will be included in a civic area.

Urban renewal also appears to have sparked the construction of arts facilities within project boundaries, but not on land cleared with urban renewal funds. Based on such land usage, an arts center is planned in Springfield, Ohio; Tulsa will have a new theater; and Little Rock has built an arts center.

April 1965

Arts Facilities Uplift
Urban Renewal Areas

Arts facilities included in urban renewal projects are tending to uplift their surrounding areas, and early indications are that they will also raise real estate values and increase business volume. This was concluded by *AM* from its recent survey of urban renewal and the arts, to which 95 cities responded.

Of the 43 cities that included the construction of arts facilities in their urban renewal plans, 23 had advanced far enough in their projects to venture estimates as to the effect the facilities would generally have on the city as well as the project area.

In answer to the question, "What benefits will your city realize from new or improved cultural facilities?" all cities responding indicated generally positive effects, while five specifically cited an anticipated increase in attendance at cultural events.

Pittsburgh reported that its planned center for the arts will develop its downtown area as a cultural center, strengthen the prestige and financial position of its symphony orchestra, and attract visitors to the city. In Washington, D. C., construction of the Arena Stage has "added enormously to the cultural vitality of the city."

Of the small number of cities in a position to estimate the effect that arts facilities in urban renewal projects will have on real estate values, 11 reported rising values. In addition, five cities indicated increased traffic, and three cities reported heightened business volume in the urban renewal area. No cities, however, reported a drop in any of the above.

As reported previously in *AM*, the majority of cities with populations exceeding 200,000 (61 per cent) include arts facilities in their urban renewal programs. In contrast, only 38 percent, or 27 of the 71 smaller cities responding to the survey, include the arts. Four other smaller cities report they are considering structures to house the arts as part of their urban renewal plans.

New Rochelle, New York, has submitted plans for a legitimate theater to builder–developers and hopes for responses in the near future. A theater center is planned in Hartford, Connecticut, a performing arts center is being built in Binghamton, New York, and a museum is being constructed in Lansing, Michigan. An auditorium is planned in Cedar Rapids, Iowa; Fresno, Califronia is modernizing several theaters in its cultural center; and White Plains, New York, is considering construction of a county-wide arts center.

Several cities with populations under 50,000 have ambitious plans for the arts in their urban renewal programs. An arts center and museum are planned in Brunswick, Georgia, and Williamsport, Pennsylvania plans a theater for the performing arts. Potsdam, New York, with less than 10,000 persons, plans the relocation of its Village Museum, and has already completed concert halls at the State University College, Clarkson College of Technology, and the Crane School of Music.

More than a quarter of the surveyed cities that included arts facilities in their urban renewal programs are being aided in the planning of these facilities by arts organizations. But the types of organizations vary. In New York, Lincoln

Center aids the city's Housing and Redevelopment Board in plans for its urban renewal area.

Rochester, New York has a Committee for the Performing Arts to help it plan its urban renewal projects. Pittsburgh works with various organizations interested in the arts, such as the Heinz Foundation, the Mellon Charitable and Educational Trust, and the Allegheny Conference on Community Development. San Francisco consults with its Museum Board, the city's Symphony Foundation and its ballet company. San Jose, California works with its Fine Arts Commission and Symphony Association.

May 1965

Visual Arts Seldom Featured in Local Urban Renewal Plans

Urban renewal projects are making limited use of painting and sculpture. In only a few instances are specific proposals for artworks written into the project; occasionally they are included without being stipulated in plans. And competitions appear to play a small role in the selection of arts works and in the design of cultural facilities.

These were the conclusions drawn by *AM* from its 1965 survey of urban renewal and the arts, to which 95 cities responded.

In answer to the question "Does your city program include any stipulation that builders must set aside a percentage of contract dollars for the purchase of art?" only 5 of the 47 cities responding answered "Yes." In each of those cities the total amount budgeted for visual art is 1 percent of the overall construction figure.

In its four urban renewal areas, San Francisco will have sculpture by such artists as Henry Moore, Marino Marini, Seymour Lipton, Jacques Overhoff, and Duane Faralla; paintings by David Simpson and Keith Boyle; a mosaic by Mark Adams; and a pagoda in its Japanese Cultural and Trade Center by Yoshiro Taniguchi.

Baltimore anticipates sculpture in addition to a fountain in its Charles Center Project. Murals, statuary, and fountains will mark Washington, D.C.'s Columbia Plaza urban renewal area. Bethlehem, Pennsylvania has selected a citizens' committee to recommend how $90,000 should be spent for art, sculpture and murals in its Civic Center. And Asheville, North Carolina will also beautify its renewal projects with artwork.

While making no specific provisions for it, three other cities include art in urban renewal projects. Chicago reported it includes art "indirectly" by basing awards of contracts to builders on criteria that state the desirability of including art and sculpture in building plans. Los Angeles says it encourages art work in design criteria. Hartford, Connecticut has a "permissive" policy; 1 percent of construction costs may be devoted to art.

Five cities—Kalamazoo, Michigan, Springfield, Ohio, Stamford, Connecticut, Chester, Pennsylvania, and Portsmouth, New Hampshire—indicated that while no stipulation exists for artwork in urban renewal projects, such a requirement is being considered.

Meanwhile, six cities have conducted competitions for design of structures or for works of art as part of their urban renewal programs. Except for Rochester, New York, these are the same cities stipulating a 1 percent budget figure for artworks in urban renewal projects.

June 1965

Cultural Building Boom to Continue *AM* Chamber Survey Reveals

This is the second part of AM's *1967 survey of chambers of commerce. Part one was based on 181 responses. An additional 40 chambers, who responded to questionnaires later, are included in the current study.*

More new buildings for the arts have been completed in the past five years than in any other period in history. This bricks and mortar boom will not only continue, but it seems likely to accelerate in the next five years, *AM's* survey of chambers of commerce reveals. The survey, which drew detailed responses from chamber of commerce officials in 221 cities, was undertaken to determine the number of cultural facilities completed since 1962 and the number of new buildings underway or planned.

More than two-thirds of the responding chambers, 141 of 221, listed some form of arts construction activity in their communities since 1962. Seventy cities completed a total of 100 new arts structures in the past five years. This list includes 36 museums, 34 theaters, 23 arts centers, and 7 concert auditoriums. The costliest of these projects was Los Angeles' $33.5-million Music Center (New York's Lincoln Center was not included in the survey).

Facilities now underway or planned outnumber those completed, according to the survey, with 98 cities reporting 126 projects in various stages of development. Cost estimates, which are given for 66 of these projects, totaled nearly $220 million. If a similar amount were projected for the 60 other projects, and if we assume that another 60 facilities were not included in the survey (colleges that are experiencing an arts building boom were listed infrequently), the national arts building bill for the next five years would easily exceed $600 million. Translated into economic terms, the building of facilities to house arts activities represents a market of considerable significance.

Motivation for many of the new facilities appears to have come from chambers of commerce. Ten chambers listed themselves as motivators, and eight other chambers claimed to have played key roles in the planning of new structures for the arts.

Two trends were evident from survey results. First, more communities are thinking about building arts centers, facilities that house several kinds of arts activities, than any other kind of structure. Of the 126 projects listed as underway or planned, 49 were arts centers. Second, many multipurpose centers are being built by municipalities and financed through bond issues and special taxes. These centers house not only facilities for the arts, but facilities for such income-producing, nonarts programs such as trade shows and conventions. Norfolk, Virginia, for example, has broken ground for an $18-million cultural–convention center which will include an arena, theater complex, and museum; Wichita, Kansas is constructing a $12.6-million municipal auditorium complex including a theater, music hall, auditorium, convention rooms, and exhibit space; Saginaw, Michigan will complete its $6.5-million civic center housing a music hall, arena, and auditorium in 1969; and Richmond, Virginia will break ground for its new $20-million coliseum in 1968. Other cities now building civic centers combining the arts and commercial activities include Denver, Charleston, South Carolina, and Monroe, Louisiana.

Centers limited strictly to arts activities range in size from Atlanta's $13-million Memorial Cultural Center and Milwaukee's $10-million County War Memorial Center for the Performing Arts, both scheduled to open in 1968, down to Cincinnati's $400,000 Contemporary Arts Center, which will be completed in 1969. Brockton, Massachusetts is planning a $5-million center; Tulsa, a $4.5-million center; San Jose, California, a $3-million center; and Memphis, a $2-million center. Colleges planning or constructing arts centers include Millikin University in Decatur, Illinois; Akron University in Ohio; Washburn University in Topeka, Kansas; and the University of Idaho in Moscow, Idaho. New cultural centers are being considered as part of core area redevelopment programs in Boulder, Colorado and Providence, Rhode Island.

A breakdown by types of facilities indicates that theaters are running ahead of museums and concert auditoriums. Responding chambers listed 30 theaters now underway or planned. Those to be completed this year include the $750,000 North Shore Theatre in Beverly, Massachusetts, the $300,000 Spokane, Washington Civic Theater, and a $150,000 theater in Cheyenne, Wyoming. Theaters scheduled to open in 1968 include those in San Jose, California ($5 million); Houston ($3 million); San Antonio, Texas ($2.5 million); and Oklahoma City ($2 million). The University of Michigan hopes to complete its $2.5-million theater in 1969, and New Orleans plans to open its $4-million theater by 1970.

New museums were listed by 29 chambers with projects ranging from Columbus, Ohio's $10-million museum, scheduled to open in 1969, to Albion, Michigan's $40,000 historical museum, which will be completed this October. An $8-million museum will open in Oakland, California in 1968, and a $3-million museum will open in Pasadena, California in 1969. Later this year, new museums will open in Clovis, New Mexico; Bartlesville, Oklahoma; Juneau, Alaska; Colorado Springs, Colorado; and Williamsport, Pennsylvania.

Only 18 new concert auditoriums are underway or planned according to the survey. These include facilities now being constructed in Cincinnati, Ohio; Amarillo, Texas; Jackson, Mississippi; Macon, Georgia; Portland, Oregon; Roanoke, Virginia; and Estes Park, Colorado, each costing more than $1 million. Huntsville, Alabama is planning a $6-million auditorium and New Orleans hopes to have its $4-million auditorium built by 1971. Orlando, Florida approved a $1.6-million bond issue for an auditorium in 1965.

In addition to new construction, the survey results indicate that large sums are being spent to remodel or enlarge existing facilities.

Summer 1967

Arts Facilities
Throughout the Nation Make News

Not since the opening of Lincoln Center have arts facilities commanded as much public attention and controversy as they have within recent months. While the big newsmaker by far has been the $70-million Kennedy Center which opened September 8, 1971 in Washington, D.C., other facilities—new theaters and renovated ones, theaters for sale and for razing—in an incredible diversity of settings, have vied for a share of the spotlight.

The Washington, D.C. area, in addition to the Kennedy Center, gained two new arts facilities this year: the Arena Stage's 500-seat Kreeger Theater and Filene Center, the $2-million concert auditorium in Wolf Trap Farm Park in Virginia. New facilities elsewhere include Midland, Michigan's $7.8-million Center for the Arts which opened in May, and several campus arts centers including the University of Pennsylvania's $5.7-million Annenberg Center for Communication Arts and Sciences which opened this spring. The University of Michigan just unveiled its $3.5-million Power Center for the Performing Arts, and Simpson College in Iowa opened a $1.25-million center.

Renovated structures have been important additions to the scene in several large Eastern cities. A former movie palace in Pittsburgh has been completely renovated and opened in September as Heinz Hall for the Performing Arts, the glittering new home of the Pittsburgh Symphony. In Philadelphia, a $2-million interior renovation and facade restoration enabled the nation's oldest theater, the Walnut Street, to reopen in October as Philadelphia's new cultural center. The Boston Center for the Arts, which will eventually provide performing, rehearsal, storage, office, and studio space for over 200 artists and arts groups, is being carved out of a group of seven old buildings at a cost of $5 million. The buildings were to be destroyed, but arts leaders led a successful effort to have the Boston Redevelopment Authority designate them as the site of the new center. In Rochester, New York, a grant from Eastman Kodak will help to pay for the $2-million renovation of the Eastman Theater where the Rochester Philharmonic performs while in Detroit, Orchestra Hall, which was scheduled for demolition, has been saved thanks to a $30,000 gift from David Elgin Dodge last month. On a less happy note, a facility built in 1965 to house the now defunct Theatre Atlanta Repertory, was listed "for sale" in a recent magazine ad.

Meanwhile, in New York, a plan under which the city would acquire Lincoln Center's Vivian Beaumont Theatre for $1, remodel it at a cost of $5.2-million to accommodate three new movie theaters and a relocated Forum Theater, and turn over its operation to the City Center erupted into a major controversy. Several cultural leaders organized a committee to save the Beaumont and its Forum Theater, and apparently their effort has been successful. [*Note:* Several years later Joseph Papp of the New York Shakespeare Festival took over the operation of the theaters, but he left after a few seasons and the theaters were again dark. During the 1978–79 season Lincoln Center announced new plans to reopen the theater.]

New York also has new arts facilities under construction, including four legitimate theaters to be housed in office buildings. Two of them, the new homes of the Circle in the Square Theatre and the American Place Theatre, are scheduled for completion this season.

September-October 1971

Buildings and Real Estate
Make News in the Arts

Cultural building activities, both actual and proposed, made major news in 1976. Interestingly, many of the new developments are pioneer activities which move arts groups into new and, at times, unfamiliar areas of operation.

In a development with far-reaching significance for large cultural institutions everywhere, the Museum of Modern Art, following a legislative battle in the state, has won approval to erect a 40-story, income-producing condominium tower atop its present facility. The New York State Cultural Resources Act of 1976, which was passed after an initial defeat in the New York State Legislature thanks to a 24-hour telephone campaign, authorized creation of a new public benefit corporation, the Trust for Cultural Resources, which can condemn a small plot of land, issue tax exempt securities, and sell air rights over the museum site to a private developer to build the tower. Instead of paying taxes on the property, the legislation will require the condominium owners to pass along the amount ordinarily payed in taxes, estimated ultimately at $1 million annually, to the trust to help meet the indebtedness incurred in expanding the museum property.

The condominium project is a unique response by museum trustees to two of the institution's pressing problems—a deficit running at about $1 million annually and insufficient space to house the museum collection and other programs. As envisioned, the income from the sale of apartments and from tax equivalency payments by apartment owners will provide the museum with additional operating income and will aid in funding the enlarging of gallery space.

In addition, to help finance its expansion and to add sufficient funds to its endowment for the operation of the expanded facility, the museum will seek $20 million in contributions. An additional contingency fund of $7 million will be sought from private foundations in order to assure the museum an appropriate return on the sale of its air rights. It is thought that some foundations might be willing to partially underwrite this kind of venture, while they might not otherwise give directly to the museum.

With the thought of substantially increasing its earned income, another New York museum is expanding its existing facility. The Metropolitan Museum will spend nearly $3 million to construct a five-story publications center within what is now a light well near the institution's grand staircase. The hopes are that the extra space will help up the $1.5-million the museum now earns annually from publications and reproductions.

Elsewhere, renovation and the reopening of existing structures, including Wilmington, Delaware's 105-year-old Grand Opera House and Lexington, Kentucky's 90-year-old Opera House, have been newsmakers. In Newark, New Jersey, Symphony Hall was reopened this spring after it had been closed for building violations thanks to the local stage employees union which contributed $10,000 worth of free labor and city government which provided materials. Miami Beach's new Theatre of the Performing Arts retains the four walls and little else of a 1950 auditorium and New York's Project Studio One, an exhibition and studio center for experimental artists, has just come to life in a refurbished 80-year-old public school abandoned 13 years ago. In Buffalo, New York, Media Study is now turning a seven-story hotel worth over $600,000, donated by a local business as a no-strings-attached gift, into an arts center. The most publicized renovation is the $5-million acoustical overhaul of Avery Fisher Hall.

Other arts groups are gathering support in the hopes of turning existing community structures into centers for the arts. The Greensboro, North Carolina's United Arts Council is leading a drive to raise $550,000 to purchase and refurbish the 50-year-old Carolina Theater; Tampa's City Council accepted the old Tampa Theater and voted to spend $150,000 to restore it; and Durham, North Carolina, arts leaders are involved in a project to turn the old county court house into a cultural center. Perhaps the most ambitious renovation project is taking place at Sailors Snug Harbor in Staten Island, New York, an 80-acre landmark site that includes a group of Greek Revival buildings used until recently as a residence for retired sailors. The new Snug Harbor Cultural Center organization is leading a battle to fund repairs for interim use of the facility until it releases its new master plan in several months. It will then launch a major fund drive for the estimated $13- to $15-million needed to turn the imposing site into a fully functioning cultural center.

Meanwhile, after months of rumors and varying press reports as to whether the arrangement was on or off, final documents have been signed that turn over operation of a building, the New York City Center, to four New York dance companies—the Joffrey Ballet, Alvin Ailey Dance Theater, American Ballet Theater and the Eliot Feld Ballet. Differences have now been resolved and, in effect, the Center is subleasing the theater for one year at $1 rental to the four companies organized as a new corporation for the effort.

Under the unprecedented agreement terms, rental, which is not automatically renewable, covers the theater, building, and the ballroom below. The Joffrey company alone will sublease the building's office tower, which includes rehearsal space, a facility it is currently using. The tower, not commercially rentable, will be operated at a net loss of between $100,000 and $150,000 which is equal to what Joffrey would pay for equivalent space.

Each of the four companies has committed itself to a season at the Center for an overall schedule of 22 weeks. Because of the lateness in concluding arrangements, however, and insufficient consecutive weeks between the four companies' seasons, only eight additional weeks are scheduled for seasons by other dance companies. With total operating costs projected at $700,000, each of the four major participants will pay a flat sum of about $23,000 for each of their performance weeks. Each company, however, will keep its own box office receipts during its season.

During their weeks as landlords, the companies as a group will keep rental income but will be responsible for theater operating costs. "There will probably be a loss absorbed by the companies, but the benefits may outweigh them considerably," a spokesman told *AM*. "What they're doing in effect is creating a dance center in New York which eventually might present a 40-week season every year." If the project works out reasonably well, the contract will be renewed and with sufficient lead time for booking and planning, the deficit can be cut considerably.

City Center Inc. as prior administrator, was not only running at a deficit but was subsidizing the costs of part of the Joffrey and Ailey seasons. If the present arrangement had not been concluded, the theater might have been closed.

Following the lead of Syracuse, where the recently opened Civic Center of Onondaga County links a county office building to three theaters, government is playing a major role in the financing of new arts centers. In Tennessee, the Governor has signed the $31-million construction contract for the new state office building and cultural complex due to be completed in 1979; in Salt Lake City voters have approved a bond issue of $8.6 million to match $7.5 million appropriated by the State Legislature for construction of a new concert hall and restoration of a 1913 theater; and in Tulsa the new $19-million arts center opening this March not only has been funded through a combination of private and public sources—general revenue sharing, a bond issue, and income from a sales tax—but will be owned and operated at a projected annual cost of over $600,000 as a division of municipal government.

Summer 1976

Renovated Buildings
Become New Arts Centers

A variety of old buildings, ranging from former movie palaces to asphalt plants, to firehouses, to railroad shops, to tenements are finding new life through reconversion into arts facilities. In Canada, the Vancouver Symphony recently played the first concert at the old Orpheum Theater, renovated at a cost of $7.1 million. The Beacon movie theater in New York opened a Murray Louis-Alwin Nikolais dance season following reconversion and will now operate as a nonprofit arts center, while the old Cheverly Theatre in Prince George's County, Maryland was transformed into the Publick Playhouse, the county's first community arts center. The Puerto Rican Traveling Theater just opened its first permanent home, in a New York firehouse.

In Greensboro, North Carolina the United Arts Council has just finished raising over half a million dollars to purchase and renovate the Carolina Theatre. It will reopen this fall on or about its fiftieth anniversary as the city's first performing arts center. In Paterson, New Jersey the country's largest former locomotive erecting shop is being turned into a combined Great Falls District arts center and historic museum, while in New York a drive to convert an unused municipal asphalt plant into a combined arts–sports center at a cost of over $1 million has received impetus with major contributions from business.

At Lincoln Center, meanwhile, where the acoustical renovation of Avery Fisher Hall was completed last October at a cost of $6.5 million, Joseph Papp of the New York Shakespeare Festival made a startling proposal. He requested approval from the Center's board to demolish the interior of the Beaumont Theater and rebuild it at a cost of $6.5 million.

Several interesting new building concepts are in various stages of development in New York, where the Museum of Modern Art selected Cesar Pelli as architect for its unique residential condominium and museum addition project. The city, which recently approved use of a large apartment development, Manhattan Plaza, as a rent subsidized housing project for performing artists, is giving approval to a plan to convert four tenements (two others already have been converted) across the street from the Plaza into Theater Row. The unique project would house six 100-seat theaters and 11 floors of rehearsal space. Importantly, the city would substitute a tax equivalency plan for real estate taxes for 20 years, with half of any profits going to the city in lieu of taxes.

Theater, jazz, and other arts activities will find an unusual performing site in one of New York's most interesting facilities when St. Peter's Church opens its new home this fall. Located at the base of the giant, new Citicorp center, the church, noted for its involvement in the arts, will house a 250-seat theater, recital room, and jazz rehearsal room under a chapel designed by Louise Nevelson and an adjoining sanctuary. The sanctuary also will serve as a 500-seat theater-in-the-round, and outdoor plaza spaces will be used for informal cultural events. The church is now involved in a major fund-raising campaign to help finance its expanded cultural program.

March-April 1977

Dancers of the Acme Company in the sportswear by designer James Berry that inspired James Cunningham's dance-fashion event, "One More for the Road." (Photo by James Berry. Courtesy of Pentacle Dance Management)

3

Funding the Arts

THE ECONOMIC VIEW

Recognition Growing for Economic Value of Arts

The economic importance of the arts is winning increased recognition. In addition to the ammunition provided by a growing number of economic impact studies, the U.S. Department of Commerce and other agencies are finding new ways to utilize the arts to spur economic growth. In its new Municipal Policy Statement, released in December 1977, the U.S. Conference of Mayors stated that "all levels of government must recognize the arts as an essential service" and urged that the arts be utilized as a stimulus to economic development.

A key force in spearheading government and private awareness of the economic value of the arts has been the Commerce Department's new Office of Cultural Resources, headed by Louise W. Wiener. Ms. Wiener not only has been a presenter of the arts case at both arts and nonarts national meetings, but she also has been involved in gathering data, developing new programs, and in providing information and technical aid to arts groups. For the recent White House Conference on Balanced Growth, she presented a paper on "Perspectives on the Economic Development Potential of Cultural Resources" which won a generally favorable reaction. This February, for the first time, cultural resources was included as one of the agenda items in the Commerce Department's high-level Roundtable meeting on business retention efforts.

Among the concerns of the newly established office has been finding ways to help arts groups better utilize such Commerce Department resources as programs of the Economic Development Administration. The EDA has committed public works funds for construction and renovation of arts facilities to help create jobs and attract business in such communities as San Antonio and Winston-Salem. Technical assistance on EDA funding has been provided by the office to arts projects in St. Louis, Newark, Fort Lauderdale, New York, and San Francisco.

Ms. Wiener forsees a far greater arts role in tourism. She has been working closely with the U.S. Travel Service, which already has made a commitment to reviewing ways to better present cultural resources in its materials, and she has been promoting arts facilities to foreign travel writers, so they in turn, may "sell" them to their readers. A "culture U.S.A." tour for foreign journalists was held in November and another group will be in the U.S. for ten days beginning February 27th. American travel writers will also be involved in the new program.

In New York state meanwhile, a legislative group, recognizing the economic significance of the culture industry to the state, will seek to determine just how great an effect the arts have on state tourism, employment, commercial development, and the retention of business as the first step towards providing greater help to the arts. In a year-long project that began in December, an eight-member special state senate committee, headed by William T. Conklin, will study both nonprofit and profit sectors of the industry as well as the program and policies of the state arts council through a series of private sessions and public hearings.

In a separate and widely publicized state effort, New York's state Department of Commerce has committed a $1-million advertising budget to promoting New York City tourism through its theaters. The initial result is a just-completed 60-second commercial featuring stars from nine different Broadway shows. The new campaign grew out of a 1977 state Commerce Department study which indicated that the cheapest and quickest way to create jobs, increase revenue from taxes, and bolster the state economy was by building up tourism. That same study showed that New York's two main tourist attractions were Broadway shows and its museums.

The arts, as a key tourist attraction, have benefited from transient hotel taxes. Last year such taxes brought San Francisco arts programs $2.5 million and San Diego arts $1 million. In Texas, a new bill gave localities the option of adding 1 percent, which could be used for the arts, to an already optional 3 percent hotel tax. Some ten cities exercised the new option with some of the funds earmarked for the arts. Houston's new arts council will launch its program with a $1 million windfall from the new hotel taxes.

Essential reading for groups interested in assessing the economic impact of the arts in their own communities, is the new study published by the NEA's Research Division (2401 E. St., N.W., Washington, D.C. 20506), *A Model to Assess the Impact of Arts Institutions: The Baltimore Case Study.* The 92-page report, available free, provides a model with a series of equations for use by groups in other areas.

January-February 1978

How Nonprofit Groups
Can Boost Their Income

The August 1972 issue of *Institutional Investor,* a journal for professional money managers, was devoted to the theme "The culture crisis: Can our nonprofit institutions be saved?" Although the focus was broader than the arts, *AM* is reprinting the following article in a slightly abridged version (copyright 1972 Institutional Investor Systems, reprinted with permission) because it discusses key trends worthy of consideration by arts managers.

Sorting Out Priorities. Despite widespread belief that government, directly or indirectly, is going to play a bigger role in financing nonprofits, the trend, needless to say, does not meet with universal acclaim. Thus, nonprofits are faced with some tough choices in sorting out their priorities. The key concern here is about the types and quality of services that would be available. And no less an authority than the Carnegie Corporation has called for establishment of a national committee to "think through and articulate" the requirements of a massive campaign to deal with the future of nonprofits. Certainly, many city museums and cultural institutions would collapse without even the amount of state support they get now, and legislation has been proposed to allow them to use larger amounts of their tax-exempt receipts for lobbying in behalf of their case. But the trick is in trying to develop a consensus on how the government could best meet the needs through direct support, grants and loans, public subsidy of user services, or through tax incentives—or some combination of the three. Muddying the water still further, notes John Jay Iselin, managing director of New York's educational TV station, which raises more than $2 million annually from "subscribers," is that "we can no longer be beholden to any one group, public or private. We must deal with the fact that we must *qualify* for support; we must prove our value to the consumer."

Going Into "Business." While nonprofits are not by definition designed to make money, there is nothing to prevent them from owning profit-making enterprises. Numerous colleges own coal mines or oil wells, and one (Knox College of Galesburg, Illinois) even owns a race track. Frank Jennings, secretary of Columbia's Teachers College, a proponent of a mixed-economy approach, points to the fact that Columbia was bequeathed the land upon which Rockefeller Center stands. Private schools, for instance, could aim for better land use, and many nonprofits—including museums, which make money from restaurants and book stores on their premises—are eyeing this approach to additional income with special interest. MIT, among others, looks longingly at the profits which result from research done in its laboratories, and other schools are also interested in the kinds of fees professors can make when they take their ideas off campus. The Stanford Research Center is cited as an example of what can be done, with its approach of conducting research and development for both private and public customers.

Better Utilization of Assets. The emergency task force at NYU has proposed week-end sessions to use its plant more efficiently, and the prospects for leverage elsewhere are almost limitless. Museums can get more mileage out of "the billions they have in their basements," according to Wilder Green, director of the American Federation of Arts, and universities have a plethora of rooms that aren't being fully utilized.

Sharing of Facilities. Every hospital in the land seems to want a cobalt treatment center, and every university an urban studies program. But some sharing is already beginning to take place, particularly among hospitals, and there is a notable increase in the number of interchanges between other nonprofits which have expensive new technologies that they can share and jointly underwrite.

"Why should the library hold art shows, and why should we have a library?" is the way a director of a leading New York museum puts it. Needless to say, there is considerable vested opposition to this, but foundations increasingly feel they will be called upon to become merger-makers among nonprofit institutions which so far have seemed unwilling to share their identities.

Moving Toward Decentralization and Specialization. "Institutions that are not individual or different will either be absorbed or go out of business," warns an eastern university president. An oft-cited example of what could be done is the old University of Paris, where traditionally the only common facilities places were meeting halls and the library. There, students took care of their own food and lodging requirements.

Tapping the Potential of the "Third Sector." A phrase coined by Amitai Etzioni, director of the Center for Policy Research, the "third sector" describes using an approach that would avoid both the too-profit-oriented business world and the too-bureaucratic government world in seeking solutions. Sample patterns are the new postal service and Comsat. A great many nonprofit organizations already fit the pattern, says Etzioni, adding, "imagine what an effective attack could be made on heroin addiction, for instance, if government funds, hospital staffs, community groups, law enforcement officials, and local business got together to tackle the problems under a well-coordinated and well-financed system."

Seeking New Financial Remedies. Clearly, economizing will not solve a problem of the magnitude of the one facing nonprofits, so many of them are seeking new ways to balance the books. Some are considering how traditional capital-raising drives can be put on a continuing basis, such as getting a commitment from university alumni to repay, over their lifetimes, the difference between what they paid for their education and what it actually cost. Various tithing schemes have been proposed, including one whereby the Internal Revenue Service would collect 1 percent of a person's income each year after he graduates and return it to his alma mater. Residents of suburban St. Louis, to cite one example of what can happen, recently imposed a tax upon themselves to help support a series of urban institutions, including the St. Louis Museum and Zoo. "Somehow," concludes one foundation administrator, "we are going to have to provide a continuous stream of support."

September-October 1972

Performing Arts Face
Continuing Cost Pressures
W. J. Baumol and W. G. Bowen

One can read the prospects of the arts tomorrow in the economic structure that characterizes them today. The evidence will suggest that the prospects offer no grounds for complacency—that there are fundamental reasons to expect the financial strains which beset the performing arts organizations to increase, chronically, with the passage of time.

It is apparent that the live performing arts belong to the stable productivity sector of our economy, offering little opportunity for major technological change.

Even if the arts could somehow manage to effect technological economies, they would not solve their long-term problem if such savings were once-and-for-all in nature. In order to join the ranks of the rising productivity industries, the arts would somehow have to learn not only to increase output per man-hour, but to continue to do so into the indefinite future.

True, some inefficiencies of operation are to be found in the field, and their elimination can help matters somewhat. Moreover, performing arts organizations can reduce the rate of increase in their unit costs by permitting some deterioration in the quality of their product by fewer rehearsals, the use of more poorly trained performers, shoddy costumes and scenery. But such a course is never popular with organizations dediated to quality and, furthermore, it may lead to loss of audience and community support. Nevertheless, it is not an uncommon "temporary" expedient, imposed by the realization that the cutting of corners may be the only alternative to abandonment of the enterprise.

There is one other important avenue for cost saving open to the performing arts. We refer to wages paid performers. The live performing arts constitute a rather special labor market, a market in which the need for great native ability and extensive training limits the supply, but in which the psychic returns to those who meet these tests often offer a very substantial inducement to remain in the field.

Performing arts organizations in financial difficulty have often managed to shift part of their financial burden back to the performers—and to the managements, who also are generally very poorly paid by commercial standards. The level of the incomes in this general field must be considered remarkably low by any standards, and particularly so in light of the heavy investment that has often been made by the artists in their education, training, and equipment.

However, there are limits to the financial sacrifices society can extract from the performers in exchange for psychic returns. One may reasonably expect that rising incomes in other sectors will ultimately produce untoward effects on the supply of talent. At what point this will occur depends partly on the income elasticity of the demand for psychic income.

In sum, the cost structure of the performing arts organizations promises them no easier future. One might anticipate, therefore, that this structural problem would produce discernible effects on pricing policy. There is a widespread impression that the arts have indeed behaved in accord with this anticipation—that ticket prices have been soaring. Yet our preliminary data indicate that the rate of increase of ticket prices has barely managed to keep up with the price level and has lagged substantially behind increases in costs. We suspect that a valid explanation is the role of a doctrine of just price in the objectives of arts organizations.

The tendency for increases in prices to lag behind increases in costs means simply that arts organizations have had to raise larger sums from their contributors, and our analysis leads us to expect this trend to continue. If, as may be suspected, there are limits to the amounts that can be obtained from private contributors, the question is obviously raised as to whether society can find other sources of support for the performing arts if they are to continue their present role, and especially if it is intended that they will expand their role and flourish.

February 1965

Philanthropy a Significant Institution, Says Noted Sociologist

Arthur Vidich

This article is a portion of a larger study, the Third American Revolution *(Harper and Row), written by Dr. Vidich in collaboration with Dr. Joseph Bensman.*

The expansion and growth of private philanthropy is consistent with the rise of the service state insofar as the philanthropic redistribution achieves the same economic ends as secondary and tertiary job expansion in industry and government. In effect, philanthropy is another mechanism by which the problem of overproduction finds a resolution counter to the Marxian prediction.

It is of the essence of modern philanthropy that it produces nothing but services, but that it produces *only* services is its major economic significance. Theoretically, the market for services, in contrast to other forms of economic goods, is limited only by man's capacity to imagine ways of marketing services. . . . Philanthropy facilitates the marketing of services by providing them for nothing or so far below cost as to allow calling it philanthropy. . . .

It is abundantly clear . . . that both the government and private sectors share in meeting the costs of philanthropy. Though absolute volume of government investment in philanthropy is incomparably greater than private philanthropic investment, the structural terms which define how the burden is shared must be specified. For example, what is one to make of the fact that even though the government carries a disproportionately heavy share of the burden, the number of units distributing these vast amounts of money is small in comparison to private philanthropic units. Of private, nonprofit *foundations* alone, there are more than fifty thousand, while the number of welfare, religious, educational, etc., charitable and philanthropic organizations defy enumeration. It would appear that on a dollar-for-dollar basis, the government distributes its philanthropy much more efficiently than the private sector, and indeed it is the case that where one committee in Washington can decide one afternoon to give a physics department in a university $1 million, it takes many more people and much more time for the physics department to spend the million, the more so as the proportion spent on services is greater than equipment costs. . . . To the extent that the government stands as the symbol for the large-scale production of philanthropic dollars, the difference between government and private philanthropy can be likened to the distinctions between industrial and preindustrial economies.

Private philanthropy is essentially preindustrial, being better understood on the model of the craft system where the item is produced for a specific client. . . . Generally speaking, private philanthropic welfare expenditures take the form of servicing the client, whereas the government as a general but not universal practice prefers bulk purchasing of units of service. . . .

It is in this sense that government philanthropy is technologically advanced in comparison to much of private philanthropy which remains in the labor intensive handicraft stage, i.e., large staffs relative to size of budgets. . . .

In the short run, it is always difficult for the government to spend money on projects that do not have a socially useful appearance. Tax dollars are supposed to be reasonably rational, to provide services which the community needs, and to have some relationship to the community's resources. In fact, at any one point in time public philanthropy will always have some number of ideologists who can justify the rationality, the necessity, the usefulness and perhaps the indispensability of the purposes for which the money is being given away. As for the public, it is wont to accept what is as if it had always been so and will be forevermore.

The picture that emerges for the long run is quite different, since with time there are great changes in the definition of social needs, the rationality of social expenditures and the proper ratios between expenditures and resources. It is at this point that private philanthropy begins to play another role. Because private philanthropy has no public accountability, it can indulge itself in the continuous and never-ending activity of creating new service needs, of embellishing and elaborating old needs, and of expanding the availability of all needs to all groups. As a result of these efforts, new areas of needs are accepted as legitimate by the public mind. Once such legitimacy is achieved, the need eventually can no longer be met by private philanthropy alone and must be taken over by government or subsidized out of tax funds. In this way we increase our range of public welfare, health, educational, and cultural programs and in the long run the tax load as well. Once the government steps in and takes over any area of new needs, the private philanthropic dollar is free to engage in the exploration and creation of other areas of need, and the whole cycle starts all over again. . . . In this sense private philanthropy . . . provides a perpetual mechanism of expansion.

The heroic role of the fund raisers must be seen in the light of the above discussion. These entrepreneurs who create new causes and then go out and collect the money to support them are capitalism's current equivalent to the risk-taking entrepreneur of an earlier stage. The philanthropic entrepreneur performs the functions of stimulating the flow of currency from the market economy into non-productive channels. The stimulation of the consumption of non-productive services supports the market economy.

February 1964

Arts Groups Spurn
Available Funding and Survive

Selling tickets and winning grants may be among a nonprofit performing arts group's most essential activities, but there are at least two theaters that *deliberately* ignored this normal course of action and survived.

The University of Toledo Theatre, for example, sent out notices at the beginning of the 1970-71 season to announce a new free-ticket policy which it termed, "legit and exciting madness." The notice read, "We're poor, so we've gone free . . . We can't afford a subscription campaign so we'll be passing the hat instead."

Dr. Bernard Coyne, the head of the university's theater department, decided to initiate the new policy in an attempt to broaden the theater audience beyond students. A highly successful small-scale free admission experiment the previous season had drawn large attendance from every area of the community including residents of old age homes, participants in vocational rehabilitation programs, factory workers, blacks, and youngsters. Under the new policy, overall attendance has increased by some 40 percent.

"Theater in Toledo has been a big society splurge," Sheila Sabrey, the theater's public relations director told *AM*. "But as an urban university we have a responsibility to break down the barrier of elitism and bring theater to all the people. The people we're getting now are the people we want."

The theater, which receives operating funds from the student union board, discovered after starting the program that it couldn't accept donations because of university auditing procedures. However, with attendance vastly increased and with operating costs pared to the bone, it is confident of operating free theater again next season.

Thousands of miles away, in Lucaya/Freeport, Grand Bahama Island, the Freeport Players Guild is awaiting the opening of its newly-built theater in 1971. However, but for the guild's desire to "make it" on its own, it could have been in a new building two or three years ago.

In 1967, when the community theater was six years old and housed in a converted shipbuilding facility, it decided to raise funds to build its own theater.

Almost immediately, the Grand Bahama Port Authority offered the group a site and a basic structure, an estimated $50,000 gift. According to one of the theater members, "The vitality of the company was based on our ability to overcome difficulties. The gift would have made things too easy." The gift was rejected.

With the fund drive moving haltingly, one of the theater's founders offered to donate $150,000 to build the theater. Again, for the same reason, the offer was rejected. Finally, after three years the fund drive raised $150,000 and construction started. Then, having proved it could fund its own theater, the guild accepted a $50,000 donation from the Port Authority to complete the project.

March-April 1971

Lowry Discusses New
Ford Foundation Survey

In Spring 1971 the Ford Foundation announced a full-scale economic survey of 200 performing arts groups, covering the five-year period ending with the 1969-70 season. In this interview with AM *editor Alvin H. Reiss, W. McNeil Lowry, Ford Foundation vice president for the humanities and the arts, discusses the program and its ramifications.*

Q: How and when did the idea for developing the economic survey originate?

A: When Ford Foundation trustees approved an arts program in 1957, one of the subjects the staff proposed for exploration was the economic and social position of the artist and of organized outlets for his career. Between 1957 and 1962, Ford Foundation staff collected a large quantity of data on the operations of nonprofit arts groups, although the data was not on a comparable basis, and it became apparent that only the deliberate construction of a uniform survey could provide the kind of information most needed. At about the same time, other agencies announced plans for performing arts studies. The Rockefeller Brothers Fund Report was one illustration; the important volume done by Professors Baumol and Bowen was another. The need for a more comprehensive analysis of the nonprofit arts sector continued to be stressed, however, not only by performing arts managers but by mahy private and public agencies, including the newly emerging national and state arts councils. In 1970 the Ford Foundation, in consultation with these other agencies, moved to undertake such a survey.

Q: What kind of advance study and pretesting preceded the actual formulation of the questionnaires?

A: Case histories of a small number of performing arts groups were prepared by the staff of the Ford Foundation and discussed in June 1970 with the foundation's trustees, who gave approval in principle to a national economic survey. From that date until January 1, 1971, with the help of performing arts managers, economists, and systems analysts, the data collection form was revised and tested by more than a dozen groups in the field. The data collection form distributed in May to 200 arts groups was the result.

Q: Do you agree that most groups will have difficulty in answering the questionnaire? Not only will they be asked to provide accurate material on seasons that were completed four or five years ago, but they must also exercise judgment in many cases. How can you be sure that the material you receive from performing arts organizations will be accurate and valid?

A: There will undoubtedly be difficulties. The responses of the groups included in the pretests, however, were more encouraging than had been anticipated. The administration of the survey includes assistance from the project staff when this is called for by performing arts groups required to exercise judgment in accommodating their own records to the data form.

Q: On what basis were the 200 participating arts groups selected? How do you define a professional group?

A: The 200 participating groups are largely those who have associated themselves in particular categories of operations in the fields of theater, dance, opera, and symphony orchestra, namely, American Symphony Orchestra League (major and metropolitan orchestras), League of Resident Theaters, Association of American Dance Companies, the Central Opera Service, and OPERA. America. In each field the groups included are nonprofit, use union personnel, and operate at a minimum budget level comparable to other groups in the same field that are embraced by the survey.

Q: How will nonparticipating arts groups benefit from this material?

A: The report, which is expected to be published and distributed in 1972, should be of great benefit even to the performing arts groups who operate at a lower budgetary level or do not have sustained performance seasons. Projections and extrapolations from the data supplied by economists and experienced performing arts managers should reveal many important trends applicable to the smaller as well as to the larger groups.

Q: Is it an intention of this program to develop a uniform system of accounting for all performing arts groups? If so, will you be making guidelines available to the arts?

A: The Ford Foundation, of course, does not presume to offer a uniform system of accounting for all performing arts groups. Reactions of managers of some of the groups in the pretests suggest, however, that a byproduct of the survey may be the development of more consistent and uniform definitions of expenditure and income categories.

Q: Considering the impact of change on the arts and the development of new kinds of programs and problems, how helpful will the material you've gathered be?

A: The first aim of the survey is to describe and analyze operations of a significant number of nonprofit groups over a five-year period. The impact of change and the development of new programs and problems should be more visible as a result of the analysis and not less.

Q: Why didn't the studies start four months later and include the 1970-71 season?

A: The time lag in financial statements and fiscal year audits at the conclusion of one season ranges between 90 and 120 days. The survey will, however, include the 1970-71 season and all seasons subsequent, since the foundation has announced its intention to deep the data up-to-date by an annual canvass of information from the same groups.

Q: Considering the many problems affecting the arts and the fact that the data bank will cost $500,000 a year to update, why did you view this program as a current need?

A: In the 14 years the foundation has operated in the arts, the demands for a better economic analysis on a national scale and for more uniform data have increased every year. The results are important not only to artistic producers and managers, but to private and public agencies at every level, local to national. A consistent theme of all writing and discussion about the arts in the United States is the tentative nature of the economic and fiscal projections. The $500,000 figure is a tentative budget estimate for all research and development activities of the foundation in the arts. We do not know exactly what it will cost to update the data bank, but it clearly will only be a small fraction of $500,000.

Q: The Ford Foundation has invested considerable money in the arts ($238 million) since 1957. Will the current program in any way adversely affect the future arts funding policies of the foundation?

A: The survey will in no way adversely affect the policies of the Ford Foundation in its support of the arts. As stated by the foundation, the objective sought by the survey is not related to grantmaking plans and policies. The large investments in the arts since 1957 testify to the sustained character of the foundation's commitment in these fields.

Summer 1971

It Is a Far, Far Better Thing to Give, Isn't It?

The following satirical comment by AM *editor Alvin H. Reiss on philanthropy in the arts, appeared originally in the April 1974 issue of* Eddy, *a magazine about dance.*

When Sybil Jackson-Johnson was eighteen, she saw an early Ginger Rogers-Fred Astaire movie which motivated her towards a career as a dancer and actress. When she was nineteen she learned to dance on point, something she's been off ever since.

Mr. Jackson-Johnson is known to thousands of poverty-afflicted dancers as the titular head of the Sybil Jackson-Johnson Foundation for the Dance as Long as It's Not Modern, a supplicator to needy causes in dance if, the cause of the causes in the first place is Mrs. J.J. herself. Perhaps no woman in America has spread her money around as freely and as recklessly as she has, and yet in spite of this, she remains.

Among Mrs. Jackson-Johnson's many accomplishments is her mastery of the one-line speech, terse in content yet saying all. Her now famous address, "I'm thrilled to be here as you are," first said spontaneously at a fox hunt held in honor of twenty visiting Bolshoi dancers, has retained its impact, if we ignore the one time the third word came out "chilled," when she was forced to introduce a former protege since dropped from her patronage.

But it would be unfair to allow Mrs. J.J.'s laurels to rest merely on her speaking ability. Any catalogue of her contributions would surely include the following:

- Mrs. J.J. donated the money to build a stage where it was most needed—in the kitchen of Arthur. There, her friends, when democratizing with the help or sampling the chocolate mousse, were able to wing off a fast grand jete whenever they were struck by the muse. Only because legions of her circle thus indulged themselves, has the now famous expression, "jete set," since abbreviated to jet set, passed into common, everyday usage.

- Mrs. J.J., a top musical figure in her own right, is the uncredited composer of the score for Jerome Robbins silent ballet, "Moves." She also served as dialect coach for Marcel Marceau, a fact not generally known.

- In spite of an impossibly busy personal schedule, Mrs. J.J. took over the artistic reins of a dance company to allow the artistic director to devote all of his time to a choreography career. Interestingly, until the moment of the takeover, the artistic director never realized that he wanted to devote all his time to choreography; nor did the deposed co-director realize that he wished to devote all of his time to job hunting.

What motivated Mrs. Jackson-Johnson to dedicate her life to dance and give so much to so few? In spite of numerous conversations with many of her associates and with those who have benefitted from her largesse, it is difficult to piece together a clear and consistent rationale for her actions. We can, however, outline, for the first time publicly, the famous guidelines that have governed not only her personal activities in the field of culture, but which have provided the Jackson-Johnson Foundation for the Dance as Long as It's Not Modern, with a plan of operation and with a basis for decision making. These five guidelines are:

1. Love the discipline you will honor with your money, and love the money that you will honor with your discipline.

2. Establish your identity firmly and unquestionably. Affix your name to everything you do and everything you support so that nobody can accuse you of noninvolvement, a horrible crime in today's society.

3. Streamline your philanthropic operation by refusing to open unsolicited letters or grant applications. It is far better to give one less grant than to chance giving a grant to someone who might be subversive or even avant-garde. You will save time and reduce the possibility of error by making your own selections of fund recipients before they apply.

4. Save the artist from his own worst enemy, egotism. If an artist's achievements are too highly praised, the favorable attention may go to his head, and prevent him from ever again doing significant work. If necessary, sacrifice yourself to save the artist, even to the point of your taking credit for his work.

5. Dispense your money with a flair. What is important is not who you give to or how much you give, but the way in which you do it. Remember that giving, like dancing or painting, is an art.

November-December 1974

The Arts Future:
A Cultural Common Market

George C. White

The "salad days" of fund raising in the arts may be over. Increasingly, those sources of support that helped seed many arts programs are turning their consideration to new and more pressing areas, such as interracial relations and ghetto redevelopment. Arts leaders acknowledge that new sources of subsidy must be found.

Many argue that business and industry must shoulder the burden, but corporate support is often tied to specific self-interest. Moreover, big business cannot be expected to experiment.

Within the business world, only one industry exists that can be expected to benefit from experimentation in the arts—the entertainment industry. The relationship between the so-called experimental and the commercial is becoming intermixed increasingly, and a growing number of productions that originated in regional theaters or Off-Off-Broadway have been purchased by major film companies. Yet, the large entertainment corporations continue to look at nonprofit performing arts groups as panhandlers rather than as product development centers. With several notable exceptions, the entertainment industry has failed to provide support to the nonprofit arts field.

If the mass entertainment media and the highly commercial "cultural" enterprises are to survive, however, let alone raise their standards, they must contribute to their own long-range development. As surely as the technologically oriented corporations must invest in the future through grants-in-aid and through the sponsorship of countless courses, seminars, and conferences, the performing arts in the nation—whether leisure-time activity or true cultural achievement—will have to be sponsored by those who will receive the greatest commercial benefits. The alternatives, stagnation or complete government control, are too grim to contemplate.

With the fear that the time is already late, I propose an "Entertainment Foundation," supported collectively by the great entertainment corporations and administered by a staff similar in character to that of a Ford or a Rockefeller Foundation.

If, for example, CBS, RCA, ABC, Paramount, Columbia, U-I, BMI, and their proliferating subsidiaries turned over just the income from a reasonable number of their shares of treasury stock—not the stock itself—to this proposed foundation, the result would be an entertainment "community chest." This growing fund would remove the support burden from private foundations which have so effectively primed the pump.

The establishment of this foundation would provide us with one central fund to which nonprofit performing arts organizations could apply for grants. In addition to centralizing the grant-giving function, this would give the entertainment giants a central bank of developing talent and a real and useful knowledge of "what's going on."

In today's world of theater, where, for example, a 90-minute television program may cost close to $1 million and an Off-Broadway "experimental" may be capitalized for $25,000, no room exists for failure, for true experimentation, or for growth. Regional theater companies are discovering daily that the gap between income and expenditures is growing wider and wider, and few can be expected to survive without outside help.

The cultural community chest I propose is highly practical and could be implemented from within the existing entertainment complex. Administration of such a program has precedent in existing foundations, and talent is available to manage it. The contributing corporations could benefit just through elimination of the "if-we-do-it-for-this-one-then-we-must-do-it-for-that-one" kind of decision making. And the projects or individuals they save today may, in many instances, provide them with their artistic strength in the future.

Here's another point for the entertainment giants to keep in mind. When government investigators point their fingers at them and ask what television and motion pictures are doing to upgrade and improve their products, here is an answer that these corporations have not had in the past: support and development of the nonprofit performing arts.

I realize that in many ways what I propose is full of problems—not unlike Churchill's wartime proposition of eventual amity between France and Germany

—but the European Common Market is a reality today. Why not a Cultural Common Market in a country which, in the 1950s and '60s, has proved it need never again take a second place in the arts to any nation on earth? The ultimate beneficiary is American civilization and its cultural heritage.

Summer 1968

PLANNING AND DEVELOPING
FUND-RAISING CAMPAIGNS

Nine Key Steps to
Successful Fund Raising

Fund-raising and development campaigns require careful timing and conscious, step-by-step planning. According to John Price Jones Company, a leading fund-raising firm, there are nine key phases in a development program.

The first is stating the case. A definitive statement of an organization's case must be prepared and then placed before the organization's leaders and its prospects. Every conceivable method of communicating this case to the public should be used.

Second is the identification of all prospects—the prospecting phase. Once the list is drawn, it must be carefully screened and evaluated. Next, prospects must be rated according to interest in the organization and potential to give.

Organizing the campaign structure is the third key phase. Leadership, especially on the top level, must be organized early in an institution's schedule of operations. Committee heads must be appointed, and the campaign headquarters must be carefully planned so that volunteers will have sufficient support and service to function efficiently.

Next comes the cultivation and motivation of prospects. A solicitor must personally meet the prospect and stimulate his interest in the organization, its case, and its needs. This calls for private luncheons and other meetings in social settings, as well as public functions to which prospects should be invited.

A fifth key phase is finding pace-setting gifts to get the campaign moving. This phase is particularly crucial. It can make or break a campaign because big gifts offer a "parade of enthusiasm which leads to others climbing on the bandwagon." Pace-setting gifts usually come from someone within the organization itself, such as trustees or other members of the organization's official family.

Timing is another essential. Ideally, each step in a campaign should follow the one before it in a natural and logical manner. Thus, prospects are best approached when a sense of urgency has been developed in them and the person who is best suited to contact them personally is found.

Momentum is equally important. Although campaigns start slowly, they will, as a rule, gradually accelerate until a point of intensity is reached. This point of intensity should be sustained as long as it is necessary to do so. In short campaigns, momentum cannot be sustained for very long unless organizations work at maintaining it. Special climax points such as organizational dinners, parties, and campaign announcements are essential to developing momentaum and sustaining it.

Soliciting, the eighth phase, is the most important. No matter how well-planned the rest of the program is, the campaign will fail unless someone asks someone else for a gift. At times, one direct call may produce results. Frequently, however, much follow-up work is necessary. If everything else fails, then a "mop-up" mail campaign may have to be used. But whatever the methods used, every prospect *must* be asked for a gift.

Lastly comes acknowledgment. By thanking prospects for their help, a doorway to continued future support remains open.

April 1964

Advice on Fund Raising

Free advice on the planning and execution of fund-raising campaigns may often be obtained from executives of health and welfare organizations who face financial problems similar to those encountered in the arts. Get to know these leaders and maintain cordial relationships with them, but avoid requesting information during their fund drives when they have little free time.

May 1963

High Standards Vital
to Fund Drives for Arts

Sound fund-raising practices are important to arts groups for the efficiency of their operation and the continued success of their fund-raising drives. Basic standards have been established by the National Information Bureau, a nonprofit consultant group that evaluates national philanthropic and cultural organizations for its subscribers—foundations, community chests, and corporations—that want to be sure the money they donate is being properly used.

AM interviewed Erich Gottlieb, a member of NIB's research staff, to find out the basis for NIB's ratings. According to NIB, the following standards are basic.

The board of directors should be an active, responsible group, and its meetings—or those of its executive committee—should take place at least five times annually, preferably eight times.

Members of the board should not be letterhead figures only; they should be well informed about all the institution's activities, discuss basic matters of policy, and participate in decisions.

NIB, in many cases, actually goes to the offices of a group it is evaluating and meets and talks with the staff. It suggests that new board members be invited to do the same, as part of an orientation program.

The arts group's purpose should be clearly defined, and it should be able to show, if asked, that it does not duplicate or overlap the functions of other groups. It should also be able to demonstrate that its schedule of events has been planned so that it doesn't overlap or compete unnecessarily with other groups.

The fund-raising practices of an arts group should be above reproach. This means there should be no payment of percentage commissions (i.e., as distinct from fees) for fund raising, no mailing of unordered tickets or merchandise with a request for money, and no telephone solicitation of the general public.

It also means that the money raised should be used for the purposes specified in the group's promotion. For instance, if a group solicits funds specifically for an orchestra tour, it should not use any part of the money raised for other purposes.

Ethical promotion is a very important part of fund raising. Promotional claims should be justified in terms of the actual services and programs offered. Specifically, if an arts group advertises that it is offering a series of first-rate performances, the orchestras, theater troupes, or soloists must indeed be first-rate. If the group cites attendance figures at events or exhibits, these figures should be based on some system of counting, rather than on loose estimates.

Who does an arts group's audit can be just as important as how well it is done, according to NIB. It should *not* be done by the treasurer of the group, by a committee of the board, or even the treasurer's company, if he is a member of an accounting firm. The audit should be signed by an independent outside firm.

The statement itself should conform to the best accounting practices. There should be no catch-all categories; all items should be as specific as possible, although lack of standardized classification has plagued the accounting practices of philanthropic groups. Instead of administrative expenses, for instance, there should be a breakdown of salaries, publicity, promotion, mail, etc. The expenses of administering a concert series, for example, should be separated from the year-round administrative expenses. Cash donations should be separated from donations of "goods-in-kind," so that a painting, for instance, would be listed as a "painting, valued at" instead of setting a cash valuation on a painting and then listing it as cash received.

Finally, says the NIB, every group must submit an annual detailed budget that projects a plan of expenditures and sets monetary limits on the various parts of its program. It is true, the NIB notes, that cultural groups often are not sure how much money they will get, and therefore find it difficult to set a budget.

The answer is that the budget need not be immutable—there can be minimum budgets, maximum budgets, and even "in-between" budgets. But there must be a plan of expenditures, and it must be seen, discussed, and approved by the board.

September 1963

How to Start an Effective Bequest Program

Bequest programs offer nonprofit groups a major source of income that is far from being fully exploited. In the following article, John Price Jones, a leading fund-raising firm, tells how to develop a successful bequest program.

One can make a strong case for bequest programs in the next few years. As taxation eats into large fortunes, bequests offer a means of offsetting this drying up of large pools of private wealth. Moreover, bequests to nonprofit arts groups are exempt from federal estate taxes.

The organizations that have set up bequest programs in recent years and stayed with them have built additional, stable sources of income in a period of increasing competition for the philanthropic dollar. Records show that bequest programs per time and dollar invested pay off better than many other fund-raising programs.

Moreover, there is less wear and tear on volunteers and their consultants in bequest programs than in campaigns. Many volunteers find such programs suit their temperament more than campaign solicitation.

Bequest programs frequently raise funds that would not, and could not, be otherwise secured. In a period of increasing taxes, bequests offer a means to the middle income person—and there are more and more of them—to make a substantial gift to the organization of his choice. Bequest giving is on the increase.

A question often raised is that bequest program results cannot be measured. This is not true. Measure them the same way you measure other fund-raising costs—by the money coming in and what it costs you to obtain it. Simply figure results over a longer period of time than 12 months. Figure them on a five- or ten-year basis.

Here are some ways to increase your bequest income. First, have a sound case—valid reasons why people can and should leave you money in their wills. And your program should be broad enough to offer a range of gift opportunities. Second, get your explanatory literature into the hands of your prospects, lawyers, bankers, and tax consultants as well as others in your area.

Third, capable volunteers are needed, and they may require technical assistance at some point in their work. Tax, legal, accounting, and other matters must be determined by qualified persons who may be employed by the person making the bequest or who may be on your staff. Both are often involved.

Fourth, make specific suggestions or presentations to your prime prospects —geared to their known interests and desires. Persistence is particularly necessary in bequest campaigns.

The volunteer who has written an organization into his own will makes its best ambassador. He is enthusiastic, and he is not asking anyone to do what he has not done himself. However, for a bequest program to be successful, it must be supported by a broad publicity campaign.

April 1965

Insuring Success

Cultural organizations named as beneficiaries in life insurance policies can realize significant future income. This kind of contribution may also have special appeal to some donors since annual premium payments, which are tax deductible, cost less than annual payments on a cash pledge of the same amount. However, it should be remembered that the organization must be named an irrevocable beneficiary, and the donor cannot reserve the right to change beneficiaries. The total value of the gift is ensured the moment the policy is enforced and remains so as long as the premiums are paid each year.

December 1964

Bequest Form .

To ease the way for bequests to your organization, keep sample bequest forms on hand for distribution. The forms should bear the name of your organization as beneficiary. In addition, printed information on the tax benefits to the testator should be made available to contributors.

October 1965

Motivating the Donor

An approach used by a college to increase donations through wills, trusts, and insurance policies may be of interest to arts groups. Swarthmore College in Pennsylvania devoted the entire March issue of its bulletin to the topic "Creative Giving and Swarthmore College." More than half of the handsome 16-page illustrated publication was devoted to a section that discussed in detail eight different forms of gifts. Through charts and hypothetical examples, it carefully explained tax benefits and advantages to the donor in each of the listed categories.

June-July 1966

A Trust Fund Program
Can Help Arts Groups

A trust fund program is one method of fund raising sometimes overlooked by arts organizations.

Trusts typically are repositories of money, securities, or property to be used as specified in an agreement establishing a trust corporation. Having perpetual life, permanent trusts continue to earn money even after the death of the donor.

Often, persons who might not directly contribute to an arts group will establish a permanent trust for it because of tax benefits and trust permanency. Contributors to a trust are entitled to a tax deduction on their gift. This rule applies when the recipient is a nonprofit organization receiving at least on-third of its support from the public or government agencies. On the other hand, no taxes need be paid by nonprofit groups on income earned from a trust. (Note: The implications of new tax laws are uncertain. Check with attorneys first.)

One trust form, the temporary trust, has a special advantage because it may be set up for as short a period as two years to benefit a tax-exempt organization. At the end of that time, the principal of the trust reverts back to the contributor. But in the meantime the nonprofit group benefits from the income earned from the trust.

Because trust take many forms, and because each state has specific statutes governing them, arts groups wishing to promote trust programs should consult an attorney first. Information on local trust laws should then be made available to potential contributors.

July-August 1965

The Special Gifts Campaign:
Eight Fundamental Preconditions for Success

No type of fund raising is more important than the "special gifts" campaign. It may be part of an overall effort that employs direct mail, house-to-house canvassing, and other solicitation methods, or it may be used by itself.

What are special gifts? In the parlance of the professional fund raiser they are relatively large donations solicited on a personal and highly individual basis. They contrast with the small contributions sought in a mass effort. While canvassers may seek $5 contributions from householders, or a street-corner solicitor may collect quarters and dimes, the special gift is usually that of $100 or more.

Measured on a dollar-spent-per-dollar-raised basis, the special gifts drive is usually the most economical and efficient of all forms of fund raising. Moreover, its special characteristics make it particularly suitable for smaller institutions.

The small institution frequently cannot solicit over a broad geographical area, or it may lack a large corps of volunteers, or it simply may not be able to afford the relatively high costs of other methods. For these reasons, the special gifts campaign has become the staple of the small organization. It is also the most important part of the effort of the larger groups, and the chief weapon in the armamentarium of the effective fund raiser.

However, not every institution can conduct a successful special gifts drive. Certain preconditions must be met before an effective push can be made. To determine whether your institution can make use of this method now, ask yourself these eight questions:

1. How strong and clear is your "case"? Define your mission and the specific purpose of the contemplated fund drive. You must show your donor how, by giving, he will be helping a cause larger than the institution itself. A fuzzy case will not convince.

2. Are your board members well known and widely respected in the community? Your board is not only a major source of special gifts itself; it is also your most important line of communication to other donors. Its strength and public repuation may compensate for other weaknesses in your situation. You may want to consider adding judiciously selected members before entering the campaign.

3. Is your board a paper body? It may include some of the most important and respected members of the community but, if it is not a working body, your special gifts campaign may never get off the ground. The brunt of the effort in this form of fund raising necessarily falls on the board. It will cost its members time and money. They must set the pace, both in terms of gifts and of effort. Without its enthusiastic support, a special gifts drive is doomed in advance.

4. How well known in the community are your activities and accomplishments? Donors hesitate to give to an unfamiliar institution. A sustained public relations drive before the campaign begins can help let people know about you.

5. What is the economic health of your community? Check with your local united fund to see whether it has met its target in the most recent campaign. Check, too, with specialized health and welfare funds. Their fund-raising results are usually a matter of public record, and you should have no difficulty getting them. A general pattern of fulfillment suggests that the community is able and willing to give; a consistent pattern of failure suggests the opposite.

6. Is the time right? Even if there is clear evidence that patronage is available, it may be foolish to start a drive just when other drives are under way that may involve your potential supporters.

7. Is the community disposed to support your kind of activity? Is it generally culture-conscious? Here any information about the success or failure of recent drives by other cultural groups can give a clue to the prevailing atmosphere. If it appears negative, it may be improved by a carefully planned, energetic public relations effort calling attention to the role of your institution in raising the quality of community life.

8. Do you have the resources? Even though the special gifts campaign is the most efficient of fund-raising methods, it can require months of close attention by one or more staff people and considerable clerical time. It will require brochures, press releases, and other such material. You will need money for fund-raising events like a banquet or a cocktail party; you may even want to engage outside professional assistance to do research, make surveys, or manage the drive. It takes money to raise money, and your institution must be prepared to foot the bills.

Realistic answers to these questions can give you a fair estimate of your chances for success in a special gifts campaign.

March 1962

The Special Gifts Campaign:
How to Rate and Reach Your Prospective Donor

The success of a special gifts campaign depends heavily on the committee that develops the list of prospective donors, rates them, and assigns them to solicitors. If this part of the campaign for large gifts is well planned, the drive can succeed; if not, it will probably fail.

The listing committee should first draw up the basic list of possible donors. Members of the soliciting organization are, of course, the first source of names. But other sources should be carefully screened for additional leads. Some of these sources are programs or publications of similar, noncompeting organizations; business and city directories; social registers; and club membership lists.

The name of each potential giver should be entered on a card, along with as much relevant data about him as possible, such as his occupation or business affiliation, positions held, record of past giving, club connections, and personal friends or interests. Omit nothing that might help determine the best approach to the individual or the appropriate size of the donation to be sought.

An evaluation committee should then study these cards. Such a committee should include people who, through their business or social position, are able to estimate each prospect's ability to give. Its members are ordinarily found in the board of trustees of the campaigning institution. It is their task, once having rated each donor's potential, to assign prospects to solicitors. In doing so, the committee should ask itself the following questions:

1. Does the proposed solicitor have the right relationship to the potential donor? A business relationship can be of great value, especially when the prospect wants to maintain the good will of the committee member calling on him.

2. Is there a committee member or solicitor in the same giving class as the prospect who has social connections with him? It is natural for the donor

to contribute an amount close to that given by his solicitor if that solicitor is also a friend.

3. Have members of the solicitation committee made "pace-setting" gifts? A solicitor is far more effective in asking for a generous contribution if he himself has made one.

No solicitor should be assigned more prospects than he is willing or able to handle. He should always do so personally, though the setting may be business or social. Some donors are best approached at their office; others at lunch, cocktails, or an intimate dinner party where there is adequate time to explain the financial needs and program goals of the institution.

It is vital that the solicitor be thoroughly familiar with the purposes, program, and financial status of the organization. He should always have printed material to leave with the donor as a reminder. Sometimes it is effective to bring with him a staff member of the institution to answer detailed questions.

Above all, a special gifts campaign must be based on personal, face-to-face contact. It has been proved through the years that other methods—mailings or telephone calls alone, for example—will not produce special gifts as large as the evaluation committee may have planned or hoped.

May 1962

Acknowledgment Vital
to Special Gift Repeats

When an organization has run a special gifts campaign for large contributions solicited on a personal basis, proper acknowledgment of the gift is often the key to repeat giving.

In fact, repetition of special gifts through the years on the part of those people who are permanently, not only temporarily, interested in the group's work is essential if the institution is to build a sound base of support. Solidifying givers into permanent friends is the goal of an acknowledgment program.

Acknowledgment can take several forms. For example, large donors, as a group, can be thanked by invitation to special events organized for the purpose, such as a banquet, an opening night cocktail party, a preview of an exhibition, or an intimate dinner party at the home of a socially prominent person of the arts.

All contributions over $25 should be acknowledged by personal letter. One letter should be sent over the signature of the person who actually solicited the gift. In addition, a formal letter signed by the president of the organization can be included. But if there are so many acknowledgments to be made that duplicated letters must be used, they should be written in the same type employed to fill in the contributor's name, address, and amount of gift.

From this point on, contributors of $25 or more should receive all informational mailings, as a step to bind them to the organization.

August 1962

Your Economic Worth

Does your community know your economic as well as artistic value? In Seattle, A Contemporary Theatre (ACT) issued a release showing production by production employment for musicians, actors and production people—78 in all. The release not only showed company and production salaries of ACT's resident troupe, but also pinpointed the money spent in the community for food and lodging by out-of-town actors employed for its summer season.

January-February 1974

Sustaining Message

A theme for a fund-raising or ticket subscription drive is most effective when it becomes familiar to your audiences. This year the Arts Council of Winston-Salem, North Carolina adopted a new theme for its annual fund drive and has since used its message—"You Gotta Have Art"—and its cartoon-like pictorial representation not only on its general brochure, but on billboards, bumper stickers, other printed materials, and in television spots.

March-April 1974

Happy Birthday

Arts institutions may be interested in one museum's approach to community service and extra income through the same program. The Museum of the City of New York arranges birthday parties for children from 5 to 12 years old on weekday afternoons. At a cost of $7.50 per child for between 10 and 15 youngsters, the museum will include refreshments, games, prizes, and a tour of the facilities.

November-December 1973

How to Plan and
Conduct a Benefit Performance

The benefit performance generates funds through the sale of tickets at prices increased to include contributions.

The first step in developing a benefit campaign is to organize a strong committee. This is usually composed almost entirely of socially prominent women and should be headed by a member of the board of the benefiting institution.

This committee should be led by a chairman, a vice-chairman for publicity, and one for planning and arrangements.

The event should be chosen with care. It may be an opening night, a preview, or a special program. Whatever event is selected should have broad popular appeal.

The group must next decide on how many tickets it thinks it can sell, and on an appropriate price structure. Guests pay the regular ticket price, plus a premium (the contribution). This premium seldom exceeds $20 per seat, although in rare cases it may go as high as $100. Ordinarily, at an event at which the top premium is $20, a section of seats are set aside at the $20 level; other blocks at $15, $10, and $5 above the regular price.

Experience indicates that the top and bottom price seats sell better than those in the middle range, and so, in planning for a sale of, say, 600 seats, the committe might set aside 200 at $20, 100 each at $15 and $10, and 200 at $5. Such a distribution would yield a gross income of $7500 if all 600 seats are sold. Of course, the price levels and particular distribution chosen should reflect the potentials of the benefiting organization.

The next step is to work up a list of sponsors—prominent business and community leaders who agree to allow their names to be used in the accompanying publicity.

Once this is done, invitation kits must be printed. These include the invitation itself, which should contain not only the time, date, place, and a description of the event, but also the names of the committee, the sponsors, and the trustees of the institution. The invitation should also carry a statement explaining the work of the institution and spelling out its need for funds.

The kit must also include a reservation card listing seats available with prices, and a return envelope for checks.

Once these preliminaries are concluded, the publicity vice-chairman should arrange for a dinner or meeting at which the first public announcement of the benefit is made. It is vital that this meeting be reported in the press, preferably in the society pages. Photos of the principals should be given the press. Releases should contain the names of sponsors, committee members, and others associated with the event.

This initial public relations effort should be followed by a continuing flow of releases, pictures, and progress reports to local newspapers.

In the meantime, the vice-chairman for planning and arrangements should call upon members of the committee to submit the names of potential ticket buyers whom they will agree to solicit. These names are put on a master list and culled for duplication. A list of more general prospects is compiled from the social register, chamber of commerce members, and similar sources. Members of the committee agree to solicit those with whom they are personally acquainted. Unassigned names are divided arbitrarily, or accepted by the committee leaders as their assignments.

Committee members then mail invitation kits, along with personal, preferably hand-written notes to each of their assigned prospects. The return envelope in each case is coded with the name of the committee member sending it out.

The committee holds periodic meetings to follow the progress of the campaign and inspire greater effort. Additional assignments are made as necessary.

As checks arrive, they should be ticked off against the master list of prospects. Return envelopes will indicate which committee member sent out the invitation, and this member should be notified so that she knows which of her prospects have made purchases and which need additional prodding.

The benefit campaign described above usually takes between three and four months. As the date of the event approaches, final arrangements for seating and other details must be worked out.

September 1962

Taxes and Tickets

Are you selling tickets to a fund-raising event? According to guidelines published by the Internal Revenue Services, only that portion of payment which exceeds the fair market value of any consideration received by the purchaser can qualify as a tax deductivle gift. This, if $25 is charged for an opera ticket that normally sells for $10 only, the $15 above the normal ticket price is deductible. The IRS urges sponsoring organizations to indicate in their promotional material what the actual amount of the gift being solicited is.

September-October 1967

Educating Donors

How well do your contributors understand your organization's financial picture? For many laymen the nonprofit economy is a bewildering world of deficits and contribution requests that few organizations have bothered to explain to them. One arts group taking positive steps to educate its audience and help itself at the same time is the Chicago Symphony Orchestra, which features an easy-to-understand series of short articles in its newsletter under the general heading of "Let's Take the Mystery out of the Symphony's Money Requirements." The April 1973 issue, Report six, featured an article explaining specified, currently expendable gifts.

March-April 1973

Follow-up Mailings

If responses to fund-raising and subscription letters are excessively slow, the postal delivery system may be at fault. At least that's what a number of arts programs have been claiming when they send apologetic follow-up letters to potential subscribers and donors. In any event, follow-ups attributed not to zeal but "to make sure that our friends know about our forthcoming concert," as one group phrased it, may be a gentle reminder for your audience.

March-April 1973

To Sell for Christmas,
Plan Card Program Early

The sale of original art Christmas cards can be effective way of promoting your cultural organization and a source of income.

However, many art groups throughout the country who are in the Christmas card field warn that it is an extensive and expensive proposition, begun when the preceding year's sales figures are in and ending when the holiday season is over. In view of this, it might be wise to initially purchase slow-selling cards in bulk quantities at a trade discount from larger institutions already in the Christmas card field.

Whether you plan to buy and sell, or to print your own and sell, the following guidelines may prove helpful.

Form a committee to select a number of cards for your collection. The number in any collection may vary, of course, but a dozen or more designs may be needed to provide buyers with an adequate choice of price and type. The Museum of Modern Art, which runs an extensive Christmas card program each year, offers 28 different cards. Museums may draw on their own art collections for card designs. Others may buy designs from museums or commission original designs from artists. (Some artists are willing to donate their services.) In either case, vary the subject matter to include some religious, some nonreligious, some nonwintery, and some humorous cards. Keep legends simple. Offer some cards with no legend at all. Divide the collection between color and black-and-white. Remember that inexpensive one-color cards are usually the biggest sellers.

Once cards are selected and purchased or printed, promotion begins. Since card promotions tend to be expensive, it is often wise to use the same promotional material for other purposes as well. Some institutions link the card drive with membership recruitment by offering members special discounts on cards.

Promotion should begin in September with a direct mail effort. The organization's subsequent mailings of schedules, calendars, and other material should carry card advertisements as well.

As Christmas approaches, try to display the cards and other seasonal material where they will get the most attention. Make sure employees or volunteers are on hand to run the over-the-counter sale efficiently.

A Christmas card sale is only slightly better than a break-even proposition at best, many institutions report. It can, however, yield nonfinancial benefits in terms of service to members and publicity for the organization. Every original card mailed out by a purchaser carries the organization's name. A tasteful design helps create a favorable image of the institution.

May 1963

How to Spot, Woo, and Win a Foundation

In making an approach to any foundation, cultural organizations should take the same professional attitude as that exhibited by the educational, health, and social welfare groups that win the lion's share of foundation money.

The primary step must be the careful choice and delineation of the project to be supported. It should be timely, important, and something that your institution could not finance in any other way.

The next step is painstaking research into those foundations that are possible sources of support for the project—not all foundations are.

Generally, larger national foundations like Ford and Rockefeller prefer to aid "risk ventures"—new departures in the grant recipient's field of endeavor. They veiw their grants as "seed money," and only rarely grant funds for maintenance needs or similar routine demands. Smaller foundations, mostly local, family, or local corporate, are more likely to help close the financial gap in a community organization's regular program.

The right foundation to approach is one whose stated purpose would be furthered by the project for which you seek assistance. Canvassing foundations whose expressed aims would not be advanced by your project is a waste of time for the applicant and potential giver. To locate the appropriate foundation in a field of 13,000, consult the *Foundation Directory*. Also, a visit to one of the six regional depositories of the Foundation Library Center offers a chance to consult conveniently a wide range of relevant literature. Keep an eye peeled for new foundations in your field opening for business and looking for their first grantees.

The first contact with a foundation may be a sounding-out session in person or a very brief description of the proposed project in a one- or two-page letter. If this piques the interest of the foundation, you will be invited to follow up with a full presentation. Although requirements of individual foundations vary widely, here are a few cardinal points no application should fail to cover:

1. The project—its significance, timeliness, and relationship to the foundation's own aims

2. Your organization—its qualifications to carry out the proposed project successfully

3. Carry-over value—the usefulness of your project results to others in your field

4. Plan for inspection and review—the foundation's opportunity to oversee work in progress and evaluate results

5. Need—proof that the foundation's aid is absolutely essential

You should also include such essentials as a description of the precise nature of your organization, its history, legal form, and controlling body. List names and addresses of officers and professional staff. Explain its financial status and provide a detailed budget for the current year, along with the name and address of the auditor and a copy of your federal tax exemption certificate. Offer to supply any further information the foundation may request.

Your presentation should take into consideration the sensibilities of the foundation and of the community. One foundation executive, for example, may be known to court projects that pay off quickly with community approval and to shun those whose results are long-range and less obvious. The more you know about your target foundation, the better.

To the old claim that "knowing the right people" can be as much help with foundations as elsewhere in our society, foundation people offer mixed comment. Jeanne Brewer, an expert on foundation relations, writes of one foundation official who remarked, "Acquaintanceship is no substitute for a soundly constructed proposal." Yet another, she says, put it this way: "Personal connections with us are important. We look for good proposal ideas first, but they're rare, so we give generally where we know the man or the institution asking us."

February 1962

Foundation File

If your organization is interested in foundation support, it will be worthwhile for you to maintain a foundation card file. On each index card list the pertinent information about each local foundation, such as name, address, and phone number, and the names of key personnel within the foundation. Then every time you come across some new information concerning the foundation, such as the size or purpose of gifts given, or a statement of policy made by an executive, jot it down on the card. Also keep a record on the card of any foundation person who is a member of your organization or a ticket subscriber.

October 1963

Foundation Supports of Arts:
A Special Study

Harlan F. Lang

What chance does an arts organization have of receiving a foundation grant? To determine the kind of support foundations give to the arts, a representative sampling of 222 foundations selected from the files of Foundation Research Service was studied carefully. The period of analysis was fiscal year 1971, the last year for which detailed information is available, and the study based its analysis on all grants of $1000 and up. (This study offers much new information since the Foundation Center's widely used indexing system does not include grants under $10,000.)

The foundations examined provide a good cross-section of the foundation world, with total assets of $4 billion and with 30 states represented, headed by New York's 59 foundations. Other states with seven or more foundations were California, Illinois, Massachusetts, Minnesota, New Jersey, Pennsylvania, Ohio, and Texas. The study did not include such major, and perhaps atypical, givers to the arts as the Ford and Rockefeller Foundations.

Collectively, the 222 foundations gave $17 million of their overall total of $219 million to the arts. Interestingly, of the 745 arts grants recorded in this survey, 511, or about 70 percent of the total, were under $10,000 and 454, or about 60 percent, were $5000 or under. The $1000 grant was the most common, with 130 of the 745 included in this category. This was followed by the $5000 gift with 96 grants; $2000 with 59 grants; $2500 with 55 grants; $10,000 with 44 grants; and $25,000 with 31 grants. Other gift sizes were: 27 grants of $3000; 20 of $50,000; 19 of $15,000; 16 of $20,000, and 16 of $4000.

The accompanying table shows the distribution of art grants by size of gift and by category of recipient. (In this table the following symbols are used: A—Arts support organizations such as arts councils; O—Opera and other nonsymphonic music groups; S—Symphony orchestra; PA—Performing arts including theater and dance; M—Museums.)

Size of grants	A	O	S	PA	M
$ 1,000	24	17	23	40	28
$ 2,000	16	5	12	14	10
$ 3,000	12	7	8	21	9
$ 5,000	22	11	13	31	22
$10,000	14	9	6	7	9
$15,000	4	2	3	6	4
$20,000	1	1	1	8	6
$25,000	7	2	4	11	7
$50,000	1	1	6	4	8
$50,000 and over	8	6	13	8	18
Totals	99	61	89	150	121

The table shows that the performing arts won most grants of the categories sampled, with museums a close second, and, support organizations, orchestra and operas and other music groups following. Most noteworthy is the obvious fact that there is not too much variance among the five categories as to size of grant apportionment, although museums and orchestras clearly received more of the very large gifts.

This sampling, with its wide number of smaller grants, seems to disprove a prevalent impression among nonprofit arts organizations that foundations only give grants for total programming support. If foundations do indeed support portions of programs, arts groups might learn a lesson—that it is better not to be too ambitious when seeking grants unless a group has been to the foundation previously.

In an attempt to determine the degree of multidisciplinary giving to the arts and the willingness of foundations to give to new areas, the grant patterns of 175 of the 222 foundations were examined in greater depth. Of these 175, 81 gave to the performing arts category, 77 to arts support groups and programs, 73 to museums, 63 to orchestras, and 40 to opera and other musical groups. Although only 12 foundations gave to all five categories, there was a fair degree of multiple giving, with 21 giving in four categories, 23 in three categories, 35 in two categories and 32 in a single category. Fifty-two of the foundations did not give to the arts in 1971.

A two-year comparison showed that 45 percent of these foundations gave to arts disciplines in 1971 that they had not given to the previous year. Dance and theater received the most new gifts, 28; followed by museums, 26; support organizations, 22; and orchestras and other music organizations, both with 14. These results would seem to indicate that an arts organization has a good chance of convincing a foundation to support it even if that foundation hasn't given to a similar group before.

As one arts expert remarked, "The real trick is to get a foundation to give to the arts for the first time." Clearly, foundations are not standing still on their past giving records in regard to both size of grants and categories of giving, and the astute arts administrator has a challenge well worth the trying.

March-April 1973

Foundation Data

Arts groups that regularly seek foundation funding may find the Associates Program of the nonprofit Foundation Center (888 Seventh Avenue, N.Y., N.Y. 10019) a useful resource. For an annual fee of $200 plus charges for photocopying, computer time, and extended research, an Associate may request photocopies of IRS returns of private foundations and other microfiche and printed materials; phone or mail answers to specific questions; library research; and custom computer searches from the center's computerized information books. Included in the service is use of a toll-free WATS line.

Summer 1975

Learn About Funding

Groups seeking to strengthen their fund-raising programs now can learn from the best examples of others. A slide-cassette program, "Fund Raising for the Arts," created and narrated by *AM* editor Alvin H. Reiss employs a 35-minute audio cassette synchronized with an 80-slide carousel tray to demonstrate some of the innovative techniques used over the years by Canadian and American arts groups to win support from individual and corporate donors. This is the first in a new Arts Management Audio-Visual Series, with programs on audience development, business aid, and publicity to follow. For information, write to *Arts Management,* 408 West Fifty-seventh Street, New York, New York 10019.

Summer 1977

Researching Grants

The Foundation Center (888 Seventh Ave., N.Y., N.Y. 10019) has come up with a COMSEARCH printout service that breaks down more than 50,000 annual grants of $5000 or more into over 55 subject categories, including art and architecture; dance, theater, and performing arts; music; museums; and historical projects. Paper printouts are $10 plus $1 postage for each category, and microfiche copies are $3 each.

Summer 1977

How to Maintain Ties
with Old Contributors ·

A new fund-raising drive logically begins at the conclusion of the old one. During the period preceding the start of a new campaign, every effort must be made to maintain a friendly and continuing relationship with contributors. Too often, in the understandable zeal to discover new prospects, institutions neglect the constituency that has already demonstrated an interest. However, past contributors already "sold" on the institution may become bigger givers if properly cultivated. Moreover, they are excellent possibilities for future volunteer work and can become effective fund raisers themselves.

The first step in developing a continuing relationship with a contributor is a suitable acknowledgment of his gift. This should be done as quickly as possible after the gift is received. Donors of large gifts should receive personal acknowledgments from top leaders in the campaign. In the case of exceptional gifts, the board of directors might consider a formal resolution of thanks.

Since it is impossible to acknowledge all gifts personally in a large campaign, form acknowledgments should be drafted with care. They should be attractive, and the wording should impart the feeling that the institution is sincere in its appreciation of the gift, whatever its size.

After acknowledgments have been sent, the institution should have a prepared program to assure continued report-back to contributors. Initially, contributors should receive an accounting of the funds raised and an explanation of how these funds are being used. Regular written reports, inexpensively prepared in newsletter or simple letter form, should go out under the signature of a top officer of the institution to keep the donor aware of the continuing program of the institution. These should be supplemented by verbal reports at periodic organizational functions to which donors and/or volunteers are invited.

Although extra work and money is involved in maintaining relationships with past contributors, such a program will more than pay its way when the next drive rolls around.

March 1964

The Personal Touch

As a change from the coldness of the typical acknowledgment card sent to donors, the head of an arts organization might try sending out one with a personalized look. This can be done by reproducing a pen-and-ink message on a card that bears a printed heading—the reproduction of the handwritten message and signature could be in a typical blue-black ink that gives the impression of a personal thank-you note.

January-February 1968

Progress Report

A record of organizational growth should be an important part of any fund-raising case statement, but too many groups either forget to include it or don't present it to its best advantage. A good example of how to emphasize progress is found in an eight-page brochure recently issued by the Indianapolis Symphony Orchestra entitled "State of the Symphony." The report includes a description of all current orchestra activities, but also features a "then and now" comparison between its program and budget in its early days and today. The brochure's two-page centerspread dramatically demonstrates the orchestra's rising income and expense picture by featuring a color graph of the period between the 1965-66 season and the 1970-71 season, which uses actual figures for the completed seasons and estimated figures for the current and coming ones.

January-February 1969

Tax Deduction

Taxpayers often have difficulty recalling exactly how much they gave to charitable, nonprofit groups months before. If the receipt given donors at the time of giving is plainly marked with a reminder that the gift is tax deductible, it will help the busy donor place it with records he will need at tax time. A standard phrase imprinted on receipts and a reminder in acknowledgment letters should be automatic.

August 1962

Like It Is

To explain its case to prospective donors, including many in the business community, the Minnesota Orchestra decided to speak in the language of its audience. In a slim brochure with the cover line reading "One very solid investment Sylvia Porter would probably never recommend," the orchestra briefly discusses such topics as "bringing our product to market," "the in-go and the out-go simplified" (along with appropriate charts), and "the return on your investment."

Summer 1976

Who Gets the Check?

A campaign to raise funds for a health charity recently mailed elaborate printed material to potential contributors. But along with all the handsome literature came a mimeographed card clearly made necessary by the failure of someone to indicate how checks were to be made out. Often contributors and those ordering tickets by mail are left in doubt on this point. Organizations can save themselves and the public trouble by remembering to print clearly in bold type or capitals: "Please make checks payable to . . ."

April 1964

How Professionals Maintain
Records in Fund Campaign

Keeping accurate and adequate records may be unglamorous, but it is an important part of any fund-raising effort. Some large campaigns require that literally thousands of individual accounts be kept up-to-date and within easy access. In one $15 million campaign, for example, fund raisers maintained 15,000 regular accounts plus thousands of additional ones for direct mail respondents. The women's division of the campaign maintained records on still another 25,000 prospects solicited by its members. In a drive of this magnitude, punch card systems are almost a necessity. But even small campaigns require detailed attention to the record-keeping function. Good record keeping one year can be of inestimable help in the following year's drive.

A typical master file of 4 x 6 inch index cards ought to contain the following information for each giver or prospect: name and address; name of person to be interviewed, if the account represents a business; up-to-date information on the type of business, and number of employees.

Many professional fund raisers keep a ten-year giving record on the card, indicating the size of the gift each year, the date of each gift, and the name of the successful solicitor. Space should also be provided in which the solicitor can jot down the reasons given for a refusal to contribute.

Where there are a great number of very small contributions, it may be wise to establish a cut-off point for record keeping. Thus, while every contribution must be posted somewhere for bookkeeping purposes, it may be uneconomical to bother with additional data on those who give under $5.

While such painstaking record keeping takes time, it is essential to effective fund raising.   *July 1963*

Cautious Use of Surveys
Can Help Gauge Fund Potential

Many cultural organizations reach a point in their development at which they need professional help in gauging their fund-raising potential. To do this they often call on a professional fund-raising firm to undertake a study that will help them plan realistic fund drives.

Some studies, designed for organizations with very large constituencies, are based on questionnaires sent by mail. These are simple, and responses are given in yes-or-no form. A survey of this type may reveal which aspects of the institution's program are most "saleable" in the fund campaign. However, this type of survey cannot indicate the depth of individual commitment to the organization.

Another type of study focuses on a relatively few individuals, but attempts to probe their reactions to the institution in depth. For this type of survey, interviewers spend from one to three hours with each interviewee, attempting to provoke value judgements about the institution's program and effectiveness. Such interviews can indicate the degree of support the institution can expect during its drive. Sometimes, interviewers cannot only elicit information, but can obtain a significant campaign pledge then and there.

Success of either type of survey depends heavily on careful drafting of questions and thoughtful evaluation of responses. In the interview type, much also depends on selection of interviewers. Organizations should not rush into a survey without careful consideration of its objectives and cost. Interview studies are costly, and may range in price from $1000 for a one-month study based on 25 interviews, to $10,000 or more for a three-month study of a larger sample.

                                        November 1963

Variety of Printed Literature
Needed in Fund-raising Drives

Booklets, fact sheets, handbooks, and other printed materials are vital tools of every fund-raising campaign. They are important for explaining the reason for the drive, for helping cultivate donors, and for supplying factual information.

What is needed and how it is used depends on the purpose of the campaign and the group appealed to. According to the John Price Jones Company, a New York-based professional fund-raising firm, the following paragraphs describe the most used printed materials.

The case statement, the first piece, is basic. It explains what service the institution provides, why this service is needed, what opportunities exist for greater service, and what funds are needed. Subsequent publicity is often based on this statement, and it can be used to indoctrinate campaign leaders. Since it is not for general distribution, it is usually mimeographed or duplicated rather than printed.

The second major piece is a pamphlet intended for the general public. It contains the same material as the case statement, but sets the institution's goals within a larger framework by explaining the community's problems and then noting the institution's role in helping solve them. Since it is meant for mass distribution it should be printed and made attractive with pictures of present activities and various kinds of art work.

Each campaign worker should receive a handbook that contains tips on effective canvassing, a chart of the institution's needs, and a list of campaign committee members. It may include a section presenting the questions most often asked and their answers.

A preliminary campaign announcement is usually the first notice sent to prospective donors. It lists the institution's needs and the details of campaign preparations.

There are several categories of specialized campaign pieces. Many groups prepare a tax leaflet that lists the various forms that gifts can take. Sometimes there are personal appeals to more important prospective donors. These often list separately the special purposes the funds will benefit and are usually hand-typed or otherwise personalized.

Many drives prepare leaflets for particular groups, such as business.

For building drives, a gift and memorial opportunity leaflet presents the prorated cost of each unit, such as a meeting room or gallery, along with floor plans and a text pointing up the opportunity to name a unit after a donor.

Careful attention to the preparation of printed materials can make an important contribution to your fund-raising drive.

July 1963

Cultural Stocks and Bonds

The Winston-Salem Arts Council used parchment type paper for a fund drive promotional letter. A three-part folder, the outside is printed in green and is made to resemble a share of stock. The text in the folder informs the recipient that "The holder of this share is entitled to the benefits of a rich community life through the varied and ever-expanding facilities of the Winston-Salem Arts Council and its members. Very negotiable." The reverse side refers to "The Arts: Winston-Salem's Unique 'Growth Stock.' "

April 1964

Making a Date with the Donor

A New England school for the deaf has used an unusual and effective fund-raising reminder that places its appeal before potential givers 12 times annually. Every year it sends out a calendar with each month printed on the back of a business reply envelope. When the user tears off a month, he finds himself holding the institution's message and a self-addressed contribution envelope.

February 1962

Sense of Humor

A humorous approach can help to promote a fund-raising event successfully. When the Art Gallery of Toronto, initiated a "Happening" to raise funds, attractive posters proclaimed, "Make your own junk sculpture right in the Art Gallery of Toronto. (Junk available cheap at the Gallery.) Learn the truth about Pop. It's a wise child who knows his Dada."

April 1965

More Arts Groups Hire Fund-raising Pros

Richard C. Trenbeth

Although cultural organizations have lagged behind most nonprofit institutions in hiring professional counsel to help with their financial development, many more are turning to skilled firms and consultants to guide their volunteers and executive staff in their promotional and fund-raising efforts. Lincoln Center in New York, the Los Angeles County Museum, the Lyric Opera of Chicago, the Stratford Shakespearean Festival Foundation in Canada, and the New York Museum of Modern Art are among those that have successfully used professional help.

Far from being an admission of inadequacy on the part of the organization's board, the hiring of professional development counsel is a forward-looking, efficient approach to a problem as demanding of specialized help as a medical or legal problem. Effective money raising is a business. It makes use of the marketing, sales promotion, and advertising techniques with which board members are familiar from their own business interests.

Almost any cultural group can make good use of counsel, but the following conditions virtually demand it:

1. When capital funds are needed for new construction, rehabilitation, endowment, or other specific purposes
2. When annual gift support is inadequate to meet budget needs
3. When membership or subscription enrollment is lagging

Capital fund drives generally require the complete services offered by large firms specializing in campaign management. Most of these are members of the American Association of Fund-Raising Counsel, a highly regarded professional association with offices at 500 Fifth Avenue, New York, New York 10036. Smaller firms specializing in continuing annual support appeals are to be found in most large cities. Still other consulting firms tell their clients how to organize their own development programs, then guide them through the first three or four years.

Some cultural organizations have employed the part-time counseling services of professional development men working for similar organizations. An increasing number are creating their own development staffs, with or without outside counsel.

Whether hired for a capital campaign or a continuing annual appeal, most consultants start with an extensive study and survey of the organization, its needs and potentials. Sometimes they conclude that an intensive campaign is not feasible; in other cases they decide that the tentative goal is unreasonably low. Campaign management firms next project a timetable and preliminary strategy, working at the same time with staff and volunteers on list analysis and rating of prospects. This is followed by the organization of committees, the recruiting of volunteer leadership, and the assignment of duties. Then specialists are called in to write campaign literature, form letters, set procedures, and handle publicity.

Continuing counsel, after the initial survey, builds for the long pull. It stresses definition of objectives and cultivation of prospects through published information, orientation meetings, and special events. It sets up personal solicitation plans and works out regular direct mail solicitations to broaden the base of support. Extensive direct mail promotion always requires expert counsel from the first planning stages through each step, including gift acknowledgment.

Where membership or subscriber promotion is needed, counsel suggests sales techniques and list-testing procedures to get the maximum benefit from the promotional budget. Volunteer trustees are reminded at this stage that the money they are spending now may not produce substantial profits until a renewal pattern has been established.

Where there is an acute or impending financial need, counsel can usually save both time and money through orderly, economical planning and skillful direction. Further, counsel brings to the organization an objective, practical point of view, playing the disturbing "role of the stranger" who candidly points out weaknesses that may have been swept under the rug for years. Seasoned counsel shares with the organization years of experience in all aspects of fund raising and promotion, providing sound rules for judging success or progress, offering reassurance, or prodding, when necessary.

Counsel's greatest value often lies in bringing skilled communicators to bear on publicity and promotion. They know when to drop false modesty and how to obtain invaluable public service space and time from communications media. But experienced counsel is also the first to warn that even though good and continuing publicity is essential, it is not a substitute for one person asking another for money.

Perhaps most important of all, hired counsel stimulates trustees and other volunteer leaders to act immediately to protect their investment in counseling fees and campaign expenses. Sometimes this changes a board's concept of who its own members should be in the future to assure continuing financial support. Finally, counsel provides continuity of direction, offering the services of skilled professionals of higher caliber than most organizations can afford for their own staff.

January 1963

Fund-raising Counsel: The Cost is High, So Choose with Care Before Hiring

Richard C. Trenbeth

The main objection to hiring professional counsel for a fund-raising drive is the cost. Often small organizations are in such a bad way financially that a large promotional effort is needed to prevent untimely death and speed the patient on the road to recovery. There are natural fears that there just isn't enough money on hand to pay the doctor's fee.

Costs are usually substantial, but well worth it in view of the alternative. It must be kept in mind, too, that the initial expense is compensating for years of neglect of orderly work at building a sound financial base.

Counseling fees and campaign expenses must be faced long before any practical returns can be expected. Most reputable firms, and that includes all member firms of the American Association of Fund-Raising Counsel, refuse to work on a commission basis. They evaluate the potential through their initial survey, estimate the time and manpower required to accomplish the goal, and charge a fixed fee plus reasonable expenses.

Almost all firms charge for the initial survey, whether they are eventually hired for a campaign or not. Fee for an adequate survey can range from $500 to $10,000. Few qualified consultants will agree to work for less than $250 per day per principal executive. The client also pays a premium for experienced short-term help to carry out details.

Many organizations not familiar with development planning and operations ask for a program with a price tag attached, without defining their goals and true needs or authorizing an adequate study by the prospective counsel. Such a procedure is unfair both to the client and to the counseling firm. When a campaign is required, absolute candor is necessary on both sides if the costs are to be balanced by results.

An arts group considering counsel should be careful to evaluate what type of counsel will best accomplish its objectives at the most efficient cost (not necessarily the lowest) over the period when counsel is required. Does it need a major gifts campaign for capital funds? Or is the main problem to obtain regular annual support for a fairly stable budget plus minor improvements? Does it have on its staff a qualified but inexperienced person who can be given full-time development responsibilities? Or does it need a new person with experience?

Often it is wise to invite several counseling firms for short interviews, and eliminate those which would not be interested. Serious applicants should be asked to present their record in similar campaigns and submit references from groups they have served. Perhaps most important of all, they should bring for personal interview the account executive to be assigned if the firm is hired, because he is the one the client will be working with.

In checking references, try to ask for opinions from at least three people in the organization previously served; at least one should be the top staff executive. This is to reduce the chance that you may get a false picture from one person who may have had a personal difference with the account executive, or generally denigrated the value of counsel.

Good sources of names of fund raising counsel are the A.A.F.R.C. mentioned above, staff executives of community fund drives, and college and university development executives. As firms are interviewed, do not be discouraged by lack of definite promises or estimated costs at the first meeting. Most reputable firms will not make a commitment until they do some investigating of their own, or until they are hired to make a preliminary survey.

When costs, promises and services are compared and a choice of counsel is made, insist that the contract state clearly what services the fee covers and any limits to be placed on expenses. Reputable firms ask the client to pay actual costs in addition to their fee. It is up to the client to place a realistic limit on these expenses, subject to review. But the organization should make provision for swift authorization to spend more in an emergency.

It should be clearly understood at this point that all major policies recommended by counsel are to be cleared quickly with one or two officers, or a small executive committee. Nothing cripples counsel more than indecision. Precision timing is a fundamental of effective development.

February 1963

Counsel May Cost 10 Percent of Funds Raised

Richard C. Trenbeth

If your fund-raising counsel recommends an intensive campaign at first, to be followed by a long-range development program, don't be surprised. The really sound organization should expect years of strong support long after the campaign ends.

Some indication of the length of the campaign itself may be found in a recent survey by the American Association of Fund-Raising Counsel, covering thirty-seven recent campaigns for colleges, universities and professional schools. In campaigns for goals under one million dollars, counsel service averaged 13 weeks in preliminary work and 16.6 weeks of active campaign period. Campaigns for $1,000,000 to $7,000,000 averaged longer—34 weeks in preliminary work and 45 weeks in the active period.

The same survey of campaigns under a million showed costs ranging from a high of $68,080 for total contributions of $600,000 to a low of $13,832 for total contributions of $294,830. In the larger goal group, costs ranged from a high of $290,681 for total contributions of $7,070,161 to a low of $39,245 for total contributions of $1,748,461.

For arts groups, costs may be expected to run as high as ten per cent or more of the goal, especially if there has been little or no development activity in the past.

Firms or individual consultants handling continuing annual support programs usually work on an annual contract basis, although some may insist on a minimum initial contract of at least two or three years. They bill on a monthly basis in terms of agreed-upon services usually ranging from eight to 40 hours per month, plus fees for special writers or analysts as needed. Total fees might range from $250 to $1,500 a month or even more.

Annual support programs are based on careful planning, a detailed time table, and professionally prepared printed material and letters. Such consultants usually offer sound advice on the buying of printing, envelopes, lettershop services and other requirements, and these recommendations eventually add up to substantial savings.

Annual drives for an arts group always involve considerable effort on the part of the organization's own staff and trustees, but with able counsel the effort is put to more effective use and usually requires far less time, which must also be considered in computing true costs.

For the very small organization or one just getting started, the independent counsel or the part-time services of someone already working fulltime for another organization may be the best alternative. For as little as four hours a month such a consultant can often save the organization many times the amount of his fee, and though some may require contracts of at least two years, others may agree to work for six months or a year.

Don't expect miracles from a short-term agreement. It usually takes a competent staff department under the most capable supervision at least a year to show any kind of results from a standing start, and often longer to do more than get expenses back. Under a limited counsel arrangement, the organization's own staff must be prepared to do all the work except planning, major writing, and other creative work.

A growing trend in organizations fortunate enough to have a qualified staff development executive is to employ outside counsel on a limited basis. The outsider, with an objective point of view, can make the staff man far more effective by pleading his case and his recommendations before the board or other policy group.

The old saying that it takes money to make money certainly applies in development or fund-raising work.

March 1963

How to Select a Staff Director to Head a Development Program

To meet expanding financial needs, many arts institutions have reached the point in their growth at which they need a staff director of development. This is one of the most crucial positions in the organization.

In searching for a staff fund raiser, you may find it useful to explain your needs to a professional organization, such as the National Society of Fund Raisers or the American Association of Fund-Raising Counsel, Inc., both in New York. Similarly, a large employment agency specializing in fund-raising personnel may also be helpful.

Fund raisers, unlike lawyers, doctors, and scientists, are not required to have formal training. Therefore, it is much harder to determine their competence. In choosing the right man for an arts institution, one must rely on good judgment, intuition, and a thorough analysis of the candidate's qualifications and experience.

There is no standard questionnaire that can be used to measure the candidate's capabilities, although success in other campaigns, even those conducted for unrelated kinds of institutions, may be a valid indication of competence. Be sure to check on a candidate with both the executive directors and lay leaders of organizations he cites in his employment record.

Each institution, of course, will have its own criteria for selection. However, a staff director of development should have a knowledge of fund-raising techniques; a knowledge of community life and organizational structure; an ability to interpret and sell the institution's program; the ability to communicate to top echelon leadership through a direct approach and through written materials; the capacity to establish effective working relationships with important community leaders; aptness in selecting the most pertinent aspects of the program for exploitation; and the ability to write brochures, speeches, and presentations for corporation and foundation prospects. Although no individual fund raiser will possess all the above qualities, a good one will be a synthesis of many of them.

April 1964

Check Ten Points when
Choosing Fund Drive Head

Planning a fund-raising campaign? A basic decision that must be made is the choice of your drive chairman. G. A. Brakeley & Co., Inc., of New York [now Brakeley, John Price Jones, Inc.] , a leading firm of professional fund raisers, has devised a ten-point test to help select an effective chairman. Score candidates from one to ten points for each item. A score of 85, says Brakeley, makes a good chairman. However, the firm warns, if a two-man team is involved, the score should total 95 or better. Here are the ten checkpoints.

Does the candidate have:

1. A thorough familiarity with and understanding of the basic philosophical and practical reasons why the cause or institution should be supported; a consequent conviction and desire to do the job.

2. The calibre of a good trustee (if not a trustee at the time), a "leader" or "leader-designate."

3. Ability to make an important gift personally—if not sacrificially, at least the top level proportionate to his means.

4. Ability to get a leadership gift from his corporate affiliation(s)—assuming this to be a cause to which corporations can logically give.

5. Ability to obtain leadership gifts (or to assure this through others) from the trustee group and wealthy "friends" of the cause or institution.

6. Enthusiasm in asking for big gifts—in most instances, by amount or at least "range"; often teaming up with an institution president, a top researcher, or department chairman, and often with the idea of identification of the donor with a specific project.

7. Willingness and ability to enlist and work with a top-level team ("executive" or "steering" committee) for policy decision, planning, organization, and delegation of authority where necessary.

8. Availability for periodical meetings of the "executive" committee, probably weekly to begin with, but tapering off as the organization and delegation of responsibility proceeds; adequate time for key enlistments and solicitations, also tapering off. (How much time? Tremendous variations, but we generalize for the average capital campaign at between one-and-a-half

and two working days or their equivalent in time per week, including lunch, later afternoon, and occasional evening meetings.)

9. Willingness to accept "professional" advice and adhere to a responsible and prepared plan schedule.

10. Ability to preside with enthusiasm and inspiration over meetings of his associates.

December 1963

CASE STUDIES IN FUND RAISING

Telethons Can Play a Key Role in Boosting Financial Support

Cultural organizations seeking to bolster their fund-raising programs might consider sponsoring telethons. Although telethons require long planning, careful coordination, and an advance outlay of funds, they can yield major financial returns.

Telethons have been successfully used by health and welfare organizations for a number of years, and the techniques employed by such organizations as the Muscular Dystrophy Associations of America, Inc., for example, can offer helpful guidelines to arts groups. On a 20-hour MDA telethon held on WNEW-TV in New York beginning on Labor Day, more than $1 million was pledged. By November 1, MDA had received 85 percent of this amount.

According to Lila Brigham, Manhattan district director of MDA, planning for the recent telethon began more than a year in advance. The first step was finding a television station that would commit free air time. Choices were limited to local independent stations with strong records of public service. WNEW-TV met these criteria, and a top MDA volunteer helped win station approval for a Labor Day airing.

Next, a host had to be found. In January, the organization asked its national chairman, film star Jerry Lewis, to be master of ceremonies. His early acceptance motivated many others to participate.

Although talent and a variety of services were contributed, the organization decided to hire a top television producer to recruit celebrities and mount the show. MDA recognized that a professionally presented production would help to attract and hold an audience, and thus spur donations. Next, the organization rented four floors of the Americana Hotel at a discount rate for the week preceding the show and for the telethon.

With confirmation of station, date, place, producer, and star, the organization, under the overall supervision of its director, began the tremendous task of coordination. An organizational chart was prepared, headed by the director, who was responsible for budget, purchasing, and contract negotiations. Three separate divisions were established under the director—operations, promotion, and show production.

About six weeks prior to the telethon, the operation moved into high gear. The paid producer began lining up his talent and assembling the production. The promotion division, manned by paid staff members, began an all-out campaign geared to motivating stay-at-homes to watch the Labor Day telethon. A printing firm donated posters which were distributed to stores and supermarkets throughout the city, and 750,000 fliers were posted in large housing developments, enclosed with rent statements, and distributed through other organizations. Also, spot announcements featuring Jerry Lewis were aired regularly on station WNEW, Lewis and other celebrities "plugged" the telethon in radio and television interviews, and scores of newspaper stories were released.

The operational division, headed by staff members, coordinated the efforts of more than 2000 volunteers recruited from within the ranks of the organization through publicity, and through specially established suburban offices.

Well in advance of the telethon, cards were sent to volunteers informing them of their four-hour work shift, their specific assignment, and where and when to report.

The telethon, which began at 10:00 P.M. on September 4, 1966 and ran till 6:00 P.M. on September 5, proceeded according to advance planning. The producer kept the show moving while batteries of volunteers, armed with written instructions, handled the pledges phoned and wired in. Calls were taken both at the Americana and at 12 regional centers. During the show, everyone who phoned in a donation of more than $100 was immediately called back for verification. Volunteer drivers picked up pledges from out-of-the-way areas. Figures were totaled and announced on television following verification.

Follow-up was essential. Within 24 hours after the telethon, staff and volunteers had mailed out cards to everyone who had made a pledge.

Although telethons can be highly lucrative, Mrs. Brigham offers these cautions to arts groups: never anticipate receiving everything that's pledged; be prepared to spend money to make money (MDA budgeted $200,000 in advance for the program); and anticipate some difficulty in working with celebrities.

November-December 1966

A Three-day Radio Marathon
Is Effective Fund-raising Device

Radio marathons can be effective fund-raising and promotional tools as several symphony orchestras, Boston and Cleveland among them, have discovered within recent months. In Dallas, a 72-hour marathon organized by the Dallas Symphony Association in June 1971 raised nearly 50 percent more than was anticipated and helped provide the orchestra with vital exposure during "Dallasound Countdown 30," the orchestra's final 30-day campaign to enable it to qualify for a $2 million Ford Foundation endowment grant.

Key elements in the marathon's success included advance organization, enlistment of support from local leaders and business, and a simple and workable formula, in this instance the playing of records in return for contributions. Beginning at 6:00 A.M. on a Thursday morning and continuing through midnight Saturday, listeners to WRR-FM, the city-owned classical music radio station, were invited to pledge specific amounts to the orchestra and, in return, to dedicate musical selections to a person or an organization of their choice. For $5, unspecified selections could be dedicated; for $10, specified selections up to 15 minutes in length could be dedicated; for $20, 30-minute requests; and for $50, 45-minute requests. Those pledging larger amounts were given such extra benefits as multirecord symphonic albums or the opportunity to be guest disc jockey on the program. Single LP records donated by commercial recording firms were offered as incentives to callers throughout the marathon.

To maintain interest, local celebrities served in three-hour shifts as guest disc jockeys. In addition, such special guests as the city's mayor and orchestra officials appeared.

Of the $150,000 the orchestra needed to raise during June, the three-day marathon realized $7500 and provided an extra publicity base for the month-long fund-raising effort. Commenting on the marathon, Robert H. Alexander, public relations director of the Dallas Symphony, said, "The station was delighted with the results, and to have your name mentioned on the air for 72 hours is worth more than any amount you actually collect in the marathon, although $7500 is sweet to think about."

September-October 1971

Groups Learn TV Auctions
Are Not Always Successful

Televised auctions may look like a fast and easy way to raise money, but if the experience of seven Brooklyn, New York cultural groups is any indication, the arts path may be paved with unseen stumbling blocks. A televised auction for the benefit of the organizations in March 1976 was widely publicized, drew a celebrity-packed audience of some 700—mostly paying guests—and created excitement for weeks in advance. Moreover, most of the televised time was donated, as was the facility where the auction was held, and volunteers manned phones and handled bids. Yet when the smoke cleared, only 40 of the 250 contributed items had been sold and the result, according to Charlene Victor, director of the Brooklyn Arts and Culture Association, was "a most magnificent financial fiasco."

What went wrong? First of all, there were a number of unforseen costs, including the "up-front" TV production expenses needed to professionally present the program. The sponsors were unaware of the extent of these costs when the project was conceived.

In the final analysis, however, the confusion caused by fake telephone bids was the most serious problem since bidding on each item was not only open to everyone present in the studio but to viewers as well. The second item presented, a handmade rug worth $400, attracted frenzied bidding, and when it went over $2000 it seemed obvious that something was wrong. However, bidding was allowed to continue until it reached $59,000. This kicked off a rash of crank bids.

Although the seven sponsors were soured by the experience, they were not defeated and still hope to salvage real dollars from the effort. A nontelevised event is being planned to auction off the remaining items.

However, some Brooklyn arts leaders are still thinking about another TV auction, with most bidding limited to the paying audience attending the auction. About every 15 minutes the program would switch to phone bids, but none would become final until a special check and call back had been made. Meanwhile, live bidding would continue in the studio. "We'd verify bids before we'd accept them," added Ms. Victor.

In spite of the negative financial results, the March evening wasn't a total loss, according to Ms. Victor. "The exposure did a lot for Brooklyn's cultural groups," she told *AM*. "In addition to weeks of advance publicity, each participating group had three-minute on-the-air promotions to tell their stories. But the next time around, money will be nicer than publicity.

March-April 1976

Radio and TV Raise Funds, Promote Programs

Radio and television are proving to be lively and rewarding media for arts promotion and fund raising. Although radiothons and phonoramas have been around for some time new variations on old themes plus strong support from local broadcast stations are resulting in outstanding successes for symphony orchestras and other arts groups.

Station salutes of arts groups include WEFM—Chicago's week-long, 24-hours-a-day presentation of recordings by the Chicago Symphony, some of which go back to 1916, when the orchestra began to record commercially, and WQXR's special "Metropolitan Opera Week." Initiated to raise funds for the opera company, "Opera Week" spotlighted the Met on all WQXR feature programs and concluded with a unique gala concert broadcast live from the opera house. Open to the public at a tax-deductible $10 per ticket, the concert featured company stars who donated their services, singing to piano accompaniment. The station promoted the Met's fund needs during the broadcast and volunteers took phone pledges from listeners.

In Detroit, a live telecast of interviews with Symphony Orchestra leaders on the Detroit Today Show, provided Women's Association volunteers, with a vehicle for selling season tickets. More than 50 women hosted coffee hours in their homes on the morning of the telecast for friends, acquaintances and interested people—nearly 1000 in all—to listen to music director Aldo Ceccato and executive director Marshall Turkin discuss the season.

A broadcast phone solicitation campaign over WBEN in Buffalo tested a new and interesting concept—live performances by nearly 50 high school orchestras and bands for two days around the clock as a salute to the Buffalo Philharmonic. To increase interest, music director Michael Tilson Thomas of the Philharmonic participated in the broadcasts and related the school music programs to the orchestra's overall program. In Minneapolis, the Minnesota Orchestra's recent 18-hour "Phonerama" over KTWN-radio, sponsored by a local bank, was designed specifically to promote subscription sales rather than to raise funds. Listeners were invited to visit Orchestra Hall, where live Phonerama interviews with orchestra figures and local celebrities were held.

Buoyed by the success of radio marathons in Cleveland and Boston, which raised more than $100,000 each in 1975, the Chicago Symphony will participate in its own 60-hour marathon over WFMT next May. A feature of the new program will be special premiums offered to contributors including such services donated by orchestra players as cooking a gourmet diner, private recitals and lessons, an evening of bridge or scrabble, and a morning of jogging or cycling.

In spite of many successes, some broadcast promotions, especially those tried for the first time, don't work out quite as well as anticipated. However, as the Albany Symphony Orchestra discovered, a less than total success need not negate the attempt at a second effort, especially if the problem area can be pinpointed and corrected.

In January 1975, the Albany Symphony was approached by the area's top audience radio station, WROW, with the idea of a station give-away benefit for the orchestra, "WROW Night at the Pops." The first phase of the promotion featured a drawing for 100 pairs of symphony tickets over WROW for listeners. Next, at "WROW Night," the station orchestra tie-in was promoted through a program editorial and an intermission address by the station manager on the importance of the project. Finally, an over-the-air appeal for funds on WROW was made every half hour on the Monday and Tuesday nights following the Saturday concert. Although interest was aroused and money was raised, the total was far below expectations.

What were some of the miscalculations that orchestra and station personnel noted? First, the promotion was presented only a week before the area's public service classical music station WMHT presented its own two-day marathon for funding. According to orchestra public relations director Ilene Klinghoffer, "we knew that theirs would be happening at almost the same time, but felt that listeners to WMHT and WROW did not overlap in any substantial numbers, and that the WROW audience is considerably larger anyway. With 1000 percent hindsight, we now suspect we were wrong."

Other miscalculations included a weekday rather than weekend fund appeal time slot which prevented many husbands from listening; the nearly one-week lag between the give-away and donation portion of the project; and a misjudging of the attitudes of station advertisers, who were asked to donate opening and closing news tags to the orchestra and didn't. Also there wasn't sufficient advance promotion by the station on the giveaway and fund appeal.

Despite the lack of financial success, the promotion was deemed a positive move by both station and orchestra, and plans are now underway for a new promotion which will correct last season's mistakes. "Our ties with the station have grown even stronger this season," added Betsy Kennedy, the orchestra manager, "and we're beginning to discuss the next promotion. We may change the format or try another type of fund-raising event, but they'll still be with us 100 percent."

September-October 1975

Win-an-Orchestra Contest
Builds Community Support

Radio station WRYT in Pittsburgh is known within its coverage area for its unusual contests and off-beat promotional stunts, but one of its most notable contests was a 1962 event benefiting the Pittsburgh Symphony Orchestra.

In effect, the listener-winner got the Pittsburgh Symphony Symphonetta for her own personal concert by writing a letter to the station and enclosing a contribution to the symphony orchestra's annual maintenance fund campaign.

The contest idea came from Bob Stevens, Program and Operations Manager of Pittsburgh's good music station, WRYT. Stevens serves on a Campaign Advisory Council for the Pittsburgh Symphony Orchestra. His scheme was to ask WRYT listeners to write letters to the station explaining why they would like to have some of the symphony's musicians play a special concert for them. Each letter was to include a contribution to the orchestra's maintenance fund campaign.

The program began in mid-summer and ended just before the opening of the fall concert season. It called listeners' attention to the fact that a symphonic concert would be just fine on a patio or in a small neighborhood. The private concert idea caught fire, and soon entire communities were sending entries through civic officials. Hospitals, schools, housing developments, churches, building superintendents, and industries also sent entries with cash. One entry even asked the orchestra to play for a wedding.

Letters were considered by an impartial board of judges. A young supervisory nurse at Presbyterian University Hospital was declared the winner. She wanted the Pittsburgh Symphony Symphonetta to play a concert in the hospital auditorium so that shut-ins and hospital personnel who could not hear regular concerts would be able to enjoy a performance.

A quartet of musicians was dispatched to the Western Pennsylvania School for Blind Children to play for the youngsters there, in response to a second letter that was judged the runner-up.

In addition to raising funds for the orchestra, the WRYT contest served the very useful purpose of keeping the orchestra in the public mind through its off-season.

When the concert season began in October, residents of the station's listening area were well keyed to its activities. In consequence, campaign officials believed they were better able to approach potential ticket buyers and contributors because of the frequent spot announcements carried by WRYT.

January 1963

Cultural Groups Play Games
to Win Funding and Members

Running an arts institution is a serious business but, as many administrators have discovered, some creative gamesmanship can help to promote programs and raise money. Moreover, the light touch, properly applied, can lead to happy audiences and satisfied donors.

In Louisville, Kentucky, for example, a game board provided both theme and setting for a 1977 annual symphony ball that drew double the attendance and income over the previous year. Faced with the prospect of coming up with an unusual and interesting setting for the Louisville Orchestra Ball last winter, chairperson Jo Ann Gammon focused on an unused 120-year-old city water company enginehouse as a site. Following months of discussions, Ms. Gammon finally won approval from the Board of Water Works to use the abandoned facility for a $1 rental, provided she agreed to get it cleaned up for public use.

Aware that "Water Works" is one of the stops on a Monopoly board, Ms. Gammon and her committee prepared fold-out invitations with the word "Go" and a red arrow on the cover. Invitations opened accordian style to show familiar Monopoly tokens and invited recipients to advance tokens to Water Works, which occupied the back cover of the invitation. Enclosed were two cards. "Chance," when accompanied by a $50 per person check, allowed recipients to advance to the water works on June 11. "Community Chest" carried the message, "I wish to donate but cannot attend."

Since the facility hadn't been used in years and was something of a shambles, hundreds of volunteers from the Women's Committee had to spend weeks cleaning it up and getting ready for the party. "We hustled everyone we knew in town for donations and materials," Ms. Gammon told *AM* "and virtually everything we used was donated." At the party itself, a giant game board was drawn on the floor of the facility with Monopoly name places adapted to actual locales in Louisville, and some fun elements added. Community Chest, for example, was drawn to resemble a well-proportioned local belle.

In addition to attracting some 400 people—including crashers because of the tremendous publicity—and raising over $23,000, the party brought an unexpected benefit to the people of Louisville. Pleased with the way water works looked after its metamorphosis, local preservationists and arts center leaders undertook a campaign to insure its use as a permanent community arts facility to house crafts and other activities.

Another game, this one devised by the staff of the Chrysler Museum at Norfolk, Virginia, has helped to up attendance, increased interest in the objects on exhibit, and led to a small rise in membership. On September 15, the museum introduced the "Art Game," asking museum visitors to correctly identify ten different art works from clues in rhyme provided in entry forms. One such rhyme read, "Round and round on a vase of green, fixed grey elephants can be seen." According to a museum staff member, the clues weren't difficult, but they did force visitors to focus on the collection in order to answer them. All entries were thrown into a container at the entrance, and new games and prize drawings were held weekly with contestants vying for such donated prizes as concert and opera tickets, works of art, free vacations, and gift shop items.

Because the promotion involved a contest, local radio and television stations felt they couldn't give the museum free public service time. With no budget for advertising, the museum decided on a new ploy—it prepared thousands of inexpensive fliers and had them distributed at the checkout counters of five local supermarket chains. The resulting publicity was exceptional, as was overall newspaper coverage.

One direct benefit was that some 100 museum memberships were taken out by gameplayers. Although the game was to have ended after three weeks, the museum is continuing it and offering memberships as prizes.

In New York, meanwhile, the Lincoln Center Student Program has discovered, as it expected, that adults as well as children love to play with new toys. In place of its usual announcement inviting school administrators to participate in its program, center officials mailed giant color posters which not only listed esssential information, but which also served as a cut-out board. With it, students could assemble their own Lincoln Center complete with all the buildings, trees, people, and even cars and buses. Some 20,000 were mailed and the response was overwhelming.

"We had three or four times as great a response as we've had to any mailing," Mark Schubart, the program's director, told *AM*. "The posters were effective not only as a toy, but as a way of getting across information."

September-October 1977

Arts Groups Try a Fun Approach
to Win Dollars and New Friends

In an attempt to attract new audiences and win friends, arts groups throughout the country are developing fund-raising events that emphasize informality, excitement, and fun. In fact, in many communities such traditional offerings as black tie dinners and formal balls may be a thing of the past.

In Wichita, Kansas, for example, the Symphony's Women's Association, aware of declining interest in the annual symphony ball, decided to do something different for its 1971 event. The long-closed main waiting room of Wichita's Union Station, with its three-storied ceiling and once-elegant Harvey House dining room, presented both a unique setting and a party theme. Following months of discussion with railroad officials beginning in the fall of 1970, permission was given to reopen the room the following spring for a benefit, the "Symphony Station Stop."

On May 27, after a 15-year accumulation of dirt and dust had been removed, a capacity crowd of more than 400 people assembled in the restored waiting room, illuminated by kerosene lanterns, for an evening of fun and entertainment. Dressed in everything from overalls to white tie, the guests, who paid $15 per couple, arrived in a driving rain and experienced two tornado alerts during the evening. "It was one of the worst nights in memory," Wichita Symphony manager Dewey Anderson told *AM*. "There was a tornado on the other side of town, but it didn't bother anyone—they were having too good a time."

Although the weather prevented the use of railroad handcarts, which were to have transported guests from the parking lots to the station, the old-fashioned railroad theme was in evidence everywhere. Old station scales, shoe-shine stands, and outdated baggage carts served as bars, and a large ice sculpture of a train dominated the buffet table. Entertainment included dancing to the Kansas City Philharmonic Rock Band, banjo playing in the lobby, tours of a restored caboose and nearby Historical Railway Museum, and continuous showings of two silent films, *The Great Train Robbery* and *Freddy Takes the Throttle*. Guests posed for pictures in front of a large train mural and purchased antique dining car silver from a benefit boutique. They feasted on the buffet in the old Harvey House and quaffed draft beer.

Publicity before and after the event was excellent, and although it was planned "as a fun event involving many new people and good will for our organization," according to Anderson, about $1500 was raised. "I think that we learned from this event," he added, "that the old Symphony Ball is now past history in a city like Wichita."

November-December 1971

Museum Salvages Fund Benefit
and Boosts Image

What does a financially hard-pressed arts group do when it has built a benefit around a heralded new Broadway musical—*Working*—developed a theme based on the musical's subject matter—" 'Working' for the Hudson River Museum"—did a good job promoting the event, sold tickets, and then, just several days before the benefit is to take place, learns that the musical has closed? If the organization is the Hudson River Museum in Yonkers, New York, it rounds up volunteers for rush telephone duty, keeps the theme and date, makes necessary program changes, and then goes ahead with the benefit, reaping some unexpected dividends in the process.

The story behind the benefit's ultimate success goes back to January 1978 when a board member, seeking marketing and promotional help for the museum, arranged a meeting between museum staff members and top advertising executive Mary Wells Lawrence of Wells, Rich, Greene, Inc. Ms. Lawrence was so impressed with the museum's potential and the enthusiasm of its staff that she loaned the museum several executives from her agency on a part-time basis to help it develop an overall marketing program. Personally committed to the museum, Ms. Lawrence also made the use of her office available for a pretheater cocktail party when the idea of a benefit was first suggested and agreed to serve as an honorary chairperson. She also was helpful in recruiting noted illustrator Milton Glaser to design invitations and graphic materials.

Although the closing of *Working* in mid-June 1978, just a few days before the scheduled benefit was a shock, everyone agreed that too much had been invested in the effort to cancel it. Following Ms. Lawrence's offer to hold the entire benefit in her office and a commitment from *Working* composer and director Stephen Schwartz to present selections from the show at the party, the wheels quickly began to turn. For three evenings, staff and volunteers called every ticket purchaser to explain the program change and to ask them to attend the benefit. Out of a total of nearly $8700 in ticket sales, only 12 individual tickets were refunded. Overall, the party cleared more than $6000.

The event itself was a tremendous success with six cast members performing with Schwartz. Area publicity was also outstanding. As public relations director Jane Cohn told *AM*, "The benefit was a lift to our morale and image. We won new memberships from those that were there and from those who read about it. Everyone was so enthusiastic that already we have a base of support for our next benefit."

Summer 1978

Orchestras Use Giveaways as Fund-raising Tool

In an attempt to raise substantial funds through a continuing promotion, several symphony orchestras are giving away free prizes every month. For the past few years, the Denver and Pittsburgh orchestras have run successful giveaway promotions, raising more than $30,000 a year each, and now the Sacramento Symphony is jumping on the bandwagon.

Since November 14, thousands of Sacramento citizens have been invited to "support your symphony the fun way" by donating $10 to it. In return they received coupons for a monthly "Opus '74" prize drawing and a coloful calendar listing each of the prizes. Promotional material clearly indicated that it was not necessary to make a donation in order to be eligible for a prize. On January 21 and on the third Monday of each following month throughout 1974, the orchestra will draw a coupon for prizes valued at upwards of $500, including a week-long cruise to Mexico and a 12-foot catamaran. In addition, a year-end grand prize worth more than $9000 will be awarded.

Planning for the event, which set its first year goal at $20,000, began last spring with the naming of a chairman and co-chairman and solicitation of gifts for prizes. "We were very selective," orchestra manager Barbara Boudreaux told *AM*, "because the quality of the gift offered is related to the campaign's success." The promotion also was cleared with the district attorney and the county to make sure that it didn't violate local laws and one result was the provision that participants did not have to make contributions to be eligible for prizes. (Statutes differ from place to place, and all such campaigns should be cleared in advance.)

The campaign was launched with a coordinated promotion drive including the use of ten billboards, spot announcements, newspaper stories picturing symphony leaders with prizes, concert program stuffers, and a giant public mailing. A separate mailing to orchestra league members asked them to take two Opus '74 calendars at $10 each and send calendars as Christmas gifts. Within two weeks of the first mailing of 5000 announcements, $4000 in donations had been received. Donations were not required in order to receive coupons, but only four percent failed to send them.

Although each coupon is eligible for all 13 drawings, the orchestra hopes to push hard on new sales through the end of its season next April. Promotional help will be provided by Sacramento's two major daily papers, who will publish winners' pictures in alternate months. Pictures also will appear in symphony programs.

The experience of orchestras using giveaways has shown that first campaigns have been the hardest, especially in finding suitable prizes, but that participation later has been easier to find. "Without solicitation we already have three gifts for next year," Ms. Boudreaux said. The Sacramento orchestra plans to make the giveaway an annual event, with end-of-the-season drawings promoting the following campaign.

November-December 1973

Orchestra Rummage Sale
Breaks All-time Record

A well-organized rummage sale sponsored by the Women's Committee of the Toronto Symphony Orchestra netted the organization $27,000 in a single day in 1963.

The event grossed $35,000 from the sale of thousands of articles selling for as much as $95 (a mink jacket) and as little as 5¢ (a piece of costume jewelry). Expenses ran to $8000, of which $3000 went for rental of space at the Canadian National Exhibition.

An estimated 15,000 people attended. Some 600 bargain hunters were lined up in rows four and five deep hours before the doors opened at 10:00 A.M. Early birds were rewarded with such bargains as a lamp for 35¢, a pair of ski boots for $1, a suitcase for 50¢, and a large radio priced at only $1. Yellow-smocked volunteers worked in shifts until 9:00 P.M. when the sale culminated with the auction of one-of-a-kind small appliances contributed by retailers and individuals.

The women's committee is responsible for raising $90,000 of the orchestra's annual $250,000 deficit. Other means used by the committee to raise funds include a cocktail party, a large ball, and a theater benefit. A canvass by the women picks up $40,000, and the Junior Committee this year raised an additional $5000 by presenting Captain Kangaroo during the Christmas season.

In addition to fund raising, the committee engages in other activities. It promotes students' concerts and gives suppers for the student councils and music directors of the secondary schools. Also, three musicales were held in members' homes to promote younger artists. A subcommittee arranges parties for visiting artists and, in an effort to keep in touch with symphony members, a party is given for orchestra members and their wives at the end of each season.

Participation in the rummage sale—this was the tenth one sponsored by the committee—has become a social status symbol in the community. Each of the 1000 volunteers (over and above the committee's 200 regular members) is screened and instructed carefully.

Preparations for the next sale begin almost as soon as one is completed. This gives the committee a full year to do its work. Activity reaches its peak eight days before the sale opens, when volunteers begin sorting the contributed goods. Articles for sale are picked up by trucks of major companies in the community. These companies also make warehouse space available until the time of the sale, and, as an additional service after the sale, arrange for delivery of the goods to the homes of purchasers willing to pay a $1 delivery fee.

At the sale, goods are placed on tables or on the floor, and the would-be customers—only 600 at a time are allowed in the building because of fire regulations—use pushcarts borrowed from a supermarket chain. They check out their purchases at cash registers manned by cashiers loaned by local banks.

The committee permits its volunteers to take first crack at the goods on sale. Volunteers may do their buying in the eight days before the sale, but pay a 50¢ premium on each item. This special privilege is not publicized, however. On the day of the sale, volunteers work in three shifts.

Mrs. Arnott Parrett, organizer of this year's affair, summarizing the lessons learned, said that the evening auction created so much enthusiasm it will be extended next year. Also under discussion is the possibility of renting additional space. The sale this year occupied 20,000 square feet.

May 1963

Museum Uses a Garage Sale
to Clean Attic, Make Money

The garage sale, that staple of American suburban and small town life designed to recycle trash—or better unwanted items—painlessly and sometimes profitably may have a positive application to the arts. In Orlando, Florida, the John Young Museum and Planetarium was faced with an interesting problem as the result of a changeover in its focus some time ago, from a general museum to an institution specifically concerned with science and techology. Over the years the museum had accumulated masses of items that were no longer relevant to its new interest, and, with museum space at a premium, something had to be done.

That something, conceived by Ken Hobbs, the museum's executive vice president, was the "First Super Colossal John Young Museum and Planetarium Garage Sale and Auction." With agreement on the concept in late spring 1976, the wheels began to move quickly. The first step, accomplished with the aid of a local antique dealer and auctioneer, was the selection, cataloguing, and appraisal of the items to be included and a determination of which of them would be auctioned (the more valuable ones included original art) and which would be included in the garage sale. Next, to dramatize the event and capture the interest generated by the three-day Bicentennial weekend celebration in the city, July 3 was selected as the date.

Three weeks prior to the event the public relations campaign opened with news stories, spot announcements, and the distribution of thousands of circulars to key spots in the city. The idea of a museum garage sale captured media fancy and, helped by a limited budget advertising push the week prior to the event, the museum was able to make the entire city aware of the sale.

The auction, held in an auditorium a few steps from the museum, maintained an average attendance of 300 people between 10 A.M. and 6 P.M. The garage sale, which included items ranging from old desks to knives, was held in tents outside the museum and drew some 3000 active customers until early afternoon rains forced its closing. As an added plus, many of the shoppers also visited the museum.

How successful was the event? According to museum publicist Jack Martin, exposure was excellent with publicity reaching about a million people. "We anticipate this becoming a yearly event," he told *AM*. Best of all, perhaps, was the fact that while everyone had a good time and the museum became better known, the event itself cleared over $15,000.

September-October 1976

Unusual Funding Techniques
Tried by Arts Institutions

Beset by growing funding needs, arts groups are finding new and unusual ways to raise money. In Montreal, Les Grands Ballets Canadiens asked 100 Quebec artists to contribute personal statements on the arts in their own handwriting. Each statement was reprinted on a 7 x 10 inch parchment in a limited edition of 1000, signed by the respective artist, and each was sold for $2.

On a somewhat similar, but far larger scale, the Oklahoma City Performing Arts Cultural and Industrial Development Trust issued tax-exempt revenue bonds to help finance a theater center. Printed on art paper, the bonds, on their reverse side, featured limited edition prints by local artists. When mature, the bonds can be redeemed at their face value of $500 or, hopefully, from the theater's viewpoint, be retained for their art value. In New York, the Creative Artists Public Service, which provides fellowships to artists in a variety of disciplines, is helping to fund its program by selling a limited edition portfolio of 14 original prints by CAPS artists for $650.

Elsewhere, the Los Angeles Philharmonic is flying to Nice, where the players will board the luxury liner M.S. *Danae* for an unusual concert tour with tremendous fund-raising potential. Between May 2-19, the players will be nonpaying guests on a Mediterranean cruise—they'll receive regular orchestra salaries during the period—and will stop off and perform at ports along the way. A key aspect of the cruise is that fares for other cruise passengers, which begin at $1775, will include a 25 percent contribution to the orchestra. This will pay for the players' air fares and other tour expenses and, hopefully, add something extra to the orchestra's general kitty, an estimated $90,000.

During the cruise, guests will have the opportunity to attend orchestra rehearsals and chamber recitals at sea, as well as scheduled concerts in port. Although this is the first time that an entire symphony orchestra has ever participated in a cruise, Exprinter International of New York, which operates the *Danae* and the M. S. *Daphne*, regularly schedules thematic cruises, including many this year dealing with the arts. Scheduled are visual art, theater, literary, and jazz cruises featuring programs and performances by artists, actors, musicians, and writers. In September, Exprinter will run a North Sea Tour featuring the Israel Philharmonic.

A unique partnership between Affiliate Artists and the 13,000 local General Federation of Women's Clubs throughout the country will pump money into professional artists residency programs. The fund-raising vehicle is a specially made RCA album of songs by Sherrill Milnes, which the clubs and the GFWC's 650,000 members will sell for $6 each. The money raised from this project will be used for local arts events.

Records are being used elsewhere to attract donors in high-giving categories. The Metropolitan Opera is offering contributors of $100 or more an historic recording of Verdi's *Otello* with Martinelli and Tibbett, a price that seems a real bargain when compared to a Carnegie Hall offering. The latter is a limited edition recording—1000 numbered records will be sold at $500 each—of the complete performance of Carnegie Hall's fund-raising "Concert of the Century" last May.

While most groups are seeking huge sums, at least several are following in the footsteps of the Brooklyn Academy of Music's "very reasonable request" campaign, including the Fort Wayne Fine Arts Foundation. A mailing sent to members of the Foundation's member organizations this fall with a request for "5.00!! No More, No Less" drew better than a 10-percent response. In Stratford, Connecticut, the American Shakespeare Theatre's "Bill for Will" grass roots campaign, has raised about $10,000 in the past few months and in Staten Island, New York, the Snug Harbor Cultural Center has launched "The Buck Stops Here" campaign with the hopes of selling nearly 350,000 raffles at $1 each.

One group faced with foreclosure of its mortgage, the New York Jazz Museum, held a nonstop 60-hour fund-raising "Jamathon," featuring continuous playing by volunteer jazz musicians. The $15,000 raised will enable the group to keep its doors open.

January-February 1977

Volunteers Man Parking Lots, Raise Thousands

An arts organization with a large number of male volunteers can raise considerable sums of money by following the example set by members of the Kiwanis International. Starting seven years ago, Kiwanis members took over the parking concession at tent theaters operated by Music Fair Enterprises, a commercial theatrical producing organization. The lodge members collect donations from showgoers for expediting their entry and exit from parking lots. After paying expenses, the Kiwanis clubs use the net proceeds for their charitable, educational, and youth activities.

At one of the newer chain locations, Shady Grove Music Fair near Washington, D.C., manager James O'Neill worked out a seven-year parking contract with the Kiwanis Club of Silver Spring, Maryland. Under the agreement, Kiwanis agreed to furnish manpower to handle traffic at every performance during the summer tent season and to repay the show company for having the parking lot paved with gravel. Kiwanis furnished uniform caps, reflective vests, and signal lights for its crew.

Except for one regular, paid employee, Kiwanis adult members and boys from the Kiwanis-affiliated Key Clubs in local high schools man the parking areas as volunteers. Usually, each volunteer serves one evening a week and is admitted to the show gratis after cars are parked. Eight to ten persons are required to handle the parking job on crowded nights.

The Silver Spring Kiwanis draws on two other neighboring clubs for manpower, as well as on the high school boys. "You need about 70 active people to do the job right in a place this size," President Thomas G. Owen of Silver Spring Kiwanis told *AM*.

In its first (1962) season at Shady Grove, Kiwanis took in about $1000 weekly from parking donations, over a 15-week season. The 1963 gross should be above $20,000, Owen said, because the tent seating capacity has been expanded, and the season lengthened to eighteen weeks. Owen expects Kiwanis to net $8000 from parking this season, compared to $4000 last year. It should go higher in 1964. According to James Hay, manager of the Westbury Music Fair in Westbury, New York, these sums are comparable to the money collected at his fair.

From the showmen's viewpoint, O'Neill told *AM*, "The Kiwanis club has taken the parking problem off our hands, and is raising money for a good cause while doing it. We both benefit."

July 1963

Industries and Bank Aid Novel Fund Drive

A nonprofit organization seeking funds, a packaging firm searching for new business, a bank eager to attract depositors, and seven manufacturers looking for free publicity all combined in a new form of fund raising that can be successfully adapted by arts groups wishing to raise considerable sums of money.

When the Association for the Help of Retarded Children sought a new and effective fund-raising device it turned to James J. Harris, a board member who also heads Guest Pac, a product packaging firm. He came to their aid with an idea used successfully by his organization to gain new customers for banks. As a result, depositors at any of the eight branches of the Lincoln Savings Bank in the Metropolitan New York area were offered gift sets of cosmetics and drugs worth $15 in return for contributions of $3 or more to the AHRC.

Tying in the sources that both supplied and promoted the offer was Mr. Harris, who convinced manufacturers to contribute their products and induced the bank to advertise the offer free on behalf of the Association.

The key to his approach, Mr. Harris told *AM*, was assurances made to manufacturers that their products would receive prominent mention by name in all promotions of the offer. Moreover, it was pointed out that they would enhance the image of their companies by being linked with a nonprofit organization.

The promotion was given added impetus when the bank offered to compound interest on savings from a date as much as two weeks prior to the date of deposit. Thus, potential depositors attracted to the bank's interest rate advantage were exposed to the gift set offer in the same advertisement. This was especially important since any person wishing to receive the gift set by contributing $3 to AHRC had to become a bank depositor first. The promotion did not disrupt bank services since only a handful of volunteers were needed to man a single table placed prominently on the banking floor, where the kits were exchanged for donations.

To attract the public to the offer, the bank placed advertisements in leading daily New York newspapers. The association, which did not contribute toward the cost of the advertisements, thus received valuable free publicity.

While considerable funds were expended in the drive by the AHRC, the organization expects to profit by more than $200,000 from the campaign. Gift Pac, which charged the nonprofit group less than $1 per kit for the collection, transportation, assembling, and packaging of 100,000 kits is also realizing a profit from the promotion.

Items in the sets were handsomely boxed, and care was taken to acknowledge each link in the offer with stickers on the outside of each package. A thank-you note enclosed in the kits read in part, "Items in this kit have been provided through the courtesy of the manufacturers. The Association for the Help of Retarded Children has paid for the assembly and distribution." By detailing the sources of the offer and the expenditures involved, contributors were quickly informed of the Association's stake in the drive.

Initial responses to the offer have been excellent, and most depositors indicated their delight at receiving such a fine bargain in return for their contribution. Moreover, the association, in addition to the prospect of raising considerable funds, has also laid the groundwork for future fund drives. Bank advertisements told the public that the AHRC is an organization having "a varied program which has dramatically demonstrated that the mentally ill can lead fuller lives."

July-August 1964

Checks from Checkrooms

Why lease checkroom concessions when a profit can be made by operating them yourself? In Salt Lake City, the Utah Symphony Debs, a volunteer service organization, staffed the checkroom at concerts. Proceeds realized from charges of

15¢ per person and 25¢ per couple, went into the sustaining fund of the symphony.

August 1963

Thrift Shops

Any charitable thrift shops in your community? In New York, the Nearly New Thrift Shop accepts donations of clothing, furniture, antiques, and household items and turns over the proceeds from the resale of these items to the American National Theater and Academy (ANTA) and other nonprofit organizations. Donors, who may claim tax deductions, can specify which of the participating charities should receive the proceeds from the sale of their gifts.

March-April 1967

Volunteers Raise
Money with Ad Supplement

The production of a special supplement about a cultural organization, published as part of a major newspaper, can effectively publicize the group while at the same time bring in substantial revenue through the sale of advertising space. In Toronto, Ontario, for example, the Women's Committee of the Toronto Symphony Orchestra Association raised more than $27,000 by selling advertising in a 20-page Sunday photo supplement on the orchestra. It appeared as part of the October 31, 1964 edition of the *Toronto Telegram,* which has a circulation of 800,000. The supplement was sold to the committee by the newspaper at cost.

In a well-coordinated and carefully planned campaign, members of the women's committee sold advertisements to 100 leading businesses in Toronto. Although the women had no previous newspaper experience, they also wrote text for the advertisements, wrote feature articles on the Toronto Symphony Orchestra, and participated in all the editorial functions that went into putting the special section together. In some cases, businesses made donations to the orchestra instead of buying space in the supplement.

The volunteers began selling space in the special section to advertisers about a year ago, and by last January they had completed the selling phase of their work. To insure the success of the campaign, the committee initially lined up about 30 leading companies as pacesetters, firms that agreed to purchase advertisements but did not commit themselves to the amount of space they would buy. The names of these companies were then used to influence other local businesses to purchase advertisements.

As an inducement to advertisers, socially prominent women and their families modeled for the advertisements. Most of the models were members of the women's committee. In a number of instances, businessmen's wives modeled for their husbands' products.

Advertisements identified the models, some of whom were photographed in their own homes with the products advertised, and told of their role in supporting the orchestra.

A totally diversified set of advertisers was featured in the section including major automobile manufacturers, radio stations, department stores, textile firms, a brewery, music publishers, and a bank.

Members of the orchestra cooperated with the committee by appearing in the photographs. In one advertisement, for example, Walter Susskind, who directs the orchestra, thanked a manufacturer of concert pianos for his support.

In addition to the advertisements, the supplement also featured a number of stories about the Toronto Symphony Orchestra. Articles summarized the orchestra's history, discussed the program for the coming season, and told readers about special orchestra events, the orchestra staff, and the work of the volunteer committee which put the supplement together.

Stressed throughout the section was the orchestra's need for funds. One article outlined the orchestra's financial picture, emphasizing the fact that $325,000 was needed for the coming season which runs from late October through mid-April.

Barbara Heintzman, who headed the committee, told *AM* that other arts groups wishing to undertake a similar project "should allow at least a year" from its inception to date of publication.

December 1964

Volunteers Raise $11,000 a Year Selling Books

A one-week sale of used books that nets $11,000 for a college scholarship fund depends on techniques adaptable to the needs of many arts organizations. The sale, sponsored by the Vassar Club of Washington, started in 1949 and has since become an annual institution in the nation's capital. In its early years it yielded only about $1000 a year. But tight planning and hard work has made it increasingly profitable.

"A primary reason for the success of the book sale is its institutionalized character," Mrs. Mary Randall of the Vassar Club told *AM*. "We hold the sale at the same time every year, in the spring. People have come to expect it." But good management is important, too.

The club calls upon members to solicit book contributions all year long from among neighbors and friends. About 30 of the club's 700 members volunteer to pick up donated books and deliver them to a central storage point—the basement of a member who has willingly made this her contribution to the organization every year since the sale began. About 30 more volunteers sort and price the books. A few of the women have become "real semiprofessionals" at pricing, *AM* was told. Occasionally, a member's husband is called in for advice on pricing of books in a technical field with which he is familiar. During the week of the sale itself, about 50 members turn out to help as sales clerks and cashiers.

Costs are kept to the bare minimum, making the event a low-risk way of raising funds. Total expenditure for the sale is about $1200—roughly ten percent of the gross income from the sale of an estimated 50,000 books per year. Biggest items of expense are publicity, mailings, and advertising, and transportation of the books by a professional mover from the storage point to the site of the sale. Except for the one moving bill, the entire project is carried out by volunteer labor. Also vital to keeping costs down is the club's securing a centrally located, yet vacant, downtown store rent-free for the week required.

"This project has been a success not only because we have developed expertise over the years," says Mrs. Randall. "It is a project that appeals to our members, and the cause—college scholarships—is appealing to the community. But we also work consistently at publicity."

Postcard reminders are mailed to people who left their names and addresses at the previous year's sale. (Everyone leaving the sale is asked whether he wishes to be notified of the next one.) In addition, local newspapers carry publicity pictures of preparations for the sale as well as advertising. The store windows are used, too. Some of the finest bargains are displayed in the windows a few days before the sale opens.

A tribute to the quality of the Vassar book sale is the determination shown by numerous book dealers in elbowing their way to the front of the crowd that presses around the door on its opening morning.

November 1962

Enlarging the Garage

The garage sale is a fund-raising staple of smaller organizations with limited funding goals. However, the garage sale, multiplied into a series of coordinated sales could put goals of $25,000 within reach. This was the approach of the Seattle Opera which scheduled 500 different garage sales during April and May, 1975, an average of 45 per weekend. More than 5000 opera subscribers donated sale items, and the sale raised $30,000.

March-April 1972

Foreign Flavor

Planning a benefit program with a foreign theme? Support may be available from foreign companies or government agencies in your area. The recent Pro Arte Symphony Orchestra Ball in Long Island used its "Carnival in Rio" theme to win support from the Brazilian Government Trade Bureau, a Brazilian jeweler, H. Stern, the Brazilian Coffee Institute, and Varig Airlines.

Spring-Summer 1969

Celebrities Playing Star Roles as Fund Raisers

A growing number of nonprofit arts groups seeking to raise funds or build audiences are turning to popular entertainment celebrities for help as benefit performers or program sponsors. Harry Belafonte, for example, donated his services for a whirlwind benefit tour of Canada in December 1977, performing with nine different Canadian symphony orchestras in nine different cities. The tour raised over $300,000 for the orchestras.

On Long Island in New York, the PAF Playhouse cornered the celebrity market in April 1978 with a unique, two-pronged fund-raising event that, in a single evening netted almost $175,000 for the resident professional theater company. Aided by the efforts of board chairman Harry Chapin, who as a noted singer and songwriter is a popular celebrity himself, and a team of top Long Island business leaders, PAF put together a benefit concert preceded by a $125-per-plate fund-raising dinner. On a wave of tremendous publicity, and aided by the fact that dinner hosts included such notables as Robert Redford, Jose Ferrer, and radio personality John Gambling, more than 1100 supporters were drawn to the dinner.

The benefit concert, which drew 8000 people to the Nassau Coliseum at ticket prices ranging from $10 to $25, had its own drama. Reunited for the perfformance for the first time since 1972 (due to the persuasive efforts of Chapin) was the noted folk group Peter, Paul, and Mary, who appeared along with Chapin and singer Kenny Loggins. The fund-raising event was part of a continuing PAF effort to meet a $571,000 Ford Foundation match.

Other celebrities have been lending their names and talents to nonprofit arts groups. During the past year, for example, Elizabeth Taylor served as gala chairman for a Wolf Trap benefit, Joanne Woodward worked with the Dennis Wayne Dance Company and supported the Connecticut Arts Commission in its drive for increased funding, and Carol Channing helped the Detroit Symphony launch its fund-raising radio marathon. Stage South, South Carolina's state theater, drew on the support of Celeste Holm, Gregory Peck, and Richard Chamberlain among others to launch a volunteer support organization.

The Chicago Symphony even found a way to use absent celebrities in its fund-raising radio marathon in April 1978. Such one-of-a-kind celebrity premiums as a Harpo Marx painting, Marcel Marceau ballet slippers, Bob Hope golf balls, and Frank Sinatra's working sheet music for "My Kind of Town, Chicago Is," were offered as premiums for sealed bidding.

March-April 1978

Fund-raising Event Achieves Social Status

The active participation of community leaders in the planning and execution of a fund-raising event can transform it from an institutional function to an important social occasion. In New York, the participation of leading department store executives, fashion editors, and designers helps make the 1965 "Party of the Year," held by the Metropolitan Museum of Art's Costume Institute, an outstanding social as well as financial success.

The seventeenth annual party drew a turnaway audience of more than 800 persons and raised more than $74,000 in net profit for the institute. Tickets sold for $100 a person, and not a single ticket was distributed free of charge. Some persons not attending the event nevertheless sent contributions to the institute.

A key to the success of the event was that leaders in the fashion industry, who benefit from the work of the institute, were involved in virtually every phase of it.

Leading department store executives encouraged attendance and participation in the event. Invitations to the party were signed by John S. Burke, general chairman of the party committee and president of B. Altman & Co., and the two party cochairmen, Melvin E. Dawley, president of Lord & Taylor, and Adam L. Gimbel, president of Saks Fifth Avenue.

A highlight of the festivities, which were held at the museum, was a show produced and mounted by persons prominent in the fashion industry, including leading editors. Top fashion models contributed their services free of charge to the show.

Funds raised at the annual function help further the work of the institute which, in addition to serving the public, makes its resources available to the fashion industry.

March 1965

A Fashionable Evening Program
Helps Arts Groups Raise Funds

Fashion has provided an arts group with an unusual setting for a successful annual fund-raising effort. For the past three years, the United Arts Fund of Greensboro, North Carolina has been the beneficiary of Fall Fashion Concert, a combined fashion-entertainment show, sponsored by the Greater Greensboro Merchants Association and presented in the auditorium of the city's coliseum.

The fashion extravaganza idea was initiated by Greensboro merchants five years ago as a means of calling attention to the city's importance as a fashion center. Although tickets were only $1 each, attendance was disappointing until the third year, when Merchants Association officials asked the chairman of the United Arts Fund to head the ticket sales effort. He agreed, but only on the condition that all proceeds from ticket sales would go to the arts fund. Since then, between 2200 and 2600 tickets have been sold annually, although the auditorium seats only 2400, and the arts fund has realized better than $2000 each year.

The event itself, which comes after the arts fund has completed its own annual drive, features local personalities modeling fashions as well as music and entertainment. In addition to its monetary importance, Fall Fashion Concert ties local business to the arts and focuses attention on community arts groups. It also prepublicizes and sets the stage for the coming United Arts Fund campaign, which this year has a goal of $130,000.

The Detroit Symphony Orchestra is another arts group that has tied fashions into its fund-raising picture. This March the orchestra's Women's Association, in cooperation with the J. L. Hudson Company department store, presented "Fashionscope Symphorama" as a benefit for the orchestra's mainenance fund. The showing of men's and women's styles featured well-known Detroiters as models, including several top professional football and hockey players. A small contingent from the orchestra performed in a musical portion of the program.

Fashions are included in still another Detroit Symphony activity, the Coffee Concert series. These very successful Friday morning programs have been presented under the sponsorship of the National Bank of Detroit since 1970, both to attract shoppers downtown and to help support the symphony. Along with the concert performance by the orchestra, each program includes a complimentary continental breakfast and a short fashion show.

Summer 1972

Fashion and Beauty Fields
Source of Growing Support

The fashion and beauty fields are providing the arts with new funding and promotional opportunities. Increasingly, noted designers are lending their names and talents to cooperative arts ventures, fashion manufacturers are developing interesting tie-ins with cultural groups, and some arts organizations are incorporating fashion into their artistic programs.

Fashion shows featuring the latest collections by "name" designers have become fund-raising staples for many groups, including such events in the past year as Bill Blass benefits for the Detroit and Jacksonville Symphonies, Adolpho's benefit for the Museum of the City of New York, and the Elizabeth Arden Salon benefit for the Joffrey Ballet. In Houston, jeweler Harry Winston donated a golden diamond clip worth thousands of dollars for auctioning off at the recent Houston Ballet Ball and also hosted a preball party. In October the prestigious Council of Fashion Designers of America's evening of fashion and theater will benefit the Eugene O'Neill Theater Center.

Several designers have developed close working relationships with performing arts groups, including Rudi Gernreich, who collaborated with Bella Lewitsky on a work for her company, and James Berry, whose T-shirt collection based on international road signs inspired James Cunningham to create a new dance for his company, "One More for the Road." Pierre Cardin has ventured more deeply into the arts, serving as both producer and underwriter for the Pilobolus Dance Theater and the Ondeko-Za Company from Japan.

Fashion provided a theme for a well-publicized exhibition, "The Great American Foot," which recently opened at New York's Museum of Contemporary Crafts. The exhibition, which cost over $50,000 to mount saluted the foot through works by noted artists and craftsmen, and found a not unlikely sponsor in the Kinney Shoe Corporation. A $75-per-person benefit, cochaired by Kinney president Richard Anderson, preceded the exhibit opening. American Express sponsored another current exhibition, the Museum of the City of New York's "Best Bib and Tucker," which featured fashion costumes from the museum collection.

Dance has attracted the attention of such fashion firms as Danskin, Capezio, and Apollo, who have made dance groups beneficiaries of events introducing new collections or the opening of store departments. To introduce its new perfume Cabriole last season, Elizabeth Arden sponsored benefits for six ballet companies in cities around the country including the American Ballet Theatre, the Los Angeles Ballet, and the Boston Ballet.

In still another use of fashion, several theater groups have used costumes from productions to raise funds or promote programs. The Manitoba Theater Center has held costume sales—over 1000 were sold one year with the help of Eaton's Department Store in Winnipeg—and Milwaukee Repertory Theater volunteers have promoted the company and raised funds through a traveling 45-minute fashion show featuring MRT costumes.

The link between fashion and the arts was reinforced recently when the Parson School of Design honored Joan Mondale at its annual Fashion Critics Awards Show. An award was given in recognition of "Mrs. Mondale's deep support for American art and design."

March-April 1978

Imaginative New Approaches
Help Groups to Raise Funds

Cultural groups continue to show imagination in their quest for new funding. The New York Public Library, which was beneficiary of a unique bank promotion several years ago (the East New York Savings Bank encouraged new depositors to contribute the value of free gifts to the library rather than accept them) came up with an interesting idea of its own.

From November 16 through December 16, 1977, the library, as part of its campaign to match a Humanities Endowment $1.5-million grant, asked the public to donate gold—any gold—including jewelry, gold teeth, and coins to its fund drive. Every weekday between 10:00 A.M. and 4:00 P.M., goldsmith Charles Cafarella, ensconced in the third floor rotunda of the library, appraised the donated items and gave evaluation certificates to the donors.

The Gifts of Gold campaign was the brainchild of new library board chairman Richard Salomon, who, having lost one gold cufflink, wondered what he'd do with the remaining one. The answer was to donate it to the library. With the help of an anonymous donor who paid for the goldsmith's services, the campaign was launched at a well-publicized party at the library. To tie in with the fund drive, the library presented a modest exhibit of books, decorated or illuminated with gold, in its rotunda.

The campaign captured the public imagination, and everything from wedding rings to a golden horseshoe was donated. A set of gold coins worth $1000, donated by a coin dealer, was the largest gift. When the campaign ended, about $20,000 had been raised, and the library was the recipient of excellent publicity, including feature stories in all New York papers. The gold items have been sold to a refiner who paid the firm's published price for gold.

In Durham, North Carolina, the American Dance Festival received a gift as good as gold. The Duke University Development Office and a local corporation, the Liggett Group, pledged to raise a $1-million trust fund to enable the festival to move there next summer.

The American Museum of Natural History in New York, which will honor celebrated staff member Margaret Mead with a chair in her name, capitalized on a rare double occasion to launch its fund drive for the chair. Because 1977 was Dr. Mead's seventy-fifth birthday year and fiftieth year at the museum, donors to the new Fund for the Advancement of Anthropology, were given the opportunity to sign their names and add a birthday message to Dr. Mead in their contribution envelopes. The names and messages were part of a mile-long birthday card to Dr. Mead.

Elsewhere, several funding events with successful histories outdid their past efforts. The Metropolitan Opera's third annual bazaar and auction raised $43,000 from the bazaar and over $100,000 from the auction. The Association of American Dance Companies took over Roseland Dance Hall for the second year in a row and invited the public to dance with the dancers. The $50-per-person invitation was in the form of dance card listing such "partners" as Mikhail Baryshnikov, Melissa Hayden, and Cynthia Gregory. Over $6000 was raised.

November-December 1977

Old Treasures Help Dance Company Funding

A desire by auctioneers and appraisers to uncover forgotten objects of value and an arts group's interest in promoting its program and raising money can be parlayed into a successful and relatively painless fund-raising event. In San Rafael, California, the Marin Civic Ballet drew overflow audiences to its two "Antiques Critiques" this year and raised over $3000 in the process.

Aware that many people have heirlooms and antiques whose worth they may long have been curious about gathering dust in their attics, the ballet company asked a respected San Francisco appraisal firm if it would donate five or six hours of service by several of its professionals in the hope of finding objects of value. When Butterfield and Butterfield agreed to the proposition, the dance company opened shop at its ballet school one Thursday morning and, through a strong promotional campaign, invited the public to bring up to ten items per person for appraisal. Fees, in the form of donations to the dance company, were $3 for the first item and $1 for additional items.

On a wave of publicity, about 1000 people showed up with such items as silver, old books, porcelain figurines and works of art. Following registration—to help build up the company mailing list—each person waited in turn to see an appraiser who indicated the fair market value of the item and told something about its history and identity. Company volunteers copied the information on special forms which also reminded patrons that the ballet would receive a finders fee of 15 percent if items were offered to the appraisers for auction. Although many items had limited value, there were a few surprises, including one Tong vase worth many thousands of dollars.

Pleased with the program's success, both the appraisers and the ballet company held a second event, although the maximum number of items was limited to five at $2 per item. Again the program was a great success. In fact a group of local decorators was so impressed with the project that it offered a tour of its showrooms as a ballet company benefit.

September-October 1975

Tickets to Art Raffle Party:
Taking a Chance for Art's Sake

A fund-raising raffle with works of art as prizes has netted an average of $12,000 for a New York settlement house during the three years it has been held. The Collector's Choice Art Benefit, a creation of the Hudson Guild Neighborhood House, can be adapted to the money-raising needs of cultural groups on a wide scale.

Key points in the successful Hudson Guild raffles are selecting art work prizes judged as especially attractive to the organization's friends, limiting the number of tickets sold, setting the right price per ticket, and organizing the ticket sale with precision.

In 1960 and 1961, the art benefit offered three prizes, both sculpture and paintings, to 200 subscribers at $100 per ticket. This year's drawing offered four art prizes to 225 ticket buyers at the same rate. The ticket admitted a couple to the gala cocktail party at which the drawing was staged.

For the three years, the total price of the art works averaged $3000 and were obtained by a committee of collectors from galleries for the best value in terms of price, quality, and importance of the artist. Gross receipts averaged $17,000 per yearly raffle; other expenses (cost of the drawing party, printing raffle brochures, and mailing) averaged $2000—producing a net for the beneficiary of $12,000.

A group following the art raffle formula must determine at the outset how many tickets at a given price can be sold, and what price tickets will bring the optimum result. The Hudson Guild set up a committee of board members and friends to sell tickets. Prospects were singled out and a seller assigned to each. As the sale progressed a publicity committee was active in the society, art, and social work fields.

Meanwhile, the drawing party was planned at the home of a prominent guild member, and the point was stressed by ticket sellers that the cocktail party would be a memorable social occasion,offering buyers the opportunity to mingle with distinguished art lovers.

Initial expenditures in a raffle of this kind can be considerably reduced if one or more prizes are donated by a local art patron. The donor should be given a receipt for the value of the art work to be used as a tax deduction.

July 1962

Anniversary Cards to Donors

Arts groups seeking new donations from past contributors might be interested in a successful approach used by the Seattle Opera Association. The opera's revolving sustaining fund appeal is based on the theory that for many donors one particular time of year, the month in which they previously contributed, is the most convenient giving time.

Acting on this premise, the group sends out personalized, auto-typed letters each month to all the previous season's donors on the anniversary of their gifts. Each letter mentions the exact amount of the last donation and frequently offers the contributor some incentive for increasing the size of the gift. Letters, three or four paragraphs long, include information about the current or previous season, the growth of the opera company, its key accomplishments, and the need for additional support.

Following a description of company achievements one typical letter read in part, "Á great part of this success comes from your loyal support of our Sustaining Fund. We were very grateful for your gift of $90 last season. Because each year's goal must be higher than the previous year's attainment to match our rapid yearly growth, I hope that you can do even more for Seattle Opera this year by increasing your gift."

According to staff member Ellen Blassingham, "This method seems to be successful for us. A large percentage send in their contributions immediately and the number of follow-up letters needed is decreased."

March-April 1973

Audience Appreciation

Looking for a dramatic and effective way to thank your contributors and members? You might consider honoring them with a performance. The Wichita Symphony, which successfully matched a Ford Foundation Endowment Fund grant by raising more than $600,000 from the community, thanked its contributors with a "Gala Appreciation Concert" this February. Invitations for the free concert were sent in advance to all donors of record. Later, tickets not reserved by contributors were made available without cost to the general public. Further recognition was given in the concert program, which listed all Ford Fund donors.

March-April 1972

Chain Party

Would you like to pyramid donations? You might try using an old fund-raising idea that worked well for the Indianapolis Symphony last season—the chain party project. The initial step is to find someone to host a part and collect $1 from each guest as a donation to your organization. Each guest then hosts his own party within the next three weeks, inviting one less person and collecting a $1 donation from every attendee. The Indianapolis Symphony pyramid was launched by Indiana Governor Whitcomb, who held a dinner party for eight couples. Then all eight couples hosted their own parties for seven couples who in turn had parties for six couples and so on down the line. Parties ranged from picnics to teas to formal dinners. Although in theory a party beginning with eight should eventually involve 109,600 people contributing $109,600, don't plan on the chain remaining unbroken for too long. Nevertheless, the Indianapolis Symphony was more than delighted with the $14,000 the pyramid raised.

November-December 1971

Orchestra Employs
Novel Fund-raising Methods

An all-out publicity and promotion drive, which employs new techniques yearly while retaining successful ones from the past, is a vital ingredient in the continuing success of the annual fund and membership drive conducted by the Rochester Civic Music Association. The CMA, which supports the Rochester Philharmonic Orchestra and other community musical activities including the Civic Orchestra, Tiny Tot Concerts, and radio concerts for the public schools, raised nearly $250,000 in its 1963 fund drive. While this was 2 percent short of the quota, it still established an all-time record for funds raised in the regular CMA campaigns dating back to 1931. Moreover, with 17,000 individual pledges, CMA officials believe that among comparable organizations it has the broadest base of support in the United States.

While emphasizing a strong and continuous public relations program through normal publicity channels, CMA officials do not neglect to investigate any new approaches that come to their attention. For example, although television coverage has always been excellent, the CMA went a step further this year in arranging for the local American Broadcasting Company outlet to donate a full-hour program in prime evening time to the CMA. On a Sunday evening just prior to the campaign's kick-off, the program, featuring filmed interviews with top musical figures who had performed in Rochester, including Arthur Fiedler and Benny Goodman, was broadcast to a large audience. In addition, major local companies such as Rochester Gas and Electric donated commercial time on the programs they sponsored.

Another new device was the use of a four-sided display booth erected in Midtown Plaza, a covered downtown shopping area built by two leading department stores. The plaza management donated the space and the telephone company donated four telephones set up inside a display which also included pictures of musical activities in Rochester. When a visitor picked up a phone he heard a recorded message urging support of the CMA from Eddy Meath, one of Rochester's leading disc jockeys.

Past approaches used again successfully this year included messages on billboards donated by outdoor advertising companies, the display of posters in 900 stores throughout the city, and the use of 200 car cards in public transportation vehicles. For the fourth straight year, the Blue Boy Dairy imprinted solicitation messages on every bottle of milk it processed during the drive. The message, which appeared on more than 250,000 bottle caps, read, "In Rochester there is music for everyone. Join the Rochester Civic Music Association."

As a climax to the promotional effort, thousands of notes were sent to children in Rochester schools near the end of the campaign. The notes, which were brought home by the youngsters, reminded parents that in case they had not yet given, there was still time to contribute to the CMA.

April 1963

Vacation with Profit

Seeking a fund-raising device with family appeal? An arts group in Roslyn, New York, is raising funds and promoting ties with members and their families through its sponsorship of hotel weekends. Several times a year the North Shore Community Arts Center contracts for all the rooms in a small hotel at reduced rates for a weekend, and then rents them to members at slightly higher rates. Fine arts programs are featured throughout the weekend.

February 1966

Movie Premieres

Premieres of major movies can be used by cultural organizations to raise funds and win wide attention. Whenever possible, however, the film should be viewed beforehand to determine its suitability. Several arts groups in cities throughout the country recently sponsored benefit opening night showings of Twentieth

Century Fox's *The Agony and the Ecstasy,* a motion picture based on the life of Michelangelo. The film company arranged for the appearance of celebrities at the openings and provided publicity, advertising, and promotional materials. While offering these services, the company specified that the sponsor purchase all the seats in the theater for the premiere night. In New York, the film's opening was sponsored by the Metropolitan Museum of Art, and tickets purchased by the museum for $3.25 were sold for $100 each.

January 1966

The Art Express

Looking for a unique setting for a fund-raising event such as an art show? One organization in Long Island, New York recently sponsored an Israeli art festival in three parlor cars borrowed from the Long Island Railroad. On four consecutive Sundays the trains were moved to locations in four different communities where townspeople were invited aboard to view the paintings, which were hung in the cars. The public flocked to the showings and purchased many paintings.

October 1964

Arts Groups Using
Food to Whet New Appetites

In funding, promotional, and subscription campaigns, arts groups have used food as a lure to eat their way into the affections of their audiences. An American Museum of Natural History ad in the *New York Times,* for example, urged readers to "Follow Peking Duck with Peking Man." In Dallas, eating is built into a concert series. The Dallas Symphony's Friday Morning Series is preceded by a complimentary continental breakfast and followed by a buffet lunch.

The Chelsea Theater Center in Brooklyn, New York is offering donors of $500 or more this season, not only personal delivery of Chelsea T-shirts by artistic director Robert Kalfin, but a special invitation to dinner for two with Kalfin. The opportunity to "Lunch with Beverly," was an offer made to season subscribers by the Houston Opera this year. "Order season tickets by June 1," said the brochure, "and you may win lunch with a Season Star. Five stars (including Beverly Sills) and 25 winners."

Food is also a fund raiser in Poughkeepsie, New York, where the Dutchess County Arts Council has joined in a promotion with the Global Menu Club, an organization which sells annual memberships in a "two meals for the price of one" program. For every $20 membership sold through the council, Global is contributing upwards of $5 to the arts group.

Music critic Harold C. Schonberg had an unusual and pungent commentary on the arts-food relationship in an October 19, 1977 *New York Times* article entitled, "With Poached Turbot, Make Mine Handel." Noting the fact that music and food share a distinguished history, Schonberg lamented the inappropriate music frequently accompanying dinners in restaurants and homes today. The article included a box suggesting a progam of music to accompany a formal dinner in the home. With each course suggestion it listed the appropriate wine and music, including the names of record companies and disc numbers.

September-October 1977

Fast Food Funding

Fast food franchises often cooperate with local nonprofit organizations to show their interest in the community. If a franchise operation in your area has an upcoming anniversary, you might suggest that a share of the franchise proceeds on that day be contributed to your group. Federated Arts of Manchester, New Hampshire was one of three community groups to split 50 percent of the proceeds from Dunkin' Donuts recent fifteenth anniversary celebration, "Donate with Donuts."

November-December 1977

Gourmet Dinners Woo
Donors to Eat for Benefit of Arts

Arts groups are discovering that the way to an audience's heart and to its pocketbook may be through its stomach. Gourmet dinner parties, restaurant raffles, food served in unusual settings, and even special fund-raising diets all are proving useful funding devices.

In Ontario, Canada, Theatre London raised nearly $30,000 at its annual Gourmet Dinner Auction in April 1978, which featured bidding on such items as a six-foot salami and restaurant dinners. Following a silent auction and cocktail party and preceding a live auction, about 400 contributors, who paid $50 each, sat down to a dinner described by the theater as a "gastonomical gorgy." In Akron, the Ohio Ballet raised over $13,000 from its "Epicurean Evening" for 359 patrons in June. The tripartite event opened with a cocktail party at the home of a volunteer, followed by dinner at one's choice of any of 11 different homes. Tickets were $45 per person for the entire evening.

Each volunteer host and hostess offered contributors a different ethnic meal, with the choices including French, Mexican, Lebanese, Southern, Hungarian, and Texas barbecue. Following dinner the patrons, along with their respective hosts, rejoined forces at still another home for a "Grand Dessert."

The Opera Theater of St. Louis, which set up a tent as a bar this season, made extra use of it during its last program week when it introduced "A Night at the Opera." The promotion, available only to ticketholders—100 each night at an *extra* $15.50 each—included a gourmet dinner in the tent, with menus tied into the setting of the evening's opera, a free cocktail, free parking in a preferred space, and an informal discussion with cast and musicians after the performance. The promotion did well, with an overall 80 percent capacity for the five nights, including three sold-out evenings.

What might be the most unusual and light-hearted gourmet event of all will be held on October 6. The Pennsylvania Ballet will host a benefit, "Culinary Capers at the Granary," at a former railroad grain elevator, with the party designed to appeal to "closet cooks and happy hoofers." With renowned choreographer George Balanchine—whose hobby is cooking—serving as honorary chairman, the gala will feature cooking demonstrations by top celebrities. Drinks, buffet dinner, and disco dancing will be included in the evening. Befitting their professions, Philadelphia judges and lawyers will preside at the bar.

The evening's top event, a gastronomical auction, will feature bidding on such unique prizes as a picnic in a Goodyear blimp, breakfast at Tiffany's with Jack Kelly, a built and stocked wine cellar, a dinner for ten served by Philadelphia celebrities enroute to Lincoln Center, a tour of the White House followed by lunch there, a private plane ride for six to dinner anywhere in the Eastern United States, and dinner in a different Philadelphia restaurant every week for a year. Tickets are priced at $25 and up. Patrons, at $50 and "Patron Saints," who gave even more, are offered such additional gourmet activities as a picnic at a Main Line estate and a penthouse dinner party. The overall fund-raising goal is about $20,000.

In Riverhead, New York, an innovative yet inexpensive fund-raising event designed to involve scores of volunteers and local businesses helped the East End Arts and Humanities Council raise nearly $3700 and win good publicity. "Adventures in Dining on the East End" was a restaurant raffle that offered meals in 104 different area eating establishments, ranging from posh restaurants to coffee houses to fast food spots, as prizes. Raffles at $1 each, or $5 for a booklet of six chances, offered dinners, lunches, brunches, breakfasts, pizzas, and desserts. A key to the program's success was the organization of committees in several local communities and solicitations by volunteers of the restaurants they regularly patronized. Raffle-book covers listed each of the restaurants and their prizes.

Dinner settings at times have been stronger attractions than the meals themselves. The Lyric Opera of Chicago once again held its annual business meeting and dinner for patrons on the stage of the Civic Opera House this May before a backdrop from the opera, *Lorenzaccio*. Earlier last season the Metropolitan Opera honored Sir Rudolf Bing at a Benefactor Patrons dinner party on the stage of the opera house before a setting from Act II of *La Boheme*. In Cleveland, 175 patrons of the Great Lakes Shakespeare Festival assembled in a DC 10 parked on an airport runway for a "First Class Party" with plane, drinks, and dinner all contributed by United Air Lines.

In several instances, noneating has proved as important to fund raising as eating. In Madison, Wisconsin, "Big Joe" Wilfer, the 5-foot 8-inch, 215-pound director of the Madison Art Center, vowed that he would lose 50 pounds be-

tween June 1 and September 1, 1978 and challenged supporters to pledge anywhere from a penny to a dollar or more to match each pound he lost. Pledge
cards included the statement, "I understand all proceeds will go toward MAC's
Building Fund and a more fashionably slim image for the director." With less
than a month to go, 38 pledges totalling $30 a pound had been received and Wil-
fer, on his way to his goal, had shed 24 pounds.

Elsewhere, Stouffer's Cincinnati Towers Hotel celebrated the opening of
its new tower by *not* hosting a dinner-dance and, instead, donating $10,000 to
the greater Cincinnati Fine Arts Fund. In an "invitation" announcing the contribution, the hotel's general manager requested "the pleasure of your absence at a
Grand Opening Celebration of the hotel's new tower for the benefit of the
Greater Cincinnati Fine Arts Fund, which will not be held on Monday evening,
the twenty second of May at eight o'clock, No R.S.V.P. No Black Tie." The non-
event was well publicized. One news photo showed two sleeping "nonchairwom-
en" who, according to the caption, were "pursuing their responsibilities."

Summer 1978

In Writing

Local visual artists can help to capture your program and raise funds in the process. The Wilmington, Delaware Opera Society Guild commissioned artist Cyn-
thia Doney to sketch scenes from four different operas performed by the company. The sketches were then printed on attractive paper and along with matching envelopes sold in sets of eight for $2.25 per set. Each set featured two scenes
from each of the four operas.

January-February 1977

The Personal Touch

In addition to program listing, the Montclair, New Jersey Chamber Music Society offers a special bonus for contributors of $25 and up—a special reception and
evening of "Chamber Music in the Home." According to manager Mimi Cohen,
the concept has been successful and popular "because it seems to be in keeping
with the more personal and intimate character of chamber music."

January-February 1977

SPORTS AID ARTS

Horse Sense

Race tracks may be an unexpected source of support for your program. In Arkansas, Southland Greyhound Park donates all the gate receipts from two separate evenings to the Arkansas Arts Center. Another track, Pimlico in Maryland,

honored a local arts institution by designating a race as the "Baltimore Museum of Art's 60th Birthday Race."

November-December 1974

Arts Groups on Right Track
as Horse Racing Offers Aid

Horse racing, the sport of kings, is bringing king-size financial benefits to the arts. In a growing number of instances, cultural groups are developing new, unusual, and lucrative relationships to thoroughbred racing.

In Canada, Toronto Arts Productions netted over $50,000 from "The Run for the Arts" May 28, 1977 at Woodbine Race Track. The first-time program was conceived by the nonprofit arts group, a major producer of plays, concerts, and public affairs programs in Toronto, not only as a way to help itself, but as a promotion that could benefit the race track as well. The track was competing for attendance with a new major league baseball team for the first time this year, and was looking for ways to bolster its image and attract attention. "They needed us as much as we needed them," Linda Zwicker of TAP told *AM*.

Patterning their idea somewhat on British Heart Fund Day at Ascot, the group won approval from the Ontario Jockey Club, which administers the track, to print and sell their own tickets to the nine-race program and to find sponsors who would pay for the privilege of having races named for them. In spite of the potential benefits, the run was still something of a gamble because Toronto Arts Productions, without sufficient volunteer help, had to hire additional professional staff, lay out money for printing and promotion costs, and develop an entertainment program for presentation at the track between races. Up-front costs totalled nearly $30,000, but this amount was recouped in advance when TAP sold sponsorship of six different races for $5000 each to six corporations.

Months in advance, TAP laid down a promotional barrage which included costumed actors selling track tickets at open air markets, fashion previews of clothing to be worn at the track, and a softball game between TAP actors and Ontario jockies in a Toronto park. Over 5000 of the 15,000 tickets printed by the arts group were sold with TAP keeping $6 from each $7 ticket and $3.50 from each $4 ticket. Additional income as raised through the raffling of $15,000 worth of donated prizes at the track, and the sale of food, drink, and souvenirs in the paddock area by volunteers and a $30-per-person luncheon at the Turf Club for invited guests. Overall, the Run for the Arts grossed $78,000.

On event day, the festivities began at 11:30 A.M. with continuous entertainment in the paddock area, followed by an official opening by Toronto Mayor David Crombie at 1:00 P.M. Raffle drawings were held following seven of the races—the Canada Dry Cup, the Colonel's Plate, the Winco Steak N' Burger Steaks, and Beethoven's Ninth, the last race, among them. In addition to advance and follow-up publicity in all media, TAP benefitted from several pages about it in the official program and continuous promotion at the track.

In assessing the event, Ms. Zwicker found the pros far outweighing the cons and, with some changes, it will be held again next year. "The program got most of our board involved," she said, "helped make us better-known, and identified a base of volunteers on which we can build." Fittingly, next season's program will be called "Son of a Run."

In Indianapolis, meanwhile, the Indiana Repertory Company's annual fund appeal resulted in an unusual response from Russell Fortune, Jr., a local arts patron. In lieu of a cash donation, Mr. Fortune, who raises thoroughbreds, gave the theater title to one of his yearling horses worth thousands of dollars. He will board the horse until September, when it will be sold at auction in Lexington, Kentucky, with all proceeds going to the theater.

In other cities, arts groups have been involved successfully with horse racing for some years. The Louisville Orchestra has presented Kentucky Derby Festival concerts since 1972 as part of Derby activities and, since 1974, Brown and Williamson Tobacco Company has sponsored the free event. Another "bluegrass" group, the Kentucky Opera Association, has presented its own Hard Scuffle Steeplechase for the past three years as a day-long fund-raising event, a six-race program sanctioned by the National Steeplechase and Hunt Association.

In Saratoga, the Performing Arts Center has benefitted from both the flat and harness tracks, which run special races honoring festival artists and programs and join the center in cooperative advertising projects, group sales programs, and special promotions. The flat track maintains a festival ticket booth, and the harness track's April opening has been a benefit for the festival on several occasions.

In Arizona racing dogs rather than horses may provide the key to the financial stability of Tucson arts groups. In an unprecedented move, a coalition of local cultural organizations is seeking state government approval to purchase dog-racing tracks in Tucson and Amado (which, by law, present owners must sell by 1978) through the issuance of government-underwritten industrial revenue bonds. The proposed plan, developed by two board members of the Arizona Civic Theater on behalf of the arts groups of Tucson, would enable a new nonprofit corporation of Tucson arts groups to take ownership of the tracks over a long period of time through a lease-purchase arrangement paid for from track proceeds. Estimates indicate that participating cultural organizations could split annual track revenues of from $200,000 to $500,000.

Because present state laws prohibit industrial development authorities from financing sports facilities, plan proponents, amid a flurry of local controversy, have been seeking legislative approval for a change in the law. An attempt this May to amend the present law failed, but supporters are pushing for statute changes early in next year's legislative session.

Summer 1977

Musical Touchdown

In an effort to help the St. Louis Symphony recover losses suffered when the orchestra cut its 1965-66 season by four weeks (due to a strike by orchestra members for higher pay), the St. Louis Cardinals, a professional football team, made the musical group the beneficiary of proceeds from an exhibition game held prior to the start of the 1966 football season.

The benefit game, played between the Cardinals and the Baltimore Colts, raised $58,000 for the orchestra. This enabled the orchestra to lengthen its 1966-67 season by one week and place the remainder of the proceeds into a fund for orchestra players' salaries. The football team handled the bulk of the promotion and publicity for the game, although the orchestra hired a publicity specialist for two months prior to the game to help increase attendance.

January-February 1967

Campaign Kickoff

Looking to add some extra interest to your season ticket or fund-raising campaign? You might select your chairman from an area not normally associated with the arts, such as sports. Try, however, to choose a personality who has had some involvement with your group. Theatre Calgary in Canada recently named its first honorary season ticket chairman, Fred James, defensive tackle for the Calgary Stampeders football team. Releases noted that Mr. James was "a season ticket holder of several years' standing."

Summer 1972

Gambling on the Arts

In California, horse racing at Santa Anita has enriched the coffers of performing arts groups in Los Angeles. According to California Horse Racing Law, Chapter 4, Division 8, each racing association other than state, county, or district fairs must designate from three to five days as charity days, with net proceeds on these days contributed to nonprofit organizations approved by the state racing board. In 1967 and 1968, the state distributed over $2.5 million from races to various charities. Santa Anita alone this year distributed $470,000. Among its recipients was the Performing Arts Council of Los Angeles, which received $20,000 for distribution to its member groups.

September-October 1969

A Sporting Deal

If you have a professional athletic team in your area, you might find them a willing source of support or promotional aid. A professional basketball team, the

Utah Stars, gave $2500 to a dance company, Ballet West, as a way of thanking Utah citizens for the recognition and support accorded to the Stars. Said the team, "It is our pleasure to give this recognition to another Utah-based professional company that has received international acclaim for the excellence of their performance—Ballet West."

January-February 1973

Sports Events Aid and Promote Cultural Groups and Programs

Cultural groups are finding a new and unlikely ally in the quest for support—organized sports. Over the past few months, baseball, football, tennis, and track have promoted or helped raise funds for arts organizations.

In California, the Monterey County Symphony Guild has raised thousands of dollars through an ambitious undertaking which has since become an annual event—presentation of an International Senior Open Tennis Tournament at Pebble Beach. Featuring such top players in the 45-and-over category as Bobby Riggs and Pancho Segura and prize money donated by corporations, the tournaments, held in 1972 and 1973, have been well publicized and drawn large crowds. The symphony, in addition to receiving the net profits, is promoted through several pages of pictures and text in the official programs. This year's benefit tournament, sponsored by Almaden Vineyards, will be held in October. Tennis has been a fund raiser in Pittsburgh also, where a Symphony Benefit Night was held this spring at a match featuring the Pittsburgh Triangles, the city's new entry in the World Team Tennis League.

Several recent sports-arts involvements have had an international flavor, such as the giant North Carolina arts festival in Durham this July, which was built around the much-ballyhooed U.S.A.-USSR two-day track meet. Located adjacent to the track stadium, the festival grounds featured a specially commissioned sculpture in its center, music from three bandstands, a pavilion with art works from the Soviet Union, tents and booths in which 150 state craftsmen exhibited works and offered demonstrations, and a nearby performing area for free concerts.

The 1976 Olympics, to be held in Montreal, have helped make a major art commission possible—the U.S. Olympic Editions by Kennedy Graphics. Original graphics and posters interpreting the spirit of the games have been designed by 15 American artists and will be offered for sale this fall, with part of the proceeds benefiting the U.S. Olympic Fund. In Canada, track star Bruce Kidd helped organize the Artists-Athletes Coalition for the Cultural Celebration of the 1976 Olympics and has been touring Canada and holding public meetings to make provincial cultural authorities aware of the arts community's concern for expanding cultural programming during the Games period.

Meanwhile, a college theater director, frustrated at the limited exposure his group receives as compared to the school's football team, has decided to join forces. During the coming season, Dr. John Marshall Stevenson, of A & T State University in Greensboro, North Carolina, plans to have his theater group accompany the football team to out-of-town games and present productions at each "away" campus on the Friday night preceding the Saturday night football game.

One of the most sports-minded arts groups has been the Indianapolis Symphony, a participant in a first annual "Symphony Day at the Ballpark" this spring. Held as part of a double-header between two professional International League teams, the Denver Bears and the host Indianapolis Indians, the event featured a pregame softball match between the Indianapolis Symphony "ISO-Metrics" and the Cincinnati Symphony "Fantastiques" and a between-games pop concert by the Indianapolis Symphony. Throughout the professional games the orchestra, seated in the grandstand, presented segments of works. To heighten the sports identification, Indianapolis 500-mile race winner Johnny Rutherford played softball with the ISO-Metrics and led the orchestra in the playing of the National Anthem. Months earlier Rutherford had conducted the orchestra in a pops number at Clowes Hall.

This first joint venture of the orchestra and the baseball team was arranged with the help of the manager/president of the Indianapolis Indians, whose father had once played with the orchestra. A city grant, which encourages free community concerts, paid for the orchestra's services. As a result of interest in the event, the baseball team has agreed to host future games between the orchestras and donate a winner's trophy.

In addition to winning over ball fans, the orchestra found a new supporter in race driver Rutherford. In an *Indianapolis News* interview following the game, Rutherford said of the orchestra, "I've gotten a greater respect for those people because of my experience with them. If people would just take time to listen to the symphony . . . it doesn't cost that much . . . I think they'd find it would be very relaxing and very enjoyable."

Summer 1974

TV Sports Shows Aid Arts

Ballet West, aided by a $25,000 NEA grant and donated time from a local advertising agency, launched a prime-time television ad campaign on three commercial Salt Lake City stations. The Sacramento Ballet enlisted the services of local sportscaster Steve Somers for a three-minute TV film designed to demonstrate the athletic qualities of ballet dancers. The film was aired on local TV sports shows.

November-December 1975

Sports Stars Help

Professional athletes making their contribution to culture include four Carolina Cougar star basketball players. At a September fund-raising benefit for the United Arts Council of Greensboro, North Carolina sponsored by the Greater Greensboro Merchants Association, the athletes modeled as well as entertained. Earlier this year, quarterback Bill Nelsen of the Cleveland Browns participated in a televised fund appeal for the Cleveland Symphony Orchestra.

Fall 1970

A Good Sport

Looking for involvement in another field to help promote your program and attract new audiences? You might focus on sports as the Indianapolis Symphony has over the past few years. The orchestra, which participated in "Symphony Day at the Ballpark" in the summer of 1974, took the program to its own locale with its first "Sports Night at the Symphony" held in November, 1975. The light-hearted program featuring sports celebrities appearing with the orchestra as singers, instrumentalists, and narrators attracted a lively audience and good attention in the local press.

January-February 1976

Cultural Groups Find Sports a Useful Resource

Sports, a field seemingly far removed from the arts, is proving to be a useful resource area for cultural groups.

During 1977 both the Seattle Symphony's Women's Association and the Oregon Museum of Science and Industry used World Team Tennis matches as fund raisers. The museum netted $2000, including 10 percent of all season ticket sales, as beneficiaries of the Sea-Port Cascades opening match of the season. For the last home game of the season in August, the tennis team gave the museum a free block of tickets, which it sold at half price.

A professional baseball team cooperated with a museum in a unique season-long program. The Philadelphia Phillies gave the Franklin Institute Science Museum use of its scoreboard during the 1977 season to present a series of "Do-Its," simple science experiments that fans could do from their seats. Early in the season the museum presented a live science demonstration before a Phillies game.

The relationship between dancing and athletics has been explored in a series of lecture-demonstrations given last fall by New York City Ballet star Edward Villella at such universities as Bridgeport and Adelphi. Mr. Villella's concepts, as demonstrated in his television film, "Dance of the Athletes," proved to be the stimulus for a special ballet techniques course given at the New Jersey

School of Ballet for 100 Montclair High School athletes last summer. Another noted artist, concert pianist Eugene Istomin, chronicled his life-long love affair with baseball in his bylined *New York Times Magazine* article (October 9, 1977) "Conversations with Fingers."

Several noted artists have incorporated sports themes into their work recently. Claes Oldenburg's giant baseball bat sculpture, *Batcolumn,* installed in Chicago last year, may be the most visible work, although Robert Indiana's contribution may be more provocative. Indiana recently completed a $27,000 commission for the Milwaukee Exposition and Convention Center, his design for a new Center basketball court. In New York, to introduce a Parks Department table tennis tournament in December 1977, business sponsor White Rock Beverages commissioned a work by composer George Costinesco, "Tournament Overture for Flute, Cello, Synthesizer, and Two Ping Pong Players."

Basketball and dance have cooperated in several instances recently. After dancer Tom Rawe of Twyla Tharp's Company did several workshops for the Polytechnic Institute of New York's basketball team last spring, the team demonstrated to its fans the dance techniques they had learned and were incorporating into their practice sessions. Just this past month, "Arts Night" was celebrated at a basketball game of the University of North Carolina at Charlotte, with the Charlotte Regional Ballet presenting a new work based on basketball movements between halves.

The magic of famous sports names has proven helpful to arts programming and fund raising. A year ago Muhammad Ali boxed an exhibition in Boston to benefit the Elma Lewis School of Fine Arts, and this past season members of the Buffalo Bills football team, including star O. J. Simpson, tended bar and signed autographs at a Buffalo Philharmonic benefit. Orchestras, including the Cincinnatti, Houston, and Indianapolis Symphonies, have featured big league baseball players as guest artists at Pops concerts. The athletic abilities of volunteers and trustees has also proven useful to the arts. In Chemung Valley, New York, 235 supporters raised over $4000 for the local arts council in a charity Bike-A-Thon, while in Phoenix, volunteers will run a half-length marathon race this March, wearing Phoenix Symphony T-shirts.

While the sports-arts ties were being strengthened, the National Endowment for the Arts may have taken a backward step with its survey proclaiming that more people attend arts than sports events. That theme was reinforced in the NEA's public service commercial featuring manager Billy Martin of the New York Yankees in the Metropolitan Museum asserting that the arts have more fans than the Yankees, Knicks, and Nets. Taking note of the NEA survey, a *New York Times* editorial not only questioned the survey figures, but more importantly questioned the "versus" aspect of the survey. Said the *Times* in an editorial.

> More invidious is the proposition, suggested by the either-or style of
> the report, that Americans go to a football stadium or a museum,

but not both. We prefer to believe that substantial numbers of football fans also enjoy the theater, even that some hockey fans may be aficionados of ballet. . . . In the meantime, we suggest that the promoters of the arts relax and leave the heavy competition to the athletes.

January-February 1978

MERCHANDISE SALES

Symphony Association Finds that Time Really is Money

On the face of it, the Women's Association of the Dearborn Symphony has done a good job in raising funds. The face in this instance belongs to a watch—more accurately over 500 watches—which the Association had emblazoned with the Dearborn Symphony name and then sold to raise funds and promote the orchestra.

A symphony supporter got the idea for the project following a discussion with a friend who had taken over business management of the World Wide American Time Company in Detroit. The executive suggested that his company print up the symphony name on the watch faces for a very nominal fee. The Women's Association then would buy the watches at less than $8 each and resell them for $15. The association enthusiastically endorsed the project and went to work developing a saleable design, which was then executed by a member's architect husband.

Initially, 1000 faces were printed and a total of 75 watches were made up in three different styles—men's with alligator band, ladies, with round black case and matching strap, and ladies, with clear lucite in a square shape. In November 1974 the watches were offered to the public and they sold without effort, resulting in a net profit of $7 per watch for the association. Pleased with the response, the group added two new pendant designs, and had additional watches made up.

Thus far some 550 watches have been sold at a profit of nearly $4000, and orders have come in from all over the world. Watches are continuing to sell and, according to Women's Association president Joan D. Irwin, the group is trying to decide "whether to form our own corporation for their promotion and sale or go with a commission per watch from the company."

March-April 1976

T-Shirts, Ingots, and Ties Reap Good Profit for Arts

An increasing number of cultural groups are selling specially designed items of clothing and accessories featuring their logos or institutional messages as part of their fund-raising programs. Both T-shirts and sweat shirts emblazoned with such messages as "Culture's My Bag," or "Support Your Local Artist" are becoming increasingly ubiquitous at prices ranging from $2 to $7.

Lately, however, new and varied items are moving onto the scene. Wilmington's Grand Opera House which also sells T-shirts, recently introduced loom-woven neckties at $7.95 each, which feature miniature images of the Opera House facade set against a blue, maroon or green background.

Although it can only loosely be considered an accessory, the most intriguing new item in the arts showcase is the silver commemorative ingot now being sold by the Chattanooga Committee of the Tennessee Performing Arts Foundation. Offered at $50 each to help support the $4-million statewide endowment campaign for the Tennessee Center for the Performing Arts, the ingot is made of .999 fine silver and features a sketch of the planned center and brief information about it.

September-October 1975

Bountiful Ballet Boutique
Rings Register With Sales

During its fall 1975 season, the City Center Joffrey Ballet will be advertised all over New York City by a legion of fans who have paid handsomely for the privilege. The advertising will contain such moving messages as "The Joffrey Is a Time for Joy," "Dance With Me," and "New York Export, Opus Jazz," on scarves, pendants, T-shirts, needlepoints, umbrellas, and other wearable and transportable items. Some items, such as tote bags, will contain no words, just rows of dancers' silhouettes, a familiar Joffrey image. These items will enrich company coffers by thousands of dollars.

Since 1974, the Joffrey Circle Boutique has "been in business" and has become a familiar retailer to dance audiences. Through intermission sales counters at performances, tables at street fairs, a growing direct mail operation, and local stores in cities where the company's on tour, the Boutique sells hundreds of items directly and reaches a mailing list of 2,500 purchasers all over the world. In its two five week 1975-76 New York seasons alone, the Boutique made over $20,000 for the company through theater sales.

Although Joffrey started its sales program in 1973 when it sold some 300 T-shirts, business really didn't pick up until Joan Abramowitz joined the ballet as head of audience development in January 1974 and decided to expand the sales picture. "I had an idea we could sell a lot of stuff," she told *AM*. "Our audience is somewhat cultish and are very proud to promote the Joffrey name." To launch her effort she had a needlepoint design made up and packaged and expanded the T-shirt line to a variety of colors. During the following year she added scarves, jewelry, umbrellas, pendants, tote bags, and a calendar and initiated the mail order business.

"Our biggest initial problem was dealing with manufacturers who didn't want small orders," she added. "I had to make money first in order to have money for purchases, and it took a year and a half to reach that point. Now I keep part of the money we make to invest in other items." Ms. Abramowitz advises arts administrators considering similar programs to deal with manufacturers they know. "I go to friends or friends of friends," she added "who are interested in helping."

In spite of its success as fund raiser for the company, the operation has its problems, including bookkeeping, money handling, inventory, design (her biggest headache), and exchange. "We always must remember," she adds, "that it's not as important to make money as it is to spread good will." Thus, returns are made willingly. The mail-order business, which brings in much less income than direct sales, has special problems such as shipping—goods must go out in three weeks—and returns. Ms. Abramowitz handles the entire mail order herself, which cuts down on overhead. "If we had a rented store and paid help," she claims, "we couldn't afford to sell T-shirts at $4 each." Mail order business has been helped by good publicity, including shopping column mentions in such magazines as *Seventeen*.

Because the boutique is only one small part of Ms. Abramowitz's overall audience development job, she must rely on a volunteer force of 100 for direct sales. During the two five-week New York seasons, three volunteer leaders are at the theater every night to supervise the 11 volunteers who work at intermission booths in exchange for free admission. Also, whenever anyone hears of an interesting street fair, volunteers are asked to go and set up tables.

In analyzing the entire operation, Ms. Abramowitz sees it as an excellent audience development tool "with people paying you money to advertise you" and as a good money-maker which could be even better, although she does caution against automatic economic success. "Never sell an item unless you can make double the price it costs you," she advises. She suggests starting with easy items such as T-shirts, "but even they won't last forever" or buttons, "we bought them at 8¢ each several seasons ago, sold them at 25¢, and made $1600," and getting plenty of volunteer help. Scarves and tote bags have been other good Joffrey sellers, while jewelry is good for mail order but too small for theater sales. On the negative side, umbrellas have been difficult to ship, and wool scarves flopped because they cost too much.

To keep interest high, Ms. Abramowitz must introduce several new items each season. Scheduled for this fall are Joffrey cards, which should do well at Christmas, three new T-shirt designs (including an All-American, naming every American choreographer included in the company's repertoire), football jerseys, and perhaps a Joffrey pen to be worn around the neck.

Summer 1976

The Shirts on Their Backs

Arts groups might cash in on the T-shirt craze by involving their volunteers and audiences in the design process. In Washington D.C. the Friends of the Kennedy

Center recently held their first T-shirt competition and came up with "Culture Vultures" as winner, "I Blow My Horn at the Kennedy Center" as runner-up, and "Good to the Last Prop" as honorable mention. All three slogans with their appropriate designs have been made up and are now being offered at prices ranging from $3 to $5 each.

March-April 1976

In the Bag

The Chicago Symphony has discovered a fashionable way to raise funds and promote its program. Specially designed symphony tote bags, imprinted with the orchestra's musical logo in red, blue, and green, are being sold by the women's association for $10.50 each. The cream-colored canvas bags, 13-inches wide and 14-inches long, feature shoulder-length straps and an inside zipper pocket. In an extra promotional touch, each bag quotes the words *sine qua non* that *Time* magazine used in its cover story last year to describe the orchestra.

September-October 1974

Unusual Gifts Increase Museum Shop Revenues

Museums interested in bringing in additional revenues can learn from the experiences of the Gallery Shop in the Brooklyn Museum, New York. By stocking imaginative merchandise closely allied with the museum's exhibits, the shop does a thriving business that requires four paid, full-time employees and many part-time volunteers. Many of the 750,000 yearly visitors to the museum stop to buy unusual toys or original handcrafted sculpture and jewelry imported from 61 countries all over the world. Some of the most unusual offerings come from remote places visited by friends of the museum, who bring back arts and crafts suitable for exhibit as well as for sale.

The idea for the shop came from Carl Fox, its present manager, who was an administrative assistant in the museum's art school. Mr. Fox knew that 250,000 children visited the museum yearly, and he wanted to stimulate their interest in collecting works of art. In 1953 he organized the Gallery Shop and filled it with toys, arts, and crafts from many foreign countries. Prices started at 5¢. Today the shop still sells toys, but also carries merchandise for adults, such as handmade jewelry and primitive African and Peruvian sculpture and masks. Prices now range from 5¢ to $200, but the toys still outsell everything else.

The shop is open seven days a week, 364 days a year—it is closed only on Christmas. Hours are 10-5 daily, and 1-5 Sundays and holidays.

According to Mr. Fox, other museums have tried the same merchandise formula and have been equally successful.

September 1963

Wrapping Things Up

The Women's Committee of the Indianapolis Symphony has tied together the orchestra's fund need into a small package aimed at prospective purchasers and wrapped it, literally, in paper. Sold at $7 per roll, the musical wrapping paper features excerpts from a John Melcher composition printed on the 100-feet-long by 30-inch-wide paper, enough for wrapping over 50 gifts.

Summer 1976

TAPPING DONORS

Group Taps Small Givers with a Small Request

A "very reasonable request" for donations by the Brooklyn Academy of Music has brought over 2000 new givers and more than $10,000 into the arts center's fold. The request in this instance was for $5-donations, no more or less, and the direct-mail approach was made to a carefully pruned list of nongivers who had purchased tickets for academy events or had asked to be placed on its mailing list. Within two months of the 15,000-piece mailing, a 14-percent response was realized.

In planning the campaign, the academy based its approach on its own successful ticket-selling pitch which offers tickets to top events at only $5 each. "The $5 sale was turned into the $5 request," Academy public relations director Charles Ziff told *AM*. Once the concept was developed, two different approaches were pretested—one requesting $5 and the other asking for $5, but leaving the option open to recipients to increase the amount of the gifts. The tests showed clearly that audiences responded to the unique appeal of a $5-only gift. "It's easy for people to write a check for $5," said Ziff. "In fact, many donors called or wrote us to comment on how delightful and refreshing our approach was. There was a sense of fun and good will about the approach."

The mailing piece itself added to the audience delight. A "soft sell" letter was accompanied by the "$5 reasonable request" card which contained a list of responses, several tongue in cheek, from among which donors could check the reason they were contributing to the academy. "Pennsylvania Ballet," "Henry V," and "the leaks in your roof" were among them. Many donors filled in their own reasons for giving. Each donor received a thank-you card which began, "Dear One-of-our-largest contributors."

The academy will now keep a purchasing history of each new giver to determine future ticket purchases and donations, and subsequent campaigns will be based on this history.

Summer 1976

Check-in

To make sure that potential contributors don't have to search for checks, the Wisconsin Youth Symphony mails them sets of preprinted checks made payable to the orchestra. Each check, in the amount of $5, includes spaces where donors print name, address, bank name, and checking account number. As the orchestra notes in its accompanying letter, the checks are bank-approved and totally tax deductible.

January-February 1973

How to "Fix" a Parking Ticket

A unique fund-raising method is suggested by the recent campaign of the Mooreville, West Virginia Red Cross blood bank to collect 120 pints of blood.

Through an arrangement with local authorities, one 24-hour period was set aside as a day on which tickets issued for parking meter violations could be "fixed" by motorists. A violater could cancel out his parking ticket by contributing a pint of blood in lieu of paying his fine.

The method may be adapted to a fund-raising campaign for the arts where city fathers are cooperative. It not only can bring in a sizable sum on a single day, but reap wide publicity at the same time.

September 1962

Orchestra Wins 80,000 Donors in Six Weeks

Arts groups seeking to broaden their base of support might steal a leaf from the pages of the Sacramento Symphony's unique and succesful Roll of Honor. The orchestra, which raised all but $50,000 of its $500,000 Ford Foundation matching grant by March 15, 1971, went soaring over the top in an unprecedented six-week Roll of Honor drive which added nearly 80,000 individual donors to its roster and $120,000 to the campaign treasury.

The Roll of Honor was conceived by Carlyle Reed, publisher of the *Sacramento Union* and an orchestra board member, as a way of involving the total community down to, and especially including, the $1 donor in the drive. This appeal to the smallest contributor was symbolized by an actual book—the Roll—which contributors were told would be inscribed with the name of every $1-and-up donor and permanently displayed in the foyer of the city's community center, with a different page to be spotlighted daily.

A small committee of four planned the entire campaign and maintained control of all phases of its development. To reach various segments of the community, seven committees were organized in advance, and were composed of cultural and civic leaders, labor union presidents, college students, business leaders, military officers, representatives of men's service clubs, and officials of the state employees association. A week before the actual solicitation began, a coordinated all-out publicity drive was launched featuring donated billboards and car cards, bumper stickers, frequent broadcast spots and features, and extraordinary coverage by all three local newspapers. In the *Sacramento Union,* which sponsored the campaign and paid its costs, at least one major arts story appeared daily.

The campaign officially opened April 14 with a press conference and mayor's proclamation. During the following weeks, to the accompaniment of a barrage of publicity, large contribution envelopes with spaces for 50 names were circulated throughout the city, to stores, schools, and companies, and the *Sacramento Union* distributed enrollment envelopes among newspapers.

With most letters bringing in $1 contributions, the original $50,000 goal was reached in less than two weeks, and within six weeks the $100,000 mark was passed. The 78,682 names are being computerized now prior to their inscription in the Roll.

November-December 1971

Patrons Bid for Auction Gifts as Arts Groups Bid for Donors

By adding a few frills to an old-fashioned American selling device, the auction, cultural groups are opening donors' pocketbooks and winning attention in their communities.

In Binghamton, New York, the Roberson Center for the Arts and Sciences, an arts council, has just completed its second annual "building blocks" campaign, an art auction of donated works for the benefit of its building fund. To assure attendance and a precommitment of funds, the center sold building block certificates several months prior to the date of the event, which were redeemable in lieu of cash at the auction at twice their face value. Adorned with a special drawing by famed local cartoonist John Hart, the certificate showed the Wizard of Id and B. C., Hart comic strip characters, piling up building blocks. The cartoon was repeated in posters and in other promotional materials.

According to Roberson Center director, Keith Martin, "The building block made the purchaser aware of his participation in a building fund drive, while the promise of doubling his money made his advance commitment irresistible." The irresistibility was evidenced by the fact that last year a sales promotion team of about 40 men and women helped sell some 600 certificates before the auction took place. This year, with $10 and $25 certificates sold also, overall receipts, including auction sales, increased by 10 percent to $6000. A black-tie preview of the art, held several days prior to the auction for purchasers of $25 building blocks, helped spur the sale of the higher priced certificates.

Although artists donated works to the auction in the past, the success of the event will now enable the center to guarantee artists 50 percent of the established value of their works in future auctions.

Another successful auction with a novel twist was held in Boston, Massachusetts for the benefit of educational television station WGBH. This year's event, the third annual, raised $282,000, more than 5 percent of the stations's yearly operating budget. The auction was presented on the air for seven consecutive evenings, with viewers phoning in their bids for the merchandise they saw televised. A key reason for the event's success was the participation of top Boston area businessmen. Not only did corporations donate nearly all of the merchandise—6000 items ranging up to $25,000 in retail price were offered this year —but their board chairmen, presidents, and vice presidents acted as on-the-air auctioneers.

Meanwhile, a committee of prominent St. Louis civic, business, and cultural leaders is actively involved in finding unusual gifts for its "Cultural Auction of Many Extraordinary Lots of Treasure," Camelot, for short, which will be held on November 1 and 2. The auction, under the general sponsorship of Famous-Barr, a department store, will benefit the Arts and Education Council of Greater St. Louis. Among the items which have been suggested for the auction are an African safari, a walk-on part in a Broadway play, a gold mine, and dinner with a movie actress. Similar auctions in San Diego, Seattle, and Portland have raised more than $100,000 each for cultural groups.

Summer 1968

House Call

Doctors are good targets for fund-raising campaigns, and the chances for success with them may increase if appeals relate to their areas of interest. This spring, Wilmington's Grand Opera House went after doctors in its major fund drive with a specially organized medical committee spearheading the drive. An on-target approach letter from doctors on the committee recalled the association between music and medicine, and read in part, "Freud analysed Mahler in one afternoon (presto analysis). Illness pervades the last act of more operas than can be quickly counted. One can imagine the disastrous last act of *Boheme* had Mimi, instead of wasting away, sustained a sudden cardiac arrest. In short, medicine has been there when music needed it. Now there is a new call for our help."

Summer 1975

Doctors Celebrate Centennial
by Funding Local Arts Groups

Four Ohio cultural groups are in "better health" as a result of a unique contribution made by over 200 local doctors. In Youngstown, Ohio, the Mahoning County Medical Society celebrated its centennial anniversary late last year with a $31,000 donation to the Youngstown Symphony, Youngstown Playhouse, Butler Institute of American Art, and Youngstown Ballet Guild.

When planning for the medical society's November 1972 centennial commenced some 18 months earlier, a committee composed of all the organization's past presidents developed such special projects as a design contest for a centennial emblem, expansion of the monthly bulletin to include an historical article in each issue, and a history of medicine exhibit at the annual country fair. The biggest idea to come from the committee, however, was a two-fold event—a giant "meeting of the century" for Society members and a birthday gift. "We decided that since it was our birthday," said Howard Rempes, the society's executive secretary, "we would give a birthday gift to the community." Although no formal ties existed between the Medical Society and local cultural institutions, one committee member suggested arts groups as recipients in appreciation of their contributions.

To broaden the celebration and help make the birthday gift possible, the society made the "meeting of the century" an event for the community at $25 per couple. Then it turned to its doctor-members for the bulk of the gift. "We started by making all members give $100 (a dollar for each year) toward the birthday gift," added Rempes. "We kept after them and kept reporting the results in the Bulletin under the heading of 'The Century Club.' " Over 200 doctors, two-thirds of the membership, contributed $100 each.

For months preceding the gala "meeting," held on a Saturday evening in early November, local media promoted the event and the overall centennial program heavily. The recipient arts groups, in addition to sharing publicity and the birthday gift, also shared in the program, with the symphony performing and the playhouse presenting a one-act play starring hometown movie star Elizabeth Hartman.

One final event marked the happy relationship between the medical society and the local arts groups. During the entire month of November, the Butler Art Institute featured a "Medicine in Art" exhibition.

Summer 1973

Arts Group Tries "Hard Sell" and Boosts Financial Support

Faced with a growing budget and a moribund fund-raising program, a Canadian arts group instituted a step-by-step "hard sell" campaign to win increased financial support. The new approach, conceived two years in 1964 by the Royal Winnipeg Ballet, set a chain reaction of giving into motion, which resulted in greater financial assistance from government at every level and new and important support from business and industry. This same approach has provided a continuing framework for the organization's now-successful fund-raising program.

According to George Coroneos, the ballet's general manager until recently, the organization had "a kind of defeatist attitude until 1964." Recognizing then that a coordinated effort was necessary to meet an anticipated annual budget of $200,000, the group's leaders developed a program that began with a pragmatic approach to the city government.

Documenting its case with concrete information—how the ballet company helped to keep money in the city and how it promoted the city through its outside tours—the group's leaders asked for $25,000 from a city government which had given it only $3000 the previous year. Pages of statistics were presented to the Winnipeg Metro Council, an official municipal agency. The presentation showed how the company created employment not only for its own members, but for independent local contractors, and it indicated how much money remained in the city through the purchase of goods and services by the ballet. Also, scores of press clippings demonstrated how the company promoted the city of Winnipeg nationally and internationally. The hard-hitting presentation was successful, and the ballet received a grant of $18,000.

Following the same basic approach but broadening the case to include the entire province of Manitoba (charts showed anticipated cultural growth with the opening of a new arts center in 1967), the ballet asked the provincial government for greater support. An increase to nearly $13,000 was granted. Next, a presentation to the Canada Council pinpointed the national benefits of the company's activities and resulted in a grant of $42,000.

Bolstered by its success in winning increased government support at every level, the ballet prepared its case for local business, which had contributed less than $40,000 the previous year. The Metro Council grant in particular had been well-publicized in Winnipeg, and it provided the ballet company with a weapon to prod the community to give more.

In advance of any direct approach to business, the ballet's board prepared a detailed profile of corporations in the area, rating them according to their actual and projected incomes and their past giving records. Next, two-paragraph letters "selling" the ballet were sent to key local corporations. The letters emphasized four essential points: what the Royal Winnipeg Ballet was; what its future prospects were; how much it had to raise to achieve this goal; and how much it expected to raise from the people of the city. Each letter indicated a specific date on which representatives of the ballet would call a company executive to arrange an appointment.

Aware that many corporations thought of ballet as an "esoteric activity," the dance company selected a group of practical, business-minded board members and aggressive staff people to make oral presentations to each corporation. To strengthen their case they brought a specially prepared brochure with them, which pinpointed the current and future financial picture of the organization.

A major business breakthrough came when the ballet received a grant of $50,000 from the head office of the largest investment brokerage firm in Canada, James Richardson and Sons. According to Mr. Coroneos, the brokerage house, which had contributed only modest sums to the ballet previously, was influenced by increased government support and the approval that that support implied. The business-like approach to the company also helped. "For the first time," he told *AM*, "they were clearly able to see the ballet's long-range plans."

Although the Richardson grant was not publicized in the press, it was used by the ballet in its approach to other local businesses, and it started a chain reaction of business contributions. As a result, a total of $118,000 was raised from local business. Also, the size and number of individual contributions increased.

Using the same approach in its 1965 fund campaign, and with its budget upped to nearly $250,000, the ballet company again increased the total amount of money it raised.

April 1966

Naming Donors

Cultural groups are using novel methods to win friends and raise money. Theatre Calgary in Canada introduced a "Wall of Fame" (four plywood panels 7 feet high by 4 feet wide) which lists the names of contributors. Business donors can have their names inscribed or their logos printed on the wall for donations ranging from $25 for a 2 x 4 inch space to $100 for a 4 x 12 inch space. Used initially as part of the group's television auction, when hundreds of viewers phoned in donations to have their names listed, the wall has since become a permanent part of Theatre Calgary's home.

Fall 1970

New Credit Cards for the Arts
a Reward to Fund-drive Donors

There's a new status symbol in the arts—credit cards. In St. Louis, a select group of arts patrons can now say "charge it" when they purchase tickets or works of art from ten local cultural organizations.

The plan was conceived by the Arts and Education Council of Greater St. Louis as a way of showing appreciation to the 1300 people who contributed $50 or more to the 1968 united arts fund campaign, which topped its goal for the first time in the fund's five-year history. The drive drew $776,584 from 10,500 donors.

Issued in September, and valid through December 31, 1968, the wallet-sized green and white cards list the names, addresses, and phone numbers of all participating organizations, which include the St. Louis Symphony, the Repertory Theatre of Loretto-Hilton, and the Painters Gallery.

In a separate attempt to raise the sights of donors, the council has, for the past two years, sent a "wheel of tickets" to everyone who contributed $25 or more to the fund. The wheel, a circular piece of paper with eight sections, each devoted to a different local organization, offers free tickets to events sponsored by the participating groups.

November-December 1967

Visual Persuasion

Arts groups are taking more aggressive steps to dramatize their financial cases. The Long Island Symphony recently mailed the bottom third of a letter to remind supporters that "subscriptions and ticket sales pay for only part of any performance—at most 1/3 of the total cost. The balance must come 1/3 from grants and 1/3 from contributions—contributions from people like you." The Winston-Salem Arts Council superimposed a message in black ink over its contribution form reading. "We'd hate to end this performance at intermission" and then went on to explain that tickets pay only part of the performance cost. The United Performing Arts Fund in Milwaukee mailed two parts of a torn ticket that fit together, with the second half reading, "Your contribution will complete this ticket."

March-April 1976

Local Arts Group Cooperation
Wins Funds, New Audiences

Unusual cooperative ventures between arts groups in the same community are providing participants with new means of raising funds, winning audiences, and promoting activities.

In Hartford, Connecticut, the women's committees of the five leading local arts organizations—the Connecticut Opera, Hartford Ballet, Hartford Stage, Hartford Symphony, and Wadsworth Atheneum—have joined together for the first time to sponsor what may be the largest and most unique fund-raising event ever attempted in the community. On the evening of April 12, some 2000 people will assemble on and around the green of a small New England village for Hartford's first "Country Fair." The village, with its green, shops, trees, livery stable, church, livestock exhibit, and operating carnival, is actually a fantasy, totally constructed by volunteers within a giant aircraft hangar donated by the United Aircraft Corporation. The evening's goal has been set at $125,000, with all funds raised to be equally divided among the five participating organizations.

The idea for the event gradually developed over the years. The women's committees had often talked about cooperating on a major joint venture, and three years ago the opera, symphony and ballet had presented a much smaller fund-raising program. When Country Fair finally crystallized late last spring, it was greeted enthusiastically and it received strong encouragement and support from the Greater Hartford Arts Council, which, according to director Philip A. Mallet, "has been pushing for this kind of cooperation."

A key to the fair's hoped-for success is its careful organization, its all-out promotional effort, and its premise that all materials, services, and professional skills must be donated if possible. In addition to the nearly 400 volunteers working on 31 separate committees, top local professionals and consultants are offering their services without charge, including the architect who is designing the floor plan and mechanicals, the theater designer who is planning the individual stores where goods will be sold, the United Aircraft technicians who will supervise lighting and sound, and a G. Fox and Company display man who will plan decorations and centerpieces. In addition, Hartford Federal Savings and Loan Association will donate cash registers, cashiers, a payments supervisor, and an armored car to take cash receipts to the bank, and United Aircraft will donate security personnel.

To reach its fund goal, the event has several money-raising aspects, including tickets sold at $50 per couple ($25 per single ticket) for regular admission, $100 for patrons, and $250 for sponsors; concession booths where donated crafts and specialty foods will be sold; and games of skill in an amusement area.

A special Country Fair calendar in a handsome hardcover book with a color print on its cover will be given free to each couple attending, but some 4000 extra copies will be sold at $5 each following the event. Featuring local advertising and 18 months of event listings, the calendar will also include descriptions and membership blanks for each of the five participating groups, a telephone directory of all local arts organizations, and color prints of works from the Wadsworth Atheneum.

The event itself is planned as a fun evening beginning at 6:00 P.M. with an open bar and homemade canapes served inside the specially constructed town. Moving lights and calliope music will be part of the setting and at 8:00 P.M. guests will be summoned by a musical chorus to the sit-down, family-style church supper. Social and square dancing will continue throughout the evening, and following dinner guests will be able to shop in the town's stores, stroll through the carnival area with its game and rides, or visit the livestock show.

With local enthusiasm high, the arts council has used the event to help engender greater business involvement in the arts. Some six weeks prior to Country Fair, the council will host a meeting for public relations officers of Hartford Area companies where the topic of discussion will be the fair and the contributions of women's committee members.

Elsewhere, other arts groups are discovering the benefits of cooperation. The Pacific Science Center and the Oregon Museum of Science and Industry have joined in a mutual membership program which permits members of one institution to visit the other on the presentation of membership cards. Also, the Science Center allows PSC members reduced-rate participation in field trips, science classes and summer camps.

In Phoenix, members of cultural groups in two different disciplines recently shared in an exchange activity, as the first step towards a larger cooperative program. Art museum members attended a dress rehearsal of a Phoenix Symphony subscription event while the symphony members attended the museum's reception and preview—including a jazz performance and informal artists' talks—of the touring Whitney Museum exhibition, "Twentieth Century American Painting and Sculpture."

January-February 1975

Then Mayor Paul Jordon, M.D. (right) and New Jersey State Commissioner of Community Affairs Patrick Kramer take the first ride in a balloon launching "Jersey City Awake" in 1972. (Courtesy of Department of Health and Social Services, Jersey City, New Jersey)

4

Government and the Arts

CITIES

Cities to Play More
Important Role in Arts

Alvin Toffler

I think we can sketch some of the new relationships between art and the city that seem likely to take shape in the next decade and a half. In this exercise in conjecture, I am speaking of cities with populations of about 500,000 or over, of which we will have a good many more by 1980.

1. Any such city without *professional* theater, or music, or dance, without a first-rate art gallery, or bookshops, museums, and a culture-oriented radio or television station, will be regarded as an embarrassing relic of the past. States and, perhaps, the federal government will rush to provide technical assistance to these culturally underdeveloped areas.

2. By 1980, virtually all such cities will have something that passes for a culture center. New facilities will have been built in part with public funds.

3. Every such city will have an arts council.

4. By 1980, most cultural centers and arts councils will be regarded by many artists as being already hopelessly ossified. New arts groups will spring up outside, and in opposition to, the centers and councils. Each city will have a "culture establishment," and around its edges, the start of an antiestablishment movement.

5. One reason for this breakaway will be the explosion of new artistic media and forms made possible by the technological revolution . . . plastics, computors, video tape. Experimenters with these will be represented in the main cultural institutions, but will rebel and demand more time, money, and attention. These artists will continue to face a difficult struggle because most philanthropy will be channeled through the "arts establishment."

6. Newspapers, radio, and television will devote more attention to the arts. Critics will be more specialized. Local critics will be more respected and powerful.

7. Local universities will become much bigger; the dollar volume of educational activity will climb. All schools will be enormously more important in the economic and political life of the city.

8. The dollar volume of cultural activity will also increase sharply. Arts groups will be linked more closely with the ascendant power of the educa-

tion system. Taken together, educational and cultural activity will constitute a very significant factor in the city economy. This economic significance will be relfected in sharply increased political influence.

9. Every city will have a culture lobby that will parallel and often work together with a local education lobby. Arts lobbies will pressure city councils for various subventions and concessions. City officials will be increasingly receptive to them, because by 1980 arts lobbies will enjoy the active support of business, labor, and other politically potent groups in the community.

10. Virtually every city government will have some agency devoted primarily to the coordination and encouragement of artistic activity or to maintaining liaison with private groups performing these functions. This agency will channel funds from counterpart state and federal agencies into the arts institutions of the city, most likely in support of riskless culture, the safe, and the traditional. It will also compile detailed data about local arts activity and review all contemplated municipal decisions from the point of view of their potential impact on the arts. Cities can also be expected to levy a variety of imaginative taxes and charges to raise money for the arts.

As culture becomes legitimate grist for the local political mill, it is predictable that many groups outside the culture industry will make their weight felt in decisions concerning the arts.

If these predictions have any validity, it is clear that public agencies will play a far more important role in the development of the arts. Cities, by becoming more important as patrons, will further reduce the already declining significance of the individual donor—the only real source of support for venturesome arts projects.

This imbalance in the patronage structure can be offset somewhat by the city offering tax incentives to individual donors and by offering aid directly to artists, including—and especially—those not affiliated with any institutions. Loft studios could be designed into public housing projects and offered to painters at minimal rents. Similarly, cities could offer special low-rent apartments to composers and performers.

Another way for cities to help creative artists is to give them some institutional connection as, perhaps, artists-in-residence attached to libraries or to school systems at teachers' salaries. Cost would be minimal.

Concern for the quality of life will deepen in the next 15 years, mainly because powerful economic and social forces, acting on our value systems, are going to compel it to happen. People will care about their cities and will demand a higher level of cultural activity than ever before.

None of this means that utopia will have arrived. Each change has consequences not immediately visible and not necessarily good for the arts or the city or society.

September 1965

"Culture Vote" Can
Prod Cities to Assist Arts

The role of municipalities in culture is becoming increasingly important. Although the kind of assistance city governments give to the arts varies widely from community to community and their overall contribution is still relatively small, the potential of municipal support cannot be dismissed.

In Los Angeles, for example, the city supports programs in both the visual and performing arts. This includes sponsorship of band, choral, and chamber music concerts, ballet recitals, and support for the Hollywood Bowl, the Los Angeles Philharmonic, and several community orchestras. In addition, a Municipal Art Commission incorporated into the city charter since 1911 budgeted nearly $300,000 out of a total 1963-64 city budget of $271,025,417 for cultural purposes. The commission operates an all-city art festival in Barnsdall Park, and is responsible for the design of all public buildings and for the acquisition and location of the city's art works.

What role can arts leaders play to encourage municipal support of the arts? Eddy S. Feldman, a member of the Los Angeles Board of Municipal Art Commissioners, suggests the following four-point program:

1. Citizens should find out what cultural facilities the city provides and use them.

2. Citizens should concern themselves with the work of municipal agencies concerned with the arts. They should attend meetings, make suggestions and wherever possible participate in the work of the agency.

3. Citizens should demand from their city the cultural programs which they cannot provide for themselves. Even if budgetary problems exist, claims Mr. Feldman, the creation of imaginative programs can have the effect of mobilizing both legislative and popular support for them. In addition, every part of the city, not just a few fortunate sections, should be exposed to high level cultural programs.

4. Citizens should impress their needs through demands on city officials and upon those who are running or plan to run for municipal office. According to Mr. Feldman there is such a thing as a "culture vote" and this was demonstrated in the 1963 mayoralty campaign in San Francisco when the arts became a campaign issue. "Culture voters," says Mr. Feldman, "will lend prestige to office holders and seekers, will work hard for their elec-

tion, and provide them with financial support. The culture voters have only to be encouraged."

Mr. Feldman points out that it is the city administration's responsibility to lead the way in creating and expanding cultural programs. "It is not elected simply to follow tested and unimaginative pathways," he says. "The administration may not always be aware of the desires of the populace to be involved, yet all that may be needed is simply the inspired call to action."

March 1964

Arts Prove Key
Resource to Troubled City

A part-time effort to develop a summer cultural program proved so beneficial to a troubled city that the city has since established an official office on the arts, instituted a year-round program, and helped launch a new community theater group.

The story of Jersey City, New Jersey's involvement with the arts began less than two years ago, shortly after its new mayor, Paul Jordan, who is also a physician, took office. An ethnically diverse municipality of 260,000 located across the river from New York, Jersey City had all the familiar symptoms of urban unrest—crime, poverty, racial problems, and loss of industry—plus a 75-year history of political corruption. Elected on a reform platform, the new mayor pledged to bring back life and vitality to the city, a message that had been heard too often by a skeptical populace.

To convince people that change was really taking place, the mayor saw the need for developing programs in areas that would involve the total population and enliven the city. The arts was such an area and the mayor recruited Charles Robinson, an energetic, young Jersey theatrical producer to develop a program. Mayor Jordan offered to "open doors" and provide whatever moral support he could to help Robinson get the program off the ground that summer, but since he pledged fiscal austerity in his campaign, he couldn't make an outright commitment of public funds.

The mayor's interest was enough, and Robinson set out to find money for the program, symbolically named "Jersey City Awake." Beginning in May 1972, he raised $9000 from local business in several days by convincing companies that a thriving cultural program which would reduce tensions and help build a new image for the city would be in their own best interests. This demonstration of local support helped win a $7500 grant from the state arts council. Next, with the mayor's approval, he went through the city budget and by enlisting various agencies as program cosponsors he was able to find another $25,000 in money, materials, and services.

To attract attention, Robinson decided to kick things off with an exciting visual event—a symbolic balloon ride by the mayor and state commissioner of community affairs over the heart of the business district. Although the event attracted tremendous public interest and front-page headlines, Robinson recognized that it was a "gimmick" and not really tied to culture. "So," he told *AM*, "you decide that your next visual must be cultural." That turned out to be the commissioning of four major "city walls," which permanently added attractive art to four different areas of the city, pleasing four neighborhoods and making those people part of the support constituency.

Planning the program was a major challenge. "In a city deprived of 'high culture' for three generations," Robinson said, "you find that reeducation in the arts is your first major task. To that end you forget about contacting Hurok's office for a world-famous violinist or presenting a series of ethnic unknowns just because they're ethnic and inexpensive. Instead you spend $5000 for an evening in the park with Duke Ellington, who attracts all segments of the population, leads to editorials in papers which previously ignored your program, brings a turnout of nearly 5000 people, and generates the revival of the urban spirit you're seeking."

During its first summer in 1972, beginning with the Ellington concert, Awake sponsored 30 concerts in city neighborhoods, four theater performances, the first annual Jersey City jazz and art festivals, a UNICEF festival with dancing by 20 ethnic groups, a three-night Italian street festival, arts and crafts workshops in the public schools, and the city walls project.

Although Awake was successful, it was planned as a summer program and Robinson didn't return to it until the following year. By the time an expanded summer 1973 program was concluded, however, (with a concert by the Metropolitan Opera Studio, a performance of the Off-Broadway musical "Godspell," an appearance by the Newark Boys Chorus, and a ten-day visit by folk singer Peter Seeger in his sloop *Clearwater* added to the previous year's events), Robinson and the mayor both realized the need for a continuing year-round arts program. This January, Mayor Jordan named Robinson to the newly created, full-time position of Jersey City's cultural coordinator, operating under the Department of Human Resources.

Since undertaking Awake, Robinson has learned some key lessons about representing the city in the arts, including the inescapable conclusion that the best way to overcome apathy by both press and government is to personally involve their leaders in your project. He has, for example, given women's editors, along with wives of government leaders, advisory program roles. Government officials have been credited publically for their support and have been asked to participate in press photos announcing major donations or state grants. "But most important," indicated Robinson, "they are asked for their personal opinion before final decisions are made on events arrangements."

In soliciting business, Robinson's learned to develop support programs that meet a company's public relation needs. Colgate-Palmolive, for example, which has the city's largest riverfront factory and has been blamed—unjustly, they feel —for river pollution, sponsored visits by Peter Seeger's sloop *Clearwater* to the Awake program. Not only did press stories cite the company's contributions in cleaning up the Hudson River, but Mr. Seeger, known for his interest in ecology, endorsed their efforts.

With his new year-round job, Robinson looks to full development of his newest effort. Jersey City's community theater, launched last December with city support but now functioning on its own. Although progress has been made, dealing with a bureaucracy has presented problems. "I face the constant necessity," he added, "to remind government leaders that cultural programs must function independently of recreational and social programs."

March-April 1974

Civic Pride

In Jersey City, New Jersey, where an all-out effort led to the formation of a permanent city cultural office, Jersey City Awake, city arts endorsement has become highly visible. Awake now issues and distributes free of charge brightly colored 15-by-3-inch bumper stickers proudly proclaiming, "Bravo Jersey—Support the Arts in New Jersey."

January-February 1975

Port Authority
Sponsors Orchestra Tour

A commercial reason for supporting the arts was acknowledged by the Delaware River Port Authority, which sponsored a month-long, seven-nation European tour by the Philadelphia Orchestra this spring. According to reports, the Authority underwrote the tour cost of $150,000 to promote European shipping to Philadelphia and other Delaware River ports. In each of 12 cities where the orchestra performed, Authority executives and Philadelphia Mayor James H. J. Tate greeted European shippers at preconcert receptions. Prospective customers were given concert tickets, a booklet on Authority ports, and a new album recorded by the orchestra for the trip, which featured the Philadelphia waterfront on its jacket.

Fall 1970

Legislative Aid

To encourage continued support from your local legislators, you might honor them for their help or even involve them directly in your activities. Recently, the

Bronx Council on the Arts hosted a cocktail reception for the borough's seven councilmen and two councilmen-at-large and presented them with certificates of appreciation for their support of local cultural programs. The event also included a complete briefing for the lawmakers on the organization's plans for the 1974-75 season.

Summer 1974

Community Interest Sparked by Lectures on City Redevelopment

A free series of lectures, sponsored by a museum with the active support of local arts and business leaders, helped spark community-wide interest in the revitalization of downtown Portland, Maine, and increased local awareness of the importance of good architecture and the arts to the city's future well-being. These positive reactions were especially significant at a time when local arts groups were urging the construction of a performing arts center in downtown Portland.

The program resulted from a request by the Portland Museum of Art for assistance in developing an important lecture series. A local committee, including representatives of the Greater Portland Arts Council, selected the theme "Rebuilding Portland" as one that would have the greatest community significance. Planning began in February 1965, a year prior to the presentation of the series of five lectures. The program was strategically timed to precede the issuance of a report by Victor Gruen Associates on downtown Portland redevelopment.

During the entire planning period, the support and cooperation of community leaders helped the committee stay within its budget of less than $1500. A public relations firm volunteered its assistance, five local commercial banks underwrote the hiring of Frye Hall where the programs were presented, news media offered their full cooperation, and most of the speakers, who were well-known city planners and architects, waived lecture fees. Also, local television station WGAN made a film and videotape of the lectures.

With community interest high and with excellent prepublicity, the lectures, held on Wednesday evenings in February and March, attracted full houses of about 500 people each. Most attendees were men. The series consisted of lectures on the mid-century city, mid-century urban design, Portland today, Portland tomorrow—downtown, and Portland tomorrow—regional metropolis. Large dinners preceded the first and fourth lectures and informal parties at the museum followed the other three lectures. The museum also featured an exhibition related to the series.

According to Mrs. Sidney W. Thaxter, cochairman of the lecture series and president of the arts council, "The series was very successful in opening the minds of the people to the many facets of redesigning a city today. The lectures really awakened several important business leaders to a new perspective." She told *AM* that since the series ended, one building was bought and repaired and a colorful restaurant was installed in it.

An equally important result, especially with the arts council attempting to engender interest in a new downtown arts center, was the positive reaction of civic officials. "City councilmen," Mrs. Thaxter told *AM*, "have said they now realize the importance of downtown activity at night in the center city, a point emphasized by the lectures."

As a subsidiary benefit of the series, the arts council gained 200 new members following the completion of the series, representing a 50 percent membership increase.

October 1966

Convention Bureau

St. Louis, through its Touring and Convention Bureau, gave $50,000 to the St. Louis Symphony for a special program designed to promote the city as a convention and tourist site. Some of the money was used by the orchestra for two out-of-town concerts, in New York's Carnegie Hall and at Washington's Kennedy Center. Between 500 and 1000 New York and Washington business leaders were invited to each of these concerts and to receptions following them, which promoted the attractions of St. Louis. The rest of the money provided St. Louis conventiongoers with tickets to the orchestra's local concerts.

March 1963

Printing Help

Need flyers and press releases printed? Perhaps a municipal agency can help you. In San Francisco, the Art Commission has established a community printing service that all local cultural groups can use to promote their upcoming events. Charges are minimal, and when organizations can't afford to pay, the service is free.

Summer 1971

Arts Move to Increase Support from Cities

Although arts aid has been included in many city budgets for years, the pattern has been irregular from community to community and an overall national focus has been lacking. At the U.S. Conference of Mayors meeting in San Diego in June 1974, however, the arts were not only given a national platform, but a strong resolution in their behalf was passed by the delegates. In Canada, meanwhile, arts leaders organized a fall seminar with key mayors as a prelude to a national effort designed to increase city aid to the arts.

At the conference in San Diego, a first-time panel—"the Arts as Part of City Living"—chaired by Mayor Wes Uhlman of Seattle outdrew concurrent sessions on labor relations and urban transportation. The audience of some 100 city officials at the nearly three-hour-long session heard Uhlman and fellow mayors Robert LaFortune of Tulsa and Lawrence Cohen of St. Paul describe the kinds of support their cities provide to the arts and the rationale for that support and then listened to three Arts Endowment program directors—Stephen Sell of Special Projects, Bill Lacy of Architecture and Environmental Arts, and Brian O'Doherty of Visual Arts—discuss developments in their respective areas and the ways in which they relate to the interests of cities. Joseph Farrell of the National Research Center of the Arts discussed findings from his firm's recent attitudinal survey.

In a discussion period, most comments from the floor focused on the need to better articulate the arts rationale to city councils and the public. "There was no doubt expressed by any questioner or speaker," said Sell, "that involvement in the arts made good political sense."

As a capstone to the panel, a plenary session of mayors approved a resolution sponsored by Mayor Uhlman of Seattle on the "Quality of Life in our Cities." That resolution was drawn from a 14-point "Bill of Rights for the Arts in Our Cities" written by *AM* editor Alvin H. Reiss who, last May, had visited Seattle and met with Mayor Uhlman. The resolution read:

WHEREAS, surveys, public demand and increasing private support and participation indicate that citizen-involvement with the arts is strong and growing; and

WHEREAS, continued growth of the arts in quantitative and qualitative ways can no longer be sustained by traditional support resources; and

WHEREAS, the arts are an essential element providing the opportunity for a quality urban environment.

NOW, THEREFORE, BE IT RESOLVED that the United States Conference of Mayors adopts the following principles as guidelines for city action:

1. That city governments recognize the arts as an essential service, equal in importance to other essential services, and help to make the arts available to all their citizens.

2. That every city have a public agency specifically concerned with the arts.

3. That the physical appearance of the city, its architectural heritage and its amenities, be acknowledged as a resource to be nurtured.

4. That a percentage of the total cost of every municipal construction budget be set aside for the purchase or commission of works of art.

5. That city governments working together with the public at large shall help to effect a new national goal: "That no American shall be deprived of the opportunity to experience (or to respond artistically to) the beauty in life by barrier of circumstance, income, background, sex, remoteness or race.*

Meanwhile, across the border, the Canadian Conference of the Arts has developed a long-range program aimed at increasing municipal funding. This November at a seminar with municipal officials and the Canadian Federation of Mayors and Municipalities, the CCA will introduce a working paper pinpointing the difficulties the arts face in winning city aid. The city representatives then will outline their problems in funding cultural programs. Based on the exchange, the working paper will be revised and used as a discussion document at meetings between city and arts representatives to be held in a major city of each Canadian province early in 1975. A final document including concrete recommendations to cities on their arts involvement would be presented to the Mayors Federation for consideration at its April 1975 meetings with a response to the recommendations requested within a year.

At the local level, all Calgary candidates in the then upcoming federal election in Canada this June were invited by city arts leaders to a public forum—the first such program in Canada—to discuss their policies on cultural development and their parties' platforms on the arts. All 19 came and two of the parties sent arts policy statements. In New York, a report on cultural policy for the city, with possible national implications, will be released in September by a special panel appointed by the mayor.

Summer 1974

Arts Role in Revitalization of Cities is Growing

The growing role that the arts are playing in the revitalization of cities and their downtown areas is receiving increased attention. New studies are under way, a major first-time conference is in the offing, and models indicating new and different kinds of arts-city relationships are beginning to emerge. Also, in President Carter's recent Urban Policy statement he called for "a new arts and cultural program to promote community and human development in our urban areas"

*Alvin H. Reiss, Culture & Company, Twayne Publishers, Inc., New York, 1972.

and proposed providing $20 million for a "Liveable Cities" program from HUD, in participation with the NEA.

The revitalization of two of America's best-known streets, one in New York and the other in Minneapolis, symbolizes the new arts role in restoring decaying thoroughfares to their former prominence. In each instance, street revitalization is expected to exert a tremendous economic impact upon the surrounding areas. In New York an entire block of West Forty-second Street between Ninth and Tenth Avenues will be closed off on May 13 for a day-long "Salute to Forty-second Street Theatre Row." The Row is a group of older buildings, former porno cinemas, burlesque houses, and massage parlors, which, following a $1-million fund drive by the Forty-second Street Local Development Corporation, were purchased and renovated for theater use under New York City's Business Investment Incentives Program. Eight theater organizations are now housed in the Row.

In Minneapolis, the remodeling of the 1888 landmark Masonic Temple Building into the Hennapin Center for the Arts will kick off an effort to restore an eight-block strip of Hennapin Avenue, linked to the downtown City Center and the nearby Butler Square. The new center, which opens in 1979, will include three performing spaces, an exhibition area, office and classroom space for arts users and some commercial space.

Another major Minneapolis development is the Arts Commission-led drive to convert an underutilized warehouse district into a revitalized area combining commercial space with low-cost housing for artists and others. Under the plan, selected warehouses would be renovated to accommodate low-cost housing units on the upper floors and commercial facilities on the first floors. Through a public grant revolving fund, a nonprofit developer would perform basic renovations, with acquisition and renovation costs payed back through commercial tenant rents. Artists and other low-income resident tenants on the upper floors would provide their own labor to renovate their raw spaces, helped by materials purchased through the revolving fund. The Arts Commission is applying through the city for a $3-million Urban Development Action Grant from HUD to initiate the revolving fund.

Elsewhere, support from varied levels of government, including the Economic Development Administration and HUD, has helped change the appearance of downtowns. In Aurora, Illinois, a major downtown urban renewal program included renovation of a 1931 movie palace into the just-opened Paramount Arts Center, while in Wichita, both artists and the city have benefitted from a less permanent arrangement. The local urban renewal agency gave "All of the Above," a group of Wichita artists, free use of buildings scheduled for demolition as temporary art spaces. The artists used the buildings for environment rooms, work space and exhibition areas and for a nine-day performing arts festival. When two of the buildings were demolished, they moved into other buildings provided by the city.

In Seattle, the City Council recently legalized artist live-in space in commercial areas through a change in the local zoning ordinance. New revenues for the arts have been authorized in Buffalo, Lackawanna, and Tonawanda, New York, where a sales tax redistributing plan will allocate 11.4 percent of the local share of sales tax revenues to increasing services, "particularly in the area of library services and support for cultural and public benefit agencies." Also, a new traveling exhibit, "We the City," organized by the Association of Science-Technology Centers, will focus on urban planning and the role of people in it. An exhibition core will circulate throughout the country in 1979, with sponsoring museums plugging local components into the core.

Two studies nearing completion could be key resources in strengthening arts involvement in cities. *Local Government and the Arts* (ACA, N.Y., N.Y. 10018; $12.50), ready for publication this summer, will include pragmatic data for municipal officials to help them assess ways to use the arts in their programs. A UCLA study under the direction of Architecture and Urban Planning Dean Harvey Perloff focuses specifically on the arts impact on urban areas and promises to go beyond economic value in pinpointing use of the arts in city transformation.

The upcoming development with perhaps the greatest potential for spurring future action, is the October 4-7, 1978 conference in Minneapolis, "A New Currency: The Role of the Arts in Urban Economic Development." Planned as a working conference for participants from middle range cities (populations from 100,000 to 1 million), the meeting hopes to draw over 500 elected city officials, planners, economists, corporate leaders, funding agency representatives, and arts administrators for sessions designed to help participants develop approaches and program plans directly applicable to their individual situations. Sponsored by Minneapolis' Arts Commission and Industrial Development Commission, along with HUD, the Department of Commerce, the National League of Cities and the NEA, the conference will utilize various "tracks," targeted to the different experiential levels of participants.

March-April 1978

Mayor's Proclamation

Do you have an important event coming up? A proclamation from the mayor of your city, properly publicized, may be helpful in focusing attention on it. When suggesting a proclamation to a civic official, however, be sure to emphasize the community-wide significance of the event.

April 1966

Mayor Gives Unexpected
Support to Local Arts

As arts leaders in an upstate New York community have learned—quite happily in the final analysis—assumptions can be misleading and counterproductive. In Plattsburgh, New York, the cultural community had assumed that the city was not interested in supporting the arts because a previous municipal arts agency had been allowed to die and because, since his election two years earlier, Mayor Roland St. Pierre had not given overt aid to arts programs. Moreover, Mayor St. Pierre, the only Jesuit priest in the nation serving as a mayor, was not known to have a personal background in the arts. Yet, until late fall, 1973, nobody had personally approached the mayor to ask for his help.

Faced with a critical fund need, however, leaders of the local Clinton-Essex County Council on the Arts and cultural programmers at the State University of New York College at Plattsburgh, met with the mayor late last year to determine his attitude towards arts support and to see if he might be able to offer some financial assistance, even if token.

To the surprise of the contingent, the mayor greeted them with an aria from *La Boheme*, and following a discussion of cultural needs promised initial city funding. He also pledged to work with county legislators to win their support. "Nobody from the arts ever bothered to work with him before," claimed Clyde Kuemmerle, a college cultural programmer, "and when we did we were pleasantly surprised."

The initial sums won by the arts were small, $500 from city and county, but pledges were won for increased funding in coming years. Also, a major barrier was broken when for the first time arts representatives were appointed to the board of the civic center, which opened in May, and to several other city-county commissions. This summer, the city gave the arts council rent-free use of the center for a concert and promoted an expanded community arts program.

"We think the breakthrough is here," added Kuemmerle, "and we've been promised increased city involvement from now on."

September-October 1974

City Helps Artists

The city of Seattle, which passed a "1 percent for arts ordinance" for municipal construction projects in 1973, broke new ground this fall with the introduction of a unique and perhaps precedent-setting "artists' rights" contract which provides special protection for the artist. The city also has developed a clear set of guidelines and administrative procedures to govern implementation of the ordinance.

One of the contract's key features is its clause that stipulates that if the city sells a work in the future, the artist will receive 15 percent of its appreciated value. The contract also gives the artist the right to borrow a work for 60 days for inclusion in a public exhibition once every five years and gives him the first opportunity to make necessary repairs and alterations. Also, the contract specifies the city's responsbility to maintain the work and keep records of its conditions and location.

Seattle's first city department to take advantage of the new 1 percent ordinance was City Light, which commissioned $20,000 worth of art for two auditoriums from 22 local artists.

September-October 1974

STATES

State Programs Reach Out
to Reach New Audiences

Aware of the growing need to professionally market and promote their arts programs and reach publics not as deeply involved in the arts as they might be, two states have launched major new projects. In North Carolina, the Division of the Arts named Ted L. Cramer, a former marketing and promotion man for consumer products, as director of marketing, while in California, Arlene Goldbard, former coordinator of the San Francisco Art Workers Coalition, became coordinator of the Cultural News Service, an ambitious statewide communications project.

Cramer, who until earlier this year was responsible for the Lark Cigarettes marketing program will, according to a state announcement, "market the arts like other consumer products." Hired on a one-year pilot basis, Cramer hopes to develop a specific marketing plan which can be instituted by the beginning of the next fiscal year in July.

"Nobody's really doing market planning in the arts," Cramer told *AM*. "We need it to help us forecast and program and to overcome the crisis atmosphere in the field." Specifically, Cramer began his program by initiating surveys for each of the four divisions of North Carolina's Department of Cultural Resources—Theater Arts, the State Arts Council, the North Carolina Symphony, and the State Art Museum—to determine the market for each. When the data is collected by late January, Cramer will meet with division heads and their staffs to analyze the findings and set out objectives based on them, prior to developing strategies and specific tactics for marketing each program.

Because the resulting effort will be a major one, Cramer hopes to develop a volunteer corps of top professionals in advertising and public relations who will assist in a statewide campaign. "We'll be twisting some arms," he added, "to get the highest quality business pros to work with us."

In California, the Cultural News Service, functioning as an independent agency with state funding through next July, was specifically organized to reme-dy communications problems among artists and the community. The program, with a staff of four, has two broad objectives—providing information and techni-cal assistance to state artists and promoting arts activities and needs to the gener-al public, legislators, and government agencies, including the California Arts Council. In the latter area, in addition to disseminating news widely and working with all media, the CNS will facilitate development of broadcast programming on the arts.

In its artist aid program, the CNS is compiling a registry of artists, facili-ties, sponsors, funding, employment prospects, and legislation, among other areas, and will pull out this data for use as needed. Also, it will organize regional conferences for artists, provide consultants and consulting aid to arts groups, and act as matchmaker between artists and organizations. Those with projects need-ing support can send short descriptions about them to the CNS and receive a list-ing of possible funding sources in return. To make its program really functional, CNS will work with 20 "information conduit organizations," groups around the state that will act as distribution centers for its material and transmitters of local artist information.

Interestingly, in her prior role as a representative of artist interests in the San Francisco area, program director Arlene Goldbard was frequently at odds with government agencies and established arts institutions. "I guess they wanted a troublemaker to do this job well," she told *AM*.

Meanwhile, state arts agencies elsewhere have been finding ways to im-prove existing information programs in the hopes of bettering communications with their arts constituency and the general public. This past summer, the Center for Arts Information was established in New York with state council funding to serve as a clearing house for information on the arts in the state. The center maintains an arts research library of books and periodicals open to the public, responds to requests for information on a wide range of topics, and publishes special reports—one on county arts funding recently—and news bulletins.

November-December 1976

State Uses Orchestra
to Attract New Industry

Although it is not uncommon for corporations to promote local cultural groups as part of their employee recruitment programs, it is not often that arts organi-zations become active partners in a program established to lure new industry to a state. Yet the state of Utah has acknowledged the fact that it is helping to underwrite out-of-state tours by the Utah Symphony as a means of influencing leading corporations to relocate in the state. According to James N. Kimball, deputy director of the state's Coordinating Council, Department of Development Services, "I feel confident in saying that the Symphony tours have played a significant part in the attraction of many new industries to our state."

In June 1968, Utah will underwrite about one-third of the cost of the orchestra's first concert tour to four Pacific Coast cities—Los Angeles, San Francisco, Portland, and Seattle. A press release from the symphony board, which announced the new concert program, credited Utah Governor Calvin L. Rampton with originating the idea for the tour and quoted him as saying, "In today's intense competition for industry, music, and cultural events, such as those provided by the symphony orchestra, are important factors that help sell this area. The June tour will again focus the attention of thousands of people on Utah."

The state's Coordinating Council for Development Services will help to coordinate concert arrangements in each of the four cities in cooperation with the orchestra and local committees composed of former residents of Utah. Committees will direct the local sale of tickets and will help in arranging buffet receptions immediately prior to each concert for invited corporate executives and other guests. The "sell Utah" theme will be inherent in each reception, right down to the food served—all of which will be Utah-produced under the supervision of a state consumer marketing specialist.

Milton L. Weilenmann, managing director of Utah's Coordinating Council, views the upcoming tour as an important means of reaching industrial leaders. "It has been our experience," he said, "that through the cultural exposure provided by the symphony on such tours, we have been able to meet successfully the national leaders of business and industry and thereby better tell the story of our state's phenomenal economic development. Tangible results of the Utah Symphony's assistance in the industrial growth of Utah were the contacts made in New York City prior to the Orchestra's concert at Carnegie Hall last fall."

Queried as to the "tangible results," Mr. Kimball mentioned the decision of General Instruments to locate an electronics facility in Salt Lake City. "It was during the September 1966 Utah Symphony concert at Carnegie Hall," he told *AM*, "that we made our initial contact with General Instruments. They attended a reception held by the state of Utah at the Waldorf-Astoria prior to the concert and expressed an interest in relocating one of their research plants in our state. The decision was consummated in subsequent meetings."

November-December 1967

State Council Song

Recognition came to the New York State Council on the Arts when it became the subject of a song in a professional theater production, perhaps the first government arts agency in history to earn this singular distinction. New York's Equity Library Theatre, in its between-the-acts appeal for funds held during the entire two-week run of *One for the Money,* featured an original number written by composer-conductor Fred Roffman. A cast member, lamenting the fact that the future of the Equity Library program was in jeopardy because the state council did not renew its grant, sang such lyrics as, "I've got the New York Council on the Arts blues/Can't lose 'em/Because the New York Council cancelled their dues."

March-April 1972

Paintings in Artmobile
Tour Throughout State

An "Artmobile," which is actually a traveling wing of the Arkansas Arts Center of Little Rock, is rolling through the Arkansas countryside bringing an exhibit of original paintings to the people in the manner of a library bookmobile.

The Arkansas Artmobile cost $65,000. It is the gift of Winthrop and David Rockefeller and of the Barton Foundation of Arkansas. Gasoline to keep the Artmobile on the road is donated by the Lion Oil Refining Company, founded by the late Colonel T. H. Barton of the Barton Foundation.

Dedicated on December 13, 1962 with an address by Winthrop Rockefeller, the unusual vehicle has set out on a two-year tour of the state. Stops are scheduled for one, three, or five days in a given town. It carries 17 paintings from the Netherlands.

Air-conditioned and heated for visitors' comfort and for protection of the paintings, the Artmobile maintains constant temperature and humidity. The precious canvases are mounted on specially constructed walls, screwed into place with heavy steel rods holding their backs firm.

The unusual appearance of the Artmobile itself acts as promotion, as its shining steel sides are lettered with its name and the cargo it carries. Blue and green pennants fly from two poles attached to the roofed rear platform, which when opened extends the length of the Artmobile to 67 feet.

February 1963

State Arts Report

In Spring 1972, the New York State Commission on Cultural Resources, which was organized following the record $18-million legislative appropriation to the arts in 1970, issued a detailed report titled "State Financial Assistance to Cultural Resources." The commission, in addition to voicing its approval of the state arts council program and recommending an increase in council staff and regional offices, issued a series of other suggestions and recommendations, 15 overall. Among them was the recommendation that the state's emergency aid to the arts program be continued on a permanent basis and that the $18-million appropriation, which it deemed inadequate, be increased to $30 million.

Now, several months later, another specially created state arts study group, the Advisory Commission on Financing the Arts in Illinois, has issued its report. Unlike the New York report, however, the Illinois study does not recommend an immediate and drastic increase in state aid to the arts. It suggests instead what commission chairman Joel F. Henning terms, "bread and butter recommendations—most of which can be implemented *now*, at the current level of state appropriation." In a statement accompanying the report, Henning says,

> The Commission recognizes the very desperate need for substantially increased arts appropriations. . . . Realistically, however, we know that additional funds will not be available from the State until the crushing weight of the welfare burden is lifted. We therefore recommend that the appropriation for the Illinois Arts Council increase over a five year period from its current level which amounts to $.05 per Illinois citizen to $1.00 per citizen, or from $600,000 to $11-million.

Among the 27 additional recommendations were several key proposals relating to the operation and program of the state arts council. The basic thrust of these was that the council change its program orientation and concentrate its efforts on providing facilitative services and technical aid to arts groups and artists instead of making grants or producing its own arts activities. Included in the recommendations was a proposal to reorganize the state council to meet the suggested new objectives.

Another provocative recommendation related to the state's major established arts institutions. The commission asked these groups to reconstitute their boards of trustees and committees to "give more than token representation to men and women who can help attract new sources of support as well as to youth and labor, and increased attention to ethnic and cultural diversity."

September-October 1971

Communications Link

A pilot project in New York is providing the state arts council with an important communications link to scores of small cultural groups throughout the state. At the same time, it is providing the small groups with a day-to-day informational resource and an ear receptive to their needs and problems.

The project, which is being undertaken for the state council by the Performing Arts Association of New York through a council grant, underwrites the part-time services of six young arts administrators from different areas of the state. As the association's regional representatives, they are charged with learning everything they can about their areas and about the arts groups within them.

Since the program began in May 1971, the representatives have become known to scores of arts groups and have helped them by pinpointing available local resources and by explaining the state council program and how its various services can best be utilized. They have also acted as catalysts, consultants, and as information gatherers on arts programming. In one community a representative encouraged the library to provide meeting space to arts groups; in another, the representative helped expand the reach of an arts council by bringing cultural groups in nearby cities into its program.

The representatives maintain weekly phone communications with a program coordinator. In addition, they send the coordinator monthly written reports on their activities.

November-December 1971

COUNTIES

Arts Groups Rely on
County Recreation Agency

When performing arts groups in a Washington, D.C. suburb need help, they turn to their county recreation agency and, invariably, they receive it. Unlike park and recreation departments whose concern is limited to the avocational aspects of culture, the Recreation Division of the Arlington County, Virginia, Department of Environmental Affairs is seriously involved in day-to-day arts activity. The division, in fact, through its full-time performing arts section, acts almost as an arts council does in providing local art groups with varied services and, in some instances, funding.

The recreation division's involvement with local cultural groups dates back to the 1950s when a children's theater and ballet group both grew out of classes it was conducting. Several years later, the division helped organize a new opera program and agreed also to pay part of the salary of the Arlington Symphony's music director. In 1967, the division decided to go "all the way" in the arts. The performing arts section was reorganized to include six full-time arts professionals, and nonprofit Arlington County arts groups were invited to affiliate with the section and draw upon it for services and salaries.

The performing arts section, whose staff includes a technical director, costume coordinator, production and program supervisors, and a part-time publicity coordinator, operates on an annual budget of $104,000 [1971 figure] ; 80 percent of which is for salaries and 20 percent for programs. Part of this is used to pay the full or partial salaries of the directors of affiliated arts groups. Throughout the year the section conducts workshops, discussion programs, classes, and helps present about 25 to 30 public performances of its affiliated groups. Administrative and technical services include training volunteer workers in the technical aspects of theater, working with boards and artistic directors, and developing community support and outside funding.

In addition to its regular day-to-day activity, the performing arts section is involved in short and long-range special projects. Last spring, for example, it helped develop and find outside funds for a pilot program in dance which resulted in the Arlington Dance Theater becoming a professional company. Currenty the group is engaged in a special 30-week county residency.

September-October 1971

Culture Thrives in a
Former "Arts-poor" County

A poor rural area considered something of a "cultural wasteland" in 1969 has since developed an ongoing program that within three years has brought the arts into the daily life of the community. In Marlboro County, South Carolina, an area of 27,000 residents with the third lowest per capita income in the state, and a county seat, Bennettsville, located 100 miles from the nearest city with available arts activity, three years of effort have resulted in such achievements as the organization of several permanent cultural groups; the introduction of arts programs into the schools; a regular calendar of performances, workshops, and exhibitions, including the first local concerts ever given by a full symphony orchestra and a ballet company; remodeling of the school auditorium; initiation of a regular newspaper column and radio program on the arts; creation of a county arts commission; and the continued involvement and support of individuals, local government and business.

The spark that lit the local fire was an experimental $5000 grant by the South Carolina Arts Council to pay the salary of a community arts coordinator who, it was hoped, could spur cultural activity in the county. At the time, in November 1969, the only county groups were some music clubs, dance bands, and church choirs, and there was no organized force to promote the arts, hold workshops, and sponsor performances. Within three months local leaders, with the help of the coordinator, Mrs. W. H. McIntyre, Jr., the mother of eight, had organized the Marlboro Area Arts Council in Bennettsville, and in April 1970 the new council, as part of the state tricentennial week, sponsored an arts festival, presented a full symphony orchestra concert, helped coordinate a three-performance historical pageant created by local citizens, and supervised a participatory collage by townspeople that was installed in the Bennettsville town square.

In subsequent months, the new council helped organize two new arts groups—Marlboro Players Theater and Marlboro Arts and Crafts Guild—sponsored additional performances, and developed a range of projects designed to involve the entire area in the cultural program. As a result of a clean-up of the four-acre, city-owned gardens with the help of the Jaycees and Boy Scouts, the City Council voted to hire a leading landscape architect to further improve the gardens. Summer classes in the arts were introduced, and the Marlboro Players initiated weekly workshops for teenagers. The local Merchants Association co-operated on a sidewalk art exhibit, and the Recreation Department worked with the council on a parks and recreation study. Involvement with the school system resulted in county education authorities using emergency assistance act funds to start a program of arts instruction in the schools, and council initiation of a program to remodel the 1902 school auditorium for performances won the active support and participation of local industry, schools, and organizations.

A major test for the embryonic organization came in 1971 when it initiated a membership and funding campaign to supplement funds granted by the state council on a decreasing three-year basis (a total of $8660). The resulting drive brought in 650 members—the largest enrollment of any organization of any type in the county. In addition, both new organizations founded by the council, the Players and the Arts and Crafts Guild, conducted their own separate membership drives successfully.

According to coordinator Lucy McIntyre, the effects of three years of "analyzing, planning, pursuing, hoping, and backing up" are really beginning to show. "Marlboro County had little of this before and I think it improved our area. People are asking to help," she told *AM*, "and are casting aside personal prejudices to work side by side." Small signs indicate the progress. The movie theater owner, for example, scheduled good children's films all summer as a result of discussions with the council. The county began sending arts council resumes to industries considering the area for the location of new plants.

Currently, the council is engaged in its largest undertaking—sponsorship of a concert by the Atlanta Symphony Orchestra on January 12 in Bennettsville, a program that will cost $2000. An all-out campaign was launched in late November with the appointment of "ticket ambassadors," development of in-school programs on the symphony orchestra, a poster contest, and a ticket sale program offered by service and civic clubs in the area. On the first ticket sale day, one-fourth of all tickets were sold. The council is optimistic that the performance will be sold out well in advance.

Even with its record of success thus far, the council isn't sitting still. Future plans include a broader art and music program in the schools, greater professionalism in arts undertakings, a yearly cultural festival, regular Saturday workshop programs in the crafts, and presenting several high calibre concert groups as well as opera, ballet, or symphony programs every season.

November-December 1972

Politics and Art

In December 1971, the Erie County Legislature voted to withhold a $25,250 grant from the Studio Arena Theatre's school unless the theater guaranteed not to sponsor "morally objectionable presentations." At issue was the theater's ear-lier sponsorship of several performances of *Hair* by a touring company. Studio Arena's board stood up to the challenge and issued a public statement support-ing the management and artistic direction of the theater. It asserted that "great art is free art" and asked the legislature to reconsider its action and "grant us funds without contingencies." Buffalo newspapers, in their editorial coverage of the situation, were strongly critical of the legislature's stand.

In the following months, when the legislature's Education and Cultural Af-fairs Committee reviewed the grant situation, it received a statement from thea-ter trustees declaring that the school "never sponsored or produced 'morally ob-jectionable presentations' and has no intentions of doing so in the future." This statement apparently provided a way out of the situation. The committee rec-ommended approval of the grant without strings attached, and several days later the legislature concurred.

In New York, a leading arts institution unwittingly became involved in a political tale involving a movie, the mayor, and money. The film *The Hot Rock,* which raised more than $300,000 as a controversial benefit showing for the Lindsay for President campaign, had been shot at the Brooklyn Museum. (Twen-tieth Century Fox reportedly paid the museum an $8000 fee plus overtime for personnel.) According to reports, the political benefit killed the possibilities of a planned museum benefit in Brooklyn, which would have netted about $40,000.

January-February 1972

CANADA

Government Agency in
Canada Becomes Impresario

In its first full season, 1974-75, Canada's newest impresario will do over $1 mil-lion a year business. In an ambitious and unusual undertaking, the Canada Coun-cil, the country's official government agency for the arts, established a Touring Office this April that combines the services of a booking agency with those of an information bank, tour coordinator, press agent, and subsidy source. As its pri-mary activity, the office will organize, publicize, and in some instances subsidize tours by Canadian performing companies and artists to communities throughout the country. Also, it will coordinate and promote the tours of foreign companies in Canada and cooperate with the government's Department of External Affairs in broadening touring opportunities abroad for Canadian companies.

The need for a national booking office has been growing since the centen-nial year of 1967, when with the opening of Expo '67 the government gave addi-tional money to the arts and sent some dozen leading Canadian companies on tour around the country. Since then, many Canadian companies expressed interest in greater touring opportunities if funding could be made available, and communities not on the regular tour path demanded visits by groups their tax dollars helped support. (When the National Ballet of Canada toured *Sleeping Beauty* last year, it did not perform in such large cities as Edmonton, Calgary, Regina, and Winnipeg.) Because Canadian impresarios weren't large enough to serve communities throughout the country, the council, following consultations with arts leaders, decided to take on the job itself.

"We're not trying to take over from the private impresario," Andre Fortier, the Canada Council's director told *AM*. "Where a commercial manager has the necessary organization, we will work with him and eventually hope to forge a link with him."

Although the Touring Office is just getting organized this year, it will aid and service tours already set for the coming season and in some instances provide money for additional performances. Also, the Office's own publicity department will at times produce special press materials including window cards, biographies, advertising mats, and releases. "There's no point in touring the provinces," added publicity coordinator Helga Stephenson, "unless you back it up with publicity. Our aim is to develop local sponsors and to make small communities self-sufficient." The office, which will provide advice on every aspect of touring from the central information bank it is developing, also plans to publish a detailed directory of organizations, facilities, and individuals in the arts in Canada. Operating with a staff of seven, it anticipates a budget of approximately $1 million.

While developing the Touring Office, the Canada Council is concerned also with a variety of other major new projects. Through "Explorations" the Council will make grants to a wide range of innovative programs in the arts, humanities, and social sciences, with applicants chosen through national competition. Under its Art Bank program, the Council will spend $5 million over the next five years to purchase works by professional Canadian artists for rental to departments and agencies of the federal government. As its programs expand, the council is also making major efforts to strengthen its relationship with the arts community. "Our whole approach now," Mr. Fortier told *AM*, "is to expose ourselves to the public. Operating from the national capital our presence really wasn't visible. We're trying to change that now. We're going on the road more."

Going on the road means more frequent visits by Mr. Fortier and council staff members to different areas of the country where open meetings are held. "We'll be criticized at the meetings," added Fortier, "but that's what we get paid for. And if the criticism is valid, we'll bow to it." This June, for example, Fortier, his chairman, and vice chairman spent a week holding public meetings in the maritime provinces.

In addition, council staff members normally visit a different province every quarter, and the entire council of 21 members, annually visits one province for a week of open meetings with artists, heads of cultural groups, the press, and anyone else who wishes to attend. This October the council's visit to Ontario will include open meetings in Toronto, Hamilton, and London.

As its program grows, the council has become increasingly concerned with finding ways to increase arts funding from all sources. Currently, the council's 1973-74 budget of $20 million for aid to all aspects of the arts excluding museums—they are funded by a separate government program—is supplemented by an additional $20 million in arts aid by provinces, municipalities, and the private sector. "What I foresee by the beginning of the eighties is the need for $150 million in aid to the arts from all sectors," Mr. Fortier said. "If we believe we should spread the arts and bring art to people, then organizations like ours must quadruple our funding."

One result of this kind of prognosis is that for the first time there is a definite interest by the council in stimulating new areas, such as business, to support culture. Currently, business in Canada gives less than $4 million annually to the arts.

September-October 1973

FEDERAL GOVERNMENT:
A CHRONOLOGY OF DEVELOPMENTS

Arts and Humanities
Foundation Established

Federal subsidy to the arts is here. After Congress rejected financial aid to the arts for more than a decade, it passed a bill establishing the National Foundation on the Arts and Humanities in September 1965.

The bill authorizes, but does not guarantee, up to $10 million a year, for three years for the arts and an equivalent sum for the humanities. In addition, up to $500,000 per year for three years will be available to the Commissioner of Education to strengthen instruction in the arts and the humanities. Although funds have been authorized, they have not been appropriated. A request for funds is expected to be submitted to Congress soon.

In signing the bill on September 29, President Johnson pinpointed as Foundation priorities the creation of a national repertory theater; support of a national opera and national ballet company; creation of a national film institute; commissioning of new musical works by American composers; support of symphony orchestra; and grants to bring artists-in-residence to schools and universities.

The legislation, which its Senate manager, Claiborne Pell of Rhonde Island, termed "the most meaningful of its kind we have ever considered" establishes two fund-granting agencies under the new Foundation, a National Endowment for the Arts and a National Endowment for the Humanities. The chairman of each arm has complete authority to make grants in his area.

A newly established Federal Council on the Arts and Humanities will "advise and consult" with the two Endowments and will "promote coordination" between them.

The National Council on the Arts, established by Congress in 1964, will review applications for financial assistance made under the act and will make recommendations on them to the Arts Endowment chairman. Neither the national nor the federal council, however, will have veto power over grant-giving decisions made by the chairmen of the two Endowments.

Under provisions of the Arts Endowment, grants-in-aid will be available to nonprofit, tax-exempt arts organizations, state agencies, and "in appropriate cases" to individuals. Although the legislation primarily is aimed at support for professional arts activities, funds are also available for amateur "workshop" activities.

Most often, grants to groups will be on a matching basis, and will not exceed 50 percent of the total cost of a project or production. In some instances, however, groups may obtain more than 50 percent if they can show they were unsuccessful in attempts to raise funds equal to the amount they requested of the Arts Endowment.

Projects eligible for Arts Endowment support, as outlined in the bill, include artistically significant productions emphasizing professional excellence and "American" creativity; professional productions that would be unavailable to many citizens without such support; projects that help artists to achieve standards of professional excellence; workshops encouraging public appreciation of the arts; and other relevant projects including surveys, research, and planning in the arts.

The Humanities Endowment will award grants, loans, and fellowships to institutions and individuals for training and workshops in the humanities and support research, study and the publication of scholarly works.

Of the approximately $20 million a year authorized to be appropriated equally between the arts and the humanities, $5 million may be available immediately to each. In addition, the Endowments, which are eligible to receive donations of money and other properties, may receive funds matching the gifts received—up to $5 million a year for the humanities and $2.25 million for the arts.

An important beneficiary of the Arts Endowment will be state arts council's; $2.75 million a year can be allocated to their programs, with each state council eligible to receive up to 50 percent of the total cost of an approved project. In addition, those states without councils may receive up to $25,000 for the purposes of conducting a study that will lead to the establishment of a council.

According to the law, the chairman of each Endowment will have, in effect, complete control over his operation. In addition to grant-making powers, he will have the authority to accept gifts, order payment withheld if recipients of grants fail to comply with provisions of the law, appoint employees and consultants, establish an office, and "make other necessary expenditures."

The chairman of the Arts Endowment, who will have a four-year term of office, will be "the individual appointed as Chairman of the National Council on the Arts." Roger L. Stevens is the first council chairman.

The law authorizes specific funds only until June 30, 1968. After that date, Congress will have to authorize additional funds.

Of special importance to arts leaders who fear government control is Section 4(c) of the legislation. This prohibits government supervision or control over the policy or administration of any nonfederal agency, institution, organization, or school.

October 1965

Government Groups
Question Arts Program

Several events in April 1966 raised anew the question of whether government support of the arts might mean government interference in program content. In California, the Los Angeles County Board of Supervisors demanded that several of the tableaus of artist Edward Kienholz, in his exhibition at the Los Angeles County Museum of Art, be altered on the grounds that they were pornographic in nature. The board threatened to withdraw public support from the museum or order closing of the exhibition if the suggested alterations were not made. The exhibition opened as scheduled with one alteration made—the door of one of the works, *Back Seat Dodge,* remained closed. However, the museum refused to remove a reclining figure from the work *Roxy.*

In a unique response to the situation, the California Arts Commission, a state agency, issued a public statement deploring the county board's action. It read:

> In view of the recent effort to censor work of Edward Kienholz in Los Angeles, the California Arts Commission wishes to reaffirm its policy with respect to the freedom of artistic expression. The Commission declares and strongly condemns any efforts on the part of any political or legislative bodies to control or censor the free expression and exhibition of artistic works. It contends that the decisions and appraisals regarding performance and exhibitions be left to the discretion of the boards and professional staff of artistic institu-

tions, organizations and museums, and to the discernment of the public.

Meanwhile, in Washington, D.C., some congressmen questioned the content of the program of the National Endowment for the Arts. They contended that, among other things, the Endowment was not telling them in advance how funds were to be disbursed. In a report to the House of Representatives on the Endowment's budget requests, the House Appropriations Committee suggested that "extreme care must be exercised that those responsible for the administration of the program do not unduly influence through the award of grants the type of style of art which is to be cultivated in this country." The report also recommended that "in the early phases of this program more emphasis be placed on the award of grants to established foundations, organizations and institutions rather than to numerous individuals in the field."

May 1966

Roger Stevens Reviews Endowment Program

The National Endowment for the Arts initiated its program under the direction of Chairman Roger L. Stevens. In this exclusive 1967 interview with AM *editor Alvin H. Reiss, Mr. Stevens discussed the Endowment's past program and examined its future prospects.*

Q: Mr. Stevens, are you satisfied with the progress made by the Arts Endowment?

A: Yes, considering the small amount of money we were given. In our first two years we've granted $6.5 million for programs and $2 million to state arts councils. For fiscal year 1968 our budget will be $4.5 million for programs and $2 million for states.

Q: Do you anticipate problems with budget appropriations in the future?

A: I think that congressional support for the Endowment is growing. One of our handicaps has been that the big deficit in the entire government program affects us, and for this reason it is difficult to secure the full authorization.

Q: How big a budget would you need to do the job you would like to do?

A: About $150 million a year. This is not an unrealistic figure, when it is considered that the Science Foundation receives $500 million a year. By fiscal year 1969, we will ask for $25 million and the following year we will ask for $50 million. It is reasonable to think that we can get these amounts authorized, but whether they will be appropriated is another question.

Q: What are your future program plans?

A: Up till now, the one area of the arts that has received insufficient attention is music, and we would like to undertake some important programs in this discipline. We are organizing a completely separate music panel to examine what can be done. Ideally, we would need $25 million for music alone. The Ford Foundation has helped to stem the tide, but there are still many needs.

Q: How have art leaders responded to the Endowment program thus far?

A: On the whole, the response has been excellent. Specifically, our visual arts program has been highy praised, and the establishment of the so-called laboratory theater groups has been very well received. We are now planning to establish another such group in the Watts area of Los Angeles.

Q: The development of state arts councils has been slow until now. Do you think it was correct to authorize study funds before state councils had proven themselves?

A: The appropriation of funds for state council studies was included in the legislation creating the Endowment, and it is something that we have to honor. By July 1 we will review all of the state council reports, and we will tell the councils if we think they are making mistakes in their planning. We do not plan to dominate the councils or impose our thinking on them, but we would like to exercise our right of review and be as helpful as we can, in an advisory capacity.

Q: What about the Endowment's relationship to private organizations, such as foundations? Can this be strengthened?

A: We have research and staff facilities in the arts far surpassing anything the foundations have. We encourage foundations, and corporations also, to come to us and we will be very happy to work with them in the development of programs. Not enough do so now. In order to develop better coordination between our office and large foundations active in the arts, we've held several meetings with them recently.

Q: The Endowment has been slow in developing programs in the area of arts administration. Why is this so?

A: The only two times I have been turned down by the National Council on the Arts has been when I suggested arts administration programs. For some reason the council is not attuned to the needs in this area. I still have hopes that the situation will change and that arts administration programs can be developed in the near future.

Q: What are the remaining unsolved problems facing the arts?

A: I think that the most pressing problem is education, and everything relates to this. For example, let me illustrate four separate areas of concern. First, teachers in primary and secondary schools generally do not have a good background in the arts. Second, most colleges do not look favorably on high school arts credits. Third, except for those who specialize in the arts, the average college graduate isn't sufficiently exposed to the arts. Last, we are not sufficiently educating the audiences we're trying to develop. The public must realize that preparation is needed to fully appreciate the arts. We hope to work closely with the U.S. Office of Education in a coordinated approach to these problems.

Summer 1967

Nancy Hanks Discusses Endowment Program

Shortly after Miss Nancy Hanks assumed the chairmanship of the National Endowment for the Arts, AM *editor Alvin H. Reiss interviewed her. Three years later, in 1973, Mr. Reiss again interviewed Miss Hanks to discuss the Endowment's progress since 1969 and its future prospects.*

Q: How would you evaluate the progress of the Endowment in the past three years? What do you think were the most important accomplishments during this period?

A: We feel there was much progress made toward greater public awareness of the needs of the arts, and the great potential they have for improving the quality of life. This change in attitude may have been the most important accomplishment of this period. In addition, Congress and the president continued to give strong bipartisan support to the arts both in public statements and with greatly increased funding for the National Arts Endowment.

Q: In regard to programs, what do you consider to be the major developments?

A: A number of important new programs were established. The Museum Program, which began in 1971 with $1 million, last year accounted for more than $4 million of our budget. The Expansion Arts Program, designed to encourage community-based, professionally directed activities, began in fiscal 1971 and in one year went from $307,600 to $1,137,088. We hope that funding for this area will continue to increase. During the same period, we undertook a new program in public media, and we are now beginning to see some very excellent results from it. We were also pleased with the growth of the Artists-in-Schools program and the tenfold development of the Jazz Program.

Q: The Endowment will be up for reauthorization in the next few months. What would be the ideal kind of action that could be taken in Congress regarding authorization and funding?

A: We hope that we will be reauthorized for three years and that Congress will continue to give us the kind of firm support that it has in the past. Since fiscal

1971, our budget has been increased nearly fivefold. Our experience of the past three years has confirmed our belief in the basic validity of the legislation as originally drawn by Congress and, therefore, we would hope it would remain substantially the same.

Q: A figure of $200 million in federal funds for the arts by 1976 has been suggested. Do you consider this to be a realistic goal?

A: The "art of budget" at the Endowment is designed to be responsive to the demands of people and the arts. We are hardly through our planning for fiscal years 1974 and 1975, and planning for fiscal 1976 is in a very preliminary stage.

Q: What do you feel are the greatest challenges facing you and the Endowment now?

A: The challenge to maintain the flexibility to be responsive to the greatly changing demands of the public and the resultant needs of the arts. I am speaking both in terms of policies and procedures.

Q: What is the possibility of arts workers throughout the country having a greater voice in the Endowment's future policy planning?

A: We are constantly looking for new ways to involve people, and welcome ideas and suggestions from anyone. The staff is always glad to talk with people when they are in Washington and when they are out on field visits. Much of our work is accomplished with arts councils at the state level, and we plan to continue our strong emphasis on input from this source with meetings and conferences held in regional areas. We also rely on our advisory panel members, who are listed by name and area in our annual reports. They are all distinguished practitioners in their respective fields, and we find their insights and advice to be based on very practical experience.

Q: What are the prospects for increased state funding of the arts?

A: There have been significant breakthroughs in funding for the arts in several states in recent years, which appears to be a trend. Funds for the councils and commissions in the states themselves have gone from $2,664,640 in fiscal 1966 to approximately $23,600,000 in the current fiscal year, a figure that will probably be increased in coming months. In addition, there are a number of special projects funded from the Arts Endowment through the states, particularly the Artist-in-Schools program and the Coordinated Residency Touring program.

Q: Are there any new plans for increased attention to the funding of programs to train arts administrators at every level?

A: Yes, we would hope there would be more recognition from the field of the important need for this training, which we feel is a very critical area. We are very pleased with the pilot training programs we have established, and hope to see them expanded.

Q: What do you consider to be the remaining major unsolved problems facing the arts?

A: It is not "the problems facing the arts" that I am worried about; there will always be problems and they will always be solved. What concerns me most is the continuing lack of understanding of the potential of the arts for all of our society.

Q: What can arts groups and individuals do in the coming months to help the Endowment best state its case to Congress?

A: Write on!

January-February 1973

Government Involvement

With arts planks in both major party platforms and specific pro-arts statements made by both presidential candidates, considerable excitement was generated in the arts community during the recent campaign. This was in marked contrast to 1972, when the arts were virtually invisible politically with a few scattered exceptions such as special statements published in *AM* by George McGovern and by Leonard Garment, who responded on behalf of President Nixon at the President's request.

Also, President Ford used the occasion of a Medal of Freedom presentation to Martha Graham at the White House to announce that he would ask Congress for $50 million more over the next three years for challenge grants for the arts.

In more local situations, such as in the state of Washington, where five gubernatorial candidates responded to four specific questions asking for their positions on arts issues, candidates seemed to have a new awareness of the arts. Local arts funding, however, as indicated in the recent Survey 3 of the Council on Foundations, is a growing problem, with severe cutbacks expected and already evident at city, county, and state levels. In two key New York counties, for example, the situation was critical with budgets under consideration proposing to completely eliminate arts support. In Erie, the Buffalo area, more than $2 million is at stake, while in Suffolk on Long Island, the potential loss is $200,000. Arts leaders in both areas were rallying support, attending public sessions in force, and meeting with legislators in attempts to get the cuts restored.

On the legislative front, there were several significant developments. Nationally, the first copyright revision since 1909 was passed, as was a tax revision bill which, in its final version, dropped a provision favoring credits for artists' charitable donations of their own works. Reauthorization for the Arts and Humanities Endowments for the next four years also passed, with provisions for appropriation ceilings of $93.5 million for fiscal 1977 and $108 million for 1978 for each Endowment. The legislation also approved challenge grants on a one-to-three match up to $18 million for fiscal 1978.

Perhaps the most significant news at the state level was passage of California legislation providing royalty payments to visual artists of 5 percent of the resale price of works selling in excess of $1000 if the resale is at a profit. Royalties are payable when sellers reside in California or the resales occur within the state.

September-October 1976

Politicalization and Popularization

With the naming of Livingston Biddle, Jr. to head the National Endowment on the Arts in October 1977, a long period of rumor-mongering and uncertainty finally ended. Events leading up to the decision, however, precipitated some internal struggles within the arts that brought the hitherto serene arts-government relationship into the public eye and introduced such words as "politicalization" and "popularization" into the general vocabulary.

Early in October, Michael Straight, the NEA's former deputy director, charged that both the Arts and Humanities Endowments were being politicized by the Administration and by vested interest groups, citing the appointment of Joseph P. Duffy as NEH head and Joan Mondale's preeminent role in the arts as examples. A week later, Vice President Mondale used the swearing-in ceremony for Duffey, who also has been appointed chairman of the Federal Council on the Arts and Humanities, to lash out against politicalization charges.

Meanwhile, the kind of behind-the-scenes government-arts activity that is seldom brought to public view provided the basis for three long articles in the Sunday, October 16, 1977 issue of the *New York Times,* all of which carried real or implied criticism of government's role in the arts at the federal and state levels. Under the heading, "Will Government Become the Modern Medici?" the *Times* ran articles dealing with the presumed threat of politicalization, the funding of both "high and low" culture by the New York State Council on the Arts, and the way in which Livingston Biddle was chosen as Nancy Hanks' successor.

Developments elsewhere, including the opening of new Washington offices by arts advocacy forces and the stepped-up lobbying activities by organizations fighting for increased government funding, have led to suggestions of internal differences among arts groups. One thing seems certain: the arts, more than ever before, have gone public. In spite of the negative overtones of some of the recent reports, an *AM* spot check of several top administrators showed a general feeling that the public airings were healthy and were perhaps the best safeguard against real politicalization.

September-October 1977

New Directions Seen
for Arts Endowment Programs

The National Endowment for the Arts is moving to strengthen its relationships with two key minority groups—blacks and Hispanics. Although his duties have not been totally defined as yet, Gordon Braithwaite, former director of Special Projects, will move to a newly created post as the Endowment's liaison to the black community. In general terms, Braithwaite will work with all of the NEA's program areas to insure their consciousness of black needs, act as a kind of ombudsman for black groups who feel their funding needs haven't been given adequate hearing, and represent the chairman in meetings with black and other minority groups, many of them small and struggling, throughout the country.

At the same time, the NEA is moving towards greater recognition of the needs of the Hispanic community. A task force in Hispanic arts, established by the National Council on the Arts in 1977 at the urging of Hispanic leaders, has held several meetings and regional sessions since April 1978 and will report to the National Council this November. The force, which includes some 25 Hispanic arts leaders in its membership, hopes to present a full series of recommendations to the council by next May. The creation of a national service organization is expected to result from the present activity.

Meanwhile, two other NEA task forces are moving towards completion of their efforts. The final set of conclusions will be presented by the arts education group to the November meeting of the National Council, with a public report expected to be issued shortly afterwards. A major focus of the education force is on that training of both artists and arts educators. A task force on Fashion/Design, which will come up with a series of recommendations for NEA support, was organized following an April 28, 1978 meeting in New York attended by NEA representatives and fashion designers, historians, journalists, and educators. Other constituencies also have been knocking at the NEA door. In August, 14 national and regional service organizations based in New York met with Chairman Biddle and other top NEA staffers to explain their programs and present a case for increased funding.

In an area of major impact, Federal-State Programs, a draft of new program policy recommendations has been introduced. The recommendations, which still are subject to further review, will most probably be adopted for "Transition Year" use since full adoption must await Congressional reauthorization of the Endowment in fall 1979. A key concept is the movement towards multi-year state program design, with plans calling for about 18 states annually to each present three-year program plans for review. Also, a small portion of state funding would be dependent upon that state's record of appropriations to the arts. A recommended budget formula would set aside 82 to 85 percent for basic state operating grants ($275,000 per state in Fiscal 1979) 12 to 14 percent for basic regional operating grants, and 3 to 5 percent for government support services funds including national service organization functions and pilot projects.

Summer 1978

Organizations of
Government Officials Aid Arts

Recognition of the arts by organizations of officials at virtually every level of government continues to grow. Although official recognition through resolutions or program platforms has not been an automatic trigger for increased support, it has helped engender legislators' awareness of arts needs and provided a useful first step to more active involvement by government groups in the arts. At the same time, it has provided an opening wedge into different levels of government for opportunistic arts administrators.

In November 1978 in Denver, for example, the National Conference of State Legislators, which represents over 7500 state legislators and their staffs, will host the first meeting of its new task force on the arts. Headed by Senator Alan Sieroty of California and funded by a $25,000 NEA grant, the task force will develop a clearinghouse of information on the arts for legislators and make recommendations on where and how state legislative support to the arts can be increased. The NCSL passed a resolution on arts support in August 1977.

The National Governors' Association, at its meeting late in the summer of 1978, passed a nine-point policy position paper on public support of the arts. Presented by its Subcommittee on the Arts, headed by Governor Brendan Byrne of New Jersey, the paper included references to increasing state appropriations, exerting influence on corporations to up arts support, and supporting educational programs that integrate the arts into the curriculum. The paper also indicated concern that Congress has not provided separate funding for mandated statewide conferences on the arts and humanities. City managers also gave recognition to the arts. At the annual meeting of the International City Management Association in Cincinnati in October 1978, the organization held its first sessions on arts support and agreed to promote the arts through its publications.

At its annual convention in Atlanta in July 1978, the National Association of Counties adopted a resolution on the arts, a five-point statement patterned after the arts resolution written by *AM* editor Alvin H. Reiss and passed by the U.S. Conference of Mayors in 1974. The convention also marked the first meeting of the NAC's arts task force, whose activities are being supported by an NEA grant. NAC also was collecting and analyzing data from its survey on county involvement in the arts which it distributed to 3500 members.

Meanwhile, the U.S. Conference of Mayors, through its Urban Arts Project chaired by Mayor Maynard Jackson of Atlanta and supported by the NEA, released a position paper in reaction to the passage of Proposition 13 in California titled, "The Taxpayers' Revolt and the Arts." The document, which provides succinct arguments for local government support for the arts, is available from the project at 1620 Eye Street, N.W., Washington, D.C. 20006. The conference will meet again in St. Louis November 24, 1978, with a wide range of arts activities built around the meeting.

Greater local government interaction with the arts on a pragmatic basis may be one result of a recent first-time conference held in Minneapolis on "The Role of the Arts in Urban Economic Development." The four-day meeting involved participants in working sessions which tackled such specific areas of concern as development of special arts districts, rehabilitation with a focus on arts use, and city-sponsored cultural programs. The meeting drew nearly 40 percent of its participants from areas of urban involvement including city planners, legislators, and community development specialists.

September-October 1978

*A Union 76 gas station attendant helps to promote
Seattle Opera performances. (Courtesy of Seattle Opera Association)*

Business and the Arts

RATIONALE FOR SUPPORT

Sorensen Sees
New Corporate Obligations

Theodore C. Sorensen

I congratulate those firms with the vision to recognize—and the initiative to act upon—the unmistakable fact that corporate support of art or culture, or corporate wars on poverty or prejudice, are indeed in their enlightened self-interest. Their actions are not only profitable—they are commendable. But are they enough? Is self-interest, no matter how enlightened, ever enough? Is a corporation to support the arts, or to engage in other public-spirited activities, only when it can find an economic benefit? Are there no broader motivations, no higher obligations?

I believe there are. I believe that gradually, almost imperceptibly to many of those closest to the scene, the modern corporation has evolved into a social as well as an economic institution. Without losing sight of its need to make a profit, it has concerns and ideals and responsibilities that go far beyond the profit motive. It is no more expected to confine itself to economic issues than the modern clergyman is expected to speak only of religion, or the modern educator only of education. It has become, in effect, a full-fledged citizen, not only of the community in which it is located, but of the country and world we all inhabit. And what would become of that country and world if all of its citizens acted only out of self-interest? What if every citizen supported art or public charities or took part in public affairs only in the expectation of an economic gain?

When I was a student of law, the old casebooks on corporation law laid the same stress on economic self-interest as the literature pertaining to this conference. The old common-law rule required the showing of a direct corporate economic benefit before the corporation's funds could be used for any outside purpose.

Today, as a lawyer, I am willing to predict that the courts of our time, if necessary, would uphold corporation expenditures for the public good even without a showing of even indirect economic benefit to the corporation.

The trend of the law merely reflects the trend of history. Two world wars, a depression, a civil rights revolution, the effects of industrialization and automation, and a host of other changes have impressed upon our corporations their obligations of citizenship. The decline of kings and clergy as patrons of the arts and the reduced proportion of great personal fortunes as the result of tax structures have combined to increase the role and responsibility of the corporation. Business enterprises, like all other citizens, recognize now more clearly than ever that they can survive and succeed only in an atmosphere of liberty, progress, and prosperity—and that that amosphere must be nationwide, not merely local.

No doubt, in this age of specialization, many business leaders will plead that they have no interest in problems outside their business. That we cannot afford. We are all citizens first and businessmen or lawyers or doctors or whatever second. The corporation's influence upon our country, its power for good and for progress, imposes upon it obligations of citizenship and leadership, which it has no choice but to accept—in support of good art, yes, and in support of the good society as well.

May 1966

Gingrich Cites Stanton Talk on Business and Arts

Arnold Gingrich

Speaking before a joint meeting of the Arts Council of Columbus, Ohio and the Columbus Area Chamber of Commerce, Dr. Frank Stanton of CBS observed that business is learning that "it is not an island unto itself and that it both nourishes and is nourished by all those other activities that give any society character, richness, variety, and meaning."

No more eloquent answer than Dr. Stanton's has been given to the isolationism of those die-hard "business firsters," whose heads are still stuck ostrich-like beneath the barren sands of such bleak dicta as Cal Coolidge's "the business of America is business" and Engine Charlie Wilson's "What's good for General Motors is good for the country." In the Columbus speech, Dr. Stanton forecast a new degree of empathy between commerce, industry, and the arts, "fostered by a new breed of American . . . a breed in league with the arts"—one who "rejects an environment that says that the only concern of business is the 30-day balance sheet."

Those in the field of financing and managing of the arts who must still contend with specimens of the old breed can find not only consolation, but also ammunition in some of Dr. Stanton's remarks.

Here are some of the cogent reasons he cited to explain why alert business managements are now expressing greater interest in the arts: to attract a larger share of the country's graduating college students to business than the mere 12 percent of them who now make it their first choice; to provide added incentive in recruiting able employees for plant communities; to earn and keep the respect of the nation's public and private sectors; to better the understanding of the human values of business; and to elevate the level of business communications.

Citing the great wave of corporate support of education in the eight years from 1956 to 1964 when it rose by 127 percent, Dr. Stanton foresaw a similar wave in the offing of corporate support of the arts:

Education, generally, has a much more easily observed relationship with all other institutions than the arts do, but I don't believe that it has an any more valid one. And I am not sure that the arts are not ultimately the meeting ground where liberal education and progressive business come together. The purpose of liberal education is, basically, to enable us to make distinctions. The essence of successful business practice is to operate on distinctions. The arts carry distinctions to their logical, and very often their illogical, extremes. And so the first place to worry about American life losing its vital qualities of individualism is in the arts. If this happens, no liberal education will save our kind of society, and no business enterprise will long prosper in what is left of it.

In Dr. Stanton's view, "Art is not a remote thing, responsibility for which can be bucked over to some far center of funds or authority. It is the thing that preserves for all life—including business life and perhaps, in a complex industrial society, especially business life—the human scale."

These are brave words—and heartening—for they underline the fact that Dr. Stanton himself exemplifies the new breed of businessman, the rise of whose influence he foresees.

March-April 1967

American Corporations Overseas Create New Image Through Arts

Robert E. Kingsley

We live in an era that is moving towards what McLuhan calls the "Global Village," where the proliferation of mass media offers unprecedented opportunities and perils. But, paradoxically, the communications gap between nations, between cultures, grows. Words have become weapons or, at best, too often are used to frustrate understanding and to magnify differences. Fortunately, we are coming to see that the arts and their creators can play a mediating role by forging links of mutual respect and appreciation.

It is not surprising that the modern business corporation abroad, which can survive and prosper best in an atmosphere of international good will, has come to be an enthusiastic patron of the arts. The example of my own company is cited only because it is familiar to me. Esso affiliates throughout the world have been leaders in sponsoring the plastic arts, literature, music, and other art forms.

Our motivation has been clearcut: to establish, through the arts, a community of interest wth the host nation, to become a part of its cultural life as well as contributing to its economic well-being. We bring to these countries our capital, technology, and management skills; in return, we hope to enrich *ourselves* by supporting the artists and intellectuals whose contributions to the future are as significant as our own.

Quite honestly, the overseas U.S. corporation is at times victimized by un-reasoning nationalism which rejects everything foreign. The other side of the coin is the widespread belief, especially in underdeveloped areas, that the U.S. expatriate or businessman has little interest and less respect for the national cul-ture. Yet both industry and the arts are needed if a nation is to develop to the full its material and cultural life.

I realize that in many ways Esso and other progressive U.S. corporations have been subversive in undermining the stereotype of callous and exploitive business. Our support of the arts has been one element in shattering the false image of U.S. business abroad. But it has brought us, more than any other effort has, closer to the creative people who are fashioning the new world in which we all want to live.

September-October 1968

Public Relations Counsel Helps
Spur Corporate Support of Arts

William Ruder

The public relations counselor is becoming increasingly effective as a manage-ment member of the American corporation. This gives him added leverage in the role he plays of helping to shape the relationship between the corporation and the arts. Furthermore, the "corporate conscience" has become more and more an area of public relations responsibility. Finally, the corporation has faced the inescapable fact that it must participate in the arena of public issues. It must take a stand. It must be involved in the social turmoil around us. This set of in-volvements is also part of the responsibility of the public relations counselor.

Some of us in the public relations field have discovered that the arts can become an important instrument through which corporate commitment to good citizenship can be expressed. We have also discovered that the arts speak in a uni-versal language—and this can be most helpful in an environment in which the noise level is as high as it is in America.

We have found that through the arts we can express both our good citizen-ship and also develop a technique for communications that can reach individuals and groups as perhaps no other technique can. If the arts speak a universal lan-guage and have an ability to reach and touch as does nothing else, and if the cor-poration can build a communications program that includes art of real quality and integrity within it, then there is a unique set of forces at work.

These discoveries have been made only lately by some of us, though of course the objective facts have been there waiting to be discovered for many years. But perhaps these are the times that will tend to encourage a little ven-turesomeness and a little discovery.

The public relations field, as "keepers of the conscience," as corporate communicators, and as participants in the development of corporate policy where it becomes part of public policy can help to encourage a relationship between the arts and the business enterprise which can become one of the few clear channels through which society's and the corporation's interests can mutually be solved.

November-December 1968

LABOR

Organized Labor Backs Pilot Arts Program

Greater support of the arts by organized labor is in the offing. As a first step in this direction, the AFL-CIO's Department of Community Services, headed by national director Leo Perlis in cooperation with SPACE, a group of unions representing scientific, professional, and cultural employees, is sponsoring a one-year demonstration project in the arts which is being launched in four cities this year—New York, Minneapolis, Louisville, and Buffalo. If successful, the program will be expanded to include other cities throughout the country. According to Mr. Perlis, "This is the first time in the history of the labor movement that the involvement of labor in the arts is being organized in a disciplined fashion."

The current program traces its beginnings back to the annual meetings of the AFL-CIO in San Francisco two years ago when a resolution calling for greater labor participation in the arts was adopted in principle. The resolution was then referred to the organization's executive council, which appointed a special subcommittee to study labor's relationship to the arts. The subcommittee, after surveying the activities of labor unions in the arts, recommended the current program. Recently, Harlowe F. Dean, who will work out of Washington, D.C., was named overall administrator for the program.

The cities picked for the demonstration program were selected from a list of 12 original possibilities on the basis of interested central labor leadership, an active community services program, good local cultural resources, and geographical location. In each of the cities, the labor leadership will take inventory of cultural facilities in the community, survey the current status of local labor participation in the arts, organize two-day seminars bringing together arts and labor leaders, and then develop a list of practical projects. Among the projects which Mr. Perlis told *AM* would be undertaken were labor support in financing cultural programs; its sponsorship of special arts programs in schools and in poverty areas; the free use of union halls for performances; the organization of labor tours to museums; greater labor involvement on cultural boards; and arranging for arts leaders to speak regularly at local union meetings.

In Minneapolis, for example, Frank Sugrue, a representative of the national Department of Community Services, spent three days speaking to local arts leaders and union members recently to win their support for the program there. Plans for a seminar involving the arts and labor have been developed, and business agents representing all member groups of the Central Labor Council have been meeting with officials of the Minneapolis Institute of Art in the hope of developing a joint program.

Although funding of each demonstration project will be the responsibility of organized labor in the participating cities, the AFL-CIO, in its original resolution, appropriated $10,000 for the project. The national organization is now attempting to find additional funds for the project from various sources, including the Endowment for the Arts.

The program is a modest one, but as Mr. Perlis pointed out, "This is not a one-shot idea. We want to do a thorough program on a continuing basis." He admitted to *AM*, however, that the project is not on the high priority list of the AFL-CIO.

January-February 1968

Arts and Labor Groups
Seek New Coooperative Ties

Local labor unions are developing new and interesting ties with arts programs in their communities but, on a national level, a long-hoped-for alliance between the arts and organized labor has not yet materialized. Despite a growing movement towards a shorter work week, increased leisure time, and the generally positive results of a labor demonstration project in the arts some years ago partially funded by the Arts Endowment, AFL-CIO national leadership has not endorsed the arts as a priority concern. However, increased local activity, NEA support, and the emergence of arts-minded labor leaders could lead to significant breakthroughs.

One recent development that promises to bring the fields closer together is the creation of a new arts-labor study group in New York headed by former Labor Secretary W. J. Usery, Jr. The panel, with Ford Foundation funding, will study relations between management and labor and explore development of a continuing forum.

In Cleveland, a new Labor Arts Committee formed by the United Labor Agency last September has commissioned a play about the late labor leader, John L. Lewis, as its first major project in an overall community arts program. The one-man show, "John L. Lewis: Disciple of Discontent," written by Clevelander James A Brown, will be produced by the labor group and funded entirely by it. All profits will be turned over to the committee to help fund other art projects for the 250,000 Cleveland area workers served by the labor agency.

The committee, which is now seeking a top actor and director for the production, is taking a grass roots approach to its overall program in an attempt to open the doors of cultural programs to workers, show them what's available, and then help them to get involved. As its initial activity, it sponsored a labor night at the Playhouse Square Association last fall, which attracted 350 officials from 24 unions to a play and a party preceding it.

In Baltimore, one of the nation's most ambitious labor-arts efforts is bringing cultural programs to workers at the places they work and at union meeting halls. Begun two years ago under the aegis of a newly organized committee on arts and culture of Baltimore's AFL-CIO Council, the program has brought unionists to performances by Center Stage and the Pickwick Players and sponsored a slide show of workers art which ran for two weeks at the Baltimore Museum of Art.

The most significant and far-reaching program aspect, however, has been the Music Appreciation Project conducted by players of the Baltimore Symphony Orchestra in cooperation with the committee. Beginning with a voluntary four-session music appreciation course for interested union members in the summer of 1975, the program expanded into additional courses and free lunchtime concerts for workers in such varied settings as a garment factory, a distillery, and a telephone building cafeteria. Last year the program applied for and won an NEA grant for a two-year project which is enabling Baltimore Symphony players to present 45 lunchtime concerts—one every two to three weeks—and 12 music appreciation courses for workers. The grant also frees Jack Hook, the orchestra's second trombonist and an originator of the program, for half-time duties as project coordinator.

ILGWU official Jerome Breslaw, who chairs the arts committee for the AFL-CIO Council, thinks that the Baltimore experience could be duplicated elsewhere. He advises arts managers to visit their local Central Labor Council to suggest setting up joint programs to reach workers as an audience. "But don't just go to ask them for money," he adds. "It won't work."

In New York, where the AFL-CIO Community Services Committee sponsored the review "I Paid My Dues," last year—it later played the Ford's Theater in Washington under sponsorship of the National AFL-CIO Department of Community Services—the program of the Labor Theater has been growing. A private troupe not affiliated with a union, the theater presents productions oriented to working people and receives free services, rehearsal space, and performance fees from several local unions. In Silver Spring, Maryland, the George Meany Center for Labor Studies, which sponsors courses for union members who come from all over the country, has included both visual and performing arts activities in its program for the past five years, including NEA-sponsored weekly performances. The center will initiate its own ten-week theater season this summer with future plans calling for the development of a touring company.

Ultimately, however, a national arts-labor program must come from a co-ordinated effort between national leaders in both areas. Leo Perlis, head of the AFL-CIO's National Community Services Department, has met with NEA officials from time to time, but nothing concrete on a national level has happened as yet. Labor, he told *AM*, is interested in the arts, but "not to the extent of raising sufficient amounts of money to finance artistic programs on a continuing basis. Labor's money is limited and labor leaders still feel that first things come first, and first things are still union organization, collective bargaining, political action and legislative lobbying."

The NEA, meanwhile, has "substantial interest" in developing labor-arts programs, according to staff member John Clark, and is entertaining proposals for new projects. Also, an intern is now working on a labor-arts booklet. Leo Perlis, who has aided and encouraged many arts-labor programs over the years, is keeping his door open also. "We're here," he told *AM*. "We'll speak to people if they want to speak to us. They may not get money, but we'll try to help."

March-April 1977

VOLUNTEER EXECUTIVE HELP

Corporate Planners Help
Arts Identify Needs

Top corporate planning executives have joined lawyers, accountants, and other business professionals who have developed programs of voluntary aid to the arts. As the precursor to a possible national effort, corporate planners in New York are helping three arts groups with their long-range planning.

The concept of a public service project that would transfer the planning methodology used in business to nonbusiness areas on a voluntary basis was conceived late last year by members of the New York chapter of the North American Society for Corporate Planning. The Society, with ten chapters in the United States and Canada, has nearly 1000 members overall.

When the idea took shape, R. J. Allio, director of corporate planning for Babcock & Wilcox and president of the New York chapter, began to seek out nonbusiness groups that had a need for planning and had a leader who recognized the need and was willing to work with volunteer consultants. Personally interested in the arts, Allio discussed the project with Nancy Hanks and asked the Business Committee for the Arts to suggest several groups. Of the seven projects later undertaken by the chapter, three were for arts groups—Hospital Audiences, Inc., the Municipal Art Society, and the U.S. Institute for Theatre Technology.

According to Allio, the job of the corporate planners (20 volunteer chapter members worked on the seven projects) has been to provide primary skills in planning methodology in order to focus on what an organization's goals were to determine with the organization the strategies needed to reach these goals, and to ascertain if the group had the skills to reach them. "We don't do the planning," Allio told *AM*. "Groups must do their own planning. We give them the format and provide advice and guidance. They try to fill in the empty spaces."

Participating New York arts groups have been unanimous in their praise for the expert volunteer help they've received over the past few months. In conversations with *AM* their directors have talked about the practical scenarios and plans prepared by the consultants which have helped their groups formulate new strategies and develop long-range organizational plans. Said Michael Jon Spencer of Hospital Audiences, "The corporate planners have helped us to clarify priorities and think through solutions."

Meanwhile, across the country, a rehearsal room became a "war room," complete with charts and graphs earlier this season, as top local businessmen helped the Seattle Opera to determine its priorities. One evening a week for three months the executives worked voluntarily with opera staff on a detailed management study which included the analyses of more than 50 different opera projects in production, administration, and education, to determine their community reach, potential for success, and cost in relationship to possible return.

Summer 1971

Executive Help for Fund Drive Offered to Groups by Industry

Need trained and talented executives to help with your fund campaign on a free but full-time basis? Health and welfare organizations for many years have been asking and getting precisely this kind of assistance from business organizations. The New York chapter of the Arthritis and Rheumatism Foundation, for example, has used personnel from such companies as the Metropolitan Life Insurance Company, the New York Telephone Company, IBM, and Sperry Rand in recent fund drives for a month or more of full-time work. Executives-on-loan have been used to meet with prospective donors, to handle clerical work, or to perform tasks demanding special skill, such as accounting.

Some concerns, such as the New York Life Insurance Company, have a regular plan for making retired employees available to nonprofit organizations. These workers are paid full salary by the company. Other companies send young employees whose brightness and energy compensate for a lack of experience. According to one official, corporations rarely send out secretarial help.

The best approach to a corporation for the loan of executive help is a personal visit by a top official of a cultural organization. If nobody within your organization knows an executive of the firm, and if the company is a large one, outline your proposal in writing and send it either to the personnel director or the vice president for public relations of the company. Requests to smaller companies should be addressed to the president.

Be specific about your needs. Tell the company how many employees you require, what skills are most needed, what the duties of assigned workers will be, and the approximate length of time for which workers are needed. Larger corporations generally lend workers for a one-month to six-week period; smaller companies may send employees for several days. If a company requests that a specific worker be used only for certain kinds of duties, it is important that this request be honored.

May 1963

Borrowing Businessmen

Business executives can be key cogs in a fund-raising campaign, especially if they are able to devote full time to it, as 100 of them did in Boston. The executives spent eight weeks working on the 1965 Massachusetts Bay United Fund Campaign, with their salaries paid by their employers. Participating corporations indicated that this action helped them because executives received good training and experience, developed contacts and generated good will for their companies.

June-July 1966

Lawyers Form Organization
to Aid and Counsel the Arts

Legal aid for the arts is a reality. After a year of organization and planning, a New York-based group known as Volunteer Lawyers for the Arts has acquired offices, found seed money for a three-year program, formulated a set of operational guidelines, and served its first "clients." Although one of VLA's principal activities is to provide free legal counsel to nonprofit cultural groups that can't otherwise afford it, the organization also issues publications of interest to the arts and undertakes investigations of arts-related legal problems.

According to VLA president and founder Paul H. Epstein, a New York lawyer, the organization has developed a pilot program, which, if proved successful, can be adapted by lawyers in other states.

Fall 1970

Donated Services

Is your arts group looking to receive expert free counsel and service from lawyers, accountants, architects, personnel executives, or other specialists? You might point out to them that they may be able to deduct a donated service as an advertising expense. According to the IRS, the expenses incurred by executives engaged in civic activities are a deductible business expense if these activities are of a type normally engaged in by their firm, and if they are undertaken primarily as a means of indirect advertising—a way of keeping their name before the public.

September-October 1969

Business Donates Key Personnel
to Community Cultural Programs

In Columbus, Indiana, a corporate personnel executive has just completed a three-month assignment as an acting arts council director while on loan from his company. In Oklahoma City, a former museum education director recently became a full-time arts-business liaison for a local foundation. In both instances, the services of the new cultural administrators were underwritten by interested community business leaders.

Until the end of May 1973, P. E. Braskett was manager of professional employment at the Cummins Engine Company in Columbus, Indiana, a concern long involved in spearheading and supporting cultural development in its community. When the long-brewing idea of creating a local arts council gathered force about two years ago, the Irwin Management Company, a concern in which Cummins board chairman J. Irwin Miller has a direct interest, paid for the services of an outside consultant to survey the local cultural picture. This led directly to the organization and incorporation of the Driftwood Valley Arts Council in August 1972.

Although the council initially operated without a professional staff, it soon became apparent to its leaders that executive help was needed. Since the seed funding available to the council precluded the hiring of a full-time executive at that point, the council turned to Cummins Engine, a firm that had "loaned" executives to organizations before, although never to the arts, for assistance. Fortunately, Cummins had in Braskett an executive who was not only an able administrator, but one who also had been actively involved with the cultural life of the community as a founder of Columbus Pro Musica and as a former president of the Columbus Art Guild.

Serving as acting director of the arts council while continuing to draw his full salary from Cummins, Braskett set out to accomplish three specific goals during his brief tenure as a businessman turned arts manager. By September 15, 1973, when he had returned to his corporate duties, he had accomplished all of them: setting up a permanent headquarters office and installing operational procedures; coordinating a recruitment effort for a new full-time paid director; and organizing and conducting the council's first major fund drive, an effort that topped its $80,000 goal.

Meanwhile, in Oklahoma City, John Kirkpatrick, the head of the Kirkpatrick Oil Company, saw both the need and the possibility for drawing business and the arts into a closer working relationship as a logical follow-up to several in-state seminars organized by the Business Committee for the Arts during the past year. A major supporter of local cultural institutions as well as a BCA member, Kirkpatrick decided to speed up the rapprochment between corporations and cultural groups in the city by placing Mrs. Joseph Smelser on the full-time payroll of the Kirkpatrick Foundation. As the executive director of Business and Arts Development, she will "provide local assistance to businesses who wish to get involved or expand their present involvement in the cultural life of the city."

In her new position, Ms. Smelser, former education director of the Oklahoma Art Center, already has begun to develop a number of special projects, including one designed to use business to help circulate "buried" museum collections. A new Corporate Performing Arts Ticket Program, currently being tested in behalf of the Oklahoma Theater Center, will seek to sell tickets in bulk to companies for distribution to their customers and employees and among children, senior citizens, and the disadvantaged. In return for a company's participation, Ms. Smelser's office will help its ad agency market and promote its involvement.

"We're beginning to identify the needs of businesses in terms of their own self-interest," Ms. Smelser told *AM*, "and package special programs which meet those needs while meeting the needs of the arts as well."

As a liaison between business and the arts, Ms. Smelser hopes to develop a year-round flow of business-arts information—a newsletter will commence publication soon—and hold a series of meetings on such special topics as the involvement of corporate branch offices in the arts.

September-October 1973

Business Skills of Executives Aiding Arts Groups

Increasingly, business executives are utilizing their professional skills and backgrounds on a volunteer basis to help cultural organizations. In Hartford, Connecticut, an Advocate Action Committee has been organized by the Greater Hartford Arts Council to help arts groups with management and technical problems.

Created in 1974, the program already has enlisted some 40 executives on loan from eight major corporations including United Aircraft, Aetna Life, and Heublein to tackle such varied assignments as an accounting project for the Artists Collective; a study on job descriptions, management flow, and pay schedules for the Wadsworth Atheneum; and a study for eight major local cultural groups, including the arts council, on the feasibility of developing centralized administrative services. As another aspect of its activity, enrolled volunteer executives are being used also as speakers and advocates to promote increased funding for the arts at the city, state, and federal levels.

The Arts and Business Council of New York City, meanwhile, is about to initiate an ambitious program which, if successful, could become a prototype for similar projects elsewhere. The Skills/Services/Resources Bank will not only help to bring volunteer corporate consultants to arts groups, but through a special arrangement with New York University, will first train them to understand the operations and needs of cultural institutions.

A curriculum for a course for business volunteers, to be given at NYU has been developed by ABC in cooperation with NYU's Graduate School of Business, School of the Arts and School of Education. Four weekly sessions of two hours each are planned. The project also will tap local business for free secretarial and clerical help for arts groups and for contributions of mechanical services and materials.

In Chicago, executive skills in fund raising are being put to the test this spring through a new all-out campaign on behalf of the Chicago Symphony. A "blue ribbon" committee of businessmen plans to contact every Chicago firm of 50 or more employees in an effort to raise business giving to the orchestra from last year's $450,000 to $700,000. A donated full-page ad in the *Wall Street Journal* and a new businessmen's newsletter will back up personal and mail solicitations.

March-April 1975

Business Volunteer Programs for Arts Growing

Programs to recruit and train business executives and professionals as arts volunteers and board members are growing, especially in New York. The New York Society of Certified Public Accountants, which instituted a volunteer financial advisory service for minority businessmen several years ago, now has expanded the program to include arts groups, In addition to providing accounting aid, volunteers also will serve as ongoing advisors and board members. In management, the Volunteer Urban Consulting Group, which provides the free services of qualified business volunteers to nonprofit groups, recently instituted a clearinghouse program to refer businessmen interested in cultural board membership to arts organizations.

Organizations patterned after New York's Volunteer Lawyers for the Arts are on the increase with Atlanta becoming the tenth city outside New York State (where the program originated) to have such a group. An Iowa Lawyers for the Arts is also in the planning stage. Although a VLA-type Boston office is now defunct, VLA is administering services there through a cadre of Boston volunteer lawyers. In Minneapolis a special legal education program on the arts will be presented on May 20 by the Arts Legal Assistance Program of the Affiliated State Arts Agencies of the Upper Midwest. Topics will include artist rights issues and development of estate and deferred giving plans.

In other arts-business developments, the United Arts Council of Puget Sound in Seattle, one of the first united funds aimed specifically at business, was dissolved and then reorganized as a new Corporate Council for the Arts in the hopes of doubling annual giving from the current $300,000 level. Recipient arts groups are no longer represented on the board but now serve in a separate arts advisory council. In New York, the 65-member Off-Off Broadway Alliance is exploring the initiation of a united fund drive aimed at business, and the Museum of Modern Art has organized a special 12-member business committee with the specific objective of raising $200,000 annually from corporations.

In New Jersey, a statewide Business Arts Foundation has been organized to provide active corporate support to cultural groups. Organized as a membership group with annual business dues ranging from $250 to $5000, the group already has enrolled some 20 members and hopes to attract $100,000 in membership income by late fall. The group's board of businessmen will provide operational and project aid to arts organizations and might consider capital funding as well.

March-April 1976

FREE GOODS AND SERVICES

Free Transportation

Importing something for an exhibition or show? If it's of considerable value or importance, a transportation company may carry the cargo free of charge in return for the publicity value. The Home Lines Steamship Agency of Canada provided round-trip shipping from Europe to Canada for the important "Heritage de France" art exhibition. The same principle can be applied to local hauling as well.

May 1962

Conference Room?

Need a free meeting place for a regional get-together, a seminar, or other group session? Many businesses—newspapers, particularly—offer cultural groups free use of their well-appointed conference rooms if arrangements are made well in advance.

May 1962

Need Staff Members?

A major company in your community may be helpful in easing your personnel woes. Some companies will provide personnel services for you. They will work up job definitions, tell you prevailing wage scales, even conduct interviewing for you. Western Electric in Winston-Salem, North Carolina provides services such as these for the Winston-Salem Arts Council.

April 1963

Movie Theaters

If your group lacks facilities appropriate for fund-raising events, you can often find the space you need in local movie theaters. For example, in West Springfield, Massachusetts, Cinema I & II invites community groups to use their auditoriums for fund-raising events during nonoperating hours. The service is provided to nonprofit organizations without charge.

February 1965

Corporations Lend Aid
to Leading Art Museums

Although many corporations have provided services to arts groups on a one-time basis, there are relatively few examples of corporations that have provided continued assistance over a period of years. One exception is the Baltimore Federal Savings and Loan Association.

In January 1963, the bank agreed to provide three large display cases in its West Room for exhibitions of works from the Walters Art Gallery. The idea originated because of the gallery's acute shortage of display space and its desire to reach a portion of the public who might not otherwise come to the gallery. At the time the program began, the gallery was launching a public drive to raise funds for a building expansion.

Although the program began as an experiment, it has continued regularly since its initiation, with the bank sponsoring six exhibitions annually, each lasting two months. In January and February 1968, for example, the art of the locksmith was featured in an exhibition titled "Under Lock and Key." "Japanese Lacquers" and an exhibition of clocks titled "Timepieces" followed.

The bank, which is a regular member of the gallery, pays for transportation of the art, the insurance and publicity costs of the exhibition, and the printing of exhibition brochures. Located in the heart of the Baltimore business district, the exhibitions have been viewed by thousands of visitors since their inception.

Another museum that is benefiting from corporate support is New York's Museum of Modern Art. For some time, the museum has offered corporate members its Art Advisory Service, a consulting program in which the museum, on a fee basis, selects works of art for companies interested in either purchasing them or borrowing them to display in corporate headquarters. Now, for the first time, a corporate member, the posh Four Seasons restaurant, has used the consulting service to assemble a collection for public display. The exhibition, titled "Five Works in Light and Movement," features works on loan from leading private galleries. Mr. Charles Hesse, who is in charge of corporate relations for the museum, told *AM*, "We hope that the idea of corporations using our service for public exhibitions may start a new trend, and may even encourage some firms to become corporate members."

In Canada, meanwhile, the Montreal Museum of Fine Arts leased nine paintings by young artists to Benson & Hedges, Ltd. The large abstract and pop paintings are now hung high above machines in the cigarette factory, where the 250 workers on the floor can view them daily. In addition to rental fee, the company pays all insurance costs.

March-April 1968

Free Furniture

Do you know local businesses that are moving to new quarters or refurbishing existing ones? They might be willing to give arts groups chairs, desks, and other pieces of furniture they no longer need. When the Exxon Corporation refurnished its offices, it donated, through the Arts and Business Council of New York City, Inc., furniture and business equipment in excellent condition to some 40 different art groups.

March-April 1974

Textile Mill Remnant Bargains
Slash Set and Costume Costs

Theater and opera companies can slash production costs by buying material for costumes and draperies directly at the mill as remnants, rather than through local retail outlets.

One East Coast community opera company told *AM*, "We saved about 90 percent on our material costs for our last show. The bill could have run to $600 or even $700."

In the textile industry, mill remnants are frequently on hand in lengths of a dozen yards or more, and in a variety of styles and shades. Mill managers are glad to turn such remnants, too small for commercial sale, into cash-and-carry deals. A Pennsylvania mill opened its plant on a Saturday recently to show its wares to a theater director. The latter made a 500-yard bargain purchase.

In the immediate vicinity, textile mills can be found through city directories and classified telephone books. For the larger surrounding area, a quick way to locate mills and determine the types of fabric they produce is to consult *Thomas' Register of American Manufacturers*.

March 1962

RETAILERS AID ARTS

Alert Arts Groups Get Help
from Local Department Stores

Department stores represent an important source of potential help to cultural organizations, far beyond giving financial aid in fund drives. Because retailing is highly competitive, stores are constantly searching for new ways to make friends and build prestige in the communities they serve.

An energetic and alert arts manager can suggest many avenues of service to department store executives that can benefit his arts group and the store at the same time. For this reason he should learn as much as possible about local stores, their record of community service, and who in their executive hierarchy makes decisions in such matters.

A community cultural group should make every effort to obtain the active service of a top executive of a leading store on its board. Not only can he guide the organization in work with store people who direct public relations, advertising, and sales promotion, but he can also provide insight into the business community as a whole.

Among the ways department stores can help the arts is to provide free window displays saluting an organization or a special event; feature organizations in pictorial institutional ads; provide volunteer workers; sponsor concerts and exhibitions; provide ticket sales booths; lend rooms for meetings; raise funds; and permit arts groups to use their mailing lists.

Among the many cultural activities of stores that have come to the attention of *AM*: Abraham & Straus in Brooklyn, New York, has started a series of theater seminars for high school students in cooperation with the American National Theatre and Academy that attracted 300 students to its first program; Burdine's in Miami will sponsor an International Art Show in cooperation with the University of Miami; and R. H. Macy in New York recently helped finance a youth concert for 2000 students presented by the West Side Symphony.

The National Retail Merchants Association has given a great impetus to retail store cooperation with the arts by joining *Reader's Digest* in sponsoring an annual awards competition for outstanding community service. The winning entries present fine examples of aid given cultural groups by stores.

In Inglewood, California, the Boston Stores devoted a special sales day to raising funds for local organizations. A store in South Carolina led a campaign to build a regional museum, and a South Dakota store helped build a community auditorium. Ackemann Brothers, Inc. in Elgin, Illinois helped lead a fund-raising drive for a community band shell to be used by local music groups and the civic theater.

The grand opening of Walker-Scott Company in San Diego was used as a fund-raising occasion to assist the local symphony orchestra. The New Orleans Symphony received a tremendous publicity boost from the Krauss Company, which spelled out messages to the community in behalf of the orchestra in lighted letters six-feet high above its marquee.

One of the most unusual services offered by a store is that provided by Loveman, Joseph and Loeb in Birmingham. The store added a children's drama consultant as a full-time member of its public relations staff. Employed by the store since 1957, this specialist tours schools throughout Alabama, Mississippi, and Georgia, conducting workshops in creative drama for teachers and providing free consultative service in formal drama for children.

October 1962

Department Store
Offers Free Ads to Arts

Department stores can be important sources of free advertising for the arts. In Brooklyn, New York, for example, Abraham & Straus, a leading department store, places about 25 advertisements in six major metropolitan newspapers each year promoting cultural events. The advertisements, offered without charge to the arts institutions whose events are featured, generally include noncommercial messages about the department store.

Such organizations as the Delacorte Mobile Theater, the Brooklyn Ballet Guild, and the Brooklyn Academy of Music are among the institutions that have benefited from the store's advertising program. In addition to paying for the cost of the advertisements, A & S also prepares the art work for them.

While advertisements vary in size, they are usually two to three columns wide and 150 lines long. At times they fill an entire page. A full-page advertisement in the *New York Times*, one of the newspapers most frequently displaying the advertisements, costs the store more than $5000.

Furthermore, the store has sponsored performances by several of the organizations featured in the advertisements. This summer it presented the Delacorte Mobile Theater's production of Shakespeare's *A Midsummer Night's Dream*, which was held in Brooklyn's Prospect Park.

William Toby, vice president in charge of advertising, public relations, and sales promotion for the store, told *AM* that his company pays for the advertisements to "identify itself with programs that arouse community interest." He said that letters received from the public indicate a warm response to these efforts.

No rigid formula exists for approaching the store for free advertisements, and each request is weighed individually. However, organizations must have an official civic affiliation and must be nonprofit.

In many cases the store's efforts to promote arts groups have reached far beyond free advertisements and the sponsorship of events. It recently donated a booth on one of its floors to promote the membership drive of the Brooklyn Academy of Music.

November 1964

Good Neighbor Store Lends
Meeting Room, Windows, Aid

One of the most important services that department stores can provide for the arts is free use of their space. In the Philadelphia area, Lit Brothers, a department store with six outlets, carries on a broad program of assistance to nonprofit organizations in which it lends them not only space, but also the use of personnel and other facilities.

Lit's has assigned a large room in each of its six branches as its Good Neighbor Room for the use of cultural and other nonprofit groups. The Good Neighbor Room may be reserved free of charge during store hours on a regular weekly or monthly schedule, depending on availability. The rooms range in size from a seating capacity of 50 to 500. They are equipped with a public address system, a movie screen, a grand piano, and an electric organ.

Each Lit Brothers branch reserves one large window for community groups on a rotating two-week basis. Those using the window send their props to the display department of the store, which then takes care of dressing the window in a professional manner.

Lit Brothers employs a full-time Good Neighbor Director at each branch store to work directly with community organizations. She sees to the use of the rooms, the provision of window displays, and the placing of weekly advertisements in the newspapers honoring individuals within those organizations that perform outstanding service to the community.

Among her other duties, the Good Neighbor Director cooperates with art centers in her locality and plans a comprehensive program of art exhibits and receptions that are held frequently in her store.

March 1963

Department Store Gives Technical Aid to Arts

Cultural groups in New Jersey seeking advice on such promotional problems as publicizing productions, selling tickets, printing programs, placing ads, and selecting media frequently find the answers to their problems in their local department store. Bamberger's, a chain of department stores in Newark and seven other New Jersey cities, offers technical assistance to arts groups as part of a comprehensive program in the cultural field.

Bamberger's active and unique program in the arts began in 1959 when it arranged for the Ballet Russe de Monte Carlo to appear at the Mosque Theatre in Newark. With the store backing the visit with an all-out promotional campaign, the performance was a sell-out, and Bamberger's became convinced that the community wanted good cultural attractions on a regular basis. The store arranged for yearly return visits by the ballet company and immediately launched a campaign to bring other top arts programs to New Jersey.

Since then, Bamberger's has arranged for many performing arts groups to visit Newark and other areas of the state where it has stores. This month, for example, it helped to bring the National Ballet Company from Washington, D.C.

to Newark and Trenton for two performances in each city. A Van Cliburn concert arranged by the store will take place in Newark soon. Although Bamberger's does not actually act as impresario for any of the visiting attractions, it does initiate many of the preliminary performance arrangements and it also pays for promotional expenses. In addition, it sells tickets, publicizes the events, advertises the performances, and prints most of the programs free of charge.

The store, which assumed all responsibility for promotion and institutional advertising on behalf of the now defunct Garden State Concerts, now lends its full support to the New Jersey Symphony. The store, in fact, played one of the major roles in the planning and administration of the orchestra's annual Symphony Ball, and Arthur Manchee, Bamberger's chairman of the board, served as chairman for the affair. The store also wrote and printed the program for the ball, printed tickets, and sold tables.

According to Martin Stuart, public relations director of Bamberger's, the store's informal program of technical aid to the arts helps two or three different cultural groups each week. Stuart and his three assistants, one in the Paramus store, one in the Cherry Hill store, and a third who travels among the other stores, see leaders of cultural organizations in their offices and advise them on promotion, advertising, and other technical matters.

In the visual arts, Bamberger's presents a "Living With Art" Show each January. This exhibition, designed to uncover new artists, is open to any New Jersey resident. Although the store retains several of the paintings for its permanent collection, most of the works are available for purchase.

The retail chain has also been instrumental in developing a monthly calendar of cultural events with the assistance of the Greater Newark Development Council. It takes a regular ad in the calendar to help support its production and mails calendars free of charge to all who request copies. "We have a stake in our customers and the community," Stuart told *AM*, "and we believe that through our program in the arts we are offering a real service to the community."

April 1964

Retailers Aid Arts

Local cultural groups can pick up added financial support by lending a hand to local retailers. In North Carolina, one successful gift shop owner gives a different arts group each year the money he would otherwise spend on 3500 customer Christmas cards. In addition, he donates 10 percent of the profits from all Christmas cards sold at his stores and 10 percent of the sales on a designated day to the cultural organization. The recipient group simply announces this policy to its members when mailing them their season tickets and thus encourages their patronage of the shop.

November 1962

Department Stores Resource
for Arts Funding Campaigns

Department stores, long a key promotional resource for the arts, have become increasingly important allies in cultural fund-raising programs. Throughout the country, a growing number of retailing outlets have made arts groups beneficiaries of funding events—many traditional, but some innovative.

When the American Shakespeare Theater was faced with a major fund crisis in 1976, Bloomingdale's Stamford, Connecticut store came to its aid. In dramatic newspaper ads telling its customers, "To be or Not to Be? It's Up to You." the store not only pinpointed the theater's urgent fund need, but also advertised its own approach to meeting that need. As outlined in the ad, the store presented an all-day Elizabethan Extravaganza as a salute to the theater and turned over 10 percent of its receipts on that day—nearly $13,000—to the theater. In San Francisco, Macy's Union Square was the site of a dramatic ballet button sale designed to help the San Franciso Ballet meet a Ford Foundation matching grant.

Although symphony orchestras traditionally have been among the most popular beneficiaries of department store fashion or design fund-raising benefits, other kinds of arts groups, some for the first time, have profited from them. In New York, nearly $10,000 was raised for the Association of American Dance Companies at a fashion show sponsored by Bloomingdale's to introduce Regine's first ready-to-wear collection. A Bergdorf-Goodman fur show benefited the New York City Ballet, the reopening of Bonwit Teller's first floor was a Museum of Modern Art benefit, and the opening of Bonwit's Hunting World section aided the International Center for Photography.

While new beneficiaries are cropping up, orchestras are still realizing huge fund gains through retail-fashion ties. Marshall Field & Co., for example, raised $50,000 for the Chicago Symphony as sponsor of a black-tie designer collection fashion show which kicked off the WFMT/Symphony marathon. A "Saks/Blass and the Symphony" fashion show and dinner dance, timed to coincide with the publication of the Detroit Symphony Women's Association annual rotogravure section, raised thousands of dollars for the orchestra. Bloomingdale's splashy benefit for the New York Philharmonic was a preview of 18 model rooms, seven dedicated to American composers.

In Huntington, Long Island, the reopening of a renovated department store at a suburban shopping mall triggered a relationship between the store and the arts council which has led to continued involvements. In October 1975, Abraham & Straus joined with the Huntington Arts Council to produce a three-day "Salute to the Arts," which included exhibits and performances by Council members, to celebrate its reopening. Following the successful festival the A & S board chairman helped the council initiate a local business-arts program by

speaking at the first dinner introducing the concept. Just recently the store sponsored a second, and more successful, arts festival with the council.

Perhaps the ultimate expression of a store's support of the arts is evidenced in London, England, although self-interest provides the motivation. The
Arts Council Shop, a nonprofit purveyer of books, posters, exhibition catalogues, records, and other arts-oriented materials, is operated by the Arts Council of Great Britain.

September-October 1976

Store Promotions

Many department stores now plan special promotions for a week or longer built
around specific themes. Alert art organizations can suggest tieing in with the
planned events. Often the stores will help to promote the organizations affiliated
with the events in advertising and publicity, and will sometimes give them window space.

May 1965

Store Windows Feature
Work of Local Arts Organizations

Cultural organizations in and around Washington, D.C. received a generous promotional boost in July and early August 1963 from Woodward & Lothrop, the
largest department store in the area. For a full month the store turned over two
show windows in its main store and 17 windows in four of its suburban stores to
exhibit the work of local arts groups and cultural institutions.

A luncheon at the store, attended by local cultural leaders, preceded the
display program.

The Woodward & Lothrop display department asked each organization to
help plan its own window and to furnish props and costumes wherever needed.
Thus, Arena Stage provided costumes and props from its recently concluded
production of *The Threepenny Opera*. Several art galleries offered either original
pieces of sculpture and paintings or good reproductions.

The most spectacular display of all was a ballet scene from Tschaikovsky's
Swan Lake, with mobile figures in brilliant costumes moving to ballet music that
could be heard by sidewalk viewers. In displays where figures in contemporary
dress were needed, the store supplied mannequins and clothed them attractively,
without labels or prices. Nowhere did the store permit a commercial note to in-
trude on the cultural displays.

Each of the cultural groups involved in the store's promotion benefited by
receiving free publicity in a new and colorful form. The event was reported in
the newspapers and stimuated a citywide, word-of-mouth discussion. People interested in the work of particular arts groups visited the stores to view the windows, and many stayed to do some shopping.

The midsummer salute to Washington cultural groups fits into a pattern of month-long summer salutes developed by the store over the past several years. The cultural project was eight weeks in the planning and execution. Woodward & Lothrop's summer display is the second longest of the year; only the pre-Christmas windows stay in place longer.

The principal benefit for the store, a Woodward & Lothrop spokesman told *AM*, is that the cultural windows attract traffic. Not only are Washington area people drawn to the displays, but tourists are attracted as well. In addition, the store benefits from the goodwill generated by rendering a public service in the community where it does business.

August 1963

Shopping Center Fare:
Groceries and Culture

Shopping centers, an accepted part of suburban life, are beginning to play an important role in promoting cultural activities in the community.

A good example is the Monmouth Shopping Center, Eatontown, New Jersey, which serves all of Monmouth County and the northern part of Ocean County.

One of the largest of its kind in the state, the center receives $100,000 per year from the Merchants Association (a group comprising the management of its 42 stores) to promote a community relations program.

Since the center opened in 1960, this fund has been used, among other things, to sponsor plays, concerts, puppet shows, films, lectures, and art shows. These events are held on the shopping center's sidewalks or in the 400-seat Civic Auditorium.

Although the auditorium was built for use by the center, commercial groups can rent it for $25 to $200 per day, depending upon the space used. Non-profit organizations are billed slightly less. The center charges no admission to any program it sponsors and makes no profit from renting the hall. The money received is used to pay for maintenance and personnel of the auditorium.

On July 13, 1963, the center will hold its fourth annual outdoor art show, and over 600 professional and amateur artists from all over New Jersey are expected to participate. No fee will be charged to enter the show. A panel of competent artists and art critics will serve as judges.

To promote events and to keep the community informed, the center publishes its own newspaper, issues monthly bulletins to the stores' 900 employees so that sales personnel can inform shoppers of what the center is doing, distributes posters, and advertises on highway billboards. The 800-member children's club, formed by the center, also receives a monthly calendar of events.

The center's stores, including Bamberger's, Montgomery Ward, and Lerner's, donate window space, lend merchandise, and contribute prizes for the various art shows.

Cultural groups seeking to enlist the aid of a shopping center should approach the manager of its largest store. If he himself cannot help, he will direct you to the proper person to whom you may present your plan for staging a performance or establishing an arts program within the shopping center.

June 1963

Arts Group Profits
from Shopping Center Shows

Smaller performing arts organizations can win new audiences, achieve widespread publicity, and realize financial gain by presenting productions in local shopping centers. Because shopping centers are highly competitive operations, their managers are constantly seeking promotional activities, such as performances, which will attract large numbers of customers. In Baltimore, Maryland, for example, the Baltimore City Ballet Company has given seven performances during the past year at a large shopping center before an aggregate audience of more than 10,000 people, many of them first-time attendees at a ballet. According to Max Yerman, president of the ballet company, "These are the few projects from which we actually make a profit."

The ballet company got the idea of performing in shopping centers in the spring of 1963, and it sent letters to managers of the larger centers in Baltimore inviting them to attend the ballet's second annual dance festival as guests of the company. As a result, a very large and profitable center, the Mondawmin Shopping Center, asked the Baltimore City Ballet to present four 15-minute performances as an Easter promotion at a fee of $500. An audience of about 3500 people attended the performances, and the management of the center was so pleased that it invited the ballet company to return for two Saturday performances at a fee of $600. Attendance exceeded 5000.

This spring the company again presented an Easter performance, and it has also been invited back to the Mondawmin Center for a two-performance back-to-school promotion in the fall. According to Mr. Yerman, the shopping center and the ballet company now have a mutually happy relationship, and from all indications the dance group will continue to work with the shopping center.

It has been especially significant to the ballet that Mondawmin promoted each of the performances to its mailing list of about 80,000 people, thus giving the Baltimore City Ballet excellent and widespread exposure.

May-June 1964

Arts Program Draws
Crowds to Shopping Center

Visitors to the Walt Whitman Shopping Center in Huntington Station, Long Island enjoyed a free performance of ballet and orchestral music on a fall 1964 Sunday afternoon. The performance presented by the Ballet Repertory Company and the Orchestra da Camera, was supported by the New York State Council on the Arts under its Professional Touring Performing Arts Program and sponsored by the Walt Whitman Shopping Center Merchants Association.

To highlight its week-long Mexican Festival, the association asked the council to support a top cultural program. Once the program was approved, the association spent about $5000 to get its covered mails prepared for the free presentation. Costs included heating the performance area, renting chairs for the audience, assembling a stage, providing dressing rooms and sound equipment, and staffing the site for the event. The performance was presented on a Sunday when the 80-unit center, with more than a million square feet of space is normally closed.

A capacity crowd of 2000 attended the performance, and 5000 additional people were turned away. Omar Lerman, the council's special consultant on the performing arts, termed the performance "one of the most successful in the council's history."

Alvin M. Goldberg, executive director of the merchants group, noted that the performance has spurred a continuing program of cultural events at the center, including organ recitals by Evan Wood on November 1 and Mark Bauer on November 8. Each of the performances drew audiences of about 1500 people.

Mr. Goldberg told *AM*, "The objective of the association is to make the shopping center a community center for culture as well as a good place to shop. We are attempting to duplicate in a small way what the council is doing." He added that "exposing the shopping center to an audience of arts lovers will ultimately pay off in good will."

To promote the event, the shopping center paid for advertisements in major Long Island newspapers.

December 1964

Supermarkets Aid Arts
at Checkout Counter

By gaining the cooperation of local merchants and their suppliers, cultural groups can create new avenues of advertising that effectively reach nearby audiences at a small cost. The Mummers Theater in Oklahoma City, Oklahoma, for example, arranged with the National Cash Register Company to let it imprint an advertisement reading "Discover the Mummers, Subscribe Now" on the backs of cash register tapes the company sells to supermarkets for use as customer receipts.

The theater group then secured commitments in writing from three chain stores with 66 branches in the Oklahoma City area to use 35 cases of the imprinted tape rolls during the summer season. Safeway distributed the tapes to 20 stores, Humpty Dumpty to 19 stores, and Seven-Eleven to 27 stores. Printing costs for the tapes were $70.00 for the logo and $6.64 for each caseload of tape, or a total of $232.40 for the entire promotion.

To guarantee the success of the promotion, chain stores needed to be assured by the tape supplier that they could purchase the comparatively small quantity of imprinted tapes used in the advertising campaign at the same price per case they paid for large quantities of clear tape. Speaking of the role played by the supplier in this aspect of the campaign as well as in the entire promotion, David Lunney of the theater group told *AM*, "the extra help of the local NCR supplier is invaluable. He can really get things off the ground—if he wants to."

Greater effectiveness was given to the advertising drive by offering increased reductions during the campaign to season subscribers. Before the campaign started, discounts of 15 percent were offered on the purchase of tickets for the eight-play season which runs from September 1964 through June 1965. However, during the month-long advertising drive, reductions were raised to 25 percent. After the drive ended, they reverted to the original 15-percent discount, which will be available until the completion of the first play in the season's repertoire.

As a result of these and other promotional efforts, including the display of the Mummer logo on 15 billboards throughout the city, the theater company has excellent prospects of reaching record subscription totals. By midsummer the group had already obtained more than 3500 season subscriptions. Included in the total were 1100 new subscribers. This figure surpasses the 3175 total subscriptions sold during all of 1963.

September 1964

Record Shop Prospers
by Giving the Arts a Hand

The record shop known as a center for good music can play a vital role in a city's cultural life well beyond that of selling fine recordings.

An example is the Discount Record Shop in Washington, D.C., which has recently expanded both its function and its title to the Discount Record, Book and Print Shop. Basic to the merchandising outlook of Robert Bialek, president of the firm, is that lovers of good music, books, and graphic art in one city are very often the same people.

While records remain the anchor of the shop's business, broadening its cultural appeal has both stimulated patronage and sales and enabled it to render greater community service. The results have been mutually profitable, since the store's name is repeatedly connected with cultural activity. The shop:

- Helps publicize performances by local cultural groups by displaying their posters

- Acts as a ticket sales point for benefit concerts
- Gives generously to fund drives by established groups like the National Symphony Orchestra and the Arena Stage
- Assists in sponsoring new organizations, such as the local opera society
- Promotes the recordings of local artists to help them gain recognition
- Publicizes visiting artists by interviews on the shop's weekly radio program carried by a good music station, WGMS

Now rounding out its eleventh year in business, the Discount Record Shop has in the past four seasons stepped out on its own as impresario. It has booked into Washington comedians like Jack Paar and Tom Lehrer, and such popular vocal groups as "The Limelighters" and "The Weavers."

This season the shop has booked the Philadelphia Orchestra for a series of five Tuesday evening concerts conducted by Ormandy, Klemperer, and Stokowski. It has also presented Peter Cook's "Establishment," a full-length topical revue from London. In its role as impresario, the shop works closely with the city's principal concert manager to avoid conflicts in bookings.

"We have a sense of civic responsibility in our business," Bialek told *AM*, "so we try to fill a cultrual need not met by others. From our experience with what sells in this shop we can tell what will go well in performance here.

"It would be very smart business for any good music store to become a center for ticket sales and arts publicity. People who come in for tickets often walk out having bought both tickets and records. But only if the store has the proper volume and the management know-how, should it try acting as impresario. Arts management of this kind is risky business."

Bialek estimates the number of customers entering his doors every week as "thousands." His mailing list, which is constantly renewed and is covered at least four times yearly with promotional material, he numbers "in the tens of thousands."

In its combined function as a retail cultural outlet and an interdisciplinary crossroads for the community, Bialek believes his shop is unique. The idea of a retail store working closely with arts groups, however, may well be applicable in a good many communities.

December 1962

TRAVEL AND TOURISM

Hotel Help

Hotels can help to promote your arts program. Chait's, an art-oriented hotel in Accord, New York, mailed postcards to its former guests announcing the American premiere of a play at New York's Renata Theatre. Headed "Dear Friends,"

the notices were signed by the hotel owners. Included on the cards were performance dates, ticket prices, and a form for purchasing tickets which could be
mailed directly to the theater.

March 1966

Resorts Provide Growing
Market for Cultural Programs

Resort hotels are becoming more involved with the arts, and cultural groups near
these resorts might well consider working with them. These hotels can help promote an arts program, gain publicity for an organization, and, in some instances,
be a source of added income.

Art galleries have been established in some resorts, others have presented
music and arts festivals, and many hostelries have added recognized art instructors to their payrolls.

A good example is Tamiment in the Poconos, Pennsylvania. For the past
three years, this resort has aided the Poconos Arts Center by donating to it all
proceeds from a chamber music festival the hotel sponsors. Concerts, held four
days a week, are free to the hotel's guests, but visitors must purchase tickets for
$2 each from the Arts Center. The Arts Center, in turn, promotes the perform-
ances. Last year this organization realized several hundred dollars from the festival.

Tamiment is probably the only resort int he country to build a special hall
just to house its annual chamber music festival. However, the hotel encourages
the arts in other ways, too. It holds frequent art shows and schedules weekly lectures ranging from psychology to art appreication. One evening a week concert
recitals are held in the Tamiment Playhouse. Plays, jazz groups, and ballet companies also are booked into the hotel.

Art groups interested in coooperating with local resorts should write or see
the public relations director or program coordinator of the hotel.

June 1963

Arts Get Free Publicity
from Travel Companies

Arts organizations may be able to obtain important promotional help from businesses in the transportation field if they plan in advance, if they are not easily
discouraged, and if they develop imaginative programs geared to the individual
needs of each business approached.

In Lake George, New York, for example, Fred Patrick, executive producer
of the Opera Festival there, received continuous free advertising space from a
bus company and an airline during his entire season last summer.

Beginning in December 1962, Mr. Patrick approached nearly 150 companies involved with transportation, including arilines, railroads, gas and oil companies, and hotels, suggesting a joint promotional campaign built around Lake George's importance as a tourist center. In each instance Mr. Patrick geared his approach to the particular promotional needs of the company. About 25 businesses responded, and two—the Schenectady Bus Lines, Inc. and Mohawk Airlines—worked out definite programs with the festival.

The bus line established a special reduced-rate service on Friday and Saturday nights for the 50-mile trip from Schenectady to the opera, and featured the opera festival in many free advertisements. The festival, in turn, promoted the concept of bus trips to the door of the opera performance.

The airline company, which flies to within nine miles of Lake George, put 11-inch stickers on the back of every seat in its planes. They read, "Lake George is an opera festival. Go there on Mohawk Airlines." It promoted the festival with the same slogan on billboards throughout New York. The opera festival gave space in its program to the airline.

Hotels, motels, and restaurants in the vicinity of Lake George also cooperated with the festival in the planning of a press trip. Mr. Patrick invited 15 writers from leading publications in New York to attend the festival, and the local facilities provided free lodging and meals to the writers in the hope that their establishments and the area would receive favorable coverage from the reporters. As a result of this kind of cooperation, the festival's only expense was in providing round-trip automobile transportation for the writers from New York to the festival at a total cost of about $200. The Opera Festival at Lake George received widespread national publicity.

According to Mr. Patrick the key to receiving promotional aid from transportation facilities lies in discovering how a cooperative program might benefit the business approached. Often, he claims the key may be an obvious one.

December 1963

Hotel Chain Creates Circulating Exhibit

The Pick Hotels, a hotel chain with 33 locations throughout the East and Midwest, is launching its own series of traveling art exhibitions.

The idea for exhibitions originated at Washington's Pick Motor Inn, where sales manager Dan Botkiss, a former art student, set aside an area in his mezzanine for a permanent display. The first exhibit featured the paintings of the Italian-born artist, Pietro Lazzari. The public received the idea so favorably that the chain's main office in Chicago decided to send exhibitions to each of its other hotels, with the chain paying for the cost of transporting both the paintings and the artist whose works were on exhibition to the next location.

Botkiss frankly admits that the exhibitions are designed as "art on the run" for guests who are too busy to visit art galleries outside the hotel.

November 1963

New Hotel Warms House
with Gala for Arts Givers

A Washington cultural group raised more than $11,000 with relative ease, and a swank, new capital hotel made hundreds of friends in a unique cooperative venture.

The teamwork formula, carried out by the Washington Ballet Guild and the Georgetown Inn, can be adapted for benefit parties wherever the management of a new hotel or restaurant, properly situated and equipped, is willing to spend money for an opening splash to attract attention.

The Georgetown Inn, a small, beautifully decorated hotel aiming at a clientele of discriminating taste, took the initiative. Long before construction was finished, Julius Epstein, Georgetown Inn operator, sought a cultural organization for which the hotel could stage an opening-week benefit, on the theory that its best friends locally would be people interested in the arts.

Mr. Epstein offered space, a cocktail reception and a lavish dinner with three wines, completely free of charge, at a cost to the hotel of more than $3000. The National Symphony Orchestra was approached at first, but rejected the proposition because of space limits in the hotel dining rooms. The ballet, a smaller group, then accepted. It promoted the benefit tickets as both an aid to the guild and as admission to a special preview of a unique hotel-restaurant, amid a gala crowd of VIPs.

The benefit dinner drew 220 friends of the ballet guild and their guests, who paid $50 apiece to attend the evening affair. An added fillip was the presence of the Duke and Duchess of Windsor. Socially and financially, the Washington Ballet Guild found the joint enterprise a great success. George L. Williams, guild leader responsible for the benefit, wrote to the hotel management:

"I don't believe there could ever be another benefit so well done because the hotel management was so lavish in their contribtuion to the ballet. We all, trustees and patrons of the ballet, are very grateful and appreciative of what you did."

Mr. Epstein, who heads a firm that manages hotels in several cities, told *AM*, "I am delighted with the results. The ballet benefit allowed us to show the Georgetown Inn to the flower of Washington philanthropy. These are the best people in the city, both from my viewpoint and that of the ballet guild."

July 1962

Hotel Helps

In Phoenix, the new Adams Hotel celebrates its formal opening in May 1975 by saluting its nearby neighbor, the Phoenix Symphony, and by hosting and under-writing the orchestra's annual ball. At an estimated cost of $35,000, the hotel donated a dance band, full use of its facilities—ballroom, main dining room, and meeting rooms—plus a cocktail reception and dinner for 2500 people.

September-October 1974

Auto Dealer Gives Art
Free Ride to Exhibits

A New York automobile agency is offering artists free studio-to-gallery transpor-tation of their one-man exhibitions. According to Curt Gruber, general sales manager of Fifth Avenue Motors, a Volkswagen dealership that has exhibited art in its showrooms, his company launched the program in the hopes of finding prospective station wagon customers among artists. First announced in Decem-ber, the promotion has already benefited 14 artists who have had one-man shows transported to the exhibition gallery.

The offer appears as a monthly pull-out coupon advertisement in a publi-cation, the *New York Arts Calendar.* Its only conditions are that the artist must accompany his works in the Volkswagen bus, dates must be made at least ten days in advance, and the transportation must be limited to one delivery from studio to gallery in Manhattan. Although artists have called and requested the movement of furniture and other items, the offer is limited to the art scheduled to appear in one-man shows. Normal automotive insurance, provided by the auto-motive dealer, covers the vehicle and its contents.

February 1964

Newspaper, Railroad, and
Stratford Festival Bring Toronto
to Shakespeare in Package Trip

Harry J. Allen, Jr.

The Stratford Shakespearean Festival at Stratford, Ontario, Canada has a thea-ter-by-rail plan that guarantees it almost 10,000 patrons a season, about $10,000 worth of free advertsing lineage, and thousands of news lines in a metropolitan newspaper. In cooperation with the Toronto *Telegram* and the Canadian Na-tional Railways, the Festival draws as many as 600 adult patrons a week for the two-hour trip from Toronto, a city of more than a million people, 88 miles away by rail.

The 1962 season offers 14 Tuesday evening trains, including one afternoon special in behalf of the Actor's Fund. For an entire evening's package, the patron pays $11.25 and gets a $5.00 theater ticket, or $9.75 with a $3.50 seat. He gets round-trip rail transportation, a festival ticket, dinner, bus transportation in Stratford, and a beverage during or after the performance. In each case the festival receives the full price for its ticket.

Victor Polley, festival general manager, says the joint promotion with the newspaper and railroad has helped to build the festival in Toronto, the large city closest to Stratford, and has encouraged many from Toronto to attend the theater using other means of transportation. Polley says:

"There are still people who prefer to buy a package form of travel, in which they are given painless attendance at the theater. We are fortunate in having a major newspaper like the *Telegram* to carry this promotion. It couldn't have been more ideal for us."

As many as six members of the newspaper's promotion staff are aboard each train to distribute booklets giving the layout of Stratford, a resume of the plays, and information about sights along the route. Attendants answer questions and pass out free roses, cigarettes, and wash 'n dry towels. In Stratford the patrons are carried by bus to a church where they are served dinner by one of the five church women's auxiliaries, and they are then taken to the theater. After the performance, the bus moves them back to the train for the trip home.

Announcement of the summer plans are made in March. The newspaper runs a three-column ad once and sometimes twice a week promoting the trains, and also provides considerable news lineage. The $10,000 value of this free advertising is equal to what Stratford spends for its entire United States advertising program.

The *Telegram* underwrites any losses incurred by the railroad. While some weeks show losses, compensating profits at other times keep the paper from losing money on the operation. The newspaper pays for its own ads, window cards, and the staff it puts on the trains, as well as for the dinner.

Tickets are sold at the CNR Toronto office, with Stratford allocating up to 500 tickets for each performance. If Stratford runs short of tickets, some of the Toronto tickets are called back, with the box office keeping in close contact with the CNR. When the plan started eight years ago, 3200 patrons made the trip; in 1959 and 1960, package patronage was close to 10,500 each year.

The *Telegram* also sponsors a student train in the first two weeks of September. This is nearly sold out, with more than 5700 scheduled to "take the classroom to the theater" in this way. There will be 12 trains running to matinee performances and two evening trains in th student program.

The *Telegram*'s promotion has been emulated by two U.S. newspapers. The Buffalo, New York *Catholic Union and Echo* charters a train and promotes through its columns some 1500 tickets sold to Catholic high schools. The Detroit *News*, in addition, runs two trains a season to Stratford charging its readers $12.75 for the package. Both newspapers provide generous news coverage for the events.

The festival sends announcements to groups that have attended before, advising them to book early, and aids in arranging accommodations in Stratford.

July 1962

PROMOTIONAL AND PROGRAM SUPPORT

Business Books Art

In Wellsville, New York, a top local corporation, concerned with the paucity of professional arts attractions available to its employees and to community residents, approached the New York State Council on the Arts in 1967 for help in developing a continuing cultural program. The query from the Air Preheater Company prompted the Council to send two staff members to Wellsville to meet with local leaders and officials of the corporation.

As a result of the meetings and the advice of council officials, the new Wellesville Performing Arts Council was established, a performing arts series of four evening concerts and four free children's matinees was scheduled, and plans were developed to use the town library for traveling art exhibitions circulated throughout the state by the council. Moreover, the Air Preheater Company agreed to underwrite all concert series costs not defrayed by ticket sales. The council has continued to assist the new venture by providing technical assistance services to the neophyte community organization in such areas as organizational development, membership campaign, box office procedures, promotion and publicity, and ticket sales.

The community reacted enthusiastically to the new program, and its three leading service organizations agreed to help sell series tickets and assist in promotion. The local newspaper responded with a long editorial calling for local support of the program and with continuing news stories. The editorial said, in part,

> This is the first opportunity in some time for large scale participation in a series of cultural performances of a high order brought here for the primary benefit of area residents. The projected series is a highly commendable response by the Air Preheater Company, together with a number of civic-minded citizens and organizations, to the growing hunger in this region for improved cultural opportunity. . . . It is now up to the residents of this area to ensure the success of the project through strong support.

November-December 1967

Win Diners

Local restaurants can help to promote cultural groups. Many restaurants may be willing to have a printed message about an arts organization appear on the back of their customer checks if the organization pays the small printing cost. When such a check is presented face down, the message of the cultural organization greets customers.

July-August 1964

Illuminating the Arts

Looking for a unique way to advertise cultural activities in your community? Perhaps a local retail operation might lend you its facilities. In Huntsville, Alabama, for example, a laundry allowed the Arts Council of Huntsville to announce cultural events on its illuminated revolving sign. In eight months the council displayed 46 announcements on the sign.

August-September 1966

Fill 'em Up with Publicity

Local gas stations may be a good source of free publicity for events your organization is sponsoring. Supply them with fliers and announcements which they can pass out to motorists along with change and trading stamps. During the summer it's wise to emphasize events with particular appeal to tourists passing through your community.

May 1963

Priming the Pump

To emphasize the potential of business support in its community, the Arts Council of Rochester devoted an entire issue of its newspaper, *Scene,* to business involvement in the arts. Underwritten by Flanigan Furniture of Rochester, the 20-page publication featured general information on business support as well as specific write-ups on the arts support programs of more than 20 local companies.

September-October 1975

Milkman Brings Publicity

Free advertising may be available from your local dairy. For example, one arts group arranged for two dairies in its community to print messages on the side of their milk containers promoting the cultural organization's season subscription program. These messages included information on ticket prices and the organization's telephone number. Although the promotion was made without cost to the group, it had to supply all the art work for the announcement.

September 1964

Business Promotions
Help Win New Audiences

New audiences for the arts can be created through the establishment of imaginative joint promotions with local businesses. For example, Martin Tahse, a theatrical producer, has successfully promoted his touring productions to audiences who do not normally attend theater by tying in promotions with chain store supermarkets and travel agents. As a result, there has been a steady upswing in attendance at his two latest road productions, *After the Fall* and *A Funny Thing Happened on the Way to the Forum.*

Advertising was aimed specifically at young nontheatergoers by including brief descriptions of play content in the copy. Mr. Tahse also arranged to have advertising placed on grocery bags used in supermarkets prior to the arrival of the shows. Coupons on the bags encouraged shoppers to send in for tickets or to inquire about theater parties. In addition, free tickets were raffled off at the supermarkets.

Another promotion instituted by Mr. Tahse was a tie-in with the National Tea Company, which mentioned *A Funny Thing* on radio and television spot commercials, in window posters, in newspaper advertisements, and in about 1.5 million promotional booklets mailed to Chicago-area families. In exchange, Mr. Tahse gave the 250 supermarket stores owned by the company a total of 5000 tickets to be awarded to shoppers.

Travel agents provided Mr. Tahse with another novel outlet for promoting his shows in communities within 75 miles of performance sites. Mr. Tahse helped put together a "package" for the agents to offer their clients. The package consisted of transportation arranged by the agent, an orchestra ticket provided at the normal price, and an original cast recording and a souvenir book, both sold to agents at cost.

The agents sold the package at a profit, but below the price the items would normally cost the theatergoer. In that way both agent and patron benefited, while Mr. Tahse attracted a new audience to his shows.

January 1965

Apartment Houses

Local realtors and builders can be a good publicity outlet for the arts. In New York, the John Adams apartment house calls attention to the cultural life in its neighborhood by listing in its rental ads the nearby cultural events. Another new apartment house, the Saint Germain, has invited groups to furnish programs and posters for display in the lobby.

November 1962

Real Estate Office

The window of a real estate office in a residential neighborhood can be a regular showcase for arts group publicity. Many real estate dealers look for new ways to attract attention to their offices through their windows, which too frequently display the same tired old snapshots of houses for sale. An arts display publicizing an upcoming event can be designed in cooperation with the dealer to promote the idea that living in his sales area is culturally rewarding.

April 1963

Business Talks

Aside from their dollar value, corporate grants can be important promotional tools for arts groups. The Buckingham Corporation, makers of Cutty Sark Scotch Whiskey, sent letters to all Seattle Opera Association subscribers announcing a $3000 program grant it had made to the opera company. Importantly, the letter lauded the opera company and the specific significance of the project supported by Buckingham.

September-October 1973

BANKING HELP

Bank Promotion
Attracts Funds for Culture

By varying a tried promotional tactic, the free gift to new depositors, a New York bank made a key contribution to a cultural fund-raising campaign and helped itself at the same time. Importantly, the technique used by the East New York Savings Bank to benefit the New York Public Library could be adapted by any company offering premiums to help cultural organizations in its community.

When East New York was planning the opening of a new branch on Manhattan's West Forty-second Street in mid-1972, it looked at its immediate neighborhood to see the local amenities with which it might identify. Foremost among them was the main branch of the city's library system, located across the street. The library was then about to launch a major fund-raising drive to match a $500,000 grant from the National Endowment for the Humanities by June 30, 1972.

With the dual objective of helping the library's fund drive and promoting its own branch opening, the bank launched two consecutive 30-day promotional campaigns beginning on May 15, the first in all nine Metropolitan area branches and the second at the Forty-second Street branch alone. The traditional free gift offer used by banks to attract new customers was varied to permit new account openers to exercise an unsual option—they could accept a gift or they could donate its price to the library. If they opted for the donation, the bank agreed to match the gift.

The promotion was backed by the usual heavy advertising barrage that accompanies branch openings. In East New York's case this meant two ads every week in each of New York's dailies, double pages in tabloids, and full pages in the *New York Times,* plus a full schedule of weekly newspaper ads and radio announcements. A typical full-page *Times* ad showed bank chairman John P. McGrath standing behind a table laden with gifts. The caption read, "East New

York Savings Bank has a gift for you, but we'd rather you didn't take it. . . . Instead—let us contribute the price of your gift to the New York Public Library. And we'll send an equal amount." Accompanying text described the library's financial needs and outlined the alternate gift plan. Library contributors were also given certificates of acknowledgment and a permanent identification label in a library book.

Although the amount raised through the bank was not a major part of the overall total raised by the library, it far surpassed expectations. During the initial campaign and the first two weeks of the second campaign, both coming prior to the matching grant deadline, 20 percent of all new depositors waived the free gift and contributed to the library. Moreover, the bank received a number of library donations from nondepositors, and its action helped to spur business contributions, some rather sizable. Perhaps most important to the library, however, was the tremendous exposure it received as a result of the bank promotion. "We received more than triple our advance expectation in contributions," the library's chief of public information, Edward White, told *AM*, "and an immeasurable amount of exposure and good will." Three days prior to the matching grant deadline the library announced that it had topped its goal by nearly $200,000.

The bank was equally pleased with the results. Its vice president for marketing, Edward J. Pfeiffer, said, "Forty-second Street was the most successful branch opening we've ever had. We exceeded our maximum projection of the number of new accounts and the amount deposited by a good degree." The bank also received tremendous institutional recognition, and its offices were flooded with hundreds of congratulatory letters.

"We feel it was a great benefit all around," added Pfeiffer. "We were able to perform a public service and still meet our marketing objectives. Any business offering any kind of substantial premium could make this kind of option available to its customers."

Summer 1972

Bank Deposits Aid Arts

When Hospital Audiences, Inc. helped find youngsters to fill the balcony for a children's classic film shown in New York's Town Hall last summer, sponsored by the East New York Savings Bank, it was the beginning of a business relationship that has not only made the national service organization $15,000 richer, but promises increased support from the bank in the future. Impressed by the HAI service and the group's organizational ability, the bank, a long-time supporter of the arts, decided that instead of offering new Christmas Club accounts free gifts, it would turn the cost of those gifts—with a minimum guarantee of $15,000— over to HAI.

By the end of the Christmas season, the bank's 12 branches had recorded the same $15,000 in club deposits as last season. Although the number of depositors was down somewhat, this may have resulted from the fact that some of last year's depositors split their deposit into two account to get two of the free recipe books offered. Importantly, none of the depositors complained about the lack of free gifts. "We didn't get any negative playback from any of our branches," Edward Pfeiffer, the bank's vice-president fo rmarketing told *AM*. "We did get a good deal of national publicity, and some of our depositors applauded our action."

March-April 1976

Bank Becomes Partner
in State Arts Project

In Maryland, the state council and the Maryland National Bank are cosponsoring performances by Baltimore's Center Stage in communities throughout the state. The council, which hopes that the example set by the bank may influence other corporations to support activities, claims that "it is the first time that a business organization and a state arts council have collaborated on a major arts project." The bank's total financial commitment to the project is $8000.

In the pilot phase of the program, the Center Stage presented performances of *Pictures in the Hallway* in Salisbury and Hagerstown in November 1967. Based on a favorable response to these performances, the council now hopes to expand the program so that performances will blanket the entire state after the first of the year. Other productions to be presented include *Waiting for Godot, Under Milk Wood,* and *The Marriage Proposal.*

November-December 1967

Bank Aids the Arts

A leading New York bank was so impressed with the results of the first arts project it sponsored that it immediately undertook sponsorship of a second program. Subsequently it voted to allot 10 to 15 percent of its 1967 advertising budget to the support of cultural programs.

Although several board members of the Trade Bank and Trust Company were personally interested and involved in the arts, the bank itself had never considered sponsoring a cultural program. However, after several bank executives attended a conference on business in the arts at Lincoln Center last spring, at the urging of its sponsor, the Arts Advisory Council of the New York Board of Trade, their interest was stirred and they asked the council if there were any projects which needed corporate support. The result, achieved after resistance by some bank board members was overcome, was the sponsorship of an exhibition of Herbert Migdoll dance photographs at Lincoln Center's Philharmonic Hall last fall. The exhibit was subsequently shown at the Museum and Library of Performing Arts, again under the bank's sponsorship, and at the bank's main office and two of its branches.

The exhibit drew a favorable response from the public and the press. As a result, the bank experienced little resistance in selling it board on sponsorship of a second program, "The Arts in Your Life," a series of six evening programs designed to introduce young people to the performing and visual arts. The programs, held monthly through May 1967 at New York's Fashion Institute of Technology, feature demonstrations, performances, and discussions by such groups as the New York City Ballet, the APA-Phoenix Theatre, and the New York City Opera. The final event in the series will feature a "happening" created by Michael Kirby.

Following the successful first performance in the new series, the bank board voted to donate a percentage of its 1967 advertising budget to the support of arts programs. "Although we had to be sold initially on support of the arts," said bank vice president Lawrence A. Meyers, "we're convinved now, In fact, our recently completed stockholders' report contained a page commenting on our sponsorship of cultural programs."

January-February 1967

Bank Floor is Unique Setting for Performance by Orchestra

The main floor of a leading bank will become an auditorium for the Buffalo Philharmonic Orchestra when it presents a concert there on December 12, 1964. The Buffalo Savings Bank has donated space on its banking floor for the event and will pay the orchestra for the performance.

In addition, the bank will advertise the event without charge to the orchestra, and serve coffee and doughnuts to the 1400 persons who are expected to attend the concert, which will take place between 2:00 and 4:00 P.M. on a Saturday. Seats for the performance are free and will be offered on a first-come, first-served basis.

Seymour L. Rosen, the orchestra's manager, told *AM* that his organization suggested the program to the bank last April and received approval for it in June. The bank will spend about $4000 on the concert, with the major portion earmarked for the orchestra's players.

The orchestra won support for the project by pointing out to the bank that it would be providing a service to the community generally and to its customers specifically. It was also maintained that community goodwill generated by the event would benefit the bank.

To gain bank approval, the orchestra's board members established personal contacts with board members of the bank. Although the bank had previously cooperated with the orchestra on limited projects such as sending out mailings on behalf of the orchestra, closer ties resulted from working on the event. The bank is now considering sponsoring other arts events.

Mr. Rosen feels that promotion of the performance will help generate interest in the orchestra since many persons who may attend the concert normally do not go to regular orchestral presentations. To appeal to a wide audience, a program of semiclassical and Christmas music is planned.

Advertisements of the presentation were scheduled to appear a week before the concert in the *Buffalo Courier-Express* and the *Buffalo Evening News,* major city newspapers with a combined total circulation of more than 590,000. In addition, posters announcing the event will be displayed in the bank lobby, and spot radio and television announcements will be used. The bank also sent direct mail to its customers telling them of the concert.

Mr. Rosen said that the bank is ideally situated for the performance since it is in the heart of the downtown shopping district.

December 1964

Bank Support

Banks, which pioneered in matching gifts for the arts, continue to develop new programs. In Boston, in cooperation with the Metropolitan Cultural Alliance, the National Shawmut Bank has committted $10,000 to match donations by its employees to cultural groups of their choice. In Tucson, Arizona, the Catalina Savings and Loan Association is making donations to nonprofit groups selected by customers who open new accounts or add to existing accounts—$5 for up to $5000 deposits and $10 for over $5000, amounts set by state law.

November-December 1973

BUSINESS FUNDING
OF ARTS PROGRAMS

Theater Wins Business Aid
by Asking Business for It

A leading theater company, with no significant record of past business support, organized its first campaign for corporate funding in 1974 and upped business giving from $2500 to $75,000 in a single year. The approach was so successful that the theater doubled the 1975-76 business goal and will soon introduce a new corporate membership program.

Until 1974, the American Shakespeare Theater in Stratford, Connecticut limited its fund-raising approach to private donors, foundations, and to a small degree, government. With fund needs growing, however, the group, with the aid of a new development director, Gerald Lennick, set its sights on business early in 1974. "We added several top corporate people to our board in 1974," Lennick told *AM*, "and we decided to go after business funds. When we built $50,000 in corporate giving into our budget, everyone thought we were crazy."

The theater's approach in the spring of 1974 was to host a series of three regional luncheons for corporate executives in communities near Stratford, with the invitations sent over the signatures of businessmen-board members. The luncheons were deliberately low-key, with the theater staff members talking about the coming season's program and the organization's goals and objectives. A 10-minute film told the Shakespeare Theater story.

Later, without any overt approach yet made for funding, Lennick called on many of the 50 businessmen he had met at lunch to personally invite them to the theater that summer. Following a night at Stratford, where they were greeted by officials, each businessman received a written proposal asking for a specific grant. Some 30 companies responded with grants. "We were shocked that in instance after instance," Lennick added, "executives told us that they had never given to the theater before either because nobody had ever asked them to or because they didn't know we needed their support."

Based on last year's breakthrough and a new relationship with the business community, the theater set this year's goal at $150,000. It expects to reach it, not only by upping the number of corporate donors, but by increasing the size of the average gift. Throughout this summer, as last year, top Connecticut corporate executives have been attending performances as guests of the theater as a prelude to a formal proposal for funds.

Summer 1975

Business Tapped for First Time
Responds to Theater Fund Drive

Faced with a fund crisis, a suburban arts group enlisted the support of local business for the first time and found a willing angel in the wings. In Huntington, New York, the Performing Arts Foundation of Long Island, which has operated a successful year-round professional theater for six years, needed $50,000 to cover the conversion of a warehouse to its playhouse 22 months earlier. With creditor pressure mounting and the board unable to raise the funds, it was obvious that immediate and drastic action was necessary. Finally, early last December the board announced an emergency fund drive. Unless $50,000 could be raised by January 29, the theater would close.

With no time for preparation, no experience in conducting a major drive, and only seven weeks in which to reach its goal, the organization had a nearly impossible task before it. However, the drive received a financial and promotional boost when the Huntington Town Board passed a resolution awarding PAF

$12,500. A leading local businessman, Robert Mitchell, former president of the chamber of commerce and head of his own Cadillac agency, helped spark support by personally buying time on radio station WGSM to appeal for funds. Mitchell, who later became president of the Huntington Arts Council, was heard twice a day for a week. The station matched his contribution with free spots.

"Mitchell's appeal had a very positive effect on local business," executive director Clint Marantz told *AM*. The Huntington Chamber of Commerce passed a resolution pledging its support. The Village Merchants Association set aside January 20 as "Save PAF Day" and asked member firms to contribute five to ten percent of their receipts to PAF that day and to place donation boxes in their stores.

Although the organized support of business had never before been solicited, the response was immediate. A leading area utility, Long Island Lighting, helped launch the drive with a $2000 donation. Over 300 area merchants helped promote PAF Day and raised more than $500 from donation boxes in their stores. Some $3000 was raised from Merchants Association members who contributed a percentage of their January 20 receipts to the Foundation. A nonmember, MacDonald's, gave PAF over $1600—50 percent of the day's gross receipts from its two stands in Huntington. Some PAF business creditors noted the drive's success and responded. They either forgave indebtedness or accepted performance tickets and playbill advertising as payment.

By deadline date the board announced that the goal had been topped by $3000. "Not only did we tap business," added Marantz, "but we developed a continuing ally. It's been decided already that the third Saturday of every January will be an annual event for local merchants—PAF Day."

January-February 1973

Company Subscriptions

If your group has a subscription season, you might develop a sponsorship program aimed at business. The Milwaukee Symphony Orchestra introduced a campaign this season which allow companies to sponsor a pair of subscription concerts at a cost of $2500. In return, the company receives a four-page program insert, program acknowledgement, is identified in news releases, and has the opportunity to purchase tickets at substantially reduced rates. At last count, 11 companies had become sponsors.

September-October 1973

Business Is Finding New Ways to Aid Local Cultural Groups

Business is aiding the arts in new ways. Increasingly, cultural groups are discovering that support concepts tested elsewhere can be adapted to their own needs.

In Phoenix, Arizona, for example, the Symphony Association initiated a "concert guarantor" program for the 1973-74 season, similar to one successfully introduced by the Milwaukee Symphony Orchestra, with local companies purchasing sponsorship of a pair of concerts for $3000 and receiving promotional benefits in return. Not only have several series been "sold," but a leading local department store, Diamond's, already has purchased opening night performances for the next three seasons. The concert program is one of the first activities to be initiated since a new organization, the Select Committee of Businessmen in Support of the Phoenix Symphony Orchestra, was formed at a kickoff luncheon this fall. The committee, composed of 25 local business leaders, has subdivided itself into ten different business areas, with each subcommittee heading an orchestra fund drive in its own business sector.

In Minneapolis, businesses that regularly entertain customers and suppliers at baseball, football, and hockey games are now taking them to the symphony hall. Through a pilot project called "Operation Sound Decision," the Minnesota Orchestra went after the same corporate ticket buyers that professional sports had cultivated over the years.

Working on the premise that business sells best to business, the orchestra asked prominent local executive Harvey Mackay of Mackay Envelopes to head a drive to sell $50,000 in season tickets to local corporations. He in turn invited 48 of this top businessman friends to a private luncheon and divided 500 ticket prospects among them. The campaign theme was direct. "If you own Vikings, Twins, and North Star seats," it asked, "why not the Minnesota Orchestra?" When the campaign ended just prior to the start of this season, 632 subscriptions and tickets, more than $60,000 in sales, had been sold to 200 local companies.

Elsewhere, businesses are using their own resources to aid the fund campaigns of cultural groups. In a recent full-page *New York Times* ad, a publisher, Viking Press, offered to send donors a free book in return for a contribution to their local libraries. Ad reprints were sent to about 3000 libraries throughout the country, and the response thus far has been hundreds of donations.

In California, business leaders played a mjaor role in launching the California Arts Commission's new $1-million grants program. On a voluntary basis, an accounting firm helped state arts groups prepare budgets and grant applications, a management consultant arranged grant procedures, public relations executives publicized the program, and the Fred Harvey Company offered complimentary hotel rooms for meetings of the commission's panels.

November-December 1973

Business Helps Neighborhood Arts

Neighborhood cultural groups in New York have found a staunch advocate in a top corporation, Standard Oil of New Jersey. The company, which contributed more than $50,000 to the city's borough arts councils last year to encourage community-based cultural activity, has since stepped up its involvement. This summer it sponsored the "Fiesta at Fordham," a two-week program of free performances by the Alliance of Latin Arts, and underwrote the cost of an outside wall mural at the Henry Street Settlement Theatre by the Cityarts Workshop.

Early this fall the company premiered a new film documentary on neighborhood arts activity. *Hometown,* a 33-minute color film underwritten by Standard Oil and produced by the Arts and Business Council of the New York Board of Trade, depicts the activities of six performing arts groups in New York's five boroughs. *Hometown* will be shown overseas by the United States Information Agency and is available without charge from the distributors, A. A. Schechter Associates, 551 Fifth Avenue, New York, New York 10017, for showings in America. A separate 28-minute version is available for television.

Standard Oil has also agreed to underwrite all administrative costs of a massive new cultural auction, "The Possible Dream," for the benefit of New York's community arts groups. The program, patterned after auctions held in St. Louis and elsewhere, will culminate in a series of fall 1973 fund-raising events including community auctions and a gala dinner auction. Incorporated as an activity of the New York Board of Trade's Educational Foundation, the "Dream" will be administered as a united fund by a professional staff, with proceeds to be disseminated by the borough arts councils to neighborhood arts activities.

Summer 1972

Artist Finds Company and Wins Studio, Materials, Commissions

A young Ohio artist interested in metal working but lacking the means to open a suitable studio systematically solicited area industries until he found one interested in giving him free space without any strings attached. While Thomas W. Taylor envisioned a studio that would always be open to employees, he didn't wish to trade his artistic services for free space.

Although they had never met, Harvey Gittler, manager of manufacturing for the Tappan Air Conditioning plant in Elyria, Ohio, responded to the unusual suggestion. In March 1972, several weeks after the initial proposal was made, Taylor moved into his new studio tucked away in a maintenance department area used mainly for storage. The studio is large enough for his needs and includes such materials as an arc welder, portable crane and hoist, work bench, and storage cabinet. In addition, virtually every tool in the maintenance department, from drill presses to abrasive saws, and tools in the plant's other departments have been made available to Taylor. "The paint line will send through anything that fits," said Taylor, "as long as I don't mind green and yellow, the color of the air conditioners and furnaces they manufacture." He also can take any material he wishes from the Tappan scrap yard without charge.

Officially identified as the company's artist-in-residence, Taylor has found the relationship beneficial both from an economic and production viewpoint. During the past year he has produced a variety of new works, including a winged form made from old boiler shells and a rotating piece made from damaged air conditioner and furnace parts. He has also been working on modular building units based on pentagons and prism shapes.

Although, as Taylor puts it, "The present involvement does not solve all the problems of survival," he has found a customer for his work in Tappan. His decorative wall sculpture now hangs in the company's training room, and a large steel form of his has been rented by Tappan for display in its front yard. Recently, the marketing department bought a large piece of his to highlight its exhibit at a trade show. The campany also hired him as a color consultant to brighten areas within the plant, and Harvey Gittler personally commissioned a steel structure and several abstract steel forms.

"Having Tom here has been an exciting experience for our employees," said Gittler. "Many regularly visit his studio, and they now see artistic form in their everyday surroundings."

January-February 1973

Companies Fund Publication

The Missouri State Council on the Arts, faced with the prospect of producing its first annual report, but lacking publication funds in its budget, turned to local corporations for assistance. As a result, seven Missouri firms underwrote the total cost of publishing the Missouri State Council on the Arts 1965-66 Annual Report, which summarizes the council's accomplishments during its first two years of operation. The report is a handsomely designed and illustrated 40-page brochure with a two-color front and back cover featuring a reproduction of a work by St. Louis artist and sculptor, Ernest Trova.

In addition to providing financial support, one of the corporations, Hallmark Cards, Inc. of Kansas City, also contributed design, layout, and production services for the report. Other firms who shared the publication costs were the Kansas City Life Insurance Company; First National Bank of Joplin; Commerce Trust Company of Kansas City; Westab, Inc., a subsidiary of Meade Corporation, in St. Joseph; First National Bank of Kansas City; and Kansas City Southern Railway Lines.

November-December 1967

Marketing Firm Finds
Corporations to Fund Arts

A commercial marketing firm, whose involvement in the arts is recent, helped to win corporate support for a costly national cultural program—and won itself an arts client in the process. The program was the first annual American College Theatre Festival, which brought together ten college theater companies for two weeks of performances in Washington, D.C.'s historic Ford's Theatre and newly built Theatre on the Mall this spring. The performing troupes were selected from 176 colleges in a nationwide competition that began last fall. The commercial firm was the National Student Marketing Corporation, which develops programs to help clients sell their products and services to high school and college customers.

Initially, the festival producers, the American Educational Theatre Association and the American National Theatre and Academy, won corporate support on their own when American Airlines responded to their proposal to become one of the festival's three official sponsors, along with the Smithsonian Insitution and the Friends of the John F. Kennedy Center. When it became evident, however, that the ambitious undertaking would require additional funds, an American Airlines public relations executive suggested that, because of the festival's college orientation, the producers ask NSMC to help. The marketing firm had recently established a creative arts division under Mitchell Nestor, a former Off-Broadway producer and director.

It was Nestor's job to put together a marketing package that he could sell to a corporate client—one that would win dollars for the festival without exploiting it, and at the same time win good program identification for the corporate underwriter. He found the package in a souvenir journal and the company in the Chrysler Corporation.

In Chrysler's behalf, National Student Marketing prepared festival journals and posters and distributed 500,000 of each of them to college campuses throughout the country, sent out releases on college productions entered regionally in the competition, and gave away tape recorders to college theater departments. Chrysler, for the considerable amount of money it invested in the festival, won the youth identification it sought. It received recognition as underwriters of the journal, had six pages of ads and editorial copy within the publication, and was identified on all the posters.

Nestor and NSMC were to play one more vital role in the festival. One of the sponsors, the Smithsonian Institution, was looking for a corporation to underwrite the $50,000 cost of the Theatre on the Mall, which was to be used for a variety of summer arts programs as well as for festival productions. NSMC found an "angel"—Pepsi-Cola.

Spring-Summer 1969

Business Approach

Approaches to business for support should be made in a businesslike manner. With this in mind, the Arts Council of Winston-Salem, North Carolina asked business to support its annual fund-raising drive in a letter accompanied by four pages of exhibits to show where contributed money would go. One point underscored by the arts council was that "many persons who make up your company's corporate family and their wives serve as directors or perform numerous of the tasks for member groups." The thought was backed with statistics.

May 1965

A Dollar a Month

Many businesses now have "Buck of the Month" clubs through which employees grant management the right to deduct $1 each month from their paychecks as donations to worthwhile causes. In plans of this type, employees are given an opportunity to select the organizations they wish to aid. Arts groups should seek out the businesses in their areas that have such plans, and then present their case for support to these companies and to their employees so as to be included in the plans.

December 1964

Annual Corporate Donations

Make sure that companies who have contributed to your fund drive in the past are gently reminded when contribution time comes around again. *AM* learned of one recent instance where a secretary, typing a corporation's annual contribution list, forgot to inspect one sheet of paper. The result? An arts group and several other nonprofit organizations failed to receive their annual contributions.

Summer 1967

Dollars from Pop

Soft drinks may bring in hard cash. The Sacramento Symphony Orchestra, through a cooperative venture with the 7-Up Bottling Company of Sacramento, realizes about $100 at each of 16 concerts through the sale of soft drinks and coffee. While the Symphony Association pays the company for the actual cost of soda supplied to them, about 4¢ a drink, the bottling company provides free coffee, equipment, manpower, cups, and ice. The soft drinks are sold for 25¢ each and the coffee for 15¢ a cup. The project was initiated at the suggestion of the bottling company to help raise money for the orchestra.

Spring-Summer 1969

Cultural Events Play Key Role
in Employee Relations Program

Local businesses are becoming increasingly receptive to the sponsorship of cultural events on their premises as part of their employee relations program.

In Philadelphia, for example, the Professional Training Orchestra of the New School of Music presented a Saturday afternoon concert in the lunchroom of the Smith Kline & French Laboratories for employees of the company and their families.

Members of the all-student orchestra were paid for the performance, which was sponsored jointly by the company and the Martha Baird Rockefeller Fund for Music, Inc. This was the first in a series of industrial concerts to be presented by the orchestra during the 1965–66 season. A performance at the Philco Corporation plant in Philadelphia followed.

Two years ago, the New School initiated its industrial program with its orchestra performing in a concert sponsored by the Krylon Paint Company of Norristown, Pennslyvania. The open-air concert, held at the local high school stadium with employees of the company and their families in attendance, was given as part of Norristown's tercentenary celebration.

According to Max Aronoff, director of the school, "The purpose of these industrial concerts is to create a greater demand for live music and to develop a larger listening audience in the Philadelphia area." In addition, he said, "such a project will also provide a 'learn and earn' program for orchestral students."

Meanwhile, in Hartford, Connecticut, the Travelers Insurance Company is offering its employees, free of charge, a series of lectures intended to spur interest in fine music and attendance at concerts, including those of the Hartford Symphony.

Lectures conducted by Mary Lane, a violinist with the Hartford Symphony, cover such specific topics as the role of the conductor, the role of solo instruments, the arrangement of instruments, the functions of a large symphony choir, and a discussion of the musical styles of the last three centuries which make up the symphonic repertoire.

Featured in the lecture series is a discussion of the major works which the Hartford Symphony will perform this season.

February 1965

Business Finds New Ways to Aid the Arts

There is an increasing trend by arts groups to develop programs based on continuing relationships with business, where the long-range potential supercedes the immediate gain.

In Stratford, Connecticut, for example, the American Shakespeare Festival Theatre developed an Industrial Council, with membership drawn from top Connecticut corporations of a thousand or more employees. Members, including such firms as Charles Pfizer and Company, Avco, and the Electric Boat Division of General Dynamics, each appointed a top executive to serve on the council, which meets quarterly with Festival executives. The purpose of the council, according to the Festival, is to link the "two most successful aspects of the state of Connecticut—its industrial growth and its cultural growth—to form a mutually beneficial relationship."

There are two key aspects to the program. First, the Festival makes it clear that membership in the council is not a request for a financial donation. Second, the Festival provides a series of special benefits to each corporate member. These benefits include making blocks of tickets available at preview performances during the Festival's student season; saluting individual member corporations at special performances; allotting a limited number of free dress rehearsal admissions to companies who place standing orders for house seats; arranging backstage tours for representatives of council organizations and providing members with in-plant lectures and demonstrations by cast members; spotlighting Council members in local and national publicity and listing them in the Festival program; and providing members and their employees with monthly bulletins on the council and its activities.

Another Connecticut arts group, the Long Wharf Theatre in New Haven, tied its first anniversary to the 100th anniversary of a local corporation, the Winchester Company. In a ceremony, which was publicized locally, Winchester presented several antique rifles from its collection as a gift to Long Wharf for use in future productions. This initial project triggered several others. The theater was invited to present a revue at Winchester's centennial dinner attended by executives of the corporation and stars of the Hollywood movie, *Stagecoach*. Also, Winchester planned a "Company Night" for its employees at a Long Wharf performance to be followed by a gala champagne reception.

Meanwhile, in New York, the City Center of Music and Drama, Inc. was the recipient of an unusual service provided free by the Interpublic Group of Companies, Inc. Twenty younger employees of the corporation, which is composed of several leading advertising and marketing companies, conducted a detailed market analysis of the City Center operation. Upon completion of the study, the employees presented a report, more than 60 pages in length, to the Center containing their recommendations on how the Center could achieve a broader and more stable base of financial support.

The employees, representing different companies in the Interpublic Group, participated in the two-month-long project as part of a special corporate training program designed to help promising employees improve their skills. The project participants made the choice of the cultural group as a vehicle for analysis, although commercial corporations are normally studied in the program. They received counselling from top executives in the corporation during the course of study and presented their findings to an Interpublic review board before presenting them to the City Center.

Recommendations included suggestions on improving the Center's direct mail and public relations programs and a plan to increase membership in the Friends of City Center. In addition, the study group analyzed various advertising outlets in the Metropolitan New York area and recommended specific media to use, and a proposed advertising schedule and budget for each. Three new radio commercials and three print advertisements accompanied the report.

According to Mrs. Nancy LaSalle, director of the City Center's Education Department, "the report was interesting as a confirmation of many things we already knew. However, several of the points contained in it may prove of use to us."

A long-range program developed by a New York restaurant, the Cattleman, may prove beneficial to various arts groups. Early this summer, the restaurant invited the public, at a cost of $9 per person, to attend a week-long series of champagne suppers saluting the cast of a Broadway show, *Half a Sixpence.* The restaurant advertised the program in newspapers and on the radio, distributed invitations at theaters, and publicized it in its own newspaper and in table tents. The Cattleman assumed all costs and turned profits over to the Actors' Fund. Beginning this fall, the restaurant plans to resume the program on a regular basis for the benefit of the Actors' Fund and other arts groups by saluting new shows and other cultural attractions regularly. To attract more people, however, it intends to substitute drinks and refreshments for supper and lower the admission price.

August-September 1966

Orchestras Gain Support from Unusual Sources

To mark the anniversary of its first year in a new building, the Northern States Power Company of Minneapolis, Minnesota engaged the Minneapolis Symphony Orchestra to present a free public concert in the plaza adjoining the building last September. The result was extra paid employment for the orchestra, its exposure before a new audience, and favorable publicity for the utility company.

The idea for the project was conceived by R. D. Furber, vice president of Northern States Power and a board member of the Minnesota Orchestral Association, the parent body of the symphony. Planning for the concert began last May when the company contracted for the services of the orchestra at a fee of $2500. A September date was agreed upon by both parties as the earliest possible time for the concert. Details of the musical program were left to the orchestra's music director, Stanislaw Skrowaczewski, who selected such works as Dvorak's Symphony No. 4, Glinka's Overture to *Russlan and Ludmilla,* and Respighi's symphonic poem, *The Pines of Rome.*

To mount the program, the corporation had to build a platform for the orchestra on top of a pool at one end of the plaza. The possibility of traffic noise was eliminated when nearby construction work closed streets to vehicles on both sides of the plaza, which is located in a busy section of downtown Minneapolis. The plaza's marble wall behind the musicians served as an orchestra shell.

Full-scale promotion began a week prior to the event, with the corporation running announcements over local television stations and placing full-page advertisements in Minneapolis newspapers. The concert, held on a Sunday on a first-come, first-served basis, drew an enthusiastic overflow crowd of more than 3000, including many families and a surprisingly large number of children. The audience sat in chairs, stood, climbed a parking ramp across the street, and even sat on sawhorses, stacks of lumber, and mounds of earth at a nearby construction site.

According to E. J. Felton of the power company's information department, the concert enhanced the symphony's prestige as a community organization and made it the beneficiary of a tremendous amount of newspaper publicity both prior to and following the event. The company, in turn, viewed the concert as a highly successful public relations activity which drew attention to its longstanding support of the symphony.

"We would like to arrange another symphony concert under out sponsorship next summer," Mr. Felton told *AM*. "We believe that our concert has prompted some thinking by other firms toward possible sponsorship of symphony concerts in the future."

Another orchestra, Hofstra University's professional Pro Arte Symphony in Hempstead, Long Island, was the recipient of an entire building. When the Donald E. Axinn Company, a local real estate firm, decided to move to new offices, it donated its former building, valued at $25,000, to Hofstra University. The one-story, 34-by-44-foot wood-frame structure was moved eight miles to its new site on the Hofstra campus, where it will now serve as offices for the orchestra and for the university's Institute of the Arts.

January-February 1967

Standard Oil of New Jersey
Is Pragmatic Arts Patron: Aiding Projects
Brings It Prestige and Goodwill

The increased use to which business has been putting the arts in public relations work is dramatically illustrated by the experience of the Standard Oil Company of New Jersey. The parent company and its affiliates, both in the United States and abroad, have been pace-setters in cultural patronage. A notable recent example is the TV series "An Age of Kings," which brought Shakespeare's histories, as acted by the Old Vic company, into American homes.

Carl Maas, art director of Jersey Standard, told *AM* that the company is completely pragmatic about its activities in the arts. Its purpose is to build goodwill and prestige for the firm and to promote its products in a highly competitive field. Proof that it has been effective is seen in the flood of commendatory letters that have come to Maas and his colleagues within the Jersey Standard complex.

Local arts groups seeking patronage should approach the company through its local affiliate, Maas told *AM*. He emphasized that applicants should be prepared to state what they think the company can gain from sponsoring a particular program. Jersey Standard policy is to look for the unusual, to the end that a cultural program will attract favorable attention and thus win commendation for the sponsor. Company public relations in the arts is oriented toward thought leaders, *AM* was told.

Maas said he receives many suggestions and requests for aid, a large number of which are for projects either too small or unsuited to the company's purpose. Every project is examined, however, and where appropriate it is referred to the affiliate most likely to find a way to work it into its own program.

Jersey Standard's use of the arts as a means of visual communication goes back to 1942, when the company began to commission American painters to document the role of the oil industry in the war effort. By 1946 the company owned a sufficient number to warrant a traveling exhibition, which toured for five years and was shown in 125 university and museum galleries throughout the U. S. and Canada.

In 1944 the company started two other visual projects—the establishment of a photographic library and the production of its first motion picture. The photographs have since appeared in periodicals and books of many kinds, and some have appeared in museum exhibitions.

The first motion picture, produced by the late Robert Flaherty, was *Louisiana Story,* an artistic, highly honored documentary about a boy of the bayous and the friends he found among the men who came to drill an oil well. The film's musical score, "Louisiana Story Suite," was composed by Virgil Thomson. It was played by the Philadelphia Orchestra during a European tour and is available as a recording.

Imperial Oil Limited, Jersey's Canadian affiliate, has sponsored such films as *The Legend of the Raven* and *The Seasons,* which were distributed jointly with the National Film Board of Canada and by educational departments of Canadian provinces.

Imperial has also commissioned paintings and drawings by some of the country's finest artists for use in its magazine, *Imperial Oil Review,* and has decorated the lobby of its home office building in Toronto with two large murals by R. York Wilson, one of Canada's leading painters.

Another Imperial Oil project in the arts is its purchase of a collection of drawings by Charles S. Jefferys. The company photographed and catalogued Jefferys' work and distributed reproductions to schools.

In France, the Jersey affiliate, Esso Standard S.A.F., has employed outstanding sculptors to design figureheads for the company's tankers. In Italy, the local company has held art competitions and used works of avant-garde artists to illustrate the company magazine, *Esso Revista.* The English company has made a notable color film, *Our Native Shores,* of which the government Information Office has made versions in several other languages.

February 1963

Airline Sponsorship
Helps Concert Program Grow

A concert program for young artists, limited in scope and regional in nature during the first three years of its existence, has grown to national prominence since receiving the support and sponsorship of a leading corporation, American Airlines.

American Youth Performs, an organization that arranges paid engagements for promising apprentice singers and instrumentalists to appear with youth symphonies and choirs, served a limited East Coast area from its founding in 1961 until 1965. Many of the concerts were booked into small towns and outlying areas of large cities. Artists' fees were paid for by school and local education boards presenting the concerts, and the remaining costs were loaned to AYP by interested individuals.

In the spring of 1965, Charles Abdoo, the founder of AYP, approached American Airlines for support, after first studying the company and its basic philosophy. He discovered that the company was interested in local affairs, especially those involving the youth of a community. Also, it had sponsored good music programs on radio for a number of years. He suggested that the airline sponsorship of AYP be tested in several local markets first, as part of the company's community relations program.

The airline supported concerts in five cities initially, and it broadened its support considerably the following year, sponsoring concerts in 62 cities throughout the country. This support, including artists' fees, all travel expenses, and, where necessary, auditorium rental fees and the printing of tickets and programs, enabled local schools to present the concerts without cost. Airline support averaged about $1500 per market, covering three to six concerts in participating cities. As a highlight of its 1966 sponsorship, the airline underwrote the cost of a Carnegie Hall concert featuring artists brought to New York from 50 cities and subsidized the production and national distribution of a complimentary record album taped at the concert.

In 1967, under the sponsorship of American Airlines, AYP is presenting concerts in 60 to 65 cities. A second Carnegie Hall concert will be offered on April 20, with young artists from 99 cities performing as orchestra members and as choristers. A record album of the concert again will be released and distributed without charge to school music supervisors throughout the country. In addition, airline sponsorship has enabled AYP to add performing educators to the program —orchestral and choral conductors and music clinicians—at the high school, university, and conservatory level. These educators travel to various cities, where they work with youth orchestras.

Based on his own experience, Mr. Abdoo offers this advice to arts groups seeking corporate support: "When you get a good idea, shape it into a workable and tangible program before presenting it to a potential sponsor. When you do present it, make sure that your program is complete and that it works for the sponsor and not just for your organization. Also, try to develop programs which can be presented on a small test basis at first, and then expanded if they work. Always give credit to the sponsoring corporation, even if they don't ask for it. And finally, be persistent."

March-April 1967

Growing Business Support

The Kennedy Center in Washington, D.C. initiated a new Corporate Fund for the Performing Arts with the endorsement of President Ford. Headed by nine prominent corporate leaders—chairman Donald S. MacNaughton of Prudential Insurance and eight vice chairmen—the group set a first year goal of $1 million to be raised from business.

Elsewhere, there is good evidence of new kinds of business support. In Smithtown, New York, a group of department stores, banks, and other merchants at the Smith Haven Mlll, one of the country's largest suburban shopping centers, has agreed to provide most of the funding for a year-long arts program at the mall budgeted at about $100,000. Offered free to shoppers, the program features some 84 different cultural events, many by local groups, produced for the mall by the Smithtown Township Arts Council. In nearby Huntington, New York, the local McDonald's Restaurant gave $25,000 to the PAF Playhouse to provide a permanent home for the theater's professional acting company for children.

Orchestras winning support include the Detroit Symphony, the beneficiary for the opening of the new Detroit Plaza Hotel; the North Carolina Symphony; whose new multimedia program was funded by IBM and whose Carnegie Hall debut in March will be sponsored by R. J. Reynolds; and the Phoenix Symphony, which has upped its list of corporate guarantors for pairs of concerts, at minimum donations of $3000 each, to eight this season.

January-February 1977

Business Sponsor

Perhaps you don't have "a friend at Chase Manhattan," but if a company in your area has a quality art collection, as a growing number of corporations do, you might borrow an idea from Chase and benefit your group. In the fall of 1971, the bank presented the first public exhibition of its outstanding art collection as a benefit for the Dance Theatre of Harlem. The exhibition, held at Finch College in New York, featured a sparkling cocktail party opening with guests paying $25 each to view the collection and see a brief, informal performance by the dance company in the college auditorium. Net result? Good will for the bank and money in the bank—nearly $10,000—for the dance company.

November-December 1971

Divide and Conquer

If arts groups can't find a single corporation willing to sponsor an entire project, they might be able to entice several companies into sharing the project, especially if it is one that can be easily divided, such as the pages of a publication. The January–March 1970 issue of the four-page newsletter *Museum Matters,* published by the Orange County Community of Museums and Galleries in Goshen, New

York, had three different corporate sponsors—one for page two, another for page three, and a third sponsor for page four. Each was identified by name, address, and telephone number and credited at the bottom of its sponsored page.

Winter 1969-70

Breakfast with Business

Speeches by executives of cultural institutions at meetings of leading organizations are a good method of promoting the institution's activities. One important platform, frequently overlooked, is the business meeting or convention. Some companies, such as Prentice-Hall, Inc. in New York, have regular executive breakfasts at which experts in various fields address the company leaders.

August 1963

Business as Sponsor

If your organization is planning to issue a regular publication, you should consider asking local businesses to sponsor it on a rotating basis. Thus, no one business will be asked to assume a continuing financial burden, and the example established by one company may act as a spur to other companies. In Rockland County, New York, *South of the Mountain,* the quarterly publication of the Tappan Zee Historical Society, has been sponsored by a variety of local business organizations since its inception in 1957.

December 1963

Local Business Is Good
Source of Arts Assistance

Local businesses and franchise operations, while seldom able to give at the level of national companies, can play a key role in the funding picture of many arts groups. Moreover, once a breakthrough has been made, it can lead to increased yearly funding and the personal involvement of individual businessmen.

The Jenkintown, Pennsylvania Music School, for example, through a campaign aimed at six areas of local business and two professions, was able to win new business money, a high level of enthusiasm, and even recruit a businessman-volunteer to the board. The campaign, known as BRASS—the Businessman's Rally for Arts Scholarship Support—was built around business volunteers serving as division leaders who solicited scholarship funds from their business colleagues in the names of their respective professions. A real estate broker, for example, suggested contributions of $25 to $100 for a "Realtor's Scholarship." Other divisions included insurance brokers, travel agents, physicians, lawyers, store owners, department store executives, and bankers.

The $3000 raised was not large, but it represented for the school the first contributions from many local businessmen. Moreover, the general chairman joined the board and also accepted the job of running the BRASS campaign during the coming season on a much-expanded basis. Not only will the number of divisions be doubled, but promotional activity will be stepped up, with local businesses featuring window displays and posters.

In communities throughout the country, owner-operated McDonald's stores are proving to be strong supporters of local arts activities, especially those programs oriented to youngsters. Although the company has a national grants program—the Kennedy Center has been a major beneficiary—and underwrites the PBS series "Once Upon A Classic," store operators throughout the country have become the most accessible targets for community arts groups. In recent months McDonald's operators have underwritten Omaha Symphony concerts for youngsters, promoted the Taconic Theatre on placemats, and sponsored programs by the Great American Childrens Theatre Company in Milwaukee.

Importantly, because McDonald's owner-operators in a television market area are organized into groups for advertising and promotional purposes—there are about 100 groups drawn from the 4600 stores nationally—the combined resources of several stores in a group can up the dollar potential considerably for local arts programs. Just this June, for example, the owner-operators of 41 McDonald's Restaurants on Long Island in New York combined to give a four-year grant to the PAF Theatre for Young People. The grant, $35,000 a year or a total of $140,000, will help underwrite performances for thousands of Long Island youngsters annually.

Community involvement by local owners has been spurred by the national office which considers such involvement good business. Next month, in fact, McDonald's will distribute a specially prepared "Case History Package" to all its owner-operators and advertising people. The booklet, in a three-ring binder, will include some 15 to 20 examples of local community support and involvement, with about eight dealing with the arts and education.

Summer 1978

Broadcasters' Group Backs
Canada Drama Festival

The Dominion Drama Festival in Canada, devoted to the stimulation of theater art through national competitions, has for three years had the active backing of the Canadian Association of Broadcasters, an organization of 167 radio and 55 television stations. CAB support, financial as well as promotional, has helped make the annual festival an event of importance.

An average of 95 theater groups participate in regional and subregional drama competitions. This year eight organizations participated in the finals, held in Kitchener, Ontario. The playoff festival is held in a different city each year. Regional festivals are judged by qualified drama professionals. The national competition is judged by a prominent theater personality from outside the county.

The top judge this year was Pierre Lefevre, head of the drama school of Centre de l'Ouest, one of France's leading national theaters.

Financing has always been a problem for the Dominion Drama Festival. Each region is responsible for its own budget, and participating drama groups pay entry fees to the national body, but coordinating and running the festival program requires an annual budget of $69,000. This money goes not only to stage the national festival, but to operate a small office in Ottawa, with a staff consisting of a national director—Richard MacDonald—an assistant, and two clerical employees. The funds are raised from private contributions and a subsidy from the Canada Council, a government agency. From 1952 to 1960 the festival also had the support of Calvert Distillers, Ltd., which made an annual grant of $15,000. When this support was discontinued in 1960, however, the festival faced severe problems. It was at this point that the Canadian Association of Broadcasters stepped in.

The CAB, interested in encouraging Canadian talent and in building a better public relations image for itself, now donates $21,000 annually. This provides $1000 in prize money for each of the regional winners, and an additional $1000 for the winning drama group in the final festival.

The CAB, however, goes beyond its financial contribution. It actively promotes theater in all parts of the country, and does much to promote ticket sales for both the regional and national festivals. For the regional meets, the television and radio stations broadcast spots, flashes, news items, interviews, and feature stories on the presentations. For the final festival, the situations in the host city produce material for broadcast in the home cities of the participating groups and air their own shows about the festival. In addition, the Canadian Broadcasting Corporation, the government-owned broadcast network, usually carries a live program about the presentation of the awards.

Awards go not only for the best production, but for the best plays (one in English, one in French), for the best director, outstanding actors and actresses, etc. There are cash prizes and a $3000 scholarship awarded by the province of Quebec for the most promising artist whose mother tongue is French.

The festival program has not only stimulated new interest in theater, but promoted interest in biculturalism. In six regions, French-speaking and English-speaking drama companies compete against one another. The festival appears to have demonstrated that the two-language factor is not a barrier.

August 1963

Art Programs for Corporations
Win New Members and Audience

Cultural institutions seeking to increase interest and support from the business community are wise to develop special programs for this group. A successful activity of this nature was sponsored by the Minneapolis Institute of Arts.

An evening was set aside at the institute for a "Treasure Party" exclusively for the employees of Corporate Members of the Minneapolis Society of Fine Arts, the governing and supporting organization of the Institute. Admission was free, and the 105 business members—contributors of $100 or more to the society's annual Guaranty Fund Drive—were send handsome invitations, and companies were asked to post these on their bulletin boards.

700 persons attended the three-hour reception. Guided tours were held, behind-the-scenes visits were made to the museum workshop where works of art are cleaned and restored, a short film was shown, informal discussions took place with the museum's staff, and refreshments were served.

According to one official, "Many individual memberships were sold as a result of that night. We also know that events such as this one, which bring people into the institute for the first time, increase our attendance from that night on, as the same people bring their friends."

September 1962

International Ties

Arts groups planning a program with an international flavor may get support for the event from a local business that has international ties. For example, an American company which had its origins in Switzerland recently contributed $300 to help sponsor an exhibition of Swiss posters on loan from the Traveling Exhibition Service of the Smithsonian Institution. The exhibition was presented at a cultural institution in the company's home community.

January 1966

Corporate Gifts

The Whitney Museum in New York has developed a successful corporate gift plan which might be adapted by other visual arts groups. Corporations contribute $3000 to the museum to enable it to purchase a painting. Once the painting is selected by the Museum, it then lends that work, or up to three others, to the corporation for one year. At the end of the year, the painting is returned to the museum to be added to its permanent collection.

November-December 1967

Floral Tribute

A fund-raising technique used successfully by the Ballet Guild of Cleveland, Ohio may be of interest to smaller arts groups. Each year, the guild provides volunteers to man the display of a local florist at an annual flower show. The florist, in turn, contributes the "wages" earned by the volunteers to the guild.

March-April 1968

Joint Celebration

Seeking business support for a project? You might tie-in with a company that has a special celebration coming up, such as its 25th or 100th anniversary, and you can use your program as a means of calling attention to its special year. Last year TRW sponsored a Cleveland Orchestra concert and commissioned a work for it in honor of its 75th anniversary. This year J.C. Penney is sponsoring a major exhibition, "Turn of the Century America: Paintings, Graphics, Photographs, 1890–1910" as part of its 75th anniversary activities. The exhibition will open at the Whitney Museum in June and will then tour other museums.

March-April 1977

Culture Center Also Retailer to Help Finance Arts Program

A New England arts group has found a unique way to help finance its nonprofit operation. It has become a commercial retailer. Since April 1971, the National Center of Afro-American Artists, Inc. in Dorchester, Massachusetts, which conducts an intensive training and performance program in dance, drama, music, and art for black artists, has been partner as well as operator of the Capezio Dance Shop in Boston.

The Boston store, a long-established and successful operation, is one of six Capezio Dance shops throughout the country which are run as partnerships between the parent company, Cap-Sal-Ballet Makers of New York, and local entrepreneurs. When Herbert Tieman, the Boston operator died this February, Cap-Sal president Ben Sommers, who is also the president of the Capezio Foundation and a board member of several national dance organizations, began searching for a new local partner. Elma Lewis, a nationally known arts educator and a good friend of the former owner, was recommended. Instead of proposing herself as a partner, however, Miss Lewis suggested that the Afro-American Center, which she founded and directed along with the Elma Lewis School of Fine Arts, take over half-ownership and manage the operation. "Whatever profits we make," she told Sommers, "can go back into the operation of the center and the school."

The idea of artists and dancers running a store that sold dance supplies, shoes, and leotards had tremendous appeal to Sommers, as did the fact that both Miss Lewis and her operation were well known and respected in the Boston area. Moreover, they would have a tremendous incentive to do well because the arts center would benefit. As Sommers told *AM,* "This was a tremendous opportunity for the center, and we made it easy for them to acquire the partnership."

While it is highly unlikely that store profits will ever negate the need for center fund raising, the new arrangement does provide it with an excellent source of added income which hopefully, will continue to grow over the years. Miss

Lewis told *AM* that the store is already making plans to expand into such new sales areas as jewelry, books, and makeup.

In the first few months under the in-store managership of dancer Delores Brown, the store, according to Miss Lewis, "is doing marvelously. We're doing about twice as great a volume as the previous management, and we're very excited about it."

Summer 1971

Business Develops
New Arts Support Programs

A New York bank that several years ago asked depositors to donate the value of new account gifts to the public library instead of accepting them broke new ground again during the summer of 1974. As a means of rewarding continuing depositors, a market often ignored by gift-giving banks, East New York Savings Bank underwrote its own six-event cultural series at Town Hall and gave away free tickets on a first-come, first-served basis to more than 7500 depositors. In Boston, the opening of the "Frontier America" exhibition at the Museum of Fine Arts this January mark something of a corporate record—the eighth major exhibition to have been sponsored by Philip Morris and its affiliates since 1973.

Business publications have given their editorial support to the arts recently. On October 2, in its influential editorial page feature, "Review & Outlook," the *Wall Street Journal* ran a full feature entitled "Underwriting the Arts," which concluded, "The performing arts in America have the vitality to innovate on their own. The important task is to crystallize the economic base which will allow them to flourish." On a local level, the Greater Minneapolis Chamber of Commerce saluted the opening of Symphony Hall and the city's new fine arts complex by devoting the entire September issue of its magazine to "Business and the Arts."

In South Carolina, a model program aimed at business, the Industrial Musician program, sent classical guitarist Richard Phillips to companies around the state from October 1973 through last May. Phillips, who also appeared at local schools, gave factory concerts and was used in employee relations programs.

September-October 1974

ORGANIZED FORCES OF BUSINESS SUPPORT

Chamber of Commerce Spurs Arts in City

An important chamber of commerce program in Oklahoma City has provided a strong stimulus to the growth and maintenance of arts organizations there. Almost all the city's leading cultural institutions, including its symphony orchestra, arts center, theater, and museum, were established with the help of the chamber and have received its continuing support.

The chamber has mobilized the leadership and resources of the community to heighten local interest in the arts. "This goal has been consistently set forth throughout the years in the chamber's policies and projects, alongside the goals for industrial and commercial development," Lola Hall, secretary of the chamber's Committee on Education and the Arts, told *AM.*

As part of its policy, the chamber has frequently played an important role in leading fund-raising drives to meet the financial needs of the city's cultural institutions. In 1962, the chamber helped to organize a special Danny Kaye Benefit Concert and Symphony Maintenance Fund Campain on behalf of the Oklahoma City Symphony, an orchestra it helped to found in 1938. More than $153,-000 was raised in a single night to help the orchestra pay its accumulated debts and to place it on a sound financial footing. In addition, the chamber was instrumental in instituting the regularly scheduled network broadcasts of the orchestra which have been heard throughout the county for 20 years.

Another local group which has been aided by the chamber is the Mummers Theatre. In 1963, the Ford Foundation offered the theater a matching grant of $700,000 for a home and equipment. The chamber led an intensive two-week campaign in which the grant was more than matched by $750,000 raised from civic leaders.

The chamber also led a drive that resulted in the location in Oklahoma City of the National Cowboy Hall of Fame and Western Heritage Center, built by the 17 western states. Oklahoma's share of $1 million toward the center was raised through a drive spearheaded by the chamber.

To accelerate future cultural growth in the community, the chamber helped to establish the Oklahoma City Industrial and Cultural Facilities Trust last year. Funds from the trust were instrumental in financing the completion of the Cowboy Hall of Fame and in helping it to acquire a $1 million collection of Charles M. Russell art.

Oklahoma City University, a large contributor to the city's cultural life, has benefited greatly from chamber support and leadership. Stanley Draper, managing director of the chamber, is chairman of the school's Campus Development Committee, with which the chamber worked to develop the university's plan to expand its facilities. Currently, a $600,000 addition to the university's music school is being undertaken. This addition will include space for speech, drama, and ballet activities.

Other groups which the chamber supports are the Oklahoma City Junior Symphony, the Civic Music Association (Mr. Draper is a member of the board of both), the Chamber Music Series, and the Oklahoma City Civic Ballet. The chamber was instrumental in establishing the Oklahoma Art Center in 1935 and has given the institution its continued support from the beginning.

March 1966

Chambers of Commerce Supporting the Arts

Chambers of Commerce are asking an increasingly active role in supporting arts activities in their communities, according to the results of a recently completed *AM* survey. A detailed questionnaire drew responses from chambers in 181 cities in 44 states throughout the country. Responding chambers represent more than 125,000 business members.

Strikingly evident from survey results is the fact that chambers are establishing closer ties with their local arts groups. Seventy chambers, 40 percent of those responding to the question, indicated that they have created special committees on the arts, with 33 of them organized within the past three years. Five other chambers include the arts in civic affairs or recreation committees. An *AM* chamber survey five years ago revealed that only 27.9 percent of responding chambers had such committees. In the first three months of 1967 alone, eight chambers created new cultural committees, and others are now being organized.

As another indication of increasing chamber interest in the arts, a surprisingly high 18.7 percent of the chambers reported that they have published special brochures or pamphlets devoted to the arts of their communities. These ranged from mimeographed publications prepared at virtually no cost by two chambers in Indiana to handsome brochures costing thousands of dollars.

In Winston-Salem, North Carolina, a chamber-published arts brochure cost $5000; a report on the arts in Dallas cost the chamber $7500; and a 1963 Atlanta chamber brochure cost $12,000. The Houston chamber published brochures on the arts in 1963 and 1965, and the Minneapolis chamber has twice published cultural brochures as a supplement to other chamber publications. Some chambers, such as those in Springdale, Arkansas and Orlando, Florida have published brochures for special arts events.

Some arts groups are receiving direct financial assistance from chambers in their communities. Nearly 20 percent of responding chambers answered yes to the question "Does your chamber make financial contributions to any local cultural organization or institution?" In Dayton, the chamber contributes $6000 to local arts organizations and produces 18 summer concerts in cooperation with the city and the local musicians' union at a total cost of $25,000. The Beloit, Wisconsin chamber contributes $2500 to a local art gallery; chambers in Hollywood, Florida and Hartford, Connecticut each contribute $1500 to concert series; and the Asheville, North Carolina chamber contributes $1125 to the Thomas Wolfe Theatre.

Music and arts festivals receive financial support from chambers in North Little Rock, Arkansas, Harlan, Kentucky, Savannah, Georgia, Kirkwood, Missouri, Asheville, North Carolina, and Pawtucket, Rhode Island. The Winter Park, Florida chamber contributes $500 to the local symphony and the Amarillo, Texas chamber donates $500 to its fine arts council.

In Cherokee, Iowa, the chamber, in addition to contributing $100 to the arts council, spent more than $500 plus hundreds of hours of contributed time, to help promote a bond issue for a new community center. The Alhambra, California chamber purchases the prize for an art competition. In Flagstaff, Arizona, the chamber helps finance the printing of brochures by various arts groups.

Over 80 percent of responding chambers provide nonfinancial services to local arts groups. Although the most common form of assistance is the promotion and publicity of cultural events, chamber help is wide-ranging and varied. Chambers in Fort Dodge, Iowa; Louisville, Kentucky; and Oklahoma City, Oklahoma; for example, offer counsel in fund-raising campaigns. The Beckley, West Virginia chamber raises money for the West Virginia Historical Drama Association, and the Cincinnati chamber "highlighted the need for business support of the Playhouse in the Park."

In a number of communities, chambers furnish meeting facilities for arts groups and provide secretarial and administrative services. The McKeesport, Pennsylvania chamber provides quarters for its symphony orchestra, and the Hollywood, Florida chamber does bookkeeping for its symphony. In Denver, the chamber helped establish the western offices of the National Folk Festival, and in Orlando, Florida, the chamber is helping to organize a community arts council. Other chambers maintain arts calendars, help organize festivals, and present arts awards.

The Houston chamber, for example, conceived, organized, and sponsored the city's first comprehensive arts festival, held in October 1966. Two years of advance effort preceded the month-long program.

In Ypsilanti, Michigan, the chamber is trying to save the Greek Theatre, which presented its first season last summer, but has been forced to cancel the 1967 season because of financial difficulties. The chamber has agreed to take over business management of the theater at the request of the theater's board of directors. In an attempt to insure a 1968 season, chamber members have been contacting foundations and soliciting funds.

How important are the arts in attracting tourists to a city? Only 6.8 percent of responding chambers view the arts as a prime factor; 29.0 percent see it as very important; 46.6 percent see it as moderately important; and 17.6 percent find the arts an insignificant tourist attraction.

The arts, however, play a more prominent role in attracting new industry to communities. Although only 3.4 percent of the chambers see the arts as a prime factor, nearly 46 percent consider the arts a very important factor, and 39.8 percent indicate that cultural activities are moderately important. The other 10.8 percent view the arts as an insignificant factor.

One hundred and twenty-five chambers estimated the percentage of their member companies making direct financial contributions to arts groups. The responses were: fewer than 10 percent, thirty-one chambers; 10 to 25 percent, forty-four; 25 to 50 percent, twenty-six; 50 to 75 percent, fifteen; and over 75 percent, nine chambers.

March-April 1967

Businesswomen Aid Arts

Businesswomen are a new group to lend assistance to the arts. In Anaheim, California, 230 members of the Women's Division of the Anaheim Chamber of Commerce have developed a widespread cultural program. This year, for example, the group cosponsored and coordinated Anaheim Cultural Arts Month and the Carousel of Anaheim, a two-day community-wide arts festival. Through its cultural arts committee, the group has developed art exhibitions, sponsored an annual lecture and concert series, and assisted the local arts council. It is now planning to publish a brochure, "The Cultural Arts of Anaheim," to be based on its survey of arts activity in the community.

November-December 1968

A Chamber of Commerce
Has Ten-year Arts Plan

The main program focus of a southern chamber of commerce during the next decade will be on the arts. The Greensboro, North Carolina chamber, which celebrated its ninetieth anniversary last year, is planning for its centennial with a multifaceted cultural program which will be climaxed by the presentation of a new symphonic drama in 1977.

As the first step in its ten-year arts program, the chamber recently underwrote the engagement of Thomas Cousins for a two-year period as Greensboro's composer-in-residence. Cousins in the former conductor of the Greensboro Symphony Orchestra and former faculty member at the University of North Carolina in Greensboro. The chamber has also commissioned a work of sculpture which, when completed next month, will be placed in the downtown business area.

Among its other programs, the chamber is planning a study of the community's historic sites for restoration, a survey of Greensboro's cultural resources, and a closer liaison with the Greensboro Arts Council.

Members of another southern chamber of commerce, in Jackson, Mississippi, provided unique assistance to the American Symphony Orchestra League. When the chamber's members learned that the League had been trying for two years to find funds to purchase a station wagon for the use of its headquarters staff, they raised the funds and presented the money to the Jackson Symphony League for transmittal to the ASOL. An official presentation of the automobile was made at a board meeting of the ASOL's Women's Council in Chicago.

January-February 1968

Key Business Group
Features Arts in Program

Quietly and without fanfare, an international organization with more than 2300 top business leaders as members has developed a significant program of education and idea exchange that includes the arts as one of its key aspects. The Young Presidents' Organization, which limits its membership to men and women who became the chief operating officers or presidents of their companies before their fortieth birthday (there are qualifying requirements also as to company size and business volume), emphasizes self-development for its members in all areas of personal and public responsibility. Although primary emphasis is on business subjects, the arts are regularly included as topics in national and regional meetings, and they have been the feature subject for national symposia as well.

This fall, for example, YPO will sponsor its fourth annual symposium on the arts at Lincoln Center. Open to all members, the program includes lectures on cultural topics by arts leaders and members' attendance at performances. The four areas of discussion are theater, ballet, opera, and music.

In the spring of 1967, YPO sponsored a five-day West Coast Cultural Seminar in Los Angeles which included visits to leading museums in the area, tours of UCLA's fine arts and performing arts facilities, and a full day at the Los Angeles Music Center for tours, meetings, and attendance at a concert. Special class sessions, with faculty drawn from Los Angeles area cultural groups, rounded out the program for corporation presidents.

The annual University for Presidents, a week-long international gathering of YPO members, has included the arts as one of its four permanent divisions since 1967. The educationally oriented program features approximately 100 different courses for attendees. At this year's university, held in Puerto Rico in April, R. Philip Hanes, Jr., vice chairman of Associated Councils of the Arts and a YPO member, served as arts dean, and Ralph Burgard, executive director of ACA, was his assistant. Members of the arts faculty were Maria Tallchief, Philip Johnson, Stan Vanderbeek, Jonathan Williams, and Jules Irving, who discussed such subjects as the new theater and its significance to the community, new poetry, and architectural decay.

In addition to the programs YPO presents on a national and international level, it offers many additional meetings and seminars at the area level (the organization is divided into 11 major areas throughout the world) and at the chapter level. Each of the 35 chapters in the United States and in 30 foreign countries develops its own monthly program, independent of the international organization, and frequently the arts are featured.

Although YPO as an organization does not underwrite outside cultural activities or programs, its commitment to the betterment of the arts and its treatment of the arts as an essential aspect of everyday life is precedent-setting.

Summer 1968

A CHRONOLOGY OF
BUSINESS-ARTS DEVELOPMENTS

Group Formed to Spur
Corporate Aid to Arts

A national advisory organization of corporate executives, created to spur increased business support to the arts, has just been organized and expects to be fully operational by January 1968. Called the Business Committee for the Arts, the group traces its origins back to a proposal made by David Rockefeller, president of the Chase Manhattan Bank, in an address to the annual meeting of the National Industrial Conference Board in September 1966. Mr. Rockefeller, at the time, proposed the establishment of a national council on business and the arts to be composed of businessmen knowledgeable in the arts, cultural leaders, and representative artists whose purpose would be to broaden the base of corporate support to cultural organizations.

The positive response to his suggestion prompted Mr. Rockefeller to meet with other top corporate leaders and plan the development of the new organization. As now constituted, the committee will include 75 to 80 members, all top corporate officers at the level of executive vice president and higher. The committee, to be located at 1270 Avenue of the Americas, New York, New York, will be chaired by C. Douglas Dillon, former Secretary of the Treasury and now president of the United States and Foreign Securities Corporation. [*Note: BCA is now at 1501 Broadway, New York, New York.*]

From within the overall membership, a board of directors and an executive committee of some six to ten members will be drawn. The new group will serve in an advisory capacity, and while it will suggest ways in which corporations can assist the arts, it will not be a grant-giving organization itself. The committee hopes to support its activities through funds provided by a consortium of foundations.

Although cultural leaders and artists will not be included on the committee, as was originally proposed by Mr. Rockefeller, G. A. McLellan, who was recently hired as the committee's president, told *AM* that his organization will work closely with national arts organizations in the development of its program. Mr. McLellan, former administrative director of Plans for Progress and most recently director of public affairs at Olin Mathieson, outlined five working objectives of the committee: to research information on support of the arts for the business community; to counsel corporations interested in aiding the arts; to develop a nationwide public information program to inform corporations of new opportunities for support of the arts and to apprise art groups of corporate activity in the arts; to assist cultural organizations in presentations to corporations and encourage participation by businessmen in arts groups; and to represent business in cooperative endeavors with arts organizations and governmental arts agencies.

Most members of the committee will be drawn from large corporations, but several several smaller firms will be represented as well. Both a geographic and industrial balance will be maintained. The group plans to hold its first meeting in January 1968.

September-October 1967

Survey Shows Increased
Corporate Aid to Arts

Corporate support to the arts is increasing—it has quintupled from 1959 to 1969 —but much more is needed if the problems of the arts are to be alleviated. This is one of the conclusions reached in the nation's first comprehensive survey of business support of the arts, undertaken by the National Industrial Conference Board on behalf of the Business Committee for the Arts. The completed survey is based on the results of a detailed seven-page questionnaire sent to corporations of varying sizes last summer, with 500 of the questionnaires selected at random for inclusion in the study.

Nearly 70 percent of the respondents, 345 of 500 corporations, said they contributed to the arts. Based on BSA/NICB projections and interpolations with other studies, the report estimates that corporate contributions of funds and gifts in kind to the arts in 1968 totalled $45 million. This amount was nearly equalled, according to the report, by the additional $40 million corporations gave to the arts in 1968 through business expenses—items carried on the corporate books as advertising or promotional expenses, rather than contributions.

What kind of corporation is most likely to support the arts? A profile drawn from the survey shows it to be a relatively small, nonmanufacturing, publicly-held company with fewer than 1000 employees, which is primarily concerned with local markets. The most favored areas of corporate arts support are symphony orchestras, museums, and cultural and civic centers, in that order. Least popular are donations to experimental art forms and composers.

The survey explores many other aspects of corporate support in detail, including the rationale for giving and for nongiving. A complete analysis is contained in the BCA book *Business and the Arts '70*.

Winter 1969-70

Business and Arts Equal
Partners in New Council

A pioneer corporate aid-to-the-arts program organized by the New York Board of Trade six years ago, has been restructured to include *equal* arts and business representation within its committee membership. The new Arts and Business Cooperative Council, which replaces the Board's Business and the Arts Advisory Council, plans to promote corporate support for all arts programs regardless of size and serve as a business-arts voice on vital issues concerning the arts in the city.

As its first public action, the new committee presented a program for businessmen at Lincoln Center's Forum theater honoring neighboring arts activities and featuring brief performances by four community cultural groups. At the program, the committee announced that through it, Standard Oil of New Jersey had made a $52,500 grant to New York's borough arts councils to encourage cultural programs at the community level and to enable the councils to continue their administrative services.

Summer 1971

Canadian Firm Starts Million-dollar Arts Fund

In an unusual action which suggests a model for corporations interested in aiding the arts, a Canadian cigarette manufacturer has established a performing arts council and committed $1 million to its support over the next five years, from 1972 to 1977. The du Maurier Council for the Performing Arts, with Canadian Senator Donald Cameron as chairman and four leaders of the arts and education communities as directors, will operate independent of its benefactor, du Maurier Cigarettes, in providing grants to existing Canadian performing arts groups. Emphasis will be on broadening the general public for the arts.

Over the years, du Maurier has been an active contributor to a variety of performing arts activities. The new program will enable it to maintain its involvement and support—its coordinator of arts activities will serve as liaison to the council—while removing from it the burden and responsibility of selecting grant recipients. Moreover, the cigarette company has agreed to provide marketing and public relations help to groups sponsored by the council. Organized in December, the council will meet twice a year to select grant recipients. As one of its initial actions it announced grants to six leading Canadian symphony orchestras in support of their special "pops" concert series.

January-February 1972

Company Hires Culture Head, Nation's First

In a precedent-setting, move, a leading American corporation, Dayton Hudson of Minneapolis, has filled a new slot in the business hierarchy—corporate director of cultural affairs. The position, believed to be the nation's first corporate job with full-time executive responsibility in the arts, will be manned as of January 2, 1973 by Orrel Thompson, former director of the Art Institute of Akron, Ohio. Elsewhere, other key developments are focusing increased national attention on the business role in the arts.

One of the nation's largest retailers, with operations in 26 states and annual sales exceeding $1 billion, Dayton Hudson has long been involved in supporting cultural programs in cities where its department stores are located. One of the few companies to utilize its full 5-percent tax deductive allowance for contributions, it has twice won the Esquire/BCA Business in the Arts Award.

The decision to create the new post was reached several months ago by board chairman Bruce Dayton and trustees of the Dayton Hudson Foundation who recognized the company's growing role in cultural affairs. "We decided that our principal thrust will be in the arts," said Robert W. MacGregor, vice president and executive director of the Dayton Hudson Foundation. "Instead of giving to everyone, a concentration of effort in the arts, under the professional direction of Mr. Thompson, will help us to use our funds more effectively and bring maximum benefits to the groups and artists we help."

In his new position, Thompson will be responsible for coordinating the existing corporate arts program, after evaluating present priorities and developing sound criteria for arts support. He will establish also a program of continuing education and communications in the arts for company employees and develop, with the help of cultural groups and community leaders, new projects in a wide range of areas. He indicated to *AM,* however, that the overall Dayton Hudson arts program will take time to develop. "We can't establish a program in a vacuum," he said. "Before we can develop a serious program we will have to get out and explore where the needs are."

In a discussion with *AM,* Thompson pinpointed some of the areas that he hopes to explore in the coming months, including the development of far-reaching arts programs for shopping centers, free consultative help to cultural groups, discount ticket distribution to employees, lecture and dialogue programs in theater and music for community groups, and development of working state-wide arts–business coalitions.

"We're looking to develop an exemplary arts program," he added, "which can demonstrate to other corporations what can be done. It's our goal to establish the kind of program that can help the cities in which we're located become major cultural centers."

Elsewhere, a government agency has become interested in the arts–business relationship. The United States Information Agency is now involved in the planning stages of an exhibit on business and the arts which, when completed sometime in the spring of 1973, will be offered to the 120 USIA agencies throughout the world for their possible use. Included in the exhibit will be articles and books, films, and visual materials.

Organizationally, there are continued developments of interest. The Business Committee for the Arts sponsored pilot business–arts meetings this fall in Wisconsin, southern California, and Oklahoma and full statewide conferences in Indiana and Louisiana. Eight or nine additional meetings are expected to be held by mid-1973.

In New York, the Arts and Business Cooperative Council of the New York Board of Trade, established seven years ago as the first organization of its kind, will take on a new structure and an important new role soon. The council, an equal representation group of business and arts leaders, has just been incorporated as a not-for-profit organization and under its new name, the Arts and Business Council of New York City, Inc., will operate as an entity separate from the Board of Trade. This status will allow the council to become a tax-exempt body with a new action role—obtaining contributions from business to make grants to arts programs and cultural groups in New York.

Corporate involvement in the arts is attracting editorial attention as well. The *Harvard Business Review* is planning several future articles on the subject, and the January 1973 issue of *The American Way,* the in-flight magazine of American Airlines which is read by hundreds of thousands of businessmen, features an illustrated cover story on the subject by *AM* editor Alvin H. Reiss.

November-December 1972

Businesses Launch Pilot Arts Aid Programs

Two new business support programs with broad-based approaches are benefiting cultural groups throughout the country. The model projects, both begun in 1974, involve sizeable contributions by their respective corporate sponsors, and unlike many past business grants, aid small as well as large and established institutions.

The Mobil Foundation's $500,000 "experimental" arts program was developed to support arts activities in those communities where the company had a major interest in terms of plant location, large numbers of employees, or share of the market. Interestingly, the foundation turned to Mobil's employees to help in the selection of grant recipients. Working from guidelines sent to them—activities at the grassroots level in either the performing or visual arts were suggested—Mobil field managers were asked last July to identify projects worthy of support in their areas, including those that were new and innovative.

With an October deadline for grant proposals. Mobil managers had to move quickly to investigate and pinpoint those arts projects that they felt were most worthy of support. Managers in each of the 30 areas involved in the program were given a predetermined budget for their respective locales and permission to allocate the funding as they saw fit. The process of selection itself brought many of the managers much closer to local arts activity than they had been in the past and made them aware of important cultural programs that perhaps they and their employees had overlooked. By deadline time, 130 arts groups in the 30 areas, representing a wide range of cultural activity, had been nominated for grants of from $1000 to $3000 each. Virtually all the recommendations were approved by the foundation.

Within a month after the selection, checks were mailed to arts recipients including such groups as the Oklahoma City Symphony Society to continue its children's series; the Augusta, Kansas Public Library to set up an exhibition area for local artists; Houston's Theatre Under the Stars for performances for handicapped people; the Joslyn Center for the Arts in Torrance, California for full sponsorship of a folk art festival; and the New Orleans Opera for help with a new production in 1975.

Perhaps most important from the arts viewpoint was the fact that the program broke new ground for the foundation and could set a precedent for future arts funding. Although the Mobil Oil Corporation has funded major cultural projects, the foundation, with a few exceptions, has limited its broad support programs to health, education, and community welfare. According to a Mobil spokesman, the results of the new arts program are currently being evaluated, and although a decision for 1975 hasn't been reached yet, "it is likely that the program will be continued in some form."

In East Walpole, Massachusetts, a corporation founded in 1975 has tied its long history into a new $100,000 project of support to historic preservaton groups throughout the country. Beginning in November, Bird and Son, manufacturers of building and industrial supplies and machinery, started soliciting applications for matching grants of up to $5000 each to help local nonprofit organizations complete historic restoration projects by 1976, the Bicentennial year. Eligible projects which may include historic arts facilities such as theaters and opera houses, must be registered or under consideration for registration by the National Register of Historic Places, must be publicly accessible, and must include a proposal for an exterior improvement not yet started but possible to complete by next January.

Selections will be made regionally and then nationally by panels of architects, historians, and environmentalists. According to the company, nearly 500 letters of application had been received by early February, and although most requested the full $5000, many asked for much smaller amounts.

Meanwhile, a corporate pioneer in broadbased funding to cultural groups, du Maurier of Canada, has announced a new series of grants. The du Maurier Council for the Performing Arts recently awarded a total of $336,000 to orchestras, theaters, opera companies, and one dance company throughout Canada for projects to be presented during 1975.

January-February 1975

Support Programs Aimed at Corporations Growing

Organized programs designed to win support from business are growing. In addition to national and regional nonprofit umbrella groups which approach corporations both directly and indirectly on behalf of more than one cultural organization, local arts groups are demonstrating versatility and imagination reaching for business funding.

In Toronto, the Council for Business and Arts in Canada, organized last September with an initial grant from the Canada Council, reached its minimum target of 70 corporate members by July 1975 with representation from virtually every major industry in the country. Importantly, in order not to compete with corporate grants to arts groups, annual dues of $1000 per company have been treated as memberships and are not tax deductible. The council, which according to its president, Arnold Edinborough, already has been "instrumental in getting almost one-fourth of a million more dollars for the arts in this half year" is currently planning a series of publications for corporate donation committees, for arts groups seeking business support, and for companies starting art collections. The CBAC will hold its first annual meeting this October. The council's American counterpart, the Business Committee for the Arts, is planning its first national arts funding seminar to be held at the Kennedy Center in Washington, D.C. on October 27. Open to all businessmen who receive the quarterly *BCA News,* the seminar will discuss such topics as matching gifts, united arts funds, lotteries, and program support.

The National Corporate Fund for Dance, which conducts a coordinated business support drive on behalf of seven major American dance companies, has made major progress this year in finding new corporate donors at upwards of $500 each. New supporters include such companies as American Airlines, First National City Bank. General Telephone and Electronics, and CBS Foundation. The Fund, which is seeking $150,000 this year, or 5 percent of its participating companies' 1974-75 deficit, had raised half of its goal by August.

The Arts and Business Council of New York City, which directly solicits business on behalf of arts groups through showcase programs and publications, has more than doubled its corporate membership in the past year to 40 at an average membership fee of $1000. The council is one of the few business–arts groups to include cultural organizations as members, at annual fees of only $25 and it maintains a 50-50 balance between arts and business members.

Summer 1975

Arts Push for Increased Support from Business

The Mobil Foundation's program of local support for the arts, established as an experiment in 1974, not only has continued, but has grown every year. The program asks Mobil Oil employees, in those areas where the company has facilities or a large share of the market, to recommend new and innovative arts projects for Mobil Foundation support. Most grants are from $2000 to $5000, although several arts recipients have won $10,000. In 1976 the program will award some 140 grants, totaling $403,000 to more than 35 different localities, nearly a 35 percent increase over the first year.

In Canada, the Imperial Tobacco Company, which gave $1.3 million over

the past five years to arts groups through its du Maurier Council for the Performing Arts ($367,500 to 37 performing groups for the current season), has extended
the program and increased its funding. In its second five-year program, the council will distribute $1.5 million. Arts groups meanwhile are beneficiaries of the
Social Service Leave Program established by Xerox five years ago to allow employees to be paid by the company while they serve a nonprofit group of their
choice for three months to a year. Although only two employees chose arts
groups in the first four years, three of this year's 25 recipients are cultural organizations.

In Boston, the Metropolitan Cultural Alliance's matching grant program
for corporations has been reshaped into a matching membership. Since the program was launched in June 1976, four local companies have matched new cultural memberships by their employees on a two-for-one basis, and a fifth company,
with 10,000 employees, is on a one-for-one basis. In the three-month period ending September 30, 1976, the program attracted 218 employee memberships in
57 different Alliance groups. The average membership was $27.05, and with
company matches, the program generated more than $13,000 in new income.
The program hopes to add five businesses by January.

Elsewhere, interesting new business support programs have been initiated.
The South Carolina National Bank in Columbia awarded the largest public affairs
grant in its history, $20,000 renewable annually, to Stage South for a statewide
audience development program. In Buffalo, the nation's first Volunteer Accountants for the Arts program has been launched; in Los Angeles, Atlantic Richfield
opened the new, nonprofit ARCO Center for Visual arts; and in New York, Citi-
bank announced a $300,000 program of support over the next three years for
arts groups that lost funding in city budget cutbacks. Coincident with the grant,
the bank initiated a series of full-page color ads in the *New York Times Magazine*
pinpointing the arts need.

In Cleveland, where the Central National Bank recently sponsored a three-
month free admission program at the Museum of Art, and TRW, Inc. commissioned a new work and sponsored a Cleveland Orchestra concert in commemora-
tion of its seventy-fifth anniversary, a new arts and business council was launched
this October at a seminar–luncheon attended by more than 150 businssmen. In
the three months preceding the luncheon, arts council leaders met with 81 local
businessmen in a series of 13 luncheons.

Promotionally, the arts and business have been relating. In St. Louis, Mark
Twain National Bank gave "art-tee shirts" with original Ernest Trova designs to
new depositors; in Saratoga, New York, Price Chopper Stores gave free "Nutcracker" coloring books to children attending New York City Ballet performances; and in New York, the Boston Symphony took ads in the financial section of
the Sunday *New York Times* to suggest "a new twist on the business lunch"—
company subscriptions to its five-concert series at Carnegie Hall.

Other countries have been developing their own business–arts program patterned after the American experience. In England, the recently organized Association for Business Sponsorship of the Arts, modeled after America's BCA, named Luke Rittner as its first full-time director. The ABSA, supported through membership fees of £100 to £500 per company, will organize conferences, publish materials, but will not give grants.

September-October 1976

Business Support of Arts
Draws National Notice

Greater attention is being focused on business as a source of arts support than perhaps ever before. Spurred by the first national arts–business conference in June 1977 and the Business Committee for the Arts' survey of corporate support, leading magazines and newspapers—the *New York Times, Saturday Review, Associated Press, Washington Post, Los Angeles Times, Amusement Business,* and *Marketing Communications* among them—lavished considerable space on the arts-business relationship from May through the end of July 1977. Indicative of the coverage was the July 24 arts section of the *Washington Post,* which featured three separate stories on business and the arts—on the arts budgets of six corporations, on the BCA survey, and an evaluation of the overall BCA program. Still to come is the October issue of *Fortune Magazine* which, in its "On Your Time" column, will feature an article on business executives personally active in arts programs.

Coincident with the coverage, ongoing arts–business programs and services have expanded in several directions. Among united business funds for the arts, the Corporate Fund for Performing Arts at the Kennedy Center in Washington, D.C. organized in March, raised $850,000 of its $1-million goal by August 1; the Lincoln Center Fund reached an all-time high of $1.743 million this year; and the National Corporate Fund for Dance, which raised $126,000 in 1976, set its 1977 goal at twice that amount.

In Boston, the Corporate Matching Membership Program of the Metropolitan Cultural Alliance completed its first year this July with eight corporate participants. Nearly $40,000 was generated through the 686 memberships purchased through the program.

Support concepts, other than funding, are growing also. New York's Volunteer Urban Consulting Group has moved more deeply into the arts with its Board Candidate Service, a program designed to help nonprofit groups find board members from business. Earlier this year it published "CPA Partners and Managers" a brochure that listed background data on 22 businessmen interested in serving on arts boards and sent it to every organization on the New York State Council on the Arts' grantees list. The Arts and Business Council's Skills Services Resources Bank, also in New York, completed its fifth training cycle this spring for business people interested in serving as arts volunteers. Since its initiation in 1975, program graduates have provided free consultant help to 80 arts groups. In San Francisco, the Bay Area Lawyers for the Arts, with approval by the California State Bar, has initiated the first legal referral program of its kind. Under the program, all artist and arts organizations, regardless of income, will be eligible to receive a half hour of consultation with a qualified attorney for "only a small fee."

In dollar terms, business support of the arts has increased significantly over the past three years according to the BCA survey, although many smaller arts groups still remain relatively untouched by business largesse. The survey, conducted by Touche Ross, showed corporate giving up to $221 million last year, with 12 companies, headed by Exxon, giving over $1 million each. The role of big business in arts giving is indicated by the fact that nearly half of all business support comes from 1 percent of the companies. In Canada, where all-out arts solicitation of corporation is a more recent development, giving is up as well. A recent survey by the Council for Business and the Arts in Canada estimated 1976 business giving at between $12 million and $15 million dollars. The council's 94 member corporations along gave $6.1 million to the arts, an increase of 34 percent over 1975.

Among individual corporations, Exxon continues to lead the field as the prime giver to the arts, although several other companies have developed interesting and innovative concepts. Exxon's record of giving, $5 million in 1976, is summarized in a special section of a recently published Exxon report, "The Other Dimensions of Business" which includes a listing of all 1976 grants. It is available free from the Public Affairs Department, Exxon Corporation, 1251 Avenue of the Americas, New York, New York 10020.

Corporate advertising on behalf of the arts is an area of growing involvement. In addition to the Arts Endowment's new Ad Council campaign, developed on a volunteer basis by Doyle Dane Bernbach, Inc., several companies have developed their own interesting concepts. Mobil's series of public service ads, appearing weekly on the Op Ed page of the *New York Times,* has focused on arts groups nearly 100 times since the series was initiated five years ago. The ads, which include a sketch of the featured project or group and copy about it, have aided theater companies, museums, arts centers, and libraries among others. Although Mobil selects most of the subjects from groups which the company is aiding, it will consider outside suggestions.

In an unusual development, one aspect of Mobil's arts support program will receive special notice. "Arts for the Arts," an exhibition at New York's Museum of Contemporary Crafts from September 9-25 sponsored by Mobil, will feature a collection of art books and posters commissioned by Mobil to promote cultural groups and programs.

Philip Morris, whose arts support program formed the basis for a Harvard Business School case study, developed an ad campaign last December which was designed not only to focus on its own cultural aid program, but to spur other companies into increasing their support. The series featured six separate color ads, each devoted to an art exhibit sponsored by the tobacco company. Each concluded with the message "It also takes art to make a company great." Ads showed photos of works in each exhibit, and copy pinpointed the importance of imagination and creativity, telling readers that "sponsorship of art that reminds us of that is not patronage, it's a business and human necessity." Readers were invited to write company chairman, Joseph F. Cullman, III to learn more about corporate sponsorship of art.

The campaign which ended in June and cost $400,000 featured 90 insertions in such varied magazines as *Financial World, Black Enterprise, Art News,* and the Washington editions of *Time* and *Newsweek,* and drew responses from over 700 readers. Most letters were from businessmen wanting more information on getting involved in the arts, and many of these received personal replies. All correspondents received materials on Philip Morris's arts support program and copies of several BCA pamphlets. In conjunction with its sponsorship of a new Jasper Johns exhibition at the Whitney Museum this fall, the company is planning another ad campaign.

Summer 1977

Organized Campaigns
Reach for Corporate Dollars

Arts fund drives aimed solely at corporations are picking up a growing share of the business philanthropic dollar. The newest effort, the Corporate Theatre Fund (50 West Fifth-seventh St., N.Y. N.Y. 10019), brought together five leading professional resident theaters last fall—American Conservatory Theatre, Arena Stage, Center Theatre Group/Mark Taper Forum, the Guthrie, and the Long Wharf—to seek increased support from business. The united approach, initially suggested by some of the companies that the theaters had been soliciting individually, will concentrate on national corporations and will not negate local fund drives. With possible expansion after the first year, the Fund has set memberships guidelines at budgets of over $1 million; earned income of at least 55 percent of budget; continuous operations for ten years; and national recognition. Although a specific fund goal has not been set, contributions already have been received from such companies as Lever Brothers, RCA, Exxon, and Pfizer.

The older National Corporate Fund for Dance (130 W. Fifty-sixth St., N.Y. N.Y. 10019) has grown considerably since its organization in 1974 and has set its 1978 goal at $250,000, a figure it expects to reach. Corporate contributors are up from 14 the first year to an anticipated 90 or more this year. Membership increased to nine with the recent addition of the San Francisco Ballet and, as evidence of its growth, the Fund just opened a new Chicago office. Membership guidelines require annual operating budgets over $750,000, extensive touring in the United States, and meeting professional standards. Other fund members are American Ballet Theater, Joffrey Ballet, Alvin Ailey American Dance Theater, Nikolais Dance Theatre, Murray Louis Dance Company, Eliot Feld Ballet, Merce Cunningham and Dance Company, and Paul Taylor Dance Company.

Corporate funds organized by two leading arts centers met major goals last year. The Lincoln Center Fund, which raised $1.7 million, upped this year's target to $3 million. The Corporate Fund for the Performing Arts at the Kennedy Center in Washington, D.C. met its first year goal of $1 million recently and has set a similar goal this year. Another arts center, the Brooklyn Academy of Music, reports that corporate giving has increased 300 percent in two years, from 29 companies giving $101,261 in 1975 to 78 giving $317,452 last year.

Elsewhere, there is evidence of business breakthroughs by individual arts groups. The Chicago Symphony reported 11 corporations matching employee contributions to the orchestra in recent months, and the Detroit Symphony in its first corporate sales campaign for season tickets sold 7679 seats worth over $47,000 to 140 Detroit businesses. In Houston, the Society for the Performing Arts introduced a new concept in corporate support by asking businesses to underwrite specific events through a guarantee against ticket sales.

The Metropolitan Museum of Arts' Department of Public Education has come up with an interesting new concept designed to acquaint companies and their employees with the museum collection. Since January the department has been offering live "Art Lectures in the Office" during lunch and after work.

A hopeful sign is the emergence of companies directing major first-time support to the arts. In January 1978, United Technologies in Hartford, Connecticut announced "a major new thrust in direct support of the arts in Connecticut, involving grants exceeding $500,000." Nine Hartford arts groups were recipients.

March-April 1978

Artist Blue Sky's mural "Tunnelvision" on the 75-foot wall of the Farm Credit Bank building in downtown Columbia, South Carolina. (Courtesy of South Carolina Arts Commission)

6

Reaching Audiences

BUILDING ARTS AUDIENCES

Reach: A New Method
of Measuring an Audience

Bradley G. Morison and Kay Fliehr

The traditional measuring stick for audiences in the performing arts has been the box office—a direct reflection of total attendance. In recent years, as producing organizations decentralized and institutionalized, a second audience statistic took on added importance: the season subscription total—a measurement of the thoroughly committed audience base.

But now, with emerging interest in expanding and broadening audiences, a third audience measuring stick must be given the same close scrutiny as the familiar total attendance and season ticket count.

This third figure is one we call *reach*. It is the measure of penetration into the total community that an institution is achieving. As we define its application to the performing arts, reach is the total number of different people in the community who involve themselves with an institution one or more times during the year. The figure usually differs drastically from either total attendance or season subscription.

Regardless of the year-to-year trends in total attendance or season subscription, a healthy audience development situation demands that reach grow steadily. Intelligent analysis of and attention to reach is an important key in the fight for survival of any performing arts organization.

To illustrate, let us use a hypothetical theater, assuming a five-play season in which 20,000 people see each production for a total attendance of 100,000. Reach would be the total number of different people who saw at least one production.

If this theater had 20,000 subscribers, each seeing all five plays, then the reach would be 20,000. At the other extreme, suppose that the theater had no subscribers and none of the people who attended saw more than one production. The reach would then be 100,000.

In a real situation, actual reach would fall in between the two extremes. Assume, for instance that the theater had a season ticket sale of 8000 and that the average single ticket buyer saw two of the five plays. The statistics would look like this:

Total attendance	100,000
Season ticket attendance (8000 × 5)	40,000
Single ticket attendance	60,000
Single ticket reach (60,000 ÷ 2)	30,000
Season ticket reach	8,000
Total reach	38,000 different people

The theater reached 38,000 different people in the community. If the population was one million, the reach percentage for the season would be 3.8.

Why is it important to analyze reach figures and their trends? Because reach trends do not necessarily parallel total attendance or season subscription in either proportion or direction. It is possible, for instance to have subscriptions and total attendance increase from one year to another while reach is actually declining.

While a slight decline in reach is not disastrous, it would call for increased audience development efforts to bring new people to the theater the next year, efforts that might not be made unless an analysis was done.

It is also possible to have a situation in which season ticket sales are decreasing from year to year, but where reach is actually increasing steadily. While a downward trend is not desirable in season tickets, the situation where reach is increasing is less disastrous than one where it was declining along with subscriptions. The people who make up the single ticket reach constitute the best possible potential for season ticket sales. Unless single ticket reach is substantial and growing, it is difficult if not impossible to make season subscriptions grow. In the declining subscription situation, the increased reach trend is enlarging the pool of prime potential for reversing the down-trend in season tickets.

The ideal, healthy audience growth situation demands that all three figures —total attendance, subscriptions, and reach—be increasing. Total attendance is an important measure of box office success and the drawing power of a particular season. Subscripton totals are a measure of hard core, dedicated base support. Reach, and the percentage of the population it represents, is the measure of the degree to which the institution has really touched and influenced the main body of the community. It tells the institution how much it is growing in importance and meaning to the community it is dedicated to serve and that it must serve if it is to survive.

The people who comprise the total reach represent the institution's potential for growth. They are the word-of-mouth communicators, the receptive audience that can be educated and introduced to more adventurous theatrical experiences, the untapped reservoir for deeper commitment to season tickets, and the friends who can be called upon for help in time of crisis. This group must be kept growing.

Calculating the reach of an institution requires research and additional record keeping. An accurate figure on the number of times the average person is involved with the organization each year must be determined. But the institution that wants a lucid, valid indication of how successfully they are reaching into their community—the institution that truly wants to extend its reach—will find a serious analysis of reach figures well worth the effort.

January-February 1968

Museum Attendance Boosted
Through Cake Box Promotion

In a dramatic move to increase attendance, a Philadelphia science museum "piggybacked" on such familiar media as food packages and newspapers to carry its program into the homes of its potential audiences. Built around "DO-ITS," on-paper descriptions of simple science experiments, the relatively inexpensive campaign initiated a little more than a year ago already has resulted in 34 million exposures and has boosted attendance and interest substantially at the Franklin Institute Science Museum. Moreover, through the use of no-cost commercial distribution channels and a well-planned volunteer distribution program, the entire campaign has been conducted within a $10,000 budget made possible by a grant from the National Endowment for the Arts.

The idea for the "DO-IT" program came about during an informal staff meeting at the home of museum director Joel N. Bloom which was called to consider ways to boost an attendance that had dropped because of gas shortages. The concept that emerged was to provide actual museum experiences to children and their parents in their own homes through the widespread distribution of instructions for simple experiments which could be conducted with readily available materials. While familiarizing at-home audiences with the museum's field of interest, the DO-ITS would also provide such incentives for visiting the institution as information on institute exhibits relating to the DO-IT experiments and coupons for reduced price admissions. Most importantly, the program developers recognized that while they would be educating the public, the tone had to be light.

The first four DO-ITS, featuring such experiments as "What do you see?" and "Mathamagic" and utilizing such commonplace props as pencils and coins, were distributed through free handouts by institute volunteers and through newspaper reproductions. The initial response was excellent—over 350 people who requested the first DO-IT through a newspaper announcement visited the institute—and during one evening alone, Super-Sunday inter-institutional cultural festival, more than 50,000 DO-ITS were distributed.

The program really went into high gear when the Franklin Institute joined forces with Tasty Baking Company, the makers of Tasty family packs. Under the arrangement, the institute staff provided general copy and Tasty artists executed the layout and design of the colorful experiments on the backs of six-pack boxes of cakes. Printing and distribution costs were paid by Tasty, which has since distributed 12 different DO-ITS—each featured on a different Tastykake produce box—to 32 million people. Featured have been such experiments as "Make your own sundial" and "Does white light have any color in it?" Because Tastykake is regionally distributed, boxes do not carry reduced rate admission coupons, but the museum has received letters of commendation from Tastykake eaters all over the country.

"The program's role in increasing public awareness of the Franklin Institute has been overwhelming," according to project manager Eileen Reynolds. Future planning also calls for the development of adult experiments for public places. An initial adult DO-IT, used as a vehicle for the institute's school group educational program, was distributed successfully at cocktail parties at local educational conferences.

September-October 1975

Offbeat Promo by Upbeat Kids
Woos Young Audience to Opera

Bumper stickers reading "Bravo Opera," buttons proclaiming that "Opera Lives," and flyers describing *La Boheme* as "four old-time Hippies in an attic," are only a few of the techniques being used by the Seattle Opera Association in Washington in a campaign aimed at encouraging young people to attend opera performances.

Long interested in attracting youth to the opera audience, Glynn Ross, general director of the association, decided earlier this year that the best way to reach them was through their contemporaries. In April, 1976 he placed an advertisement in the University of Washington Daily which read: "Seattle Opera Wants Three Washington Whiz Kids. Definition: A young adult, either sex, who can make the Seattle Opera Success Trip. . . ." Of the 64 who responded, Ross selected five to develop the youth-oriented promotional program.

The new program got off to an impressive start. The immediate advice of the Whiz Kids was that the association forget old traditions and speak to young people in a language they could understand. Thus, beginning in May, scores of "What is Boheme" flyers, with copy referring to the "old-time Hippies," were distributed in the university district. Two hundred passes to a May 11 performance were given away to students, with each resident house on campus receiving two tickets. Following the performance, letters signed by Mr. Ross were sent to all the students who attended the performance, telling them about a new subscription series and suggesting they let their friends and parents know "what is really going on."

Mr. Ross's letter said in part, "As you now know, and contrary to what many people choose to believe, it is not a single star that makes opera grand. It is the blending of acting, singing, costuming, lights and music. It surpasses the popular light show as a galactic happening—a trip into the world of total art."

In June 1967, the Opera imported an impressive 12-foot-high piece of "junk sculpture" titled *Warrior* as its principal exhibit at the Seattle Teen Spectacular. Although the sculpture bore no relationship to opera, it was a success in two ways, according to Mrs. Erna Husak, public relations director of the association. "First," she told *AM*, "it caused hundreds of young people to stop and consider opera as a living and dynamic thing with some sense of humor. The goal of trying to tie the general concept of opera with the youth revolution was achieved. Secondly, the rise in ticket sales during the period of the Teen Spectacular and the few days following accounted for 16 percent of the total sales for the opera series which followed."

With this as a beginning, the Whiz Kids flew into high gear, carrying out the entire project in much their own way. Pamphlets, letters, and ads were written by them and printed by the association. Buttons, bumper stickers, and posters were prepared and distributed. The message of opera was brought to students through meetings and phone calls.

Two of the Whiz Kids have already written a series of advertisements for this year's season of productions. The ad for *Don Giovanni* reads, "Well . . . What can you say about Don Juan—He's Don Juan—Right?! Seducer, murderer, and general rake. Seductions, mistaken identitites, and a statute who invites himself to an all-time dinner. Supernatural flames and sinking palaces. A crowd of beautiful women all chasing a man who wants one thing—and gets something else— All with sounds by Mozart."

When the campaign for fall season subscriptions was completed, the youngsters began to develop projects designed to sell opera to elementary and junior high school students. In discussing the campaign's success and the reasons for undertaking it, Mrs. Husak said, "We are continually open to new ideas, no matter how flippant or strange, that may serve to promote understanding and appreciation of opera."

Perhaps the best justification for the campaign is contained in the flyer for youngsters advertising the low-priced Fall National Series, which suggests "an opera date for the price of a movie." "Why opera for teens?" it asks. "Why not? Opera is a total experience, a cosmic happening of sight and sound. Opera is NOW. . . . Are you prepared to dig opera? It's not for the conventional; it's for the beautiful people of NOW. . . . people who can grasp life. Can you?"

September-October 1967

Theaters Seek Out Communities and Win Support and Audiences

Two communities more than a thousand miles apart have the beginnings of new and possibly year-round theater programs, thanks to the organizing ability and perseverance of two outsiders—one uninvited and the other invited but initially overlooked. In Bradford, Vermont, an economically depressed area in the Upper Connecticut River Valley, Terry Schreiber, who has operated his own New York acting studio and theater since 1969, is beginning his second summer as head of the Bradford Repertory Theater. Since barely surviving its first month as a summer theater last year, the company has won an audience, received strong local support, and developed a growing program in the schools.

Before Schreiber came to Bradford, the Junior Chamber of Commerce, working with a company of midwestern theater students, produced two summer seasons of commercial theater at a local church. The 1970 season was moderately successful, but dissension broke out among the company the following summer and the season was cancelled. With some subscriptions unredeemed and an unfavorable atmosphere hanging over the community, the arts-minded minister of the church decided to try to save theater for the community by finding a serious-minded director to present a season in 1972.

When Schreiber arrived in Bradford last summer with six actors and six apprentices to present a season of four plays in repertory, he found organizational chaos awaiting him. A nonprofit organization had been put together hastily to sponsor theater and other arts, and there was advance promise of season subscriptions and several grants. However, following a full house in the 176-seat theater for an opening night benefit, things immediately went downhill. "We never saw most of the first-night audience again until the end of the summer," Schreiber recalled. Without local promotion, attendance for the first three nights was 16, 11, and 12. The second week with a new production didn't do much better.

Threatened with closing, the theater found unexpected support from a local businessman who liked the group's work. Raymond Green, head of an explosives company and chairman of the school board, voluntarily took over the business end of the theater and found a local woman to undertake public relations. Then Green won a loan for the theater's sponsor, on the basis of a promised grant, to insure the season.

Community interest was awakened almost immediately with a series of educational and fun promotions, successful in large measure due to the cast's willingness to cooperate. Attendance also picked up dramatically, and although there was a $3000 deficit by season's end, the theater had become a force in the community. To insure continuity, the board was reorganized into a completely new nonprofit organization, the Bradford Repertory Theater, and plans were formulated for an in-school program. In October and January the group came back to present a week of theater games at seven area schools, and in April it presented an area tour of "The Diary of Anne Frank" with makeup and set design demonstrations for 12 schools in Vermont and New Hampshire. Two adult evening performances also were presented. The response by fifth and sixth graders according to Schreiber was "fantastic."

During the winter and spring the theater won additional local support with the formation of the Friends of Theater and a fund-raising cabaret program. Now in its second summer and doing much better than a year ago, Schreiber told *AM*, "We're 65 percent on the way to being fully accepted, and support is growing." Already, plans for a three-production tour of local schools this fall, winter, and spring are near completion, and some funding has been assured from both the Vermont and New Hampshire arts councils.

Even more dramatic is the experience of 26-year-old Louis Ambrosio. Without prior professional theater experience and without financial backing or "big names" in theater behind him, Ambrosio, in nearly unbelievable fashion, sold his concept of professional theater to a community selected sight unseen.

Ambrosio's saga began late in 1971, when, studying for his M.F.A. degree in theater at Brooklyn College, he started to think about developing a professional resident company outside New York. Uncertain as to location, he developed criteria for a potential home base and then sat down with an atlas and other reference works to find a city. Among his requisites were over 250,000 area residents, demonstrated receptivity to the arts, strong business base, easy accessibility to other medium-sized cities, and a local sparkplug.

By June 1972 he selected Augusta, Georgia, a city serving an 11-county area of a million people which was located 136 miles from Atlanta, and he interested a small group of theater associates in his plan. Still, the idea was unknown to a key partner in the venture—Augusta itself. Quickly, however, he moved his plan from the concept to the action stage, spending the next few months speaking to everyone he could find to gather information and win support. At the suggestion of the U.S. Institute for Theatre Technology, he met with Nancy Breslin of Junior Leagues of America, and since the idea looked promising to her, she wrote the Augusta League about it.

When that letter resulted in an invitation from the Augusta League to discuss the idea further, the wheels really began to turn. On his first visit to Augusta this past January, Ambrosio not only won support from the League's arts coordinator, but had doors opened by her to key people in the community—school officials, government representatives, and leaders of the chamber of commerce and local industry. Several days with state arts officials and theater people in Atlanta followed before he returned to Augusta and received an important boost when a local leader, Mrs. Lilly Lake Stephenson, gave Ambrosio a six-room house to use as company headquarters, rent free, and won support from others for him.

After a month in Georgia the young producer headed back to New York to meet with his nucleus group—five actors, one technician, and his associate, Joanne Sockle, to refine the concept and shape the projected plan to the specific needs of Augusta. Although there were still no funds in hand, by March Ambrosio won a commitment for a pilot in-school theater program for the fall and promise of a summer rent-free residency at the Performing Arts Center of Augusta College this summer. With these assurances, the promise of additional local support and the development of a program involving the theater as a resource center for such nearby cities as Savannah and Macon, Georgia and Columbia, South Carolina, plus a full season of four productions at Augusta College set for next June, the Augusta Repertory Theatre was incorporated this spring and joined the Augusta Arts Council.

"All of us will live on our savings from August to October," Ambrosio told *AM*, "when our school program begins. In the meantime we've had indications of help from the state, and we're busy writing proposals."

Summer 1973

Birthdays Bring Arts
Groups Dollars, Good Will

A milestone in the life of an arts organization can provide that group with a unique opportunity for reaching new audiences, raising funds, or enhancing its public image. In Philadelphia, the Museum of Art, which celebrated its one hundredth anniversary several years ago, found a new occasion to mark in 1978, the fiftieth anniversary of the opening of its current home. The museum building, an imposing structure located at one end of one of the city's major parkways and set atop a flight of 101 stairs, received national attention as a key setting in the film *Rocky*.

Because its classic architectural style and its location away from downtown gives the "Acropolis on the Parkway" an appearance of aloofness, museum leaders decided to combat that image with a fun celebration. "We wanted an event that would make us seem a little more human," said museum publicist Sandra Horrocks.

For the museum, fun meant hosting a week-long birthday celebration including special programs and exhibitions, a free birthday party for the public, and a birthday-cake decorating contest. For the latter event, leading local professional bakers were invited to submit cardboard mock-ups of museum birthday cakes. The three winning entries and eight runners-up were placed on display in the museum during the birthday week in an exhibition titled, "Ornamental Icing: The Art of Cake Decoration."

The highlight of the week took place on its next to last day, Saturday, April 1, when the museum opened all its galleries to the public without charge and the first 200 visitors received free slices from the prize-winning cake, specially baked for the occasion. A birthday magic show followed. Other free events designed to relate to the museum's long history, included a band concert of early twentieth century music and a showing of an uncut, hand-tinted print of D. W. Griffith's "Intolerance."

The museum received tremendous attention during the entire week, and virtually every newspaper and television station in the city covered the highlight day, when over 4000 people came, double the usual attendance.

Another arts organization, the Opera Company of Boston, will use its twentieth birthday this May as the peg for a major fund-raising drive, with the help of a leading Boston department store, Filene's. For the first time in its history, Filene's will host a fund-raising event in its downtown store and will pick up the entire cost of the mammoth "Operathon Ball" set for May 18. On that evening 400 people will contribute $75 each to attend a cocktail party and dinner at Filene's in honor of the opera company. A little later in the evening, 400 more people, paying $25 each, will gather at Filene's for dancing, birthday cake, and a toast to the company's distinguished director, Sarah Caldwell.

The publicity for the ball will give added impetus to a second day's fund raising activities. On May 19, WCRB-FM will present an all-day tribute to the opera company, and will take bids on prizes contributed for the event. The Opera Company anticipates raising $100,000 during the two-day celebration.

March-April 1978

Right Times and Prices
Help to Lure Audiences

Arts groups are making it easier for audiences to attend their program. This summer Whitney Museum in New York changed its weekday visiting hours from the usual 11:00 A.M. to 6:00 P.M. to 2:00 P.M. to 9:00 P.M. to take advantage of the longer summer daylight hours. The new summer hours were in effect from July 1 through September 2, from Tuesday through Friday evenings. The new program, which didn't cost the museum anything extra, drew many people around 6:00 P.M., immediately after work, and resulted in accolades from scores of museumgoers.

The New York Shakespeare Festival has reached one step beyond the student rush concept to provide a wide range of theatergoers with an opportunity to see productions at its Public Theater at reduced prices. Every evening, the Festival sets aside 25 percent of the tickets for each production at the Public Theatre for sale at less than half price to *anyone* who wishes to attend. "Quik-tix," available at 6:00 P.M. each evening, bring weekday prices down to $3 from $8 and weekend tickets down to $4 from $9.

The Museum of Modern Art is luring out-of-town groups to its crowded Cezanne exhibition with a new "People to Pictures" program. The program allows groups of up to 30 to visit the museum for a group fee at hours when the museum is closed to the public, all day Wednesday and Thursdays before 11:00 A.M. The cost, which includes a lecturer, is $135 on Wednesdays and $125 on Thursdays.

Artists are reaching out for new audiences. In San Francisco, some 700 street artists now hold city licenses, and in Atlanta the new MARTA transportation system, which will open next year, will include works of art in each of the system's stations. In New York, the Organization of Independent Artists has used the recently passed Public Buildings Cooperative Act, which encourages community use of public facilities for arts and other activities, to place exhibitions in nine different public locations in the city, including several court houses. The group hopes to develop similar programs elsewhere.

September-October 1977

Cultural Samples Help Spur
Membership and Attendance

Arts groups throughout the country are offering audiences an enticing variety of cultural "samples" in an effort to boost attendance and promote membership. In Albany, New York, the League of Arts initiated a Performing Arts Sampler Series this fall [1975] in an effort to attract new audiences to the programs of its 22 participating member organizations and, at the same time, increase its own individual and family memberships.

For a $10 fee, which covered annual membership in the league, purchasers were entitled to attend 17 free programs of member groups and buy two-for-one tickets to ten different events, mainly those presented by bigger, more professional groups. A special PASS book dramatized the program, and as an additional promotional touch, ten of the participating groups agreed to offer free miniperformances or "samples of the sampler" to local social, cultural, and ethnic groups on request.

The program which has helped up league membership from 175 in September to over 500 by December is a continuing promotion which allows it to be sold for a good part of the season. With new lists of free and "two-fer" events published quarterly, the league was able to launch a special Christmas gift campaign featuring 21 tickets to 21 different performances. Through December, subscriptions were coming in at a steady rate of about 25 or more a week.

Although the program has attracted good attention locally and won seed-funding from local businesses, it's still too early to assess its success in developing larger audiences, according to league executive director, Carol Bullard. "we won't really know for sure until next year," she told *AM*. She indicated that if the project continues next season, she would urge all participants to offer the same kind of sampler—two-fers instead of free performances.

Elsewhere, Theatre London and the London Symphony Orchestra in Ontario, Canada joined forces to offer a combined subscription package for the current season—seven plays and five concerts for $25. In Fort Wayne, the Fine Arts Foundation offered donors of $25 and up to its annual fund drive a sampler of one ticket to one performance for each of four cultural groups participating in the drive. Also, volunteers who made at least 1200 calls during a fund drive "Phone-A-Thon" were rewarded with samplers.

Young audiences are the target for a unique sampler effort in Atlanta. In an effort to acquaint children and their parents with the various arts programs presented at the Atlanta Memorial Arts Center throughout the year, the High Museum of Art initiated the Children's Spring Festival five years ago. The one day program, held in and around various areas of the center, features a nonstop schedule of simultaneous events from 10:00 A.M. to 4:00 P.M. including concerts, art exhibits, children's theater, puppet shows, tours, and dance recitals. Most events are free, although two productions charged $1 each this year because of union rules. Program participants include the center's five resident organizations as well as invited outside groups who perform at the center. This year's progam, featuring 13 groups, drew a record attendance of 13,000.

November-December 1975

Civic Ballet Draws Huge Crowd
with Free Tickets for Christmas

An unknown, pent-up desire to see and enjoy good ballet flooded over the Atlanta Civic Ballet, to its delighted surprise, once the price dam was broken by the staging of a free performance on December 27, 1962.

The enthusiasm generated by the announcement that free tickets were available resulted in a rush for tickets by 15,000 people. The experience proved to certain unbelieving citizens that Atlantans—in large numbers—really want art.

The idea of staging a free performance for all comers as a Christmas gift to the city of Atlanta from the dance group, the oldest civic ballet in America, originated with Dorothy Alexander, the founder of the company.

After discussions between the ballet leaders and the mayor of the city, the mayor agreed to donate use of the municipal auditorium free of charge for the performance. Immediately, hundreds of volunteers went to work to raise the money to cover the cost of costumes and sets, payment of union scale to stage and lighting men, and rehearsal and costume rental expenses for the Choral Guild of Atlanta. Businessmen responded with an impressive number of gifts ranging from $100 to $1000.

A grant was received from the Music Performance Trust Fund of the Recording Industry, covering 75 percent of the rehearsal and performance costs of the Atlanta Pops Orchestra. The Atlanta Civic Ballet, from directors and staff to dancers, contributed their services free.

By December 20, a week before the scheduled performance, more than 9000 ticket requests were received. Yet the auditorium held only 4800 seats. Within the final week another 5000 requests arrived at the ballet office. Hundreds of letters of gratitude poured in, many from people who said they had never before attended a ballet.

A capacity audience attended a special dress rehearsal, and the December 27 performance, featuring *The Nutcracker,* played to a standing-room-only audience.

On the momentum of the recent success, the ballet company is already planning three "Holiday Gift" performances for next Christmas, and a fund-raising effort to finance them has begun. Even in advance of this, however, spontaneous gifts had reached the dance organization.

January 1963

Sampling the Arts

Audiences that taste your programs may come back for full portions. Operating on this principle, Dance Associates of Durham, North Carolina presented a "Day for Dancing" recently. Utilizing nine different areas, Dance Associates presented continuous classes throughout the day in everything from ballet to modern to belly dancing to creative movement. An overflow audience was attracted by both the low prices—$.50 per class, $2.00 for the day, with senior citizens free—and the opportunity to sample from the variety of programs offered.

September-October 1975

Show Tempts Audiences
with a Free First Act

In an attempt to stimulate waning attendance caused by unfavorable reviews, an Off-Broadway producer recently instituted a free first act policy, with theatergoers paying for seats only if they stayed to see the concluding two acts. Bro Herrod, producer of *The Chief Thing*, at New York's Greenwich Mews Theatre, initiated the policy one week after the play opened.

Although people heard about the plan, few took it seriously, and nobody took advantage of the offer. The show closed a week after the policy went into effect. Herrod told *AM* that the plan didn't work because it wasn't promoted prior to the show's opening, before the reviews were published. He intends to reinstate the policy again with a full pre-opening promotion for a new production later this summer.

June 1963

Student "Reps" Help
Build a Theater's Audience

Arts groups seeking to attract students from nearby colleges to performances can profit from the experience of the Charles Playhouse, Boston's resident professional theater. Since 1959, the playhouse has conducted a comprehensive student representative program which has resulted in increased student ticket sales, widespread publicity, and has also helped to establish direct lines of communication between the theater and some 40 New England colleges.

The idea for the program resulted from the theater's inability to reach the more than 100,000 potential theatergoers at colleges in the state through normal communications channels. To find an answer to this problem, Miss Nance Movsesian, publicity director of the playhouse, recruited a group of student representatives eight years ago through the drama and English deapartments of local colleges. The emphasis at first was on sales ability, with representatives receiving

10 percent commissions for selling subscriptions and organizing theater parties among campus groups.

Over the years, however, the progam has broadened greatly, and its emphasis has shifted from direct sales to promotion of the theater's productions. Although representatives still receive sales commissions, other benefits, which involve them directly with the theater and its productions, have proved more significant. Each of the representatives now receives two free tickets to every opening night performance, invitations to attend open-end panel discussions during the run of each play, invitations to attend playhouse social events, a copy of the theater's annual journal, and special permission to attend final production rehearsals. In addition, the theater's artistic and technical staff frequently help student representatives with their theater projects. As a result, the program has attracted many students interested in theater as a career.

The functional phase of the program begins about a week prior to the opening of each playhouse production. Student representatives, headed by their elected president, meet at the playhouse with the theater's staff to discuss the production, exchange promotional ideas, and receive posters and other materials for distribution. Guest speakers from various areas of the theater frequently address the group. Minutes of the meeting are mimeographed immediately by the "rep" secretary, who then sends them to any representatives unable to attend the meeting.

Back on their own campuses, the 40 representatives hang playhouse posters at key locations, contact college newspapers and radio stations to arrange coverage of productions, distribute complimentary tickets in exchange for advertising, discuss upcoming productions with department heads, and send the playhouse any reviews or pertinent clippings that appear in local papers. In many instances, reps recruit volunteers on their own campuses to help them with their work.

During subscription campaigns, representatives distribute brochures on campus, sometimes so zealously that the playhouse claims to have reached every student, faculty and staff member at several colleges. Students also are indirectly responsible for increasing the number of theater parties through their collection and maintenance of up-to-date lists of all campus organizations, which are turned over to the theater's group sales department.

January-February 1967

Rock Group and Arty Party
Help Orchestra, Museum Reach Youth

A symphony orchestra that appointed a rock music group, Tranquility Base, as a "resident" unit last fall plans to continue and perhaps broaden the association during the coming season. According to Elizabeth Webster, executive director of the Hamilton (Ontario) Symphony Orchestra, the rock sextet's informal affiliation was "based on the desire to explore the musical potential of such an association, and to work together as closely and creatively as possible."

The association resulted in four well-received joint concerts—two in the student series, one in the pop series and a free outdoor performance sponsored by the city council to commemorate Hamilton's 125th anniversary—which featured several new and specially commissioned works, including Steven Gellman's "Odyssey," a piece for rock group, piano, and symphony orchestra. Tranquility Base also appeared with Hamilton Philharmonic conductor Boris Brott when he led the Toronto Symphony. The audience response was excellent, especially among youngsters. "Tranquility Base's participation has definitely brought out many people to our concerts," Mrs. Webster told *AM*.

The affiliation with Tranquility Base is only one of a number of efforts by the Hamilton Philharmonic to develop programs aimed at new and young audiences. This past season, in addition to its two subscription series, the orchestra has presented 450 in-school ensemble concerts and has gone out into the community to present concerts in libraries, on street corners, and in restaurants at lunch hour. One result of its educational effort is that students now comprise one-third of its subscription audience.

Both the Hamilton Philharmonic and Tranquility Base are seeking and developing new material for the coming season. They will appear together in a pop series program which will be repeated out-of-town, and there is a possibility that the city council may reschedule the outdoor concert, which attracted 30,000 people but was rained out after half the performance had been completed. Also, the rock group will perform at library concerts.

The reaction of both adult audience members and orchestra players to Tranquility Base has been surprisingly favorable. Mrs. Webster says of them, "This is a particularly attractive and talented group of highly trained musicians who have awed the symphony players by their versatility and improvisational ability."

Another arts organization that has successfully reached out for young audiences is the Seattle Art Museum. Each year during its Northwest Annual exhibition the museum has hosted an "Arty Party" for students, featuring free refreshments, music by a youth combo, and attendance by participating artists.

The party idea was conceived by museum volunteers in 1966 as a way to introduce young people to the museum and its collection and at the same time provide a social event for young artists and art history students. Held on a Sunday afternoon in the fall when the juried Northwest annual is presented, the party has drawn between 1200 and 2000 students annually.

Volunteer planning begins early with posters, designed by local artists, duplicated by a "generous" printer, and distributed to schools. Local merchants provide free beverages, cakes, and other refreshments. When contacting schools, the museum requests that a few students from each act as hosts during the party and spread the word about it in advance. Publicity is usually excellent, with downtown and suburban papers providing good coverage and radio stations contributing free spots.

Summer 1971

Group Sponsors Musical Picnic;
Wins New Audience, New Image

A unique cultural event, presented for the first time, helped a Rochester, New York arts institution to favorably change its image; uncover a new and untapped audience; sell out the house; attract hundreds of congratulatory letters; bring its own staff, students, and performers much closer together; give the community an unforgettable evening; and reap scores of other direct and indirect benefits. The event was the Eastman School of Music's first Musical Picnic, a smorgasbord evening of activities for family groups presented in November 1970. Billed in advance as a low-priced music/fun event, the progam included box suppers, prize drawings, costumes, a children's playroom, films, a music wheel, and strolling minstrels, all combined with its basic ingredient—good music, and lots of it.

The picnic was conceived during the previous summer by Eastman's concert manager, Mrs. Ruth Glazer, who was seeking a way to win new audiences for student performances. Perhaps, she thought, the answer was a change in format and concert time, an event that could bring in whole families who otherwise couldn't afford to buy tickets and pay for dinner, parking, and baby sitting. According to Mrs. Glazer, a casual remark by a young Rochester mother provided the final impetus for the resulting program. "I think of the Eastman School," she had said, "as a rather forbidding place where a layman like myself has no place."

Planning for the new event proceeded with three goals in mind: to change the "forbidding" image that some local people had of the school; to develop a new audience; and to present a congregation of the arts in a relaxed atmosphere of fun and gaiety at a reasonable price. Although there were many performing units at the school, including student ensembles, it was decided to make the picnic a community event by also inviting such groups as the Brockport Dance Company and the Brickler Marionette Theater to participate in the program.

With banks and leading local corporations aiding in the effort, thousands of Musical Picnic brochures were distributed in advance. Recipients were invited to bring friends, dates, wives, kids, plus their love of music, their appetites, and their sense of humor. "We'll furnish the parking, the music, the food, the prize drawing, the fun," the brochure promised. Tickets at $4 were good from 5:30 to 9:00 P.M., and $3 tickets were honored from 6:30 to 9:00 P.M. Childrens' tickets good for the entire event were only $2 each. More than a week in advance the entire house was sold out.

On Friday November 13, an overflow crowd of better than 3300, including nearly 2000 children, descended on Eastman, colorfully decorated for the occasion with ribbons, balloons, and toy animals. Volunteer hosts and hostesses costumed as opera characters greeted the audience. Those with 5:30 tickets sampled the marionette show, the dance performance, and the Imagination Playroom, where Eastman students entertained youngsters. At 6:30, everyone assembled in the big theater for box suppers.

The supper entertainment opened with a color movie, *The Great Concert Hall Caper,* which described the adventures of two children locked in an auditorium after hours. Then music took over for the rest of the evening, beginning with a Philharmonia Orchestra concert, which included Saint-Saens "Carnival of the Animals" narrated by Mayor Stephen May, while artist David Majchrzak, also on stage, sketched the animals. Children selected th order of the next four works by spinning a giant musical roulette wheel on stage, and the audience then listened to a jazz quintet, an opera aria, the school's trombone choir, and its chorale. The Eastman Wind Ensemble completed the concert with three selections, the last an audience participation version of the "On the Mall March" with clapping and whistling.

How successful was the event? The low ticket cost precluded a profit, but the outpouring of good will more than compensated for this. Here's how Mrs. Glazer described the progam's benefits to *AM*: "We more than accomplished our purpose. We completely changed the image of the school from a cold, forbidding, mausoleum-like place to a warm, open-hearted one peopled by friendly, attractive students. We made hundreds of friends and most of the community suddenly woke up to the enormous contributions which the school makes to its cultural life. Best of all, the whole school—faculty, students, and maintenance personnel—worked together on a creative project." The program now becomes an annual event.

Cultural groups interested in developing similar programs must be careful not to call them "Musical Picnic," "A Musical Picnic," or even "Music Picnic." Eastman has copyrighted all three versions of the title.

January-February 1971

Careful Plan, Total Campaign
Helps University "Up the Arts"

Six years after a similar attempt failed, a midwestern university successfully introduced a major professional artist series and stimulated new campuswide interest in the arts. Long and careful preplanning, on-target promotion, and an easily remembered and heavily publicized campaign slogan, "Up the Arts," were key ingredients in the launching of the 1974-75 International Concert Series at Western Michigan University in Kalamazoo.

Although the university is located in a city that actively supports a variety of year-round cultural programs, campus leaders felt the need for developing a series of "great" events specifically aimed at its own university audience and utilizing its excellent 3500-seat facility, Miller Auditorium. Popular entertainment series had been presented regularly at Miller, but a major artists series initiated in 1968, the auditorium's first season, was poorly attended and a second season was never attempted. The thrust for a new series intensified following the establishment of a new College of Fine Arts in 1972.

Following a long period of planning and the booking of a five attraction-series for 1974-75, the promotion wheels began turning in February when concert brochures were mailed to the entire student body, faculty, and staff. In addition, promotion letters signed by the fine arts and arts and science deans were mailed to their colleagues, and a letter from the Student Concert Committee president was sent to 20,000 fellow students. The latter pinpointed discount prices, delayed payment plans, and a phone reservation service, and urged students who "attend the rock concerts and special shows" on campus to also "give our support to this excellent artist series."

The campaign went into high gear on March 11, two weeks prior to the public sale, when subscriptions were opened to the university community. Five large "Up the Arts" kiosks were strategically placed around campus and four special information centers manned by volunteers dispensed information and "Up the Arts" buttons, bumper stickers, and brochures. The all-out media effort included a special "concert issue" of the university newsletter. Extra materials were given to each of the 1100 College of Fine Arts students so they could promote the series to their friends.

A week later, to coincide with an appeal letter mailed by the university president to "students and colleagues," the faculty women's club launched a telephone "blitz" campaign to every faculty member at home. Finally, when the entire campus had been reached by mail, phone, in print, or in person, season ticket sales were opened to the general public. By the end of March, about 800 season tickets had been sold, with nearly one-fourth purchased by students.

During the late summer, "Welcome to Western" letters sent to all new faculty and staff members by the cultural events committee chairman and fine arts dean urged subscription purchases, but pragmatically recognized that "joining a new faculty involves all kinds of extra expenses." The letter emphasized the 18 percent faculty discount and the payroll deduction system spreading costs over 18 pay periods throughout the academic year. A congratulations letter to new students offered them 25 percent discounts on subscriptions. To catch those not reached, "Up the Arts" bookmarks were distributed in front of the campus bookstore during the first week of school.

By the time the season opened, the goal of nearly 2000 subscriptions had been reached, with some 70 percent sold to the primary audience—students, faculty, and staff. Moreover, the promotion proved so effective that the first three series attractions—the London Symphony, the Alvin Ailey Dance Theatre, and the Soviet Georgian Dancers—all were sell-outs, with sell-outs also expected for the remaining two events—Richard Tucker and Robert Merrill, and Loren Hollander.

An additional benefit according to Robert Holmes, dean of the College of Fine Arts, was the fact that the series led directly to campus residencies by members of the London Symphony, who gave master classes for college music majors and high school music students, and the Ailey Company. Loren Hollander will be on campus for three days this February in conjunction with his concert.

Although the campaign was more expensive than the average promotion because of the volume of materials mailed, it was not costly. On campus mailing was free, and off-campus mail was sent at bulk rate. Also, the university administration partially subsidized program costs and guaranteed to make up the difference if income was below a given level.

"We're delighted with the results," added Holmes, "and we've insured continuity of the series. Everyone now knows about it, and the cost of promoting future series will be much less."

November-December 1974

Museums Test Pilot
Cultural Voucher Plan

A pilot program with national implications is testing an approach to reaching thousands of people not traditionally served by arts institutions. In New York, Museums Collaborative, a cooperative group of museums and other cultural agencies affiliated with the City Department of Cultural Affairs, initiated a "cultural voucher" system in July 1973 to enable community groups to participate in a series of arts programs. Thirteen city institutions including the Metropolitan Museum of Art, the Studio Museum in Harlem, and the Whitney Museum serve as resource centers.

The concept of cultural vouchers—making tickets, program participation, or admissions available to audiences through special vouchers which after their use are redeemed by participating arts institutions—has been eyed by arts leaders for some time. Yet aside from the voucher exchange used by the Theatre Development Fund for the past few years, there has been limited use of the concept. The current test is perhaps the first communitywide voucher plan to involve so many diverse cultural institutions in an across-the-board visual arts program.

The pilot project titled "Museum Summer '73," enables community groups and in some instances individuals to sign up on a first-come, first-served basis for one of 26 programs offered by participating institutions. Each is designed for a particular age group or groups, from preschool through senior citizen, and is offered on varying schedules throughout the summer.

The way the voucher system works, each participating cultural institution receives paper credit in advance for the cost of the program and is reimbursed later according to the actual number of enrollees. Thus, although a particular project might be budgeted at $5000 based on an enrollment of 50 participants at a cost of $100 each, the sponsoring museum would receive half that amount if only 25 participants enrolled. Enrollment not only is free, but includes, in some instances, transportation costs to enable participants to travel anywhere in the city for programs of their choice. The pilot effort, budgeted at $95,000, is supported by grants from the Arts Endowment and six foundations.

The idea for the program grew out of meetings first held a year ago between representatives of New York museums, the state arts council, and members of the Museums Collaborative Staff. As the plan developed, cultural groups were invited to submit proposed programs for screening by an evaluation panel composed in part of community people. Of 31 submitted, 5 were rejected, 20 accepted, and 6 more accepted after they were revised to make them more applicable to the needs of their intended audiences. Following approval, colorful posters outlining each of the programs—concept, meeting times, kinds of participants, sponsoring institution, and contact—were prepared and sent to a list of community organizations. Day care centers, senior citizen groups, community art centers, homes for the blind, and religious centers were included on the list. Sponsor institutions were urged to follow-up with potential participants to insure full use of all available vouchers.

It is still too early to evaluate the success of the new program, but Museums Collaborative hopes for a full enrollment of 4000 this summer involved in an average seven days participation each. "This is a unique program," Collaborative director Priscilla Dunhill told *AM*. "Not only can we begin to reach audiences that no museum alone could possibly reach, but we hope to develop a prototype cultural voucher system with wide applicability."

Based on what is learned from this pilot voucher program—an NYU evaluation team will report back by September—the Collaborative hopes to design a "true" voucher system, a three-year project that could place cultural coupons in the hands of users to be spent on a wide range of programs of their choosing.

Summer 1973

Holiday Party Brings
Publicity, New Audiences

A Boston arts group has started to think about New Year's Eve early, and with good reason. The Handel and Haydn Society's first combination New Year's Eve concert and follow-up party in 1971 not only drew huge audiences, half of them first-timers at a society concert, but resulted in outstanding publicity and good will.

According to society manager Margaret May Meredith, the idea for the New Year's Eve celebration grew out of a desire to do something imaginative "on a night when entertainment is getting pretty mundane." What resulted was a nonsubscription performance at Boston's Symphony Hall of Haydn's oratorio *The Creation*, with soloists, chorus, and orchestra conducted by Thomas Dunn followed by a bring-your-own-bottle party at Horticultural Hall across the street. There were separate admission charges for the two events—the concert was scaled from $3.25 to $7.25 and party admission was $1.50. People could attend the concert or the concert and party, but *not* the party alone.

The concert, which drew outstanding critical notices, ended about 10:15 P.M. in the evening, and about half the audience of 1800 crossed the street to attend the party. The society discovered just how popular the event was when the crowd, swelled by party crashers, reached over 1000. "We could have sold at least another 400 party tickets if room had been available," said Miss Meredith.

Although partygoers brought their own liquid refreshments, the society contributed food, noisemakers, and entertainment. In the hall's larger room, donated records were played. In the second room there was live entertainment by chorus members doubling as barbershop quartets and do-it-yourself piano playing and singing by audience members. Decorations, helium-filled balloons, and large tropical palms were lent or donated. In keeping with the festive holiday spirit, advance fliers had described the party as a "do-it-yourself creation" and had invited the guests to "dare to dress as you care—White Tie to Tie-dye." Many did.

Although the event occasioned several problems, foremost among them party crashing and high refreshment costs, the society viewed the evening as an unqualified success and received scores of "fan" letters. "It certainly gave us a lot of publicity including television interviews and spots," commented Miss Meredith, "and helped promote the rest of our season. Also, it gave us a good focul point for an outstanding choral work and seemed to enhance our image of imaginative programming."

Planning for this year's concert and party has started already. Although the party will again be held at Horticultural Hall, there will be some changes made based on last year's experience, including higher admission prices, better security against gate crashers, and allowing the public to bring in more of the food.

Summer 1972

New Theater Involves Public
and Scores Box Office Success

By totally involving a community in its program, and by emphasizing sound management practices, a new resident theater will be "in the black" when it ends its first full season later this spring. Behind the success of New Haven, Connecticut's Long Wharf Theatre is the drive and philosophy of Harlan P. Kleiman, its executive director. Mr. Kleiman, who holds a combined master's degree from

Yale University in industrial administration and drama, contends, "Arts groups must compete in the fiscal market." He has woven this belief into a bold program of management that strikes out into almost every avenue of audience development. Consequently, more than 85,000 persons, including 8000 season subscribers, are expected to see the company this year.

Every step in the growth of the theater was carefully planned. Even before the organization gained its nonprofit status it began to develop the nucleus of a resident company by starting a commercial summer theater in Clinton, Connecticut in 1964. That fall Mr. Kleiman conducted a detailed survey within a 50-mile radius of New Haven to determine if a professional resident theater was feasible there. The survey showed that there was a sufficient number of professionals, educated people, and people with annual incomes of $6300 to $17,000, the groups most likely to support a resident theater. Based on these and other positive results, plans were made for organizing a professional theater in New Haven headed by Mr. Kleiman and Jon Jory, artistic director.

"There are three keys to having a successful theater," Mr. Kleiman told *AM*. "Make yourself important to the community, it won't let you down; present it with good plays; and make seats hard to get."

Relying on the strategy that by involving the community it could later approach it for funds, the theater organization asked for advice from persons in the area as to the kind of theater they desired, the plays they wanted to see, and the ticket price structure they preferred.

In addition, more than 140 lectures were presented to community groups by about nine speakers trained by the neophyte organization. "You get more by talking to 40 persons," Mr. Kleiman maintained, "than you do from a half-page ad."

A goal of $125,000 was set in October 1964, to initiate the full-time theater. Pledge cards were used initially in lieu of collecting contributions. When the pledges showed that the theater was well on its way to its goal, contributions were collected. By July 4 the goal was reached.

To prepare for its first full season, which began last fall, the company first presented a summer season in New Haven. The summer theater sold out 99 percent of its seats, with 93 percent of the audience subscribers.

Prior to the opening of its first fall season, the theater recognized that it was virtually impossible for a new arts group to receive grants from national foundations. Therefore, it devised programs that would bring special groups to the theater through grant support from government agencies like the Office of Economic Opportunity. It also helped local schools to prepare Title III proposals utilizing the services of the company.

To pursue this progam to its maximum effecitveness, Long Wharf hired a full-time director of theater development to help groups get grants to come to the theater. "She made back her salary in two weeks," Mr. Kleiman said.

Thus far, the theater has developed a program to bring groups of elderly persons and adult literacy students to the theater; a program to bring economically disadvantaged students to the theater; and a school program, including touring, which in its first three months involved 89 schools from 57 towns. A new program, which would involve the mentally retarded, has been proposed and is awaiting approval It is essential to the operation of these programs that participants are not seated in a special section of the theater but are integrated with the regular audience.

The theater receives additional help from active volunteers like The Long Wharf Hands, a group of 250 women who raise money, help backstage, and are responsible for selling 25 percent of the season subscriptions.

Advertising has helped the theater pay for much of its literature. Mr. Kleiman said, "Our playbill makes a fortune." Furthermore, a special study guide distributed to 10,000 youngsters participating in the touring progam was paid for through advertising.

February 1966

The Older Audience

If you offer special performance discounts to senior citizens, remember that many of these people cannot attend the theater or concert hall without a younger person providing transportation. Recognizing this fact, the Studio Arena Theatre in Buffalo, New York, which offers weekday reduced-rate tickets to older people, allows them to purchase two tickets, instead of just one, upon presentation of senior citizen identification cards.

March-April 1968

Hot Lines

Telephone services that provide information on events and programs are becoming increasingly popular in the arts. Recently introduced services include the ARTS Hot Line sponsored by the Arts Information Center and manned by volunteers who provide information on events in the Greater Los Angeles area, and the new Poets and Writers telephone service. The latter service, which provides information on how much to reach more than 3000 fiction writers and poets, may be contacted between 9:30 and 5:30 P.M. weekdays and will even accept collect calls from any of the 50 states. Dial (212) PL 7-1766 for the service.

September-October 1976

Hold That Line

Arts groups are discovering new twists on a familiar theme—the recorded telephone message that provides callers with information on cultural events. In Red

Bank, New Jersey, ARTS-phone callers hear cultural event listings from "James Cagney," "Groucho Marx," and other well-known Hollywood personalities. In reality, the voices all belong to the same person, local actor and impressionist Mark Kineavy, who is lending his services to the Monmouth County Arts Council for the promotional experiment. The Brooklyn Museum, meanwhile, uses telephone waiting time as a promotional tool. While callers are "on hold," a one-minute recording gives them one of three different messages, depending on who they are calling, and the information sought—a weekly event listing, general information on the museum program, or a special exhibition message. In the near future a fourth message, directed to schools and other groups, will be instituted. The service is especially useful on weekends when the phone load is heavy.

Summer 1977

Punny but True

A catchy name can help draw attention to your program. The Louisville Fund for the Arts drive was built around the theme, "The Dough Must Go On;" the Syracuse Symphony's special July and August season was titled the "Summer's Hear" campaign, and the Minnesota Orchestra's rug concert of eerie and ghoulish music was promoted under the title, "To Hell With Music."

Summer 1977

Military Post Audience

Civilian employees residing on a military post some distance from town can be effectively reached for reserved seat performances through an on-post ticket agency. The Olney Theatre (Olney, Maryland) arrangement with the Fort Meade personnel service to collect money and phone in ticket reservations has been a gratifying success to the theater management.

July 1962

Theater Celebrates Anniversary
with Full Week of Free Events

If your organization has a key anniversary or landmark date coming up, you might let the whole community celebrate with you and reap new audiences and widespread publicity in the processs. In Winnipeg, Canada, the Manitoba Theatre Center celebrated its fifteenth anniversary in September, 1972 with a carefully planned week-long series of free events culminating in a giant all-night birthday party at the theater, open to the entire community. Not only was Open House Week a huge promotional success, but it helped MTC launch a new season effectively, increased the mailing list by serveral thousand, encouraged new season subscriptions, and importantly, wound up costing the theater nothing.

Following an offical proclamation of Manitoba Theatre Centre Open

House Week signed by the mayor of Winnipeg in a public ceremony at the theater, the week opened on Sunday, September 10, 1972 with the release of thousands of balloons (some containing ticket vouchers) from the theater roof. From Monday to Friday between 1:00 and 8:00 P.M., the theater, manned by volunteers and staff, was open to the public for free guided tours which included costume and prop displays and a slide showing of past productions. Coffee and tea were served in the lobby. With the incentive of free single seat and season ticket drawings, visitors filled out forms listing name, address, phone, category—student, adult, or senior citizen—and whether they were new to the theater. Among the visitors were some 3000 not previously on the mailing list.

Although attendance was open to anyone, special days were designated for certain audiences. Tuesday, for ladies, featured a fashion show of MTC costumes and a wig styling demonstration. Senior Citizens' Day, Wednesday, included bingo games hosted by a local television personality and a bake sale. Saturday morning was set aside for activities and displays for children, followed by a family barbeque at noon. Later in the afternoon, an auction of MTC costumes from past productions realized $700 for the theater.

Although the closing event, the free all-night party on Saturday, was the most expensive on the week-long agenda, with orchestra and food costs about three-fourths of the $1000 spent during the entire week (posters, daily refreshments for visitors, and the opening ceremonies were the other expense items), the proceeds from bar sales paid back part of the cost. In fact, because of bar and auction proceeds, contributions of prizes and equipment made by local business and the fact that activities were manned by volunteers and staff, the week actually wound up costing the theater nothing.

The publicity value of the event was excellent, according to Penelope Burk of the theater's public relations staff. "As we run from October to May," Miss Burk told *AM*, "there is, naturally, a slump in publicity over the summer months. This week is valuable to us because it helps, in a soft-sell sort of way, to announce that MTC is back in business again, and that people should get ready to come back to the theater." The fact that the event is free gives it an interesting twist, according to Miss Burk. "For an organization which spends most of the year trying to get the public to give their leisure money to MTC rather than put it somewhere else, a turn-about, where the theater invites the public to come and have fun free of charge (or at the theater's expense) is a welcome change for both theater and public."

September-October 1972

Arts Groups Seek New Ways to Lure Potential Audiences

Cultural groups continue to experiment with a variety of techniques designed to make the arts experience more convenient, accessible, and inexpensive for potential audiences.

In Indianapolis, ten conductors appearing with the Indianapolis Symphony are participating in a new "Symphony Seminar" series prior to each of their opening concerts. Cosponsored by the Jewish Community Center, the series is available at $1 per ticket at the door. In Los Angeles, the County Museum of Art initiated a weekly one-hour open discussion this summer, with the public invited to question museum officials on virtually any aspect of museum policy.

The Houston Opera not only initiated two new subscription series of opera in English exclusively for high school and college students this season, but found a new, and hopefully more convenient, time to present the performances. The 7:00 P.M. Monday and Tuesday series supplement regular matinee programs for younger students. The Albany Symphony, meanwhile, has extended its student discount policy to anyone under the age of 25 in response to a letter. The writer complained that many young nonstudents are no better off financially than students are and should be given the same opportunity to purchase tickets at $2.50 each. Younger audiences will benefit also from better productions if a New York State Council on the Arts program has its desired effect. In an attempt to strengthen and improve children's theater, the council is offering grants of up to $5000 to enable theater companies to commission new plays by professional writers not previously involved in the medium.

At the opposite end of the age spectrum, one of New York's leading revival and art film houses, the Elgin Cinema, initiated a new policy admitting anyone over the age of 62 to the theater for 25¢. The policy is unique in that admission is good for all shows every day of the week.

In Los Angeles, a barrier of sorts was broken when the Music Center presented its first dance festival before audiences seated on the floor of the Dorothy Chandler Pavilion. The six-week season, featuring two local companies every Sunday and guest celebrities in informal audience talks prior to each concert, was offered without charge and drew overflow crowds. Columbia, South Carolina, meanwhile, will make its own bid to attract the attention of overflow audiences through local artist Blue Sky's mural—"Tunnelvision." Under a grant from the state arts commission, Blue Sky will paint a view through a tunnel on the three-story, 75 foot wall of the downtown Farm Credit Bank Building. According to the artist, "Cars in the parking lot in front of the wall will blend into the mural on precisely the proper scale to form an important prelude to what one sees on the wall."

November-December 1974

Educational Services Develop
Interested Cultural Audiences

A midwest arts council is offering two radio series to its audience, an Eastern drama school is sponsoring a workshop for directors of nearby community theaters, and a state arts council is underwriting an experimental program designed to help public school teachers learn how to look at art. These and a mushrooming number of similar activities are all indicative of the educational services that organizations are offering in the hopes of developing knowledgeable and interested audiences.

The Arts and Education Council of Greater St. Louis, for example, has presented a weekly "Living Calendar" radio series since November 1967 as a supplement to the monthly calendar of events that it publishes. Aired on station KFUO, the progam highlights cultural events for the coming week and includes "in-depth" interviews with cultural newsmakers. In an effort to stimulate critical thinking locally, the council initiated a second weekly radio series, "Armchair Critic," presented over the NBC affiliate, KSD. This program is an informal discussion by four informed and intelligent laymen, not necessarily experts, who have seen four local cultural events in advance of the program. The thirteen-week series featured in its initial progam a discussion of the Pulitzer art collection at the City Art Museum, the film *The Graduate*, a recent Public Broadcast Laboratory program, and the Loretto-Hilton production of *Six Characters in Search of an Author.*

In Buffalo, the Studio Arena Theatre School inaugurated a twice-weekly workshop for community theater stage directors, with an enrollment of 22 local directors. According to Maurice Breslow, director of the School and instructor for the 30-hour program, "the workshop represents an important step toward establishing the type of relationship that a professional resident theater should have with its community, one in which the theater and the community work together to raise the level of theater throughout the area."

A pilot project in New York, started in February, 1968, is designed to help school children and their teachers respond to and enjoy art and other visual experiences more fully. Sponsored by the New York State Council on the Arts and the New York State Education Department, a "Workshop in Looking," conducted by art critic Katharine Kuh, is bringing together 52 elementary and high school teachers from all subject areas for a series of 12 weekly meetings featuring open discussions and individual experiments. Orthodox lectures and technical terminology are taboo in the meetings.

March-April 1968

Informed Audience

Arts groups striving to develop an informed and interested audience might benefit from the experience of the Hartford Stage Company and its "Sunday at Six" program. The hour-long panel discussion program for subscribers is held between the matinee and evening performance of a production as it nears the end of its run. Panel participants include the director, producing director, a designer, three actors, and several others, including a moderator. Since most of the audience has already seen the production, the questions are frequently provocative. Summaries of each program are included in issues of the theater's magazine.

November-December 1968

New Group Attracts
Patrons of Tomorrow

An organized approach to a special arts audience—educated and affluent young adults—is meeting with initial success in New York. Through programs of a new organization, Young Friends of the Arts, men and women between the ages of 25 and 45 are exploring a variety of new arts experiences and are not only returning to buy tickets and subscriptions on their own, but are becoming increasingly aware of the funding needs facing cultural institutions.

According to Sandra Sanderson, who founded Young Friends in January 1976, the program is reaching out for what she terms "a neglected audience," educated and successful young executives, in the hopes of making them the arts patrons of the future. Ms. Sanderson, manager of publications administration and secretary of the contributions committee at American Airlines told *AM*, "Nobody's really focused on the untapped potential of educated and affluent young executives who have disposable income and are looking for new and interesting activities and involvements. We felt that many of these people, including some newly transferred to New York by their companies, didn't have a familiarity with the arts, but with a little education and prodding could become deeply involved."

In an attempt to provide that familiarity, Young Friends has thus far recruited nearly 125 members—individuals at $25 and couples at $35—and brought them a range of services in the arts including a monthly newsletter on cultural activities, opportunities to attend performing and individual events as a group, arts education programs, and meetings with artists. Having won its tax-exempt status this fall, YFA plans a major membership drive early in 1977 and hopes to recruit up to a thousand members.

As part of its program, the organization regularly purchases group-rate tickets to events and offers them to members as a "performance plus" package. Normally, the "plus" involves a talk with an artist or administrator the same night as the event, although an Alwin Nikolais performance was preceded by a visit to his studio a week earlier. Other events this year, 22 in all, have included exhibition and lecture tours at the International Center of Photography and the Metropolitan Museum of Art and an Eliot Feld Ballet performance at the New York Shakespeare Festival's Public Theater, preceded by a discussion of the Festival's program and operation. Attendance has averaged between 30 and 40 at an event, with some open to guests, serving as membership recruitment programs as well. The program also included two out-of-town tours.

Also planned is a monthly series of afterwork cocktail seminars at midtown locations with leading arts figures discussing such topics as the economics of the arts and audience development. Also, the membership will visit arts service organization offices—the Theater Development Fund will be first—for cocktail seminars with administrators.

A program now in the works will ask companies such as brokerage houses, who train out-of-town employees in New York to take out YFA corporate membership for all its trainees. Hopefully, according to Ms. Sanderson, a three- or four-month involvement with Young Friends will motivate trainees to become involved in local arts activities when they return home.

Ms. Sanderson has noted such initial results as several members becoming arts organization volunteers and frequent member return to cultural programs following initial exposure. Also, although arts fund raising is not a specific organizational activity, Ms. Sanderson finds members becoming increasingly aware of funding needs. "Once we get them to become part of the regular arts audience," she said, "their contributions will increase. Our function now is to introduce and educate members in the arts." Looking to the future, Ms. Sanderson hopes to find out two things—that follow-up attendance at events has doubled or tripled and that the majority of members are involved with arts groups as board members, volunteers or supporters.

November-December 1976

Museum Offers Tour Information on Nationwide Arts Attractions

An information service by the Walters Art Gallery in Baltimore, Maryland, keeps vacationers and travelers posted on museum activities in other cities. Information on current exhibitions, displays, and lectures at museums throughout the country is available from Walters.

In spring 1963, Geoffrey W. Fielding, Walters' public relations director, wrote to museums asking to be put on their mailing list, and offering to reciprocate. Material came in regularly from museums in more than 50 cities on their current shows and events. All sections of the country were represented.

News of the service was publicized in the Baltimore press. Individuals were invited to call the gallery from 9:30 A.M. to 4:30 P.M. to get news of events in museums in other cities, or to stop in and consult an up-to-date file in the first-floor office of the membership secretary.

According to Mr. Fielding, requirements for the service are minimal—about a foot of file space, and a few minutes of a secretary's time daily to keep the file current and answer phone calls.

July 1963

Solving a Puzzle

Crossword puzzle enthusiasts can be indulged in their hobby, while at the same time learn more about your arts group and its programs. The Studio Museum in

Harlem in New York featured a specially designed crossword puzzle in its newsletter recently, with all definitions dealing with topics of interest to the museum program. Instead of being published in the newsletter, puzzle answers were available only on a bulletin board in the museum.

March-April 1975

Baby Sitters

Do you want young parents in your audience? St. Paul's Community Theater in Brooklyn, New York did, and to entice them into coming it offered a special baby-sitting service at the theater on selected weekend dates. Telephone reservations for the service, available at $1.50 per child, were accepted in advance.

Summer 1971

Question Mark

A lively forum can help to draw public attention to the arts. In St. Louis, a leading newspaper, in cooperation with the Arts and Education Council, is providing just such a forum. A regular question and answer column about the arts appears in the *St. Louis Democrat* under the title "Queries on Culture."

Spring-Summer 1969

Study Groups

Cultural groups attempting to spur public interest by organizing study groups on their programs should seek to include men as well as women in the sessions. The Seattle Symphony, which organized afternoon study groups conducted by university teachers and members of the orchestra 15 years ago, added Sunday evening meetings to its schedule. As a result, many men now attend these programs.

November 1965

Behind the Scenes

Arts groups can encourage a direct interest in their activities by initiating behind-the-scenes tours of their facilities. If the organization's work is diverse and extensive enough for an interesting tour, the group can even charge a fee for the visit. In New York, for example, the American Museum of National History offers annual "Behind the Scenes" tours where it shows visitors how its staff simulates a natural effect in displays. The fee is $2.00 for nonmembers and $1.50 for members.

June 1965

Special Effects

A dramatic offstage touch can help to call extra attention to an unusual event or exhibition. When Theatre Calgary in Alberta, Canada presented a production of *Dracula* this season, it had nurses from St. John's Ambulance on duty to heighten the play's atmosphere. During the production's run, however, one audience member fainted and four became hysterical, necessitating aid from the nurses and resulting in some added publicity for the play.

March-April 1971

Happy Time

An occasional fun event can be a pleasant experience for both the arts group and its audience. As part of its "Six for the Show" concert series during the 1970-71 season, the Indianapolis Symphony presented "Mystery Night at the Symphony." Printed programs, instead of listing the works to be performed, asked the audience to identify them by filling in blanks or selecting from multiple choice answers. Most of the 11 works were legitimate, if unusual and unfamiliar, and the program was highlighted by a performance of Malcolm Arnold's "A Grand, Grand Overture for Orchestra, Organ, Rifles, Three Hoovers [vacuum cleaners] and an Electric Floor Polisher." Guest artists on the nontraditional instruments included Indianapolis's deputy mayor, a mayoral aide, local broadcasting personalities, a soprano, and the orchestra's harpist, publicist, and manager.

March-April 1971

Free Bus Lures Tourists
to Cultural Institutions

By working together, cultural groups can use nearby tourist attractions to increase attendance at their own facilities. In 1964, for the second straight summer, Philadelphia's Academy of National Sciences and the Franklin Institute, its neighbor across the street, joined in the sponsorship of a free bus service bringing visitors from Independence Hall, a prime tourist attraction, to the museums and then returning them to Independence Hall. The bus service ran on a regular hourly schedule from Tuesday through Sunday of every week.

The idea for the promotion was conceived as a means of boosting lagging attendance at each of the museums during the summer months. It was considered successful in its first season when more than 4700 tourists used the bus service. During its second year, the Philadelphia Museum of Art joined with the academy and the institute in sponsoring the project, which was launched as a climax to "Museum Week" proclaimed by Mayor James H. J. Tate of Philadelphia.

Busses were rented from Philadelphia's public transportation company and the overall costs, including rental, flyers, and signs, were prorated among the three museums, based on the previous season's attendance figures. Thus, between June 16 and September 5, the height of the tourist season, the museums shared the bus rental charge of $50.50 per day and $44.00 on Sundays, with the academy paying 24 percent, the institute paying 35 percent, and the Museum of Art paying 41 percent.

Independence Hall was helpful in publicizing the service. It placed a signpost announcing the tour at its regular bus stop, and it displayed posters and bus schedules at its information counter. Guides ended their tour of the hall by mentioning the service to tourists.

A cooperative promotional campaign by the three sponsors included radio and television spot announcements, news releases, and attractive flyers sent to hotels, motels, tourist agencies, and other museums in the area. In addition, each of the sponsors promoted the tour in its own institution with posters and schedules, and guards and cashiers invited tourists to visit the two other museums. The tour bus itself was an effective promotional device with two large banners attached to each of its sides.

Although the free bus idea has great potential, Mrs. Libby Demp Forrest of The Academy of Natural Sciences noted that dealing with a public transportation company subject to union demands has also created several problems. "I would caution other institutions," Mrs. Forrest told *AM*, "to carefully study all the aspects before they institute a similar service."

July-August 1964

Dinner Stop

Performing arts groups with inadequate parking facilities may be able to arrange parking at hotels and restaurants with a free bus link to their door. To attract dinner guests, two hotels in Minneapolis offer these services to preconcert diners later attending performances of the Minneapolis Symphony Orchestra.

June 1965

At Your Service

Is your facility located in an out-of-the-way, impossible-to-reach-by-foot area? The Long Wharf Theatre in New Haven, Connecticut, located a mile from the town's center and directly off a highway connector, worked out a way to attract those people who would not ordinarily attend performances because of the transportation problem. A limousine, rented for a nominal $15 per hour, shuttles audience members to and from a center city hotel and the theater. Since the distance is short, there is not much waiting, and the two to three trips necessary take under 15 minutes. The house manager coordinates loading of the limousines.

September-October 1968

Charter Bus

Attendance at downtown auditoriums with limited parking area can be increased through charter bus service provided for ticket holders. In addition, riders will be in their seats on time. The Utah Symphony in Salt Lake City runs a special bus which stops at six convenient locations to transport passengers to and from the concert. The charge is 50¢. Advance reservations are made by phoning the orchestra office.

February 1963

Audience Eats Dinner on
Lawn and Stays to See Shakespeare

If visitors to your arts festival complain of crowded conditions in local restaurants, you may be interested in the arrangement that the Oregon Shakespearean Festival Association in Ashland, Oregon has worked out with a local hotel.

The hotel's management, aware of the pressures upon local restaurants during the summer festival, devised a plan by which visitors to the Shakespeare plays can eat in the relaxed atmosphere of the 100-acre Lithia Park (where the performance is held) and still attend the theater without a last-minute rush.

The theatergoes reserves a "gourmet basket" by calling the hotel and giving his seat number, the date, and time, then picks up a take-along ticket. On the night of the performance he presents his ticket at the hotel, picks up the picnic basket (priced at $2.75 each or $5.50 for two), goes to the park, selects a quiet spot, and eats his dinner in the park. Then he strolls to the theater.

Although the Oregon Shakespearean Fesival is not directly involved in this promotion, festival officials voted on the idea at a regular board meeting. The consensus was that the gourmet picnic would indirectly advertise the Shakespearen plays and allow visitors to take advantage of Lithia Park or the mountain forest regions that surround Ashland.

May 1963

The Way to
an Audience's Heart

Monticello College in Godfrey, Illinois, helped make the appearance there of the Sahm-Chun-Li Korean dance group a particularly memorable and gala evening by arranging with a local restaurant for it to serve a specially prepared Oriental dinner the night of the performance. The arrangement resulted in good local publicity as well. Ticket prices did not cover the cost of the meal, but college announcements made a point of advertising the dinner menu at the cooperating restaurant.

March 1964

Food Becomes Promotional
Aid for Varied Cultural Programs

Arts groups, experimenting with varied promotional techniques, have found that one way to an audience's heart may be through its stomach. In New York, for example, the American Place Theatre presented four short plays divided by a food break. Advertised to subscribers as a "festival, with comedy, drama, food for thought and sustenance for the soul," the program featured two short plays— one appropriately named *Cream Cheese*—followed by audience movement to the theater's cabaret area, where box suppers at $2.50 each were offered. Two very short plays, the "desserts," were then presented.

Several cultural groups have developed beneficial ties with local restaurants. In Minneapolis, Charlie's Cafe Exceptionale features special menus to coincide with Minnesota Orchestra concerts and Guthrie Theater programs. Scheduled this season were Mozart Viennese dinners, Berlioz French dinners, and Michael Langham English dinners, with all including free bus rides to the theaters. Hartford Stage Company ticketholders receive a free bottle of wine with their dinners at the Hearthstone Restaurant, while concertgoers showing their stub from any program that evening receive a free drink at the Home Bar in New York. Ticketholders at the low-priced Midday Medley series at New York's Town Hall received a practical benefit—a free preperformance hot dog or hamburger at Nathan's Famous.

Inexpensive lunch-hour programs are bringing arts events to working people. In San Francisco, the "Brown Bag Opera" program has been presented several times weekly by the San Francisco Opera in Veteran's Auditorium. Tickets for the hour-long program are 50¢ and audiences may bring their own food or purchase brown bag lunches for $1. "Eine Kleine Noonmusick," a series of free lunch-hour concerts sponsored by the Cleveland Area Arts Council every Wednesday between September and June, is held in the indoor mall of the historic downtown Arcade Building. Featuring a wide range of performing events, the program attracts as many as 3500 passersby weekly. The Phoenix Symphony outdoor "Sandwich & Pop" concerts on the Symphony Hall mall included box lunches with $2 tickets.

Food suppliers or manufacturers seeking product identification have tied in to arts events. At the end of a recent performance of *Albert Herring*, the Bronx Opera Company treated its audience to free herrring snackes, courtesy of the Vita Company. Similarly, when the Chicago Symphony fearured Brazilian music at a "University Night" concert, it presented—courtesy of a Brazilian sponsor of the program—a postconcert coffee-tasting reception on stage.

March-April 1974

Orchestra,
Audience, Meet and Eat

One way to strengthen the ties between a performing arts group and its public is to bring artists and audience together in an informal setting. An organization that does this regularly is the Seattle Symphony Orchestra, which holds a Tuesday night open house at a local restaurant. The public is invited to come and meet its conductor, Milton Katims, and the guest artists of the evening. Started in 1961, the program has won enthusiastic response according to Mrs. Hugh E. McCreery, manager of the orchestra.

The symphony group takes over most of the space in a first-class restaurant immediately after the Tuesday evening concert. Those who hold a ticket stub from the performance are granted a 20 percent discount on any food purchased. The restaurant is happy to offer the discount because it receives an increased flow of business at an hour when turnover is usually slow.

No formal program is presented, but everyone has a chance to meet and chat with the artists. Attendance averages 60 to 75.

April 1962

Arts Try Cocktails
to Reach New Audiences

The search for new audiences has taken arts groups into such unlikely performance settings as prisons and hospitals. It is doubtful, however, if many American performing organizations have ventured into nightclubs, as the Halle Symphony Orchestra in England did. Beset by financial difficulties, the orchestra looked for a new and untapped source of income and found it at a nightclub in Wakefield. Audience response was excellent, as was the fee, and the orchestra signed for four more dates.

The cocktail audience, but in a more traditional setting, is a target of Town Hall in New York, too. It initiated a series of Wednesday programs aimed at businessmen, which begin with cocktails in the lobby at 5:00 P.M. followed by a one-hour performance at 5:45 P.M. Tickets are priced at only $1.50, thanks to support from the New York State Council on the Arts. The varied program featured such groups as the Paul Taylor and Arthur Mitchell Dance Companies and Jazzmobile.

January-February 1972

Cooperation Among
Arts Groups Reaps Benefits

Cooperation between a theater and a ballet company in Philadelphia has expanded the promotional reach of each group and has resulted in dollar savings on pooled services. The Theatre of the Living Arts and the Pennsylvania Ballet Company exchange program advertisements, feature each other in lobby displays, pool recreational personnel, insert each other's brochures in programs, and jointly purchase printing supplies. In addition, the groups share a press agent with a third organization, the Philadelphia All-Star Forum, which presents touring attractions at the local Academy of Music. Acting on behalf of the three groups, the press agent was able to convince the Philadelphia Tourist and Convention Bureau to send out a national press release promoting the performing arts in Philadelphia, the first time the Bureau had ever done this.

Recently, the theater and ballet company joined with the All-Star Forum in sponsoring the publication of an eight-page newspaper supplement designed to promote all three groups and sell tickets to their programs. Titled "Crescendo," the supplement was published as part of the *Jewish Exponent* (circulation 70,000) with an overrun distributed with the *Jewish Times* (circulation 28,000). An additional 100,000 copies were mailed to the list of Philadelphia Cultural Communications, a nonprofit organization that maintains a computerized mailing service for 13 local nonprofit organizations. The $6800 cost of the cooperative effort was divided among the groups.

The initial returns were good, although it is too early to determine the overall effectiveness of the promotion. Moreover, there were some surprising side benefits. John Bos, producing director of Theatre of the Livng Arts, told *AM*, "We stirred up a lot of local interest. We also received at least 100 letters from people who read *Crescendo,* and assuming it to be a permanent publication, requested subscriptions."

As a result of this reaction, and other positive benefits resulting from the cooperative effort, the three supplement sponsors invited representatives of the Philadelphia Orchestra and the Temple University Music Festival to join them at a meeting designed to explore pragmatic ways they could work together in such areas as ticket sales, promotion, and winning greater support from city agencies. Also on the agenda was a plan to make *Crescendo* a regular publication of Philadelphia performing arts organizations.

In another city, Youngstown, Ohio, a symphony orchestra and ballet company joined together in a "marriage" that brought great benefits to both groups. In 1967 the Youngstown Symphony Society invited the then four-year-old Youngstown Ballet Guild to join its organization as an affiliate. After board approval by both organizations the merger was completed. Although the guild still maintains its own board and operates autonomously in programming performances of its dance company, the affiliation has helped to solve many problems encountered by a young regional ballet company.

The Symphony Society, for example, now includes the ballet budget within its own, coordinates all publicity, and assumes responsibility for such business details as insurance. Several times a year the ballet company and orchestra perform together, with the society handling ticket sales and other arrangements.

January-February 1969

TICKETS AND SUBSCRIPTIONS

Symphony Orchestra Sails Up as Frisbees Entice Students

In an attempt to sell season subscriptions to college students, a symphony orchestra initiated a special on-campus campaign highlighted by the use of a promotional tool familiar to students—the frisbee. The Indianapolis Symphony approach was so successful that students wound up buying some 2000 special subscriptions at half price, out of a total of 6000 sold.

The campaign began in August, 1976 during registration periods at Butler and Indiana-Purdue Universities. With the cooperation of school authorities, orchestra volunteers manned tables in the registration area and passed out thousands of subscription brochures to students. At Indiana-Purdue, authorities allowed the orchestra to stuff 14,000 brochures into official registration kits, which volunteers did by hand.

To call attention to the campaign, volunteers also handed students about 2500 Humphrey Flyers (costing less than 50¢ each in quantity), decorated with the orchestra logo in black and bearing an inscription reading, "Go Symphony."

"The frisbees really called attention to the campaign," said Sue Staton, the orchestra's director of audience development, "and gave us an identification with the students. We had an added bonus, although we didn't plan it. Students have sailed symphony frisbees in unexpected places, including over the heads of audience members at a jammed rock concert."

November-December 1976

A Good Taste

A really eye-catching poster is one of the best promotional tools you can find. The promotionally minded Seattle Opera came up with a poster that's not only attention-getting, but mouth-watering. The 24- by 33-inch color poster shows a robust motherly type holding a huge silver tray much wider than she is, dominated by a gigantic serving of spaghettti and meatballs. The legend underneath reads, "You'll eat it up. Seattle Opera's 76/77 Season."

November-December 1976

The Wively Arts

Cultural groups might begin to think about Monday night programming for wives if the inferences drawn by the Yale Repertory Theatre have validity. This season the theater introduced a new low-priced subscription series on Mondays, the same night that millions of Americans stay home to watch the televised football game of the week, and discovered that nearly 70 percent of its Monday audience was women. In a release headed, "YRT's New Monday Series: Salvation for Football Widows," the theater suggested that theatregoing may be emerging as a new form of entertainment for many women "who, having joined with other similarly imaginative and liberated women, are taking the big step out of their domestic Monday night doldrums, and heading for the Yale Repertory Theatre."

September-October 1974

Ticket Campaign in Store Window a Success

With the cooperation of a local store, arts groups can increase ticket sales by staging a telephone "marathon" promotion. In Atlanta, Georgia, volunteers made telephone calls from the window of one of the country's leading department stores, Rich's, and sold over $2500 in season tickets for the Atlanta Symphony Orchestra in a matter of hours. Only subscriptions to the entire 12-concert season were sold.

"More tickets were sold than on any previous single day in the orchestra's history," Mrs. William Robertson, Jr., the orchestra's publicity director, told *AM*. Sales during the marathon were bolstered by a 16,000-piece mailing that went out to new ticket prospects prior to the marathon date.

Volunteers, including members of the orchestra's board of directors, women's committee, and local celebrities, sat in the department store window during the promotion. Manning six telephones for three-hour shifts, the volunteers called prospects and aroused their interest by opening the conversation with the provocative sales line, "You won't believe this, but I'm sitting in a window at Rich's selling tickets to the Atlanta Symphony."

Mrs. Robertson told *AM,* "The marathon was a great success, and one that can be highly recommended to other communities. Even then, it takes the proper combination of enthusiasm, timing, and people."

The only expense incurred in the marathon was the cost of local telephone calls. While this was the first time such an event was held, it success has spurred the group to plan another one next year. It is planned to run for two or three consecutive days instead of only one day.

February 1965

Telephone Blitz Sells
Season Tickets for Theater

A gigantic telephone blitz campaign, undertaken by more than 300 volunteers on behalf of a year-round legitimate theater in Canada, resulted in the sale of more than 5000 season ticket subscriptions.

In Winnipeg, Canada, the Manitoba Theatre Centre, a nonprofit organization, begins its intensive fall ticket sales campaign during the summer. Brochures describing the productions to be presented during the coming season are mailed to a list of about 30,000 prospective customers in August. About a week later this is followed by a reminder letter.

Shortly after Labor Day, the week-long telephone blitz campaign begins. The Theatre Centre's women's committee recruits between 300 and 400 women as volunteers and sets up a switchboard and more than a dozen telephones in the theater's lobby. The women then make personal phone calls urging the purchase of season tickets to every prospect on the list who has not responded to the previous mailings. In the evening, members of the organization's board of governors often relieve women at the phones. In one instance, an enterprising board member sold two season tickets by bringing together a man and woman over the phone who both claimed they wanted to buy tickets but had nobody to go with.

According to Lucile Fleming, the publicity director of the Theatre Centre, the telephone campaign is tied in with an intensive advertising drive in all media. In addition, a comprehensive publicity program, which includes the airing of radio spots made by actors scheduled to appear during the forthcoming season, insures total saturation in the community.

January 1964

New Promotional Techniques
Draw Audiences and Members

In an unusual promotion campaign, the Nikolais Dance Theatre reached out to attract the same audience twice in a single day. As part of its two-week season at New York University, the modern dance company promoted the concept of "dance doubleheaders." Audiences were offered, at a discount, tickets for a matinee and evening performance at substantially reduced discounts. Surprisingly, of 8300 seats available for the entire run, 1000 went to those who took advantage of the offer.

Originally, the promotion was designed with a third component, a discount dinner at a neighborhood restaurant, and the offer was featured in newspaper ads and in a direct mail drive. When no restaurant was willing to make an attractive enough offer, however, the company decided to run the promotion without the dinner. As Nikolais manager Peter Obletz told *AM*, "Dinner wasn't important as things worked out. Of the 500 separate purchasers, only seven even asked about restaurants."

A key to the offer was the fact that two completely different programs were offered to afternoon-evening performance purchasers, so that the novelty of seeing six different works in one day and night was highlighted.

Summer 1975

Installment Buying

Cultural organizations may increase season ticket sales by offering subscription purchasers the option of either paying the entire price at once or buying tickets on a time payment plan. The St. Louis Symphony Orchestra allowed buyers of season tickets to make a one-third down payment in September. The balance is payable in equal installments in November and January.

October 1964

Last-Minute Changes

Last-minute program changes in a previously announced season series can cost a performing arts organization ticket renewals the next season. After a series is announced in print, every effort should be made to adhere to the schedule; otherwise, ticket subscribers may be disappointed and lose confidence in the organization. They will be cautious when renewing, remembering that the program to which they subscribe is not necessarily the one they will attend.

November 1965

Return Stub

Arts groups can ease the way for holders of season tickets to renew their subscriptions. Stage Centre of the Manitoba Theatre Centre in Winnipeg, Canada issues season tickets in strips. A renewal stub is included between the penultimate and last ticket in the strip. The stub can be mailed or handed in at the box office, assuring subscribers of automatic seat renewals for the next season. Should subscribers prefer a different seat location, they merely notify the box office when sending in renewal stubs.

May 1965

Program Change

A mid-season change of program is often confusing to season subscribers unless the change is clearly explained to them. To inform subscribers that the order of two productions had been switched, the Long Wharf Theatre in New Haven, Connecticut, printed little four-page folders titled, "There've been some changes made . . ." Inside, the new performance schedules were noted.

January-February 1967

Daytime Numbers

Ask for a daytime telephone number from ticket buyers on your mail order blank—with it you can talk your way out of many a ticket snarl. Without it you may have no way of reaching the purchaser during working hours to straighten out misunderstandings or other difficulties. Orders arriving in a rush frequently impose arbitrary decisions on the box office staff. Sending tickets for alternate performances, price classes, or separate seats can lead to ill-will and empty seats. Quick phone contact helps arrange a full house to everyone's satisfaction.

March 1962

Explaining Subscriptions

If the logistics of season subscriptions are confusing to your audiences, then take the trouble to explain your policies to them. The Studio Arena Theatre in Buffalo, N.Y., in response to inquiries from subscribers who wondered if the theater was attempting to oversell the house, issued a release headed, "Once again—the subscription dilemma." The release explained in detail how a 509-seat theater could accommodate 14,000 season subscribers, the announced goal of the organization, and still sell single tickets. "Scrutiny of the mechanics," it stated, "will show our goal to be mathematically viable."

November-December 1967

Groups Try New Approaches
to Reach and Tap Audiences

In an effort to up attendance and increase support, arts groups throughout the United States and Canada are reaching out, frequently into a variety of publics. Mobile exhibitions and performances, imaginative promotional techniques, the development of new ticket distribution methods, and sampler programs, often in unexpected settings, all are maong the "reach" devices used by cultural groups recently.

Students, from elementary school through college, have been a target audience. The Seattle Opera initiated a training program in "the history of rock" so that volunteers could learn to communicate better with young rock audiences, while the Whitney Museum, through a Helena Rubinstein Foundation grant, has admitted college students free since May 1978. Both the High Museum in Atlanta and the Young People's Theatre Center in Toronto are attracting younger students through newly developed learning kits which instruct in an entertaining manner. The Museum's "Eye-Openers" are packets of games for children to play in the museum, and are available at 50¢ each. The center's instructional tools are specially packaged in envelopes reading, "Neat Stuff Inside."

Tickets are being distributed in new ways and in new places. In Albany, New York, the League of Arts, which has operated a successful community box office and arts awareness display center in a busy central area of a major shopping center since the beginning of last season, recently won an NEA grant for continuation of the project. The pilot effort, initiated by the community arts council on behalf of its member groups at the Colonie Center, proved a spur to single ticket sales and during peak arts activity periods took in about $2500 weekly. In New York, the seven Off-Off Broadway theaters comprising Forty-Second Street Theatre Row along with two other nearby theaters opened Ticket Central, a centralized box office which accepts credit card phone reservations, a rarity for Off-Off Broadway, as well as walk-in direct and credit card ticket sales. In an effort to reach new audiences, Theatre Row also initiated a new sampler program which for $15 entitles purchasers to attend one performance at each of the seven theaters.

The ticket voucher concept, initiated by Theatre Development Fund and now operational in five cities in addition to New York, has been adapted for use by corporate employees. The National Corporate Fund for Dance makes vouchers, redeemable for discount priced tickets, available to employees of corporations that support the fund. Vouchers are distributed by each corporation, and employees can then turn them in at box offices for reduced price tickets for specified performances by fund dance companies. Rochester's Business Committee for the Arts distributes special booklets of discount coupons for arts events to its member companies to distribute to their employees. Booklets, which offered free and reduced-rate admissions to 15 different Rochester arts programs last season, are being offered in a larger version this year.

Elsewhere other kinds of free and low-priced sampler programs have been aimed at a variety of audiences. In Minneapolis, CityWide, a progam that ran from August through October 1978 under the sponsorship of City Art Productions, a CETA Title VI arts company of the Greater Minneapolis Chamber of Commerce, featured dozens of free performances, events, and exhibitions. Albany, New York sponsored its second annual Arts Sampler Fair in October, a day-long event featuring previews, displays and segments of upcoming works by over 50 arts council member groups. The event drew an audience of over 15,000 last year.

Other "awareness" spurs have included St. Louis' Arts Awareness Day in February, Illinois' Arts Week in September, Buffalo's "Salute to the Arts Month" in October, and Knoxville's first annual Artfest in October which included a Mayor's Week and Mayor's Ball for the Arts labeled by Mayor Randy Tyree "an effort to heighten the art awareness of everyone who lives here."

Free events have involved new audiences. The American Symphony Orchestra, which donated a 12-hour-long Wall to Wall Bach Marathon to New York last January, followed up six months later with a Wall to Wall Music Festival which invited amateur musicians to sit down and play with orchestra professionals. The Detroit Symphony, recognizing "the role of the church as the single strongest insitution, both past and present, in the black community," presented a free public concert at the Bethel African Methodist Episcopal Church in Detroit this October. The program, entitled "Classical Roots," traced black American musical heritage through works by black composers and nonblacks influenced by blacks, and featured along with the orchestra a 75-member chorus drawn from black church choirs in Detroit.

The reach of the arts is indicated by several moveable programs. The Denver Symphony, with support from Union Pacific, Chevron Oil, and government arts agencies, toured Wyoming and Idaho this September in a specially furnished train to give performances in smaller communities. In Canada, 27 specially commissioned posters representing works of art from Canadian museums are being displayed throughout the year on railroad trains traveling across the country.

In Peoria, an "Art on a Bus" project in April featured six prize-winning drawings by children from among 1749 entries received which were reproduced on 30 large panels—five copies of each winner—and placed on the backs and sides of Peoria buses for a two-month period. In Philadelphia, the Rouse Company, developer of Philadelphia's downtown Gallery shopping mall, is providing storefront space there for two local museums—the Franklin Institute and the Academy of Natural Sciences' Please Touch Museum—for a year's trial run at a cost of $106,000.

September-October 1978

Getting to Know You

Members and contributors may identify better with performing arts groups if they can identify with the performers first. Aware of this, the Indianapolis Symphony Orchestra mailed out new brochures showing an extended hand on the cover under the legend, "It's a pleasure to meet you." Inside its elongated 12- by 13½-inch pages, the brochure featured pictures and brief biographical data— including training, experience, length of orchestra service, and marital status—on each of the orchestra's 82 players, its conductor, Izler Solomon, and its associate conductor. The back cover showed a handshake with the legend above it reading, "Nice to have met you."

March-April 1974

Matching Gift

If your group is planning to offer a free gift as a reward to subscribers, members, or contributors, it will be more effective if the gift itself relates to your program. To promote its minisubscription "Mixed Bag Series," for example, the Grand Opera in Wilmington, Delaware announced that "we'll throw in the bag . . . free." The throw-in was a tote bag inscribed with the group's name. The Monmouth County New Jersey Arts Council's free insulated carrier for new sponsor members lived up to its name. It was hand-carried by volunteers to members, since it couldn't be crushed and mailed.

January-February 1977

Family Night

Parents can be induced to take their children to performances if the ticket costs aren't too high. The Great Lakes Shakespeare Festival in Cleveland, Ohio sets aside several evenings at a special price for families. Single admissions are $3.00 and $3.50, but a family, regardless of the number of children, pays only $6.00 total. On family nights, all seats are reserved on a first-come, first-served basis.

September-October 1968

Keeping Them Posted

If you're offering subscription and membership benefits, you'll want your supporters to remember what they are and how to use them. In its publication, *On the Scene,* the Hartford Stage Company included a pull-out Subscribers' Guide page with perforated margins marked "clip and save." One side had information on box office, parking, ticket exchange, restaurants, and special theater programs. The other side listed performance dates and included a map of the area around the theater pinpointing the location of the seven restaurants participating in a subscriber discount program.

September-October 1978

Flexible Subscriptions

Performing arts groups seeking to attract new audiences with flexible and convenient season subscription plans might be interested in the Guthrie Theater's Hot Line membership. Under the plan, subscribers purchase a membership for two for $20 and receive in return 14 coupons, two for each of the season's five plays and four "free choice" coupons for use at any play. Each coupon is worth $2 toward the purchase of one ticket in any of the theater's three price categories. A key selling feature of the plan is the members' special Hot Line phone number. When subscribers select a performance date they call Hot Line, give their membership number, and reserve tickets in any price category they wish. On performance night they bring their coupons to the theater's new members' window, pay the difference—"with a $2 coupon, the lowest-priced ticket will cost only $1.45 in cash," states the brochure—and pick up their tickets. In promoting the program, the theater stresses its advantage to subscribers. They save money by paying only $20 for $28 worth of tickets; they have flexibility in being able to purchase tickets at different prices for different plays; they are able to bring friends with free choice coupons; and they have the convenience of attending the theater when they wish without going to the box office in advance or paying the total price in advance.

Summer 1971

Subscription Miss

Because seasons subscribers purchase their tickets far in advance, they often experience date conflicts which cause them to miss performances. To maintain the good will of its subscribers. The Loretto-Hilton Theatre in St. Louis has initiated a policy to help subscribers attend performances they missed when there wasn't sufficient advance time for them to exchange their tickets. Under the "dead seat" policy, the theater recommends those performances for which seats are likely to be available. Subscribers then may come to the theater and if seats are available before curtain time, they are given them gratis.

March-April 1975

Seasonal Calendar

Although most performing arts seasons coincide with the academic year, September through June, most printed calendars cover the year from January through December. Why not help your subscribers seee your season at a glance with seasonal calendars? The Seattle Opera distributed handy little plastic cards featuring on one side a 1971-72 calendar running from a mid-year to mid-year. On the reverse was a smiling soprano and the legend, "Season's greetings from Seattle Opera."

November-December 1971

Satisfaction Guaranteed

What happens when a performing arts company offers a money-back guarantee to its audience? The Atlanta Symphony, which has offered such guarantees occasionally, has never yet been asked for a refund. Another group, the Saint Paul Opera, took a half-page ad in the *St. Paul Pioneer Press* this October offering money-back guarantees to two performances in the hopes of attracting new audiences to its "new era in opera" performances. The result? No requests for refunds, the largest single ticket sales in the company's history for one of the two performances, and greatly increased corporate support for group sales.

September-October 1969

Arts Gift

Promoting tickets as gifts? You might try selling gift certificates that offer purchasers discounts on events. The Fort Wayne Fine Arts Foundation sells "handsome, parchment-like Gift Certificates" for $10. Each certificate contains $10.50 in discount coupons that can be redeemed for a variety of arts activities in Fort Wayne. Seven of the detachable coupons offer $1 discounts and seven offer 50¢ discounts. To promote the gift idea, certificates are personally inscribed to whomever the purchaser designates and also bear his name as the donor.

September-October 1971

Season Subscriptions

Want to increase your sale of season subscriptions even after the first performance in a season series has already been presented? Single ticket holders may be your answer. In Winnipeg, Canada, the Manitoba Theatre Centre invites nonsubscribers to take their ticket stubs to the theater box office where they may apply the cost of a used single ticket toward the purchase of a subscription membership. The savings to be realized—15 percent over single ticket purchase—is emphasized in the promotion of the plan.

February 1964

A Sound Offering

Hearing is believing. The 1976-77 season subscription flier of the American Symphony Orchestra is a four-page booklet which includes within it an inexpensive, pull-out, 33-1/3 rpm record which includes excerpts from three orchestra works. The brochure cover invites potential subscribers to listen and, according to the orchestra, they have, with the result that subscriptions have increased.

September-October 1976

An Arts Diet

You can make the arts appetizing to your audiences and increase ticket sales. The Montclair, New Jersey State College calendar of activities is headlined, "The Arts Menu, 1976-77" and the four-page folder, about the size of *AM*, lists an "appetizer," "the autumn entree," and "for the classical palate" four different musical events. The menu ends with "just dessert," a listing of films.

September-October 1976

Call Number

Looking for a simple and inexpensive way to remind potential audiences of your program? You might try using telephone stickers. In a recent season subscription mailing, the Guthrie Theatre in Minneapolis included red peel-off stickers to be placed on phones and on phone book covers. Each read, "How about the Guthrie tonight? 612 377-2224."

Summer 1974

Theater Offers Trading
Stamps as Box Office Bait

Trading stamps, most commonly used to promote patronage in grocery stores and filling stations, have been extended to the arts. An Off-Broadway theater producer in New York, faced with the loss of audiences due to an extended newspaper strike, offered trading stamps with the purchase of tickets. His audiences increased by 25 percent.

Ned Hendrickson opened his production of *The Wide Open Cage* at the Washington Square Theatre shortly after the New York newspaper strike began on December 9, 1962. Because normal advertising and publicity channels were closed, he turned in desperation to the E. F. MacDonald Company, distributors of Plaid Stamps. Since January 14, every ticket buyer at Hendrickson's theater has received 30 Plaid Stamps with the purchase of a $3 ticket. Some people have even come to the box office specifically requesting stamps.

In addition, Hendrickson arranged for Plaidland redemption centers to distribute coupons entitling purchasers to receive a bonus supply of 500 stamps by presenting the coupons at the box office.

Although Hendrickson pays $15 for each pad of 5000 stamps, he believes that the increase in his audiences following his offer of trading stamps proves that the stamps are paying for themselves. He therefore intends to continue using Plaid Stamps even after the newspaper strike ends. In spite of Hendrickson's apparent success and the fact that he recommends stamp programs to other theatrical producers, it should be remembered that he issued stamps as a desperation measure in an unusual situation.

A check by *AM* of several leading trading stamp companies indicates that the use of stamps by cultural organizations is a rarity. An official of S & H Green Stamps, one of the oldest and largest companies, is pessimistic about their value to the arts because, he said, "Stamp plans work best only where there is a very high volume of trade."

H. T. Goodenberger, a district manager of E. F. MacDonald in the New York area, is more optimistic about the possible success of stamp programs in the arts, although he cautions that plans work only if there are a large number of outlets in one area that offer the same brand of stamp.

Companies that issue stamps generally do so under a licensing arrangement. They provide identification signs and other promotional materials boosting the stamp they distribute. The Plaid Stamp organization will also on occasion design and print mailing pieces at their own expense for a customer's use.

Plaid Stamps, as an example, cost $15.00 per pad of 5000, and $12.50 for each pad after the first five. Stamps must be paid for on delivery, although the MacDonald company guarantees to refund any leftover stamps at the price paid. Stamps must be issued by the user at the rate of one stamp for each 10¢ purchase, although bonus arrangements similar to the one used by Hendrickson are permitted.

March 1963

Tickets on Consignment

To help build audiences, some organizations send tickets to lists of potential buyers with a request that they either pay for them or return them by a given date. Because most recipients feel a sense of personal responsibility and respond one way or the other, the system can be quite effective. But it must be employed with discretion. Use lists of names of individuals who have proven interest in the organization. Always record both the address and phone number of recipients. Set the deadline for payment or return early enough to follow up with those who fail to respond.

December 1962

Bulk Ticket Sales

Looking to sell blocks of tickets? The college student union in your area may be a good outlet. As part of their programs, college unions often arrange student visits to nearby cultural attractions. The University of Delaware union, for example, purchased large blocks of tickets for monthly concerts at the Academy of Music in Philadelphia. The Trenton State College union in New Jersey arranged student bus trips to Off-Broadway theaters in New York.

April 1966

Alumni Groups

College alumni groups represent a generally untapped market for block purchases of tickets. Many are looking for cultural programs to offer their members. In New York, the Wisconsin Alumni Club sent a mailing to its members informing them they could obtain preferred seats for summer concerts by the Metropolitan Opera at Lewisohn Stadium if the group purchased a block of 20 tickets.

June 1965

Taped Promotion

Arts groups faced with an upcoming program and lagging ticket sales might try a technique used successfully at the University of Indiana in Bloomington. With a concert for the benefit of Czechoslovakian relief less than a week off, and tickets moving slowly, the school's concert office asked a group of distinguished local citizens for their help. The community leaders taped 30-second phone interviews in which they explained why they were attending the concert. A Bloomington radio station then aired the tapes as public service spot announcements. The result? Local interest was engendered, and the concert was a great success.

January-February 1969

Attractive Tickets

One way to promote the sale of tickets is to enhance their appearance. In Woodstock, New York, when the Woodstock Artists Association, Inc. was planning an art raffle, it arranged for artist Bernard Steffen to execute an original drawing for the tickets. The drawing was printed on a detachable portion of the tickets.

September 1965

Symphony Sells Seats with a Coloring Book

An unusual promotional device, a Symphony Coloring Book, is helping to attract young couples to concerts of the Atlanta Symphony Orchestra. Published by the Junior Committee of the orchestra, the eight-page booklet describes in whimsical fashion the 11 special concert evenings sponsored by the Junior Committee. Each of these evenings begins with cocktails at a leading Atlanta country club at 6:00 P.M. Dinner, at a cost of $3.00 per person, follows at 7:00. At 8 P.M., waiting buses whisk diners from the country club to the concert auditorium for 50¢. The committee reserves an entire section of the auditorium for each of the 11 subscription concerts ($23.18 for each season subscription) so that couples who eat together can also sit together at the concerts.

The theme of togetherness is emphasized in the coloring book. The first page has a cartoon depicting a couple slumped in front of a television set. The caption underneath says, "See the dreary people. They never go anywhere. They never eat out. They are missing all the fun. Color them bored." The next page, which shows an unhappy couple driving a car, suggests that traffic will detain the couple and that they will be unable to find a parking space. Opposite this page is a cartoon of smiling people seated at the concert. The caption reads, "See the smiling people. They are at the Symphony. They are with their friends. They ate dinner with their friends. It was good. They cleaned their plates. Yum.

Yum. The nice bus brought them right to the door—on time. Color them happy."

October 1963

Seating Plan

At the orchestra hall or theater box office, both ticket buyers and sellers save time when the seating plan is prominently displayed at the point of sale. People can decide on their preferences while standing in line. Seating plans should also be included with mailings soliciting advance purchase of tickets and given to newspapers for publication at the season's end.

June 1962

Sell Tickets in Suburbs

Organizations seeking to increase ticket sales or promote membership in suburban areas might consider the use of a "ticketmobile." Libraries, museums, and commercial enterprises have had great success in serving hard-to-reach groups of people through mobile units. A symphony orchestra, for example, might send out a truck or station wagon equipped with orchestra recordings, pictures, programs, and ticket and membership information. Notify in advance neighborhood publications in the communities you are visiting to insure maximum publicity. If shopping centers are visited, arrange for the distribution of posters announcing the visit or notices to be placed in shopping bags.

September 1962

Ticket Sales

Selling tickets? Make it easy for the audience to buy them. The Arts Council of Greater St. Louis bound a ticket order form into the center of its monthly calender of events, offering readers the opportunity to purchase tickets to 39 performances sponsored by nine different arts groups during a single month. With one order form and one check, purchasers could buy tickets for any of the programs.

November-December 1966

Apartment House Tickets

Apartment buildings seeking new tenants may be good outlets for the purchase of tickets in bulk. In Washington, D.C., for example, the Park Plaza Apartments offered an inducement to new tenants—a pair of complimentary tickets for Arena Stage's 1966-67 season. The offer extended also to current lease-holders who bring in new tenants.

May 1966

Pocket Promotion

Would you like to have your audience in your pocket? Then put yourself in their pockets. The Old Globe Theatre in San Diego, California developed a wallet-sized promotional piece printed on both sides of a 9½- by 3½-inch sheet which folds twice into a convenient 3½- by 2½-inch card. When folded, the front page lists box office information, subscription and single ticket prices, and performance times. The middle pages detail information on each of the nine productions offered in the eight-month season, and the full 9½-inch-long reverse side contains a calendar listing every performance.

November-December 1968

A CHRONOLOGY OF TICKET-SELLING AND SUBSCRIPTION TECHNIQUES

New Ticket-Selling Techniques
Winning Audiences for Culture

Arts organizations throughout the country are experimenting with a variety of ticket distribution methods in an attempt to increase attendance, develop new audiences, and attract members. In many instances, the approaches used are variations of techniques that have proved successful elsewhere.

In Dayton, Ohio, the Miami Valley Arts Council introduced a Membership Privilege Book in an attempt to enlist new members. The book, similar to the "two-fers" used by Broadway theaters, offered members a set of coupons that could be exchanged for two tickets for the price of one. The book's attraction was that it included coupons redeemable for programs presented by 14 diverse cultural groups, including the Cincinnati Symphony Orchestra, Playhouse in the Park, the Dayton Civic Ballet, and the University of Dayton's Arts Series. The purchase value of the tickets was about $40.

All 14 participating groups combined their mailing lists for the initial direct-mail campaign. Within three weeks of the first mailing, a successful ten percent return had been achieved, and 500 new members, at $5 per year each, were enrolled. According to the arts council, the campaign achieved three important results: the $2500 raised through new membership dues enabled the council to expand its services; coupon redemptions helped to sell tickets that otherwise might not have been sold; and by offering a variety of performances in different disciplines, a crossfertilization of arts audiences took place.

Coupon redemption was the key also to the Corporate Coupon Program designed to win business support for the Alley Theatre in Houston, Texas when it opened its 1968-69 season in its newly built theater. A similar program initiated the previous year by the Guthrie Theatre in Minneapolis resulted in the sale of 2000 corporate subscriptions to 37 Twin Cities corporations.

Under the program, Houston firms were offered the opportunity to purchase as many books of five coupons as they wished, with each coupon redeemable for one ticket to each of the five plays presented during the Alley season. Books were priced at only $13.75 each, or $2.75 per individual ticket, although the normal single ticket price ranged from $2.80 to $6.90. When redeeming coupons for tickets, coupon holders were guaranteed seats in the best locations available for the performance they chose.

There were two keys to the campaign, both carefully outlined in a detailed brochure mailed to 140 selected local firms prior to the season's opening. First, corporations were told that they could use the coupons successfully in their employee relations programs by either selling them to employees at cost or at a discount. In either instance, employees would purchase tickets at the lowest price possible. The second key aspect was the group of services offered by the theater to coupon holders, including special box office attention when calling for reservations; free Alley posters for corporate bulletin boards; free payroll envelope inserts; photographs and news material for employee publications; theater staff help in selling tickets ro employees; and a free coupon book for every 25 purchased by the company.

To promote the concept to corporations initially, seven young bank executives, under the direction of Lewis A. Brown, vice president of the Texas National Bank and the program's chairman, personally visited all of the corporations that received brochures. The results were impressive, with 1500 coupon books sold to 40 corporations. According to Paul E. Stroud, the theater's director of board relations and special events, the program will continue next year and, hopefully, the services offered to business will be broadened to more fully involve corporations.

Elsewhere, the old question of which is more effective—selling season subscriptions or individual tickets—was explored by the City Center Joffrey Ballet, and the results, although not conclusive, proved interesting. When the dance company mailed brochures for its spring season, it suggested in the same mailing piece that purchasers could buy individual tickets for any performance or they could purchase subscriptions. The responses, when analyzed, showed that subscriptions and individual ticket sales were almost evenly divided.

January-February 1969

Arts Groups Experiment
With Subscriptions

Greater flexibility, extra benefits to subscribers, and monetary savings are some of the features of subscription ticket plans being tested by performing arts groups throughout the country. In New York, the Shakespeare Festival introduced a new Public Theatre pass for $15 ($7.50 for students and over 65's) which admits holders to one performance of each of the productions planned for the 1971-72 season, a minimum of eight. Each time a subscriber exchanges his pass for a ticket, either in person or by mail, one of the 12 dots printed on the pass is stamped to indicate the specific performance for which it is used. Because the Festival has four performance facilities, the subscriber can visit the theater without making prior arrangements, and be fairly certain of getting tickets for one of the productions. When the idea was conceived, the theater set its goal at selling 5000 passes. By the first week of October more than 10,000 had been sold.

Across the river, the Brooklyn Academy of Music introduced its first flexible subscription program. The $25 coupon book—$20 each for two or more—guarantees subscribers orchestra or mezzanine seats to up to 14 different events. Subscribers redeem coupons for any performance of a particular event on a first-come, first-served basis. In New Haven, Connecticut, the Long Wharf Theatre is giving audiences the option of purchasing either traditional season subscriptions, with performance dates for all eight productions specified in advance, or flexible admission cards. The cards, at $27 for eight admissions, are exchangeable for any weekday performance and can be used singly for each performance or all in one night. The Indianapolis Symphony, in response to what it terms numerous requests for greater flexibility, has given Thursday night subscription series audiences the option of purchasing either a winter or spring "half series" subscription.

Theaters elsewhere are wooing subscribers with a variety of extra benefits. In San Francisco, the American Conservatory Theater is offering subscribers a $5 "Bonus Benefit Package" featuring inexpensive parking, special dining privileges from several nearby restaurants, and discount coupons for extra tickets to ACT productions and special events. Thus far, about 20 percent of the subscribers have purchased packages, and $4000 of an anticipated $10,000 has been realized. Buffalo's Studio Arena Theatre is offering its season ticket purchasers free subscriber discount cards with these dividends: 10 percent discounts on additional ticket purchases and on bar tabs in the theater's lounge; a 15 percent discount on performance nights at six top restaurants; and a 30 percent discount on parking.

One of the more interesting and apparently successful experiments is the Guthrie Theater's "Five Plays for the Price of Six" season subscription. The new plan, conceived by the theater with the help of Arts Development Associates, reverses the usual policy of offering extra productions as a bonus and asks subscribers instead to contribute the price of an extra ticket to the theater. "Subscribing members" receive five tickets for the price of six and "investing members," who pay $125 for two subscriptions, not only purchase five for six, but also subsidize student memberships. According to a spokesman, "the response has been extraordinary."

September-October 1971

Varied Approaches Used by Arts to Reach Out for New Audiences

Arts groups are continuing to find new ways to reach relatively untapped audiences. In Omaha, Nebraska, for example, the symphony orchestra helped draw interest to a coming concert series by encouraging the general public to attend free open rehearsals. The rehearsal times were widely publicized in advance.

To attract young audiences, the American Place Theatre in New York instituted a new ticket card for those 21 and under this season. The card, which makes 32 theater visits possible at a total cost of only $9, features eight punches for eight different performances. A single punch, however, admits not only the cardholder, but up to three other youngsters to the same performance. Under the plan, reservations are accepted on the afternoon of each performance. In Duluth, Minnesota, the symphony orchestra called on its own supporters to help make youth attendance at concerts possible. Under a "Symphony Parents" plan initiated this season, 51 individuals and business firms purchased season tickets for 74 local music students nominated by their high school teachers. In Maryland, a unique presentation concept that places the orchestra and conductor on videotape has enabled the Eastern Opera Theatre to tour "full orchestra" opera productions economically to schools throughout the state. The Opera Theatre, an educational subsidiary of the Baltimore Opera Company, initiated its tour in March 1973 after Baltimore Symphony musicians requested and received union permission to make the videotape recording of Donizetti's *Rita*.

Symphony orchestras are using convenience and informality to reach younger audiences. The Detroit Symphony included among several new subscription offerings a Zodiac series for those under 30 featuring special events, such as instrument demonstrations, preceding each concert. Recently, the orchestra presented a special audience-choice April Fool's Day Concert at which concertgoers selected the program after they were seated from among 50 works in the orchestra's repertory. New York Philharmonic audiences will have their own informal fling on the orchestra floor of Lincoln Center's Philharmonic Hall where all the seats are being removed. The "Rug Concerts" will feature the orchestra performing on the auditorium floor surrounded by members of the audience seated on rugs.

Factory workers are the special target of the Seattle Opera Company. For the past year, the opera has used a morning preceding each of its productions to present two minipreviews at the giant Boeing Company plant. Attendance by both plant personnel and executives has averaged about 250 people, and the small expense involved has been more than justified by fine word-of-mouth promotion and articles on each program in the potent *Boeing News,* which reaches 35,000 company employees. In Fort Worth, Texas, the new Kimball Art Museum included taxi drivers and construction workers among the audiences invited to a series of special preopening events last October. Cab drivers who attended the Sunday afternoon party, and hopefully would be taking fares to the new museum frequently, were given brochures, tours of the facility, and were feted with refreshments and entertainment.

A new and continuing program designed to woo suburbanites to arts programs has been initiated by the Metropolitan Cultural Alliance of Boston. Between March 17 and April 8, 1973, the alliance booked a daily schedule of cultural events into the Walnut Hill School for the Performing Arts in suburban Natick. Groups performed for 90 percent of the box office—the alliance used the rest for publicity, management, and box office—and included such attractions as the Boston Ballet; the Theater Company of Boston; the Chorus Pro Musica; Collage, the contemporary music ensemble of the Boston Symphony; and the Pocket Mime Circus. Evening performances were scheduled at 7:30 P.M. to attract entire families, and additional weekend matinees for children were also presented. The pilot program, whose ultimate goal it was to establish permanent suburban locations where arts groups could be booked regularly, will be expanded to other locations and will include weekday matinees for children.

Meanwhile in Raleigh, North Carolina, the North Carolina Museum of Art has been aiming its promotional guns at entire communities throughout the state. In a repeat of a program last attempted in 1967, the museum in cooperation with the North Carolina Art Society, has scheduled a series of "community days" designed to bring people closer to the museum "their tax dollars are helping to support" and to alert legislators to the service provided by the museum.

March-April 1973

Concept of Cultural Vouchers is Growing

The cultural voucher concept is growing. This fall, new programs have been launched in several East Coast cities, and the voucher idea is being seriously studied by arts groups in several other communities. Although program implementation may vary from place to place, the basic concept—making no-price or low-price tickets and admissions available to audiences through vouchers which after their use may be redeemed by participating arts groups, and the purpose—audience development—is generally the same.

In New York, a pilot program tested by Museums Collaborative in the summer of 1973 became operational, thanks to a noncompetitive renewal grant of $105,000 for each of the next three years by the Department of Health, Education and Welfare's Fund for the Improvement of Post-Secondary Education.

The collaborative is a cooperative group of museums and other cultural agencies.

Under the program, vouchers will be issued in block amounts of up to $8000 to selected community groups such as senior citizen centers, ethnic societies, settlement houses, and drug rehabilitation centers for the purchase of existing museum services and new programs specially created by the seven participating cultural institutions. Existing services include memberships; admissions to lectures, exhibits, and special events; the purchase of publications and other materials; and the use of educational facilities. New programs—many have been pretested by the collaborative over the past three years—will help community groups develop educational projects incorporating local traditions and skills.

The seven museum participants will be selected soon from among cultural groups throughout the city, not just collaborative members, and the list will include both large and small institutions. Each will receive a salary stipend to enable it to add a community liaison person to its staff.

In the performing arts, a new voucher plan introduced in Buffalo, New York by Arts Development Services, the local arts council, is patterned after the model created by the Theatre Development Fund in New York. Vouchers, costing $1 each and sold in sets of five to union members, retirees, teachers, and others normally unable to pay regular box office prices, can be exchanged for tickets to programs of 25 different local performing arts groups half an hour prior to performances. Purchasers receive fliers each month describing upcoming performances and may phone in reservations.

Through a $100,000 fund raised by ADS, participating arts groups will receive $2.50 for each voucher they accept. The program's administrative costs will be covered by the sale of $1 vouchers.

In Boston, a limited but successful voucher experiment undertaken by 12 local theaters last season has provided the impetus for the development of a broad citywide voucher program. In an attempt to reach untapped audiences, member companies of the Metropolitan Cultural Alliance's League of Local Theaters introduced a two-for-one voucher last season which allowed purchasers to attend two different theaters for the price of a single ticket. Now, the league and the alliance, with help from the Theatre Development Fund and the Massachusetts Council on the Arts, is planning to introduce a coupon book next summer which, in addition to theater, would include vouchers for dance and music events.

Impetus for the voucher movement has been provided by the Theatre Development Fund which introduced the reduced-price ticket concept several years ago and has since seen its mailing list grow to more than 23,000. Since July it has sold 35,000 theater vouchers for Off-Off Broadway plays and 15,000 for dance concerts at $1 each. TDF director Hugh Southern has advised many cities, including Boston and Buffalo, on initiating programs, and by next season vouchers may be introduced in several new areas. Because of the growing interest,

TDF, at 1501 Broadway, New York, New York 10036, recently named a full-time director of development services, Vincent Marron, who is available to cultural groups seeking advice and information.

September-October 1974

Groups Try Varied Methods to Reach New Subscribers

A portable ticket booth, set up each day for a week at the same busy New York site, became a prime weapon in a theater's campaign to sell subscriptions. The effort, undertaken during the last week of November 1975 by the Phoenix Theater, reached large numbers of passersby and proved a useful public relations and advertising medium, or as one staff member termed it, "an incredibly cheap billboard."

The idea for the booth grew out of the theater's desire to carry its message directly to the public in a dramatic way. It selected a location familiar to theatergoers, Duffy Square, which already houses the Theatre Development Fund's popular half-price ticket booth. The city granted a permit to erect a temporary booth in back of TDF and facing in the opposite direction. While Phoenix subscriptions weren't actually sold at the booth—the city permit didn't cover sales—scores of brochures on subscriptions and individual plays were given away, and the staff and volunteers who manned the booth provided information on all aspects of Phoenix activity. According to Liz Gordon, Phoenix's subscription manager, "We don't have direct sales figures, but judging from the reactions there's no doubt that the promotion was successful."

A factor in the booth's success was that it served as an attraction for those waiting in line to purchase half-price tickets from the nearby TDF facility. Thus, each day the inexpensive booth was transported to its location and set up, usually while lines were beginning to form at the discount ticket center. Made of four foldable stage flaps painted in vinyl and held together by pin hinges, the easily transportable booth cost less than $250 and not only lasted the entire week, but is doing double duty now as a sales stand in the theater lobby for such promotional materials as T-shirts.

A plastic "credit card" proved a subscription tool for another New York theater that wanted to "get away from issuing tickets." The WPA, which sold season subscriptions for the first time in 1974, wanted an attention-getting device for its second subscription season to attract newcomers on a vastly expanded mailing list. It settled on a simulated credit card, the WPA Express Card, which was described in an accompanying letter as "a remarkable little card which can enable you and up to three guests to see some of the most exciting theatre in the world today." The card, which had to be returned with a check to be validated by the theater, offered subscribers three series choices for the six production seasons. Cardholders were offered last-minute phone reservation service and a choice of several dates.

According to coproducer Daniel Dietrich, the card has had its desired effect. "It's convenient and flexible, and people are into plastic cards," he told *AM*. "We've had a lot of artists tell us that they like to carry it in their pockets." In practical terms, the card has not only attracted attention from subscribers and the press, but has brought in new subscribers. "We've more than doubled last year's subscriptions," added Dietrich, "and about 75 percent are new to the theater."

Meanwhile, the Indianapolis Symphony offered a powerful "come-on" to the first 2182 subscribers who ordered first or second night tickets for its full 16-concert series. Budgeted into its season ticket expense, just as brochures and other items are, was a Van Cliburn concert for which tickets were not sold, but were given away to early subscribers. The campaign was a record success—and according to assistant manager Fritz Kumb, "the free concert seemed to be a drawing card that pushed our full season subscriptions."

November-December 1975

Groups Use New
Inducements to Woo Audiences

Arts organizations are giving more to get more. In the hopes of expanding their audiences, groups are offering such inducements as restaurant discounts, sampler tickets, and attention-getting devices.

A "$100 Circle Saver" coupon book, offering subscribers discounts on restaurants, garages, cultural events, and nonarts activities, worth upwards of $100 in savings, is Circle in the Square's new season subscription tool. The cost of the program is practically nill since restaurants and others offering discounts do so without charge to the theater, and many in fact make contributions to Circle to help cover printing costs.

Over the years, Circle has offered discounts to stubholders in addition to usual subscription benefits. For 1977-78, the New York-based theater company decided to place the discounts, including free tickets to several nonsubscription Circle events, into a single 72-page booklet offering some 50 discounts, and promote and advertise it heavily. The results thus far have been good, with subscriptions up 15 percent, although it's difficult to know how much can be attributed to the Saver. The booklets include 11 bonus coupons for savings that the theater will announce later in the season.

In Worcester, Massachusetts, the City's Office of Cultural Affairs published and distributed 80,000 free copies of a "Sampler" booklet this past season in an effort to boost interest in local cultural events. The miniature booklets, which devoted a page to each of 46 different programs, offered users discounts, free passes, half-price memberships, and coupons for prize drawings—each arts participant chose its own offer—as well as more unusual rewards including an art slide show viewing, bumper stickers, T-shirts, and participation in an evening of choral singing.

According to Pat Ewald, the Cultural Affairs Office director, the promotion was much talked about and very successful, and "focused tremendous awareness on the arts locally" with many people using the booklets as cultural directories. The promotion also brought local groups together since it represented the first time that all had participated in a joint project.

An old hand at promotional ploys, the Indianapolis Symphony, decided to "play with fire" in its latest subscription campaign. In an effort to involve both volunteers and professional staff, the orchestra, which has used buttons and frisbees in the past, adopted a new subscription giveaway—an elegant red and silver matchbox, emblazoned with the symphony name and logo. Volunteers manning subscription renewal tables in the orchestra lobby during March through May performances were urged to display banners and signs based on the matchbox theme.

Some of the resulting slogans, used at booths as well as in subscription brochures, included "a subscription offer you can't match"; " the hottest ticket in town"; "your renewal strikes just the right note"; "you and the ISO, a perfect match"; and "don't get burned, send your order today." By summer most of the matchboxes had been distributed, and the "fired up" organization had sold several thousand seats more than at the same time the previous year.

The Seattle Opera, meanwhile, promoted its summer 1977 *Ring* cycle with a "Wagner Orgy Kit," a giant color mailing piece featuring cut-out dagger, helmet, and spear as well as an "orgy goer's" map to the northwest.

Summer 1977

One of the many billboards in Detroit heralding Maestro Antal Dorati's first season as music director of the Detroit Symphony. (Courtesy of Detroit Symphony Orchestra)

7

Public Relations in the Arts

PUBLICITY TACTICS AND
TECHNIQUES, AND PRESS RELATIONS

How to Cope with
Controversy—and Survive

At some point in the life of almost every organization it must face the problem of public controversy. This may arise because of its programming or because of the failure of a major fund-raising effort, or as a consequence of personality differences, or for many other reasons. Whatever the cause, public controversy presents special problems for the institution's public relations staff.

Should cultural organizations avoid controversy? The temptation is to answer "yes." But many experienced arts managers and public relations experts agree that avoiding "hot" issues in an effort to sidestep controversy is not necessarily wise. Some issues must be faced head-on, even at the cost of becoming unpopular with sectors of the public. But whether the institution consciously adopts a controversial policy or finds itself embroiled in a controversy not of its own making, it should be prepared for criticism at any time and should know how to cope with it.

An institution that has carried out a thoughtful and continuing public relations effort emphasizing its services to the public will, of course, be in a far stronger position when a "crisis" arises than one that has neglected its public relations. Community understanding and respect for the organization, once developed over the long haul, will help immeasurably in its time of trouble.

Here are some suggestions that may make coping with controversy easier:

1. Anticipate it. Not everything is predictable, but sophisticated organizational leadership will only rarely be caught by surprise. In setting policy, or in programming, bear in mind local sensitivities, the policies of other cultural organizations, the traditional "image" of the institution.

2. Discreetly avoid it, if possible, by meeting in advance with potential critics, trying to win them over, perhaps even inviting them to serve on a committee to help solve the problem in question. But do not necessarily retreat if you fail.

3. In making a decision that may spark controversy, the organization should know exactly why it is doing so. The reasons should be cogently hammered out in advance, and communicated to all levels within the organization, board, staff, and even, when possible, members and volunteers. The institution whose "family" is united will be far less vulnerable than the one that enters a controversy with its own house divided or confused.

4. Clearly define authority and responsibility for the duration of the "emergency." Decide on a single spokesman to present the institution's positions.

5. In statements, be brief, clear, but not truculent. Anticipate objections and attempt to meet them.

6. Act quickly to disseminate information or to answer charges. An announcement of an unusual or controversial policy or a reply to public criticism may call for a press conference to which all interested news media are invited. Exclusive interviews or statements to a single press outlet should be avoided unless it clearly is the only one of importance.

7. In replying to charges it is usually best to maintain a tone of moderation, but there are times when indignation is justified. Reply quickly or not at all, since delay weakens the effect. But do not attack individuals. Address the response to issues, not personalities. Avoid sounding defensive, but do not be afraid to apologize if the institution has indeed, made a mistake.

8. Finally, remember that losing a battle may mean that the organization deserved to lose it—that the position it adopted was wrong. Clear away the debris and get back to constructive work.

Controversies may be unpleasant at times. But a good, healthy spirited public debate over clearly defined issues can be a great boon to the cultural institution that is not afraid of it.

April 1963

Arts Organizations
Must Reach Many Publics

Many arts groups gear their public relations program to a single undifferentiated audience. Yet the fact is that every cultural organization, regardless of its size or the extent of its program, serves many different publics. For its public relations program to be fully effective, an organization must consciously indentify the publics it wishes to reach, then attempt to determine the attitude of each toward the organization. Only then can a comprehensive program be planned that will influence not merely the "public at large," but also each of the organization's constituencies.

A public can best be defined as any group, organized or not, that shares certain interests or whose members bear roughly similar relationships to the institution or organization.

Let's analyze the publics of a typical cultural institution. Starting with the organization itself and working outward, the first public is the institution's own staff and its policy-making bodies. This includes all paid employees, the board of directors, and committee chairmen. Does every staff member fully understand the goals of the organization? Are board members up-to-date on its activities? Before an organization attempts to conduct a systematic external public relations campaign, it should put its own house in order.

Next come the volunteer workers. This large and important public is frequently neglected in overall public relations planning, but, especially because volunteers have direct contact with the broad outside public, their importance should not be minimized. Special events and publications should be utilized to guarantee that volunteers understand the long-range aims of the institution, as well as its immediate problems.

A third public is, of course, the audience that attends performances or exhibitions of the institution. This, being a more diffuse public, is harder to analyze. But the more that is known about the tastes and socioeconomic characteristics of this audience, the more effectively will the institution be able to serve it, and the more effective will its public relations program be. Some institutions have learned the value of audience research and make use of it. Is the audience satisfied with the institution's programming facilities and services? Should changes be made to eliminate dissatisfaction? Positively, what elements of programming or service should be emphasized in public relations efforts to reach this audience? Because this public is larger and more diffuse, methods for reaching it necessarily differ from those used to reach your internal publics.

Similarly, members and contributors represent two additional publics. Although few institutions neglect these publics, few take enough pains to study the differences between them. Analysis of reasons for giving or for joining should be the basis for any public relations effort directed at them. The analysis will suggest the kind of services or programs to provide for them. It will also suggest the "tone" and character of communications directed at them.

Still another public is the business community. No public relations effort aimed at this public will be harmed by a bit of simple "research" consisting of half a dozen personal interviews with business leaders to sound out their attitudes toward the institution. Such interviews with businessmen who have no connection with the institution may reveal much about widespread community attitudes. Remember, too, that businessmen, especially if favorably inclined toward the organization themselves, are powerful levers for influencing the opinions of others in the community. It is wise to discover what important services your institution may be able to offer them, or their constituencies, and then to center the business-oriented public relations program on such services.

Government at each level is still another public. The story of your institution's work with schools, or at hospitals and similar institutions, can help favorably influence this public. Other cultural institutions, too, may require special attention. Their attitude toward the work of your institution helps condition the attitude of other publics.

This does not exhaust the list of constituencies that a well-defined public relations program takes into consideration. The degree to which the public relations program reflects the differences between them is a good measure of its overall effectiveness.

July 1963

Press Calendar Aids
Organization and Editors

Cultural organizations planning for the start of a new fall season are wise to include in their advance efforts the preparation of a yearly or biannual press calendar for dissemination to all press sources prior to the season's opening. Press calendars not only help editors plan coverage in advance, but also serve to remind an organization's public relations staff of the work to be done during the year.

Press calendars differ from the ordinary calendar of events sent to the public in that they include, in addition to performances and exhibitions, the dates for all special events such as the opening of a fund drive, an annual banquet or ball, a rummage sale, the scheduled arrival of a noted personality, and the dates of any other organizational activity that might interest the press. Next to the chronological listing, include a brief description of the event and a comment on its story and picture potential, along with a notation as to the exact date when an editor will receive a detailed press release or other material. If you plan to send pictures, mention this, too.

For example, a museum planning to publish an annual report in January should include the approximate date of the report's issuance. Similarly, if an important staff member is to assume his position in the late winter, list the effective starting date along with brief background information. Although a publication may have announced the appointment previously, it might consider interviewing the appointee just before he takes office.

Obviously, many organizations will not have a complete list of the year's events confirmed by the end of the summer. However, even an approximate date, if it is so identified, can be helpful advance information to a busy editor, who must sometimes plan for Sunday supplements and special sections weeks or even months in advance.

When preparing press calendars, remember that they are merely a prelude to press releases. Keep each item short and to the point. Mail mimeographed calendars not only to cultural editors and critics, but also to editors of other sections who might be interested in some of your activities. Send copies to the program and news directors of your local radio and television stations. Be sure to include the name, address, and phone number of an official of the organization who may be reached if additional information is needed.

For the public relations director of an organization, the press calendar is of great value in helping him to assess in advance the work to be produced during each month of the year. Moreover, it serves as a constant reminder to send press releases and photographs out on time. Similarly, the journalist confronted with an immediate need for an item or story may refer to the press calendar for ideas.

June 1963

From the Source

Arts organizations should avoid the temptation to use published material, whether copyrighted or not, in their own publications without obtaining prior written approval from the publisher. Unauthorized use of such material can lead to law suits. However, the right of fair use permits you to quote a short portion of a published article, provided you attribute it to its source. If in doubt, ask your attorney.

December 1965

The Art of Holding a Profitable Press Conference

The press conference is perhaps the most misused of all publicity techniques.

Before calling a press conference, an arts manager should answer two questions affirmatively: Are there enough news reporters and photographers within reach who would be interested in attending? Is there an announcement important enough to justify calling them?

If there are only two or three persons who might attend, the organization's needs can be served better by giving the story directly to them without calling a press conference. A "press conference" at which the hosts outnumber the few newsmen present in a room of empty chairs is a humiliating experience for the group calling it.

To be worth calling in the press, an announcement must be important and question-provoking. The list of programs for the coming season, for example, can be adequately announced in written form alone. But if an orchestra has chosen a new conductor whom the press has not met, a conference permits him to discuss his background, plans for the season, and anything else about which the press is curious.

The press conference should be held during newsmen's normal working hours. In practical terms, this means between 10:00 A.M. and noon, or between 2:00 and 4:00 P.M. If held during lunch hours, the press conference may be resented. If it starts after 4:00 P.M., there is danger that some newsmen will have to leave before it is finished. If there are both morning and afternoon papers in town, alternating the starting time of each conference will give each paper its chance at printing the news first. Try not to choose a day when a major scheduled event may compete for the attention of the press.

An up-to-date press list is the first requirement for calling a conference. Each newsman should be notified either by phone or a mailed announcement a few day in advance. He should be reminded by phone on the day of the conference. In cities with a news ticker service, notification to wire service clients should be made over the ticker the day before the conference.

Still photographers should first be given the chance to get posed pictures so they can leave to develop them. The conference host should cooperate fully with professional photographers by agreeing to pose as they ask, within the bounds of propriety.

Reporters, meanwhile, should have been given a duplicated statement summarizing the main purpose of the conference to prepare them to ask informed questions. Every detail the host wants to appear correctly in print, such as exact spelling of proper names, dates, and amounts of money, should be in the duplicated release.

The person holding the conference may make an oral statement supplementing the release, or he may invite questions at the outset. It is essential that he be well informed and articulate. Sometimes the president of an organization can best make the announcement with the manager or executive secretary at his side to reply to questions he cannot answer. No question should be slighted.

If the organization wants to get a certain point emphatically across to the public through the press, it should prepare in advance a colorful way of putting its point in a few words. This precise wording should be used both in the written statement and orally through the spokesman. In this way it can often guide the headline and lead paragraph on the story appearing in the papers.

The conference should be decisively ended rather than permitted to drift along with some reporters impatient to return to their offices, yet afraid to leave for fear of missing something. The spokesman should remain available, however, to answer afterthought questions or make further arrangements for pictures or additional data. A complete list of those present should be compiled for future reference and follow-up.

November 1962

Press Conference Sent by Mail
a Convenience to Busy Editors

Arts groups with important news to communicate can effectively reach the press in distant areas by holding a press-conference-by-mail. The technique is particularly suited to the needs of small organizations with resources too limited for holding large and costly press conferences. But all groups can benefit from it because editors are grateful to receive important news gathered without the burden of long and time-consuming trips to press conferences.

A press-conference-by-mail is actually an expanded press kit which contains all the material usually supplied in a press kit, such as news releases and photographs. It should also include two other items, however. One is a prepared question-and-answer interview with your organization head that provides general background on your group. It should state your organization's purpose, its recent activities, and details of the event you are promoting.

In addition, a form addressed to your organization's head along with a stamped, addressed envelope should be enclosed. The editor should be invited to submit his own questions on this form with the promise that they will be promptly answered.

When preparing such kits, remember that they are not a substitute for a press conference that keeps editors informed of fast-breaking events, and they must be disseminated well before the date of the event you are promoting. Mail them not only to cultural editors and critics, but also to other editors who might be interested in some phase of your activities.

In addition to reaching far away press sources, the kit may be used as a convenient way of disseminating information in your hometown when news of no immediacy is being made by your group. Editors will be more inclined to use a short story about your event when they do not have to leave their offices to obtain answers to their questions.

The kit also has the advantage of giving a group time to ponder and effectively answer questions that in a press conference might receive an off-the-shoulder reply which would not serve an organization's purpose. The editor, on the other hand, has the advantage of conducting a press conference at his desk and at his convenience. It permits him to zero in on questions of import to his own readers without "tipping his hand" to his competitors.

September 1964

Toot Your Horn

If your organization has achieved a difficult-to-reach goal recently or reversed a negative picture, be sure to tell your audience about it—provided you can substantiate your contentions. Positive releases noticed recently included "Dallas Symphony Orchestra Ends 1974-75 Season in Black," "Ballet [Pennsylvania] Triples Ticket Sales," and "The Turnabout Year for the San Francisco Ballet."

November-December 1975

Trumpet Your Cause

Getting a good press? Be sure to let your members and friends know about it. Young Audiences, whose twenty-fifth anniversary celebration attracted national attention—Rosalynn Carter attended the anniversary concert—prepared and mailed a special 12-page collection of clippings under a page-one banner reading, "Extra, National News, Extra."

September-October 1977

For the Record

Looking for an impressive promotional mailing piece to send to prospective donors and members? A Congressman sympathetic to your program and goals may be willing to insert material on your organization into the *Congressional Record*. Inexpensive reprints of such articles make fine mailers.

September-October 1973

The Name Is . . .

An eye-catching headline on your release or an easily remembered name for a program or publication might give you a publicity edge. The University of California at Santa Barbara titled a recent arts program guide "The Plain Brown Rapper," while the Saratoga Festival heralded a full-length version of a New York City Ballet work with the release headline, "Uncut 'Jewels' Return to SPAC." Museum Collaborative's all-day workshop in December was billed and promoted as a "$9.98 Conference."

November-December 1975

Critic Advises Arts
Groups on Press Releases

Gail Stockholm

When Ms. Stockholm, music critic of the Cincinnati Enquirer, *was asked by a leading local arts group what, from a newspaper's viewpoint, constituted a good press release, Ms. Stockholm responded with a detailed six-page letter which included examples to illustrate her points. Although every arts organization presumes to know how to prepare and use press releases, many received by AM demonstrate that this presumption is often erroneous. With this in mind, an excerpt from Ms. Stockholm's response, excluding portions relating to the rudiments of form, is reprinted below.*

It is a good idea to check with the newspaper before you write the release to find out exactly how far ahead they need the release, and to check on which aspect of the program may interest the paper most—the musical or entertainment, the civic, or the society aspect. Most papers today will not use the same story in two or three sections, so the release should be aimed toward one particular section in hopes that that section will give the event special treatment. If in doubt on the matter of which section is most appropriate, the best thing is not to decide yourself, but to ask the features editor or the women's editor where he would recommend you submit the story. This serves two purposes: to alert one of the more important editors that the story is coming, and to get your release to the person who is most likely to be interested in it. Most papers are glad to advise you on such matters and would prefer that you consult them rather than turn in your release in an incorrect way. Always imply that you think your music story would interest many people.

In the release itself, try to attract the reader's attention with a short, snappy first paragraph that tells why the event merits attention, and include its Who, What, When, and Where. Next in order, for all amusement and entertainment pages and for the purpose of selling tickets as well, the complete musical program and the major performers should be listed, identifying the performers with their offical titles as you go along.

Ideally, the basic information and the program information should be in the first two paragraphs of your story. If you wish, you may simply list the program in the second paragraph and then add the identification of the conductor or soloist in the third paragraph. If you then wish to add some further background about the area artists series or about the orchestra's history, this should follow the listing of the program and soloists. After this basic information has been presented, go on to mention local support of the event (full committees need not be listed unless the paper or society editor asks for it).

Some papers have a policy that prevents printing ticket prices or ticket information. Put it in the release anyway, so the newspaper can give the details to interested persons who may call the newspaper with questions about where to get tickets for the concert. Be very specific about full names, including for each, Miss, Mr., Mrs., Jr., and III, and such details. Most papers also prefer the middle initial and the full street name. Addresses won't always be used, but papers need them for identification purposes.

An important point of courtesy: Do not try to force your newspaper to use the story, run it on a certain date, use a picture of the women's group, etc. This is their decision. After waiting a day or two for mailing time, it doesn't hurt to follow up your release with a telephone call to the newspaper. But don't say, "Well, are you going to run our story Sunday?" Say, "I called to make sure you received our release and that it included all the details you need. Is there anything else we can do for you?" Be sure to stress that you feel this is big news for the community—that both young and old will be interested, that people may come from miles around to attend, etc.

It is advisable to give your first story to the newspaper before running an advertisement or announcement anywhere. If the public doesn't know about it yet, it's a better news story. As soon as it appears, you can distribute posters and run ads if you wish. Also, give the release to all papers, TV, and radio stations at the same time. A paper won't use the story if it has been broadcast by local stations before you give it to them. This sometimes means the paper should get it sooner than the stations, because it takes the paper longer to prepare the announcement. Some papers prefer exclusive releases—this means giving first to one paper only If you do this, you must ask them for a commitment that they will run the story and give it thorough coverage. This usually is best done in person by a visit to the reporter.

Finally, whatever coverage the paper provides, however small, call and thank them for it. Some papers have a very hard time getting cultural news printed, and a reporter may have to fight for even a few inches. For additional stories you should come up with a new angle to give the reporter—"Record-breaking 1000 tickets sold" or "Musicians will talk personally to our students while visiting," etc. Remember—when in doubt, ask the paper. They know the answer!

November-December 1972

Editors Critical of
Publicity Effort in Arts

Communications between arts organizations and newspapers have improved, although they are still far from ideal. Moreover, the publicity efforts of cultural groups are less than professional, ranging in most instances from fair to good. These were among the conclusions emerging from *AM*'s 1968 survey of newspaper cultural editors throughout the nation, which drew responses from 27 editors in 23 different cities. In a similar survey undertaken by *AM* in 1962, there was near-unanimous agreement by editors that cultural groups did a third-rate publicity and promotion job.

Although 18 of the editors noticed an improvement in communications, eight noticed no change since 1962, and one, Harold V. Cohen of the *Pittsburgh Post-Gazette,* thought that communications had actually deteriorated. According to Conrad Wolfson of the *Jersey Journal,* "There certainly has been an increase in volume, but as far as I can determine, no increase in quality." Barbara Funkhouser of the *El Paso Times* noticed a vast improvement, but added, "There is still much to be done."

How well do arts publicists do their job? Asked to estimate what proportion of local cultural groups worthy of news coverage take the initiative to inform newspapers of their activities, 23 editors replied "almost all," and four indicated that only about half do. However, the arts scored poorly in regard to the quality of their informational program as indicated from responses to the question, "Of those that do keep you informed, what percentage do it in a manner that you would judge excellent, good, fair or poor?" More than 35 percent of the responses listed fair, 31 percent good, 19 percent poor, and only 15 percent listed excellent.

In substantiating the contention that cultural publicists are still less than expert in their work, 24 of the 27 editors indicated that major groups often did not receive coverage because they failed to submit materials, and 23 of the editors said that big organizations received less space in print than their activities warranted because their publicity work was faulty. In contrast to the opportunities missed by large groups, 24 editors claimed that small arts groups had received maximum coverage by virtue of their excellent liaison with newspapers in their communities.

Although time is a precious commodity to editors working against a deadline, nearly half of the respondents spend a fourth of their work week or more pursuing cultural groups to get facts that should have been sent to them. Hamilton B. Allen of the *Rochester Times Union* and Harold V. Cohen of the *Pittsburgh Post-Gazette* claim that whatever time they spend is "too much." Several editors echoed the view that they can't spare any time and groups who wanted stories "must come to us."

Editors were frank and frequently brutal in listing the most common faults they found with arts publicity material sent to them. Words like "overblown prose," "flowery," "verbose," and "arty" were liberally sprinkled through the questionnaire responses, and the lack of "know-how" and amateurish approach of many groups was severely criticized. Robert Jennings of the *Memphis Commercial Appeal* said, "The organizations attempt to dictate what, when, and how the material dealing with them is displayed, often without any knowledge of news value, mechanical limitations, and courtesy. The professional publicist is no problem. The volunteer for the myriad of other endeavors is often a hellish individual interested only in his or her conception of the job." Sharing this feeling was E. B. Radcliffe of the *Cincinnati Enquirer,* who faulted groups that "try to do a big job with low-cost amateur workers."

High on the list of faults noted by most editors were such obvious errors as the omission of facts, failure to adhere to deadlines, inaccuracy of material, poor organization of material, lack of consideration, inferior photographs, and what one editor termed "lack of comprehension of what is worthy of copy and what is pure baloney." Norman Nadel, cultural writer for the 16-paper chain of Scripps-Howard newspapers, said that most of the material he received "is unimaginative, incomplete, banal, and not directed at any particular requirements."

A continuing problem that plagues almost every editor is the fact that few arts publicists know how to write a press release. Irving Lowens of the *Washington Evening Star* objects to "puffery," while Mal Vincent of the *Norfolk Virginian Pilot* takes to task the publicist who is "much too flowery and too 'arty,' with too many superlative adjectives." Harold V. Cohen of the *Pittsburgh Post-Gazette* claims that releases are "so poorly written for the most part that they have to be rewritten. When there is little time for this they lose out completely."

Not the most frequent, but certainly the strongest criticisim that editors have of arts groups is that they often try to "pressure" a publication into using a story. Barbara Haddad of the *Denver Post* referred to two different kinds of pressure situations. "One," she said, "is the attitude that 'our story is the most important story of the year,' resulting in unrealistic and unfair demands for photographers, space, and follow-up stories. The second situation is that of the organization with a board of directors which includes the so-called socially prominent. Paid or volunteer staff often have no compunctions about letting these members (often rather badly informed ones) descend on the publisher or managing editor to seek special treatment or to right imagined wrongs by the staff. This does not endear the group to employer or employee, although it may produce temporary results. It is a weak and dangerous ploy in the long run and does a disservice to the organization."

A consensus among editors indicates that they are looking for help from arts publicists but too often fail to find it. According to Rolf Stromberg of the *Seattle Post Intelligencer,* the result is that "most of the cultural news is deadly, dull as a corpse. It should be stimulating, which seems easy enough when one considers all the startling ideas being utilized today."

November-December 1968

Be Factual, Terse, and Controversial, Say Editors

An awareness of what makes news, the accurate and terse presentation of facts, proper timing, and the ability to develop offbeat or even controversial angles are the chief ingredients of the arts stories that editors most want to publish. These conclusions were drawn from part two of *AM*'s 1968 survey of 27 cultural editors in 23 cities throughout the country.

Asked to advise arts publicists on "the story I will print," an overwhelming majority of editors cited the need for a brief, factual presentation of material which they could then evaluate themselves. "Give us everything and let us decide what's worth printing," suggested Dudley Saunders of the *Louisville Times.* "Avoid adjectives," advised both Dick Wooten of the *Cleveland Press* and Glenna Syse of the *Chicago Sun-Times.* "Present the facts without bally-hoo," added Barbara Haddad of the *Denver Post.* In addition, nearly every editor stressed the importance of knowing newspaper deadlines and adhering to them. "Don't wait until the last minute" was a refrain echoed by many editors.

Not enough arts publicists are aware of what legitimate news is, according to the editors. Phrases like "interest our general readers," "include facts the public wants to know about," and "find a local angle," cropped up repeatedly in questionnaire responses. Robert Jennings of the *Memphis Commercial Appeal* found some cultural groups using press books nearly three years old and deplored their "country weekly attitude" in dealing with metropolitan daily newspapers. E. B. Radcliffe of the *Cincinnati Enquirer* summed up his requirements for the good story briefly: "One that shows knowledge of the paper's style, space conditions, and news sense."

Nearly all the editors cited their continuing interest in receiving feature story suggestions with strong human interest angles. "Unless the story has news value of sufficient interest to stand by itself," said Peter Bellamy of the *Cleveland Plain Dealer,* "it should have an off-the-beaten-track feature handling or an eye-catching picture." Duane J. Snodgrass of the *Omaha World-Herald* recommended that arts publicists "be alert to bright feature ideas and attempt to find something unusual that will attract readers," while Mal Vincent of the *Norfolk Virginian Pilot* called for stories that have "an angle grounded in news value."

Two of the editors strongly urged arts publicists to be more adventurous and even controversial in their story suggestions. Rolf Stromberg of the *Seattle Post-Intelligencer* gives preference to "groups that lend themselves to controversial issues in the arts or attempt something out of the ordinary." Del Marbrook of the *Winston-Salem Journal and Twin City Sentinel* cited a problem shared by many other newspapers. "We continue to receive too many routine announcements," he said,

> when, in almost every instance, there is some interesting aspect involved that has been ignored. We are glad, as a public service, to publish announcements, but we should be happy if publicity people, and they are almost always volunteers, would be more alert to the offbeat, more willing to risk what they might consider controversy, when, in fact, it might merely lead to a good story and good publicity. There is too much second-guessing, too much image-worry amont the arts groups. We expect to find it in industry and government; we are always a little saddened to find it in the arts.

Gerald Ashford, of the *San Antonio Express and News,* who claims that the material he receives from art publicists has "all the possible faults in about equal proportions," has taken a positive step to correct these errors—he's written a 25,000 word book on publicity in the arts, published by Law-Arts Publishers.

January-February 1969

Publicity Aid

A simple guide listing essential publicity information can be an invaluable tool for public relations directors and volunteers. The Winston-Salem Arts Council published an inexpensive handbook for publicity chairmen that included such practical data as media contacts and deadlines and listings by name of outlets for placement of billboards, banners, and posters. Also included were instructions for preparing publicity and advertising materials.

September-October 1972

Immediate Release

Arts groups sending stories to editors marked "For Immediate Release" should be sure that the releases indicate the date on which they were sent. Editors will often put releases aside if they can't use them on a given day. On picking them up a day or two later, they'll have no way of knowing how old the news is if releases are undated, and they'll probably discard them.

April 1965

Colorful Releases

What's in a color? Perhaps a negative reaction by an editor to a press release. According to a survey of editors conducted by the Luce Press Clipping Bureau, over half those polled said they disliked receiving press releases on colored stock. One editor pointed out that the use of colored stock made the work of typesetters more difficult.

August-September 1966

Dual Interest

Although a single story on your organization may be of interest to several newspaper departments, avoid the temptation to send it to more than one editor. Should the story appear twice in two different sections of the newspaper, you may have two angry editors on your hands. If you think that more than one editor may be interested in the same release, it is proper to send duplicates only if you clearly indicate on the releases that this is being done.

January 1966

Clean Press Releases

Press releases should be presented as clear, clean copy. Recently, *AM* received a release from a major Eastern cultural instituion containing six penciled strikeovers, deletions, and additions. Newspaper editors will not take time to read such a poorly presented release. Remember that your arts group is in competition with other news sources for precious editorial space.

July-August 1964

Swiss Cheese Releases

Local names make local news. If you're planning an event to be attended by important people from a number of different communities and you wish to send press releases to the hometown newspaper of each of the attendees, you may use a "Swiss cheese" press release which has a blank line in place of a name. The individual name can then be typed in on the blank line, although the rest of the release remains the same.

May-June 1964

Press Kits Handy Tool—
But Use Them with Caution

Organizations planning events of major importance frequently use press kits to supplement the releases normally issued. A press kit, depending upon the event, may include all or some of the following: photographs, news releases, a general fact sheet or backgrounder, biographies of principals, feature stories, and booklets or other printed material.

Because press kits are far more expensive to compile and mail than press releases, a number of important questions should be answered affirmatively before a cultural group commits itself to their use:

- Is your story so complex that it demands additional information that cannot be provided in a press release? For example, if your institution is planning a ground-breaking ceremony for an important new building, architect's plans, pictures of the site, biographies of figures associated with the undertaking, background on your institution, and a chronological history of the building effort would all be vital components of a press kit. If you are simply announcing that a study is under way to prepare for a building program, a press release is probably enough.

- Is your story important enough to warrant the detailed coverage? The appointment of a concertmaster to an orchestra, for example, is an important news item, but does not ordinarily require a kit. A simple release is preferable.

- Is the event you are planning of interest to editors outside your immediate community? If your story is strictly a local one, a press kit is unnecessary. Invite local editors to your institution and discuss it with them.

- Do you have the time and the personnel to organize and issue a press kit? Because there are many components to a press kit, it requires considerable time to assemble. A competent person should supervise the entire project. Try to allow a month.

- Finally, do you have the finances to udertake the preparation of a press kit? Material must be inserted into the pockets of a heavy folder, and a large envelope is required for mailing. Before preparing a kit you must decide on the total number to be mailed, the number of inserts needed, the cost of photographs, and the weight of the entire package. Measure the cost against the kit's potential usefulness.

April 1962

Hometown Story

Organizations with a broad geographical reach might use committee members or active volunteers to help tap community newspapers with feature stories. When an article on how to listen to an Indianapolis Symphony concert appeared in the Greenfield, Indiana *Daily Reporter* under the byline of women's committee member Carole Arthur, the orchestra sent copies to other volunteers with the suggestion, "This copy could very easily be edited to fit your local situation—then submitted to your community's newspaper under the byline of one of your local committee members."

November-December 1977

Weekly Newspapers

Weekly newspapers, frequently ignored in publicity programs, are an excellent source for promoting arts events. There are thousands of weeklies throughout the country, and their editors are constantly searching for stories with local interest and color. If, for example, a member of your organization resides in or is a native of an area served by a weekly newspaper, prominent mention of his name in a press release may insure publication of that story. However, because the publishing schedules of weeklies vary, make sure that you know each paper's deadline so that your event can receive proper editorial consideration.

September 1964

To Tell the Truth

If your organization's building is old and unattractive, don't be ashamed of it. In fact, by contrasting vibrant activity inside the building with its facade, you may be able to turn the structure's appearance to your advantage. One arts institution recently sent out a mailing that informed the reader that its building's exterior was admittedly weather-worn and architecturally dull. However, it went on to say that inside the building there was bustling activity. To prove this point, a long list of activities sponsored by the institution accompanied the letter.

July-August 1964

Giving Awards

The granting of awards to notable persons who have made some contribution relating to an arts organization's field of interest can provide the group with a springboard for publicity. However, care should be exercised in making such awards. An impartial and respected panel of judges should choose the winner.

January 1965

Quid Pro Quo

When planning an announcement of an exhibition or event, bear in mind the special needs of monthly publications. Because their columns must be closed long before the weekly and daily press, they appreciate receiving advance notice of future events. In return for this favor, monthly editors will usually cooperate in avoiding disclosure of your announcement before your chosen release date.

July 1962

Publicity Exchange

Regular and informal meetings between cultural publicity directors and local media people can not only help to improve relationships, but can quicken the flow of information. In Boston, the Metropolitan Cultural Alliance, an arts council, sponsors monthly meetings between public relations directors of its member groups and local newspaper, magazine, radio, and television reporters and editors.

March-April 1975

Of National Interest

Local news bureaus or "stringers" could be your key to national publicity. The *New York Times,* which has national distribution, frequently publishes articles referring to arts activities in cities throughout the country. "Special to the New York Times" articles, featuring cultural developments in such cities as Detroit, Louisville, Galveston, and Portland, appeared in recent months.

November-December 1977

City Please

Are you sending event notices or invitations to a national press list? Be sure to include the city where the event is taking place. As hard as it is to believe, *AM* received a concert notice which named the participating group, the works to be played, and other details including the street address of the concert hall, but failed to indicate the specific city.

March-April 1972

Fact Sheet

You may have a good story for the business page or another non-arts section of the paper, but you must make sure that the editor you're dealing with has the necessary background data on your group. Prepare a simple one- or two-page fact sheet that contains key information and figures on your group in easy-to-read fashion. He'll appreciate that much more than pages of material.

September-October 1971

News Series

A newspaper feature is always welcome, but a four- or five-part series is even nicer. Remember, however, that the subject must have sufficient scope and interest to keep readers "hanging" until the next installment appears. You may have better luck with an editor if you suggest a cultural subject much bigger than your own group, but one in which your group could be featured. Recently published local series have included a four-parter in the *Boston Globe* on survival of the arts and a four-parter in the *Seattle Post-Intelligencer* titled "The Huckster," about Glynn Ross of the Seattle Opera.

March-April 1971

Foreign Language Newspapers

In many communities, ethnic groups are an untapped potential audience and may be especially interested in exhibits or performances that deal with their countries of origin. Foreign language newspapers, of which there are 600 in the United States, including 70 dailies, provide you with the means of reaching these groups. Although it is ideal to translate publicity material into the language of the newspaper, if this is impossible, send short and simply written releases and avoid colloquialisms.

September 1962

Contest Brings Publicity

A contest, specifically related to a performance, can help to win publicity for an arts group. The Old Globe Theatre in San Diego crowned "Miss Juliet" at a special Teen Night performance of *Romeo and Juliet*. Prior to the actual crowning, a publicized search to find the titleholder was conducted among teenage girls.

June-July 1966

Favorable Reviews

Arts groups that present performances of the same program over and over again should capitalize on favorable critical response. One way to do this is by collecting a series of critical quotes and immediately circulating them through direct mail. In Washington, D.C., when the Arena Stage received praise from critics for its presentation of Jean Anouilh's *The Rehearsal,* it quickly mimeographed highlights from the reviews and sent them to persons on its mailing list as well as to the press.

January 1965

Quoting the Critic

When quoting a critic in an advertisement or promotional mailing piece, be sure not only that the quotation is accurate, but also that the critic's name and publication are listed correctly. A midwestern theater sent out a promotion piece quoting a review by a *New York Post* critic, Richard Watts, and erroneously identified him as a writer for the *New York Mirror.* Discerning members of the audience quickly catch such mistakes, to the embarrassment of the sponsoring organization.

March 1963

Advance Notice

Is your organization planning to issue a major study or report? If so, it is wise to let the press know about the report in advance of its actual release date. Send the press a simple mimeographed announcement several weeks beforehand telling them when they will be receiving a copy and when information about the report may be released to the public. In this way, publications may plan to hold space for a story about the report.

February 1964

Pruning a Press List

Cutting down on a press release mailing list may often be a more difficult task than building one up. One way to make sure that interested people receive your material is to adopt a system used by the University of Michigan News Service. On the outside of envelopes containing their press releases, three lines of reduced size copy are printed in the lower left hand corner. They read, "If you do NOT desire to continue receiving material of this type, please check here and return in a separate first class envelope."

February 1964

Critical Disagreement

Disagreement among critics can sometimes be turned to the advantage of an arts group. In Washington, D.C., for example, the Arena Stage capitalized on the difference of opinion aroused by its production of Thornton Wilder's still controversial play, *The Skin of Our Teeth.* The company sent out publicity releases titled, "23 Years of Controversy Erupts Anew at Arena Stage," followed by nine published reviews of the play—five in praise of it, four panning it.

January 1966

The Right Name

Many people whose names are not of English origin go through life hearing them painfully mispronounced in North America. Increased use of local radio announcements by arts groups magnifies the effect of improper pronunciation. Announcers are much more likely to get a name right if the correct pronunciation is added in parentheses in every press release in which a non-English name is used. For example, if a symphony orchestra was listing the conductor Jorda in a radio release, it should read "the Spanish conductor Jorda (Hor DAH)."

March 1963

Weekly Arts Supplement

Arts groups wishing to reach a larger audience might benefit from the experience of the Nassau County Office of Performing and Fine Arts in Long Island, New York. Although the office had published an arts calendar ten times a year in co-operation with Hofstra University, it was "comparatively useless to those organi-zations it was trying to serve." Seeking to broaden its audience and promote the arts on a wider and more regular basis, the county arts office joined with Hofstra and an area newspaper, the *Long Island Daily Commercial Review,* in the publi-cation of a weekly supplement to the newspaper, a leisure guide. Costs are shared by the three participants. The weekly supplement provides extensive cov-erage of the local arts scene and a greatly expanded cultural calendar of events. It reaches twice the number of people the calendar did, including all of the news-paper's regular subscribers.

March-April 1967

Feature Stories for Newspapers
Expand Possibility of Coverage

The newspaper feature article, which emphasizes the background of a personali-ty, event, place, or institution, rather than spot news, offers excellent publicity opportunities for an arts organization. A straight news story, pegged to a definite date, has to compete with "hard" news on that date, and may be crowded off the page if important news stories break. But the feature article, the colorful or anecdotal story that can appear at anytime, may prove to be a boon to a hard-pressed editor.

Because few organizations are able to present news of real importance fre-quently, the imaginative public relations director of an arts group should try to develop the kinds of feature articles and possible picture layouts that editors look for. How can a feature article be developed?

1.   Examine your organization and its experiences carefully. Have you reached a significant milestone in your history? Are any of your activities unique? Has an orchestra, for example, acquired a rare instrument? Has a theatrical company historic costumes in its wardrobe?

2.   Look at the background and job responsibilities of your staff and per-formers. Is a woman doing an unusual job, such as managing an orchestra or handling the business affairs of a museum? A recent feature story in the *New York Times* described the work of the woman who managed the phy-sical arrangements for the Lewisohn Stadium concerts.

3.   Initiate research for possible features. What buildings, for instance, occu-pied the site you now use? A check into the records might reveal a fasci-nating history. Perhaps a museum has recently acquired a painting by an artist who lived in the area in the past. His background might uncover some little-known information about his life and work that would interest an editor.

4. Create features by initiating your own surveys. Interesting statistics seldom
    fail to captivate an editor. A theater might survey its audience on the con-
    temporary playwright it most admires. What kind of arts training are the
    youngsters in your community receiving? (An orchestra might survey its
    own members to get the answer to this question.)

5. Look beyond your immediate "family" to the outsider who has been in-
    volved in your work. Perhaps a local businessman has presented concerts
    by your orchestra for his employees. Why has he done this, and what is his
    estimate of the value of fine music for his employees? Perhaps a museum
    art class has an entire family—father, mother, and children—all taking a
    course together.

When presenting a feature story idea to an editor or writer, it is wise to
establish the special story and picture layout value of the suggestion in your lead
paragraph. The remainder of the letter should be used to provide additional
background information. Remember, too, that feature suggestions are not news
releases. In most instances an editor will assign a reporter and, if needed, a photographer, to follow up on the suggestion, if he thinks it has merit. Therefore,
when suggesting a feature story by letter, be concerned only with presenting
your suggestion briefly and with clarity, and with convincing the editor of the
merits and picture possibilities of the story. If you have pictures that illustrate
your suggestions—even snapshots —be sure to enclose them.

August 1963

Editorial Fillers

By preparing material that busy editors can use as "fillers," your organization
may increase its press coverage. Several lines of editorial copy, giving a single significant fact on your arts group, can fill an empty space in a newspaper. They also may spark a full-sized feature story or be filed for later use as background on
an interpretive story about your organization. The Utah Symphony in Salt Lake
City recently issued a press release, "Just a few facts about Utah Symphony musicians," which contained a wealth of filler possibilities.

November 1965

Updating the Press

Press books are important publicity tools. They must be updated annually, however, or their value is negated. The Indianapolis Symphony Orchestra, for example, sent revised press books, featuring background on the orchestra, biographies
of the conductor, associate conductors and concertmaster, plus quotes from recent reviews, to its press list. Attached to the folder was a note from the orchestra's public relations director reminding editors to discard any old press materials
on the orchestra that they might have in their files.

September-October 1968

New Publicist

Although it is not particularly important to the public, the appointment of a new publicity director by a cultural group is of special interest to those in the news media who cover the arts. A printed announcement card mailed to reporters will alert them to the change. It may also stimulate those who know the new publicist personally to take the initiative in getting in touch with him about writing a feature story or discussing the long-range aims of the organization.

December 1963

Arts Coverage

One of America's best-read and most prestigious newspapers, the *Wall Street Journal,* initiated a regular weekly arts page on January 13, 1978. Leisure and the Arts, which appears every Friday, features three arts articles and should be required reading for your businessmen board members. Dan Henninger at the *Journal* (22 Cortland St., N.Y., N.Y. 10017) is section editor.

January-February 1978

Special Stories

Editors are constantly looking for pictures and stories for use in conjunction with a special day or national holiday. Now is the time to start planning newsworthy ideas for upcoming holidays such as Labor Day, Columbus Day, or Thanksgiving. Also give some thought to such special dates as the birthday of a famous composer, the anniversary of a noteworthy event, or the last day of summer.

July 1963

Events Listing

If your organization is planning a major event that is open to the public, such as an annual art exhibition or an arts festival, be sure to release this information to the press well in advance of the date the event actually takes place. Newspapers and magazines, for example, which publish special listings of important events, may need such information weeks ahead of time, since this kind of news is frequently collected and edited before other sections of the publication.

April 1964

Hiring a Publicity Firm: The Pros, Cons, and Costs

In recent years cultural organizations have made increased use of professional public relations firms or consultants. While the majority of arts groups still rely wholly on their own publicity departments, composed of volunteer workers or staff members, many organizations, including the Indianapolis Symphony, the Whitney Museum, the Philadelphia Chamber Orchestra, and the National Cultural Center, to name a few, are or have been represented by outside public relations counsel.

What are the advantages and disadvantages of this practice?

A volunteer amateur publicity director may get his group into the local papers and see that its posters are distributed. But he often has no idea of the way to induce a national magazine, a wire service, or a network television producer to take a look at his organization. He may not know the name of a single out-of-town editor or writer. His effectiveness is thus strictly local, as a rule, and the picture in *Life*, the story in *Look*, the appearance on a network show are beyond his capability.

The professional outside publicist is not a miracle worker. He cannot automatically "deliver" an article in a national magazine or an appearance on radio or television. Arranging this takes considerable time and effort, and a really firm promise of delivery should make the client cautious. But the professional public relations counsel should know how to accomplish this, and he should have the necessary contact with editors, writers, and producers.

He should know how to present news, and even to create news that reflects favorably on the client. He should know how to find freelance writers likely to be most interested in the client's story. He should know how to help them prepare the story, how to dig up appropriate facts and anecdotes. He should know where the story is best told, and when. He should know how to set up a press conference—and when not to. Above all, he should know how to shape a campaign to fit the objective of the organization, whether the objective is to build audience, recruit volunteers, attract out-of-town visitors, or boost contributions in fund raising.

These talents are not necessarily limited to outside publicists. Some cultural institutions employ full-time staff professionals who are thoroughly qualified, too. But for the smaller institution that cannot afford the salary, administrative cost, and overhead of a full-time inside public relations operation, for the group that is geographically isolated from major press, radio, and television centers, for the group that needs help for only part of the year or for a special campaign, or for institutions with unusual requirements, the sensible answer may be outside representation.

Some cultural institutions, of course, do not need an extensive public relations program. They may be reaching their audience, filling the house, and suffering no financial pangs. But for those not in this enviable position, professional public relations can provide an important boost. Each cultural organization should analyze its own situation carefully, to determine first of all if it needs outside help.

The main objection to professional representation is cost. Not all groups can afford it. Even the smallest public relations firm will hesitate to take on a full program for an organization paying it less than $300 monthly. While it is difficult to name an average fee (such figures are generally confidential), the range is usually between $400 and $800 per month. For large organizations, with heavy requirements, however, the fee may exceed $1200 per month.

If a group has made the decision that it can afford the fee, it should not necessarily assume that it will receive the constant, around-the-clock attention that it might from a member of its own staff. On the other hand, some public relations firms may place a representative on the premises. There should be a clear understanding in advance of the firm's availability and the time it is prepared to give to the client.

An additional difficulty is that many public relations firms are not equipped by experience or instinct to serve a cultural account. Their entire experience may have been commercial, and they may have neither an interest in nor an understanding of the arts. Representation by such a firm may prove ineffective or undignified or both. Other firms, capable of serving a cultural group effectively, may not wish to, since such accounts are rarely as lucrative as straight commercial work.

June 1962

How to Choose and Sign Up a Public Relations Firm for an Arts Campaign

Before an arts group decides to hire an outside public relations firm, it should first determine what its primary objective is. Is it to increase audiences at performances? Is it to attract out-of-town visitors? Or to gain members? Or to win national recognition for excellence? Or perhaps to bring in financial support? What, in addition, are its secondary objectives?

Once the institution has thought these questions through and agreed upon the need for outside help, it should invite letters of application from as many public relations firms as possible. Board members should be polled for names of agencies they know, and it is wise to ask others close to the organization to make suggestions. Firms may be local, they may be in a nearby city, or they may be in New York, where access to the national publications and networks is easiest.

Applicants should be asked to state their accomplishments, their specialties, their past and present clients, and record of activity in the cultural field. Replies should be carefully screened by a committee that narrows the list down to the most appealing applicants. These can then be invited to a personal meeting, one at a time, to discuss the client's specific needs.

After the public relations firm representative have been briefed on the objectives of the organization, the latter has the right to ask for a written presentation listing services the firm proposes to furnish, its suggestions for an overall program, the proposed fee and expense schedule. The organization also has the right to meet and talk with a client already served by the agency.

Before making a final choice, the client should get the answers to several questions: Is the firm equipped to handle a cultural organization? How much time will the agency give the account? Who will work on the account? Will the supervisory personnel and heads of the firm contribute their talents, or leave the job to subordinates? Does the agency have regular and intimate access to press, radio, and television at a national as well as local level?

The arts group should be wary of a firm that tries too hard to impress outsiders with the size and magnificence of its office. This sort of thing does not mean results. Of twenty people in a firm, only two or three may be actually working on the account. The new client should be especially skeptical of the firm that claims to have certain freelance writers or staff editors "all sewed up." Although a few unscrupulous firms indulge in excessive gift-giving to writers and editors, a good firm does not buy contacts. It is instead sufficiently creative to do constant research, and thus learn what kind of stories particular editors and writers are looking for and offer them leads appropriate to their editorial interests.

When the organization is satisfied with the presentation, all questions are answered, and the staff who will work on the account is known, a contract must be drawn up. Contracts do not have to be complicated legal documents. Many firms use simple letters of agreement that specify, among other things, the length of the contract, conditions for terminating, the fee, and the restriction on expenses. A client should not expect a contract to state the actual publicity placements to be made, since no ethical firm can state this in advance.

Most public relations firms prefer to work on a year-long contract, with fees payable monthly, in advance. The minimum period for most firms, particularly where national representation is important, is three months. This is so because the placement of a story in a national magazine may take months to accomplish, inasmuch as the magazine may work on issues long in advance of publication. For the client's protection, it is wise to limit a first contract to a trial period of three months before committing the organization to a longer term.

Expenses to be paid by the client over and above the monthly fee should be carefully limited. These normally include only extraordinary costs, such as out-of-town travel, long-distance telephoning, printing, art work, photographic costs, and modest entertainment for the press. The contract can be written to fix a monthly amount, say $50, which the firm can spend at its own discretion, with the stipulation that all expenses over that amount must be approved by the client in advance.

The outside public relations program costs money. But a dignified and imaginative one, carried out with professional skill, can prove itself in prestige gained and more than pay for itself at the box office or in the fund-raising campaign.

July 1962

Helping the Editor

Small organizations of similar type can all get guaranteed space in the newspaper by uniting to compile their program information and deliver it to a busy newspaper editor in one package. Otherwise, the individual announcement can be lost. Community theaters in the area served by the Long Island (New York) *Daily Press* have delegated one person to get their week's programs to the paper, where they appear under the heading "Long Island Playbill." In addition, the newspaper guarantees to allot one photo to each theater per season, with the theater group arranging the schedule of pictures for the paper.

October 1962

Too Much, Too Soon

Advance publicity for arts events is premature if you are not prepared to meet the interest it arouses. Announcement of a recent music festival, for instance, including an exciting schedule of events with time, place, and the ticket price scale, stirred great local interest. But the first and most eager people to respond found tickets not yet printed, and the staff unsure of how many seats there would be in each price class, nor even where they would be in the hall. Then the place of several concerts was shifted, and later the location of auxiliary ticket sales points was announced before they were ready to sell tickets. Annoyance caused would-be patrons could have been avoided by proper timing of arrangements and announcements.

June 1962

Free Press Directories

Some national clipping services publish directories listing newspapers by state and city. These directories often are available to customers or potential customers at no charge. Check the classified telephone directory for the names of the clipping services in your area.

June 1963

Motorist Magazines

You may be missing a good publicity outlet if you bypass the motorist magazines published by many state branches of the American Automobile Association. These publications, some of which have circulations in the hundreds of thousands, are interested in material of use to motorists. For example, the *Connecticut Motorist* carried a detailed story on the Connecticut Opera Association's 1965-66 season.

December 1965

House Organs

Looking for new publicity outlets? House organs, magazines published by corporations for their employees and stockholders, some with circulations of hundreds of thousands of readers, are constantly on the lookout for newsworthy stories. For complete listings of over 4000 corporate publications, see the *Gebbie House Magazine Directory,* which is available at many libraries.

Summer 1968

Photographers and Writers

Looking for a top freelance writer or photographer to help tell your organization's story to a national magazine? There may be one living in your area. The American Society of Magazine Photographers, at 205 Lexington Avenue, New York, New York 10016, publishes a directory which lists more than 1700 members, both alphabetically and geographically, and includes their addresses, phone numbers, and specialties. A directory of leading freelance nonfiction writers is available from the American Society of Journalists and Authors, 1501 Broadway, New York, New York, 10036. Each annual edition lists members' addresses and phone numbers, their present and former connections, writing specialties, and magazines to which they contribute.

January-February 1967

Financial Pages

In publicizing your organization, don't overlook the nonarts sections of your local newspapers. The Seattle Opera in Washington benefited from a detailed article titled "Non Profit Opera Profits Seattle" which appeared on the financial pages of the *Seattle Times,* next to the stock market report. The story, written by a member of the newspaper's business staff, outlined the opera's fiscal picture and indicated why private contributions were necessary.

June-July 1966

Well-Laid Plans, Many Helpers
Needed for Festival Publicity

Careful planning and enlistment of the aid of others are important factors in the success of publicity campaigns for festivals or community-wide arts projects.

This was the experience of Mrs. Leona Flis, volunteer publicity chairman of the Tri-City Ballet Guild, which hosted the 1962 Northeast Regional Ballet Festival.

Mrs. Flis' committee established early contact with the Downtown Merchants' Bureau, an organization of 250 Schenectady businessmen, which agreed to publicize the festival at its own expense. The merchants printed, distributed, and displayed store window posters, cardboard table tents for restaurants, and a huge banner on the prominent railroad over-cross in midtown.

Ten cultural organizations in Schenectady and the nearby cities of Troy and Albany helped publicize the ballet festival through their own channels and sold tickets to their own members.

Special events that called attention to the ballet festival included a visit (with photographers) to Governor Rockefeller of New York by leaders of the Tri-City Ballet Guild to receive a proclamation. The mayor of Schenectady declared a local Ballet Week during the festival, and a department store carried a week-long window display in its honor.

Newspaper publicity was planned with the five daily papers in the area to avoid conflict and duplication. Mrs. Flis and her aides set up an advance story schedule, listing all the news possibilities by subject matter and date. This was broken down into five lists, one for each paper, the first story going out in mid-March.

The system was so effective that each paper used an average of two stories or pictures a week, increasing the pace to one daily during the week before the ballet festival opened.

Ten radio stations in the Schenectady-Albany-Troy area used more than 500 spot announcements. Television programs featured festival posters and interviews. One station filmed a dress rehearsal, which it put on the air twice.

"It was a wonderful experience," Mrs. Flis told *AM*, "but it was very hard work. If I were to do it over again, which I don't think I could, I would start planning even earlier than I did."

July 1962

Tell the Truth

Maintaining good press relations is a key to the success of an organization's public relations program. One sure way to rupture these relations is to place the same kind of feature story with two rival publications at about the same time. If an editor approaches you with a story idea similar to one already planned by another publication, tell him about the article that is in the works and suggest a completely different story. Your honesty will save you embarrassment later and will pay off in the long run.

April 1964

Praising the Press

If good press coverage has helped to fill the house, let writers and editors know that you appreciate their support and interest. One organization, the Little Theatre of Alexandria, Virginia, sent a thank-you letter to people on its press list last month, following the successful run of one of its productions. The letter read, in part, "Your unstinting response resulted in an unprecedented full house for each night of the production. Thus, we are eager to share plaudits with press, television, radio."

October 1964

Press Passes

Press passes issued by an arts group can help develop good relations with editors. The Academy of Natural Sciences in Philadelphia mails such passes to the press, admitting editors and their guests to the academy, its lectures, and its special events. The passes are signed by its public relations chairman, who in a covering letter invites the press to "stop by the P.R. office whenever you're in the Academy." Included with the pass is a list of academy events.

June 1965

New Information

Often, the material gathered by an editor in an interview is not of sufficient interest to warrant its publication. If this happens, don't bother the editor constantly to check on the story's status. Wait until you have some important new data and send it to him. It may result in the story's use.

September 1964

Off the Record

In dealing with the press, much confusion can be avoided if you understand the distinction between "off the record" and "not for attribution." If a member of your organization is merely giving information to a reporter as private background and does not wish that information published at all, then the conversation is "off the record." On the other hand, if an interviewee wants the information to be printed but does not wish to be quoted as the source, then it is "not for attribution."

November 1963

Keeping the Editor Posted

If you have promised written material or information to an editor and learn that you will have difficulty in obtaining it by the deadline date, let the editor know the true situation as soon as possible. By warning him in advance, he may be able to reschedule the story for a later date. If you wait till the last minute, however, he may never use the story and will be reluctant ever to call your organization again.

June 1963

Good Press Relations

Want to remain in the good graces of local reporters and editors? Keep unannounced visits to them to a minimum, and never drop in to their offices at deadline time. Learn the copy deadlines of local publications and honor them.

September 1965

Thanking the Writer

A thank-you note to a writer or editor who has featured your organization in a story lets him know that you appreciate his interest. While notes may be short, even handwritten, they should be sent immediately after a story appears. Such a gesture of courtesy may encourage the writer or editor to look to your group as a source for future articles.

March 1963

Museum Perks Press with Novel Present

An unusual Christmas greeting sent by a museum to the press achieved a resounding critical reception.

In Philadelphia, Mrs. Libby Demp Forrest, chairman of the public relations department of the Academy of Natural Sciences, was looking for a pleasant yet inexpensive Christmas greeting to send. Because she had hundreds of fossilized sharks' teeth, inexpensive items sold at the museum's sales desk, she decided to affix a tooth to each of serveral hundred specially printed letterheads and send them out as Christmas cards in 1962. A note on the card said "Unequivocally, this is the oldest thing you'll get for Christmas." The card ended by inviting the recipient to visit the museum and see many more fossils and specimens.

The card was greeted with favorable letters and local publicity. But during the year Mrs. Forrest was continually asked what she would send out in 1963. When the card arrived, it said, "Many people wanted to know what we were going to send this Christmas. In the back of our mind was the thought how could we surpass a single superb shark tooth. This Christmas we send you two."

January 1964

Good Humor

Humor can be used effectively by a cultural organization, especially if it is closely related to the objectives of the group. Philadelphia's Academy of Natural Sciences consistently promotes its function as a natural science museum in its mailings to the press. Last year the museum sent Christmas cards containing two fossilized sharks teeth. This year it sent amusing cards which featured a handdrawn "autographed" footprint of Dolores—a dinosaur.

January 1965

Deadline Calendar

Publicity directors will find it useful to post a calendar carrying the deadlines of every publication to be serviced with news and pictures. The calendar should be divided into two columns covering copy and picture deadlines for each of the following outlets: radio and TV stations, daily newspapers, Sunday editions of newspapers, weeklies, monthlies, and annuals. The calendar should be referred to regularly so that each outlet will be served on time. Of course, the special deadline requirements of any outlet varying from the general pattern should be noted on the calendar.

February 1963

Pictures for the Press

Planning to send photographs to illustrate a story? Here are some tips to keep in mind. Editors want glossy prints, preferably 8-by-10 or 5-by-7 inches in size. Pictures, other than "head" shots, should show action by having the subjects informally doing something. Generally, no more than four persons should be included in the picture, with two or three the best number to be shown. Also, be sure to attach an identifying caption to each picture. When mailing, place cardboard around the photographs to protect them.

March 1965

Photo File

Whenever possible, an arts group should maintain a file of photographs for use by the editor who finds last-minute space for a picture story. In addition to "mug shots"—i.e., portraits—of leading performers or staff, the file should include action shots, preferably candid, of your people at work. Pictures of cornerstone layings, award presentations, and other formal ceremonies are of far less interest to a good editor, as a rule, than shots that portray spontaneous activity or emotion. It helps to keep a file of negatives, too.

April 1962

Photo Enclosed

When placing a newspaper story about a personality associated with your organization, send his picture to the editor along with the story. A poll of managing editors, conducted by the Luce Press Clippings service, noted that 92 percent of the editors wanted a photo with the personality story. However, only 51 percent of the editors polled felt that photos should accompany news stories about events. If you send a picture, be sure that it has an identifying caption attached.

August 1963

How to Get Help
in Guest Artist Promotion

An effective publicity campaign for a visiting artist need never be a solo performance. There are organizations and businesses in each community ready to help arts managers by putting their publicity resources at their disposal. Cultural groups using guest artists can draw on others to achieve maximum publicity results.

Many businesses and organizations outside the cultural field have public relations representatives or people responsible for sending out releases, distributing pictures to newspapers, or arranging interviews. They are seeking press attention, and if your guest can somehow be linked with their interest, they may prove eager to cooperate.

Of course, it is important not to damage the prestige of an organization (or of the artist) by participating in stunts of dubious taste or by allowing it to become too closely connected with individual commercial enterprises. But it is possible to work well within the bounds of simple good taste and still draw valuable assistance from these outside publicity experts.

Arts groups can work effectively with railroads and airlines, hotels, retail stores, service organizations, record companies, church groups, businessmen's clubs, restaurants, athletic teams, ethnic groups, women's organizations, and many others.

The first step in conducting a cooperative publicity campaign is to learn as much about the visiting performer as possible. A letter to his management firm or to the individual himself will often answer questions about the groups of which he is a member, his hobbies, personal interests, and general background. It is also wise to find out early in the game how much time he is willing to give to publicity activity.

Top-ranking artists may not have the time or need to give much effort to promotion, but most secondary performers, including many with familiar names, are eager or willing to cooperate in publicizing their visit.

After carefully checking the artist's background, notify as many organizations as may be interested in his appearance in your community—consistent, of course, with the time he has available. For example, if an actor who is a member of Kiwanis is due to appear with a theater company, Kiwanis may be interested in honoring him at one of their luncheons.

Checking the guest in at a local booster club, chamber of commerce, or advertising club meeting not only exposes him to many potential ticket buyers but can, if there is time, lead to retail store tie-ins—such as window displays devoted to the artist and his local appearance. If the artist makes recordings, the local record store can arrange for window displays and a token appearance. In many cases the store will take ads in the local paper announcing the event.

Hotels are an excellent source of free publicity. Those that are members of a chain generally employ a publicity director who is eager to make news of the fact that the celebrity is staying at the hotel in question. He will often take pictures, make calls to newspapers, and arrange interviews. In smaller hotels without a full-time public relations person, the sales manager may frequently be of help.

Robert Windt, publicity representative of Pepsi Cola, has won a great deal of favorable publicity for his company from this kind of cooperative local effort, particularly through the use of Joan Crawford as his visiting star. He counsels cultural organizations to use the same sources.

Most newspapers devote sections to the activities of hospitals, religious organizations, and society groups. The performer's appearance, however brief, at a function of one of these groups can result in an excellent story. A visiting dancer photographed with a bedridden child who has dancing ambitions of her own makes a pictorial feature. A huge basso eating chicken legs at a church supper may have human interest value to a photographer.

An artist can throw the first ball at a game, appear at a fashion show, have a special dish named for him at a restaurant, have his photograph placed on the wall, or can do any of a number of other things that require little time, but which all mean free newspaper space.

Working with others to mutual benefit requires imagination, planning beforehand, and efficient follow-up. Successful publicity not only gives your event the immediate coverage it needs, but also sets up a working relationship with people who can help you in the future.

March 1962

Publicity Resource

Smaller groups looking for good publicity tips may be interested in "For Immediate Release," a how-to press guide written by Jeniva Berger as a series of articles for *Scene Changes* magazine of Theatre Ontario. Copies, at $1 each, are available from Theatre Ontario, 8 York Street, 7th floor, Toronto, Ontario M5J 1R2 Canada.

November-December 1977

PROMOTIONAL EFFORTS

Community-wide Celebrations
Rewarding for Local Sponsors

Major community-wide celebrations involving several weeks of special events and performances can, if planned carefully, be produced inexpensively and achieve specific goals not otherwise attainable. In Providence, Rhode Island, for example, the Trinity Square Repertory Company used a 12-day Holiday Celebration, which officially opened its new home, the Lederer Theatre Project, not only to publicize the company and its unusual facility, but to develop a community and national consciousness of the company's ability and versatility.

Director Adrian Hall conceived the celebration last summer as the facility was nearing a completion. The project is actually two separate flexible theaters, one atop the other, converted from a crumbling 56-year-old legitimate theater at a cost of about $1.5 million. Hall set aside the period from December 26 through January 6 for the official opening celebration and then planned a revolving repertory of five productions to be presented in the two performing spaces, a schedule that would permit seeing all the plays within a two to three day period.

Since the celebration was designed to involve the total community, special events, many free to the public, were planned for presentation outside the theater, in its lobbies, and in its rehearsal hall. In all, 24 different events were held including a print exhibition; three concerts; showings of an upcoming Trinity Square ETV production; such pre-performance "lobby events" as a puppet show, choral recital, and band concerts; presentation of the Governor's Art Award to Trinity Square designer, Eugene Lee; and two seminars with Trinity Square staffers and national arts figures as panelists. In addition, several days were set aside to honor six Rhode Island communities for their support, and presentations were made to them during performance intermissions.

From the moment the celebration opened with dedication ceremonies attended by top dignitaries, area interest was tremendous and publicity was excellent. Calendars and celebration posters were widely displayed, and the *Providence Journal* gave continuous coverage beginning with the publication of a special issue of its *Sunday Magazine* two months in advance of the celebration. In addition, members of the national press covered performances, and a major story in the *National Observer* called Trinity Square "the liveliest, most adventurous regional theater company in the United States, with an acting company to match."

An important aspect of the celebration was the fact that the Trinity Square staff was able to handle most program arrangements. "Costs were negligible," Tom Griffin, producer of special events, told *AM*. Tickets for performances were sold at normal prices, and there were frequent full houses. Since groups presenting special events either performed without charge to the theater or received grants, no extra expenses were incurred.

In addition to its obvious benefits, the massive undertaking had some hidden ones. "Along with the interest and coverage," said Griffin, "it was perhaps equally important what the celebration did for our own company. The people who came together to work together now have a sense of accomplishment that can't be equalled."

Elsewhere, a 75-year-old symphony orchestra was "discovered" thanks to an effective yet inexpensive community celebration which took the orchestra directly to the people. Over a 16-day period last fall, the Peoria Symphony Orchestra and a smaller ensemble drawn from its players gave free performances in open air locations throughout the city and, as a result, increased season and individual ticket sales dramatically, received tremendous publicity, and won support and interest from unexpected areas of the community.

For some time the orchestra had been looking for an effective means of arousing greater community awareness. "With only a $100,000 budget we couldn't afford much promotion," claimed manager Donald B. Kramer. "Yet we felt support was out there. We had to let them really know that we were here." With a new conductor about to begin his first season last September, the need for a tasteful yet effective way to bring the orchestra to public attention became even more important.

Borrowing the concept of a 24-foot mobile home for street performances from another orchestra, but expanding the basic idea greatly, the orchestra last June began planning a pre-season celebration to begin September 21. A five-member committee of women's guild volunteers working with manager Kramer found city support for the project, received funding from the Musician's Performance Trust Fund (two-thirds of the cost of performances), and won such donations as a carnival tent and free ads contributed by two banks.

The celebration opened on a busy closed-off downtown intersection with the Mayor proclaiming "Symphony Week," followed by a full orchestra concert under the tent. For ten of the following 16 days, including three weekends, orchestra players were all over the area, with the mobile unit bringing brass quintets to shopping centers and to nearby campuses and communities. For the youngsters, puppet shows were presented and during periods when live players didn't perform, stereo tapes of performances were played along with tapes telling about the upcoming season. Symphony Days ended in a giant riverboat party attended by a capacity crowd of 400 people.

Publicity exceeded all expectations. "Because we spent $3000 on the promotion," Kramer told AM, "we were forced to cut our normal newspaper and TV advertising drastically. Yet we still wound up with more lineage than we ever had." In addition to scores of news and feature stories, the new conductor appeared on local talk shows and Sears Roebuck took a front page ad in its own newspaper supplement to tell about the orchestra. "Actually," added Kramer, "we ran a $25,000 promotion for $3000."

The specific benefits were many, including "the sale of several hundred extra season tickets directly attributed to the drive" and a virtual doubling of individual ticket sales. Also, although the orchestra was selling its season and not fund raising, sponosr donations increased by about 25 percent.

Because of the program's success it will become an annual event, but with some changes, including a longer planning period and more volunteer help. Most important, based on this year's success, the orchestra anticipates contributions completely underwriting next year's program.

January-February 1974

Special Theater Week
is Useful Promotional Tool

Official proclamations that honor local arts groups seldom result in dramatic increases in either ticket sales or contributions. Effectively merchandised, however, they can be useful promotional tools that help a group to reach difficult markets, publicize its programs, or revive flagging volunteer interest.

The mayors of Hartford and West Hartford, Connecticut, for example, proclaimed the week of September 7-13, 1969 as Hartford Stage Company Week and urged all citizens to support the group. The special week followed a very slow subscription campaign lagging far behind the previous year's, due in part to increased ticket prices. "It was necessary to jolt our volunteers into action," said William Stewart, the theater's managing director. "A kick-off party for Phase II and the proclamation of Stage Company Week seemed the most effective method."

The kick-off party which opened the week was a gala champagne and pizza "turn-on" at the Hartford Insurance Group's Tower Suite attended by the city's top business, educational, and cultural leaders. Special guests included playwright Robert Anderson and his wife, actress Teresa Wright, and actor Morris Carnovsky. Later events that week included a series of in-school programs in nearby communities featuring company members; talks by company representatives before service clubs and business groups; subscriptions parties arranged by the women's committee; and a series of radio and television appearances by the Stage Company's staff and board members.

Publicity on Hartford Stage Company Week was excellent, and the theater was able to win coverage in newspapers and on radio and television, which without the impetus of the proclamation, it would not have received—like a special article on the Sunday business page. The company also was able to present a strong case for support to local business through speeches delivered at Rotary Clubs.

Asked to eavluate the effectiveness of the week, managing director Stewart told *AM*, "I think the week succeeded. We had excellent coverage and cooperation from the newspapers and radio and TV. And we revived a rather tired and sagging group of volunteers and created a climate to generate renewed interest from many people."

September-October 1969

Special Month-long Promotions
Can Bring Arts a New Audience

Cultural organizations performing an outstanding service for the community and seeking recognition by a wide segment of the public might consider establishing a special "week" or "month" for that purpose. Although advance preparation and careful coordination are necessary, such promotions may yield great benefits.

Special weeks and months have been highly successful public relations and fund-raising vehicles in the health and welfare field, and many of the techniques employed there can be adapted for use by nonprofit cultural organizations. For example, the Jewish Chronic Disease Hospital in Brooklyn, New York has sponsored such a program for a number of years. Under the direction of its public relations counsel, Edward N. Mintz, the hospital's special month promotion has been a model of what may be accomplished in a carefully planned campaign.

The first step in such a program is to get official approval for the desired week or month. The Chronic Disease Hospital, for example, receives a proclamation from the mayor of New York each year designating September as "Chronic Disease Hospital Month." Once this approval is obtained, the sponsoring institution can then request the support of city agencies and key private groups. Thus, the hospital has received permission from the licensing authority in New York to place more than 5000 stickers in local taxicabs proclaiming the month. It has also placed free advertising car cards in more than 1200 New York buses and posted free announcements on city billboards.

The selection of a chairman to head the week or month is another important step which should be taken well in advance of the actual campaign. The hospital, for example, generally names a leading celebrity from the entertainment field as chairman. It then features his name and his picture in announcements, correspondence, and publicity. Other key entertainment figures are asked to donate their time to record radio announcements and film television spots.

The support of prominent national and local political figures and leading private citizens should also be solicited, and letters and telegrams from them can be cited in direct-mail campgians or they can be read aloud at dinners and other special events. In response to letters acquainting leaders with the problem of chronic diseases and the role of the hospital, the institution received assurances of cooperation and best wishes from the White House, the governor of New

York, the secretary of Health, Education and Welfare, both New York senators, and many other top leaders.

Special committees composed of people prominent in a particular field should be formed early. In 1962, the hospital's radio and television committee for Chronic Disease Hospital Month was headed by the vice presidents of New York's two leading television stations. In addition, officials of more than 200 radio and television stations in New York and eight surrounding states, the bulk of them solicited by mail, agreed to serve on the committee. This kind of cooperation resulted in the use of more than 100,000 written, recorded, and filmed announcements on radio and television during the special month and afterwards, which reached an audience in the millions. Many of these announcements featured top personalities who contributed their time and services.

Although a special week or month can reap widespread benefits and be helpful in raising vast sums of money, it need not be an expensive undertaking if it is carefully organized and if maximum cooperation is forthcoming. In one of its most successful special months, the Chronic Disease Hospital spent only a little more than $3000 on the entire program. Included in this amount were the costs of making recorded and filmed announcements and printing material for car cards, taxi stickers, and billboards. Space and time were generously given by advertising media, and celebrities contributed their services.

May-June 1964

How to Plan for Specially Proclaimed Week

Careful step-by-step planning, selection of a newsworthy honorary chairman, good use of volunteers, and several promotable feature events were among the ingredients that helped the New York City Chapter of Young Audiences, Inc., reaps widespread benefits from a week officially proclaimed in its honor.

During the summer of 1970, the New York chapter decided that a week honoring Young Audiences would provide a good promotional prelude to organizational fund-raising efforts. Letters were sent to New York's Mayor Lindsay and to commissioner of Cultural Affairs Dore Schary requesting proclamation of the week of November 30 as Young Audiences Week in New York. Accompanying the letters was detailed information on the organization, with special emphasis on its benefits to the city's schoolchildren. Later that week several key board members phoned the commissioner's office to offer additional background.

When city confirmation of the honor and date came within a week, the organization was ready. Immediately, each of its volunteer committees was notified and asked for promotion and progam suggestions. One volunteer came up with the idea for one of the feature events, a week-long exhibit of children's art inspired by Young Audiences concerts. Her husband won a commitment from the presitgious Seagram Building to house the exhibit in its lobby.

On October 5, Miss Marian Anderson agreed to serve as honorary chairman. Her early acceptance was crucial, since letters and invitations to events could be signed by her, she could be prominently featured in printed material, and her testimonial to Young Audiences could be incorporated into upcoming announcements and releases.

By mid-October, the suggested wording for the official proclamation had been prepared and sent down to city hall. Also, Commissioner Schary had agreed to appear at the opening event, a Young Audiences demonstration concert at an elementary school, to present the mayor's proclamation to Miss Anderson. Letters were sent to broadcast media to prepare them for later releases.

Special attention was given during the first weeks of November to the three events that would highlight Young Audiences Week. For the opening Monday event, the official presentation, a list of 40 top dignitaries was prepared, invitations were mailed, and volunteers followed up with notables they personally knew to insure attendance. At the same time, arrangements were made with the city school system's art superintendent for the second event, "What Color is Music?" the week-long exhibit of schoolchildren's art scheduled to open on Tuesday, December 1. With cooperation from the superintendent, chapter volunteers worked with local schools to get paintings for the exhibit. The third event was a week-long series of in-school Young Audiences demonstrations.

By mid-November, the publicity machinery was in full operation. Some 400 posters were mailed to contributors and friends to place in prominent locations. Press releases were sent to weekly newspapers for use in "What's happening" columns. National magazines received long letters describing the week's activities and the organization's program. When it was discovered that Young Audiences Week coincided with National Children's Art Month, it gave chapter publicists a national angle which they turned into an ABC network television feature.

A week prior to the event, full attention was given to daily press sources. Radio and television spots were prepared and mailed. The city itself sent press releases to dailies on November 23, followed two days later by more detailed releases from the chapter.

The official week opened on a wave of prepublicity including Young Audiences store windows in Lord and Taylor and Creative Playthings and advance stories in leading dailies. The special events received excellent coverage in the papers and on television news programs, public service spots were used frequently, and feature interviews with Marian Anderson were aired on television. National magazines who couldn't do stories on the Week, became interested in the organization.

One unexpected yet important blessing also resulted from the program— Young Audiences was able to purchase ABC news films featuring Miss Anderson and have them converted at minimal cost into an excellent 60-second television spot. Prints will soon be distributed to all Young Audiences chapters.

In assessing the week's benefits, national excutive director Gerry J. Martin said, "Both city officials and media people know us much better now and so do many potential supporters. Considering the benefits, the costs weren't great, since many of them fit into the normal promotional budget." He added one word of caution, however. "Don't go into the week thinking of immediate and direct fund-raising rewards. They may come, but over the long run."

As evidence of its success, the Week will become a national event this fall, with all 40 Young Audiences chapters participating.

March-April 1971

How a Symposium Can Help a Cultural Group

If your organization is new or little known, or if it is embarking on a major change in its program, or if it is seeking to shift from a local to a regional or national base, it should consider the advantages of presenting a symposium. The symposium can be an excellent fund-raising event. Equally important, it can lay the basis for a major shift in the "image" of your organization and in its sources of financial support.

These uses of the symposium are best illustrated by the experience of the Manhattan School of Music, which was pressing an $8.5 million capital fund campaign and trying to establish itself as a national institution rather than a local one.

The event, held in November, 1973 presented a panel of prominent speakers including Supreme Court Justice Arthur Goldberg, former White House Arts Consultant August Heckscher, critic Kenneth Tynan, and Secretary of the Interior Stewart Udall. Held at the New York Hilton Hotel, it attracted a glittering audience of potential contributors. It also received widespread press coverage. Among its results were a perceptible improvement in the public image of the school, the recruiting of a top New York executive to head its business division in the fund drive, and new financial support. Although no fund solicitation took place at the symposium itself, a single contributor who until then had made only a $100 gift to the school stepped forward with a gift of $50,000.

One prerequisite for a good symposium is careful selection of the subject matter. The Manhattan School chose as its theme "The Quality of Life in This Technological Age." This permitted the school to relate its own private needs to those of society at large. In effect, the school was saying that by contributing to its cause the patron would be helping all of society.

Typically, a symposium will last one day and consist of morning and afternoon sessions and a wind-up dinner. The institution's case is usually presented at the dinner. Guests should be encouraged to participate in the event through panel discussions or question and answer periods.

Planning for a major symposium should begin six months to a year in advance. Since success depends heavily on the prominence of the speakers and their willingness to say something new or controversial, it is essential that great care be employed in their selection. Invitations should be tendered by prominent community leaders from four to five months in advance.

About three months ahead of time, a committee of prominent local figures should be enrolled as sponsors of the symposium. The Manhattan School listed 60 distinguished sponsors for its event. Their names should appear on all mailings and programs.

Approximately two months in advance, an informational mailing should be sent to a carefully selected list of potential donors announcing the event. Five weeks in advance, the R.S.V.P. invitations should be sent out. A good rule of thumb is to send out ten times as many invitations or announcements as the number of guests desired. No other public invitation should be made until results of this mailing are determined. It is best to fill the hall with preselected potential donors rather than with the general public. However, if returns indicate that not all available places will be filled, the general public may be invited through a public announcement a week or so in advance.

Whether or not guests are charged for meals or admission will depend upon the local situation. In a small city where the event can be scheduled at a time when it will face no competition for audience and where name speakers ordinarily "pull" well, it may be possible to recoup part of the cost of staging the event by charging admission or for meals. The Manhattan School charged for luncheon; dinner was free.

Total costs for a symposium may run from a few thousand dollars to as much as $50,000, depending on its scale. Chief cost items are honorariums for noted speakers (these may range from $250 to $1000), travel expenses for speakers, meals, printing, and mailings.

Smaller organizations can keep costs down to a bare minimum by using their own facilities and volunteers and, perhaps, by eliminating the dinner. Often, speakers who are convinced of the worthiness of the institution will waive the honorarium. Similarly, local businesses may be asked to contribute space, goods, or services.

It is important that the event be smoothly run. Thus, lighting and sound technicians should be paid to stand by, and the registration desk should be manned at all times. A press room should be provided, if possible. One person should be delegated to work with radio and television reporters if the event is to be broadcast. A telephone should be installed at the registration desk and in the press room. It is important that such details not merely be left up to the hotel or school at which the event is held. Volunteers should be available for last-minute assignments.

By working carefully, with adequate time, and by choosing the right speakers, the right mailing list, and the right theme, the sponsor can reap long-term benefits from the symposium. It can raise levels of support measurably and attract wide attention.

February 1964

Speakers Are Essential in Good Public Relations Program

Organizations lacking a pool of experienced speakers should seek to develop them from within the ranks of their volunteers. Very often, opportunities to address small but specialized segments of the public, who may be difficult to reach in any way other than through a direct talk, are wasted. Organizations without volunteers to address these smaller groups cannot continually ask their business board members or executives to assume these assignments. However, volunteers who profess not to be speakers can often be very effective in addressing smaller groups if their confidence is not destroyed at first attempt. The following points should be considered by the neophyte public speaker:

- Know your audience and know what it is interested in. Be sure to address yourself to those interests.
- It's better to cover one subject well than to ramble across a whole series of undeveloped subjects. Find your main theme and then develop it. If you have charts, slides, or other visual aids, use them.
- Address your audience in a natural conversational style. If you're writing your speech in advance, write it in the way you normally talk. Keep sentences short.
- Speak more slowly than you ordinarily do. A rate of about 120 words a minute is normal for speaking before an audience. Time yourself in advance to make sure that you don't exceed the pace.
- Know what you're talking about. Do some basic research on your organization first. Use facts and statistics. They aren't dull if they're presented in the right way.
- Enjoy the experience of speaking before people. If you do, the chances are that the audience will enjoy listening to you.

November 1963

Long-Distance Talk

If one of your speakers misses travel connections because of bad weather, he might try using the telephone. Director Alan Schneider did, when he was grounded in New York on the night he was scheduled to discuss the Ithaca Festival before a gathering of 100 people in a Rochester, New York home. Local sponsors of the event had the telephone company connect the phone lines to two speakers. Schneider then talked for about 40 minutes, explaining the festival and answering questions. The telephone call cost $72.

April 1966

Publicity on Speeches

Is an executive of your organization delivering an important speech before a key organization in your community? If so, by sending mimeographed copies of the speech to the press in advance, you may receive publicity on the speech immediately following its delivery. Be sure to include, along with the copy of the speech, pertinent background material as to its time and place. Also send biographical information on the speaker. Mark your material for release after the speech is given.

October 1963

Speakers Kit

Members of an arts organization's speakers bureau will perform more effectively if they are given printed materials from which to prepare their talks. The Studio Arena Theatre in Buffalo, New York has prepared an extensive speakers kit. Included are such materials as a schedule of events, subscription applications, theater party discount rates, an industrial sales plan, flyers, posters, and a ten-page outline of the organization's activities and its history.

March 1966

New Marketing and Promotional Programs Initiated

New pilot projects designed to develop effective marketing concepts and programs in the arts have been initiated at both national and regional levels. Models resulting from these efforts ultimately could benefit scores of cultural institutions.

In Madison, Wisconsin, a national arts marketing program has been recently launched by the Association of College, University and Community Arts Administrators and the University of Wisconsin's Center for Arts Administration. The ambitious two-year project, which hopes to develop a working text on marketing the arts complete with a wide range of models and sample materials, will be staffed by marketing specialists from the arts, business, and academia. The materials to be developed include publicity and advertising samples, audience and economic impact surveys, market evaluations, and model market plans for varied budgets and institutions. The project hopes ultimately to develop a wide variety of models in these and other areas from which arts groups can select prototypes adaptable to their local needs.

Currently, the study staff is doing a comprehensive review of available literature and existing resources. Within the next few months, a team of 30 experts—10 academicians, 10 arts practitioners, and 10 marketing professionals— will come together for several days to review the issues each sees as significant and plan further project activities.

In Denver, an extensive interdisciplinary marketing project with ramifications for groups elsewhere was initiated this fall by the Western States Arts Foundation with support from local business. During the initial two-part research phase, emphasis was on audience crossover between different art forms. A project survey revealed, for example, greater mixing within the visual arts and performing arts than between them and indicated that 8 percent of the audience was "superactive," with 20 or more attendances annually, and 12 percent "active," with 11 to 19 attendances. "Potentials," 26 percent attended 4 to 10 times and "inactives," 54 percent attended up to three times. In a second research phase, due to be completed by April, a more in-depth profile of "actives" and "potentials" will be compiled.

During the following action phase, a series of marketing workshops, based on research findings, will seek to help Denver's 165 arts groups identify and reach specific audiences. The foundation plans to work with arts groups in other cities interested in utilizing project findings and models.

As backup help to the new marketing efforts, a more professional approach to arts promotion seem to be developing. One resource proving increasingly helpful is the growing breed of nonprofit consulting firms in major cities throughout the country who have expanded their focus in recent years to include the arts. Public Interest Public Relations in New York, for example, has in the past two years helped such groups as the League of Resident Theatres; the Bronx Council on the Arts in development of "the Bronx is Up" promotional campaign; the NEA; and Acting by Children Productions. This past year, PIPR developed a year-long marketing and promotional program for the Alliance of New York State Arts Councils as a major part of a three-day state arts council technical assistance assignment. The firm, which like most nonprofit companies offers its services at low cost, has applied to New York's arts council to develop a comprehensive public relations program for state groups.

In Washington, D.C., the Support Center, which also has an office in San Francisco, is initiating a major new arts aid program this spring. Under a grant from the D.C. Arts Commission, the center is offering an Arts Management Resource program which will include free consulting services to area arts groups and a series of seminars and workshops. Other nonprofits providing promotional and management services to the arts include Artservices and HI Enterprises in New York, the Philadelphia Clearinghouse for Community Funding Resources —which provides free services to groups with budgets under $50,000—and the Minneapolis Communications Center.

One of the more interesting and comprehensive arts promotional programs has been developed by Multi-Arts Media Assistance in Buffalo, New York. Established in 1977 as a major component of a $300,000 one-year CETA project, MAMA operates as the nonprofit public relations and advertising agency of the local arts council, Arts Development Services. In addition to providing help to arts groups throughout Erie County, MAMA's 15-person public relations team developed the "Culture is Contagious-Catch Some" promotional campaign, which included creation of a series of animated cartoons as television spots. A major MAMA project is publication this spring of *A People's Guide to the Arts in Erie County*.

January-February 1978

How It Sounds

A catch phrase can be very helpful in promoting a program or imparting a new meaning to a familiar subject. At Wesley College in Dover, Delaware, a new series is titled, "Humanities—A Brand New Song and Dance," while in Phoenix the symphony is selling T-shirts reading "Stick it in Your Ear." In Arkansas the state legislature finally agreed to finance poetry classes in prison, but only after retitling them "Reading and Language Arts."

January-February 1978

A Good Title

A good title or slogan can focus attention on a cultural program. Arts efforts show such interesting phrasings as Affiliate Artist's business support slogan, "Join the Industrial Revelation." In Delaware, the state arts council has titled its brochure on traveling state arts resources "Shows to Go," while Nassau Community College has developed a popular lunch-time exhibit/lecture program, "Art on Rye." A Rochester New York group communicates its concern to the public through its name, Esthetic Give A Damn, known familiarly as EGAD.

January-February 1975

No Name

While a good name can help promote an organization or program, no name might be just as effective. At least that's the reasoning in Fort Wayne, Indiana, where a volunteer group, formed to help the Fine Arts Foundation promote programs and raise funds, calls itself "The No Name Group." The title has stuck because "the thrust of the group is so varied that we couldn't think of a fully descriptive name."

March-April 1977

The Light Touch

Issuing a calendar of events? Perhaps a light and humorous approach to this routine and practical kind of publication may increase its readability. The Greater
St. Louis Arts Council in its first monthly calendar of events, urged readers that
"a calendar is to tear," should they become fond of a particular feature in it. It
also made a key point in a light manner by requesting "tell us at the end of the
month whether the paper is tough enough to withstand vigorous daily wear."

November 1963

What's in a Name?

Issuing promotional material? Sometimes a name, a person, or some special element in your organization's program will lend itself to effective and imaginative
promotion. For example, the Paper Bag Players, a children's theater group in
New York, took advantage of its name by sending out their program announcements printed on small brown paper bags a little larger than a letter-size envelope. The low-cost mailing not only drew attention and reinforced the image
of informality that the group wanted to emphasize, but also helped underscore
the name of the organization in visual terms. Caution: make sure promotional
effforts are in character with the general tone of your organization.

March 1964

Arts Win Applause and Dollars
from Some Unexpected Sources

Arts organizations are discovering that funding and promotional help may be
available from totally unexpected sources, like "pop" disc jockeys and nonclas-
sical music stations. In Philadelphia, the Pennsylvania Ballet won new audiences
and received tremendous local publicity due to the promotional efforts of Tom
Brown, one of the city's most popular "deejays."

Brown, who played records for Philadelphia Metromedia station WIP until
July 1969 when he moved to station WPEN in the same city, first became interested in the dance company early in 1968 when it was preparing for its debut
week at the New York City Center. Along with the station, he promoted a tour
for two busloads of Philadelphians, including many who had never seen ballet
before, to see the company perform in New York. Later, Brown and the station
promoted a raffle, with the winners receiving free tickets to ballet performances
and a reception hosted by Brown at a leading local restaurant. This summer he
promoted excursions from center-city Philadelphia to ballet performances at a
suburban music festival. During this entire peiod, Brown publicized every ballet
performance on his radio show.

According to Eugene Palatsky, the dance company's publicist, Brown's efforts as the unofficial radio voice of the Pennsylvania Ballet won new subscribers, including some of the bus excursionists and raffle winners, and attracted great local attention. "A blast on the radio from Tom," he said, "and our phones promptly go roaring off the hook."

How does Brown feel about his help to the ballet company? While at WIP, he engineered the preparation of a flyer describing his activities which was sent nationally to all Metromedia stations and personnel. And although he's now at a different station, he has continued to promote the Pennsylvania Ballet. His real interest, however, can be summed up by the fact that several months ago he joined the dance company's board of directors.

Another prominent Philadelphia arts group, the Philadelphia Orchestra, was the indirect beneficiary of an unusual gift from an elderly spinster to the state of Arkansas. Miss Lily Peter of Marvell, Arkansas wanted to do something important for the state's territorial sesquicentennial celebration in June, 1969, so she commissioned Norman Dello Joio to compose a new work, "Homage to Haydn," and hired the Philadelphia Orchestra to perform it at two gala sesquicentennial concerts in Little Rock. Miss Peter mortgaged one of her two farms and paid the entire $53,000 program cost herself.

September-October 1969

The Light Touch Helps
Sell Cultural Programs

A light or humorous touch can help promote cultural programs, according to the experience of several arts groups. In Indianapolis, Indiana, for example, the symphony orchestra has used a series of 16 one-minute radio spots, irreverently titled "Symphony A-Go-Go," periodically since late 1965 with considerable success.

Written and produced for the Indianapolis Symphony by local radio station WATI, the spots feature dialogues between a husband and wife. Each begins with the same narration, "Now we take you to the living room for another traumatic episode of Symphony A-Go-Go." The background sounds of a football game on television are heard as the wife, Martha, attempts to convince her very reluctant husband, John, that he should attend a Sunday afternoon concert with her instead of watching football on television. As the dialogue ends, with John still a holdout, the voice of the television sportscaster is heard. A typical spot ends with the announcer saying, "Will the Packers lose? Will John go to the symphony concert? We think so, but tune in tomorrow for another exciting episode of Symphony A-Go-Go."

The Arena Stage in Washington, D.C. applied its light promotional touch to print media through a series of newspaper advertisements in the *Washington*

Post and the *Washington Star* aimed at selling subscriptions for the 1967-68 season. Each of the ads featured a production photograph with the words of the characters emanating from a balloon, comic-strip style. One ad, for example, showed an austere-looking man saying, "A season of plays to amuse me?" The copy below the picture read, "Yes, even you . . ." and then briefly described the coming season, including "three of the funniest plays in the theater."

Another ad in the series, showed a character about to be run through with a sword saying, "All right . . . all right . . . I'll subscribe." The copy below read, "If a thrifty Scotsman like Macbeth can see the value of subscribing to Arena Stage's 1967-68 season, need we say more . . . except to urge you to subscribe."

In direct mail promotion, the Something Else Press, a company of artists and writers devoted to publishing avant-garde materials, recently mailed a balloon along with its catalogue. When inflated it read, "Concrete poetry is something else."

November-December 1967

A Vote for Theater

Civic interest in Election Day triggered a tie-in promotion by the Southwark Theatre Company in Philadelphia. Season subscription forms, printed to resemble campaign fliers with an order "ballot" at the bottom, were sent to the organization's mailing list. The flier read in part: "Defeat inflation. . . . Subscription ticket guarantees 10 per cent savings. . . . Conservative ticket prices. . . . Liberal exchange policy." In addition, the theater sent a "campaign" truck around the city with a message on its side asking citizens to vote for the subscription ticket. The announcements noted that advertising was paid for by "The Philadelphia Citizens for Better Theater."

November-December 1966

Arts Wins Friends with New Promotions

In Seattle, Washington, where student "Whiz Kids" helped the Seattle Opera successfully woo young audiences several years ago, it is now gas pump operators who are selling the Seattle Opera-going idea to family groups. During August and September, all Union 76 service stations throughout western Washington have been promoting the October 2 performance of *Madame Butterfly* to their customers. Motorists pulling into the stations can't miss seeing large orange and blue posters proclaiming "Opera's a Gas!" and attendants wearing buttons reading "Join the Opera Union." Along with gas and oil, attendants dispense opera ticket order envelopes.

As part of the cooperative promotion, the Seattle Opera is supplying station operators with weekly humorous reminders for posting. These have included "Come to the opera and bring Ethyl" and "Opera moves your inner tube."

Throughout Pennsylvania this summer, liquor purchasers have been reading all about community arts festivals. Featured on the front and back of one of the state's best-scanned, if not best-read, publications, the State Store Price List, Number 107 of the Pennsylvania Liquor Control Board, are striking color photographs of Pennsylvania's arts festivals, "where the arts and the artists meet the people in a grass roots cultural explosion." Following 12 pages of price listings for whiskies, wines, and cordials, the inside back cover includes information on and listings of Pennsylvania arts festivals during 1970, plus an order blank for a 74-page report on state culture published by the Pennsylvania Council on the Arts.

Fall 1970

More Gore

A good promotion can always take a workable idea at least one step further. Several years ago, *AM* cited Theatre Calgary's successful attempt to heighten the impact of its *Dracula* production (see *AM*, No. 70) by having local nurses on duty in the theater during the run of the play. When the University of Delaware presented the same drama last season it used "Count Dracula" himself to stir audience interest. Not only was Dracula photographed in a hospital blood donor room, but a special promotional letter from the Count inviting readers to join the Blood Bank of Delaware won members for the bank and publicity for the production.

March-April 1973

Promotional Ploy

If an event has some unique aspect, you might find a promotional ploy a useful attention-getter. Recently, the Yale Symphony presented a fund-raising concert of Tchaikovsky works that, according to a release, was so Russian that "free vodka will be served at intermission."

March-April 1978

Your Schedule Makes Good Copy

Schedules of cultural events are eagerly sought by editors of the many weekly and monthly magazines distributed free in the hotels, restaurants, and taxicabs of many cities. These periodicals, addressed to travellers, tourists, and others, reach large numbers of readers who are looking for events to attend. Harried editors may not have time to seek out your schedule, but if it is delivered to them on time, they are likely to welcome the assistance and insert it in their "what's-on-around-town" columns. To get names and addresses of these publications, check a few hotels or major restaurants on your next trip downtown.

May 1962

Arts Kiosk

Looking to attract attention in your community? You might follow the example set by arts groups in Winnipeg, Manitoba. Five of Winnipeg's leading cultural organizations—the Royal Winnipeg Ballet, the Manitoba Theatre Centre, the Winnipeg Symphony Orchestra, the Winnipeg Art Gallery, and the Rainbow Stage—joined in sponsoring a 12-foot-high cylindrical structure that stands at the corner of Portage and Main Streets, one of the busiest intersections in the Canadian city. The kiosk, similar to those found throughout Paris, is decorated with colorful posters promoting the activities of all five groups. To heighten interest, the kiosk will be moved to a series of new locations throughout the year.

January-February 1969

The Telephone Directory

The covers of local telephone directories frequently feature pictures of places of interest in the community. Arts groups using one physical facility throughout their season thus have a unique publicity outlet which is seen throughout the year. Competition for this space may be keen, so get your request in to the community relations director of your local telephone company at least six months prior to the publication date.

May 1963

Press Clubs

Social affairs and entertainments held by press clubs in various cities provide an advantageous showcase for local performing arts groups. A performance at the press club is not only noted in the local papers, but also makes and cements friendships that can help in the future. Press clubs can be found in most big U.S. cities as well as in such smaller centers as Anchorage, Charleston, West Virginia, Fort Wayne; Las Vegas; and Madison, Wisconsin; and in the Canadian cities of Montreal, Ottawa, and Toronto.

July 1962

Scholarship Program

An arts organization can focus public attention on its efforts to raise artistic standards in the community by offering scholarships to outstanding young artists in its area. By establishing an endowment fund for scholarships, a group may often receive extra financial support to help it develop the program. The Winston-Salem Arts Council in North Carolina, for example, in the second year of its scholarship program gave three cash awards to students of music, dance, and art. It received local publicity as well as a number of individual contributions to the program.

October 1964

On Exhibition

If your organization's service activities are of community interest, you might consider an open exhibition to tell your story. The Chicago Symphony Orchestra presented a day-long "show and tell" in a ballroom exhibition area of Orchestra Hall to demonstrate its educational program. Demonstrations of the orchestra's preconcert training and in-school concert programs were presented along with an open rehearsal of the symphony chorus.

November-December 1975

Arts Group Wins New Audience
Through House Party Program

By sponsoring "house parties" where its representatives can meet the public face-to-face, an arts group can engender interest in its work while laying the foundation for such future activities as fund raising and ticket sales. Although house parties have been successfully used by many established cultural organizations, they also can be extremely helpful in launching a new organization or a new project.

In Ithaca, New York, the Ithaca Festival, preparing for its first season of repertory theater in 1965, mounted an extensive house party campaign to win support for the project.

Since the program started in January, volunteers recruited by the group have given over 100 parties in their homes for more than 2000 friends, and the guests they were asked to invite. Parties, attended by 25 to 30 persons, served the dual purpose of promoting the festival concept in the community in advance while conditioning guests for fund solicitations later mailed to them.

Two devices were employed to spark parties and vary programs. First, an amateur speakers bureau of local citizens was organized and trained by the festival. J. Wesley Zeigler, managing director of the group, told *AM*, "The use of volunteer speakers has been successful because party guests appreciate being approached by members of the community whom they know and to whom they can relate. The personal approach puts guests at ease, and volunteers are encouraged to answer questions from guests, but only on those aspects of the festival with which they are familiar."

Second, visual aids played an essential role in heightening party success. Until summer, slides of the festival site were shown at the parties. During the summer, parties were held on patios, and attracted large numbers of guests. To spur guest interest, a 40-minute film on the Shakespeare Festival in Stratford, Ontario, a small Canadian city the size of Ithaca, was shown. Departing guests were also given literature on the festival.

Success of the parties in Ithaca sparked an expansion of the program to neighboring cities. Since May, half the parties sponsored by the group have been held in nearby New York cities including Olean, Elmira, Watkins Glen, Geneva, and Cortland.

The parties also spurred publicity. Newspapers reported on them, and a local station televised a staged party. The television show attracted additional volunteers who offered to give parties for the festival.

October 1965

New Residents

One way to introduce new residents in the community to its cultural activity is to distribute free tickets through the Welcome Wagon organization, which is maintained by local merchants. In addition, lists of addresses of houses in newly built middle and upper-income subdivisions can be obtained from the builders or from the telephone company.

December 1962

Local Directory

Business associations that compile an annual local directory to promote the town or area usually want to list arts organizations because they are a community asset. Check to see that your group is included and its activities listed.

December 1962

Bookshelf Promotions

If the program to be promoted is multifaceted, if the information is of continuing rather than immediate benefit, and if your organization can afford the cost, you may find that hardcover "bookshelf" pieces, with pockets or openings for inserted materials, can be an effective way to promote your programs and keep them before your audience. The Smithsonian Institution promoted its International Salute to the States program with a bookshelf binder that holds three brochures, each in a different color. The Ontario Arts Council's Ontour Kit, a free arts directory for potential sponsors of touring programs, is an attractive multicolored folder, with an opening on top from which four different program brochures may be drawn.

Summer 1975

Eye-Catching Kits

Looking for an unusual way to capitalize on a successful season? The Seattle Opera Association in Washington sent out eye-catching kits about twice the size of those usually used. They contained a variety of materials on the organization including copies of press reviews, articles, brochures, and even a poster. When opened, the kits, with a cover photograph of the opera house, measured 26 inches wide. They were 16 inches long.

February 1966

Museum Highlights Major Show with Series of Related Events

Arts institutions planning a major event can dramatize its importance by building an entire program around it. The Art Gallery of Toronto, for example, highlighted its exhibition of the eighteenth-century Venetian landscape painter, Canaletto, with a full program that featured special guests, luncheons, a lecture series, and gallery talks. It altered its usual schedule of events to arrange most of its fall calendar around the exhibition, which was held from October 17 to November 15, 1964.

The comprehensive Canaletto showing, the first of its kind, contained more than 140 paintings, drawings, and etchings assembled from England, Germany, Switzerland, the United States, and Canada.

To focus public attention on the event, the Gallery arranged for Sir Philip Hendy, director of England's National Gallery, to appear at the museum and officially open the exhibition.

For this exhibition, the Gallery charged a special admission price of $1 for adults and 25¢ for children. However, regular members were given special free tickets to admit them and their guests. It was hoped that such an offering would help to attract new members. To accommodate the extra visitors expected, the gallery remained open on weekdays until 10:00 P.M., except on Wednesdays when it stayed open until 10:30 P.M. The usual closing time is 5:30 P.M.

An unusual promotion used to highlight the exhibition was a series of special luncheons organized by volunteers and featuring Venetian dishes. The museum area surrounding the dining room featured displays of art books on Canaletto. An admission price of $1.50 was charged for the luncheons.

To lend greater significance to the exhibition, a series of three monthly lectures was scheduled. An international group of speakers was selected to present the talks, whose scope was wider than the exhibit, but nevertheless related to it. Admission to the lectures was 50¢.

Gallery tours of the exhibit were presented by a member of the institution's staff four times each weekday during the period of the show and twice on

Saturdays. In addition, a different Canaletto painting was analyzed at the museum each Wednesday evening by an expert.

November 1964

Milestone

Passing an important milestone in attendance can be turned to publicity advantage by an arts organization. The Walters Art Gallery in Baltimore called public attention to the fact that sometime between 2:00 and 3:00 P.M. on December 6, 1963, the 100,000th visitor of the year entered the gallery. The Walters announcement noted that 1963 was the first year in which attendance had reached six figures, and pointed to its exhibition of King Tutankhamen Treasures as the big attraction of the year. Local publicity resulted from the announcement.

December 1963

Happy Anniversary

Anniversaries can mean extra publicity for cultural organizations, particularly if they are marked by some special event that calls attention to them. For example, the Brooklyn Children's Museum in New York highlighted the celebration of its sixty-fifth anniversary with a program of special events, including a sale of dolls and toys from all over the world and two special shows.

March 1965

Theater Offers Patrons
Discounts on Local Movie Tickets

Cooperative programs with local art film houses offer cultural organizations an excellent promotional device.

In Oklahoma City, Oklahoma, a legitimate theater has worked out a cooperate promotion with a motion picture house specializing in foreign films. The program provides an extra service for theater patrons and helps to increase the size of the audience at the movie. The Mummers Theatre offers its ticketholders a 25¢ credit, good anytime, for films being shown at the Trend Theatre. The discount is made available upon presentation of a Mummers ticket stub at the movie box office. The response to the offer has been excellent.

According to David Lunney, a Ford Foundation administrative intern at the professional repertory theater, the promotion is tied in with an inexpensive advertising campaign conducted by the theater at the movie house. The Mummers runs a three-phase trailer between films. The first phase is a theater announcement. Next is a clip on the current Mummers production, and third is an announcement of the ticket stub credit plan. Each clip costs $7.50, with the

Mummers paying for the first two and the art film house paying for the third.

February 1964

Fashion and Film
Help Promote Art Exhibit

Cultural events with a specific theme can often provide the basis for unique publicity tie-ins with businesses and other organizations if public relations directors
are alert to the many possibilities.

An exhibition of the works of Vincent Van Gogh at the Nelson Gallery of
Art in Kansas City, Missouri resulted in several unusual and important joint promotions. A local movie theater, the Rockhill, reissued the film *Lust For Life*, a
fictionalized biography of Van Gogh, in conjunction with the opening of the
museum's exhibition. Advertisements and publicity for the movie in local newspapers called attention to the exhibition.

A major department store in Kansas City, Harzfeld's, used the occasion to
introduce a new high-fashion color to its customers. Women's dresses, coats,
shoes, handbags, and hats in a yellow often found in Van Gogh's works were featured in half-page color newspaper ads which also prominently showed a Van
Gogh farm scene in yellow.

An editorial in the local daily newspaper, the *Kansas City Star,* also stirred
additional interest in the exhibition. Accompanied by a Van Gogh drawing, the
editorial discussed Van Gogh and his work and urged readers to attend the exhibition.

April 1963

Place Mats Tell Diners What's
Cooking—Until Dinner is Served

An unusual way to publicize your arts group is to print your message on place
mats used in restaurants. Many restaurants and lunch places use paper place mats
printed with descriptive messages on a variety of topics. If you can prepare an
interesting mat promoting your organization, you may find new patrons for
your exhibitions or performances.

Arrangements for printing place mats and the exact cost can be checked
with local printers. It is essential, of course, to discuss the place mat promotion
with one or more restaurants first. The operators who agree to use your printed
mats with your message may be able to tell you what kind of message is most appropriate for their patrons.

December 1962

High Visibility

How visible is your organization in the community? The Indianapolis Symphony
is seen all over town now with its new Express Wagon, a 28-foot vehicle that car-

ries instruments, music, stands, and other items for the group's 170 away performances. Special orchestra graphics appear on all sides of the wagon. Purchased with the aid of two donations, the trailer, when viewed from the rear, reads, "Indianapolis Symphony Orchestra—'On the Go'—" and in smaller letters, "Courtesy of the Penrod Society and American Fletcher National Bank."

March-April 1976

On the Road

Automobiles are good vehicles—for arts promotion. Among the bumper stickers to turn up recently was one used by the State University of New York at Stony Brook reading "I Brake for Actors, Summer '76 Playhouse, July 6-Aug. 14 Stony Brook." In North Carolina, John Soldano, head of the Goldsboro Arts Council, came up with decorative license plates for use by arts agencies showing silhouetted ballet dancers and a legend reading "North Carolina, State of the Arts, 1776-1976." Soldano's check with authorities indicated no restrictions on use of the plates as long as the official license was visible.

November-December 1976

Bumper Crop

Tailgaters might become audience members if they bother to read some of the bumper stickers on the cars in front of them. Among the arts stickers noticed recently were "I Believe in Music by the Saint Louis Symphony" and "North Carolina is Art Country." The latter was produced and distributed by North Carolina's arts council with help from Wachovia Bank.

January-February 1978

Art Exhibit

Interest in a performing arts organization can be attracted by an exhibit of graphic or plastic art works executed by members, subscribers, and contributors. Such an art exhibit mounted in the lobby of a concert hall or theater will make news in the local press. The Boston Symphony Orchestra presents an annual exhibition of paintings by subscribers to the Boston and Cambridge concerts.

February 1963

Prepare Summer Promotions

Cultural organizations, planning for their summer programs, should give careful attention to their printed promotional materials. Descriptive brochures can be highly effective if they contain specific information of a service nature for the potential audience.

In Ashland, Oregon, the Oregon Shakespearean Festival sends out brochures that, in addition to program and ticket information and background on the festival, contain special sections on dining, travel, area sightseeing, and lodgings. Each of the service sections, although tersely written, contains specific information that will be helpful to festival visitors.

The lodgings section, for example, lists twenty motels in the surrounding area by name and includes information on their precise location and the facilities they offer. In addition, the brochure points out that transportation from each of the listed motels to the festival is available nightly on special "Bard's Evergreen Busses" which run on frequent schedule directly to the theater.

Another promotional device, particularly well suited to the institution or festival that has a steady stream of visitors and that can be captured visually in an attractive photograph, is the picture postcard. Inexpensive to print, cards can nevertheless be an effective means of calling attention to an organization. Arena Stage in Washington, D.C., for example, has published its own black-and-white photographic postcard, which theater patrons may pick up free from display racks in the lobby. The attractive exterior view gives a striking impression of the modern theater building designed by Harry Weese, distinguished Chicago architect. The sign "Arena Stage" above the glass doorway can be clearly read.

Although no one knows how many of the cards have actually been mailed, Arena Stage told *AM* that 15,000 of the cards were taken from the racks in the first four months of the 1964-64 season. An average of about 100 cards per performance are taken by playgoers. The theater seats 775.

The previous season, when the postcards were left in unattended racks with a sign stating they were on sale for 5¢ each, only 5000 were taken in more than six months. *AM* was told that money for only about half the missing cards was deposited in the slotted coin boxes. The theater concluded that the cards did more good as giveaways in promoting Arena Stage than on a paid basis, since it was not economical to have an attendant collect nickels. Before special performances for high school groups, the cards are withdrawn from the racks.

Cost of the postcards is less than 1¢ each. Arena Stage found that local printers could underbid large houses doing a national business; it paid $7.50 per 1000 in an order of 100,000 cards. The theater had considered a color postcard, but found the cost prohibitive.

"Although we can't measure the result exactly, we think the picture postcards have been a good investment for publicity," an Arena Stage spokesman told *AM*.

March 1964

Put the Arts on the
Map for Summer Vacationers

When summer approaches, millions of families begin planning vacation trips and deciding where they will go and what they will do while there. One way to attract such tourists is by making certain that the arts enterprise is properly listed in tourist guide books and on oil company maps. This publicity is completely free.

The leading guidebooks for North America are those of the American Automobile Association, which publishes thirteen regional tour books annually.

To be listed in an AAA tour book, an organization should first notify the local or regional auto club affiliated with AAA. Consult the tour book entry for your city to observe the facts included and the space limits into which your item should fit. The local auto club reviews the proposed entry and then forwards it to the AAA national office in Washington.

As a backstop, send the information directly to the National Touring Bureau, AAA in Washington, D.C. A field representative may call on the institution to see if it meets AAA tour book standards. The primary concern is that it be of genuine interest to the touring public and that it be fairly represented. The tour books distinguish items of special worth with a star (*).

One can also write to the national editor asking to be included in the AAA Calendar of Events. This is an internal bulletin used by affiliated club travel counselors, who advise their own members on attractions in other regions and guide out-of-town visitors on what to see locally.

The way to put an organization on the maps published by oil companies and distributed free to millions of motorists at service stations is to insure that the local chamber of commerce knows all about it. Do not write to the oil companies.

Most maps are published by three large mapmakers: General Drafting Company, Convent Station, New Jersey; Rand McNally, Chicago, Illinois; and H. M. Gousha, San Jose, California.

The editorial departments of these mapmakers collect their data from local chambers and from national and regional organizations of various kinds. They prefer not to be solicited for listing by individual organizations unless the listing would be quite new or changed, or if notifying the chamber has brought no result.

March 1962

Promotion in Airports

Travelers in and out of airline terminals often have time between planes. Many enjoy spending some of this time looking at rotating collections from local museums or at photographic displays featuring local performing arts groups. The displays promote the institutions to local residents and to travelers and help to encourage attendance.

September 1963

State Listings

Many state Departments of Commerce issue calendars of events designed to lure tourists to the state. Since material from cultural organizations may be used in these publications, it is suggested that you write or check the Director of the Travel Bureau of the Commerce Department in the state capital

June 1963

Tourist Attraction

Passing motorists can be motivated to visit cultural institutions through a system of directional signs posted along major thoroughfares in an organization's area. In Winston-Salem, North Carolina, the Gallery of Fine Arts and Old Salem cooperated with a number of other institutions in posting a "view-way," a series of signs that directs tourists to the major attractions of the community.

November 1964

Tourist Displays

Visual displays at tourist attractions can be useful in promoting the programs of arts groups. For example, in New York, 20 of the city's museums, religious, and educational institutions were represented in a display case on the second floor of the Empire State Building. The display caught the eyes of the many visitors who passed through the building each day.

July-August 1965

Theater and Manufacturer Join in Unique Promotional Venture

A theater producer joined with a candy manufacturer in a unique promotion which won wide publicity for a drama playing Off-Broadway in New York.

Nimara Productions, aware that *Do You Know The Milky Way?* incorporated the name of a well-known candy bar, wrote to Mars, Inc., manufacturer of Milky Way candy. An agreement was concluded under which the confectionery firm displayed 10,000 cards paid for and printed by Nimara Productions, advertising its production on candy counters throughout New York in time for the March 14 opening of the play. In return, the theater's management gave free tickets to its production with the presentation at their box office of a Milky Way wrapper and the purchase of one ticket at regular prices ($3.50 top week days; $4.50 top weekends)—in effect, a "two-for-one" sale of tickets to bearers of the wrapper.

Mars, Inc., which publicized the promotion in its trade press, also set up a display in M. H. Lamston, Inc., a large five-and-ten-cent store. Similar displays were planned by Mars in cigar stores in the downtown area.

Although only 55 wrappers were presented at the box office, the publicity director of the show believes that the free publicity the play received was well worth the $210 spent for printing the signs.

May 1963

Arts Homecoming

When old grads think of homecomings, it usually means one thing—football. At Rice University in Houston, Texas, however, the theme for the 1972 homecoming was "The Arts at Rice." The program included a concert, play, film shows, and art exhibitions. While the idea is worth adopting at other colleges, perhaps community cultural groups as well might be able to convince former residents and supporters to return for an arts homecoming.

September-October 1972

Reverse Psychology

A promotional idea in Seattle, Washington attracted citywide attention. The Seattle Opera Company, which distributed "Bravo Opera" bumper stickers some years ago came up with backwards opera posters. The black and white 17- by 22-inch posters bore the twin messages, "Opera is Alive and Well in Seattle" and "Opera Lives," but the type was reversed. Viewers had to look carefully to read the message—which probably helped them to remember it.

Spring-Summer 1969

Alumni Promotion

College alumni groups may be good audiences for your programs. The Columbia University Alumni Executive Committee of Atlanta and the Members Guild of the High Museum of Art cosponsored the second annual "Columbia in Atlanta" program, with an arts theme, "The Arts in the Age of Anger." The University of Wisconsin Alumni Club in New York sponsored an "Evening at the Metropolitan Museum of Art," for $1 per family, featuring a private gallery tour.

Fall 1970

Common Market

A regular voice or common gathering place for all the arts can help the entire cultural community. In Providence, Rhode Island, 15 groups joined forces to open a new performing arts information service in the lobby of the Trinity Square Repertory Company. Operated by volunteers provided by each of the cooperating groups with the help of one full-time coordinator, the service was open daily from 10:00 A.M. to 9:00 P.M. to provide information on the functions and performances of each of the groups.   *January-February 1977*

Seeing the Light

The small fliers that frequently accompany the monthly electricity bills mailed by public utility companies can be significant publicity outlets for cultural organizations. These pocket publications, which reach virtually every home in a given area, regularly feature public service information. A recent flier from the Public Service Company of New Hampshire, for example, was devoted to summer theaters in the state, while Con Edison in New York promoted Lincoln Center Festival '67.

September-October 1967

Local Libraries

Your local library can help stimulate interest in your programs. In Washington, D.C., the Arena Stage published a small flier in the shape of a bookmark which listed the seven productions in its season. On the reverse side it printed a list of "Suggested Background Reading on Sixteenth Arena Stage Season by the D.C. Public Library." Included in the list were ten books written about the plays' authors or subject matter.

November 1965

Looking Out for the Arts

Temporarily vacant storefronts can be put to good promotional use by arts groups. In Durham, North Carolina, the Downtown Revitalization Foundation tells the Durham Arts Council when a local store is vacated and then, after requesting permission from the owner the council takes over. For several months, the council has been using a "window on the arts"—two windows in a vacated downtown store—to promote festivals, school arts programs, exhibitions, and other events.

Summer 1976

The Looking Glass

Does your group have a window area at the entrance to its office? If so, you might use it to let passersby know what you're doing. The Cleveland Area Arts Council's "Artswindow" has become an attraction with slide shows of artists and community cultural activities. The program changes weekly.

January-February 1976

Joint Presentation

A cooperative program presented by several arts groups can attract great attention and thus increase audience potential. In Baltimore, Maryland, for example, audiences were drawn to each of three institutions which joined in presenting *Two Thousand Years of Calligraphy*. The show was divided into three chronological parts, and the Walters Art Gallery, the Baltimore Museum of Art, and the Peabody Institute Library each presented a separate part simultaneously.

September 1965

Visual Performances

Performing groups interested in reaching children might use the visual arts as some symphony orchestras do. Both the Cleveland and Indianapolis orchestras sponsor contests in which children submit original drawings inspired either by attendance at concerts or listening to orchestra tapes. In Indianapolis, the Museum of Art showed the best 100 pictures in a special exhibition, and in Cleveland the 50 winning entries were displayed in Severance Hall. The Chicago Symphony publishes a calendar featuring drawings, one for each month, executed by children who've attended orchestra concerts and sells them at $4.50 each.

March-April 1977

Foreign Flavor

Planning an arts evening with a foreign theme? You might try a technique used successfully by the Boston Swiss Club to sponsor its Swiss music festival. Several weeks prior to the event, everyone on the organization's mailing list received an artistic postcard directly from Switzerland reminding him of the event. Because of the promotional value, foreign tourist services and overseas airlines may be helpful in supplying your group with free postcards or handling the mailing. For added flavor, interesting foreign postage stamps, with arts motifs, can be used on the postcards.

June-July 1966

Foreign Festivals

Arts organizations sponsoring festivals with a foreign theme can create additional interest in the events by working with officials of the countries represented. In some instances, foreign officials—eager to promote their country's arts—may be helpful in obtaining materials for the occasion. Often dignitaries of the country may enhance the event by attending its opening. The Roberson Memorial Center, an arts council in Binghamton, New York, held a Danish Festival of the Arts featuring a touring art exhibition sponsored by the Ambassador of Denmark. The festival preview was attended by the consul general of Denmark.

July-August 1965

Pennies from Heaven

Tie-ins with newsmakers, such as a penny shortage, can promote your program.

In cooperation with Bankers Trust, New York's Town Hall placed a wishing well in its lobby with a sign on it reading "Toss Your Pennies to Town Hall. Banker's Trust will toss us 10% more. All pennies, nickles, dimes and quarters will help to support Town Hall programs." Although the amount raised wasn't substantial—several hundred dollars in the first month or two—the promotional value was significant.

Summer 1975

Poster Promo

With the growing popularity of posters, arts groups might consider using them not only to promote single events, but as calendars or information resources that can describe continuing programs in detail. The Theatre Development Fund in New York, for example, lists the more than 120 theaters participating in its voucher program on a single poster. The Western States Arts Foundation published a large and attractive poster which not only listed its entire 1974-75 dance touring program, but included information and an application form at the bottom which could be cut off by prospective sponsors without marring the poster. The foundation also sponsors a dance poster series which commissions designs by regional artists.

November-December 1974

Meter Made

Postage meter advertising may be old hat to many cultural groups, but it can be old hat to your audience as well if your message is a tired and unchanging one. New messages that relate to current campaigns, performances, or special events can provide groups with additional and inexpensive publicity. Included among the meter ads seen by *AM* are "Don't Just Applaud—Send Money" from Milwaukee's United Arts Performing Fund; "Music Can Be Seen" from the Minnesota Orchestra; and a college theme, "Wherever You Want to Go, You Can Get There from the University of Akron."

January-February 1974

Stamp It Out

New U.S. postage stamps that have art themes can, with cooperation from your local post office, be promotionally useful. For example, when the New York Cultural Center initiated a George Gershwin Film Festival, a postal worker was on hand for the evening opening to sell and cancel Gershwin stamps, which were affixed to souvenir programs.

November-December 1973

Promoting to Business

One cultural organization struck a unique blow for widespread recognition with a promotion aimed at businessmen, sports fans, and other nonarts audiences. Thanks to a contribution from one of its board members, Young Concert Artists, Inc., a nonprofit organization that helps talented youngsters launch their musical careers, placed full-page advertisements in regional editions of eight leading magazines during March and April, 1972. The ads, which featured a picture of 11 young artists beneath the heading "Let them be heard . . . Before they've been heard of," appeared in such publications as *Fortune, Time, Sports Illustrated,* and *Newsweek.* According to director Susan Wadsworth, the response varied from the receipt of contributions to requests for information on booking artists.

March-April 1972

Outdoor Artists

Your local outdoor advertising company may give you the use of a white billboard on request. Get a group of volunteers to paint a message on it, with some first-rate artwork if possible. Not only will the billboard publicize your activities, but the work of the volunteers may make news as well.

March 1963

Publicity in Matchbooks

Local companies who advertise on match covers may be a source of free publicity. Often there is additional space in a matchbook for a message about a cultural organization. A Swiss cigarette manufacturer, Rio, includes a picture and message about the Museum of Natural History in Berne in its matchbooks.

April 1963

RADIO AND TELEVISION

How to Arrange Guest
Interviews on Radio

Radio interviews offer excellent publicity potential for cultural organizations. However, before suggesting a possible guest, it is important to understand the specific needs of the program you are approaching.

To find out which progams use guests and which staff people affiliated with these programs book guests, check with the program director or station manager of your local station. Then listen to two or three broadcasts of the programs to determine their guest requirements and orientation.

What special factors must then be considered? It is important to know what kind of audience the program appeals to. Generally, daytime programs attract housewives and evening programs appeal to the entire family. Within this framework, programs may appeal to narrower audiences, such as the intellectual woman or the businessman. Which audience does your organization want to reach? Who is the person within your organization best equipped to speak to this audience?

Next, how long are the interviews? Some programs interview two or three guests within a 15-minute period, while others feature extended interviews with one guest lasting half an hour or more. The guest you suggest must be able to tell his story within the allotted time.

Before approaching an interview program, it is wise to ask a whole series of questions. For example, is the program consistent with the dignity and image of your organization? A symphony orchestra might not want one of its members interviewed on a disc jockey program that features rock 'n 'roll music. How frequent are the commercial messages? Are they used in the middle of an interview?

Who is the host and how large a role does he play in each interview? Some hosts dominate interviews and barely allow guests to develop their thoughts.

What is the program's format? Are interviews only a small part of the program? Do listeners phone in questions?

Lastly, is the program live or taped? Taped programs are often edited and important remarks can be erased. Some guests, however, give a better interview when they know the program is being taped and erasures can be made.

After analyzing a program and determining who your best guest possibility is for that program, write to the specific person who books guests for the broadcast. Relate the contributions your guest can make to the program's needs. Be explicit in listing the topics the guest is prepared to discuss and include biographical information about the guest. If you do not receive a reply within a week, follow up with a phone call.

Once an interview is scheduled, make sure that your guest speaker is familiar with the program and is completely up-to-date on the activities of your organization. Ask him to listen to the program first and brief him on the length of his interview and on the topic to be discussed on the program. If you have written a letter about him to the program, be sure that he reads a copy of that letter before going to the interview so that he will know precisely what the interviewer knows about him and what he expects him to talk about.

October 1963

Orchestra Boosts Image
with Marketable Maestro

A renowned conductor not only gave an established symphony orchestra an artistic "shot in the arm," but also gave it a marketing and promotion vehicle —himself—which helped increase ticket sales, up donations, and open doors to a recording contract, foreign tour, and television series.

When the appointment of Antal Dorati as music director of the Detroit Symphony was announced late in 1976, nearly a year before he was to assume the post, it triggered off great excitement locally. Dorati, a famed conductor who has worked with some of the world's most acclaimed orchestras and was noted for his ability to turn situations around, was a key element in an overall upgrading program developed by the board.

The orchestra's publicity staff was quick to recognize that the Dorati name and the artistic program he was planning—including a season-opening Beethoven festival, the orchestra's return after several decades to the recording field, and a European tour—were all marketable developments. Thus, every piece of news concerning Dorati was carefully merchandised, with press releases increasing by about 300 percent. The 1977 fund drive drew upon the Dorati name and the excitement that he would be bringing to Detroit. Dorati sparked further publicity when he came to Detroit to meet with fund drive and season ticket committee members in the spring.

With Dorati's arrival for his first season, the campaign went into high gear and Dorati himself was a willing participant. "He has the energy of a young man," a staff member said of the 72-year-old Dorati, "and when he came here his energy really spread."

Dorati's debut in the two-week Beethoven festival was a critical success, and the staff was quick to build on it. The city was blanketed with giant billboards featuring a picture of the conductor and the words "Dorati/Detroit Symphony." A line of smaller type at the bottom read "Ford Auditorium—961-0700." Feature stories doubled and publicity efforts reached out for national publications. The local convention bureau was tapped to make symphony tickets available to visiting businessmen. Throughout the season Dorati was highly visible, sitting for interviews and kicking off such events as the corporate fund drive.

As publicity grew, the Dorati name became increasingly recognizable and even inspired commercial adaptations. One discount store specializing in stereo equipment aired a TV spot showing a conductor dressed as Dorati leading a group of stereo sets in concert.

The effects of Dorati's first season were visible in many ways and still continue into this season. Overall ticket sales increased greatly, especially single tickets which jumped from sales of $78,200 in 1976-77 to $273,900 in 1977-78.

Both the amount of money raised and the number of donors also increased, with individual donors nearly doubling to over 5,000 and corporate donors growing by 25 percent.

In March 1978, due in large part to the Dorati name, the orchestra signed a contract with London Records and in April recorded three albums. Thanks to a $325,000 grant from the Ford Motor Company, a nine-program series on the Beethoven festival events was filmed for PBS, and its airing will mark the orchestra's first participation in a national television series. The telecasts include all nine Beethoven Symphonies plus actor E. G. Marshall's informal chats with Dorati in landmark locations throughout Detroit. As a capstone to the excitement, the orchestra announced another major first, a 25-concert European tour in the fall of 1979. As one staff member summarized Dorati's influence for AM, "Ninety percent of what happened was due to Dorati. He was the touchstone from which everything else developed."

September - October 1978

Radio Alert

Is your organization receiving national attention? If so, be sure to let your members, volunteers, and supporters know about it. To promote an ABC television documentary about its program, the Puerto Rican Traveling Theater sent large picture postcards to its entire mailing list. Featured on the back was a photograph showing a scene from a company production with a large headline next to it proclaiming "The Puerto Rican Traveling Theater Goes National!"

March-April 1975

It's Punderful

Running an arts organization may be a serious business, but that doesn't preclude the use of humor or even outrageous puns in promotional material. Channel 13, the educational television station in New York, promoted its August airing of "Albert Herring" by the Opera Theater of St. Louis with the advance on-air plug, "Just wait until our 'Herring' gets pickled." Atlanta's High Museum publicized a recent benefit as a "Monday Night High," and Artpark in New York State termed its season ticket for lawn seating "Grasspass."

Summer 1978

Publicize Radio Appearances

Many hosts of radio and television programs regularly send out preprinted postcards on which they fill in the names of their guests. If a member of your organization is to appear on a program where the host follows this practice, obtain enough cards from him in time to do a thorough mailing. The host will cooperate because he wishes to reach as wide a listening audience as possible.

July-August 1964

Personal Approach to Station
Results in Broadcast Publicity

Many cultural groups plan publicity campaigns with undo emphasis on newspapers, leaving other communications outlets, such as radio and television, stepchildren of their efforts. However, an energetic approach to broadcast media publicity, such as employed by the Seattle Opera Association in Seattle, Washington, can result in interviews, spot announcements, and special features.

Recognizing the importance of maintaining a well-rounded publicity program, the association has established a special four-member woman's volunteer committee devoted exclusively to radio and television publicity. The volunteers work under Mrs. Erna Husak, the organization's publicity director.

The committee divides its labor so that three of its members each are responsible for covering one of the combined radio-television stations in the Seattle area. A fourth member covers ten other radio stations as well as the University of Washington's educational television facility.

By establishing individual relationships with broadcast officials, the volunteers "put the publicizing of the association on a person-to-person basis, and they get much better results than we could by mail and telephone alone," Mrs. Husak said.

After Mrs. Husak provides the stations with background material on the opera company, its productions, and its stars, the committee members visit station personnel to see if they are interested in an interview or feature. Members maintain virtual day-to-day personal contact with station personnel during each stage of a publicity effort, providing additional information for interviews, attending the interviews, and following them with thank-you notes to broadcasters and program directors.

This personal approach has resulted in widespread radio use of free spot announcements on the opera which committee members hand-deliver to the stations.

The publicity program has paid off with intense and varied coverage of opera productions. In the week before this season's opening, 13 interviews with company members were broadcast on radio and television. Television news announcements were aired frequently.

As a result of the committee's work, a 20-minute television program highlighted opening night at the opera. Later productions were also spotlighted with interviews and news announcements. The most recent production was sold out a month early.

Mrs. Husak told *AM*, "Members never push anything; they try to be available at all times. It's a soft sell and is growing more effective."

April 1965

Make Use of Free
Broadcasting Announcements

Much free time for spot announcements is available to arts groups for the asking these days. Such announcements call attention to programs and events as well as lay the groundwork for fund-raising campaigns. Health and welfare organizations have long made use of opportunities for using the airwaves.

An outstanding example of a successful spot-announcement campaign is that of the Jewish Chronic Disease Hospital in New York carried out by its public relations counsel, Edward N. Mintz. Spots varying in length from ten to sixty seconds were sent to East Coast stations in a drive to honor the hospital during September 1961.

One hundred and forty-five stations in seven states used more than 12,000 announcements in the month, and some stations are still broadcasting them. Although the hospital is local, it was able to extend its message outside New York because the work it is doing has national significance. At a conservative estimate, the cost of these free spots, if purchased, would have amounted to $120,000.

The first step in seeking free radio or TV time is to consider the audience to be reached and the message appropriate to it. Decisions on these points will also determine whether to aim at local stations only, or to include others, too.

The next step is to get up a list of the stations selected and the names of their directors. Directories with such listings are available at most libraries.

Then prepare copy for the spots. They may take the form of short scripts to be read, recordings to be played, or pictures or visual cards for display on television. As a rule, spots are in 10-, 15-, 20-, 30-, 45-, and 60-second lengths, with the minute and half-minute lengths used most often.

In wording copy, be terse and crystal clear. Read the message and time the reading to make it fit the appropriate length. It is a good rule to make up at least six different messages for each time length so that a station preferring a single length can deliver your message many times without deadly repetition.

After this they are ready to be mimeographed. Each spot should be marked "public service announcement" and should include the name, address, and phone number of someone the station may call for additional information. Then clip, do not staple, all the spots of the same length together, each marked as to time, and send them in a flat envelope to the station. (To help check on results, include a self-addressed return postcard on which the station director can indicate the number of spots he has used.)

If you are dealing with one or a few local stations, phone or meet the station managers or directors personally, if possible. This will help assure their cooperation.

Some stations prefer recorded announcements to scripts. These should be 33-1/3 rpm discs, not tape, although to make a disc it may be necessary to first make a tape, since it can be edited. A 10-inch record can carry two 20-second spots, one 30-, one 40-, and one 60-second message with adequate spacing between each of them.

The record label should be marked with the name of the organization, the person reading the message, and the length of each spot so that station engineers can tell at a glance what each record includes. (Incidentally, if the institution can get a celebrity to deliver the message, it will increase both its acceptability and its impact.)

The "telop," an inexpensive means of putting a message on TV, may also be useful. This is a picture—usually 3- by 4-inches—made on matte paper so it will not reflect light. The cost of making a telop varies according to the photographer's fee. A telop may contain a written message—in effect, a sign—or it may show a picture of some activity at the institution to be shown while an accompanying announcement is read.

Nonprofit cultural institutions, even those that charge admission, can reach vast potential audiences by getting on the airwaves free.

March 1962

A Date with the Arts

Calendars can be potent promotion and funding tools because of their year-long use, especially if they're well-designed and informative. In Fort Wayne, the Fine Arts Foundation prepared and distributed a "Giving Calendar" for the 1978-79 season based on the theme of the city's arts heritage. The handsome calendar not only has 8½- by 11-inch full-page listings for each month from September through next August, with upcoming arts events printed in small type on the appropriate dates, but devotes each month's facing page to a different arts group and includes a montage of photos and clippings of historic events associated with the group. The Fort Wayne Philharmonic page, for example, describes the orchestra and its history and includes a 1945 news clipping about it, a 1946 ad, and a current photo. The calendar also includes the Arts Foundation's annual report, messages from its leaders, a list of top contributors, brief bios of local arts leaders, and a pull-out contribution envelope.

September-October 1978

Hot Items

By tieing in with a current fad or major event, arts groups can help to promote their programs. For the 1978 Mostly Mozart Festival, Lincoln Center added emblazoned Mostly Mozart jogging shorts, at $7 a pair, to the T-shirts, mugs, and other items on sale at the festival gift shop. A street poster promoting the new item told audiences that "Mostly Mozart is off and running." The Seattle Opera linked its Festival of the Ring, presented both in English and German, with the record-setting King Tutankhamun exhibit at the Seattle Center. A flier including sketches symbolizing both cultural events proclaimed, "Only in Seattle, the Ring and the King." A $20-per-person reception following the English version of *Das Rheingold* included a backstage tour, meeting with the cast, a drink and canapes, and a tour of the Tut exhibit.

Summer 1978

Guest Artist Publicity

When arranging for a visiting artist to speak before a group or to appear on radio or television, plan to have the public relations officer of your organization accompany the artist. This serves as insurance in case last-minute emergencies throw the plan off schedule. In a pinch, the public relations staff person may even have to fill in for a guest who fails to show up at the appointed time or place. The staff person should be adequately briefed to take this possibility into account.

March 1964

Video Series Boosts Local Cultural Groups

An imaginative television series conceived by a Washington, D.C. station helped sell season tickets and gave a major promotional boost to three of the city's leading performing arts groups immediately prior to the start of their seasons.

On four successive nights early in September 1966, Washington's station WTOP-TV preempted one to two hours of network programming in prime time to present its "Pageant of Performing Arts." The first program on Tuesday, September 6, featured the National Ballet in performances of *Swan Lake* and *Con Amore*, which were videotaped by the station earlier in the year. This was followed on the next two evenings by videotaped performances of the National Symphony and the Opera Society of Washington. The final program in the series was a concert by guitarist Charlie Byrd. During program intermissions, host Roy Meachum interviewed representatives of the arts organizations and discussed their forthcoming seasons.

The series was conceived by the station earlier in the year as a means of providing excellent programming for its viewers while at the same time motivating them to purchase tickets to regular performances by the groups. In announcing the series, George F. Hartford, the station's general manager, said that the series would "dramatically point up the fact that these organizations, year in and year out, are available to Washingtonians throughout the season at their regular performances. I am certain that thousands of people who will see these televised productions have never attended a single performance of these groups."

Presented as a public service, the series cost the station a considerable a-mount of money. In addition to bearing all production costs, the station, by pre-empting network programming, lost income that it normally received from the network. WTOP also publicized the series, and included in its series of releases background on each of the participating organizations and information on their plans for the forthcoming season.

Although there was no direct solicitation for tickets on the programs, Robert M. Adams, the station's promotion director, told *AM* that the series acted as an important stimulus to the viewer. "The response was excellent," he said. "We received approximately 200 letters and 240 phone calls from viewers, following presentation of the series. Some were from people who had never be-fore seen the groups perform, but who now planned to attend programs. The National Symphony had eight or ten calls from viewers interested in obtaining season concert tickets. Some of our letters indicated that the writers had never been to an opera, but after seeing *The Magic Flute* they were planning to get sea-son tickets to the opera."

October 1966

Radio Station "Spots"
Promote Arts Funding

Large and small musical groups throughout the metropolitan New York area benefitted from a public service program that called attention to their growing financial ills. Throughout the month of April 1973, WQXR, the station of the *New York Times*, gave all the time normally allotted to public service announce-ments of every type to performing musical organizations to allow them to de-scribe their programs and ask for funds. In addition, the station took full page advertisements in five leading area publications in April—*the New York Times, Sports Illustrated, Time, Cue,* and *New York Magazine*—to highlight the needs of two of New York's leading musical organizations, the New York Philharmonic and the Metropolitan Opera.

The idea for the month-long fund drive for music originated with Walter Neiman, vice president of the good music station, after he had read a major story in the *New York Times* spotlighting the fiscal woes of the Philharmonic. "I was taken back when I heard about the Philharmonic," Neiman told *AM,* "and I thought the station might be able to do something. We do have a lot to gain from our identification with musical groups, and as something of an institution, WQXR should take the lead."

Once the idea crystallized, Mr. Neiman sent letters outlining the free time offer to some 50 to 60 musical groups known to the station. Other groups were reached through frequent on-air mention of the offer in March by program hosts and commentators and through a story in the *New York Times*. The guideline for spots was simple. Groups had to be non-profit, tax-exempt metropolitan area organizations specializing in music performances. Their messages were to be 60-second spots, about 125 words long, focusing on their background, service to the community, and current financial need. As the WQXR letters explained, "The messages may be informational only or may solicit contributions from the public, but the announcements may not be used to advertise specific box office attractions." The offer was limited to performing groups and did not include arts centers and similar institutions.

By mid-April some 50 different musical groups of every size had responded, with most of the requests coming from the smaller, less well-established groups. Recipients included such groups as the After Dinner Opera, Master Chorale, Oratorio Society, Pro Musica, the Little Orchestra, and the Wagner College Symphony. Each spot received was assigned a place in a rotation, with the messages being repeated once the turn came again. Although the station had a commercial commitment to many sponsors, it aired some 300 spots during April.

In Boston several months earlier, another broadcast station, WCVB-TV, helped the arts cause. Over an eight-day period in December, the station aired eight different editorial messages four times a day in support of the arts.

March-April 1973

Museum Seeks Audience
Through Radio Concerts

A museum seeking to interest music lovers in its art collection introduced a special "picture of the week" service which is broadcast during the intermissions of concerts it sponsors.

In Washington, D.C., the National Gallery of Art uses the intermissions during its Weekly Sunday night concert series to discuss a single great painting. To help listeners follow the discussions, the gallery offers them reproductions of each painting printed on 11- by 14-inch heavy paper, suitable for framing. Individual prints are sold for 25¢ each. A subscription, which provides listeners with one reproduction a week for the entire 22-week series running from October 4 through February 28, is $5.50. Each picture is accompanied by a short text and a checklist of all the pictures in the series. The service was described in detail to listeners during the intermission of the season's first concert.

According to John Walker, director of the gallery, a similar idea was a great success in Holland. He hopes that listeners' curiosity will be so stimulated by the discussions that they will visit the gallery to see the paintings they have heard described.

Tying in with the discussions is an added service offered by the gallery. During the week following each broadcast, two discussions a day are held at the museum in front of the painting desribed over the radio the previous Sunday.

October 1964

Broadcasts Help
Build Audiences for Arts

Radio or television programs created by arts groups can help build audiences and support yet cost little or nothing to produce. Such programs play an important role in the promotional campaigns of cultural organizations in Washington, D.C., Binghamton, New York, Greensboro, North Carolina, and Fort Wayne, Indiana, among others.

Groups queried by *AM* devote relatively few hours to the production of a series. The programs can be sponsored either commercially or supported by radio or television stations. In the latter instance, stations may welcome such programs since they attract listener interest while helping stations meet a federal requirement that a portion of air time be devoted to public service programming. And program formats can be simple, consisting of discussion or commentary on cultural themes.

In Washington, D.C., the Arena Stage, a theater group, used its 1964-65 season as a springboard for 13 weekly half-hour shows entitled "The Sounds of Theater," presented on Sundays on an AM and FM radio station. Programs featured music, biography, discussions, and dramatic presentations tied into the group's productions.

Each show cost about $105 to mount, and was paid for by a sponsor, the Savile Bookshop of Washington, which linked commercials to program content. Programs took about five to 12 hours each to produce, including preparation, recording, and editing time. Audience reaction was good.

A simple format marked a weekly hour-long television program reaching 750,000 persons produced by the Roberson Memorial Center in Binghamton, New York, an arts council. Air time was donated to the center by the station, and the series cost the group $200 to $300 annually to produce.

The center has produced radio and television shows since 1956, when it featured a five-minute daily cultural calendar, a format used by the Greensboro Arts Council in North Carolina.

Speaking of his television series, Keith Martin, director of the center, told *AM*, "It does not have to be scholarly or probe deeply, but it should be authentic and informal. Often you can improvise when on the air."

Another approach to radio programming was taken by the Fort Wayne Fine Arts Foundation, another arts council. Its program, "Adventures in the Arts," is heard on four different local AM radio stations each week. Air time is donated by the stations.

Programs include announcements of cultural activities in the city and recordings, with commentary. Nat Greenberg, business manager of the Fort Wayne
Philharmonic, conducts the series and is paid by funds from a local foundation.

June 1965

Air Time

If your group is seeking to broaden your exposure on radio and television,
you'll want to read a free booklet published by the Public Relations Department of the National Association of Broadcasters. *If You Want Air Time* is a
concise booklet listing publicity do's and don'ts and including sample
public service spot announcements and news releases.

Summer 1976

Cable Television May
Mean Income to Arts

Performing arts groups looking for new sources of income might cast their
eyes   at the growing cable television industry. Although local cable systems
throughout the country have incorporated cultural presentations in their programming from time to time, the arts involvement has been low-keyed and
cultural benefits have been promotional rather than financial. Some arts groups,
for example, have taken advantage of an FCC regulation that requires cable
systems to provide one free non-commercial channel for public access. The
start of a new kind of relationship may have been signalled, however, when
Teleprompter Manhattan Cable TV presented the New York City Opera's
Le Coq D'Or live and in color direct from the stage of Lincoln Center's New
York State Theater on November 9, 1971. The production, with Beverly Sills
and Norman Treigle, was viewed by an estimated 12,800 of the 80,000 Teleprompter and Sterling Manhattan Cable subscribers in New York.

The project was conceived by John Goberman of the New York City
Opera, who approached Teleprompter with the idea. The cable company was
extremely interested, and after an agreement was reached, the opera company
worked out the complicated special arrangements with unions and performers.
"We were interested in doing live productions for our audience," Teleprompter's general manager Joseph C. Groth, told *AM*. "We did a number of audience
studies, and opera, ballet, and theater always came out high."

Both the opera company and the cable system were delighted with the
arrangement. Teleprompter promoted and advertised the event heavily in advance and was able to use it as a lure to sell its service to new subscribers. The
New York City Opera received a fee from the cable system for the performance,
and everyone on the company payroll was paid once again for participation.

Moreover, the production presented no special technical problems and neither theater audiences nor cast was inconvenienced.

November-December 1971

In cable television the response to an experimental 13-week 1973 series on the arts, designed as a model for noncommercial cable stations throughout the country has been positive. "A for Art," developed with support from the New York State Council for the Arts, was aired on New York City's Municipal Channel A, with a new program presented each Sunday and then repeated nightly throughout the week. According to host and producer Russel Connor, the series will be rerun in some format in the near future, perhaps nationally, and funding for a new series is being made available by the state council and the National Endowment on the Arts. In a separate development, the Arts Endowment is providing nine one-year apprenticeships in cable TV beginning this January in cooperation with cable companies throughout the country.

In educational television, "Vibrations," the series of 20 hour-long programs of music and dance produced by WNET/13 in New York with support from Exxon, has been edited into seven 25-minute programs for instructional use on educational TV stations. Another Exxon-supported ETV series, "Theater in America," featuring 18 plays, will be aired beginning in January 1974.

The stunning public television special, "American Ballet Theater: A Closeup in Time," which won wide acclaim when it was aired this October, may have marked the opening of a new TV focus on dance. In one of the largest projects of its kind, German producers brought the entire New York City Ballet to West Berlin this fall for six weeks of filming at a cost of $1.7 million. The resulting 6½ hours of color film, featuring 15 ballets, is earmarked for European and perhaps American TV.

November-December 1973

Arts Look to TV
for Dollars and Promotional Aid

The move towards greater use of television by arts groups, both from performance and promotional aspects, grows. At stake is a reach into new audiences and donors, as well as new dollars in performance fees for artists and financially pressed cultural organizations.

A breakthrough has come with Lincoln Center's announcement that it is ready to move into the potentially lucrative business of marketing live performance experimentation, Lincoln Center developed techniques for televising live arts events with clarity and intimaxy and with stereo sound under natural performance conditions. Moreover, through unobtrusive placement of cameras and microphones, neither performers nor audience are disturbed.

Potential markets include pay television and public broadcasting. "We're open to markets," John Goberman, Lincoln Center's media development director, told *AM*, "although the key issue here is live broadcasting. We're in the business of selling performances, not tapes." Goberman added that the effort has been a cooperative one with artists, unions, and the constituents all contributing their services.

November-December 1975

ADVERTISING

Know Media Before
Advertising or Promoting

Cultural organizations rely heavily on publicity to promote their performances, membership, and fund-raising drives. The arts manager who understands the media for publicity and advertising and can differentiate among them will be able to do a more effective job than the one whose knowledge of them is haphazard.

An important first step in systematic publicity or advertising work is a survey of the media serving the community or region in which the arts institute operates. Usually the newspapers (morning, afternoon, and weekly) and the radio or television stations are the most important media. But it is important not to overlook local or regional magazines, business publications, the newsletters of other organizations, and similar specialized outlets.

The public relations or advertising staff should determine the circulation and territory covered by each publication. It should likewise learn the wattage and coverage of radio or television stations, as well as something about their equipment (e.g., can they cover a live performance, can a cameraman film an interview outside the studio?).

Next it is important to analyze each medium—its policies *vis a vis* cultural groups; its editorial point of view; its standing in the community; its special following among different sectors of the public; the age, income, and educational characteristics of its readers, viewers, or listeners.

It is important to know, too, how, where, and at what time readers, viewers, or listeners are likely to receive your message, and how the medium is geared into the work habits of the community.

If you decide to buy advertising space or time, remember that media managements and their representatives respect the buyer who tries to get full value for his money. Most media see that their rates are published and respected, and they have standard quantity discounts that are well known.

Print publications will usually establish a discount schedule based on how much total space is contracted for over a 12-month period. Radio and TV stations offer similar reductions. Some media offer cash discounts that are worth looking into if you are in a position to pay cash. A published rate card that differs markedly from the actual prices charged is often the sign of a weak medium.

Some of the best sources of information—apart from published directories like *Standard Rate and Data*—are local media representatives and salesmen. They are usually well informed about local markets and can often provide considerable statistical data about the audience of the media they represent. Remember that media representatives are interested in making your program a success inasmuch as their livelihood depends on the continuing use of the media.

Tell them, as completely as possible, what your problems are and what your resources are. Get their recommendations on size and frequency of ads, and time and length of radio and TV announcements. Then use your own judgment.

September 1963

Symphony Lauded Elsewhere
Campaigns for Local Notice

In an effort to make itself as well known in its home community as it is elsewhere, a symphony orchestra undertook an unusual promotional campaign that neither raised funds nor sold subscriptions directly. Under the overall theme of "Hearing is Believing," the Syracuse Symphony, with the aid of a professional advertising agency, bombarded local residents with posters, bus cards, bumper stickers, direct mail, paid advertisements, billboards, buttons, and radio and television spots to create a community-wide impact. When the month-long campaign ended on February 28, 1975, there were few if any local citizens who could claim to have missed hearing or reading about the orchestra.

The idea for the promotion grew out of a general feeling among the orchestra staff that, as one member put it, "we were better known in Plattsburgh than in Syracuse." For the past few years, the symphony has won widespread acclaim for its performance and touring concept which frequently has involved breaking up the orchestra into smaller components to serve different kinds of audiences. Yet in spite of the recognition won elsewhere, Syracuse residents generally were either unimpressed or unaware of its orchestra's success.

Recognizing that only a provocative, professionally planned advertising and promotion campaign—one beyond the normal scope and means of the orchestra—could break the log jam, orchestra manager Sandor Kallai applied for and received a $30,000 grant from the New York State Council on the Arts. Interestingly, to help prepare the unusual grant application, Kallai brought in the advertising agency Paul, John & Lee, which had created materials for the orchestra's 1974 fund drive and was very much "in tune" with the orchestra's program, philosophy, and needs.

Once the grant was assured, the ad agency prepared an overall written communications program that outlined the campaign's basic objectives, its primary and secondary audiences, campaign direction, areas of promotion, and creative direction. The primary audience, for example, defined as those with ticket purchasing power and influence, was broken into three categories to be reached: those unaware of the orchestra; those aware, but not of its high musical quality, and those aware of all the orchestra's qualities. The "Hearing is Believing" theme was chosen, the ad agency indicated, because "the most basic objective is to get more new people to hear the orchestra. This theme encompasses, in an inviting, almost intriguing manner, a positive statement that connotes high musical quality. It also, to our minds, suggests that if you hear us once, you're going to want to hear us again."

Although promotional saturation was vital to the campaign's success, there were other key factors including consistency of theme, visual appeal of printed materials, and the enthusiasm of the advertising agency. Although Paul, John & Lee took the assignment on a paid basis, its involvement, especially that of its president, Paul Bihuniak, went well beyond the normal agency service. "The longer he worked with us, the more involved and interested he became," Richard Detwiler, the orchestra's director of development, told *AM*. "Twice in the past year he has donated his creative services for the production of annual fund television announcements."

From the campaign kickoff on January 15 until its completion, there was scarcely a corner of Syracuse that wasn't reached. More than 5000 envelope stuffers were distributed at concerts, mailed, or left on store counters; 2000 posters were placed in store windows and public places; 3000 bumper stickers were given away at concerts; and 3000 lapel buttons reading "I heard! I believe!" were distributed at children's concerts. Drivers and pedestrians were confronted with "Hearing is Believing" billboards throughout the city and on the sides of some 50 buses.

Bolstering this effort was a giant print and broadcast campaign, featuring a variety of messages with a consistently light overall approach. To increase usage, a kit of ten different ad reproductions placed in a folder headed "Run us, Please" was sent to every newspaper within a 50-mile radius of Syracuse asking for their use as public service announcements. Typical of the messages was a full-page ad that ran in a regional edition of *Time* magazine. It posed the question, "What is the Syracuse Symphony" and answered with 15 cartoonish responses including such rejoinders as "it's a child's miracle" and "it's a cultural resource."

Another print ad showed a couple with bored expressions on their faces washing dishes. The caption read, "Ho hum." In a second picture the couple, with broad smiles on their faces, was shown leaving a symphony concert. The caption read, "Hum home."

Several of the "Hearing is Believing" radio and TV spots took a humorous approach. One, accompanied by visuals simulating the kind spoofed by the spot, asked, "Do you know where your parents are tonight?" The answer? "We hope they're at the Syracuse Symphony." In the radio spot, a man, responding to his wife's suggestion that they go to the symphony Saturday night, answered, "La-de-dah! I'd rather go to the dentist." His wife's rejoinder was, "You should. You have a big cavity. The one between your ears." A voice over then told the audience, "The Syracuse Symphony is a delightful alternative to a few rubbers of bridge, the world's worst bestseller, or another dull cocktail party [all themes, incidentally, were emphasized in print ads.] For what may be the first time in your life, come to the Syracuse Symphony."

How successful was the campaign? Because there were no direct ties to fund raising or subscription sales, definitive measurements were difficult. However, in many ways the orchestra noted a tremendous new public awareness. Comments such as "Something's going on with the Symphony" or "We're hearing a lot about you" were frequent and commonplace. Advertising executive Paul Bihuniak thought the impact was substantial. "The results to date," he indicated, "have met with the success we sought."

There was one unanticipated but extra benefit of the campaign. It served as a perfect prelude to a major symphony announcement early in March—the appointment of Christopher Keene as the orchestra's new music director.

March-April 1975

How An Orchestra Profits from Program Advertising

Programs distributed free of charge at performances can bring in substantial revenue through the sale of advertising space, while at the same time providing arts groups with effective and handsome informational tools. In Salt Lake City, for example, the Utah Symphony Orchestra publishes 16 attractive issues of its program magazine for distribution at concerts each season, many with four-color covers, and realizes a net profit of $500 per issue.

The key to the success of the Utah Symphony's program is the organization's approach to local advertisers. All advertising is solicited from the office of the symphony by a member of the staff who works on a flat salary basis. According to Herold L. Gregory, manager of the orchestra, advertisers seem to prefer knowing that the full amount of the ad goes to help the orchestra and that no portion of the fee is paid as a commission to a salesman.

In selling space, the orchestra's representative emphasizes the fact that it is good business to advertise in the program because there is full advertising value for each dollar spent. No program advertisement is ever considered a contribution to the orchestra. It is pointed out that 5000 leading citizens read and save the program.

This approach has been so successful that every program is brimming over with advertisements, many of them from repeat advertisers. In spite of this heavy schedule, however, the publication has a strict policy of never burying an ad under other ads. "Every ad in the program," says Mr. Gregory, "is adjacent to editorial copy. We maintain a general ratio of advertising space to editorial space, and although this fluctuates somewhat, we keep the general rule of thumb in mind at all times."

Advertising page rates in the program, of course, depend upon frequency of use. A full-page ad is $80 in a single issue and $60 if taken in all 16 issues. Ads are also sold in half-page, quarter-page, and eighth-page sizes, the latter costing $25 per single issue. The center spread is $150 and the back cover is $75 on a 16-issue basis. With this rate schedule, the program realizes advertising revenue of $1300 per issue. The complete cost of production including the prorating of staff employees' salaries is only $800 per issue.

Editorially, while the program promotes the orchestra and events sponsored by the organization, it also includes special features of general interest and articles on current topics. Generous space is also given to the activities of the Utah Symphony Guild and the names of active workers are frequently listed. As an editorial policy, the orchestra does not invite contributions of articles from the general public. In this way it avoids any chance that key donors or members may feel slighted because articles by them were not published.

At concerts, one copy of the program per couple is generally distributed, although requests for extra copies are never refused. Special efforts are made to provide individual copies to the section in which advertisers are seated. "They must never feel we skimp on the printing of programs," said Mr. Gregory. "There is no worse public relations blunder than to run out of programs."

It is an orchestra policy never to permit the use of a stuffer or advertising insert in the programs. "Why," says Mr. Gregory, "should any firm or organization upstage our regular advertisers and clutter up the program with extraneous circulars?"

January 1964

Arts Stretch Ad Dollar

Arts Council members in Winston-Salem, North Carolina are getting more advertising space in their local papers at lower cost through a service set up by the council office.

The Arts Council signed an advertising contract with the local newspapers, guaranteeing a minimum of one column inch of advertising weekly. Council members, who had been paying the transient rate, now get the benefit of the reduced contract rate. The savings range from 34 percent on a Sunday-only basis to 38 percent on a combination of Sunday and Monday, or Saturday and Sunday advertising. Members still get their 6 percent discount in addition.

The newspapers keep the names of the member organizations and use their ads when they receive the insertion order and ad copy. They bill the council monthly. The council adds this additional billing to its regular quarterly statement to members, prorating each organization on the basis of the space used.

In the weeks when no one buys advertising space, the council authorizes the papers to use, in rotation, one of its standing ads featuring several members.

The council and the newspapers have set up several rules to make the operation work. The papers insist on filled-in insertion orders with the ad copy. Duplicates of these orders and copy go to the council office and must arrive at least 24 hours before the newspaper's deadline. This notifies the council that one of the members is buying space. If no order is received, the council specifies that a standing ad is to be used.

According to William Herring, executive secretary of the council, "None of the organizations is spending less money for advertising, but they are getting more for their money in the medium which I personally consider the most effective for the cost involved."

February 1963

Advertising Aid

Local advertising agencies may provide aid to community arts groups that are planning advertising campaigns and do not have experienced staff members to implement them. In New York, for example, the Fred Wittner Company, an advertising agency, prepares and places advertisements for the Westchester Symphony Orchestra. The agency does not charge the group its usual service fee. As a means of saying thank you, the orchestra gives the agency free concert tickets.

January 1965

Special Newspaper Supplement
Promotes Museum's Collection

A special Sunday newspaper supplement, paid for by "noncommercial" advertisements, helped the Wichita Art Museum in Wichita, Kansas promote its collection and its membership program. Called "A Sponsor's Tour of the Wichita Art Museum," the section featured photographs of its "advertisers" viewing works from the museum's collection. Credits were limited to a line identifying advertisers, who were business and community leaders. The section, which was published last September, 1965 was devoted entirely to the collection, exhibits, facilities, and programs of the museum.

The idea for the 32-page supplement, which was published by the *Wichita Eagle* and the *Wichita Beacon,* was conceived last May by Paul Miner, assistant advertising director of the newspaper. He worked in cooperation with Sebastian J. Adler, Jr., director of the museum, on developing the project.

After the museum approved the concept of the supplement, test layouts, promotional material, and presentation letters asking for advertising sponsorship were prepared. Writing, editing, and laying out the issue was performed by the newspaper's staff, working closely with Mr. Adler. In cooperation with the museum, Mr. Miner sent out 300 letters to prominent members of the community suggesting they advertise in the issue.

The letters elaborated the details of the projected issue. They included a copy of the section's proposed layout and information concerning the basic theme and the goals that the section would achieve. Cost information was also included. Advertising sponsorships were offered at the rate of one-third of a tabloid-sized page for $116, one-half for $170, and two-thirds for $250. Prospective sponsors were informed that they could select an art object from the museum's collection with which they would appear in the issue.

A typical "ad" read, "Edgar E. Turner, Jr., partner and general manager of Head Shoe Co., stands before John Singleton Copley's oil portrait, *Mrs. James Otis*, one of a pair of Copley portraits owned by the Museum." The rest of the ad was devoted to a description of the painting.

To maintain good relations with sponsors of the issue, after it was published, a thank-you note was sent to each, along with a copy of his photograph and a copy of the section.

In addition, about 3000 copies of the section were sent to museums throughout the country and abroad. "Community reaction was tremendous," Mr. Miner told *AM*. "The museum received numerous congratulatory phone calls, and I personally received dozens of letters and phone calls."

March 1966

TV Commercials Used by Museum to Increase Exhibit Attendance

Television and radio advertisements are being used to boost museum attendance in Virginia. With paid commercials, the Virginia Museum of Fine Arts in Richmond, a state institution, is attracting record numbers of visitors to its Artmobile II, an art exhibition mounted in a trailer that travels throughout the state.

One indication of the campaign's success is that following the commercials, 2197 visitors saw the artmobile during its one-week stay in Martinsville, Virginia, compared to only 517 persons who saw it during the same period last year. David Hudson, the museum's public information assistant, told *AM*, "We believe you can sell art the way you sell anything else."

Throughout the artmobile's 13-year history, the museum has relied on free public service radio and television spot announcements to promote its tours. However, although these announcements gave the artmobile excellent exposure at no cost, there was no way to guarantee when or where they would be aired.

When the museum staff conceived the idea of using paid commercials, it obtained approval from its director and its board of trustees, with the stipulation that a private source underwrite the cost of the campaign. An anonymous donor contributed $26,000 to cover all production and time costs. The commercials, produced locally in Richmond, were written and narrated by a member of the museum's staff.

During Artmobile II's present tour, which runs from September 1 to January 22 some 300 television and 1000 radio commercials will be aired on ten television stations and seventeen radio stations in Virginia, in areas which the Artmobile visits.

For television, 60-second and 20-second commercials are being shown about three times daily for a week prior to the artmobile's arrival at one of the 21 towns and cities of the museum's chapters or affiliates. Then, two different commercials of the same duration are substituted during the artmobile's week-long stay in a community. About 60 radio spots are used in the same two weeks.

Television time cost ranges from $500 to $3500, and radio time from $100 to $300 per station. Interestingly, most of the stations have matched the purchased time by also using the commercials free, as public service announcements.

One of the 60-second television commercials used during the artmobile's residence in a community says, "Walk into the spacious, air-conditioned gallery-on-wheels and 3000 years of art come alive in a magnificent collection. For example—stand before the glowing masterpiece by the incomparable Rembrandt. Truly a Blue Ribbon Artmobile collection from the galleries of America's most exciting museum—the Virginia Museum." A special slide announcing the artmobile's location in a community is inserted into each commercial.

December 1965

Ad Agency Aid

The New York Jazz Museum enlisted the volunteer aid of a leading advertising agency, J. Walter Thompson, to help it initiate the museum's first corporate membership program. Introduced at a series of three informal sandwich luncheons, each lasting only an hour, the $1000 membership offered corporations publications and posters, film showings, attendance at openings, lifetime individual memberships, and a choice of four special programs for corporate employees and clients—a jazz puppet show for children, a special monthlong jazz exhibit at company headquarters, an audio-visual performance of jazz history, or a corporate night at the museum.

With ad agency help, the museum developed a unique promotional mailing piece, an original multicolored record jacket which on its illustrated back cover told the story of the museum and its new corporate membership program. Inside the jacket were fliers on other museum programs, a booklet on the history of jazz, and a jazz record, one of a number of old 78 rpm jazz records donated to the museum.

Summer 1975

Advertising Industry
Helps to Promote the Arts

Madison Avenue is helping to promote the arts in America. With growing frequency, advertisers are spotlighting their local cultural institutions in prominent national ads in order to demonstrate the quality of life in their city or area. Also, a leading industry-wide association, the Advertising Council, is about to take its first organized step in behalf of the arts [1970]. While it is a small one, it could become the precursor for a mammoth promotional campaign that would solicit arts support throughout the country.

The Advertising Council conducts major national public service advertising campaigns on behalf of carefully selected causes, worth millions of dollars to the beneficiaries in the form of donated advertising services and contributed media space and time. Current campaigns include "Help Prevent Crime" for the U.S. Department of Justice, "Traffic Safety" for the National Safety Council, and "United Community Campaigns" for United Community Funds and Councils of America.

Initially, the arts will be included in the council's *Public Service Advertising Bulletin*, a publication listing council-approved public service subjects that media and advertisers might wish to support by contributing free time and space. The council will evaluate the overall response to the arts listing for some six months following its inclusion in the bulletin, and could then decide, if the response has been favorable, to make the arts the subject of a full-scale, major campaign. In such an event, the council would supervise an overall program which could be worth several millions of dollars in free ads to the arts in magazines, newspapers, television, radio, outdoor billboards, company publications, and other media.

The current project had its genesis in 1969, when national arts leaders representing the group known as "the President's Council" joined the Business Committee for the Arts in suggesting the arts as a public service theme for the Advertising Council. The Business Committee has since followed up and has agreed to act as the sponsoring agency responsible for preparing materials on the arts and providing them to media that request them.

Elsewhere, full-page color advertisements promoting arts groups are being used to help "sell" specific markets. In a *Business Week* ad, the Southern Company termed its four-state area America's action frontier in the arts, and called attention to the region's 15 symphony orchestras, 6 opera companies, 18 community art museums, 17 civic ballet groups, 60 theater organizations, and more than 100 art associations. In *Advertising Age*, the *Miami Herald and News* pointed to the Miami Philharmonic as proof of the importance of its market. "Remember when South Florida 'culture' meant some bathing cuties warbling en chorale?" asked the ad. "Forget it! Nowadays we thrill the air with Philharmonic excellence. You only see activity like this in a mature community. The kind of community that makes a rich market." In large black and white ads which appeared in the *New York Times* and other publications, the Massachusetts Department of Commerce and Development pictured Leonard Bernstein and a caption stating, "Leonard Bernstein would be in the Boston Symphony audience if he had become a mathematician."

Perhaps the most unusual print media ad on a cultural theme appeared last fall in *Business Week*. The full-color, two-page ad placed by Bankers Trust Company showed views of Olana, the nineteenth-century estate of Frederic Church, last of the Hudson River School of painters. It described how Banker's Trust, an executor of the estate, went against banking convention and saved Olana from destruction by allowing a preservation group time to raise money to buy the estate and preserve it as a museum.

Winter 1969-70

Ad Approaches

Televised public service spots can be very effective if they're eye-catching or, in Milwaukee's case, pie-in-the-eye-catching. The Milwaukee Repertory Theater's 30-second spot featuring an actor giving himself a pie in the face not only won tremendous local attention, but also received a bronze medal at the International Film and TV Festival of New York. In North Carolina, meanwhile, every community arts council joined together to make February, 1976 arts-funding month in the state. The campaign theme, "Come on in, the Arts are Fine," is being heralded in print ads and TV spots in cities throughout the state.

January-February 1976

Arts in Commercials

An arts group found huge new audiences and an extra payday through television. For several months during the 1971-72 season, a television commercial sponsored by the Foundation for Full Service Banks featuring the Detroit Symphony enjoyed frequent prime-time network exposure. The commercial, one of a series designed to show how local banks serve their communities, was made in one afternoon this fall, with orchestra players receiving a fee for their participation. The 60-second vignette focused visually on the orchestra while telling viewers how the National Bank of Detroit sponsors morning coffee concerts by the orchestra to bring shoppers downtown and makes loans to its players for the purchase of rare instruments.

January-February 1972

Cultural Groups Reach Far
Out for Support and Audiences

Increasingly, arts groups are reaching out to audiences not part of their regular public to win program support and funding. The City Center Joffrey Ballet, for example, received a $25,000 grant from the New York State Council on the Arts (which conceived the project) to test the viability of commercial radio as a ticket-selling medium.

The result was an intensive radio advertising campaign which began two weeks prior to the opening of the Joffrey's fall 1974 season at the New York City Center and continued two weeks into the season. Commercials ran over nine different stations, AM and FM and pop as well as good music, and utilized two entertainment figures not normally associated with ballet, comedienne Joan Rivers and singer Bette Midler. To the background of upbeat music composed for *Trinity*, a company ballet, the two stars tried in a funny and earthy fashion to convince general audiences that Joffrey was a company they would enjoy seeing. The campaign, which featured over 500 spots, was created by the Grey Advertising Agency, and all radio time was purchased rather than contributed. The two stars donated their services.

Although results were difficult to measure, the many phone calls and comments indicated that the spots reached their intended audiences. Moreover, according to one Joffrey administrator, single ticket sales during the season's first week were up by $8000 over the previous year. Pleased with the project, the dance company is considering similar commercial campaigns out-of-town.

Meanwhile, the New York City Opera and the New York City Ballet, in their joint all-out drive to match massive $6.3 million Ford Foundation grants, launched a "We Can't Live on Love Alone" campaign. To capitalize on their slogan, the companies emblazoned it on T-shirts, posters, and buttons, all available for purchase, and had company members deliver the message in public places. For variety, and for star identification, the New York City Opera sold buttons with such other messages as "Beverly Sills is a Good High" and "We Stand Pat With Brooks."

The San Francisco Ballet, which announced a month-long "survival" campaign on September 1974, used virtually every means possible to tap the public for funds. The campaign was undertaken when the board decided that to open its season it had to raise $283,000 within a month and $500,000 by December 14, 1974.

Attacking both with in-town promotional activities to reach local citizens, and network and wire service stories to attract national attention, the company missed few possibilities. In San Francisco, dancers performed on downtown street corners and in the windows of such leading stores as I. Magnin and City of Paris and passed around ballet slippers. Wherever they went SOB (Save Our Ballet) buttons were sold.

Nationally, stories were telecast by such leading network newsmen as Walter Cronkite and John Chancellor. Both the Associated Press and United Press ran stories, as did *Time* and *Newsweek*.

One of the major fund-raising events was the "Fill the Slipper—Save the Ballet Day" held at the popular family entertainment center, Marine World/Africa USA, which included such benefit activities as a barbecue, auction, banquet, and raffle. A special attraction was the ballet company's three performances of its adaptation of *Beauty and the Beast* featuring live wild animals.

Although difficulties still lay ahead, the company had met its initial $283,000 goal by late 1974.

September-October 1974

Culture Woos a New Audience
with TV Commercial Campaigns

Cigarette commercials on television are gone forever, but cultural commercials may be here to stay. In North Carolina, an unlikely "sponsor" has been promoting culture. The North Carolina Arts Council, seeking ways to broaden the state's cultural audience, conceived the idea of producing and presenting a series of television spots. With actors and announcers donating their services and a top Charlotte film company contributing much of its time, the council was able to produce five sound-on-color commercials for only $5000. In October 1971 they began distributing a different commercial every month to each of the 15 major television stations in the state. Stations have since used them frequently as part of their public service commitment, and the response has been excellent.

A key to the success of the commercials has been their light and somewhat irreverent approach to culture. In one 60-second spot set in a diner, a truck driver is about to begin eating when a voice-over says, "If everything has become just a matter of routine, it's time to let yourself go and grab hold of something real." The truck driver then tries to squirt some ketchup on his French fries, but hits his shirt instead. Enjoying the result, he squirts ketchup on himself, the waitress, and all over the diner. The scene changes to show the truck driver at an easel, painting. As the voice-over says, "You need a new way of living—North Carolina, the State of the Arts," the logo of the state council appears.

Another 60-second spot shows a muscular man exercising in a locker room. As a voice says, "Gyula Pondi is one of the greatest athletes in North Carolina," the athlete puts a towel around his neck and walks out. In the next scene, done in slow motion, he is shown in dance movements and acrobatic leaps. "He works hard to master his profession," says the announcer, "and it's no easy business either. But who cares—North Carolina, the State of the Arts." Again the council's logo is flashed on the screen.

The commercials, which will run through February, also include another 60-second spot titled "The Writer," a 30-second spot called "All the Arts," and a 20-second commercial with a rock music background, no narrative, and a series of quick-changing scenes showing people enjoying many different arts forms.

A light touch has proved equally effective in print advertising for some cultural groups. The Cincinnati Zoo Opera, in an attempt to entice new audiences, used bold and different types of ads. One, headlined, "Why I hate opera," portrayed four "hate opera" reasons, including "opera is fat ladies with horns." The copy then proceeded to refute each of them.

In New York, the Hunter College Concert Bureau for the second consecutive year ran a series of quarter-page ads in the Sunday *Times* featuring cartoon drawings and boldfaced headlines to call attention to its special program and ticket policies. One of its six ads, used to introduce its avant-garde "New Image of Sound" series, showed a pianist fending off a thrown tomato. The headline read, "They laughed when I sat down to play the piano, Ludwig van Beethoven." The text explained that "to the squares of 175 years or so ago, Beethoven was not considered to be such hot stuff. . . a little wild. . . a little outre. But somebody gave him an opportunity to be heard."

January-February 1971

How Corning Blended Self-Help, Public Service

Why does a major corporation sponsor a cultural event? How does it combine public service with self-interest? The experience of the Corning Glass Works of Corning, New York in sponsoring last fall's telecast of the opening of Lincoln Center gives insight into the increase in business activities in the arts.

Corning manufactures 35,000 different glass products, mainly for industrial and technical use, but also for the consumer market. It spends a considerable amount on national advertising and retains Batten, Barton, Durstine and Osborn as its advertising agency.

Last summer, BBDO proposed that Corning sponsor a "CBS Special" on the Lincoln Center premiere. It gave as its reasons:

1. The program would strengthen the company's identity. Customers now using one Corning product might think of Corning's name in connection with other products as well.

2. Dignified advertising could inform the industrial audience that Corning was capable of solving special production problems for them by making glass goods for specific purposes.

3. Since many of Corning's products are relatively new, and it is likely to be introducing additional items in the future, wide exposure of its name to the public would make new product introduction easier.

4. The program would build employee morale and enthusiasm.

These objectives could, however, have been accomplished through sponsorship of many different kinds of programs. Why the Lincoln Center opening? What quality could a cultural program impart to Corning's advertising that other types of programs could not? The answer: a connotation of "excellence." According to *Printer's Ink* magazine, an advertising trade journal, Corning "wanted to define 'excellence' and then transfer that definition to the screen."

Once Corning decided to go ahead, BBDO developed a series of dignified and informative commercials—a total of 12 minutes in all.

To maximize their effect, Corning widely publicized the forthcoming telecast in advance, both by ads placed in local papers and by mailing pieces to customers, employees, and stockholders.

What were the results of the program?

1. According to Nielsen ratings and standard broadcast industry audience projections, a total of 28 million Americans viewed the dazzling premiere.

2. The company received 552 letters, almost all of them praising it for its sponsorship, over half of them specifically approving the commercials. More important from Corning's point of view, many of the letters asked about its products.

3. Widespread comment in the nation's press mentioned Corning, and some papers also took the trouble to praise its commercials.

4. Corning salesmen reported "an almost immediate" reaction to the program among their customers and potential customers.

5. Employees of Corning, according to a company spokesman, "found it exciting to be in the big league, and to be able to say, 'We sponsored the opening night at Lincoln Center.' " The company noted a new interest in "excellence," a perceptible pick-up in production, and a drop-off in absenteeism and minor injuries.

6. There has been a notable rise in attendance at the company's "Glass Center"—a museum in Corning.

Said *Printer's Ink,* quoting a BBDO official: "They got the right response from the right people."

Such results indicate that other companies can also, through imaginative cooperation with the arts, blend their own interests with programs of definite public service.

January 1963

Why Not Try a Free Billboard?

An arts message may sometimes be placed on a huge billboard at a shopping center or beside a highway completely free of charge if the regional branch office of the General Outdoor Advertising Company is asked at the right time.

Since the company was organized in 1925, it has been General Outdoor policy to donate billboard space for all kinds of public service campaigns, provided space is open. The decision on whether to donate, and to whom, is made at each of the company branches in the United States and Canada. For example, the Washington, D.C. branch office donated five billboards, including the art work, to aid the National Symphony in its 1962 fund drive. In the summer of 1960, the company promoted museum attendance on a national scale with poster reproductions of old masters.

June 1962

New Advertising Campaigns
Promoting Varied Programs

The arts are being advertised in cities throughout the country in new and unusual ways. Not only are cultural groups paying for their messages, but in many instances they are winning support from local business.

In Peoria, Illinois, outdoor advertising executive Grant Mathey, serving as a volunteer member of the "Peoria City Beautiful" program, was prompted by a discussion of arts promotion to suggest a new advertising medium—billboards featuring works of local art. Although the idea wasn't entirely new, the proposed development of it was novel. The billboards, which he offered to donate, were to feature reproductions of original works by local area artists, executed by professional pictorial painters working under the supervision of the artists.

After months of preparation, the first 14-feet-high by 48-feet-long art billboard, W. A. S. Hatch's *The Heart of the Mountain*, was unveiled on a busy Peoria street with a local bank paying the costs of reproduction. During the weeks it was on view it attracted tremendous attention locally and the interest of Peoria and national media.

By early May, a second work will have been selected, painted, and mounted on a billboard. Although there has been "no hard sell" six local businesses already have agreed to be sponsors.

One group which asked for and received free billboard space recently was the Wichita Symphony, which promoted its Ethel Merman Pops concert in March through donated billboards proclaiming "Everything's Coming up Merman." New York's Times Square is the setting for an even more unusual billboard use. To coincide with the opening of his exhibition at the Museum of Modern Art, artist Robert Rauschenberg has been given use of a 20- by 40-foot computerized billboard at 1 Times Square by the developers of the Spectacolor process. Since March, Rauschenbeg's minute-long billboard art work promoting the exhibit has been flashing hourly.

The Saratoga, New York, Performing Arts Center relies heavily on contributed advertising and promotional help from local business to get its message across. The special program to tap business support is so successful, in fact, that is now results in an estimated $300,000 worth of contributed advertising space, services, and publicity benefits annually through tie-ins, business promotions, and even sponsorship.

Initiated eight years ago by local newspaperman Ed Lewi, a consultant to the center, the program seeks to match up business marketing and identity needs with specific center programs. For the center's tenth anniversary, a local bakery made and donated a ten-ton birthday cake. Performances by the D'Oyly Carte Company weren't selling well last year, until Lewi convinced the A & P to throw a giant tea party on the center lawn in honor of a performance of *The Mikado*. Companies like Chrysler-Plymouth sponsor pop events and , according to center director Craig Hankenson, help tap markets that the program couldn't afford to reach.

Other promotional bonanzas included an Americana celebration sponsored by Price Chopper Stores last year to herald the opening of the New York City Ballet season and the Bicentennial. The program featured fireworks plus miniature apple pies and American flags for every attendee. For this year's opening on Mother's Day, Price Chopper will pay artists' fees and heavily advertise the free program in newspapers, radio, television, and all its stores.

According to Lewi, the program is open to tie-ins that will help sell tickets. Thus far, they have included everything from ballerinas driving trotters at Saratoga Racetrack to program advertising on milk cartons.

Museums are discovering that a light advertising touch can be a big help in boosting attendance. The focus of the Boston Museum of Science's first paid advertising campaign, a three-month, $30,000 program launched last summer, was a series of weekend ads in Boston newspapers and magazines designed to tempt curious readers into visiting the museum. Each of the ads asked a series of interesting questions such as "Why can't you hear an owl fly?" or "What does your voice really sound like?" Instead of answering them, the ad suggested in a tag line, "It's fun to find out. Museum of Science."

Although special measurements were difficult, museum officials estimate that the campaign won back almost $3 for every dollar spent. Richard Howe, the museum's director of development, told *AM*, "We had nearly a $60,000 increase in paid admissions and realized over $20,000 more in parking, restaurant sales, gift purchases, and memberships. The publicity was excellent, and our share of the market in Boston increased."

In New York, meanwhile, the American Museum of Natural History, with a grant from Exxon, launched a tongue-in-cheek advertising campaign which lightly spoofed its own collection. Using the nearby subway stop as a setting, the campaign featured a series of colored posters decorated with such mythical creatures as Immobilis Rex, "who was bored to extinction," and Thesaurus Rex, "a dinosaur with a vocabulary of 1000 words."

The advertising campaign with perhaps the broadest impact is the League of New York Theatres and Producers' radio series, "This is Broadway," underwritten by American Express. Beginning in March, the League sent out a series of ten different three-and-a-half minute interviews with noted theatre personalities each month to radio stations around the country for use as public service spots. Some 300 stations used the spots regularly, some as often as 40 times a month.

March-April 1977

Public Notice

To catch the public eye with your messages, put them in places where the public is sure to notice them, like out of doors. Local businesses may even help you reach your markets. Metro Transit Advertising in Detroit places bus cards on the rear of 55 of its buses to aid the Detroit Symphony's fund drive. Cards showed a hand writing out a check with the legend reading, "Write something for the Symphony." In Phoenix, Eller Outdoor Advertising donated billboards which read, "Phoenix Symphony, You should hear what we have to offer."

September-October 1977

New Advertising Approach
Used to Catch Public's Eye

Arts groups tired of billboards and bus cards might try looking out their windows. Jack Firestone, manager of the Louisville Orchestra, did and wound up with a unique public service advertising medium—a cement mixer.

Noticing a mixer emblazoned with the city's bicentennial logo driving past his window one day, Firestone wondered if the ubiquitous vehicles might offer a new way to reach people not part of the regular concert audience or those who thought of the orchestra in very elite terms. A call to the head of American Builders Supply Company, owners of the mixers, won a favorable response.

Since then, the orchestra message has traveled all over town on the sides of concrete mixers. The "concrete example" of business support reads, "Get mixed up with the Louisville Orchestra." How successful has the promotion been? According to orchestra public relations director Ellen Hall, "the comments have generally been amusement and delight."

January-February 1976

AM Survey: The Arts Get
a Free Ride on Public Transit Systems

Free advertising space on public transportation vehicles is available to cultural institutions and groups in 38 of 57 cities responding to a 1962 survey by *AM*. Space for displaying posters in buses, subways, and streetcars can be obtained at a fraction of its regular cost in 18 reporting cities. Only one transit advertising company in a single city flatly refused to offer special treatment to cultural institutions.

Members of the National Association of Transit Advertising, Inc., representing about three-fourths of the local transit advertising volume in the U.S., indicated a marked willingness to cooperate with arts groups. Many cautioned, however, that free space for poster cards is available only under certain conditions.

The first is that there is vacant space. In the words of one leading company, "Our ability to accommodate institutions . . . depends on space availabilities. Our principal business is to sell the advertising space at the full rate to regular advertisers."

Nearly all those offering special consideration to cultural groups also specify that they must be nonprofit in character. Some add that they must not charge admission to the public. Several state that applicants must be "noncontroversial." One company will not take ads announcing dates for an event inasmuch as it cannot guarantee vacant space at the appropriate time.

In general, however, there is no restriction on the content of the advertising, within the bounds of simple good taste. Nor is there a limit, except in a few cities, on the number of times a group may approach the advertising company for space.

Companies that do not offer free space but do offer reduced rates generally charge between 20 and 50 percent of the standard price. Some charge a flat labor fee of 20 or 25¢ per card placed.

In all but one case, the institution is responsible for the preparation of its own posters. Costs of these vary widely, depending upon the materials used, the number of colors printed, and the number of cards required.

Requests for free or cut-rate advertising space should, in general, be addressed to the head of a transit advertising company in your community. Many of these companies are linked through ownership or association into regional or national networks. These make it possible for national cultural organizations, as distinct from local institutions, to place a message in buses, streetcars, and subways in dozens of cities at one time—at little or no cost.

February 1962

Insurance Firm Finds Music Broadcasts Pay

A business entering its sixth consecutive year in 1964 as sponsor of a series of televised symphony concerts looks upon its sponsorship as good community relations and as a means of providing a high-level program "in keeping with the image of our company we wish to present."

In Hartford, Connecticut, the Aetna Life Affiliated Companies presents a series of four monthly one-hour concerts by the Hartford Symphony Orchestra over local television station WTIC and local radio stations WTIC-AM and FM. Each of its performances reaches an average audience of 220,000 persons in Connecticut and western Massachusetts. It costs the company approximately $50,000 each year in time and talent fees to sustain the series.

Tied in with the series is a $1000 music scholarship contest for state high school students. From nearly 300 students competing for the prize, a panel of judges headed by Fritz Mahler, the conductor of the symphony, narrows the group to three finalists, each of whom performs on one of the programs. The winner appears on the last program to perform and accept his prize.

According to Charles Dixon, superintendent of information services for Aetna, the company has reaped publicity from its sponsorship. Although executives of the company have actively worked with the Hartford Symphony and recently retired company board chairman Henry S. Beers was vice president of the Symphony Society, this had little or nothing to do with the company's sponsorship.

January 1964

Actress Diana Venora and actor Nicholas Horman perform the balcony scene from Romeo and Juliet *for P.S. 84 students in New York City as part of the Lincoln Center Institute in-school program. (Photo by Susanne Faulkner Stevens)*

8

The Arts and Education

UNIVERSITIES AND THE ARTS

College Enrolls Community
in New Campus Arts Program

A self-termed "typical academic" with no organizational experience in the arts is winning widespread support for his university's theater, dance, and gallery programs by "enrolling" the community in the effort. Through a new program initiated by Humanities Dean Thomas K. Hearn, Jr., called "UAB Arts and the Community," the University of Alabama in Birmingham is offering community supporters, for nominal $10 enrollment fees, campus benefits normally available to students. Included are community activity cards, events admissions, library privileges, special minicourses, an arts newsletter, and a subscription to the university's literary magazine. In the process the school is gathering a constituency for its future development as a center for the study of the arts, a development that may include the construction of new cultural facilities.

The new program was developed by Dean Hearn in an attempt to bring the university's arts program up to the level of involvement and achievement that it had already experienced in other areas, such as medicine. With seats available for performances by the university-sponsored civic ballet and theater company, a small gallery, and a beginning program in music, Hearn decided to develop a specific plan that would make campus arts involvement especially attractive to community people.

After winning internal support from the university administration and recruiting a local art history instructor as his special assistant, Hearn spent the summer meeting with some 30 community leaders from varied areas, including the arts, to get their thoughts on program development. Ready to move ahead, he invited a group of the city's most prominent women arts leaders to a morning coffee hour in a private home to outline his concept of a multipronged special benefit program aimed at the community. With their backing and encouragement, the program was revealed to the public several weeks later in a major *Birmingham News* story.

Capitalizing on the gathering momentum, brochures were mailed to 9000 homes, outlining the program and inviting involvement in UAB Arts to people "who enjoy poetry and music, who like to paint or act, who think you'd like to write, or dance." Within two weeks some 200 subscribers at membership fees of $10 per individual and up had enrolled, and scores of favorable letters were received. In January 1977 the effort will be expanded when 30,000 copies of the university's catalogue of nonacademic programs are mailed to local households. The catalogue includes a four-page centerfold on UAB Arts.

The key to the approach is the utilization of existing and underutilized university arts services, supplemented by special programs designed to involve supporters. One minicourse on the arts and humanities will be offered voluntarily by a university faculty member each quarter—Hearn himself will give the first—on a weekly basis for four weeks. Tickets to four ballets and four theater performances will be among the 13 performing events offered.

"The university has an outstanding reputation as a medical center," Hearn told *AM*, "and as a comprehensive institution, we'd like to extend that reputation to the arts. What we're doing is giving culturally minded citizens with a favorable predisposition towards the university an arts platform to support."

November-December 1976

University Launches
New Arts Support Program

A university arts council, still in its initial stages of development, has evolved an unusual and perhaps model approach to fostering cultural growth on its campus. The program of the Council for the Arts at Massachusetts Institute of Technology in Cambridge is especially interesting since MIT is best known not for its arts curriculum, but for its leadership in science and engineering.

The arts, nonetheless, have played a role in school life for many years—the MIT Symphony was founded in 1884—and the new program represents an effort to broaden that role to more deeply involve students, especially undergraduates, in curricular and extracurricular cultural programs. The move towards a structured program, which could promote the arts in a more organized manner and finance a wide range of new concepts, was spearheaded by an earlier Committee on the Visual Arts, headed by alumnus Paul Tishman and received impetus from the active support of Dr. Jerome B. Wiesner shortly after he became university president in July 1971. The council's potential role is perhaps best summarized in a note from a recent MIT symphony flier which read, "It is to this end—to the fashioning of an education based on scientific knowledge and analysis and balanced with the arts, the products of the imagination—that the Council for Arts at MIT is finally directed."

Publicly announced at a gathering of 900 alumni at New York's Metropolitan Museum in November 1971, and the recipient of $100,000 in gifts since then, the council has moved slowly to develop its structure and formulate its program. It has, however, several accomplishments to its credit already, including grant awards to MIT's dance workshop, its visiting poets series, the Student Art Association, and an arts and technology program, and the commissioning of a student research project analyzing arts facilities at other universities.

Its most ambitious effort thus far has been the sponsorship of last spring's nationwide tour by the MIT Symphony Orchestra to Philadelphia, Dallas, San Francisco, Los Angeles, and Chicago. Although the orchestra has toured previously, this spring's program was considerably larger in scope than previous efforts. Overall, the reviews were excellent, invariably commenting both on quality of performance and the university as well. Said the *San Francisco Chronicle*, "More than just egghead scientists and engineers are being turned out at the Massachusetts Institute of Technology. An increasing emphasis is now being placed on the arts and humanities as reflected in the institute's full-scale symphony.... The orchestra is on a par with the best of the country's metropolitan orchestra's."

As a tour follow-up, the council co-sponsored with Boston television station WGBH an orchestra concert on the campus. An hour-long videotaped version of that concert was shown three times locally and was aired in prime time on September 18 to PBS stations throughout the country. Additional focus on the arts at MIT has come from the council's widely distributed quarterly newsletter which commenced publication this spring.

Council activities will be stepped up considerably this fall as the organization enters a new operational phase with the recent appointment of a full-time director and assistant director, and the initiation of a $1.25-million drive to fund its activities over the next five years. In addition, the university has committed the half-time services of an overseer to the program, special assistant to the university president on the arts, Professor Roy Lamson.

With its 58 members drawn from prominent alumni, many active in the arts, school officials including President Wiesner and cultural leaders from the surrounding community and other areas—Sarah Caldwell of the Opera Company of Boston and Roger L. Stevens of the Kennedy Center in Washington among them—the council functions through five operational committees and an executive committee that meets every six weeks. At its second annual meeting this fall, the council will adopt a constitution and issue progress reports in each of the areas in which committees have been working.

Curriculum change is among the key concerns of staff and committees, and according to director Peter Spackman, "Ultimately, the main goal of the council is educational." Spackman, former editor of the quarterly magazine *Cultural Affairs*, sees important implications in the program. "At best," he told *AM*, "what we do here may serve others as a model, including many universities not traditionally associated with the arts."

September-October 1973

Local Citizens Spur Interest in University's Arts Program

A college performing arts series, sponsored by a group of private citizens, draws record crowds, is oversubscribed regularly, and is a "profitable" nonprofit enterprise. In Raleigh, North Carolina, the Friends of the College, Inc., have sponsored an annual "top name" concert series since 1967 in the 12,000 seat William Neal Reynolds Coliseum on the campus of North Carolina State University.

More than 18,000 individuals subscribe to the seven concert series, at $7 per subscription. Although each attraction is presented two or three times, there is a long waiting list for subscriptions.

The college provides the services of an executive director and secretary for the arts program, but the Friends play a leading role in promoting and supporting the program, suggesting attractions, and approving all bookings made by the director. In spite of the fact that the operation runs on a balanced budget and frequently shows a surplus (this year's surplus may be used to improve the facility), the president of the Friends, Charles York, told *AM*, "We've never turned down an available attraction because of a high fee. If we feel the program is worthwhile we book it regardless of its cost."

There are no reserved seats for any of the performances, and the coliseum generally begins to fill up at least 30 minutes before curtain time. In several instances, subscribers have been turned away 15 minutes before curtain time because of a full house and had to return for the second or third performance by an artist. The subscription audience is supplemented by North Carolina State University students, who receive two free tickets for each concert in the series. More than 9000 students are currently enrolled in the university.

In addition to subscription sales, income from the program is derived from contributions from many local sponsors and patrons, including leading local corporations and a variety of small businesses.

The program has become so successful that it draws subscribers from as far as a hundred miles away, and it is estimated that about 50 percent of all audiences are nonresidents of Raleigh. Attractions featured in the 1966-67 season are American Ballet Theatre; violinist Erica Morini; opera stars Anna Moffo and Richard Tucker; Jose Greco and Company; a Pops concert with Arthur Fiedler; Van Cliburn; and the Concertgebouw Orchestra of Amsterdam.

January-February 1967

Town-Gown Shares Stage

A college and a community "make beautiful music together" in Ames, Iowa, where a unique cooperative effort has resulted in a successful annual concert series. For the past five years, the Music Council of Iowa State University and the Ames Concert Association have jointly presented the Town and Gown Concert Series, a program open to both college students and townspeople.

The University Music Council suggested the partnership when the association, which previously had its own series, was about to disband following a poor season. As now constituted, the series of four programs is presented at the Ames High School Auditorium on a reserved-seat basis. The association guarantees to sell half the house, and the college used the other half for students.

According to Mrs. William McCormack, president of the Concert Association, "This arrangement gives townspeople a talent budget of twice the amount they are paying in. On the other hand, the Music Council share is purchasing for the students a value that is twice the actual cost." Additional savings are effected through independent direct buying of talent by the university's concert office. Talent is selected by a committee composed of three townspeople and three university people.

Although the details of the organization and presentation are handled by the university, the Concert Association has its own kickoff ticket drive each spring, as other civic concert groups do, to sell its half of the house. The 1968-69 series, budgeted at $7500 will present the Chamber Symphony of Philadelphia, pianist Abbey Simon, the Oberlin Choir, and the Guarneri String Quartet.

September-October 1968

College and Orchestra in Summer Partnership

A symphony orchestra and a university are cooperating in a unique summer project which extends the orchestra's season and provides the university with an important program of education and entertainment. Called "Summer Music in Minnesota," the project, initiated in 1966, features the participation of Minneapolis Symphony Orchestra players in a series of workshops, lecture-demonstrations, and concerts during their five-week summer residency at the University of Minnesota.

The program had its beginnings in 1964, when symphony representatives and the university's music department organized a two-day symposium to discuss how the orchestra might be best utilized during the summer. A plan for a broad arts program at the university evolved from these meetings, encompassing opera and dance in addition to symphonic music. It was decided, however, to concentrate on symphonic music during the first few summers and expand the program to other areas later.

The 1967 program, budgeted at $150,000, featured five Friday night "family twilight" concerts by the orchestra. In addition, orchestra members participated as demonstration units in two credit courses offered by the university: Music 60, a nine-session introduction to orchestral repertoire; and the contemporary music workshop, a five-day program codirected by Stanislaw Skrowaczewski, the orchestra's conductor, and Elliot Carter, the composer.

Two special programs for high school students and teachers utilized the talents of orchestra members. A high school musicians' project brought 141 gifted young students to the Minneapolis campus for four weeks, and a high school music teachers' workshop drew 40 teachers to an intensive five-week session.

Other facets of the program include elementary and secondary music education workshops and an opera workshop.

Summer 1967

University Becomes Arts
Patron and Buys Tickets for Students

A foundation grant has enabled a university to become a patron of the arts, and has opened an important new audience-building avenue for cultural organizations in the New York City area. Under the program, which was instituted in December 1965, the Brooklyn Center of New York's Long Island University has received $25,000 from the Youth Educational Council, a foundation. The funds will permit about 500 LIU students a year, for five years, to attend theater, dance, and musical performances in New York as part of their regular academic course. The university will endeavor to raise additional funds to extend the program beyond its original five years.

Such a program, if adopted by foundations elsewhere, could greatly aid arts groups by guaranteeing fully subsidized student attendance at performances. To attract student audiences, many arts groups now offer them substantial discounts on ticket purchases. Under this program, the university receives only slight discounts for buying tickets in bulk.

Students participating in the program are drawn from all grades and divisions of the school, including business administration and natural sciences. They attend three to five performances during the year, with special seminars at the university following each performance. A student-faculty committee administers the program and selects the events.

Dr. William M. Birenbaum, vice president and provost of LIU's Brooklyn Center, said that the program is enabling the school to use the city's theaters and concert halls as "curricular workshops." Students are attending performances this season at the city's Lincoln Center for the Performing Arts and at the Brooklyn Academy of Music. Plans call for broadening the program next fall to include performances of Off-Broadway theater groups and of other small but significant arts organizations.

This pioneering program is the Educational Council's first in the arts. During its two-year existence, it has supported programs for underprivileged children. Mrs. Marty N. Lipschutz, chairman and organizer of the foundation, expressed hope that other organizations would follow its lead in this area. She told *AM*, "The council was moved to make the grant because many courses of study, like engineering, have missed the cultural aspects of life."

January 1966

Arts are Central
at World's Largest University

Through a unique multidisciplinary program involving sponsorship and funding of residencies and tours, workshops, forums, convocations, exhibitions, consultancies, and festivals, the arts are making inroads into virtually every facet of campus life at the world's largest university, the State University of New York. With administrative headquarters in Albany, SUNY has 72 branches throughout the state, including four-year colleges, two-year community colleges, specialized schools in a variety of fields, research centers, agricultural and technical colleges, and four university centers. One of the system's newest branches, the State University College at Purchase, specializes in the performing and visual arts.

The development and implementation of a comprehensive and university-wide cultural program, which supplements normal day-to-day arts activities on each of the campuses, is the responsibility of a rotating 21 member committee appointed by SUNY chancellor Ernest L. Boyer. Composed of arts faculty members, students, and administrators, several of them college presidents, the University-wide Committee on the Arts meets about six times during the academic year as a group and dozens of times in smaller subcommittees and disciplinary committees. Day-to-day activities are carried out by an administrative staff of three with offices in Albany, headed by arts associate Patricia Kerr Ross.

Because of the many arts events scheduled at each of the SUNY branches and the number of noted artists-in-residence throughout the system, communication is one of Ms. Ross's major concerns. "We're the connecting link between the campuses in the arts," she told *AM*. "We find the mechanisms for moving resources, such as artists-in-residence, between one campus and another." Communications means mailings and announcements sent several times weekly, plus scores of letters and telephone calls which generate considerable interplay between campuses. When major university-wide events are scheduled, as many as three different mailings a day are sent. In addition, two major annual publications describing committee-sponsored university-wide programs in detail are sent to all arts department chairmen, college presidents, trustees, arts programmers, and student activities coordinators.

A key to the committee's efforts is its development of unusual arts projects that no campus would be able to initiate or fund on its own, as well as its sponsorship of residency and touring programs of special scope. Twice each year, for example, groups of 150 art students (from SUNY branches and private colleges) come to New York for three days to visit museums and galleries and meet with artists in their studios. The program, "Arts Scene," which is free to students, is organized by a distinguished critic.

In music, violinist Paul Zukofsky has held a four-day study program in twentieth century string music for 50 advanced string students for the past three years. A program initiated this academic year, the "Moveable Audience," provided funding for the theater students to visit other SUNY campuses to see drama productions. Through another new program, sculptor William King has been in residence at each of three major campuses for six weeks, sculpting rather than teaching, although students have had the opportunity to watch him work. In conjunction with his residency, a major exhibition of King's work currently is touring SUNY campuses.

Among the statewide programs available to each of the SUNY campuses are a series of art lectures and workshops, a films-on-loan series, and the University Artists Series, a program featuring resident SUNY performing artists/teachers—the Lenox String Quartet, the Cleveland Quartet, and the Brockport Resident Dance Company among them—as performers at other campuses with part of the honorarium paid by the committee. A residency and touring program of outside groups included the Paul Taylor Dance Company and City Center Acting Company this year. A new program introduced last spring is the Arts Consultant Service in which *AM* editor Alvin H. Reiss visits SUNY campuses for workshops and discussions on various facets of cultural programming and management with students, faculty members, administration, and community leaders.

A capstone to this year's arts program will be a giant four-day-long University-Wide Celebration of the Arts, from April 26-29, [1974], involving performers and programs from throughout the SUNY system. Similar programs were held in 1967 and 1969. The three-pronged program will feature workshops in all arts areas for students and, exhibitions and performances by students and faculty artists, and a series of forums on topics of broad concern to the university community. To identify topics for the discussion part of the celebration and to generate program ideas for the committee to consider for coming years, Chancellor Boyer openly solicited suggestions from the entire SUNY system.

Specifically, the celebration will include such events as an all-university student art exhibition; four or five student theater productions; a dance workshop featuring performances by as many as 12 campuses; first showings of films by four artists-in residence; and continuing events in music, poetry, film, drama, dance, and the visual arts. Also, models for sculpture submitted by faculty and graduate students will be adjudicated and seed money provided by the committee will help to get the best works built on campuses. As the major university-wide arts effort, attempts are being made to draw delegations from every SUNY campus to the celebration.

From what we've seen already," added Ms. Ross, "the ideas generated at the celebration should keep this university growing in the arts for years to come."

January-February 1974

Culture on Campus
Is Big Business at UCLA

The rise of cultural activity on college campuses has created a new kind of faculty member, the educator-impresario. This increasingly important member of the arts management profession not only must cope with such familiar problems as ticket pricing, publicity, seating, scheduling, booking, and budgeting, but must also deal with three special problems.

First, he is responsible, as a rule, for a program that combines both amateur and professional activity. Second, the program usually includes several artistic disciplines. Third, this program must in some way be integrated with the activites of the faculty.

One school that has successfully integrated a vast program through the instrument of a central coordinating agency—a kind of arts council on campus—is the University of California at Los Angeles. UCLA runs one of the most ambitious campus cultural programs in the country. Its attractions last year drew an aggregate audience of 284,155 and ran up box-office sales of about $500,000. More impressive even is the scope of the program. The 1961-62 season included 151 performances of professional theater, 89 performances of academic theater, 59 concerts, 40 film showings, 110 public lectures, and scores of other events like art exhibitions and dance recitals. This level of activity compares favorably with that in any good-sized city.

A single agency, the Committee on Fine Arts Productions (CFAP) is responsible for planning and coordinating this tremendous program. Set up in May 1954, CFAP is "a kind of holding company for the receiving and disbursing of funds needed to present student and professional offerings."

CFAP consists of eight sections. A Concert Section is responsible for presenting professional events in the fields of music and dance. These are supplemented by student productions put on by the Music section and the Dance Section. Thus, in these fields, amateur and professional activity are divided. Similarly, there is a Film Section that presents documentaries and other special movies, and a Film Production Section that completes three to six student movie productions each year. In the field of art, however, a single section is responsible for both amateur and professional shows, and a Children's Programs section stages both student and professional programs in a variety of disciplines. An eighth section for Theatre Arts is responsible for student dramatic productions.

These regular sections are supplemented by Theatre Group, a wholly professional quasi-independent drama company headed by MGM producer John Houseman and tied organizationally to CFAP. (Frances Inglis, CFAP's executive officer, sits on the Theatre Group board.)

Started in 1958, Theatre Group was given $15,000 by the university regents and told to sink or swim. Since then it has received no additional funds from the university, and has been so successful in paying its own way that it is now planning to build its own theater. The regents have given it a piece of land and authorized it to raise construction funds through solicitation. Theatre Group thus does not draw on CFAP for funds, although it receives certain services from CFAP.

In contrast, each spring, the sections present budgets to CFAP to cover their proposed programs. Student productions are only partially subsidized by university funds, so that even these usually require money from CFAP. After careful screening, CFAP makes an allocation to each section. At the end of the fiscal year each section must return to CFAP all its earned income.

Sections are expected to balance their books and turn over any profits made. Failure to repay the full amount of the allocation (which is, in effect, a loan) results in a more critical screening of the section's next budget request. CFAP provides, therefore, a reserve financial pool for cultural units on campus. Over the years, profits by some sections have balanced losses by others, so that the pool has not only maintained its level, but increased slightly.

When CFAP has a good year, the "profits" are plowed back into higher quality productions, the purchase of higher-fee artists' services, etc.

CFAP itself receives little financial support from the university. It is granted $25,000 a year to help cover administrative expenses that actually run to twice that amount. Its staff of 13 includes the executive officer; a public relations representative; three administrative assistants (one for theater, one for concert and films, one for ticket sales); a secretary for public lectures; a programmer for films; and six clerical aides. Its job—tying together the many-faceted arts activities on the campus—demands a high level of arts management. That the job is done well is reflected in the success of the UCLA program.

September 1962

Ticket Sales Pay the Full
Costs of an Unusual College Theater

A summer theater owned and operated by a women's college provides training for its students in every phase of the theater arts while supporting itself solely through ticket sales.

Stephens College of Columbia, Missouri has run the Okoboji Summer Theater outside its home state in Spirit Lake, Iowa at a profit for five summers. Its efforts have proved an artistic, educational, and commercial success that may hold lessons for colleges and arts groups elsewhere.

Stephens, in 1958, started as operator of the theater under a profit-sharing arrangement with the local group that owned it and was given ownership of the theater in 1962.

The college has taken a completely professional approach to the management of its theater. A two-year college for women, at which a limited number of students are candidates for the three-year Bachelor of Fine Arts degree, Stephens is noted for its curriculum in the arts. It combines operation of the theater with an undergraduate summer session in theater arts.

The staff for this program includes six male faculty members. During the academic year they are also members of Stephens' resident professional acting company, which presents eight productions at the campus playhouse. They are assisted by faculty responsible for business management, set and stage design, and props. There is also a counselor for the residence hall, an additional instructor for the summer courses, and a public relations specialist. The professionals direct each production and play the male roles, with female parts played by students.

During the eight-week summer session a new play is presented weekly, each production running for six nights. Matinees are devoted to children's plays. The theater holds 354 seats. Tickets, at $2, bring in the entire operational revenue of the theater.

Candidates for the new Bachelor of Fine Arts degree in theater arts spend two summers at the Okoboji Theatre. They can earn up to eight semester hours of college credit each summer from courses in acting, production, theater history, and theater management. Lecture courses are supplemented by actual work on each of the productions. The class in theater management, for example, meets four hours a week for nine weeks and covers theater organization and accounting, publicity, public relations, advertising, house management, stage management, and box office.

During the summer, students take part in all theater operations, including acting, scenery building, lighting, costuming, and ticket selling.

November 1962

Students Take Over Management and Win New College Arts Audience

With the rise of professional cultural impresarios on campuses throughout the country, at least one college is providing a contrast to this trend. At East Carolina College in Greenville, North Carolina, students have taken over the management of the campus arts program from the faculty and scored a great success.

Working with a yearly budget of almost $25,000 [during the 1962–63 season], a student entertainment committee selects guest artists for two concert series of five programs each. Students also book the artists, sell tickets, and publicize the program. As evidence of the seriousness with which student leadership is taken, the college paid expenses for two student managers to attend a recent conference of the Association of College and University Concert Managers.

Until 1961, the arts program at East Carolina was managed by a faculty committee, with a student entertainment committee providing a rubber stamp for their decisions. Then Tom Mallison, an undergraduate who later became president of the Student Government Association, was appointed head of the entertainment committee. He resolved that students should run the entire arts program aided by faculty advisors.

The student constitution was changed so as to establish a rotating student committee of eight members and four faculty advisors with authority to conduct the program. A strong student government, which administers an overall yearly budget of $130,000, provides the framework in which the entertainment committee functions.

When students took over the program in 1961, attendance had been sparse and interest was low. In two years student attendance has zoomed upward, and season ticket sales to the community have increased by 800 percent. The students courted their crowds first by engaging artists with immediate name value, but now they are gradually introducing new names into the program.

In its first year the committee operated with a $24,600 budget, a $7000 increase over the budget used by the faculty committee the preceding year. Money comes from a portion of the $15 student activity fee paid by students each quarter and students are entitled to receive tickets to all concerts in the fine arts and pops series, space permitting.

At first, student activity tickets were punched at the door. But since turn-away crowds became the rule, students must present their activity cards at the box office from three to ten days before a performance in order to obtain tickets. All tickets not picked up three days before the concert are sold to townspeople at $2 each for the fine arts series and $3 per seat for the pops series. In addition, the student committee is authorized to sell up to 500 fine arts season tickets to townspeople at $7 per subscription. All money realized from outside sales ($2000 last year) goes back into a general student fund.

Arrangements for the following year's concert season begin in the spring when at least half the artists are signed, subject to faculty approval. An approximate budget is approved by a student–faculty budget committee in May, and the rest of the programs are filled in the summer and early fall.

This year the fine arts series includes William Warfield, Alexander Brailowsky, the José Limón Dancers, Judith Anderson, and the North Carolina Symphony. The pops program includes such names as the Limelighters, Dave Brubeck, the Four Preps, and the Smothers Brothers. The budget is split 50-50 between the fine arts and pops programs.

Student fine arts attendance is thus far averaging 75 percent of capacity, up from 50 percent last year. Pops concerts are about 99 percent filled. Both figures are a great increase over the days of faculty management. The overall budget includes $1500 per year for operating expenses. Paid help is limited to students manning the box office and working as ushers at 75¢ an hour. All other services are contributed free by students and faculty advisors.

Mallison says increased publicity has been important in boosting attendance. Releases go regularly to some 75 newspapers in eastern North Carolina.

In addition to administering the arts program, the students are participating in a drive to raise $20,000 for an acoustical shell. Under a special arrangement, the students were promised a penny for each empty pack of Liggett & Myers cigarettes returned to the company. Thus far, nearly 250,000 empty packs have been collected, netting $2500 towards the shell.

"A program such as we run," Mallison told *AM*, "can work at other schools provided there is a strong student government and administration support."

February 1963

New Auditorium at
University Spurs Interest in the Arts

What happens when a campus gets a new concert hall or theater? The answer: an increase in cultural activity and arts consciousness. That, at least, has been the experience of Butler University in Indianapolis, which opened a new $3.5 million auditorium in October 1963.

The 2200-seat hall became the home of the Indianapolis Symphony Orchestra. It also booked a heavy schedule of imported cultural attractions—far more than the community or the campus was accustomed to getting. In all, during its first year of operation Clowes Memorial Hall is presenting 67 offerings. This represents an $88,000 outlay for artists' fees alone.

The availability of the big, new auditorium with its 300-seat supplementary recital hall has made it possible for many attractions to visit the city for the first time. Public response has been enthusiastic. During a single one-month period subscribers bought 1642 out of a total of 1899 tickets for a ten-attraction series. This represented an income of $71,689. Box office sales of single tickets boosted the total gross.

This season the hall is presenting, in addition to the Indianapolis Symphony concerts, touring professional performances of *Brecht on Brecht, A Man for All Seasons, Camelot,* and other Broadway and Off-Broadway plays and musicals. The National Repertory Theatre will perform in February. Community Concerts and university drama productions will help round out the program.

The size of the hall makes it economically feasible for touring productions to appear there. Thus it has been pointed out by *Variety* that, at a suggested top price of $7.50, *Camelot* would be able to gross more than $98,000 for eight performances. For a straight play giving only two performances, with a $4.50 top, the potential gross would be $15,500.

December 1963

Students a Growing
Target of Cultural Programs

Arts groups are reaching out to students at elementary, high school, and college levels, not only to involve them as audiences and performers, but to use them to sell tickets and promote programs.

The Baltimore Symphony, which has extensive programs aimed at virtually every student age level, uses student representatives recruited from some 20 area colleges to promote the orchestra season to their fellow students. To find its representatives and to insure college cooperation later, the orchestra staff recruits through college music departments and public relations offices.

After receiving a mail briefing on the orchestra season, student representatives receive posters, fliers, and special announcements and are asked to post them at key campus locations. In return for their efforts, representatives receive, on request, free pairs of tickets to orchestra concerts, as long as they're available. In addition, an annual representatives' party, with orchestra members and conductor attending, helps build student identification with the orchestra.

According to orchestra public relations director John Brain, the program is working well, and "the number of student rush tickets has increased."

In St. Louis, the Loretto-Hilton Theatre tried a new ticket sales tactic–using students as a commission sales force—to sell $20 to $40 season subscriptions. Developed by a Canadian marketing firm on a fee basis, the program involved 300 youngsters, pre-briefed on the theater and supplied with brochures and notebooks, in a door-to-door campaign last summer. Students received commissions on a sliding scale beginning at $5 for each subscription pair and going as high as $130 a week if they sold 11 pairs of subscriptions, a figure reached by only a handful. Although the students sold 1293 subscriptions in a three-month period, the theater staff was not overly pleased since the campaign was costly, too much bookkeeping was involved, and the students were easily discouraged.

A positive program aspect, however, was its role in promoting the regular fall subscription campaign, which showed greatly increased sales over the previous year.

In New Bern, North Carolina, dramatist and director Laura Hall Courter, working in the state's CETA program, developed a new children's theater company in April 1976, in which 5- to 16-year-olds do everything from acting to designing sets, working as technicians, selecting productions, even sitting on the organization's board and directing plays. The Lollipop Playhouse, which presents a season of five different productions by children and for children, is operated by a club which meets monthly and whose 35 members, all children, pay dues of $1.50 annually. The club's board of directors includes 11 members between the ages of 11 and 13, who make virtually all decisions—a reading committee selects plays—with the exception of finances, still handled by Mrs. Courter. She told AM, however, "I report back on them regularly on the budget."

Initiated with a bank loan and still solvent as a result of production income, the company presents three performances of each production with all-children casts, in addition to a day of six lecture–demonstrations in local schools. Thus far productions have been directed by older children, including one 19-year-old, but two 13-year-old boys in the club are interested in directing and Mrs. Courter thinks they'll have their own productions to direct by next season.

Prior to organization of the Playhouse there was no local theater program available to children from junior high school age down. The new group has become so popular that steps have been taken to make it inot a permanent nonprofit organization.

January–February 1977

Young People Are
Effective Salesmen for Culture

Young people from grade school through college age are helping to "sell" the arts in communities throughout the country. In Salt Lake City, Utah for example, a Collegiate Advisory Board of the Utah Symphony Orchestra (CABUS) was established in fall 1969 to promote the orchestra's activities among college students in the state. The board, like the University of Washington "Whiz Kids" who work with the Seattle Opera, is composed of college students who offer suggestions to the orchestra management on how to reach young people, and then implement these suggestions themselves. As its first project, CABUS suggested that the orchestra's president proclaim the week of October 6–11 as Utah Symphony Week on the University of Utah campus. During the well-publicized week, CABUS volunteers manned season ticket booths at three campus locations. The student advisors also have been active in the promotion and sale of "Happy Birthday Ludwig" bumper stickets commemorating Beethoven's 200th birthday.

In a separate youth-oriented program, the orchestra invited all the 2000 or more foreign students enrolled in the state's universities and colleges to attend an October 22 concert as guests of the symphony, the local Rotary Club, and the Utah Committee for the United Nations. Preceding the concert, the foreign students were feted at a reception in their honor.

At a younger age level, 10,000 elementary and secondary school students in St. Paul, Minnesota are promoting the arts council's fund drive by wearing bright green buttons reading "I invest in the Arts and Science Fund." The buttons are left in a big barrel in the St. Paul Science Museum, and youngsters can take them without contributing anything. But most of the juvenile button-takers have deposited upwards of a penny in the coin slot behind the barrel. According to arts council director Marlow G. Burt, "We view the buttons as a fun promotion gimmick which, thus far, has been extremely successful."

In Princeton, New Jersey, high school coeds helped the Princeton Chamber Orchestra reach an untapped ticket sales market and benefit an important community charity drive at the same time. The idea for a cooperative project was initiated in discussions between Gordon G. Andrews, the orchestra's manager, and Martin Lombardo, head of the local Multiple Sclerosis campaign. Lombardo had organized teenage girls to work for the M.S. drive in the past, and he thought that the same girls could be succesful in selling season subscriptions, especially to the affluent new residents not being reached by the orchestra. A cooperative arrangement was established in which the girls would sell season tickets and the orchestra, in turn, would contribute 10 percent of these revenues to M.S.

The results, according to Andrews, were "phenomenal," and a check for $560 was presented to the health charity. "Not only were we serving a community interest," Andrews told *AM,* "but M.S., in turn, was serving a community activity. The project was so successful last season that we have already finalized plans to do it again this year."

September–October 1969

REACHING STUDENTS

New Student Use of Art

Children, with some direction from professional artists and administrators, are finding new ways to participate in the arts. In Fort Wayne, Indiana, youngsters working with Neighborhood Affiliates for the Arts, a project of the Fine Arts Foundation, prepared, published, and sold for 25¢ a 16-page publication, *A Kid's Guide to Fort Wayne*. In Jacksonville, Florida, children were inspired by a symphony youth concert to sculpt the orchestra members—including at least one of every instrument—in clay. In Anchorage, Alaska, 420 students worked in 14 different one-week sessions last summer to create a 1760-foot mural on a three-block plywood fence surrounding a construction site.

The most ambitious program, perhaps, is the functioning "mini-museum" in the Hillside/Nishuane Schools of Montclair, New Jersey. Under the direction of teacher Nancy Smith, children have learned how a museum operates by setting up and administering their own museum, complete with staff, memberships, and an exhibition program. The new museum opened last November with a special ribboncutting ceremony and a preview of an exhibition featuring mobiles and clay sculptures by youngsters, prints, and other works.

January–February 1978

Sponsored Trip to Exhibitions
Important Adjunct to Teaching

A state art society is helping its public school art teachers to improve the level of local instruction by exposing them to a variety of collections and styles not available to them in their own communities. The Art Teacher Study Tour, sponsored by the North Carolina State Art Society, provides a week-long, all-expense-paid trip for selected teachers to Washington, D.C. and New York, where they visit museums, galleries, and artists' studios. Following the trip, each participant summarizes his experience in a written report to the society and also addresses groups and classes in his own community.

Community sponsors submit teacher nominations annually to the State Art Society. Each year, four are selected for the tour and the $300 cost of the week-long program is shared equally between the Art Society and the local sponsor. However, other nominated teachers are free to participate in the program at their own expense. All tour arrangements are planned in advance by the supervisor of art of the North Carolina State Department of Public Instruction.

The 1967 tour began when the group assembled in Raleigh to receive their tour materials, meet officers of the Art Society, and see the collection of the North Carolina Museum of Art. The following day the group went to Washington for visits to the National Gallery of Art and the Phillips Gallery. Four days were then spent in New York visiting ten art galleries, participating in an art education seminar at New York University, visiting artists in their studios, and seeing the collections of the Guggenheim, Cooper Union, Metropolitan, Whitney, Gallery of Modern Arts, Contemporary Crafts, and Modern Art museums.

Some of the participants were visiting New York for the first time and, as one teacher commented, "Seeing and studying first hand has put a deeper meaning into my teaching of art."

March-April 1967

School Program Brings
Art Exhibit to Students

Nearly 4000 schoolchildren in Bethlehem, New York, a suburb of Albany, are viewing original works of art daily as a series of loan exhibitions circulates throughout the entire Bethlehem school system. The unusual program, now in its second year, stems from a belief by school officials that constant exposure to fine art would be a meaningful experience for students in the six elementary schools, the junior high school, and the senior high school that comprise the school district.

The program had its beginnings in June 1962, when Hamilton Bookhout, supervising principal of Bethlehem Central Schools, appointed an art appreciation committee composed of two art teachers and a librarian from the school system to devise a visual art program. During the summer, the committee, under the leadership of Mrs. Wilma F. Collins, librarian at Bethlehem Junior High School, borrowed 50 original contemporary paintings, all of them the work of artists in the area. The Albany Institute of History and Art, for example, lent 30 paintings, including 16 that were prizewinners in the "Artists of the Hudson Valley" competition. None of these works was painted before 1945; all the artists were alive and painting. The Albany Artists Group and individual local artists also made paintings available.

Paintings were arranged by general subject matter and divided into eight different exhibits, with each of the schools in Bethlehem receiving a new exhibit every month on a rotating basis. They were displayed in libraries, classrooms, and guidance offices, and art teachers used the paintings for instruction purposes. Interest in art was so high by the end of the school year that the school system purchased a painting and received two others from grateful parents.

This year art was borrowed to create four separate exhibits, one each of oils, watercolors, prints, and photographs. It was soon discovered, however, that additional art was needed to meet the demand. Early in December the school system borrowed 16 paintings from the Albany Institute of History and Art, all of them works by artists of the Hudson River School. These have been divided into two additional exhibits of eight paintings apiece. Because the paintings have historic value, they are also being studied by history classes.

According to Mrs. Collins, chairman of the art appreciation committee, the positive reaction by youngsters has exceeded all expectations. When an exhibtion was removed, for example, she found that many of the students complained of missing paintings that they had enjoyed seeing. Mrs. Collins also thinks that the exhibitions featuring the work of local artists have been particularly significant because "if youngsters see that we esteem local artists, they will be inspired to create art themselves."

The Bethlehem art exhibitions, now considered a permanent feature of the school program, may be extended to include sculpture and mobiles in the future. Communities seeking to set up similar programs are advised by Mrs. Collins to ascertain first if there is a good source of original art available locally.

December 1963

Theater Woos Young
Audiences with Help of Student Leaders

Although many arts organizations recognize youth as an important part of their audience, few make a concerted effort to attract it to their door. One organization that has benefited greatly by aiming promotions at teenage audiences is the Manitoba Theatre Centre, a professional repertory theater group in Winnipeg, Canada. It has increased its audience and gained significant publicity by initiating a series of programs specifically aimed at high school students.

Stuart Baker, director of the Theatre School—one arm of the Centre—told *AM*, "MTC's policy has always been to build up its young audiences." A survey made by the Centre last year showed that over 40 percent of its audience was under 21 years old.

An unusual and successful project for youth initiated by the Theater School was the creation of a Drama Youth Council, composed of students who promote theater in Winnipeg. The council is student managed and financed.

As its initial project, the council held a contest for the best display of theater posters, costume designs, set designs, and programs drawn by high school students.

The contest, which ran for five weeks, was conceived by Mr. Baker, but was executed and publicized by the council. Winners of the contest had their posters displayed at the downtown branch of the Winnipeg Public Library as part of "Young Canada Book Week."

The student-publicized event received widespread coverage on regional network television and in local newspapers. Information on the winners and their exhibits was distributed to all Winnipeg schools.

The council, composed of 41 members, is also involved in other projects to promote theater to youth. It is working on the Theatre School's newsletter which is intended to better communications between high school drama clubs. It is also handling public relations and "front-of-house" work for MTC's fourth Inter-High School Drama Festival, which gives young persons working in school drama a public showcase.

Other Centre efforts aimed at youth include the presentation of plays that relate to the high school curriculum, reduced ticket rates for students, touring performances in the schools, and programs with school drama clubs.

March 1965

Advance Program Woos Students to the Theater

The National Repertory Theatre, a touring drama company headed by Eva Le Gallienne, has developed a comprehensive program of work with schools in the communities where it performs.

The detailed approach to student audiences begins several months in advance of performance with letters sent to every college, university, and high school within a 100-mile radius of a city where a performance is scheduled. Lists of relevant reading and suggestions for classroom assignments are enclosed. About six weeks prior to the performance by the NRT, the organization's advance representative visits schools and colleges interested in the program and arranges discount ticket sales for students; makes plans for displays and announcements about the performances; schedules interviews and tape discussions by cast members for use in classrooms and on radio and television; and assists teachers who wish to use the educational material developed by the NRT.

Two weeks later, a second advance representative arrives. He meets with schools who have not responded to correspondence from the NRT and attempts to make special ticket and transportation arrangements for them. He also supervises the scheduling of special promotional events and addresses classes and assemblies on the productions to be performed.

At the time of the opening, a younger member of the company who has been appointed student representative supervises final arrangements for backstage visits by students and lectures by cast members in classrooms. Eight members of the cast are available for lectures, and everyone associated with the production remains backstage after each performance to discuss the work with interested students.

October 1963

Television Commercials
Help to Sell the Arts

A famed college football coach is proving as successful in selling the arts as he has been in recruiting high school prospects. The face of Paul "Bear" Bryant, coach of the University of Alabama football team, has been a familiar sight on TV stations throughout his state as he has told listeners, "we have an awful lot of talent here in Alabama, and it's not all found on the football field. Alabama has a wealth of talent in the arts, too." Bryant cited examples of arts programs and ended by asking viewers to "support the arts in Alabama—that's where the people are."

The campaign was conceived by Ellen Dressler, then Cultural Affairs Supervisor for the Montgomery, Alabama Parks and Recreation Department and a former TV producer and promotion director who reasoned, "If Billy Martin can plug the New York City Metropolitan Museum of Art [referring to an NEA spot], why not Bear Bryant for the Alabama arts?" With the help of the University of Alabama's sports publicist, Bryant's participation was assured, and the spot was filmed in the coach's office in December 1977 by the WSFA-TV sports department. Originally planned for use by her department with a five-second promotional tag following the 25-second Bryant message, Ms. Dressler, now an arts administrator in Charleston, South Carolina, recognized that groups throughout the state could just as easily use it by inserting their own ending tag. Distribution was then arranged through the Alabama Assembly of Community Arts Councils.

Indicative of the potential of a tie-in between a top sports personality and the arts is the fact that stations jumped at the opportunity to use the public service spot following Alabama's victory over Ohio State in a post-season bowl game in January 1978. Marlo Bussman of the Alabama Assembly told *AM,* "It ran all the time for two months." With the start of football season, and without any extra promotion, TV stations in cities throughout the state began using it again without being asked. One radio station is even using the sound portion and identifies Bryant in a voice-over as the speaker.

Elsewhere, a public service spot featuring Atlanta's Mayor Maynard Jackson, chairman of the U.S. Conference of Mayors Arts Project, has been winning good air time throughout the country. The spot urges community support of the arts.

September-October 1978

Culture for Kids?

If you stage an exhibit or performance in a school, you can build interest and enthusiasm by providing teachers with a mimeographed sheet of proposed activities built around your show. The Tri-Cities Opera Workshop in Binghamton, New

York, issues a one-page bulletin. Sample from the sheet that went out before a performance of *La Boheme:* "History—what was happening in Paris or Italy or America in 1830, the time the opera was written? . . . Home Economics—Italian or French recipes. . . . Language—Students from families of Italian descent could be very helpful here in building interest." The sheet then lists Italian words and phrases from the opera libretto. Activity ideas help teachers as well as kids, and make for return engagements.

April 1962

For the Young

One way to interest more young people in the arts is to bring news to students through students, as the Warwick Arts Foundation did. The *Rhode Island Evening Bulletin* annually sponsors a Youth Awards Dinner commending those high school students whose contributions to the youth pages of the paper have been exceptional. By sponsoring an "arts award" within this competition, the foundation provided the impetus for a wide range of student-written articles on the arts during the past year. As a result of the program's success, the foundation and the paper now hope to establish annual workshops in arts reviewing for high school correspondents.

September-October 1968

Comic Approach

A comic approach with a serious purpose, turning school children onto art, is being used effectively by the Michigan Council for the Arts. To help youngsters prepare for their visits to Artrain, a museum on tracks which travels the state, the council distributes copies of "Artrain Comics" in advance to teachers and students. The booklet, featuring a comic strip about art and a story, "The Artrain Ghost," alerts students to ideas they will be exposed to on the train. The back page, "Make your own art," suggests activities that can be done in any classroom, and the whole inside is a wall poster to take home and hang as a lasting reminder of the visit.

November-December 1972

School Children
Study for Orchestra Concert

A grammar school program in North Carolina offers some lessons in developing future audiences who will understand, appreciate, and participate in the arts. It is also a good example of school support for an orchestral group.

Teachers of fifth and sixth grade students in North Carolina's Greensboro and Guilford Counties believed that their pupils get most benefit and enjoyment from something they understand. Weeks before a performance of the North Carolina Symphony orchestra the teachers began preparing their student for the concert.

Recordings of the concert's program were played to give the children a familiarity with the music. Sometimes the pupils simply listened; at other times they danced or painted their reactions to the music. They learned two songs based on the music, and those who could play simple instruments learned a score written especially for these instruments.

They learned what instruments comprise a symphony orchestra and how these instruments are arranged on the stage for a concert. Films, pictures, and live demonstrations were used to show what each instrument looked like and how it sounded.

Trips to the school library taught them something about the lives of the composers whose music they would hear. On the basis of research, they wrote reports about the composers, prepared bulletin boards showing events in their lives, and painted or drew pictures of these events.

On the day of the concert more than 400 students played their recorders, harps, and bells along with the orchestra, and the whole group joined in the songs.

July 1963

A CHRONOLOGY OF ARTS-IN-EDUCATION DEVELOPMENTS

New Government Agency to Promote Improvement of Education in the Arts

The goal of the recently established Cultural Affairs Branch in the federal Office of Education is to develop programs and activities designed to promote extension and improvement of education in the arts at all levels.

Kathryn Bloom, branch director, summed up her new agency's relation to arts organizations this way for *AM:* "I see this as a friendly adviser kind of relationship between government and the arts. We do not intend to represent a benevolent Uncle Sam intent on control."

Because the Cultural Affairs Branch is part of the Office of Education, under the Department of Health, Education and Welfare, Miss Bloom said that there must be some kind of education relevance in its activities. But this does not mean that the work of her branch will be restricted to schools, or to school-age pupils.

Attention will be given to arts education programs for adults as well as for young people, whether they are offered by community art, music, theater, or dance groups, or by museums, cultural centers, or arts councils.

Since her appointment to direct the branch in July 1963, Miss Bloom has been building her staff. Dr. Harold Arberg assists her as music education specialist. When the table of organization is filled, they will be joined by educational specialists in museum, graphic art, and performing arts work, plus research and clerical staff members. The branch budget comes from the overall appropriation for the Office of Education.

A principal activity of the branch, Miss Bloom said, will be to collect

comprehensive and definitive information regarding the state of the arts in American life and education. It is planned that a fact-finding program will be developed in order that information may be gathered in a continuing and orderly fashion, and that this will be interpreted and disseminated widely.

Needless to say, this will not take the place of research regarding the arts which is carried on by professional associations and individuals, but should provide a general and comprehensive background for such surveys and studies.

In addition, the branch will emphasize research in arts education and has funds authorized by Congress to support special projects in this area. A seminar on music education was held at Yale University last summer, with federal support, and the Office of Education is publishing the seminar proceedings.

A third area of branch activity is in publications to meet specific needs in arts education. For example, the Office is publishing *Curriculum Guides for Music,* an annotated bibliography of guides in use by states and the larger cities and counties. Branch experts also write articles for professional publications. There is no regular branch periodical in sight yet, however.

The fourth area of Cultural Affairs Branch work lies in consultative services and the exchange of information. Staff members are available to render technical assistance through interviews, correspondence, and attendance at conferences. It has already been represented at recent meetings on music education in Japan and on art education in Montreal.

Closer cooperation and working relationships with professional organizations is considered a basic part of her unit's work, Miss Bloom told *AM.*

The director is particularly well suited for her unique and pioneering position in federal government. A graduate of the University of Minnesota, Miss Bloom has been progressively an art teacher in public schools, art museum lecturer, supervisor of art education at the Toledo Museum of Art, and, from 1957 to 1963, consultant of the arts for the Association of Junior Leagues of America.

December 1963

Top Education Leader Discusses Title III

In this 1968 interview with AM *editor Alvin H. Reiss, Miss Kathryn Bloom, director of the Arts and Humanities Program of the U.S. Office of Education, dis-*

cussed the Elementary and Secondary Education Act and its past and future relevance to the arts.

Q: The Elementary and Secondary Education Act of 1965 has recently been extended by Congress for two years. Can you please explain what this extension means in terms of funding and program?

A: Because Congress feels that great progress has been made thus far, it is continuing its support of the program with a recommendation for an increase in funds. For Title III alone, $525 million has been authorized for the two years beginning in fiscal year 1969, although the money has not been appropriated as yet. During the past three years there has been a significant increase in Title III appropriations: $75 million in 1966, $162 million in 1967, and $187 million in 1968. Also, beginning in 1969, Title III administration will be phased out of of the Office of Education directly to state education agencies. In 1969, state agencies, which have been greatly strengthened by their participation in the program, will administer 75 percent of the funds, and in 1970, 100 percent.

Q: Under the various titles of the act, how much money has been expended on the arts since 1965?

A: The figures are not available for all titles of the act as yet. However, we do know that in 1966, $15 million of Title III funds went to support arts programs.

Q: The express purpose of Title III was to develop innovative programs. Has this objective been fully realized in projects involving the arts?

A: A high percentage of the programs have been innovative in terms of community need. Schools have learned what arts resources exist in their communities, and they now know how to use those resources. Broadly speaking, several kinds of innovations in education, like team teaching and flexible scheduling of arts courses, have been major advances in improving arts instruction in the schools.

Q: What are the reasons that some of the programs have been less than innovative and meaningful?

A: A major initial difficulty was the breakdown of communications between arts and education leaders. They both found it difficult to understand each other's problems. Also, on the arts side, many organizations erroneously thought of Title III grants as operating funds. Some of the resulting projects were for children, but they were not really educational; other projects were rushed into development before the participants were ready for them.

Q: What can be done to improve communications between education and the arts?

A: Professional associations in both areas can be extremely helpful in explaining needs to their constituents through programs, seminars, and printed materials.

Understanding, however, really begins at the local level, and here a catalytic agent, like an arts council, chamber of commerce, or the mayor's office, can play a key role.

Q: What is the future of ongoing Title III projects involving the arts?

A: Even though federal support for education has increased substantially, the federal government is very definitely a junior partner in providing funds for schools. The majority of financial support comes from state and local funds. Title III projects are supported on a three-year basis. Hopefully, these projects will demonstrate their value as an ongoing part of the curriculum of the schools that initiated them.

Q: Has the overall program in the arts worked out as well as your office hoped it would?

A: Overall, very much so. The kind of exposure available through the program has been very valuable. Many schools have learned how to work with arts organizations and with poets, musicians, and artists, who, before the program was initiated, were seldom looked on as resources for educating children.

Q: Some people in the arts feel that participation in Title I and Title III programs can subvert their true artistic purpose. How do you feel about this?

A: Participation doesn't have to subvert true artistic purposes. It is up to the artistic director of a group to determine how much time he wants to devote to adult audiences and how much to children. If he feels he shouldn't participate in these programs, then by all means he shouldn't. Arts leaders must remember, however, that while participation in a program is not intended to meet an arts program deficit, it can open the door to possible future funds and new audiences.

Q: What can we look for in the future of this program and in the future relationship between education and the arts?

A: A positive climate has already been established. With proper understanding, the interdependence and interrelationship between the arts and education will continue to grow. Our office (Arts and Humanities Program, U.S. Office of Education, Washington, D.C. 20202) would welcome hearing from any arts leaders who have suggestions on strengthening the ties between these significant areas.

January-February 1968

Drive to Broaden Arts-in-Education Gains

The movement to broaden the arts role in public education has accelerated considerably as a result of positive developments on several fronts. They include:

- Several pilot arts in education program have completed or are about to complete their initial funding phases successfully, and their prospects for renewed funding from local sources are excellent. Moreover, they can now provide education systems with models to be studied and emulated.

- A broad and multifaceted national arts in education program, Project Arts/Worth, has completed its initial organization and is now entering a new action-oriented phase.

- The North American Society of State and Provincial Arts Agencies has joined the campaign by issuing a strong eight-point resolution calling for an expansion of the arts in education.

- Imaginative new programs linking the arts with school systems are being developed.

- A growing number of school administrators, including some who were skeptical initially, have witnessed arts programs as part of the the curriculum and have become convinced of their value.

- A philosophical rationale for infusing the arts into the educational system is winning acceptance by many thought leaders.

The program with perhaps the greatest immediacy to cultural institutions is Project Arts/Worth, conceived and initiated by the National Council of the Arts in Education to "establish more firmly the role of the arts in general education." Funded through June 1973 by a three-year planning grant of $200,000 from the National Endowment for the Humanities, Arts/Worth, during its first year, has researched needs and planned its overall approach; gathered information on existing arts in education programs; begun to develop a network of 25 regional representatives throughout the country; organized five special consultative committees; and established its identity in both the arts and education communities.

Now the program is moving into a direct action phase with several tangible projects on the horizon. On February 25–26, 1972, for example, Arts/Worth will sponsor the first in a series of regional symposia on the arts role in education, developed with the aid of its regional representatives. These representative, according to Arts/Worth director Allen Sapp, will be "our organization's eyes and ears around the country." Upcoming in March is a White Paper on the arts role in education, which also defines the aims and purposes of Arts/Worth, and by summer the organization will begin publishing a national newsletter. Later this year, Arts/Worth will launch a national public relations campaign aimed at educators, legislators, and school administrators and finalize plans for a centralized information resources center.

Sapp, on leave from his dual post as professor of music and director of cultural affairs at the State University of New York in Buffalo, told *AM*, "We're developing a case and taking it to the people who can help to redefine priorities and switch goals in the education system—to school administrators, rural teachers, and legislators. We're also helping people to learn to use the resources on hand, the millions of untapped dollars, to develop new and permanent cultural programs in our schools. We hope that people will come to us and learn to use us."

Elsewhere, imaginative pilot arts programs in public schools funded by the Arts in Education Program of the JDR 3rd Fund have succeeded in making a positive impact on local education leaders. In University City, Missouri, for example, the foundation funded a program that incorporated the arts into the general curriculum of all classes from kindergarten through grade 12. When the three-year grant ended several months ago, the local board of education, voted to assume financial support for a fourth and fifth year.

In Mineola, Long Island, where a three-year foundation-funded project dealing with widespread student exposure to artists and arts groups ends this year, serious local attention is being given to ways in which the program can be continued. At P.S. 51 in New York, a foundation project to train teachers to teach the arts is continuing after expiration of the grant period through the initiative of the principal. As a result of the program's success, the JDR 3rd Fund has just awarded a grant to the Bank Street College of Education to develop a program aimed at training school administrators in the arts. Recently, other JDR 3rd Fund grants have been given to school districts in Oklahoma City, Oklahoma, and Jefferson County, Colorado to enable them to draw on the experiences of the pilot projects.

In five schools elsewhere, another pilot project is completing the initial funded phase of its operations this June, and here, too, the prospects for program continuance and additional funding look good. Project Impact, a $1-million program funded by the U.S. Office of Education for two years, has involved an integration of the arts—dance, theater, film, music, and visual art—into all aspects of the elementary and middle school program. Indications thus far are that the project has changed the environment in participating schools and that the arts have become a more normal part of the school day. Administrators in cities with Impact schools—Philadelphia; Troy, Alabama; Columbus, Ohio; Glendale, California; and Eugene, Oregon—have agreed to underwrite efforts to work cooperatively and seek outside funding to keep the programs going. Locally, attempts are being made to find money from community resources and state education departments.

In Rhode Island, the Arts in Education Project funded by the Arts Endowment and Office of Education has achieved positive results in communities throughout the state. Now in the second year of a three-year grant, the program uses local arts groups to provide cultural programs in schools and train teachers. A program initiated this fall by Lincoln Center is enabling each of 12 performing artists to be in residence at a city high school twice a week for 30 weeks. These resource professionals work with 150 students regularly at each school to encourage their involvement in the arts. Classroom activities, which include student experimentation in dance, music, and writing, are supplemented by discussion and by student attendance at performances and rehearsals.

January-February 1972

Pilot Program

Participation has been broadened in the pilot arts-in-general-education project of the JDR 3rd Fund and public schools of New York with the selection as program participants of all 32 schools who submitted proposals. The cooperative program, the largest joint venture between an urban public school system and a private foundation, is a comprehensive long-range school development project that incorporates all the arts into the learning and teaching process through program planning and development, technical assistance, staff training, and curriculum development.

January-February 1975

Arts-in-Education Study

Support for a stronger arts role in education will come from a $250,000 panel study initiated in 1975 under the auspices of the American Council for the Arts in Education. The panel, composed of 26 leaders from varied fields supplemented by a staff of researchers and administrators, has met twice as a body since an organizational session in June to hear "expert witnesses" discuss such areas as the significance of the arts in education and problems in curriculum and teacher training. Panel efforts will culminate in the publication of a report titled "The Arts, Education and Americans," which will include major recommendations in each of the areas covered.

Organized somewhat along the lines of the 1965 Rockefeller Brothers Fund panel on the performing arts, the current group, chaired by David Rockefeller Jr., will focus on community resources in a February meeting in Los Angeles and on financing and policy making in an April meeting in Minneapolis. In June the group will come together for a final two-and-a-half-day meeting in New York to consider the various research reports and background papers prepared for it, as well as the testimony of the many witnesses, prior to formulating the report's key recommendations.

Witnesses appearing before the panel thus far have included national arts and education leaders, critics, artists working in school programs, poets-in-residence, local and state school administrators, school board members, and heads of innovative arts in education programs in several communities.

November-December 1975

New City Arts-in-Education Coalition Formed

The movement to strengthen the arts role in elementary and secondary schools continues to grow with the development of new mechanisms. In Chicago, a League of Cities for the Arts in Education grew out of a March 31–April 2, 1976, meeting of chief administrators and arts project directors of public school education departments in six cities—Hartford, Little Rock, Minneapolis, New York, Seattle, and Winston-Salem. The group, brought together by the JDR 3rd Fund, which provides consultative and informational support for arts in education programs, will operate as an informal but united coalition to help each other solve specific problems relating to existing programs and to provide information to other cities interested in broadening the arts role in the general curriculum.

The new league is similar in its structure to the ten-member Coalition of States for the Arts in Education organized last year by the JDR 3rd Fund. In both instances, members were recruited from areas which already were involved with the fund because of their strong commitment to arts in education. Working through a steering committee, the coalition has met regularly and developed comprehensive plans for organizing arts in education programs at the state level. A free information booklet, "Comprehensive Arts Planning," is available from the JDR 3rd Fund, 50 Rockefeller Plaza, New York, New York 10020.

Meanwhile, the long-range arts-in-education program initiated by the JDR 3rd Fund in New York public schools involving teacher training, demonstration techniques, and consultative help is moving into its second successful year. "What we're trying to demonstrate," says Jane Remer, a program associate, "is that if teachers, principals, and community people really are interested in improving the quality of education through the arts, they can make it happen." The model process developed in the New York program is being adapted for use by the five other members of the new Cities League.

March-April 1976

*The Los Indianos fold dancers performing at the
1977 opening-day celebration of "Lincoln Center Out-of-Doors."
(Photo by Susanne Faulkner Stevens)*

9

The Arts and Society

RECOGNITION
OF THE ARTS

Culture's Community Role
Is Receiving Wider Recognition

The arts' battle for recognition and status in the community continues, with some positive points scored in recent months. In January 1972, for example, in a precedent-shattering move, the Chicago Press Club awarded a plaque to the 106-member Chicago Symphony Orchestra as 1971's "Chicagoan-of-the-Year." In Seattle, the County Board of Realtors named an arts administrator, Glynn Ross, general director of the Seattle Opera, as recipient of the city's coveted First Citizen award.

In April 1972, the arts case for increased federal funding was given a boost by a leading national magazine, *Saturday Review*. An editorial by president and editor-in-chief John J. Veronis strongly supported the Partnership for the Arts' priority of $200 million in federal grants by 1976.

In the education field, greater recognition for the arts has come with the granting of credits to students participating in arts activities outside the classroom. Long Beach State College in California has awarded credits for off-campus dance activities, and Hunter College students in New York are receiving credit for working with the city's Cultural Affairs Department. In Mahopac, New York, high school credits are being given to students participating in the program at the Belle Levine Arts Center.

A somewhat whimsical recognition of the growing cultural audience was found in a letter accompanying a mailing in South Carolina's February educational television program guide. The letter bore the simple heading "Dear Arts Fan."

March-April 1972

The Arts Receive
Wider Public Recognition

The arts have been major newsmakers in recent months. From international to municipal level, cultural groups have received wide attention and recognition from the press as a result of some key developments. The most widely covered of all recent arts events may have been the Philadelphia Orchestra's tour to China, with reports and features discussing everything from the performances to experiments with acupuncture to impromptu street concerts by orchestra players. About the time the orchestra returned, the Arena Stage of Washington, D.C. left for a series of performances in Russia.

In America, one of the largest individual gifts ever made to the Arts, Avery Fisher's donation of an estimated $8 million to Lincoln Center's Philharmonic

Hall [now Avery Fisher Hall], commanded considerable attention. Importantly, the bulk of the Fisher gift was earmarked not for capital expenditures, but for annual maintenance and operating deficit. Earlier, another Lincoln Center building, the Forum, became the Mitzi E. Newhouse Theater, following a $1 million donation by Mrs. Newhouse to the New York Shakespeare Festival.

Perhaps the most important newspaper coverage given the arts occurred in August when the prestigious *New York Times* ran two consecutive page-one features dealing with positive aspects of cultural activity. The stories, neither of them hard news, focused on the Arts Endowment (Aug. 12) and on New York State's Commission on Cultural Resources (Aug. 13). Within a following four-week period, from August 27 to September 28, the *Times* ran five editorials on the arts—three in a four-day period—and an excerpt from a talk by New York State Arts Council director, Eric Larrabee, on its Op Ed page.

The renomination of Nancy Hanks as chairman of the National Endowment for the Arts was an event treated with fanfare, as photographers recorded the formal ceremony presided over by President Nixon in his White House Oval office. Sixteen members of the National Council on Arts attended. Even greater public recognition is coming. *Newsweek* will devote an entire issue in December to the arts.

September-October 1973

Lobbying Activities

Because of the increasing arts concern with influencing legislation, groups should be aware of the new regulations regarding lobbying. Tax-exempt organizations with total expenditures of $500,000 or less can spend 20 percent of the total, excluding federal funds, on lobbying activities without endangering their status. In three other categories up to expenditures over $1.5 million, the percentages are determined on a sliding scale.

March-April 1977

Cultural Groups
Step up Lobbying Activities

Lobbying activity is increasing significantly in the arts. In addition to such groups as Advocates for the Arts, the National Committee for Symphony Orchestra Support, Concerned Citizens for the Arts, and the newer National Council for Arts and Education, new organizations are being formed at the state level and arts leaders from different disciplines have been coming together to plan coordinated activities. At its recent meeting, the Advocates for the Arts board voted to go ahead with plans to represent various arts disciplines in Washington and approved a move to place their staff in a Washington office.

At the state level, some 25 different advocate-style groups have been organized, some very recently. In Washington, a series of meetings earlier this year resulted in the formation of a new statewide alliance headed by a board of 32 members. In Ohio, the Citizens Committee for the Arts stepped up its activities with a series of rallies throughout the state, culminating in a final "Celebration For the Arts" in Columbus, the state capital, a week prior to the beginning of state arts budget hearings. In Massachusetts, Public Action for the Performing Arts has just adopted an ambitious three-year action plan which will include an expanded informational program, new fund-raising activities for arts groups, and development of a state advocates network.

State legislators, meanwhile, are taking a tougher attitude towards arts funding. An *AM* spot check of states indicates that although there have been breakthroughs in several instances, many states seem to be holding the line on arts funding. Where increases have been or may be voted, a key factor has been the efforts of advocacy groups.

In New York, for example, where the state council received as much as $34.1 million several years ago, a budget of $26,599,200 for the coming fiscal year, down by $750,000 from last year, was voted. The Legislature also took a tough attitude towards administrative spending and transferred some state arts programs—technical assistance, the dance touring program, and the performing organization assistance program—from the separate New York Foundation for the Arts to the Council.

A more upbeat situation seems to be developing in California. After the new council had requested a $4.3 million appropriation, triple last year's $1.4 million, Governor Brown recommended just under $4 million, and also gave his approval to a bill to place $700,000 in the state architect's budget for fine art.

March-April 1977

Recognition of the Arts Grows on Varied Fronts

Joan Mondale is helping to increase national recognition of the arts, but she isn't alone in the effort. The October 24 1977 covers of both *Time* and *Newsweek* for example, featured artists from two different disciplines, painter Jasper Johns in *Newsweek* and cellist-conductor Mstislav Rostropovich in *Time*.

In a key national development, a National League of Cities task force on the arts, headed by Mayor Frank Logue of New Haven and Councilman Joel Wachs of Los Angeles, aided by American Council for the Arts, has been seeking ways to increase the arts role in city life. One positive result will be felt in the League's annual meeting in San Francisco, December 2-4, when the arts will be included in the program to a far greater degreee than ever before. There will be Friday and Saturday sessions for city and county arts officials, who will be joined by other League members on Saturday, and a complete session for the entire league membership on Sunday. Potentially more significant is the work of the task force on the upcoming National Municipal Policy statement which is adopted by the league annually. Members have prepared recommendations to include arts involvement in virtually every area of city activity listed in the 200-plus page statement.

The United States Department of Commerce, meanwhile, has recognized the arts with the establishment of an Office of Cultural Resources headed by Louise Wiener, named special assistant to the Secretary for Cultural Resources. In her new position, Ms. Wiener will be concerned with departmental activities affecting the arts and will develop management data on departmental programs that have economic impact on arts-related industries and the general economy. Ms. Wiener will work closely with other agencies within the Commerce Department on arts-related matters.

Dance is in the limelight as it has moved into a new area of popular entertainment, film. *The Turning Point* a movie about a new soloist with the mythical American Ballet Company includes 40 minutes of dance and features Mikhail Baryshnikov and members of the American Ballet Theatre in its cast. Ann Ditchburn of the Canadian National Ballet plays a struggling dancer in *Slow Dancing in the Big City*, Rudolph Nureyev is *Valentino*, and, in *A Piece of the Action*, Sidney Poitier and Bill Cosby take their dates to a performance by the Dance Theater of Harlem.

Dance will achieve added recognition next year when the U.S. Postal Service releases a block of four different dance stamps. The Association of American Dance Companies, which has campaigned for dance stamps for several years (board member Ben Sommers has led the campaign), will launch the first National Dance Week to roughly coincide with the issuance. In another postal development, a continuing "Performing Arts and Artists" series will be initiated in 1978.

On a local level, Arts Development Services, a Buffalo, New York arts council, spurred countywide awareness of the arts with a Salute to the Arts Week from October 3-8. Built around the slogan "Culture is Contagious—Catch Some," the week featured daily performances and events at shopping malls, display materials on the arts in downtown department stores and mall retail outlets, and an arts information booth at each of the performance sites. Press coverage throughout the week, which served as a kickoff for a year-long arts promotional campaign, was excellent.

September-October 1977

Arts Policy

Policy has become a key word in the arts as conferences, hearings, programs, and reports focus on arts policy or the lack of it. Perhaps the strongest thrust towards a national arts policy is the movement for a White House Conference on the Arts for 1979. Congressman Brademas is conducting open hearings—one at New York's Juilliard School this December drew 300 people—for his House Subcommittee on Select Education, to determine interest in H.J. Res. 600.

The Carter Administration will review existing arts policy, according to reports from Washington, as part of a series of presidential reviews it undertakes for areas of national concern. The review, which probably would be undertaken by the Federal Council on the Arts and Humanities, would address itself to the role of federal government in the arts and its relationship to cultural groups and artists.

The Fifty-Third American Assembly, meanwhile, met for three days in November to discuss arts policy. The resulting report, "The Future of the Performing Arts," concluded among other things that the American people "need a more clearly understood public policy about the arts." The 19 recommendations, representing general agreement among the 61 invited participants drawn from every area of the arts, aroused some controversy as they leaned towards support of recognized and established institutions and away from education, community, and social efforts in the arts. Recommendation 6 said in part, "The financing of arts in education is the responsibility of the field of education," while recommendation 16 stated, "The direct support of the regular operations of a performing arts institution should take precedence over the funds for special projects or for social or educational goals."

The report is available without charge from the American Assembly, Columbia University, New York, New York 10027. A book edited by W. McNeil Lowry, with background papers prepared for the assembly, *The Performing Arts and American Society*, will be published early in 1978 by Prentice-Hall.

November-December 1977

Lobbying Force

The American Arts Alliance is becoming as well known in the Halls of Congress as it is to arts groups throughout the nation. Currently it is keeping in touch with legislators and its arts organization constituency on some 40 pieces of legislation involving the arts, although it has limited its major activity to four priority areas: the NEA appropriation, where it is trying to insure approval of the full $150 million for the coming fiscal year; the bill calling for a White House Conference on the Arts; postal service legislation to protect the interests of nonprofit arts organizations, and several areas of the new tax bill dealing with charitable and ticket deductions, including urging restoration of the pre-1969 provisions allowing artists to deduct 100 percent of the fair market value of a donated work.

The alliance, organized by national disciplinary arts service organizations as an action and lobbying force, has received membership applications from or-

ganizations outside its initial constituency, and in the coming months will resolve the question of whether to expand. Meanwhile, a Political Action Network
of key people around the country is being organized within its membership to
provide immediate attention to major matters.

September-October 1977

COMMUNITY-WIDE ACTIVITIES

Orrel Thompson

An Arts Need:
Public Communities Programs

Early in their battle for survival, the health, welfare, and education fields all
learned the need for developing programs aimed at building and maintaining
the support of city, county, and state agencies and elected officials—the public
communities. The arts need such community development programs now. With
growing demands for services, the implications of the energy crisis, changing
urban environments, and increased competition from other pressure groups, the
arts, unless they reserve their traditional stance of political noninvolvement, can
lose the few gains they've made in public support in recent years.

An aggressive community development program properly structured and
maintained should lead to:

- Stronger arts participation in the destiny of its community, including the
  planning, control, and creation of its visual environment
- Stronger lines of communication between public officials and the arts that, in
  turn, should result in a mutual identification of needs and resources
- Greater commitment by both parties to resolve community problems as well
  as arts problems
- The development of better tools for forecasting and planning future arts
  needs
- Recognition of the arts as a key educational resource and community priority
  (a position few enjoy today), with increased private funding a possible result
- Identification of new audiences

Granted the specific opportunities to be met, how do the arts implement
this kind of program? First, it must be understood that any public communities
program is long-range and permanent. While specific needs may be met with ease
on occasion, needs with long-term implications often demand greater patience
and commitment. Second, doing one's homework is essential since the arts are
competing with other, often more experienced, public agencies. Do not be easily
discouraged. Learn the process and rules of the game, who makes decisions, how
and when they are made, and what information must be provided. Third, re-

member that legislators can also use your support. It costs little to publicly recognize their efforts on your behalf. Say "thank you" occasionally—words often
absent from the arts vocabulary.

The arts must make greater effort not only to better understand the political process, but also to better understand the needs of those supportive of its
programs and developments. As a voting constituency, the arts can and should
assist the public community during periods of crisis. Why should the system only
flow in the direction of the arts? While these first suggestions would appear elementary, it is in these fundamentals that most people attempting to influence
decisions in their behalf fail.

Programs also must dispel the stereotype of the arts held by public officials. Many feel that the arts serve a select few, are unresponsive to community
needs, are aloof from society and seek out the public sector only when they are
in need or at a time of crisis.

To establish an aggressive community development program and unhinge
some of these misconceptions, consider organizing a community development
committee composed of selected representatives from various community arts
groups. Insist on broad representation and don't limit membership to the larger
and older organizations. This group should work directly with public officials
and agencies to bring representatives from both sectors together to discuss needs
and explore potential programming. The strongest statement will be made by a
consortium of arts groups cognizant of its leverage as a constituency. Such a consortium can demonstrate a position of solidarity and common concern for community problems with which public officials can identify.

A few letters during the year do not constitute an effective development
program. Personal experience has shown that legislators may be most interested
and appreciative of the opportunity to attend a play, reception, or social event.
Such invitations offer them an opportunity to get away from the consuming
life of politics, establish new contacts, and benefit from identification with such
new associations. Also, personally involving a community representative with
your board and including him in its normal social affairs can seldom do your
cause harm.

The social aspect of such a program is not a means to an end in itself, and
a consistent program of communications, support, and participation should be
interwoven into such social efforts:

1.   When you are in the state capitol or city hall, call at the offices of the leg-
     islator representing your district.
2.   Invite key officials to address your staff, board, or membership on impor-
     tant community issues that may directly or indirectly affect your exis-
     tence—transportation, taxation, planning, environment, parks and recre-
     ation, restoration, etc.

3. Become an information resource to elected officials. Assist them in mak-
    ing intelligent decisions based on fact; however, do not flood their offices
    with materials of marginal interest. Get to know their interests and needs
    and assist them in these areas, if at all possible.

4. Update your knowledge of the political process—how decisions are made,
    how bills pass, etc. Your odds for success increase proportionately to
    your understanding.

5. Keep contacts current, even if you have received the legislation, subsidy,
    or cooperation you are interested in.

6. Take advantage of the experience of others. Talk to your senator's staff
    and seek advice from local corporate public affairs directors. Get to know
    political consultants in the community, and enlist their volunteer aid to
    your board.

Any public communities program should include greater involvement of
arts administrators in community service activities. Chamber of commerce, service organizations, or planning committees provide new opportunities for helpful contacts.

These partnership recommendations are made with the full realization
of the problems and pitfalls inherent in such associations. The political process,
with its uncertainties, ambiguities, and, at times, irrationalities, requires astute
awareness and old-fashioned political moxie. These talents can be developed.

Many communities are enjoying increasing benefits because of their development efforts. While I would not suggest as some that the new politicians may
be the arts patrons of the future, the possibilities are worth pondering.

January-February 1974

Arts Council City Tour
Wins Friends and Funds

Arts groups in communities that attract large numbers of tourists might consider
establishing guided tours of their city to bring in extra revenue and to publicize
their own organization. The Dallas Symphony has sponsored "Face of Dallas"
tours for some time; in 1962 the Coordinating Council for the Arts in Hartford,
Connecticut initiated tours on the theme "This is Hartford."

When arts council leaders in Hartford several years ago conceived the idea
of organized tours patterned after the Dallas operation, they first investigated
the possible interest that visitors would have in such tours and the probable
number of visitors to the city. One knowledgeable local resident then volunteered to check landmarks and points of interest, draw up suggested itineraries,
and determine the approximate time for each tour.

At this point the council recognized that the job was too big and important for volunteer help. It hired a local housewife who had been active in volunteer work and who was interested in the city of Hartford and its history to serve as tour leader.

In May 1962, five regular tours for groups of 15 or more were established. They ranged from a $3.50 per person, two-and-a-half hour "Heart of Hartford" tour for the visitor with limited time to a deluxe tour by Cadillac limousine, with prices dependent upon length of time taken. The other three tours, costing $4.50 per person, were all three-and-a-half hours long.

Rather than operating on a regular schedule, tours are arranged by appointment, when there are a sufficient number of visitors interested in taking one. Mrs. Andrew Shepard, the guide, is able to adapt to this flexible schedule. She is paid $1.00 for each person taking the tour.

For a two-and-a-half hour tour of 20 people at $3.50 per person, the bus company gets $1.00 per person, admissions account for 50¢, Mrs. Shepard receives $1.00, and the arts council receives $1.00. As the number of visitors goes up, the bus price per person goes down and the council received the additional revenue.

Conventions are the mainstay of an effective tour program, according to Mrs. Shepard, since they bring large groups who are interested in seeing the highlights of the community quickly and in an organized way. Although the program has been developing slowly, and profits to the arts council are small, the tour sponsors hope that convention guests scheduled to visit Hartford this spring will help to boost attendance. A brochure describing the tour is helping to promote the program.

While few organizations may get rich on this kind of activity, its public relations benefits to the sponsoring organization and to the city can be compensation enough.

March 1963

Artists-in-Residence
Belong to Whole City

A unique artist-in-residence project, established in 1962 for an entire community rather than for a single institution, is part of a comprehensive citywide program for the arts and education in Flint, Michigan, a city of 200,000 residents.

A spur to the development of major cultural activities in Flint has been the Committee of Sponsors for the Flint College and Cultural Development, Inc., a nonprofit organization founded in 1954. Since then, in community fund-raising drives, the committee has raised more than $30 million from 12,000 donors for educational and cultural facilities. Already, nearly $8 million has been turned over to the Flint Board of Education for the construction and maintenance of such educational and cultural buildings as the DeWaters Arts Center, the home of the Flint Institute of Arts, which was completed several years ago.

In addition, several committee projects initially conceived in 1954 are now nearing realization. A theater-auditorium seating 2100 and a museum of trans- portation will be completed by 1965. The museum will be the first unit of a complex that will eventually have additional wings for a museum of history, a museum of natural history, a children's museum, and a science museum.

The artist-in-residence program originated when a group of prominent Flint residents, impressed with a concert by young pianist, Coleman Blumfield, suggested that he be brought to the community. Last year, Blumfield became Flint's first artist-in-residence in a program administered by the Flint Board of Education and underwritten by the W.S. Ballenger Trust and Charles Stewart Mott Foundation.

The purpose of the program is two-fold. First, it is designed to stimulate the cultural life of the community and its music students by providing access to a top musical talent at no charge. Second, it gives recognition to an outstand- ing young artist.

During his recently concluded first season—he has been reengaged for 1963 —Blumfield taught master classes to promising students, performed with com- munity groups, and gave concerts.

November 1963

Community Artists-in-Residence Stimulate Amateur Performers

A month-long experimental artist-in-residence program sponsored by the Fort Wayne, Indiana Fine Arts Foundation, an arts council, proved so successful that it will become an annual program. It will alternate yearly between the per- forming and the graphic arts.

In cooperation with the Fort Wayne Ballet, the city's nonprofessional dance company, the foundation engaged the First Chamber Dance Quartet as artists-in-residence beginning in May 1965. The Quartet's dancers are former members of the New York City Ballet.

During its stay in the community, the quartet presented three performan- ces, including two premieres at the Fort Wayne Fine Arts Festival, and also per- formed with the Fort Wayne Ballet. Its members taught advanced classes at the ballet's school, created a ballet for the local company, and gave lecture-demon- strations in the city's public schools.

In addition, the quartet spent four days with ballet teachers and advanced students from other cities in Indiana and from neighboring states. They led a workshop on costuming and conducted master classes.

George M. Schaefer, executive director of the foundation, told *AM*, "the Quartet gave our ballet students a new lease on life and completely won over school audiences.

"Furthermore," added Mr. Schaefer, "our experiment proved that the presence of professionals in no way lessens the pleasure of the amateur performer. On the contrary, it heightens his pleasure and stimulates him to improve his own abilities."

To enable the arts council to establish an annual artist-in-residence grant, the local Community Concert organization is booking a nonsubscription performance by the Metropolitan Opera National Company. Proceeds will go to the foundation.

Not only arts and education groups, however, are employing artists-in-residence. In an unusual development, the Norwegian Lines' M.S. *Viking Princess* named an artist-in-residence for its 106-day round-the-world cruise. John Day, an American painter, has been given studio facilities aboard the ship to prepare his one-man show to be held in New York. During the trip he will discuss painting daily with passengers.

September 1965

A Helping Hand

A community's better-known arts organizations might lend a helping hand to less-established groups and help themselves at the same time. At the beginning of the 1972-73 season, Allied Arts of Seattle, an arts council, organized a Survival Series with each of the four events featuring a different small arts group in a performance followed by a discussion. Designed to widen the audiences for the less-established groups and give them financial support, the programs were planned also to give Allied Arts members and supporters an opportunity, at bargain prices, to see groups that they had heard of but had never seen in performance. The subscription price was $10.00 with $2.00 from each single performance price of $2.50 going to the producing group. Although there were some difficulties because of the program's newness, most subscribers considered it a success. The result? An expanded series of six events was scheduled for the next season.

January-February 1973

Citizens' Arts Panels
Plan Ahead for Tulsa

A series of panel reports on the arts of Tulsa, Oklahoma may help shape that city's cultural future. The reports submitted to the board of the Arts Council of Tulsa, contained the findings and recommendations of five of the six panels appointed by the organization in 1964 to investigate the city's cultural activities. The council is expected to rely on the panel proposals in its planning.

For the first time in the city's history, the panels brought together local cultural leaders to develop a short-term as well as a long-range program for the arts. Each panel, consisting of 20 to 30 persons, met independently from four to five times during the year. Reports were submitted on the theater, dance, the literary arts, galleries and the visual arts, and city planning, landscaping, architecture, and interior design. A report by the panel on music will be issued shortly.

While each panel had specific suggestions, several overall recommendations, to which all the panels subscribed, were made. Most dramatic of these was the suggestion that a multipurpose performing arts center be built in Tulsa.

All panels saw the need for better coordination by the arts council in the planning of cultural events and in the dissemination of information.

Agreeing that audience building was a crying need of the arts in Tulsa, the panels came forth with a series of recommendations calling for greater promotional activity. Interestingly, they called for more publicity for good imported cultural events, which tend to receive less editorial space than strictly local arts activities.

Each panel found many existing problems in its specific area of investigation, and recommendations were terse and practical. Quality performances and professionalism were frequently cited needs, and in general, there was a call for increased contemporary programming—more modern dance, experimental theater, and modern art exhibitions.

November 1965

Council Sends Display on Tour
to Help Promote Its Programs

A low-cost and easily transportable traveling display has provided an arts council with an efficient and successful method of promoting its program and services to the community.

The idea of assembling the display was conceived in the fall of 1964 by the Arts Council of Columbus, Ohio during the planning of its annual "Winter Showcase of the Arts," a ten-day festival highlighting community cultural events. Originally, the display was planned as a promotional vehicle to be exhibited at specific events during the showcase period and arouse audience interest in other showcase attractions; however, the exhibit proved so popular that it has gone into year-round use, circulating from facility to facility.

The display consists of posters, programs, and photographs from each of the arts council's member organizations, representing such organizational characteristics as artists, physical facilities, and program content. These are blown up and dry-mounted on various-sized colored, flexible poster boards and then placed on an aluminum framework consisting of four triangular, curved, free-standing units, 3 feet wide by 6 feet high. There is flexibility in the use of the exhibit since the components can be assembled into one unit or set up separately in close proximity to each other.

One of the key features of the display is the low cost in assembling it and in reconstructing it. In 1965, when it was first built, it cost $175. This year when it was rebuilt for the Winter Showcase, it cost only $121, because the aluminum framework remained usable and several exhibits did not have to be replaced.

Because of the effectiveness of the display in reaching a wide range of people, including many who are not normally part of the arts audience, the council plans to continue using it indefinitely. Most recently, for example, it was shown at a library and then was transported to a neighborhood community center.

For other arts groups who may consider using a similar display, Mrs. Frank W. Bentley, public relations chairman of the council, offers this advice. "Make sure that the display is easy to transport. Ours can be dismantled and then reassembled and transported easily in a station wagon. The exhibit should also be stable enough to transport. Our units fold so they can fit into each other easily."

August-September 1966

Local Arts Council
Fights City Hall and Wins

The united voice of the arts has scored an impressive victory over the forces of City Hall in Greensboro, North Carolina. Unlike most cultural tilts with officialdom, however, this battle involved neither money nor censorship. It centered around municipal parking regulations.

When in mid-September 1968 the Greensboro Traffic Department, concerned with the heavy traffic flow, issued an edict prohibiting parking at any time on Elm Street, where the United Arts Council of Greensboro, Inc., is located, community arts leaders were visibly upset. For with street parking banned, attendance at council arts classes, lectures, and board meetings would have diminished considerably. Determined to take a stand, the council asked all its officials and the presidents of its 31-member and associate organizations to appear at a meeting of the city council the following week. Prior to the meeting, arts leaders hired a local photographer to take photographs of the street in question every hour on the hour from 9 A.M. to 3 P.M. to demonstrate that traffic was not as heavy as city engineers claimed it to be. A mathematical presentation, indicating the average space between moving vehicles, was also prepared.

Following an impressive presentation, the city council ordered a new traffic count of the street. This indicated that about 3000 less vehicles used the street daily than the original traffic estimate indicated. The result? Parking on Elm Street was restored, except for rush hour periods.

Elsewhere, parking facilities and transportation problems have spurred another cultural institution to take action. The Brooklyn Academy of Music, in Brooklyn, New York, which presents major programs in every area of the arts, is located just across the river from Manhattan, the hub of cultural activity in New York. The distance is not great, but to some members of the arts audience, Brooklyn is unfamiliar territory and parking presents a problem. So, early in October the academy launched a special bus service leaving from central locations on the East and West sides of Manhattan, with return trips scheduled 15 minutes after performances end. The round-trip fare is $1.25 per person. The service was initiated when the Living Theatre appeared at the Academy and has continued during the special season of dance, featuring many of America's leading companies.

According to Academy director Harvey Lichtenstein, the bus service which has been operating at about 75 percent capacity, has proved its value. "Although we're not quite breaking even on it yet," he said, "we think we're attracting some first-time Academy-goers."

November-December 1968

Cultural Groups Extend
Their Community Reach

Arts groups continue to seek new means to expand their community reach. In St. Paul, the Council of Arts and Sciences has taken an unusual step for an arts council by organizing a new community program agency and making it an independent and regular council member. Community Programs in the Arts and Sciences, COMPAS, which joins six performing and visual arts groups in council membership, will be housed at the council and receive operational support from it. As an independent agency it will develop "new and innovative programs to fill community needs" and initiate programs to complement those offered by other council agencies.

In New York, a new Theatre Development Fund program will help expand the audience for dance and aid scores of smaller, less established dance companies at the same time. The fund, which has pioneered in making reduced price tickets available to teachers, students, unionists, and members of youth and community groups, has just introduced a new dance voucher similar to its Off-Off-Broadway voucher, with tickets offered at $1 each to a wide range of dance concerts in the city. Some 13,000 people on the TDF mailing list will be able to purchase up to two sets of five vouchers at a cost of $5 a set and redeem them at box offices for tickets to performances by any of the more than 70 participating dance companies on the list. The dance companies, in turn, redeem the vouchers for $2.50 each.

Preliminary reports show that another TDF program, the Times Square Theatre Centre, is proving successful. According to a study, the Centre, which offers half-price day-of-performance tickets to selected Broadway and Off-Broadway shows, has increased the theater audience significantly, especially among young people, and has induced many former audience members to return to theater. Through a Ford Foundation grant, a detailed evaluation of both the Centre and voucher program will be undertaken by Princeton Professor William J. Baumol.

Another experiment in New York, the Culture Bus, has completed its pilot run successfully and will continue indefinitely. The weekend and holiday bus service enables passengers to visit many city cultural attractions for a single $1 fare, boarding and reboarding as often as they wish. The service was recently expanded to include a second line serving Brooklyn.

A successful attempt by a community arts agency to expose its audiences to the work of less-established groups has led to a new and expanded program. Allied Arts of Seattle is presenting its Second Survival Series this season [1973-74] featuring six performances by small professional groups for the $15 subscription price. In South Carolina, the Arts Resource Transportation Service, a mobile arts studio developed by the state arts council, has received a "fantastic" response since it was introduced this summer. ARTS, a truck-van accompanied by an artist-in-residence, has facilities for photography, painting, drawing, printmaking, pottery, clay sculpture, and filmmaking.

On the national level, the Arts Endowment is taking a close look at "moveable" arts programs around the country as a means of developing policies and procedures for this emerging area. Stephen Sell, who helped organize the program of the highly mobile St. Paul Chamber Orchestra, a group able to split itself into various musical groupings of virtually any size, is developing the Endowment program.

November-December 1963

Schools Join
with Town to Present Arts Series

A college, a high school, and a group of public spirited citizens have formed an alliance in Cazenovia, New York to bring a cultural program to the community of about 3000 residents. The first Cazenovia Community Series, launched in October 1963, has proved so successful that it is now envisioned as an annual event.

In the past, Cazenovia College, a two-year liberal arts institution for women, conducted its own lecture series. However, because of limited seating facilities, townspeople were unable to attend the programs. Last year a group of citizens, determined to bring cultural events to the community at large, formed a special subcommittee of the Citizens Advisory Committee for Town and Village Planning, and with support from the State Council on the Arts presented a January 1963 performance by the Metropolitan Opera Studio in Cazenovia.

The townspeople responded so enthusiastically that support was rallied for a regular community-wide program. The college offered to make its own series, supplemented by additional programs, available to everyone. The high school offered the use of its auditorium which, with 650 seats, had double the capacity of the college facility. Thus, the Cultural Affairs Committee for the Cazenovia Community Series, with four members each from college, high school, and town, was formed.

For its first season, a series of six presentations, including a ballet performance, four lectures, and the State Council-sponsored touring performance of the Irish Players in *Playboy of the Western World*, was arranged. Working as a team, the committee divided its work so that its high school and college members were in charge of staging and production and the community members were in charge of tickets, sales promotion, and general arrangements. Students helped with lighting and props, and the college service club provided free ushers.

Attendance thus far has been close to capacity. Nearly 200 season tickets at $6.50 each were sold to townspeople, and all 363 college students received season tickets as part of their school payments. High school students pay half price for all performances. As a special bonus, the committee offered a free state-council-sponsored performance of *The Worlds of Shakespeare* to subscribers.

As a guide to its future programming, the committee has been conducting an evaluation session following each performance. Both in advance of performance and following them, special educational programs relating to them have been conducted for students. The college's drama instructor, for example, led a special student symposium on Irish drama prior to the appearance of the Irish Players, and high school and college students held classroom discussions following the appearance of British lecturer, Fergus Montgomery, M.P.

According to Mrs. Dorothy W. Riester, chairman of the committee, the blending of students and adults in the Cazenovia series is proving very successful. "Students enjoy going to the lectures and performances with an adult audience," she told *AM*. "I think the series will become an important event in the Cazenovia area."

November 1963

How to Build
a Regional Base for Your Institution

Cultural institutions interested in extending their services and their sphere of interest to nearby communities can profit from the experience of the Virginia Museum of Fine Arts in Richmond. This institution, which was founded in 1936 as the nation's first state-supported art museum, has since 1960 conducted a unique program which links it with cultural groups in 18 other communities in the state.

Well before inauguration of the confederacy plan, the museum had pioneered in bringing art to scores of communities throughout the state. It invented the "Artmobile," a traveling art gallery on wheels that toured the state, and it also arranged a series of boxed art exhibits that were shipped regularly to schools, colleges, libraries, and clubs. Seeking a means of developing a closer relationship with citizens in communities outside Richmond, the museum, in 1960, sent a representative to visit arts leaders in other areas of the state.

As a result of this trip, 14 local chapters of the museum were organized, including many in communities where little or no art activity had existed earlier. In addition, four cultural organizations with already existing programs and buildings were brought into the confederation as affiliates. Although the number of chapters and affiliates has remained the same—one chapter dropped out and another was added—they have grown in size and their programs have increased.

Each of the groups in the confederation functions as an autonomous unit under local volunteer leadership and has its own programs of exhibitions, speakers, and films. Although the museum encourages the various organizations to work as independently as possible, it does urge their use of museum services, and it gives them constant programming and administrative aid. In return for its many services, including full membership privileges at the Richmond museum for each individual member of a confederate group, the museum receives $3.25 from the membership fee of each chapter or affiliate member. Thus, the confederation program is financed entirely through membership fees.

Among the services offered by the museum to all members of confederate groups are a monthly museum bulletin with news of chapters and affiliates; a subscription to *Arts in Virginia* magazine; free museum admission; preview and lecture invitations; guest privileges at the museum; ticket and sales reductions; counsel on arts programs; and admission to theater, dance, and music programs held at the museum.

In each affiliate organization's own community the museum provides two Artmobile visits a season, each featuring an installed exhibition of original art objects, noted guest speakers, art teaching kits, a loan-own art service, and bus safaris to the museum in Richmond. In addition, the museum circulates some 80 traveling exhibitions.

According to William Gaines, head of the programs division at the Virginia Museum of Fine Arts, the public reaction to the confederation program has been more than favorable, and membership in the local organizations continues to grow. "Other cultural organizations," said Gaines, "if interested in extensions of their services either through programs originating from the headquarters or by the organization of satellite organizations, would profit much from a study of our program."

May-June 1964

Federation of
11 Museums Serves Entire County

Increased attention has been focused on the efforts of museums to better reach and serve their communities. The Smithsonian Institution in Washington, D.C., for example, opened a branch museum in a deprived neighborhood under a $250,000 program financed by the Carnegie Corporation of New York. New

York's Metropolitan Museum was awarded a $100,000 grant from the New York State Council on the Arts to develop a pilot program for high school students; the Metropolitan and the Brooklyn Museum announced a cooperative program including joint exhibitions, pooling of personnel, and loans of important works; Boston's Museum of Fine Arts loaned nearly a million dollars worth of art to local banks for exhibition purposes; and finally, the Regional Plan Association, in its report on New York museum-going, which predicted a doubling of Sunday attendance by the year 2000, suggested the establishment of major museums in suburban areas.

Museums in less populated areas sharing a similar concern for service to their communities might benefit from the experience of the Orange County Community of Museums and Galleries, a confederation of 11 visual arts institutions in Orange County, New York who have banded together in an unusual countywide cooperative program. Although organized in 1961 for the prime purpose of attracting a regional museum conference to the area, the community has since expanded its activities into a variety of areas including publications, broadcasting, research, and administrative services to its members. It has helped to promote the visual arts in the county, increase attendance at local museums, and stimulate professionalism among member institutions. Moreover, the association, which started as a voluntary operation, now employs a full-time paid director and an assistant director, and has embarked upon an ambitious 11-project program.

From the period of its origin in November 1961 until 1965 when the community operated strictly on a voluntary basis, it published 11 issues of *VIEWS*, a magazine devoted to the history and culture of Orange County, doubled the number of officially appointed local historians in the county, prepared copy for brochures and travel guides, and hosted the Northeast Museums Conference in October 1963.

Paid professional help was available for the first time in the summer of 1965 when the New York State Council on the Arts awarded a ten-week research associate internship to Malcolm Booth, one of the founders of the organization and the editor of *VIEWS*. During this period, Booth, who is now director of the organization, prepared a slide program, "The Story of Orange County," compiled a bibliography of local history, and helped to develop future projects for the federation. Following Booth's internship, the organization returned to a volunteer basis for one year, during which time it developed a personnel aid program for member groups and sponsored a joint workship for museum directors and social studies teachers.

In September 1966, New York's State Council approved the community's request for a three-year grant to cover the salary of a full-time director to operate a pilot program in cooperative museum activities. Under this program, directed by Mr. Booth, several notable achievements have already been realized, including publication of a quarterly newsletter, *Museum Matters*, airing of a weekly radio series, establishment of a clearing house for county cultural events, publication of a county museum directory, sponsorship of local cultural and historic programs, and development and maintenance of a master file of organizational program chairmen for possible speaking engagements.

Other current projects include the sponsorship of round-table meetings, a consultation service to members, conference attendance and reports, abstracting articles from journals, and assistance with financial matters, including the preparation of grant proposals to foundations and government agencies. A major Title III proposal involving the establishment of a regional museum service center has been submitted recently.

Commenting on the significance of the OCCM&G, Mr. Booth told *AM*, "The museum profession has long needed a project of this type. It brings us up to the point that the library profession reached 20 years ago. New York State's pioneering steps in regional library systems is now being followed up with an experiment that, I believe, will lead to regional museum systems across the country. It's long overdue."

September-October 1967

THE ARTS SERVICE INDUSTRY

Service Organizations Expand Programs

Growth and program expansion loom ahead for several important but relatively young arts service organizations. The National Arts Workers Community [now the Foundation for the Community of Artists], for example, which was organized early in 1971 to provide key services and a collective voice to the individual artist, is on the verge of a major thrust forward. A recent recipient of its first grants from the National Endowment for the Arts and the New York State Council on the Arts—they totalled a modest $17,000—NAWC opened a permanent office on April 1, 1972 to house a full-time staff of three and scores of volunteer workers.

In behalf of artists, NAWC has initiated a fair practices agency, a discount prescription and optical supplies program, and an exhibition space project. It will soon launch a medical/dental insurance plan.

Geographical expansion is one the agenda for several organizations. Thanks to a grant from the National Arts Endowment, Hospital Audiences, Inc., which has provided arts programs for over 300,000 individuals in New York State hospitals and prisons since mid-1969, is now helping groups elsewhere to develop similar programs. As a result, HAI chapters have recently been established in Long Beach, California, Fort Wayne, Indiana, and Hartford, Connecticut, with several more to be operational by the end of 1972. Volunteer Lawyers for the Arts, whose program began in New York in 1969, has since helped organize VLA-type groups in Chicago, Los Angeles, and Washington, D.C., and has established relationships with correspondent attorneys in 11 other cities. Since its inception, VLA has found volunteer lawyers for nearly 200 artists and arts groups in New York, and its roster now lists 135 attorneys.

Another expanding New York-based program, Theatre Development Fund, whose ticket purchase program has helped scores of theater and dance groups in New York and provided low-price tickets for thousands of people (200,000 tickets are being distributed this season), is planning to branch out to Philadelphia in 1973 and provide moderate ticket subsidy for theater, dance, and musical programs there. TDF is exploring possible operations in Chicago and Washington, D.C. in coming seasons and an expansion of the New York service to other art forms including opera and concerts.

The Council of National Arts Organization Executives, a group that has been meeting regularly for more than a year, held its first interorganizational conference late this February with representatives of 15 organizations attending. The Council, now in a program development stage, plans to enlarge its membership beyond the current 10 national arts groups represented.

March-April 1972

New Service Programs
Respond to Arts Need

Two pioneer service programs, one national and one limited to New York State, are helping to meet important financial and administrative needs for cultural institutions. Since early this year, the New York Foundation for the Arts has been developing an experimental program, including the establishment of an interest-free revolving loan fund to state arts groups. In time this effort could influence the creation of similar programs on a national scale. Opportunity Resources for the Performing Arts [now Opportunity Resources for the Arts], which launched its national program in July 1972, is the first centralized interdisciplinary personnel service for administrative and technical positions in the arts.

The nonprofit New York Foundation was organized to help state arts groups out of the financial morass created by late-arriving grants and to help the New York State Council on the Arts solve an administrative problem. With a $13-million program of direct aid to state arts groups to manage during the past two years, the council found it difficult to administer its ongoing programs as well.

Since February 1972, however, efficient and economic administration of ongoing council programs has been provided by the foundation, which is not a state agency, but an independent council grantee. During the current 1972-73 fiscal year, for example, the foundation will administer council funds of $536,000 for such programs as technical assistance, touring performances, exhibitions, special programs pilot projects, information materials, and community informational services. The foundation, which has no grant-making functions, utilizes council staff members as program consultants and concerns itself strictly with administrative matters.

In its revolving loan fund program, the foundation has answered a major need of the cultural group which learns it has been awarded a grant and then waits months to actually receive it. During the period of waiting, the arts group is frequently hard-pressed to meet its existing budget and finds it difficult, if not impossible, to obtain interim financing from conventional lending institutions. The new program has filled this breach by making interest-free loans to grantees, who, as a condition of their loans, assign the foundation the grants they eventually expect to receive. When the loan is repaid in full, the total amount of the grant is released to the organization. Using available funds, the foundation made 65 loans totalling $257,050 to cultural groups through July 31, 1972. According to director Richard d'Anjou, the program has worked extremely well thus far and the default rate has been zero. All but $112,500 has been repaid, and that total isn't due until November 15. To continue and expand the program, the foundation is now seeking additional funds. "We'll accept money in any amount and on virtually any basis," d'Anjou told *AM*, "as long as we have the use of the funds at no cost."

Having established its two basic programs, the foundation is now exploring its involvement in other areas. "We're a flexible instrument," commented d'Anjou, "and we can respond to needs fast and efficiently. Having created our structure, we have the potential to undertake programs which nobody else can, provided that sufficient funding is available."

The other new organization, Opportunity Resources, already has enrolled nearly 200 individuals seeking managerial or technical jobs—full and part-time as well as seasonal—and it is currently working with 24 arts groups seeking personnel. Arts administrators using the service pay an annual $10 registration fee, while organizations pay $25. For each candidate referred to Opportunities Resources that it employs, the enrolled organization pays a small percentage of the first year's salary.

Individuals seeking positions fill out three-page forms provided by the service to indicate general skills and qualifications, employment background, and long-range goals, and then are interviewed personally by director Gary Fifield or an assistant. Following each interview, the Opportunity Resources staff member personally records his impression of the applicant. When positions are available, qualified applicants are contacted, and if they are interested their resumes and other data are forwarded to prospective employers. To reach applicants unable to come to New York, Fifield will visit several cities this fall to set up two- or three-day regional interview centers.

Organizations seeking personnel are entitled to submit an unlimited number of requests during the year's enrollment. When openings occur, they are asked to provide Opportunity Resources with job descriptions. Profiles of suitable candidates are then forwarded to them, usually within several days.

Although it's too early to pinpoint definitive trends, Fifield indicated that 90 percent of the job openings thus far were administrative rather than technical. "We've noted a great need," Fifield added, "for publicity people and fundraisers with organizations outside of New York. Also, a number of groups have been seeking experienced stage managers." Individuals and organizations interested in registering with the nonprofit service should write Opportunity Resources at 1501 Broadway, New York, New York 10036.

Summer 1972

Community Arts Councils Move in New Directions

Community arts councils, a leading force in the decentralized, grass roots art movement of the sixties, but somewhat overshadowed by state arts councils in recent years, are beginning to explore new methods of organization and new areas of interest.

In Hoboken, New Jersey, a densely populated community directly across the river from New York, a Model Cities Agency is leading the drive to organize a new arts council to serve inner city residents. By May 1, 1971, the Hoboken Model Cities Agency expects an affirmative response from the Housing and Urban Development Agency in Washington, D.C. to its request for seed money to establish the council. The request was part of an overall fund submission for the second year of a five-year program. If demonstration projects prove successful, the agency plans to request larger sums in subsequent years.

Model Cities involvement with the arts began in summer 1970 when it provided office space and facilities for a pilot inner city arts project sponsored by New Jersey's state arts council. "From the local point of view," claims Robert C. Armstrong, principal coordinator of the Hoboken Agency, "our involvement gave legitimacy to the project. People didn't know the arts, but knew us."

During the summer program, local talent in both the visual and the performing arts was discovered, but there was no framework or organization for developing this talent throughout the year. That's when Armstrong and Phillip Danzig, the projects director, began to shape the concept of an arts council. "The important thing," added Armstrong, "is that we don't want it to be an elitist council. Model Cities wants to help with seed money, but we don't want to run it."

An action with great implications was taken by the Winston-Salem, North Carolina Arts Council. According to new bylaws, effective July 1, 1971, the council will be governed by a 15-member board of trustees including five officers, drawn not from the council's member groups, but from the community at large. The decision by the nation's oldest arts council to place leadership in community hands will be watched with interest elsewhere.

Across the continent, an already established arts council has expanded its area of concern to include environmental issues affecting the community. Allied Arts of Seattle, through its committee on urban development, recently issued a widely publicized report, months in preparation, which concluded that the Port of Seattle Commission "has shown an indifference bordering on arrogance toward the city's total environment."

The report contained a series of specific recommendations to the commission, suggesting ways to safeguard the city's shoreline. It also urged Allied Arts to take an active interest in future Port activities. The council adopted the report's recommendations.

March-April 1971

Cultural Service
Industry Grows

During the past year [1975] key organizations in the fast-growing arts industry have expanded their services, broadened their geographic reach, increased their budgets, and sharpened their focus on central concerns. The seven groups informally surveyed by *AM*, share common traits to a large degree: they respond to specific and carefully defined needs; have a national impact both practically and conceptually; are pioneers in their respective areas; make their services available to organizations and individuals regardless of discipline; and, as products of recent social development in the arts, are all less than ten years old. Brief program descriptions follow:

Volunteer Lawyers for the Arts, founded in 1969, operates with a professional staff of four lawyers on a budget of $130,000, up $20,000 from the previous year. Although VLA limits liaison offices to New York State where it has four—Albany, Buffalo, Glens Falls, and New York—with three more soon to be operational, it has spurred development of similar operations in Chicago, Boston, Washington, D.C., Portland, and Los Angeles. Other offices are now forming in Miami, Cleveland, San Francisco, and in a five-state region headquartered in Minneapolis. VLA recently introduced a free newspaper, *The Arts and The Law,* published ten times a year, and is planning a new book—a tax guide—to be published this fall and pamphlets on nonprofit organization and what is tax exemption to be published this spring. Upcoming seminars will focus on trustee obligations and on the problems of working Off-Off-Broadway. Its roster of lawyers available to provide free services to arts groups and artists now numbers about 200 in New York.

Theatre Development Fund, active since 1968, operates with an in-house staff of 15 plus nine union treasurers who man its discount ticket booths in Times Square and the financial district. TDF's overall $4-million budget includes all ticket sales, receipts, and expenses. Of the previous year's $3.5-million budget, the bulk of it, or $2.25 million, represented the operation of the Times Square ticket booth. A growing aspect of the TDF program is the advice it provides to groups in other cities interested in developing ticket voucher programs similar to its massive program in New York. A Buffalo program is now operational, Boston begins in September, and the Twin Cities Arts Alliance in Minneapolis and St. Paul has just received $199,000 from the Bush Foundation for a new program. Exploratory meetings to develop voucher programs have been scheduled by TDF with groups in Cleveland, Washington, D.C., Philadelphia, and Chicago. In the next few months TDF will issue the first study of the financing of Off-Off-Broadway theater, including data relating to the impact of vouchers.

Opportunity Resources for the Arts, operational since 1972, has taken a major step forward with the recent expansion of its employment service to include the visual as well as performing arts. With a professional staff of five, Opportunity Resources operates on a budget that has grown from $68,500 to $167,000 to include expansion to the visual arts and the addition of a field service. ORA's growth is reflected in its active registrants—up to 1330 from 800 last year—increased personnel queries from organizations which come in at the rate of about 30 a week and its burgeoning role as an information center on organizational structure and staff needs. Since its beginning, ORA has filled 200 jobs—74 in 1974—and some 300 organizations are now registered with it. A new computerized retrieval system, operational this May, will help maintain present services and increase efficiency and will provide a new functional inventory of jobs to deal with a growing job range. Currently, arts councils are the largest single area of involvement, although requests for jobs in ethnic arts activities and in the visual arts are increasing rapidly. Geographically, the midwest is the fastest growing market for personnel.

Hospital Audiences, Inc., founded in 1969, operates with a professional staff of 20 on a budget of $610,000, an increase from last year's $388,000. In bringing arts programs and services to the institutionalized and disadvantaged—prisoners, the aged, the hospitalized, ex-drug addicts, and mental patients—and bringing the institutionalized to cultural events, HAI has opened up new areas of arts involvement. It now has 15 chapters throughout the country, with four more in the process of developing. Its new Norfolk chapter has been started by students at Virginia Wesleyan who will receive academic credits from the college for ther work. Currently HAI is planning a catalogue and directory of organizations providing arts services to the culturally disenfranchised. As evidence of its growth, HAI is now considered a "cost-effective" program and receives inquiries from state health commissioners and other key nonarts leaders. Because of its huge volunteer network, HAI also counsels other groups on volunteer programs.

Business Committee for the Arts, organized in 1967, operates with a professional staff of four on a $400,000 budget, the same as the previous year. Conference development is a key program aspect, with about 15 state and regional meetings on business and the arts scheduled during the current year in such cities as Miami, Philadelphia, Grand Rapids, Nashville, Boston, Cincinnati, Peoria, and Ponce, Puerto Rico. The publication program continues with a new pamphlet to be issued in April on the ways BCA member companies aid the arts, and a case study of one company's involvement in the arts to be published in hardcover later this year. A quarterly newsletter is published for members, and a monthly newsletter is available free on request, as are most pamphlets. Phone and mail consultations on business and the arts—about 1000 annually—have intensified during a difficult economic period. BCA's national advertising campaign on behalf of the arts continues with a new series of ads soon to be made available to the media. Although BCA has no regional chapters of its own, several cities, such as Indianapolis, have organized wholly autonomous groups dealing with business and the arts.

Affiliate Artists operates with a professional staff of ten on a budget of just under $1 million, up from last years $700,000. In addition to its traditional program of sponsoring artist residencies of eight weeks interspersed with additional visits—55 residencies this year—it operates a Performing Artists and Communities Together program, which offers presenters a week's service by an artist previously involved in the program and a conductor training program sponsored by Exxon. Under development are new programs for young theater directors and for concert pianists with symphonies. Its free quarterly newspaper, Catalyst, reaches 40,000 people, and it is planning a monograph on orchestra programs for young people. As an available information resource on community and campus use of artists and the training of volunteer arts administrators in programming artists' time, AA welcomes requests on information.

Advocates for the Arts, organized in 1974, operates on a budget of about $200,000 with a professional staff of five. With an action-oriented program centered on legal and legislative issues, Advocates does not sponsor seminars as such, but reaches members through its new quarterly newsletter, the Arts Advocate and local groups through its own chapters and the citizens committees it helps to organize. Currently, Advocates is assisting in a suit on behalf of

Granite magazine in New Hampshire, whose state council grant was withdrawn at the governor's intervention, and is working for increased funding of the State Department's overseas cultural program. In the coming months, it will take a more defined position on postal rate increases, testify in copyright legislation and Arts Endowment appropriation hearings, and study and develop possible legal action on behalf of the Iroquois tribes for recovery of valuable wampum belts from museums. Its study of the gross national product in the arts will be published later this year.

January-February 1975

Nonprofits Move into Commercial Areas of the Arts

Nonprofit services and programs for the arts are developing increasingly in such traditionally commercial areas as art gallery operations, artist management, and publishing. In the visual arts, for example, many relatively new organizations such as the Boston Visual Arts Union with 1000 artists as members, the Los Angeles Institute for Contemporary Arts, and Cleveland's New Organization for the Visual Arts are winning membership and support while giving exhibition and selling opportunites to local artists.

In New York, with its plethora of well-known commercial galleries, several nonprofits, most less than three years old—the Soho Center for Visual Artists, the Once Gallery, and Artists' Space among them—have been exhibiting regularly and approximating commercial galleries in the professional presentation of their work. Nonprofits do not charge artists commissions and generally do not maintain ongoing relationships with the artists. Once Gallery, for example, introduces artists in one-person shows who have not had a major New York exhibit. Yet nonprofits have found it difficult to discover and reach serious collectors since many seldom venture outside the commercial gallery world and museums normally do not make their lists of collectors available to galleries.

In a major attempt to attract collectors, however, Artists Space, which has built up a slide collection of works by more than 500 artists, will open it up to collectors beginning in the fall of 1975. According to Trudi Grace, executive director of Space, "We're going after the younger collectors. We've asked all the artists carried in our file to indicate their price range and whether they'd like visits from collectors. Then we'll invite collectors down for several slide showings and hope to arouse their interest." Artists Space is also constructing a special slide room and, in addition to the showings, will allow interested collectors to use the room during gallery hours.

In the performing arts, several nonprofit artist management firms have been organized within the past three years in New York, and there are indications that others may be starting soon elsewhere. Although services differ, the firms share a common interest in keeping client costs as low as possible, serving groups and artists "on the way up," and providing guidance in a variety of areas normally not covered by commercial management. A brief rundown on the firms follows:

Artservices, founded in 1972, represents 14 companies in dance, music, and theater, and composer John Cage. With a professional staff of five full-time and one part-time, it provides a range of services running the gamut from booking to bookkeeping in an attempt to stabilize the operations of growing groups and generate enough income for them so that eventually they can sustain self-management. Artservices receives fixed monthly fees based on budget and time spent, ranging from $75 to $500, and does not charge a percentage for booking. Funded by the Arts Endowment, New York's state arts council, and private donors, it is working at current capacity.

HI Enterprises, founded in 1972, represents five dance companies and two choreographers. With six professional staff members, it offers most of the services necessary to running a professional arts group in an attempt to bring sound business practices to its clients at minimal costs. Fees very according to the client, with some on retainer, some on percentage, but none on both. Funded by NEA, the state arts council, and foundations, HI has little turnover, and only one new artist has been added this year.

Directional Concepts, founded in 1972, represents four dance groups, two solo artists, and one choreographer. Its professional staff of three provides a range of services emphasizing career development and including booking, publicity, grant applications, and printed materials. Clients pay nothing until the first booking, except printing expenses, and then are billed on a percentage— usually 20 percent—of the fee. This charge includes management services, graphics, and publicity materials. Organized originally to provide management for talented young professional groups, Directional Concepts, with limited funding from NEA and New York's state council, can no longer afford to take groups who do not generate income. It accepts about two or three new groups yearly.

Management Services for the Arts was organized in 1974 to help theater companies stabilize their operations so that eventually they could hire their own full-time managers. Its two professionals represent six theater groups and provide a wide range of fiscal and organizational services, including bookkeeping and proposal writing, but they do no booking. Monthly bills, ranging from $50 to $500, are based on a group's budget and time spent. Its client roster has remained stable.

American Chamber Concerts, founded in 1974 by two concert artists and a friend, represents only chamber music artists and ensembles. Organized to help talented artists find concert dates, the group works almost exclusively in the booking area and sends out fliers and mailings on behalf of its ten clients. Unique in that it does not charge for any of its mailings or follow-up services, its

two artist principals who underwrite the service (they themselves are clients) justify their largesse with the explanation that it doesn't cost more to list two or
ten artists on a flier.

In still another area, publishing, a two-year-old organization is serving as
a planning and production arm for nonprofit organizations. With three professionals on its staff and a budget nearing $100,000, the Publishing Center for
Cultural Resources in New York City offers consultative services on such varied
aspects of publishing as budgeting, printing processes, color usage, and distribution, and organizes cooperative press runs for arts groups. Not a publisher itself,
the center works with prospective arts publishers to help them determine market needs and press runs and also provides free-lance editorial and design assistance. A 15 percent surcharge is added on for goods and services arranged for
arts groups (offset by savings on these purchases), but planning services are free.

In an expansion of its services, the center includes such new activities
as making interest free loans to arts groups to help them publish works that
promise recovery of costs through sales; providing a nonprofit warehouse, shipping, and billing service to help distribute worthwhile books; and acting as an
agent for arts groups in contract negotiations with trade publishers.

Summer 1975

Rapid Growth Continues
in Arts Service Industry

The arts service industry, in a beginning stage of development only ten years ago,
is continuing to grow at a rapid rate. New national service organizations have
been created within the past year [1976-1977] particularly in developing cultural areas, and the arts funding crunch has resulted in the creation of new
advocacy forces.

In the burgeoning crafts field which, thanks to Joan Mondale, has received
tremendous attention recently, the first national service organization for administrators—the North American Craft Administrators—was organized this June
during the American Crafts Council's national conference in Winston-Salem,
North Carolina. The group, run by a steering committee coordinated by Robert
Hart of the U.S. Department of Interior's Indian Arts and Crafts Board, will
focus on services to the field and craft advocacy and will include representation
from both the profit and nonprofit sectors. Its overall program will be formulated following a series of regional conferences planned for the late winter and
spring, culminating hopefully in a national conference in the fall of 1978.

Also new is the National Association of Craft Retailers. Formed at a February meeting of 80 retailers, the group plans to announce its program and priorities this fall, following a six month study by a steering committee.

In jazz, both the Consortium of Jazz Organizations (159 West 127th St., N.Y., N.Y. 10027) and the Universal Jazz Coalition (156 Fifth Avenue, N.Y., N.Y. 10010) are in early stages of development. The consortium, founded last year, has just received its second consecutive grant from the NEA to help plan and develop its service program. Because its initial focus was on New York State, the consortium has only nine organizational members now, but in a recent informal survey it identified 75 prospective members, nonprofit jazz groups throughout the country who receive funding from their respective state councils and who have paid directors. "Between a third and a half of them weren't in existence five years ago," Mari Joann Johnson, the group's director, told *AM*. The consortium will publish its first newsletter this fall.

The coalition, which received its tax-exempt status this May, aims its program at the individual jazz artist, providing a range of management, booking, and promotional services. In order to increase performance opportunities, it also produces jazz concerts.

In the ethnic area, the Association of Hispanic Arts, (200 East 87th St., N.Y., N.Y. 10028) has broadened its program considerably since its founding a little over two years ago. A nonmembership organization, the association reaches its prime audience of 285 Hispanic-oriented cultural and educational groups throughout the country with a bi-monthly newsletter. Currently, the association is involved in developing a national communications network and is doing a statistical analysis of national funding of Hispanic arts.

The excitement engendered by the publication this May of the panel report, "Coming to Our Senses: The Significance of the Arts for American Education," has inundated Arts, Education and Americans, Inc., the new organization established to follow up on the panel's recommendations, with a tremendous beginning work load. The organization is responding to information requests, providing speakers for conferences and media appearances, and will participate in an upcoming series of six special area meetings to discuss the report and its implementation. In the fall, Arts, Education and Americans, Inc., (10 Rockefeller Plaza, N.Y., N.Y. 10020) will begin publishing a newsletter.

Five national organizations with common interests—Hospital Audiences, Inc. and national therapy groups in dance, drama, music, and art—have come together to form the new Alliance of Arts and Arts Therapies. The alliance will gather and share information and hopes to initiate several key programs.

At the state level, regional coalitions of community arts councils are growing in number with 14 now in existence and seven or eight others in various stages of formation. Most have paid directors and all have growing information and service programs. With their large organizational memberships—the oldest and largest coalition, the Alliance of California Arts Councils has 210 member groups—they represent forces of some political clout. This August, New York's Alliance opened its first full-time office.

In recognition of growing state and regional arts needs, the National Endowment for the Arts recently increased the number of regional coordinators from seven to ten, and, in the process, sliced out three new regions.

Advocacy groups have been developing rapidly on a state and regional level, and the arts will have a new national interdisciplinary force on the scene. The American Arts Alliance, organized by directors and board members of leading performing and visual arts groups, following a long period of planning, will open an office in Washington, D.C.

Summer 1977

REACHING OUT
FOR SPECIAL AUDIENCES:
A CHRONOLOGY OF DEVELOPMENTS

Grass Roots
Cultural Movement Accelerates

The neighborhood and ethnic arts movement continues to grow amid signs that many emerging groups are achieving organizational stability. Moreover, government agencies are beginning to pay greater attention to programs in this area.

In Washington, D.C., the National Arts Endowment's Expansion Arts Program, which was created in 1971 to aid community-based projects, gave matching grants to 59 ongoing programs and 21 special summer programs around the country during the current fiscal year.

According to Expansion Arts director Vantile E. Whitfield, official announcement of the $1-million program last December spurred nearly 1000 requests for information and materials from nonestablished arts groups. In guidelines prepared for fiscal year 1973 applications, target participants are identified as "Blacks, Spanish-speaking persons, and other ethnic minorities concentrated in urban neighborhoods, as well as residents of the more remote Appalachian, Indian and rural American communities." The program's funding categories include instruction and training programs; community based cultural centers with multiarts programs; neighborhood arts service organizations; and special summer projects. Guidelines are available on request from Expansion Arts Program, National Endowment for the Arts, Washington, D.C. 20506.

In New York, the State Council on the Arts' Special Programs division, which since 1967 has provided funding and technical aid to ghetto arts programs—$1.5 million during 1971-72—has witnessed an impressive growth of neighborhood arts activity. "There were only a handful of continuing black and Puerto Rican arts groups in the state when we began," director Donald Harper told *AM*. "But each year we've seen a steady growth and today there are at least 100 stable and productive groups."

During 1971, Special Programs expanded its thrust into new areas. "One of our most important accomplishments," claims Harper, "is that we've taken techniques developed in ghetto communities and applied them to all culturally isolated ethnic groups."

The pilot arts program of the America the Beautiful Fund has given further impetus to grass roots arts development in New York. Under a matching grant from the state arts council and the Arts Endowment, the fund, which since 1965 has provided seed grants and technical aid to hundreds of individuals and communities seeking to improve environmental quality, has provided funds to bring arts programs to prisons, hospitals, migrant camps, Indian reservations, and rural towns. Thus far some 72 different communities have been aided with the number expected to reach 100 to 125 by June 1972.

Meanwhile, a grass roots program that has brought teams of humanists and artists into scores of remote communities around the country for presentations and discussions built around specific themes is expanding with the opening of two new regional centers. The Humanities Endowment's National Humanities Series, which has presented two-day thematic programs in 89 communities during its first two years, will now have a Midwestern Center at the University of Wisconsin and a Western Center at the University of California, Los Angeles, in addition to its continuing Wilson Center at Princeton.

Among the more ambitious grass roots projects is Aware, a mammoth, year-round program in New York designed to utilize artistic and other talents to promote harmony. Conceived by conductor Joseph Eger of the New York Orchestral Society, the program will include scores of street celebrations, ethnic festivals, and unconventional happenings, to culminate in a week-long city-wide festival. According to Eger, hundreds of volunteers, including many artists, have responded to the program.

March-April 1972

Community Arts
Organize New National Alliance

A new national alliance of community arts groups and a separate lobbying force for community-based cultural acitivities are efforts in the offing. Both have received great impetus from the week-long conference on Community Arts and Community Survival held in Los Angeles this June [1972] under the sponsorship of the American Council for the Arts in Education (ACAE). The meetings, which featured performances, exhibitions, and workships at a number of different inner city arts centers, attracted representatives of established national arts and education organizations, foundations, and government agencies as well as local community arts leaders and focused national attention on the burgeoning community arts movement.

The idea for a national association had its genesis in mid-1971 when the Los Angeles Community Arts Alliance was organized. As unifying force and information resource center for neighborhood arts groups in Los Angeles, the alliance was envisioned, even then, as the model for a larger organization, according to its chairman Victor Franco. Months later, when the ACAE was formulating plans for its annual conference in 1972, its Intercultural Committee suggested community arts as a theme and Los Angeles as a logical site. Through the proposed conference, it was hoped, representatives of ACAE's member organizations, many of them arts educators, would witness a wide range of community arts programs and develop a better understanding of how community arts centers could function within the education system.

A Los Angeles steering committee, which included in its membership representatives of the alliance, was organized, and it developed the conference format and program. Later, the alliance became a conference cosponsor, along with UCLA and Plaza de la Raza, and it prepared two important new publications— a handbook describing the goals and program of more than 50 local community arts groups and a directory of nearly 500 cultural organizations in the Los Angeles area.

The conference was an overwhelming experience for the participating Los Angeles community groups and for the ACAE members and invited guests. At its conclusion, ACAE's board passed a series of resolutions acknowledging the significance of community arts and specifically calling on legislators, government agencies, business, the education field, and funding agencies to increase support to arts organizations from minority communities. The council also recommended that "community and neighborhood arts organizations form unions or alliances that relieve the individual organizations of many administrative and fundraising responsibilities and encourage mutual assistance and solidarity."

"The conference generated tremendous enthusiasm and good will," Franco told *AM*, "and we thought it would be a good idea to develop a national meeting for community groups all over the country." Franco, who had received a fellowship to Harvard's summer institute in arts administration, took the idea east with him several weeks later and discussed it with community arts people from Pittsburgh, New York, Boston, Cleveland, Chicago, and other cities. What emerged from these sessions was the beginnings of a new organization, the National Community Arts Alliance, and a new document, a proposal for a national conference to be held in Washington, D.C. in August 1973. Conference results will determine in large measure the future structure and program of the alliance. The American Council for the Arts in Education will work with the new organization to help find funding for the two stages outlined in the proposal, a feasibility study, and the conference itself.

During the feasibility study stage, a working panel of twelve, with represensation from various ethnic areas, will direct the organization. Initially they will prepare a survey of community arts associations and send questionnaires to community organizations throughout the country. "Third World" groups will be asked to indicate their purposes and needs as well as their attitudes towards the proposed conference—its structure, duration, areas of discussion, and overall feasibility. Results of this study will help determine the conference agenda and the criteria for representation at it. Several local and regional meetings would precede the national conference.

A long-range goal of the alliance as stated in its new proposal is "to organize the community arts into an effective body, able to make its voice heard in the places of power, so that it may continue the essential development of functional arts, responsive to the great needs of its communities."

Meanwhile, another group with roots in Los Angeles, whose principals were also involved in the ACAE conference, has taken the initial steps towards organizing an active lobby for the community arts movement. The Community Arts League, formally incorporated early in the summer of 1972, has already had one full meeting of some 15 activist groups in Los Angeles who have agreed to work with the program. The league, which recently received firm commitments of support from community groups in Berkeley, Oakland, and San Francisco, plans to organize California first before becoming national.

"We're definitely a lobby group," acting president Hazel Stewart told *AM*, "because that's what is needed now." Late this fall [1972] according to Miss Stewart, the league hopes to have prepared a formal list of California groups with which it is involved. It will send this list along with a statement of purposes to communities around the country as a means of attracting more community-oriented groups to its program.

In a description of its goals the lobby group stated:

> The league hopes to influence legislation at the national and state level to provide funding which would be directly available to community arts organizations outside of the National Endowment for the Arts and the state arts commissions. In addition, the League will be active in seeking to influence legislation on municipal, county, and state levels, which can facilitate the development and funding of community arts.

If plans materialize, the community arts movement will soon be receiving increased support from the National Endowment for the Arts. In the serious discussion stage are such projects as a community arts touring program between cities, a demonstration newsletter, and a training program for the administrators of community arts groups.

Prison Arts Become
a New Area of Concern

Art for and by prisoners has become an area of growing activity. The first major touring exhibition of art by convicts, "From Within," opened at the National Collection of Fine Arts in Washington, D.C. in February 1973 and is now on tour through 1974 to major museums. Featuring work by 21 inmates of the Auburn, New York prison, the exhibition was organized by James Harithas, director of the Everson Museum and sponsored by Ruder & Finn, Inc.

In the past year the National Endowment for the Arts has given significant grants for prison programs to such groups as the Cell Block Theatre, Hospital Audiences, the Technical Development Corporation, and Theatre for the Forgotten. Recently, the Endowment initiated a study of cultural groups involved in prison programs to demonstrate how the arts can be a helpful factor in rehabilitation.

An *AM* sampling of prison arts programs throughout the country indicates a wide range of activities. The Rochester Philharmonic, for example, presented the first major symphony concert at Attica Prison this May. In New Jersey, the state arts council just published *Prison Poetry*, an 86-page book featuring works by prisoners at the Bordentown Reformatory. At the University of Massachusetts in Amherst, the Prison Theatre Cooperative recently presented an all-day workshop for individuals and groups involved or interested in taking programs into prisons or producing inmates' works.

An organization best known for its arts activities on behalf of hospital patients has become, in a short period of time, a major presenter of cultural programs in prisons. Hospital Audiences, Inc., which did not begin to program for prisons until two years ago, now devotes about 20 percent of its efforts to this area. Between March and June alone, HAI arranged 26 separate prison arts performances around New York State, and it is currently conducting year-long workshop programs in choral work, jazz, and the visual arts for the inmates of three New York City prisons. HAI also has experimented with short tours which bring a single presentation to as many as eight prisons in four days.

Summer 1973

New Feminist Arts
Movement Is Growing

Spurred by the positive results of a two-day conference held in September 1973, a women's movement in the arts is gathering force. In January 1974 the initial meeting of Wisconsin Women in the Arts, the first statewide organization of its kind, was held. In May, a ten-member steering committee of arts-involved women will meet to institute bylaws and plan the program of a new national Women in the Arts organization. Committee members include Grace Glueck, assistant metropolitan editor of the *New York Times*; Doris C. Freedman, chairman of the Public Arts Council of New York City; Harriet FeBland, director of the Advanced Painters Workshop; and Monika Jensen and Linda Heddle of *Arts in Society* magazine. In a development of equal importance, the National Organization of Women (NOW) has formed the Women and Arts Task Force, which will have a loose affiliation with the new national group.

The development of the Wisconsin organization is especially significant since, according to steering committee member Linda Heddle, the aims, purposes, and program of the emerging national organization will generally correspond to those of the state group. These purposes include developing communications between women in various fields of the arts and between these artists and cultural institutions; fostering more humanistic values in cultural institutions, and increasing their responsiveness to social needs; supporting women's career development in the arts and creating new positions for them; improving the overall image of women; challenging stereotypical and sexist views; and encouraging the development of quality in the arts pursuits of its members.

At its organizational meeting Wisconsin Women in the Arts divided itself into eight geographical districts, each charged with developing regional meetings between now and the fall to determine the kinds of activities that need immediate support. In October, following these meetings, a statewide conference will be held and officers and board members elected. Membership in Wisconsin Women in the Arts, which are being accepted at levels ranging from $3 for students to $25 for sustaining, are open to women in all areas of the arts, whether amateur or professional. Current plans for both the state and national organization include the publication of newsletters and the initiation of studies and action projects dealing with such areas as discrimination against women in the arts and emerging job opportunities. In the meantime, the steering committee is seeking bibliographies on women in the arts, talent registries, lists of women's study programs, examples of discrimination against women artists, and data on financial aid for women artists.

The NOW Task Force, which had its origins prior to the September Wingspread conference, was conceived by sculptor Suzanne Benton who serves both as its coordinator and as a member of the Women in the Arts steering committee. The task force, still in its developmental stage, will publish a newsletter soon and plans to help organize and disseminate data on women and art and raise funds for NOW and for woman artists through the use of art. Along with the embryonic national organization, the task force is working towards an International Year for Women in the Arts by 1977. "My concern," Ms. Benton told *AM*, "is in creating an environment in which the woman artist can flourish and gain independence in her community. Thus far we have received cooperation and generous responsiveness on the part of women artists, organizations and NOW chapters."

Additional attention will be focused on the women's arts movement this May when *Arts in Society* magazine publishes an entire issue devoted to women and the arts. This issue, Spring-Summer 1974, Volume 11, Number One, will provide a comprehensive report on the conference last fall that helped trigger many of the current developments. That meeting, held at the Wingspread Conference Center in Racine, Wisconsin under the sponsorship of the University of Wisconsin-Extension and the Johnson Foundation, attracted some 80 women from every area of the arts plus a few men and focused on such topics as the images of women, the woman artist's relationship to cultural institutions, and the role that feminism in the arts can play in implementing social change. The issue, available for $2.50, will feature the conferences major addresses and transcripts of workshops and discussions as well as poetry by women and reviews of books by and about women.

January-February 1974

National Program
Links Arts and Religion

A major national program linking the arts and religion in a common campaign has been launched. Under the aegis of the newly created Religious Communities, the Arts and the American Revolution [now Religious Communities for the Arts], a church-based performing arts network, is being organized in one state, arts and religion conferences are being planned in communities throughout the country, and four statewide arts and religion groups have been created.

The roots of RCAAR go back to 1970, when leadership in the United Church of Christ and the United Presbyterian Church came together to discuss the upcoming bicentennial and the need for infusing it with programs that, instead of merely recreating history, recognized the humanistic and aesthetic values. Out of this concern, an idea developed for a meeting that would use the bicentennial as a springboard, but would go far beyond it in exploring the common cause of the arts and religion in the years ahead. At a resulting three-day consultation in St. Paul in October 1973, some 200 participating artists and religionists called for the organization of the new group and development of a national program.

Although still in its organizational infancy, RCAAR has established a national office in New York under chairman Anderson Clark, senior vice president of Affiliated Artists, and executive director Grant Spradling, and it is developing a board which, when completed, will include key arts leaders as well as representation of all major religions.

Also, it has helped develop several model programs. Doane College in Crete, Nebraska, with RCAAR assistance, is organizing a statewide performing arts network which, beginning next spring, will utilize smalltown churches as cultural centers. As an outgrowth of a presentation made at St. Paul, Rocky Mountain College in Billings, Montana, is initiating a course on native American art in its fine arts department this fall, using artists from the nearby Crow Indian reservation as teachers. In Winston-Salem, North Carolina, where RCAAR helped introduce the religious community to the arts council, a church-arts week will be held this fall, followed by an arts month. Both programs will then be evaluated to help in planning a major consultation for the entire Southeast next year.

"Wherever we see arts programs affecting people's lives where they live," Spradling told *AM*, "we will encourage the religious community to understand them, become involved with them, and support them." In addition to working directly with both religious and cultural groups, RCAAR hopes to foster the development of more organizations combining an interest in both areas. Eventually it anticipates a network of such loosely related organizations similar to those recently established in Kansas, California, Wisconsin, and Minnesota. "We'll help groups design consultations and find funding for them," added Spradling, "but we will not become a funding agency."

To support its beginning program, RCAAR received a preliminary grant from the National Endowment for the Arts and seed money from the Board for Homeland Ministries of the United Church (in whose offices it is housed at 287 Park Avenue South, New York, N.Y. 10010) and from the House of Hope Presbyterian Church in St. Paul.

Summer 1974

Programs Reach Out
for Nontraditional Audiences

Cultural groups are launching major community-wide programs to reach nontraditional audiences. In the Bronx, New York, the Council on the Arts initiated a year-long pilot project during the 1974-75 season budgeted at $18,000, to involve more than 10,000 older citizens in the borough in the arts.

Funded by an Arts Endowment grant, with matching money provided by New York's state arts council, the Seniors' Program of Education, Art and Recreation—Project SPEAR—is presenting weekly lectures on cultural topics plus performances by local artists at senior citizen centers, nursing homes, and churches throughout the Bronx. Audiences are also being offered weekly mini-courses in the arts at performance locations and at the Bronx Community College.

In Tulsa, a pilot program of the local arts and humanities council is aimed at reaching handicapped residents of the area. In cooperation with the Tulsa Recreation Center for the Physically Limited, the council is coordinating an artists' residency program at the center, involving performances, lecture-demonstrations, master classes, and workshops—all aimed at the specific needs, interests, and abilities of the handicapped. Recently, for example, a professional actor visited the center twice a week for six weeks to teach voice projection, mask-making, and movement to victims of muscular dystrophy and cerebral palsy in preparation for a play to be presented by the patients. Artists and theater groups have also worked with patients. As an outgrowth of the project's pilot phase, the council hopes to encourage its member groups to establish special programs for the handicapped.

In an unusual reach into handicapped audiences, the Puppet Playhouse in New Orleans gave an unscheduled performance for patients of the Louisiana Crippled Children's Hospital. The performance was arranged when the playhouse applied for insurance coverage for its scenery and equipment. The New Orleans branch manager of Fireman's Fund suggested that instead of paying the entire premium, the playhouse could win partial payment credit in exchange for the free performance.

Meanwhile, the New York Shakespeare Festival is toying with an unusual concept to help it tap possible new subscription aduiences. If the plan goes into effect, the Festival will hire paid workers to go to movie houses, restaurants, and other popular city places where audiences are apt to be standing in line. The workers will then try to sell the waiting queues on the advantages of season subscriptions at the theater.

March-April 1975

Arts Boosting Effort
to Involve Older People

Arts programs for the aging are on the increase throughout the country. Following several years of pioneer activity by the National Council on Aging's Center for Older Americans and the Arts, local cultural groups are developing their own pilot activities.

In Iowa, a pilot arts for older people project initiated last year [1975] by the state arts council has had such great success that it will be expanded from four to ten sites this May. To date, the participatory project has worked with 160 older people between two and five hours a week for 16 weeks through poetry, painting, and music programs in three different communities. In Cedar Rapids, the poetry program, which will publish a magazine this spring, has received continued funding from a local agency on the aging. Future council plans call for ten new programs to be added every six months.

In Syracuse, New York, the just-opened $25-million Civic Center of Onondaga County, a county office building linked with three theaters, includes four newly created senior citizens' performing arts groups among its resident companies—a theater, pop concert orchestra, chorus, and vaudeville troupe. All feature performers 55 and older.

The program was conceived by Dr. Joseph Golden, executive director of the center, early last year as a way to share the talents of local senior citizens "with the rest of the community." Local agencies that programmed for older people were contacted, talent calls were issued, and by last May, following responses from performers, an advisory board including representatives of 11 community agencies was organized. By November, four arts units, each headed by a local professional, went into rehearsals under the umbrella title of Senior Citizens' Performing Arts Group. The troupes, which already have rehearsed at the new center, make their center debut on March 10, 20, and 21, 1976.

Funded by both the Cultural Resources Council, managing agency for the center, and the New York State Council on the Arts, the program has been aided by senior citizens' groups through involvement on the advisory board and sharing of mailing lists. Thus far, however, according to Gloria Romeo, the center's community relations coordinator, "none of these agencies has been successful in securing for us any funding from their budgets."

Another upstate New York community, Rochester, initiated a pilot Arts for Aging project last year based on several years of planning. Coordinated by the local arts council, and involving four cultural groups in a collaborative effort, the program has included such activities as annual free open houses for seniors at participating institutions, training courses for activities leaders, and annual senior arts and crafts courses and a free seminar in marketing at Monroe Community College.

In St. Paul, the largest arts for the aging project in the nation plans to continue its ambitious program when its pilot funding period ends in several months. Launched by COMPAS, an agency of the St. Paul–Ramsey Arts & Science Council, with a two-year nonmatching $90,000 grant from HEW's Administration on Aging, the Artists and the Aging program has focused on training professional artists to work with older participants in a variety of arts forms. Since its inception, program artists have reached an estimated 15,000 older people who have participated in regular workshops in all the arts. An additional number of senior citizens have visited studios and galleries and attended performances through the program.

Interestingly, COMPAS had developed its own comprehensive Senior in the Arts program just about the time it was approached by HEW. Designed to involve older people in the arts, the program has provided free or low-cost tickets to arts events, organized continuing courses and performing arts workshops in different arts forms, and developed performing units. Groups such as the 16-

member COMPAS Senior Stars have performed in nursing homes and have even taken shows on the road. The two programs will be merged into one when the grant period for Artists and the Aging ends June 30. New funding is now being solicited.

According to Molly LeBerge, COMPAS director, the program has been a boon not only to older participants, but to the participating artists as well. "At first," she told *AM*, "artists had to be trained to understand the physical limitations, the challenges, and the rewards of working with older people. Once out in the field and working, they've all commented on the positive effect that involvement with this audience has had on their creative output." Artist long-term residency has been a key aspect of the program, and thus artist participation has been regular and steady. According to Ms. LaBerge, artists coming to teach one workshop at a senior citizens facility often have remained for the entire day.

By mid-summer, COMPAS will have completed evaluation data on the program and also will have published a "how-to" handbook offering facts, suggestions, and guidelines. Information on obtaining these materials will be available from COMPAS, 75 West Fifth Street, St. Paul, Minnesota, 55102.

In nearby Minneapolis, a theater group enlisted the aid of older people for an unusual mission. Faced with its first solo fund-raising drive this fall, the Children's Theatre Company benefited from a "Senior Citizens March" through downtown Minneapolis sponsored by the Metropolitan Senior Federation as part of an overall "Peoples Campaign" for funds. On a fall Saturday afternnon scores of older people accompanied by their friends, grandchildren, and local dignitaries marched a four-block-long parade route in support of the theater. Many had elicited pledges for their walks or contributed themselves.

Meanwhile, senior citizens arts programs throughout the country are receiving technical aid from the Center for Older Americans and the Arts. Through a grant from the Arts Endowment, director Jacqueline Sunderland has been visiting communities to help develop local programs.

A new publication should be very useful to managers interested in arts programs for the aging. *Older Americans: The Unrealized Audiences for the Arts* (Center for Arts Administration, University of Wisconsin, Madison, Wisconsin 53706; $3) surveys developments in this area from the viewpoint of the arts administrator.

January-February 1976

New National Arts-for-Handicapped Programs Set

New national programs are reaching out to a neglected audience—the handicapped—singled out for special attention by the National Council on the Arts. In a 1973 policy resolution, the council recommended Arts Endowment support of all efforts designed to make "cultural facilities and activities accessible to Americans who are physically handicapped.

The newest and most ambitious effort is the Arts and the Handicapped Information Service developed by Educational Facilities Laboratories in New York with funding from the National Endowment for the Arts. The service, which became operational in February 1975, not only will disseminate regular information about developments in the arts affecting the handicapped—facilities, programs, legislation—but will also respond to requests for specific information and develop new materials aas needed.

The concept for the new center grew out of a study written and published by EFL under contract from NEA's Architecture and Environmental Arts Program. Titled "Arts and the Handicapped" (Educational Facilities Laboratories, New York, N.Y. 10022; $4), the 80-page illustrated study is a comprehensive round-up of 131 places and people developing program, facility, and planning solutions which remove barriers—attitudinal as well as architectural—hindering the accessibility of the handicapped to the arts. The handicapped include those with speech, hearing, or visual impairments, physical disabilities, and mental or emotional disturbances. Designed as a pragmatic tool for architects, the handicapped and arts and human service administrators, the report includes names and addresses of specific resources.

As one of its initial activities, EFL has prepared information packets available without charge that describe programs and facilities for the handicapped, the elderly, and children, and list organizations and publications involved in those areas. Included with each packet is an enrollment card with a checklist of information needs about which the service will provide specific materials. [In March 1979 the NEA absorbed the operation of the Arts and the Handicapped Information Service into its own offices.]

To coincide with the center's opening, the Arts Endowment's Architecture and Environmental Arts Program is initiating a major public service advertising campaign this March with print ads and three different 30-second spots. The spots, focusing on the need to eliminate obstacles for the handicapped, are built around the theme "No Body is Perfect" and include the box number for the new EFL program. A further indication of the NEA's interest in the handicapped is its organization of an in-house service that will refer grant proposals on arts and the handicapped to appropriate Endowment programs and to other federal agencies as well. Present plans call for the service to be operated out of the Endowment's Special Projects Office.

A separate program is being undertaken by the National Committee, Arts for the Handicapped, a private, nonprofit action force organized last summer. Committed to increasing the level of arts services for handicapped persons—including the upping of handicapped student participation in arts programs by 200,000 a year for the next five years—the committee includes the heads of several national arts organizations in its membership and supports research activity and the development of arts for the handicapped sites where model programs can be demonstrated. With limited funding through grants and gifts, the committee's basic approach is to help others to help themselves, and thus it emphasizes an information and coordination program including seminars and workshops, speeches by staff and committee members, dissemination of information and individual assistance, including helping groups to find program funds. Information, as well as a slide-tape show on the group's program, is available from the National Committee, Arts for the Handicapped, Room 2611, ROB 3, Seventh and D Streets S.W., Washington, D.C. 20202.

Television, meanwhile, is focusing attention on the needs of the handicapped. The Federal Communications Commission, acting on a petition by the Public Broadcasting Service, has proposed to reserve a television broadcast signal for television captions for the deaf. The system, developed by the PBS, would be visible only over television sets equipped with special decoding devices. Action for Children's Television, which devoted its national symposium in fall to children's television and the arts, will publish a handbook on programming and handicapped children.

January-February 1976

Arts and Religion Linked in an Expanding Program

The movement to spur increased support of the arts by organized religion is gathering force. Following two years of activity, Religious Communities for the Arts is about to move into a new and more active phase of its program.

"We went about as far as we could go with the resources available to us," claims James Buell, RCA's administrator. "Now we'll be expanding our program by working with and relating to other programs and organizations that offer us new resources and forums." One of the programs is RCA's management of the mammoth International Conference on Religion, Art and Architecture in San Antonio in 1978. RCA is also organizing a separate interfaith task force to determine the vitality of current arts programs offered by local religious groups.

Since 1974, when RCA helped develop several model programs including the organization of a performing arts network in Nebraska using churches as arts centers, the group has sponsored five national consultations on the arts and religion, has and still is circulating an exhibition of 100 works by black American artists, and has contributed arts material regularly to a syndicated radio series on social issues which now reaches some 20 million listeners weekly. Through meetings and correspondence, Buell and executive director Grant Spradling, have had some kind of working relationship with nearly half the country's state arts council directors and have become known to the program offices of major religious denominations.

Additional impetus for the national program is expected to come from two important new resource guides. In North Carolina, the Division of the Arts of the state's Department of Cultural Resources (Raleigh, N.C. 27611) headed by Edgar Marston, has published *The Arts in the Churches and Synagogues of North Carolina: A Renaissance.* The 118-page handbook is a practical follow-up to a two-day meeting of representatives from each of North Carolina's major religious denominations organized by Marston in June 1975 to explore new relationships between the arts and religion. Edited by CETA artist Jean McLaughlin, who has been working with the state's religious leaders since the meeting, the handbook offers specific suggestions to local churches on arts activities they can easily initiate as well as lists of references and resources available to them in the state. Distributed without charge to North Carolina's churches—many were accompanied by special cover letters to the local church written by denomination leaders —the handbook, which should be useful to groups elsewhere, is available at $1 from Marston's office.

A second resource is the Spring/Summer 1976 edition of *Arts in Society* (University of Wisconsin-Extension, 610 Langdon St., Madison, Wisc. 53706; $3). which devotes its entire issue to "Religious Communities and the Arts." Guest edited by James Buell, the issue offers a broad focus on its subject through papers, responses and comments of participants at several RCA consultations including a major Wingspread, Wisconsin program held in April 1975.

In an "afterword" published in *Arts in Society,* Buell summarizes RCA's special approach to its area of involvement:

> [RCA] has quite a different concern and program from other religion and the arts organizations and movements past and present. . . . What effect will the legislature's funding for the arts—or lack of it—mean to the spiritual life of the state? How can the religious community work with the business community, the educational community, and fraternal and civic organizations to improve the arts opportunities of the town or the county or the state? How can the vast real estate owned by religious institutions better serve the aesthetic life in their neighborhoods? These are the questions RCA feels are important.

Buell and Spradling welcome inquiries from arts and religious groups. Write RCA c/o the Board for Homeland Ministries of the United Church, 287 Park Avenue South, New York, New York 10010.

Summer 1976

Another Language

Do you have ethnic publics you're trying to reach? You might-with some volunteer help—try to reach them and the foreign language publications they read with releases they will understand. To tap large Spanish-speaking audiences in New York, the American Museum of Natural History sends its releases out in Spanish to Hispanic groups and the Spanish language press.

September-October 1976

10

The Arts Bookshelf

STUDIES
AND SURVEYS

Survey Research
Serves the Arts Administrator

E. Arthur Prieve

Arts investigators are beginning to show increasing interest in one type of research method—survey research. This method relies on extensive use of questionnaires and correspondence techniques for data collection along with interview schedules.

Survey research techniques applied to the arts provide a convenient, expedient means of gathering information to aid in a determination of the feasibility of programs prior to setting them up and in the evaluation thereafter; a method for assessing arts facilities, promotion, audience members' reactions, and community support; a technique that enables decision-makers to be more objective in their judgements. Although the untrained arts manager can begin by inserting an audience poll in a program, in more complex studies the advice of professionals should always be sought. The following is a method for categorization of arts survey research♦

Institutional or Organizational Studies begin with a specific problem or concern of an arts organization, and conclusions are usually limited in their applicability to that one institution. Results of individual institutional studies, collectively, may provide information with national usefulness, even though this is not their primary purpose.

State of the Arts Studies concentrate on examining a fuller spectrum of arts organizations and problems facing the arts. By providing details on arts activity on a broad scale, state of the arts research establishes a backdrop, putting more detailed studies into perspective. Data are collected about many aspects of institutions, allowing the reader to gain a general understanding of the operations and functions of arts organizations.

By taking broad-scale measurements of attendance, operating expenses, salaries of personnel, and income sources, state of the arts studies often lead to projections. For example, researchers may attempt to answer questions such as whether or not demand for performing arts events will continue to grow given certain factors such as increasing urbanization, mobility, and leisure time.

Economic Studies have examined economic variables such as earned income as it relates to expenditures and net deficit to total performing arts expenditures. In the more specific studies, researchers have focused on ticket prices as they relate to audience attendance or professional theater employment in a given year. However, the majority of economic research has dealt with such general topics as supply and demand in the theater or the effect of union wage negotiations on organizational costs.

Audience Surveys and Profiles frequently measure demographic and socioeconomic characteristics such as age, sex, occupation, and income. These measurements provide the explanatory or control variables as they relate to other attitudinal and behavioral variables in research projects.

Because attitudes change over time, such studies must be repeated on a regular basis, but can be most helpful for the manager planning a publicity campaign, determining ticket prices, or deciding seasonal offerings. For example, by determining the furthest distance an audience member has traveled to attend a production, an administrator can decide how to spread the organization's promotional efforts.

Audience surveys are particularly exciting due to the variation among audience members' responses. Individuals naturally differ, but it is a manager's responsibility to find similarities, common appeals, and reasons for unlike attitudes.

Feasibility or Planning Studies evaluate a particular situation such as starting an arts organization or building a cultural facility. They give due consideration to the individual basic decision-making factors that are important in determining whether or not to undertake a particular project. Criteria and goals still need to be defined but, once they are, research can provide hard data in setting up programs and projects to fulfill these goals. Survey of community needs and facilities are especially useful for this purpose.

Feasibility studies can be used on a local basis, or on a larger scale, for example, in the assessment of the feasibility of regional and national programs. In both cases, findings serve as a guide to implementation and, thus, such studies can be very practical planning devices.

Program or Project Evaluation Studies typically examine the extent to which programs have reached various arts audiences. By collecting data on artists' and audiences' reactions to performances, managers can identify areas of weakness and thus set long-range goals. The assessment of a particular program may be facilitated further by gathering demographic data on audience members through survey research techniques.

Although this type of evaluation research necessitates examining many factors in order to obtain an overview, it is possible to focus more directly on one aspect of an organization, such as its promotion. Evaluation studies can be done by an outside body or by organizational members themselves. In either case, informants benefit from filling out a survey instrument that is a checklist of current organizational practices. Self-evaluations allow those more informed to judge their own projects or organizations, but they could be seen more objectively if implemented by the assessment of outsiders.

One study or investigation in itself may provide few or no answers. Studies have to be repeated for verification purposes as well as to trace trends and progress over the years. However, every research project rests on studies done in the past and provides a starting point for those to come. With the advent of survey research techniques applied to the arts, there are exciting new informational possibilities.

November-December 1975

Report Focuses
National Attention on Arts

Foundations should increase their giving to the arts, the federal government should provide matching grants to meet the capital needs of performing arts organizations, and corporations should accept the responsibility for helping to support the arts in their communities. These are some of the key recommendations made in the Rockefeller Panel Report, "The Performing Arts: Problems and Prospects."

The report, based on information obtained through research, personal interviews, and specially commissioned papers, is expected to focus considerable national attention on the current and future needs of professional, nonprofit performing arts organizations.

In a chapter on foundation support, for example, the 30-member panel suggests that local foundations provide continuing operating support to performing arts organizations in their communities, while the large foundations, at the national level, should encourage experimental projects of all kinds. The report asks for flexibility in foundation giving practices and suggests that foundations which have not previously contributed to the arts can change direction if they wish. The panel urges arts groups to recognize the differences between foundations, to prepare better cases for support, and to improve administrative practices before approaching foundations.

In its discussion of the economics of the performing arts, the panel indicates that earned income, including box office receipts, can never make nonprofit groups self-sustaining, and in fact "the gap between earned income and total costs can be expected to widen in the years immediately ahead." It urges performing arts groups to broaden their base of support through programs of community service accompanied by energetic and skillful public education programs. United fund raising for the arts, a method now used by 14 arts councils, is suggested as an efficient and attractive means of increasing support from a community.

Corporate dollars, says the report, can be the difference between life and death to an arts group, and corporations should be stimulated to use the 5 percent deduction allowed them for charitable contributions. Approaches to business by arts groups should be well documented and related to the "personality" of the corporation from which aid is sought. Increased corporation giving to the arts could be stimulated, it is suggested, if an organization for the arts, patterned on the Council for Financial Aid to Education, was created.

Expansion of the professional performing arts is a key panel recommendation. "In the long run," states the panel, "it is essential to encourage formation of resident organizations. In the meantime, there is perhaps more pressing need for regional organizations designed specifically to serve large geographic areas." Envisioned by the panel as operating on a year-round basis are 50 permanent theater companies, 50 symphony orchestras, six regional choral groups, and six regional opera and dance companies already in existence. Cooperation between communities, between state arts councils, and between existing and new arts centers, which in the latter case could form regional and perhaps national networks for touring groups, is deemed essential.

Corresponding to the need for more performing organizations, according to the panel, is a need for a wide variety of service and information organizations in each art. As one of its key recommendations, the panel urges the creation of "an independent national information center that can assume an important and continuing role in the development of the performing arts." This organization would gather data, circulate bulletins, undertake research projects, and cooperate with existing national service organizations.

Stressed throughout the report is the need for better management in the arts. More effort, on a more formal basis, to provide good training for arts administrators is required—including, perhaps, a special school for arts administration.

The boards of arts organizations are not as widely representative of the community as they should be, and board members are recruited too casually, according to the report. It recommends careful screening of potential board members, and board rotation procedures. The report recommends that large arts organizations consider having a full-time paid president or chief executive.

Government at all levels should remove tax burdens and legislative restrictions on the arts, states the report. Local government should help strengthen community groups and include the arts in the school curriculum. The panel endorses the concept of state arts councils and their sponsorship of touring arts programs. Federal aid, it says, can be most effectively provided through matching grants to meet the capital needs of the arts groups.

Although the report continually stresses the fact that the performing arts today are in trouble, it also asserts that "the potential for successful development of the performing arts is tremendous."

March 1965

Study Reveals
How Theater Costs Climb

Thomas Gale Moore

Where has the audience for professional theater gone? Why are its costs skyrocketing? Is professional theater dying? These are some of the questions that the Carnegie Institute of Technology, under a grant from the Rockefeller Foundation, has set out to answer in a three-year study of the economics of the theater.

Research has focused on nonmusical productions in the professional theater, with emphasis on the factors affecting supply of plays and demand for tickets. While most of the work has been devoted to Broadway, many of the conclusions are applicable, with modifications, to the stage outside New York. Our studies cover economic changes in the theater between the 1927-28 season and the 1960-61 season. This article, giving some preliminary results based on the first year's work, analyzes the rising cost of drama production.

While theater costs in general have increased, the preopening outlays, known as production costs, have risen far more rapidly than regular weekly operating expenses after opening night. With costs of the two-season period 1927-29 pegged at an index of 100, production costs, expressed in constant purchasing power dollars, for the average straight play had risen to index 211 by the mid-1950s. But in the past six years [1956-1962] these pre-opening costs have shot up even more rapidly, to index 305 by the end of the 1960-61 season.

Why have production costs tripled? What elements have expanded the most? Building and painting scenery (the largest single item, amounting to nearly a quarter or all pre-opening costs) has a little more than doubled in the past thirty years. Costuming bills and cast salaries during rehearsals have each about quadrupled. Together these two account for about 15 percent of the total. Costumes cost about 50 percent more than the salaries paid during rehearsal and tryout weeks to the people who wear them.

There has been an upsurge of about 650 percent in relatively small items, such as cancellation of contracts, telephone, insurance, secretarial services, acquisition of stage rights, mail order expenses, health and hospitalization premiums, music and orchestration fees, and transportation of stars and directors. Expenditures for advertising and publicity, both in the pre-opening production stage and in weekly operating costs, have risen dramatically. Producers now spend eight dollars to advertise a straight play before opening night for every dollar spent in the 1927-29 period. Ten years ago, advance advertising outlays were only half the present figure.

These expenditures have been made necessary, at least in part, by a changing pattern of theatergoing. Before sound motion pictures, the stage furnished a major form of recreation; people went to the legitimate theater then as people go to movies today. In recent years television has provided another substitute.

Because of such competition, people are unwilling to attend mediocre plays. A show accordingly tends to be either a hit with a substantial run or a flop that closes promptly. A poor reception by the critics can lead to a quick shuttering of the production. If, however, enough tickets can be sold before opening night, much of the investment can be recouped, even in the face of pallid reviews. Producers have therefore pushed up advertising expenditures so as to market as many tickets as possible before the opening. The average straight show in the 1960-61 season cost more than $12,000 to advertise in advance, and another $1455 was spent for a press agent to publicize it. Together these make up about 13 percent of total pre-opening production costs.

After opening night, publicity expenses (which include advertising) take a slightly greater proportion of the total weekly operating costs—$3029 of a total of $18,055 spent to maintain the average straight show. The only item that costs more is that covering actors' salaries—$6691 a week.

Other major categories of operating cost are authors' royalties, crew and stagehands' salaries, and those of stage and company managers. Together these represent $4200, or 23 percent of the weekly costs.

The smaller expenses for productions on Broadway are multiplying in number, and the forces at work there are likely to be affecting the legitimate stage elsewhere. Taxes are up everywhere, insurance has become more important, social security must be paid, and paperwork of all kinds has proliferated. Even increased advertising is undoubtedly necessary all over the country to lure the audience from its TV sets and local motion picture bijous.

If this analysis is substantially correct, little can be done to reduce expenses in the legitimate theater. It may be possible, however, to increase attendance with greater and more certain knowledge of theatergoers. Studying them and their preferences in theatrical entertainment will perhaps point to ways to solve some of the economic problems of the professional theater.

October 1962

Survey Shows When Audiences
for Different Art Forms Overlap

To what degree is there a "general" culture public in any community? To what degree does the audience for opera or ballet overlap that for theater or symphony orchestra concerts? Such questions are of vital importance for cultural leaders planning to create a new arts institution, studying ways to expand their ticket sales, or developing interdisciplinary programs of any kind. They are questions that have fascinated arts managers in every discipline for years. Yet there is a surprising lack of objective data to help one identify the kinds and degrees of overlap.

An analysis of the first season audience at the Tyrone Guthrie Theatre in Minneapolis, conducted by the Twin Cities Market and Research Department of Batten, Barton, Durstine & Osborn, Inc., turned up some interesting facts about audience overlap, not merely between cultural disciplines, but between theater and such other entertainments as baseball and football. The results indicated a substantial overlap between theatergoers and symphony concert attenders, but a relatively small overlap between the theater audience and the audience for opera or ballet. In fact, the overlap between theater and baseball was greater than that between theater and opera or dance.

The survey was conducted by distributing 20,917 questionnaires to members of the Guthrie Theatre audience. Approximately every ninth seat holder received a form along with a request to fill it in. In all, 10,421 completed returns were submitted—49.8 percent of the total. Information on the questionnaires was transferred to punch cards and later fed into an IBM computer for tabulation.

The key question in this series asked, "Last year [1962], did you attend any of the following kinds of attractions?" A total of 8898 persons responded by checking one or more items in a list of events. The percentage results were as follows:

Symphony concerts	65.8
Pro-baseball games	55.3
Operas	33.7
Jazz concerts	19.2
Pro-football games	28.3
Ballet	24.0

Results added up to more than 100 percent because of multiple answers. As might be expected, the degree of overlap in the symphony, opera, and ballet was greater among women than men. The degree of overlap in baseball, football, and jazz was greater among men.

The survey then attempted to distinguish between overlap patterns among different occupational groupings in the Guthrie audience. (In the percentage tables below, the following symbols will be used: S, symphony; PB, pro-baseball; O, opera; J, jazz concerts; PF, pro-football; B, ballets.)

	S	PB	O	J	PF	B
Professionals	72.2	48.6	40.2	18.0	23.3	29.3
Housewives	62.0	54.4	30.9	11.4	27.1	23.2
Students	71.2	56.1	30.8	35.1	25.5	19.8
Business	53.2	75.8	29.4	16.9	50.0	17.9
Clerical	63.2	57.6	31.4	17.2	23.1	24.2
Technical and engineers	55.2	67.7	22.0	18.7	31.8	18.4
Retired	70.5	39.7	48.5	4.4	18.0	34.9

In all but one of the categories, the pattern of overlap between theater and symphony, opera, ballet, and jazz was exactly the same. There was the greatest degree of overlap with symphony, the next with opera, the third with ballet, and the least with jazz. The exception was among students, in which category the overlap with jazz was greater than the overlap with ballet.

These similarities suggest that the patterns are heavily influenced by the availability of the different attractions within a community. Thus, Minneapolis has both a big league baseball team and a pro-football team, as well as a major symphony orchestra. It does not have a nationally known ballet, opera, or jazz group. This underscores the danger of attempting to apply the Guthrie figures in another city without careful evaluation. On the other hand, the differences between the various occupational groupings and age groups (e.g., students and retired persons) may be less influenced by local factors.

The survey also attempted to show the difference in overlap patterns between season subscribers and single ticket buyers. It found that single ticket buyers were more likely to attend symphony concerts, opera, ballet, and jazz performances than season ticket subscribers, but that season ticket subscribers were more likely to attend baseball and football games than single ticket purchasers.

April 1964

Multiple Joiners in the Arts

Do symphony orchestra members also belong to the local museum, theater, or opera?

In an attempt to discover whether people supporting one arts activity also support others, a research worker for the Adult Education Department of the University of Nebraska compared the membership lists of the seven leading cultural organizations in a Nebraska community in 1962. Out of a combined membership of over 4000 he discovered the following: 4000 people belonged to only one organization; 250 belonged to two organizations; 100 belonged to three organizations; 30 belonged to four organizations; 10 belonged to five organizations; and one belonged to six organizations. Not one person belonged to all seven organizations.

Many arts managers have wanted precise data on membership overlapping, but it has only rarely been produced by exact study.

November 1962

Surveys Can Improve Programs, Reduce Costs by Predicting Size and Character of Audience

Duncan F. Cameron

The techniques of marketing and public relations research have applications in the cultural world that can lead to significant savings in dollars and cents, and, more important, to significant increases in program effectiveness.

Too little work has yet been done to say how great a role such research can play in the arts, but the few studies executed in recent years show promise. Audience-potential surveys have been carried out in connection with art center construction programs in the United States and Canada. The Minneapolis Symphony some years ago conducted a survey of audience characteristics. Some work on theater audience characteristics has been done by *Playbill*, a magazine distributed in theatres. But it is in the museum field that the most survey work appears to have been conducted.

At Colonial Williamsburg, the educational effectiveness of exhibits has been explored; at the University of Nebraska, the value of museum teaching for biology students is under investigation; the U.S. Department of Interior is concerned about studies of the effectiveness of its national parks museums; the Royal Ontario Museum, Toronto, is studying the effects of admission prices, the value of museum orientation programs for university students, and the place of museums and art galleries in the leisure patterns of the Toronto community.

Despite this list of varied research programs, audience research in the arts is still in its infancy, and is regarded with skepticism by many arts managers. These same officials will be spending millions of dollars in the next few years on programs and construction.

Industry and commerce have learned that experience and intuition are not enough, and have come to depend on market and opinion research as valuable assets in planning. For decades social welfare organizations, community chests, civic recreation authorities, and other institutions serving the public have used social surveys as an aid to planning. Perhaps it is time for the arts administrator to take a fresh look at the usefulness of surveys.

Museum audience research is not new. In the late 1920s and early 1930s, the American Association of Museums directed studies of museum visitor behavior. These investigations were supported by Carnegie Foundation grants. In the postwar era, analyses of audience composition have been made in Milwaukee, Washington, Toronto, and a handful of other cities.

Unfortunately, the earliest workers, though competent professionals, did not have the advantage of today's sophisticated techniques. Many of the postwar studies were carried out without professional help, and an unknown number of other studies remain unpublished. It is only in the last ten years that museum audience research has begun to be treated as the domain of the professional researcher, with the obligation to publish inherent.

One of the most active programs is at the Royal Ontario Museum, where a dozen studies have examined attitudes towards admission fees, the composition of the visiting audience, characteristics of frequent visitors, the museum staff's image of the audience, convenience of public hours, orientation programs, effects of special exhibitions, etc. How much has it cost? And has it proven to be a sound investment?

The best answer is that the study of attitudes toward admission fees led to fee changes that produced more revenue in the first year than the total cost of all studies, since the survey program began in 1957. Current studies at the ROM are expected to produce valuable information about the most effective advertising media for the museum, about motivations underlying museum visiting, and about public interest in different museum subject areas. The largest annual budget for audience research at the ROM including the cost of professional assistance and publication, has been less than $4000.

May 1962

Study Shows How
to Predict Museum Growth

An objective way to measure the audience potential of art museums is presented in a trailblazing 1962 study of museum growth patterns in 26 U.S. and Canadian cities. The yardstick is part of a 159-page report that can help museum directors and board members predict how population growth, increases in expenditures, provision of new physical facilities, and other factors will affect future attendance curves. Prepared for the Montreal Museum of Fine Arts by Raymond Loewy-William Snaith, Inc., under the direction of vice president Joseph Lovelace, the highly original report challenges the widespread belief that rising educational and economic levels in a community boost attendance figures significantly.

In a period in which museum attendance is increasing dramatically in both the U.S. and Canada, but in which there is a scarcity of detailed sociological and economic data on the arts, the report promises to become a standard sourcebook for museum management. Indirectly, its findings may also shed light on attendance factors in other kinds of cultural institutions, although the report makes no effort to generalize.

The study, which took eight months to complete, focuses on museum growth between 1946 and 1960, inclusive. The 26 metropolitan centers analyzed range in population from 253,000 to 4,418,000. Of these, two are in Canada, the rest in the U.S. Where one city boasts several major art museums, these were treated statistically as a single institution.

The report cites attendance figures as the most realistic measure of a museum's position in the community and the basis on which all future planning decisions should be made. Reviewing the composite experience of the museums in the larger metropolitan areas, it arrives at what it calls a "mean attendance ratio"—a measure of audience potential. The mean attendance ratio for a city of 500,000, for example, is given as 0.23. This means that an art museum in a city of that size has a potential annual attendance of 500,000 × 0.23 or 115,000. The ratio for a city of 1 million is 0.18; it drops to 0.15 for a city of 2 million and 0.13 for a city of 3 million. The report suggests that "any museum falling appreciably below the curve is not realizing its full potential in terms of attendance."

Applying the mean attendance ratios, the report lists cities like Seattle, Dallas, Cincinnati, Cleveland, St. Louis, Boston, Detroit, and Philadelphia as performing better than average. It cited Houston, Baltimore, Buffalo, and San Francisco art museum attendance as below the audience potential for those cities.

These figures bear out a significant finding: as the population of a city increases, its per capita attendance rate declines. The decrease is quite rapid at first, then levels off. The smaller the city, the more rapid the decline.

The best way to buck this seemingly inescapable trend, the report declares, is through expansion of physical facilities as population increases. To attract visitors, it is relatively more important to have a larger museum than to spend proportionately more on a smaller one.

The average museum surveyed increased its absolute dollar expenditure by 7 percent per year during the 1944-1960 period. However, per capita expenditures declined. Per capita spending between 1946 and 1960 averaged $0.1769 for the museums in which detailed financial data was available. In the 1960-61 period it dropped to $0.1560.

Museum eating facilities feed attendance figures, the report finds. Much higher-than-average attendance ratios were found in museums with restaurants. The Loewy-Snaith report strongly urges that restaurant facilities be included in any expansion move planned by a museum. It recommends the leasing of eating facilities to concessionaires in return for 10 percent of gross revenues. Experience of the museums surveyed indicates that 20 percent as many meals can be served as there are visitors—a finding that suggests excellent profit potential.

On the other hand, parking facilities do not appear to be a significant factor influencing attendance. A central location, either downtown or easily accessible to downtown is more important than parking facilities in building attendance, the report finds.

Moderately good income can be derived from a museum sales desk, the study reports. A number of museums in the sample ran their desks at a profit; one museum in a relatively small city increased its sales desk revenue by 1000 percent in three years, boosting it well over the six-figure mark.

As to floor space, "There is a direct relationship between larger per capita attendances and larger per capita areas," the report declares. It suggests that between 35 and 45 percent of total floor space should be set aside for special exhibits since there is evidence that visitors resent dismantling of the permanent collection to make room for a temporary display. A great number of special exhibits does not necessarily hike attendance, although special exhibits of out-standing quality will.

The report surprisingly finds that there is no established pattern to indi-cate that high membership results in increased attendance. It found that among museums in its sample, membership ran at a rate of between 1.5 and 2.5 per thousand in the metropolitan area population.

The report, based on questionnaires, interviews, and documentary re-search, also covers costs of museum additions, service areas, the effect of air conditioning and room dimensions on operations, and other subjects.

December 1962

Community Theaters
Pay Way Through Box Office

The preliminary findings of a 1968 theater survey offer some interesting insights into the operations of nonprofit semi professional, and professional theater com-panies throughout the country. Undertaken by the Theater Resources Develop-ment Council and the Eugene O'Neill Memorial Theater Foundation, the survey was based on questionnaires sent to 68 professional theaters, those operating with partial or total union personnel, and 57 semiprofessional groups which, al-though they sell tickets and often pay management and creative staff, use volun-teers on stage and in the front office. When the cutoff date for responses was reached, completed questionnaires had been received from about half the groups in each category.

As a general rule, semiprofessional companies pay their way through box office receipts and operate within their budgets, while the professional groups rarely cover costs through ticket sales and operate beyond their budgets. Of 27 professional theaters responding, 19 covered less than 75 percent of their expen-ses through box office and subscription income, as contrasted to the 20 to 26 responding community theaters which covered from 75 to 100 percent. Only five professional groups operated within their budgets during the past three years—15 community theaters did—and 20 went into deficit operations during all or most of this period. Obviously, with large paid staffs, the operating bud-gets of the professional groups were considerably higher than those of the com-munity groups. The average cost of mounting a production for two of the pro-fessional groups was over $50,000, five groups averaged $20,000 to $50,000, and nine averaged under $20,000. In contrast, ten of the community groups lis-ted costs under $2000, and 13 were over $2000.

The professional companies, faced with deficits, also have a greater need for outside support. Thus, although none of the community theaters reported receiving important support from government sources or national foundations, and only four indicated that local foundations helped them, the picture was quite different for the professional groups. Here, 15 companies received support from government, 10 from national foundations and 19 from local foundations. Groups in both categories, however, 15 professional and 16 semiprofessional, reported undertaking regular annual fund-raising campaigns.

Data on "bricks and mortar" provided by the companies is revealing. Of the 26 semiprofessional groups responding, 12 own the theaters in which they perform, 17 have accumulated capital funds, 11 have capital funds invested in real estate, and 13 have obtained mortgage money.

In contrast, although 11 of the professional companies own their own homes, only 6 have accumulated capital funds, only 3 have capital funds invested in real estate, and only 2 have obtained mortgage money. In response to the question "Have you any access to loans for basic capital needs?" 12 of the professional groups and 18 of the semiprofessional groups answered yes.

The number of people involved in theater activity both as paid staff and as volunteers is staggering. Cumulatively, the 26 professional theaters employ 522 actors and actresses; 207 directors, designers, and coaches; 209 stage personnel; and 246 in front office capacities. Although only two of the community groups used paid actors or actresses (the others use amateurs), eighteen nonprofessional companies use a total of 76 paid creative staff members, nine use 22 paid stage personnel, and fifteen use 53 paid front office workers. In addition, thousands of volunteers serve in creative or technical capacities, and over 400 serve as board members. Among the professional groups there are more than 800 board and advisory board members.

The professional theaters rely heavily on paid personnel for most administrative functions. Of the 27 theaters reporting, 25 use professional general managers and house managers; 23 use professional publicity managers and accountants; 20 use professional treasurers; and 19 use professionals for audience development. In fund raising, however, only 8 groups use professionals.

According to survey data, professional regional theaters average 25 weeks of continuous performances plus a significant number of extra programs including theater readings and children's school and street performances. The 27 respondents spend $7 million annually in playhouses with an estimated capacity of more than 17,000 seats. The community groups do an annual business of $2 million—mostly on weekends—in playhouses seating about 10,000.

September-October 1968

New Audience Survey
Identifies Playgoers

Thomas Gale Moore

Theatergoers are different; they go to the theater. But who are they? In the spring of 1962, an audience survey conducted for the Carnegie Institute of Technology's study of the economics of the theater attempted to learn something about the characteristics of playgoers. This article reports a few of the preliminary results of the survey which was carried out with the cooperation of the League of New York Theatres.

Since the surveying of cultural audiences is still relatively rare, the procedure used may be of interest to others contemplating audience research.

Under supervision, usherettes placed questionnaires in programs distributed to the audience at eight Broadway shows. In the case of some shows, questionnaires were handed out at only one performance. At other shows, the procedure was repeated at four performances. Large boxes into which the audience could deposit completed questionnaires were scattered around the theaters. In a trial run, I tried including business reply envelopes for playgoers to mail the forms back. This did not work well. I discovered the audience normally dropped the questionnaires off on the way out. If no box was nearby, however, they simply failed to bother with the form. All told, there were 3449 responses. These accounted for 24 percent of the audience.

Thus, to evaluate these results properly, the reader must bear in mind that a large proportion of the audience failed to fill out and turn in the questionnaire. Moreover, to draw conclusions about Broadway patrons, we must assume that those who filled out the questionnaire did not differ in any significant way from those who ignored it. What do we find?

Seventy-three percent of those who filled out the questionnaire were married; 63 percent were males; almost 70 percent were from the vicinity of New York. These percentages varied considerably with length of run and time of performance. Many more of those who responded at matinees were female, while a much larger percentage were single. As might be expected, a large proportion (70 percent) of the audience at *My Fair Lady* were from out of town.

Half of the respondents were older than 39, had a family income larger than $13,500, and had been to the theatre within the last 37 days. On average, those who were from New York or the vicinity expected to spend over 50 minutes going home that night. Again, as might be expected, the audience during weeknights lived somewhat closer to the theater than the audience on weekends. The playgoers to matinees, however, reported that they expected to take an average 71 minutes to go home; this could mean they lived further away or that travel was slower in the afternoon than in the evening.

The length of time necessary to travel to the Times Square area naturally affected how often people went; the farther away they lived, the fewer Broadway plays they saw. Two factors could explain this: first, the longer it takes to get to the theater, the less frequently people will want to go; second, those who love the stage and wish to go often may choose to live close to Broadway. Thus, it is possible that if the theater were brought closer to the suburbs, attendance from the suburban area would increase only slightly.

Sixty-five percent of local theatergoers ate at a restaurant before going to the theater. On average, each of them spent slightly over $5 for a meal and drinks. On this basis we can estimate that during the survey week New Yorkers who went to the theater contributed about $433,000 to the coffers of local eating establishments. If we assume that the average check for visitors to the metropolitan area was the same as for local people, then during the survey week patrons of the theater spent about $718,000 on food and drink. According to *Variety,* the total legitimate gross was $1,041,437. This means that playgoers paid out almost as much to restaurants as they did to theaters that week.

December 1963

Theater Survey
Shows "Ice" Overestimated

Thomas Gale Moore

There has been much speculation recently about the magnitude of "ice" in the Broadway theater. "Ice" is money paid by the ticket buyer over and above the regular price and the ticket broker's fee. A New York State investigation has led to charges that the amount of "ice" may reach $10 million a year. This is enough to pay the production costs of 20 musicals or scores of straight plays, a matter of consequence to the entire American theater. Is this figure of $10 million realistic, however?

A survey conducted during the spring of 1962 by the Carnegie Institute of Technology's study of the economics of the theater indicates that the figure is not. On the basis of what patrons reported on the survey questionnaire, the total figure for Broadway "ice" would run between $1 million and $2 million—probably about $1.75 million—per season, not $10 million. It would exceed $1.75 million in a season when there are several tremendous hits, and fall under this figure during a poorer year.

The Carnegie study drew 3449 responses from theatergoers at eight different Broadway shows. It revealed that, on the average, each person going to a straight show spent $6.25 for a seat. An individual attending a musical laid out more—on average, almost $8.00 for the ticket. People on expense accounts, as might have been expected, were more lavish—the average cost of a seat was $8.20 for a straight show and $13.50 for a musical. Note that the highest box office price for straight show tickets in $7.50 and for musicals, $9.90. Thus, the buyer paid, on average, considerably more than the official amount for his ticket.

A few visitors to New York were charged as much as $18.10 above list for their seats to Friday night performances of *How to Succeed in Business Without Really Trying* and *A Thousand Clowns.* New Yorkers tended to make smaller illegal payments—the highest, $17.20, was paid for a Wednesday evening performance of *How to Succeed.* While patrons from out of town made up only a small percentage of the audience, they accounted for over 60 percent of the total receipts of scalpers.

On the basis of these figures, we find that for the top show, *How to Succeed,* the audience paid over $80,000 a week for seats; the box office received about $67,000; $12,700 was paid to scalpers; and the remainder consisted of legitimate commissions.

Some brokers apparently receive more than the legal commission; 70 percent of those who reported paying in excess of the legitimate brokerage fee for their seats claimed they bought them from brokers.

On the basis of the figures reported in the survey, it appears that total illegal payments during the week for all shows on Broadway amounted to about $34,000.

About half the people purchasing tickets at more than the legal rate paid less than $5 above the price printed on the ticket. About one-quarter paid between $5 and $10, and the remainder paid $10 or more extra. Ninety percent of those paying over $10 above list were buying tickets to *How to Succeed.* Most of those were purchased for the evening performances, rather than for the matinees. In general, the percentage of total tickets that were sold at scalpers' rates was small. If our estimate of $34,000 is correct, however, ticket scalpers cannot be ignored; they exist and the sums they handle, while not huge, are substantial.

January 1964

Non-Newspaper Advertising Brings Few Theatergoers to Broadway Plays

Thomas Gale Moore

Why do people go to the theater? How do they choose the shows they want to see? How important is advertising? Word-of-mouth publicity? The critic? A survey conducted by the Carnegie Institute of Technology's study of theater economics explored these questions and cast interesting light on the motivations of the theatergoer.

The survey, conducted in the spring of 1962 among the audiences of eight Broadway shows, showed that the factors that affect the choice of shows are diverse. For new productions, critics are important; of the audience from the New York area attending *A Thousand Clowns* (which had been running only four weeks), almost half reported that newspaper reviews had influenced them. As shows run longer, personal recommendations become more important. For *A Man for All Seasons, Gideon, How to Succeed in Business,* and *Milk and Honey,* the percentage indicating word of mouth was 61, 41, 55, and 70 percent respectively. Except for *Gideon,* which was on cut-rate tickets and doing only fair box office business, over half of those answering from the metropolitan area indicated that they chose on the basis of personal recommendations. Critics' comments played a much smaller part in the choice of shows that had been running a few months than they did in the case of *A Thousand Clowns;* even for *How to Succeed,* only 42 percent indicated that newspaper reviews had been a factor.

The only other reason local people mentioned for attending a show was newspaper advertising. While only 12 percent of those at *Milk and Honey* and 14 percent at *A Man for All Seasons* suggested this had affected their decisions, 20 percent of those at *Gideon* and 23 percent at *How to Succeed* had been influenced by newspaper spreads. Thus, advertisements in the dailies bring a certain amount of business and good reviews give a substantial boost to a show; in the end, however, these figures suggest that the success of the show will depend on how well the public likes it. If people who see it enjoy it, they will recommend it and more people will go; without these favorable comments, good reviews and newspaper advertising cannot save a production. The survey also suggests that advertising over the radio, on billboards, or in magazines produces few local patrons.

The 30 percent of the audience that were visiting New York came to a show for much the same reasons. The importance of newspaper and other advertising, however, was somewhat less. The most significant difference between local and out-of-town respondents concerned the role of critics. While about the same percentage attributed their choice to reviewers, about half of the visitors referred to magazine critics; New Yorkers ignored magazine critics.

A significant difference exists between those who go to the theater often and those who do not in their expressed reasons for choosing a particular show. Over 40 percent of those who had been to the theater within the last week mentioned work-of-mouth as a factor in their decisions, while only 1 percent of those who hadn't seen a show in over eight months referred to it. People who go to the theater often usually credit several sources as influencing their choice, while people who go rarely give fewer reasons. From these figures we can draw one conclusion on advertising: paid publicity probably has little effect on those who go to the theater often; they would have gone anyway. Since some of those who seldom attend the theater mentioned advertising as the only reason for choosing a show, we can conclude that this group can be influenced by advertising.

In the questionnaire, the audience was asked to check the curtain time they perferred. The great majority of those responding indicated 8:30 or 8:40 P.M. But among local people—the bulk of the audience—there was a substantial feeling that a slightly earlier beginning would be nice; 32 percent of local people attending a weeknight performance wanted a curtain time of 8:00 P.M. or earlier. Only 12 percent, however, wanted it as early as 7:30. On the weekend there were fewer requests for an early start, and the number wishing a 9:00 P.M. beginning rose to almost 10 percent. A greater proportion of the visitors to New York preferred later curtains. In contrast, those at matinees who responded to the question about evening performances—whether from out of town or from the metropolitan area—were overwhelming supporters of early starts; 64 percent checked 7:30 or 8:00 P.M.

These results indicate that it might be profitable for Broadway theaters to experiment with an earlier curtain on one or two weeknights. While 7:30 P.M. was tried unsuccessfully a few years ago, the results of the survey suggest that this was too early and that an 8:00 start might be a good compromise. On the other hand, there seems to be almost no support for a curtain later than the current one.

Two practical implications can be drawn from this survey; the first is that there is a market for an earlier curtain; the second concerns the efficacy of advertising. If the responses are to be believed, we must conclude that non-newspaper advertising brings in few patrons. Radio and TV critics affect the decisions of almost no one. Frequent playgoers are less affected by advertising than by personal recommendations. Newspapers, however, have more influence on those who go casually.

February 1964

Cultural Audience in America Is Identified

Alvin Toffler

It is safe to say that since the end of World War II there has been a sharp increase in the proportion of men in the culture public. Among readers of *American Artist,* a magazine for amateur painters, 40 percent are male. And a study of the audience of the Tyrone Guthrie Theatre in Minneapolis reflects about the same distribution: 55 percent female, 45 percent male. On Broadway, where theatergoing sometimes comes under the heading of business entertainment, the audience is predominantly male. An American male is no longer regarded as a "sissy" if he shows an interest in the arts.

This shift toward increased male participation in the culture market has been accompanied, I think, by a drop in the average age of the culture consumer. A surprising number of professional administrators in the arts, who have an opportunity to observe the audience first-hand, report being struck by the presence of youth in its midst. Perry T. Rathbone, director of the Boston Museum of Fine Arts, says his museum now draws more people in the 20-to-40 age bracket than it did in years past. In Richmond, Leslie Cheek, director of the Virginia Museum of Fine Arts, calls attention to the increasing number of "young marrieds" on his membership list. Similarly, Harry Abrams, a leading publisher of art books, concludes that the largest part of his market lies with customers in the 25-to-45 age bracket, a group, he says, that is particularly alert to new trends.

One can hardly be dogmatic about the evidence, but it would seem that the increasing youthfulness of the culture consumer will affect programming deeply. For one thing, the younger the audience, the more receptive it is likely to be to all forms of innovation and experiment.

As far as income is concerned, the rich, of course, are still with us. However, the culture consumer is, most often, a member of the comfort class. In a country in which the national median income lies between $5000 and $6000, we fine the lowest reported median among a group of surveyed arts audiences to be about $9000.

Our culture consumer, it will be no surprise to learn, is also better educated than the man in the street. He may not have completed college, but the odds are roughly four out of five that he has had at least some exposure to higher education or that the head of his household has.

This does not mean that there are not in our country some poorly educated Italian shoemakers who nourish a passion for grand opera or some denim-clad ditch diggers with an appetite for abstract expressionism. What it does mean is that they form a small part of the total culture public. In fact, there is evidence that education is the single most important indicator of a person's cultural status, more important even than income.

If we analyze the culture consuming public by occupation we find that families in which the head of the household may be termed a professional or technical employee form a disproportionately large part of the culture public. They are followed by what might loosely be called businessmen or executives and their families.

There is still another discernible characteristic of the culture consumer that is worth noting: his relatively high mobility. The class we have been describing tends, in general, to travel more, to move more often, to progress up and down the social scale more rapidly than most Americans.

Another characteristic of the culture consumer is his exposure to communications. He is, through one medium or another, more "tuned in" to the world around him than his non-culture-consuming counterpart. Being tuned in implies more than just passive receptivity—it implies active interaction with the world around him.

The popular image of the reader or culture lover pictures a sedentary, home-centered person. Quite the opposite tends to be true. Generally, he is more active in community and business affairs than his next-door neighbors. Being more active, he also tends toward community leadership.

It is clear from the foregoing that that the culture consumer is a new breed. The effective arts manager must understand this new breed and the interests and motives of the culture audience if he is to appeal to it successfully.

November 1964

Institute in the Netherlands
Studies Sociology of the Arts

The Dr. E. Boekman Foundation of Amsterdam grew out of a realization by arts leaders and social scientists in the Netherlands that the development of a healthy cultural life could be realized best through a scientific study of the sociology of the arts.

Established in November 1963 under the auspices of the Netherlands Federation of Artists, the Boekman Foundation includes diverse aspects of the arts in its purview. Among them are the social position of the artist; the relationship between government and the arts; the arts audience; the formation of sociological theories of art; the function and meaning of the arts in society; and the social implications of a work of art.

Within this framework, there are four areas of concern: documentation, research, conference organization, and coordination of activities.

In its two years, the foundation has made considerable progress. It has organized an index card system listing 9000 publications from throughout the world that relate to the sociology of the arts. It is in the process of building up a detailed library in the field, with special emphasis on statistics and research projects. Also, it is publishing bibliographies on the sociology of the arts. These are available to individuals and organizations conducting research in this area.

In the research field, the foundation carries out investigations on its own initiative and at the request of others, publishing the results whenever possible. A 1964 study on the attitude of young people toward the theater in Holland, the first of its kind, was published in September 1965.

The foundation also organizes an annual two-day conference on a topical problem of the arts. A report of the 1964 conference on how the contemporary artist communicates with his public was recently published. The 1965 conference, held last month, was devoted to the changing function of public organizations and trends in the theatergoing public.

In its fourth major area of concern, coordination, the foundation seeks to avoid duplication of effort. As the central Dutch arts information agency, it collects data on developments at home and abroad.

November 1965

Colleges Surveyed on
Their Cultural Programs

Midwestern colleges and universities generally present more cultural programs than institutions of comparable size elsewhere, have larger staffs to administer the programs, and provide greater program support than institutions in other areas. These were among the conclusions reached in a survey of members of the Association of College and University Concert Managers, based on the 1966–1967 season, which was conducted by California Institute of Technology. Of the 213 respondents, 57 percent were representatives of public institutions, 37 percent represented independent private colleges and universities, and the remainder were from parochial or other institutions. Median, rather than average, figures were used to avoid distortion.

The annual number of cultural events presented by colleges and universities has increased in the part few years and will continue to grow according to the survey. The median number of events in 1966–67 was 44, an increase of 15 over the 1964–65 season. By 1968–69, it is anticipated that the median will rise to 50. The most frequent types of attractions, expressed in the median number of programs presented during the 1966–67 season were nontravel films, 12; curricular music concerts, 10; public lectures, 8; professional classical music, of which 30 percent were solo recital performances, 6; and "pop" artists, 3. The median for professional drama was 2, and for professional dance, only 1. Respondents cited "great" artist and "pop" artist concerts and professional drama productions as the most successful events, and solo recitals, chamber music, and dance concerts as the least successful.

Where are college cultural program presented? Sixty percent of the installation included in the survey have at least one major performance hall seating over 1000, and 80 percent have one or more smaller performance halls. An additional 42 percent of the ACUCM institutions use field houses for cultural programs, and 14 percent use Greek theaters.

Half of the respondents listed equipment deficiencies that prevent them from programming certain kinds of events. Among the deficiencies noted by this group (nearly all listed deficiencies in at least three of the following categories), were stage rigging, 73 percent; lights, 62 percent; stage area, 56 percent; dressing rooms, 52 percent; stage furniture, 48 percent; sound, 42 percent; projection equipment, 38 percent; and others, 28 percent.

Subsidy, in some form, is essential to college cultural programming, with only 9 percent of the responding institutions supporting fee charge events solely through ticket sales. The box office, in fact, returns only a median 41 percent of the total operating budget; 51 percent of the respondents use student and tuition fees to over deficits, and 31 percent use publications from general operating funds for this purpose. Nevertheless, ticket prices for the general public remain fairly low, ranging from a median $2.00 to $4.00 for professional music, drama, dance, and "pop" programs. For faculty and students, the median ticket range is $1.50 to $4.00 for these programs.

January-February 1968

College Audiences Surveyed

Traditional performing arts forms are finding it increasingly difficult to attract student audiences. According to a survey of professional arts programs on campus completed by the Association of College and University Concert Managers, the best student-attended programs are, in order of average attendance, rock, popular, jazz, folk music, and contemporary dance. Programs with the lowest average student attendance are vocal recitals, chamber music, instrumental recitals, symphony, opera, and choral. However, when the analysis was broadened to include the total campus audience, nonstudents as well as students, the figures showed that except for rock (72 percent), ballet and symphony have the highest average gross attendance, with 71 percent of capacity. These figures were based on responses from 170 college concert managers who spent an aggregate $5,262, 586 on the 1867 events they presented in 1969-70.

January-February 1971

Impresarios on Campus
Report Salaries, Programs, Audience

The percentage of full-time, paid college concert managers increased from 12 to 25 percent from 1965 to 1971. During the same period, there was a discernible trend towards greater professionalization among part-time managers, who constitute a majority of those in the field. In 1965 no salary was budgeted for 75 percent of the impresarios, while today [1971] only 32 percent program without either compensation or released time.

These and other conclusions relating to college arts programming and programmers were reported in the Association of College and University Concert Managers' recently released *Profile Survey IV*. Survey results, based on the 1970-71 season, were drawn from a sample of 42 percent of ACUCM's 339 member institutions.

The annual profile, which covered managers' salaries for the first time, showed a monthly average salary of $1142 and a median salary range between $1000 and $1200. However, 23 percent of the managers reporting had salaries above $1400 a month, and 6 percent were paid between $2000 and $3500 monthly.

In an analysis of concert manager salaries, the report concluded:

> If one wants to make the maximum amount of money in the concert management field, he should be male, have a PhD, be over 60, be located in a public college that has between 10,000 and 20,000 students and be a part time manager. The difference between male and female monthly salaries [male, $1193 and female, $850] many not be as significant because males have higher academic degrees than females.

In terms of budget, 64 percent of college concert fees were spent on five program types—rock, symphony, theater, popular, and instrumental recitals. The average fee for all program types was $3169, up 12 percent from $2189 a year earlier. About 46 percent of the programs cost less than $3500, and 54 percent cost more. The trend towards the use of larger facilities for all types of events continued, perhaps in response to increased fees. Happily, however, programs were subsidized at 70 percent of the institutions.

Average attendance for all events was 1335, and average gross attendance was 59 percent of capacity, down 5 percent from the previous year. Students were a significant part of the audience, representing 59 percent of the gross attendance, an annual increase of 11 percent. Moreover, at 70 percent of the institutions they helped make booking decisions through student committees.

The most popular "classical" event among all audiences in terms of average gross attendance was theater, followed by ballet, instrumental recitals, and symphony. Least popular was vocal recitals, whose existence on campus the report termed "marginal." Among students, ballet easily led the way—student attendance soared from 44 to 78 percent in a year—followed by contemporary dance, theater, and chamber music.

September-October 1971

Study Calls for Involvement of Older Americans in the Arts

Older Americans should be more deeply involved in the arts, according to a 1972 study. The report, which outlines a wide range of cultural programs for the aged, was released by a joint committee representing the Kennedy Center for the Performing Arts and the National Council on the Aging. Titled, *"Older Americans and the Arts: A Human Equation,"* it discusses approaches that can be utilized by community arts centers and other organizations.

"Many older people already make major contributions to the arts," said John B. Martin, Commissioner on Aging. "But this program, when developed, could involve millions more nationally."

The report suggests ways to encourage retired artists to share their talents with their peers and tells how arts groups can best utilize the resources and abilities of older people. According to Jacqueline Sunderland, project coordinator, its major thrust is "to alert arts managers to a potential rather than a problem."

Summer 1972

A CHRONOLOGY OF KEY STUDIES AND SURVEYS

Key Study Shows Public Receptive to Arts

The public has a far more favorable attitude toward the arts than is generally believed, and it recognizes the importance of the arts to the quality of neighborhood life and to the economic well-being of the community. In addition, an overwhelming majority of the public respects artists and views arts education for schoolchildren as essential. Moreover, if the arts were made more accessible to nonwhites and people in communities without adequate cultural facilities, attendance would increase substantially.

These are among the revealing and provocative findings gleaned from a trailblazing study of public attitudes toward the arts in New York State conducted by the National Research Center of the Arts, for the American Council for the Arts in Education. *Arts and the People: A Survey of Public Participation in and Attitudes Towards Arts and Culture in New York State,* released in 1973, is believed to be the most comprehensive attitudinal study of the arts yet undertaken. Its 200-odd pages of findings are based on 1531 interviews, averaging nearly an hour-and-a-half each, with a representative cross-section of state residents over the age of 16. This large and scientifically sound sample was broken down into 26 demographic groupings—each large enough to be projectable on a statewide basis—according to geographic region, size of place, sex, race, income, education, and age, and also broken down into a series of attitudinal groupings created from responses.

In answer to the question "How important is it to you that your community and neighborhood should have a theater where plays and ballet are performed?" 39 percent of the respondents answered that it was very important, and 33 percent said somewhat important. Only 10 percent indicated that it was not at all important. Virtually the same proportionate response held true for questions about the importance of concert halls and art museums. There was an even higher positive response to questions on the importance of cultural facilities to the community itself. Some 50 percent indicated that the arts were very important to the quality of life, and 35 percent answered somewhat important. The importance of cultural facilities to the business and economy of the community resulted in responses of 38 percent very important and 36 percent somewhat important.

In addition to choice questions, respondents were given a series of positive and negative statements on the arts and asked to agree or disagree with each. Generally, there was strong agreement with positive statements and strong disagreement with negative statements. For example, 77 percent agreed with the statement "It is important for young people to see live performances on stage," while only 33 percent agreed with the negative statement "Movies are much more relevant to life than most things you see on stage." There was majority support for live over electronically reproduced programming and strong agreement that television should broadcast more concerts, operas, and drama. Conversely, there was better than majority disagreement to such statements as "Symphony concerts are just for highbrows" (72 percent); "It's so difficult to go to a live performance that it's not worth the effort" (52 percent); and "I don't mind going to a concert in the park, but a symphony hall makes me uncomfortable" (63 percent).

In another kind of arts reaction check, respondents were asked to indicate their respect for various kinds of well-recognized professions, and the arts won a dramatically high following. Musicians came out fourth on the list, immediately behind scientists, doctors, and lawyers, and ahead of bankers. Poets were next, ahead of businessmen, with 43 percent, or a projected 5.5 million New Yorkers, according them high respect. Painters and sculptors followed businessmen by only a single percentage point. Although actors and ballet dancers were near the bottom of the list—critics were at the absolute bottom—79 percent accorded them some respect or great respect.

A key pattern to emerge from the section on public receptivity to the arts, the first chapter of the report, was evidence of the strong arts interest shown by nonwhites and those in the middle and lower middle range of the socioeconomic scale. (It was not a surprise to discover that the upper strata scored high for the arts.) The study clearly shows that the economic situation doesn't seem to change an individual's feelings as to the value of the arts or its importance to the community. Nonwhites as a whole, in fact, were more favorably inclined towards the arts than their white counterparts on a number of questions put to them and, along with women, were more concerned about neighborhood arts facilities and the general quality of life. Clearly, when the arts are brought to the public and made accessible, they receive very high interest and recognition. What this means to the arts is the demonstrated fact that there is a much larger culturally inclined coalition than had ever before been indicated and that this coalition includes good representation from the middle class. The only groups with consistently less than positive attitudes towards the arts were rural residents and those with gradeschool educations.

In addition to receptivity to the arts, the study explored key subjects in each of its other six chapters: attitudes towards children's exposure to culture; the level of individual participation in the arts; arts attendance; background of arts exposure; access to cultural events; and attitudes towards public and other funding. The highly positive reaction to education in the arts for schoolchildren was an especially meaningful finding. In spite of the fact that the majority of people think there is more arts activity in the schools than there really is, they indicated that they wanted even more exposure to the arts for youngsters. Positive interest in increasing the arts role in education was strongest among non-whites, urbanites, and young people themselves. Perhaps the best indication of the overall attitude on this subject was the fact that a majority of respondents favored credits for arts subjects in grade and high schools, thus placing the arts on an equal basis with math, science, and English.

Figures regarding attendance at cultural programs provided some positive and surprising results as the study, perhaps for the first time, developed a per capita rather than total attendance count. The results suggest, in fact, that previous estimates of the cultural audience are much lower than it really is. At least once during the year from November 1971 to November 1972, some 7.4 million of the state's 13 million people age 16 or older visited one art museum. Concert attendance based on at least one visit was 4.4 million individuals (34 percent), theater 5.5 million (42 percent), and ballet or modern dance 2.1 million (16 percent). Even more significant was the count of multiple attenders, those who visited art museums three or more times a year, or attended at least eight performances—four or more in each of two different performing arts disciplines. Over 2 million New ·Yorkers (25 percent) were multiple attenders at museums, while over one million (9 percent) were multiple attenders at performing arts programs. According to Joseph Farrell, president of the National Research Center, "the study indicates that attendance figures are most controlled by access with the socioeconomic more important than the geographic factor." He cautioned, however, that attendance figures obtained in a cross-sectional public study are rough projections, although they are accurate enough to indicate a general range of numbers.

The study shows some misunderstanding of the role of state and local governments in culture, although the public seems to favor more government support. The prevailing opinion seemed to be that arts support is more a responsibility of the federal government that it is of either state or local government.

January-February 1973

Major New Arts
Studies Nearing Publication

The arts, data-poor in the past, will benefit from the publication of three major studies early in 1974. Each is of sufficient importance to be viewed as a breakthrough in its area and each, in addition to its information uses, will have a key public relations value.

The Ford Foundation's long-awaited survey on the economics of the performing arts promises to provide the most authoritative data yet produced on the subject. Announced in 1971 and originally scheduled for completion in 1972, the survey analyzes the operations of 166 professional performing arts groups with budgets over $100,000 in theater, dance, opera, and symphony—down from the 200 originally planned—over the six-year period ending with the 1970–71 season. The standard data collection form breaks down both income and expenditures into 30 components and provides comparable data through arts disciplines. The resulting information bank will be computerized and updated regularly.

A key study aspect will be the attempt to calculate income gaps and growth rates in the performing arts. Because data has been interpolated where it has not been available, however, the study will be cautious in its projections. Although it is too early to report on definitive findings, an initial conclusion shows that in spite of a more than two-thirds rise in expenditures in the performing arts over the six years covered, from $92 million to $159 million, total income generally kept pace with increasing expenses. Earned income did also, with the exception of symphonies.

In the visual arts, a summary of the most comprehensive survey of American museums yet undertaken has just been issued. The full study itself, prepared for the National Endowment on the Arts by the National Research Center of the Arts, will be published in spring 1974.

In a 20-page booklet, "Museums USA: Highlights" (U.S. Government Printing Office, Washington, D.C. 20402), the summary offers new data on the operation, finances, programs, attendance, facilities, and personnel of 1821 art, history, and science museums that met study criteria. Survey results were projected from a representative sample of 728 museums.

Finances, obviously, are a major museum concern, Some 66 percent find that current operating budgets do not allow full use of facilities and collections. To achieve this use they estimate a median budget increase of 45 percent in the next two to three years. Also, operating costs have increased in nine of ten museums since 1966, and financial pressures have resulted in cutbacks over the past five years in 36 percent of the museums. Most museums are small, with 44 percent of the budgets under $50,000 and another 36 percent between $50,000 and $249,000.

During fiscal 1971-72, the year covered by the study, the museums received over 300 million visits. Although larger museums (budgets over $1 million) represent only 5 percent of all museums, they accounted for 34 percent of total attendance. Museums are open an average of 11 months a year and 45 hours a week. Some 59 percent have free admissions.

Other key findings were that the museum work force is 110,000, including 64,200 volunteers; of the $513 million total museum income, 63 percent came from private sources; and education is a key function, with 73 percent regularly scheduling programs for groups of school children.

The third major study deals with public receptivity to the arts and is a national follow-up to "Arts and the People," published earlier in 1973. Both were undertaken by the National Research Center of the Arts. Importantly, the findings of the new study show that nationally, just as in New York, there is a positive response to the arts across the entire socioeconomic spectrum. Some 89 percent feel that cultural facilities are important to the quality of community life, and 80 percent feel that such facilities are important to the economy of the community. In fact, 65 percent of the respondents feel that business has a responsibility to support community arts activities.

Full details of the study will not be available until publication by Associated Councils of the Arts early in 1974, but initial findings show that an unprecedented range of new, useful, and at times surprising information will be available to the arts. A section on cultural attendance reveals that it does not vary by race to the same degree that it does for other key socioeconomic factors such as income and education. In fact, an almost identical percentage of whites (10 percent) and nonwhites (11 percent) are heavy cultural attenders. (Overall, 10 percent of the public are heavy cultural attenders, 20 percent are moderate attenders, 41 percent are light attenders, and 29 percent are nonattenders.) Interestingly, some 30 million Americans with incomes under $15,000 fall into the heavy and moderate attender groups, and men and women have almost identical attendance patterns at cultural events. Childhood exposure to the arts is a major influence on later attendance.

As in the New York study, many feel that arts courses should be part of the regular credit curriculum in schools, with 78 percent citing music instrument playing, 71 per cent crafts, 70 percent art appreciation, 49 percent acting, and 46 percent dance. Also, there was strong respect for arts professions, with musicians ranking higher than bankers and businessmen, and painters and sculptors at an equal level with the latter two professions.

In spite of public receptivity to the arts, however, there is tremendous ignorance concerning the field. Thirty-three percent thought painters and sculptors earned more than salaried people, 49 percent thought musicians earned more, and 71 percent believed that actors earned more. Also, 56 percent of the public thought that most cultural institutions operate in the black, and a majority believed that arts groups (such as opera companies and ballet or modern dance companies) are self-supporting. Convinced of this, the public is less inclined to favor government support. Perhaps most incredibly, only 57 percent of the public knew that contributions to arts groups were tax deductible.

November-December 1973

Economic Studies

A 1974 study for the Lake Placid, New York Center for Music, Drama and Art shows the positive impact an arts facility can have on an economically depressed area by strongly influencing "the duration of stay of tourists and vacation home owners . . . and consequently upon their expenditures." Prepared by the Technical Assistance Center at the State University of New York College at Plattsburgh, the study indicates that the center helped generate an economic impact on the area of $1.17 million last summer—commercial establishments and government were key beneficiaries—with center visitors spending more than $730,000 on direct expenses.

"Economic Aspects of the Arts in Ontario," one of the first major Canadian studies of its kind, offers data on income, expenditures, attendance, and support during the 1971-72 season for performing and visual arts activities in the province. Some conclusions: the 77 professional performing groups earned about 65 percent of their $18 million in annual expenditures; their income gap was $6.3 million; and they drew an audience of 3.5 million out of a total potential capacity of 5 million. Worth reading in its entirety, the report is available through the Ontario Arts Council in Toronto.

March-April 1974

Ford Foundation Finance Survey

The Ford Foundation report, "The Finances of the Performing Arts," which surveys the finances of 166 performing arts groups from 1965-66 through 1970-71, speculates on a bleak economic future, including a steady widening of the earnings gap in the next decade and a need for substantially increased funding from all sources merely to maintain the 1970-71 financial position.

According to the report, the earnings gap in 1970-71 was $62 million (excluding the atypical Metropolitan Opera), with half the surveyed institutions failing to balance their budgets. Projected at the same rate, the earnings gap would increase to $180 million by 1980-81, although inflation, even at a middle range, would bring the gap to five times the 1970-71 figure—$335 million.

In a series of illustrative speculations, the study compares actual 1970-71 fundings with 1980-81 possibilities. An optimistic speculation assumes such increases by 1980-81 as (in millions of dollars) all government funding up from 8 to 133; foundations up from 8 to 23; dividends and interest up from 8 to 15; and invasion of capital down from 2 to 0. At this increased level of giving, private patronage would have to grow from $35 million to $164 million in a decade to make up the difference in the overall $335-million gap. Accompanying the report is a market research study of audiences in 12 cities.

Summer 1974

Study Probes Attitudes Toward Arts

"Winston-Salem/Forsyth County: Public Perspective on the Arts and Culture" examines in depth what people think, say, and do about the arts in the culture-conscious city where the community arts council movement was born. Jammed with interesting material, the 1974 study by the National Research Center of the Arts reaches some surprising conclusions considering Winston-Salem's highly developed arts program. Their findings suggested that a serious arts participation gap exists in Winston-Salem; there is a relatively low public awareness of local arts activities; and few people really understand the financial position of arts group or personally support them.

Moreover, while a high percentage viewed the arts role as essential to community life, favored government and business support of arts groups, and believed the arts should be part of the core curriculum in schools, the actual arts constituency was small and like many other places was young, educated, white, and with high incomes.

Viewed in light of Winston-Salem's all-out arts development program over the past 25 years, one paragraph seems particularly telling. Says the report:

> It seems certain that the potential audience for the arts among the Winston-Salem/Forsyth County population is much greater than that being tapped now. If the arts organizations wish to broaden their services to the community as well as their constituency and support, efforts must be undertaken to penetrate the feeling that the arts are

for other people not oneself, to overcome problems of inaccessibility, costs, and other factors limiting attendance. The public is strongly inclined toward the arts, but it is the arts that must make the effort to engage the public.

Also newly published was the "Report of the Mayor's Committee on Cultural Policy in New York City," which called for major restructuring of cultural organization for the city government, including the creation of an independent, professionally administered cultural affairs agency. The report also had significant data on the arts industry in New York.

September-October 1974

Report on Philanthropy

A massive report, two years in preparation, contains few major new proposals and little specific reference to the needs of the arts. Released early in December 1975, "Giving in America," the Report of the Commission on Private Philanthropy and Public Needs, is a 240-page document jammed with information on the nonprofit sector that calls for private giving beyond the current $50 billion a year in gifts of time and money to keep pace with increasing costs and a growing public need for services. Among the more than 60 studies prepared for the commission was one on the arts by Caroline Hightower.

Among commission recommendations was a call for double deductions for charitable donations made by taxpayers with incomes below $15,000 and the suggestion that all taxpayers taking the standard deduction also should be permitted to deduct contributions as an additional itemized deduction. The commission also called for detailed annual reports by tax-exempts with budgets over $100,000; greater freedom for nonprofits to influence legislation; and asked corporations to increase giving to 2 percent of pre-tax net income by 1980. The report's final recommendation called for the establishment of a permanent commission on the nonprofit sector.

November-December 1975

New National Data Bank for the Arts Established

A national data bank for the arts, envisioned for many years, finally could become a reality. In the most ambitious cultural research programs ever undertaken, detailed and sample data on some 12,000 nonprofit arts groups throughout the country will be gathered annually and made available in yearly printouts and reports. "It's long overdue," Joseph Farrell, head of the National Research Center of the Arts, told *AM*. "It's the end result of a lot of research efforts and will give us the closest thing we've ever had to an annual report on the arts and culture in America."

The project, the United States Arts and Cultural Trend Data System, has been contracted to the Research Center by the National Endowment for the Arts. Its cost, estimated at between $450,000 to $500,000 for 1976 alone, will be underwritten by grants from 12 private and corporate foundations and $200,-000 from NEA.

Within the next few months, lists of organizations will have been compiled and questionnaires developed by the Research Center with the aid of a panel of 40 to 50 consultants from the arts and other areas. Groups in every discipline will then be tapped—from established symphonies, theaters, and dance companies to craft associations, small presses, and less-established organizations—for fiscal year 1976 data on budgets, personnel, services, production, audiences, management, and expenditures. Information will be sought from groups as small as those with three-month budgets of $1000 a month. From a universe of around 12,000 organizations, 1200 will be used as the sample on which projections will be based. To ensure a high degree of accuracy, a CPA firm will evaluate budgets of survey participants.

According to Farrell, raw data will be gathered by spring 1977. The project staff will then draw an overall picture of the arts industry and next do a breakdown by disciplines.

The ramifications of the project are immense. Not only will reliable and concrete data be available annually across the board in the arts for the first time, but it will be available to a variety of sources in a variety of forms. In spite of its potential importance, Farrell indicated to *AM* that the current computerized program is only a precursor, "a Model-T version," of the kind of system that can be developed. "Eventually," he added, "we hope to be able to do state-by-state breakouts as they are needed, and perhaps take a broader view of the arts industry by including commercial theaters and galleries in our studies."

Note: As of 1979, the project still had not been completed.

September-October 1976

Research Efforts in the Arts Are Accelerating

Arts groups are showing increased interest in research—the NEA-sponsored three-day seminar on the problems and techniques of arts research in Baltimore in December 1977 drew 240 registrants—as the need for hard data on audiences and economic impact grows.

During 1977, economic impact studies have been undertaken or completed for such varied locations as Philadelphia, Fort Wayne, the state of Nebraska, and the southeast region. The San Francisco Ballet released its own survey findings showing that the company generated an economic impact of over $8.5 million on San Francisco, an annual increase of 39 percent. A terse but excellent overview of the ways arts groups have used economic impact studies is offered in the

November Theatre Communications Group Newsletter article, "The Arts: Vital Economic Reactors in the Community."

An indication of the scope and significance of audience studies may be gleaned from an important new report prepared by the Center for the Study of Public Policy in Cambridge, Massachusetts under contract from the NEA. Titled, "The American Arts Audience: Its Study and Its Character," the 221-page report to the NEA summarizes information amassed from 270 separate museum and performing arts studies, most since 1970, to reach some conclusions about the American arts audience, including: a performing arts audience median age of 35 —ballet and theater audiences youngest and opera and symphony oldest—museums, age 31; education level very high in both areas, 54 percent with four-year college degrees and 30 percent graduate training; median income for performing arts, $19,000, for museums, $17,000; men, 43 percent of the performing arts audience, 46 percent for museums; and by occupation, a strikingly high percentage of professionals—56 percent in the average audience, and only 4 percent blue collar workers.

Some other interesting conclusions were the disproportionately high number of students in all audience groups and, except for intensive theatergoers, a large crossover into other performing arts by heavy attenders in one area. The report, in a major section, assesses the quality and impact of arts audience studies and also lists information on each of the 270 studies.

National arts service organizations in the various disciplines have become a source of information on audiences and finances through the informal surveys they publish. Highlights of 1977 studies include:

- A Central Opera Service study published in the November issue of *Opera News* showed total opera attendance for 914 companies in the United States during 1976-77 up to 9.2 million from 8.85 million the previous year. For the larger budget companies—12 over $1 million, 40 over $200,-000, and 16 over $100,000—expenses rose to $79.7 million from $71.8 million, and box office receipts averaged 45.4 percent of budgets.

- The first Association of American Dance Companies survey drew responses from 90 professional companies, or 30 percent of the total, and concluded that the published estimate of 15 million dance admissions a year is reasonable. The overall budget for 84 responding companies was nearly $40 million, with tour fees and ticket income accounting for 58 percent.

- The American Symphony Orchestra League survey of 31 major orchestras with budgets over $1.5 million annually showed attendance up 8 percent to 13.4 million during 1975-76. Expenses rose to $108 million, up 9.5 percent, and for the eighth straight year, earned income was up, from 59.2 percent of the budget to 60.1 percent. Significantly, business and industry support more than doubled.

- The Theatre Communications Group study of 151 nonprofit theaters showed audiences up to 12 million and total expenses of over $77 million during the 1975–76 season. Within a core group of theaters with budgets over $250,000, budgets grew 10.6 percent over the previous year, and audience and overall earnings were up 13 percent. Audience as a percentage of capacity grew from 79.3 percent in 1975 to 82.4 percent in 1976.

Elsewhere, American Council for the Arts study of 38 united arts fundraising campaigns showed receipts of $17.1 million, up nearly $4 million from 35 such campaigns the previous year. Nearly $8 million or 47 percent came from corporations. In a separate survey of state support of the arts, ACA figures showed a 7.5 percent increase in funding by state legislatures over the previous year, bringing total state support up to $61,635,000. Appropriations increased in 43 states and decreased in six. Alaska's per capita arts expenditure again was highest, at $1.86 per person. Texas at 3¢ was lowest.

November-December 1977

CHRONOLOGICAL REVIEW OF
BOOKS AND PERIODICALS: 1969–1978

"America's Museums: The Belmont Report," had its genesis in June 1967 when President Johnson asked the Federal Council on the Arts and Humanities to "study thoroughly the status of American museums and report to me. What is their present condition? What are the unmet needs of America's museums? What is their relationship to other educational and cultural institutions?" A 16-member committee of the American Association of Museums completed the study in May 1968, and it was presented to President Johnson in November 1968 by Roger L. Stevens, chairman of the Federal Council. Now the report has been introduced into the Senate and House of Representatives as the subject of upcoming hearings.

Relying on existing data rather than new research findings, the report clearly indicates the growing demands for museum services, the key role that museums play in the educational system, and the desperate financial condition of most museums today. It pinpoints ten current priority needs and develops a cogent case for federal support of museums, "somewhere between $35 million and $60 million for the first year." The report indicates that if authorized funds are appropriated and certain amendments to statutes made, the government can help meet museum priority needs from within existing machinery.

Spring-Summer 1969

Two books, although oriented to the arts in specific cities, have tremendous value for managers everywhere. *Persuade and Provide,* by Michael Newton and Scott Hatley (Associated Councils of the Arts), is the informative story of the development of the Arts and Educational Council of Greater St. Louis as told by its directors. *The Arts In Boston,* by Bernard Taper (Harvard University Press, Boston), subtitled "An Outsider's Inside View of the Cultural Estate," is a slim yet provociative book that analyzes cultural development in the city and seeks answers to a number of key questions.

"Bricks, Mortar and the Performing Arts" (Twentieth Century Fund) is a report of the nine-member Twentieth Century Fund Task Force on Performing Arts Centers. Among the panel's key recommendations, designed to help arts centers avoid financial disaster, were that remodelling be considered before constructing new centers and that centers be made self-supporting by allocating some space to commercial ventures. The 99 page report includes a background paper on performing arts centers by Martin Mayer. Several newly published reports add immeasurable documentation to sparsely covered areas of interest. *The Arts Education and the Urban Sub-Culture,* by Don D. Bushnell, is an insightful national survey of performing arts for inner-city youngsters. The study (Grant no. OEC-0-8-071104-1742) was undertaken for the Office of Education of the United States Department of Health, Education and Welfare, Washington, D.C. *Labor Relations in the Performing Arts* by Michael H. Moskow (Associated Councils of the Arts), not only offers an excellent beginning look at a complex subject, but also pinpoints current and possible future problem areas. *The Theatre Today in England and Wales* by the British Arts Council Theatre Enquiry 1970 is a terse, on-target report on the arts scene in a foreign country. Especially interesting to American readers is the summary of priorities, the descripton of organizations, and the statistical table on subsidy.

Fall 1970

How does an art council disperse $18 million? A complete listing of the 596 cultural groups funded under the New York State Council on the Arts 1970-71 program of direct aid to cultural groups, including amounts and descriptions of funded programs, has been published by Associated Councils of the Arts. Material in the report, which also includes some important overall findings, was provided by the state council.

March-April 1971

An important publication for administrators is the Arts Endowment's *Economic Aspects of the Performing Arts—A Portrait in Figures* (U.S. Government Printing Office). The slim booklet, compiled by former Endowment staffer Sureva Seligson, offers readers a picture of the 1969-70 income and expenditures figures for 187 professional, nonprofit performing arts groups with budgets exceeding $100,000 annually and gives financial estimates for 1970-71. Among the highlights: the cost of staffing and operating the 187 groups was $144 million in 1969-70 and is estimated at $160.5 million in 1970-71, and 11 percent increase.

Earned income from subscription and box office sales and fees from services will increase 14 percent from 1969-70's $80 million to 1970-71's $90.5 million, and income from contributions, grants, and endowments is expected to increase 7 percent from $59 million to $63 million. Gross deficits, however, will probably rise 8 percent from $65 million to $70 million, and net deficits will rise 21 percent from $6 million in 1969-70 to $7 million in 1970-71.

Summer 1971

Bach, Beethoven and Bureaucracy: The Case of the Philadelphia Orchestra (University of Alabama Press, University, Alabama) was written by Edward Arian, a Philadelphia Orchestra member for 20 years and currently professor of political science at Drexel University, where he is developing an arts administration program. The short, critical work analyzes the orchestra's operation since its beginning, and takes it to task for a bureaucratic approach which the author contends has emphasized economy and efficiency at the expense of quality, artistic experimentation, the musicians, and audience development. Janet Schlesinger's *Challenge to the Urban Orchestra—The Case of the Pittsburgh Symphony* (University of Pittsburgh) is less detailed and less critical than the Arian book, but like the latter it does strongly emphasize the need for change in the future operation of urban orchestras.

Fiction, infrequently used to explore the world of the arts in the past, has made up for this oversight, and within recent months three new "culture novels" have been published. *Philharmonic* (Coward-McCann & Geoghegan, New York), written by Margalit Banai and another former orchestra player, Herbert Russcol, chronicles the activities of a symphony orchestra, at home and on tour, and the personal relationships of its players, conductor, management, and board. A concert artist and the people she works and deals with—impresarios, conductors, and personal managers—are subjects of George Selcamm's book, *57th Street* (W. W. Norton, New York). Robert A. Carter takes the reader inside the day-to-day world of a large New York museum in *Manhattan Primitive* (Stein & Day,) Briarcliff Manor, N.Y.). The novel is up-to-date in the situations and conflicts it treats, and several scenes will seem familiar to the discerning arts administrator.

The 1971 *Financial and Salary Survey* just published by the American Association of Museums in Washington, D.C. should be of interest to arts managers interested in fiscal operations. The report, based on questionnaire responses from more than 950 museums, discusses museum salaries according to discipline, geographic location, and size of budget, and lists data on such financial aspects as sources of museum funding, budgets, and attendance. Some fascinating bits of information unfold along the way, including that 44 percent of American museums ran at a deficit in 1970, and 30 percent charged admission fees.

September-October 1971

An essential work is the fourth edition of the *Foundation Directory* (The Foundation Center). The 642-page volume, which is being distributed by Columbia University Press, New York, lists 5454 foundations with assets of $500,000 and over or those that made grants of $25,000 in the year of record. Foundations are listed by state, and each entry includes such data as names of key personnel and donors, assets, grants, and purposes and activities. In addition, a useful index lists areas of interest, donors, trustees, and administrators.

    Lincoln Center for the Performing Arts (Prentice-Hall, Englewood Cliffs, N.J.) is a big and handsomely illustrated book with 32 pages of full color and 100 black-and-white photos. Following an introductory section on the development of the center, there are sections on the constituent groups. Readers looking for a guided tour rather than a social document will enjoy browsing through the book.

    Museums and the Environment: A Handbook for Education (American Association of Museums) was designed by the association for use by its member institutions and community groups. The handsomely illustrated book contains articles by experts on various aspects of ecology, followed by suggestions on how museums and other groups can develop exhibits, projects, and activities dealing with the environment. Illustrated examples of successful program are given.

November-December 1971

Museums in Crisis (George Braziller, Inc., New York) is a useful aid to understanding the complex role of museums in contemporary life and the mounting problems that threaten their survival. Edited by Brian O'Doherty with a foreword by Nancy Hanks, the book is comprised of a series of essays that originally appeared in the July-August 1971 special museum issue of *Art in America*.

January-February 1972

Lincoln Center has taken a year-long, in-depth look at its 11-year-old student program and other cultural programs for youngsters and reached some interesting conclusions. Titled, "The Hunting of the Squiggle: A Study of a Performing Arts Institution and Young People," the report, prepared under the direction of Lincoln Center's education director, Mark Schubart, envisions a new kind of performing arts organization designed specifically for young people. Such an organization would present many programs outside the formal education system and traditional performing areas. The result would be a range of interdisciplinary programs in more informal spaces, involving a wider number of participants—artists, educators, community agency leaders, and youth.

    Lincoln Center is now developing a three-year program to explore and implement the study's recommendations.

March-April 1972

Culture & Company, a book that aroused considerable interest prior to its release, was published by Twayne (Boston), in 1972. Subtitled, "A Critical Study of an Improbable Alliance," The 309-page book by Alvin H. Reiss, editor of *AM,* probes the relationship of the arts and business to a changing society and to each other. In the process, it delves deeply into such key areas as arts power; new programming and cultural tokenism; commercial partnerships between business and the arts; and the influence of government, labor, and minority groups.

Arnold Gingrich, *Esquire* publisher and cosponsor of the annual Business in the Arts Awards, calls *Culture & Company* "the definitive account . . . the most detailed and comprehensive blueprint for the still struggling movement's future—this is the one book toward which so many others have been pointing." In his preface, Alvin Toffler, author of *Future Shock,* terms the book "a piece of social reportage that will be of considerable significance to the cultural historians of tomorrow."

The ultimate cultural center, set down in the heartland of America—Culture City, South Dakota—provides the setting for still another in a recent string of novels about the arts. *Bringing Down the House,* by Richard P. Brickner (Charles Scribner's Sons, New York), is a satire, and at times is a very funny one.

The Visual Artist and the Law is the first of its kind, a terse yet surprisingly comprehensive monograph that guides the artist through such areas as copyright, publication, gallery and museum relations, sales and commissions, and tax problems. It is a joint effort of Associated Councils of the Arts, the New York City Bar Association, and Volunteer Lawyers for the Arts. *The Business of Music* (Billboard Publications, New York), a completely revised and enlarged edition of a standard in its field, is a comprehensive guide to virtually every aspect of the music record-tape industry. The 575-page hardcover includes over 100 pages of sample forms and contracts.

Anyone interested in government's role in the arts will be grateful to Francis V. O'Connor for the superb job he has done is assembling *The New Deal Art Projects: An Anthology of Memoirs* (Smithsonian Institution Press, Washington). The 332-page book, with 63 illustrations, offers the candid, first-hand observations of ten individuals who participated as artists and administrators in such important government-sponsored arts projects of the thirties and early forties as the WPA and Treasury Department programs.

March-April 1972

Management and the Arts: A Selected Bibliography (UCLA Graduate School of Management) should be a useful reference tool for administrators. The 51-page booklet succeeds a 1970 bibliography published by the school and contains many new listings among its 150 titles. Earlier, Associated Councils of the Arts published three important new directories. *State Arts Councils* includes a detailed analysis of funding and programming for all the councils as well as information on membership and staffing. The *Directory of Community Arts Councils* is a listing and survey of 254 councils throughout the country with data on their memberships, areas of activity, and funding. An updated and expanded edition of an earlier ACA publication, *Directory of National Arts Organizations,* includes data on 52 nonprofit service groups.

An 83-page publication that describes all the programs of the National Endowment for the Arts and procedures for funding will be of primary interest to arts organizations. Titled *Our Programs,* the booklet (stock no. 3600-0011) is available from the Superintendent of Documents, U.S. Government Printing Office, Washington, D.C. 20402. A guide to government activity in the arts, *Millions for the Arts: Federal and State Cultural Programs* (Washington International Arts Letter) is a reprint of a survey originally undertaken for the U.S. Senate by the Congressional Research Service. Described as a handbook for artists and art dealers, *Marketing Art* (Gee Tee Bee) deals specifically with the business aspects of the contemporary art market.

New hardcover books provide insights into several areas of the arts. Stuart W. Little's *Off-Broadway* (Coward-McCann & Geoghegan, New York) is a comprehensive and absorbing study of a key movement and its leaders. In *At the Vanishing Point* (Saturday Review Press, New York), critic Marcia B. Siegel looks at American dance activity from 1967-1971. *The History of Art for Young People* (Harry N. Abrams, New York) is an abridgement and rewriting of H. W. Janson's earlier work, *The History of Art,* tailored to the needs of students. Included in the 414-page book are 74 full-color illustrations.

Summer 1972

More and better-trained arts administrators, a broadening of the base of public support for culture, and the establishment of new arts priorities throughout the broadcast and printed media are among the key recommendations of the new Concert Environment Study. Prepared by the Association of College and University Concert Managers, the study investigated the cultural patterns of colleges and communities in 12 states. "In the broadest sense," states the report, "what this study has demonstrated is the need to integrate the arts with the total educational and social development of this country and to stimulate a national consciousness that recognizes the importance of doing so."

Summer 1972

A comprehensive study of the nonprofit cultural industry in New York State undertaken by the National Research Center of the Arts pinpoints the arts impact on the economy for perhaps the first time and should provide useful ammunition to arts administrators throughout the country. The 543 professional arts groups surveyed on their activities during 1970-71 had a total income of $168.6

million, employed 31,000 people, and attracted an audience of over 70 million. However, operating costs were $177 million, and 54 percent of the groups surveyed showed net income gaps for the year. Copies of the 194-page study are available from the Performing Arts Association of New York, Saratoga Performing Arts Center, Saratoga, New York, 12866.

"Museums: Their New Audiences," a report by a special committee of the American Association of Museums, assesses the present and potential public service role of the urban museum. Prepared under a grant from the U.S. Department of Housing and Urban Development, the report, which includes brief case studies of 16 urban museums, concludes with 16 recommendations designed to strengthen the museum relationship to the community. Included were such suggestions as community representation on museum boards and the establishment by AAM of a new urban information center. Reports are available free from the AAM, 2233 Wisconsin Avenue N.W., Washington, D.C. 20007.

The Big Foundations, just issued by the Twentieth Century Fund, is a critical study of 33 of America's largest foundations, those with assets of $100 million or more. Author Waldemar A. Nielson concludes that as a group the large foundations are neither creative nor experimental in their programs, unwilling to take risks, and tend to give preference to familiar and "generally sound" applicants. Upcoming next month (McGraw-Hill, New York) is a more positive view of foundations, *Private Money and Public Service—The Role of Foundations in American Society.* Author Merrimon Cuninggim recently resigned as president of the Danforth Foundation.

Negotiating and Contracting for Artists and Attractions is a slim but practical booklet (Association of College and University Concert Managers) written for educational and nonprofit institutions.

September-October 1972

For a book about an arts administrator, albeit an uncommon one, Sir Rudolph Bing's *5000 Nights at the Opera* (Doubleday, New York) is creating quite a stir, and deservedly so. The Bing memoir is lively, anecdotal, witty, and quite revealing of the man and the arts institution he ran.

A four-volume treatise on the legal aspects of the performing arts—theater, film, dance, music, literature, cassettes, and television—has been written by theatrical lawyer Joseph Taubman for an audience of arts producers, administrators, and lawyers. *Performing Arts Management and Law* (Law-Arts Publishers, New York) probes such areas as contracts, copyrights, related marketing agencies, derivative rights, and the law as it relates to the performer and organization. Two volumes of text at $50 are available now. The remaining volumes, forms for the television and motion picture fields, will be published later this year.

Arts in Common, the newsletter initiated as a quarterly publication for community arts councils in 1971, will be published on a ten times a year basis beginning in December 1972. Each issue will cover a different topic of interest—the initial issue on gambling for the arts discusses lotteries, and horse and dog racing.

The California Dance Directory, listing several hundred dance companies and sponsors in California, has been published by the Association of American Dance Companies and the California Arts Commission as step one of a project that will soon include a pilot artist management service. Another key reference work, *A Directory of American Poets* (Poets and Writers, Inc., New York), is now available in a revised and enlarged edition with information about 1200 contemporary writers.

A booklet prepared by the Fort Wayne Fine Arts Foundation, an arts council, may be of interest to administrators elsewhere as a discussion document on the arts and the artist's role in the community. Free copies of *A Proposal to Establish a Community Arts School* are available from the Foundation at 324 Penn Avenue, Fort Wayne, Indiana 46305. The second edition of *Grants and Aid to Individuals in the Arts* (Washington International Arts Letter) lists 1500 sources, 200 more than the first edition.

November-December 1972

The 1973 edition of the *Official Museum Directory* (National Register Publishing Co. Skokie, Ill.) is a massive 855-page volume published by the American Association of Museums in cooperation with National Register. For each of the 5100 museums listed geographically by state and city in the United States and Canada, there is concise information on personnel, governing authority, collections, activities, hours, etc. Alphabetical, categorical, and personnel indexes add to the directory's usefulness. A first-time "Theatre Directory" listing information on 140 nonprofit professional theatres has been published by the Theatre Communications Group. It is free to nonprofit theaters.

Administrators looking for fund-raising and promotional ideas may find several new titles useful. *The Handbook of Special Events for Nonprofit Organizations* (Association Press, New York) is a how-to and how-it-was-done compilation of money-making and publicity ideas. Included are over 100 case histories contributed by local and national organizations, and checklists for such events as bazaars, fairs, and fashion shows. A slim booklet, *The Anatomy of an Art Auction* (Arnold Harvey Associates, Commack, New York), presents a step-by-step program for organizing, promoting, conducting, and following up this kind of fund-raising event.

January-February 1973

A detailed description of a stunning education achievement, a pilot project that successfully integrated all the arts into the program of an entire school district, is the subject of a report published by the Arts and Education Program of the

JDR 3rd Fund (50 Rockefeller Plaza, New York, N.Y. 10020). "All the Arts for Every Child" focuses on the University City, Missouri school district where, beginning in May 1968, the JDR 3rd Fund established and supported the first of three pilot programs designed to determine whether all the arts could be made integral to the education of every child from kindergarten through high school.

Written by project director Stanley S. Madeja, the report describes key aspects of the projects beginning with the establishment of goals and continuing with staffing, development of instructional units and complementary resources, local artists and arts institutions, and evaluating progress. Although the report does not indulge in wild horn-tooting, the project's success is clearly evident from reading the report, and hopefully the document will serve as a model for school districts throughout the country. Another indication of the project's success is its acceptance by students, parents, and school administrators. The University City school district has gradually absorbed it into its regular budget, and when JDR 3rd Fund support ends in June 1975, the school district will assume full financial responsibility for permanent incorporation of the new arts program into the curriculum.

January-February 1973

Groups on the foundation trail will find the *Foundation Center Information Quarterly* (Columbia University Press, c/o Franklin Rapid Dart, 300 Boulevard East, Weehawken, N.J. 07087) of continuing interest. In addition to listing the latest available data on foundations with assets of $1 million or more, the quarterly includes guidelines on foundation funding, a bibliographical service, and announcements of the availability of computer printouts on grant listings and foundation annual reports on microfilm.

Also in the foundation area is the free annual report of the Ford Foundation for 1972 (320 E. 43rd St., New York, N.Y. 10017), with a section on the humanities and arts program, including descriptions of such key foundation projects as the cash reserve plan and the matching orchestra endowments. The Rockefeller Foundation's *RF Illustrated,* February 1972 (111 W. 50th St., New York, N.Y. 10020) includes a study of arts funding.

The Cleveland Area Arts Council and Boston's Metropolitan Cultural Alliance are mong the arts councils that have published interesting publicity handbooks within recent months. The alliance's *Getting in Ink and on the Air* is a slim booklet slanted towards local media with lists of Boston publications and resource people and some timely tips of general interest. Cleveland's *How-To Guide for Publicity Chairpersons* is divided into separate sections on print and broadcast media and includes pragmatic advice and easy-to-follow examples. A much more costly publicity publication, but one that can be very useful to the arts group that tours the country regularly, is the *National Radio Publicity Directory, 1973* (Peter Glenn Publications, New York). The spiral-bound booklet lists information by city and state on 1736 radio talk shows and their use of guests, tapes, records, etc., plus a list of college stations. Purchase price includes a summer updating.

A lively and controversial book that is causing wagging tongues among cultural cognoscenti is Sophy Burnham's *The Arts Crowd* (McKay, New York). The reader may disagree with some conclusions, but it's doubtful that he'll find the book dull.

March-April 1973

Philip Hart has taken a long and serious look at the symphony orchestra in America in his major new book, *Orpheus in the New World* (W. W. Norton, New York). Dividing his subject into five major sections, the author focuses first on key individuals whose careers helped shape the orchestra into an institution and then discusses such current concerns as economics, audience, government involvement, repertory, and education.

Several works dealing with the visual arts are new to the bookshelf, *Good Old Modern* by Russell Lynes (Atheneum, New York) takes a long and somewhat pleasurable look at the growth and development of the Museum of Modern Art. In *The New York School: A Cultural Reckoning* (Viking Press, New York), critic Dore Ashton provides an inside view into the work, thinking, and personalities of a group of artists who helped shape modern American art.

Of practical interest also is the *National Directory for the Performing Arts and Civic Centers* (Handel & Co.). Included are listings of facilities and performing groups throughout the country with data on staff, seasons, boards of directors, and architects. For drama students and those interested in amateur theater, *Organization and Management of the Non-Professional Theatre* (Richard Rosen Press, New York) will prove an invaluable resource. In easy-to-follow fashion, author Jim Cavanaugh guides the reader through every facet of theater operation.

New reports focus on the arts role in education. Jack Morrison of the JDR 3rd Fund examines *The Rise of the Arts on the American Campus* (McGraw-Hill, New York) for the Carnegie Commission on Higher Education Series. The slim report, with case studies of 17 institutions and relevant tables, is generally optomistic regarding cultural development in higher education, although it does offer recommendations for change. The Arts Endowment has published *Artists in Schools* (U.S. Government Printing Office, stock no. 3600-00015), a text and picture summary of the program sponsored since 1969.

Summer 1973

How to Manipulate the Media, produced by the San Francisco Art Commission's Neighborhood Arts Program (165 Grove St., San Francisco, Ca., 94102), is a mimeographed publicity primer for community arts groups. Written in straight-forward style, the guide is intended for groups unable to afford professional publicity services. Available from the commission, the booklet may be reproduced for use in other communities.

Summer 1973

Regional Theatre: The Revolutionary Stage (University of Minnesota Press, Minneapolis) is a historical and social study of the movement toward a decentralized theater in America. The pioneer work was written by former director of the Theatre Communications Group, Joseph Wesley Zeigler. Another important theater book, this one with a focus on acting, is Uta Hagen's *Respect for Acting* (Macmillan & Co., New York). Richard Schechner's unique and controversial concept of presenting theater—he's founder and codirector of the Performance Group—is encompassed in *Environmental Theater* (Hawthorn Books, New York) Schechner's theories are illustrated with diagrams, sketches, and schematics.

Perhaps the most useful and certainly the handsomest book yet produced for the Business Committee for the Arts is Gideon Chagy's *The New Patrons of the the Arts* (Harry N. Abrams, New York). Featuring illustrations on nearly every page, including several in full color, the 128-page book provides scores of examples and case histories demonstrating ways in which business can and does support the arts with money, services, and materials. Another book examining the arts–business relationship, but in this instance in terms of an aesthetic collaboration, is Douglas Davis' *Art and the Future* (Praeger, New York). Written by the critic of *Newsweek,* the well-illustrated book presents an insightful view into the past and present, and a look into an even greater future interrelationship between art, science, and technology. A much more modest effort aimed at the business audience is *The Businessman's Ballet Book* (available through Dance Mart, Brooklyn, N.Y.), by Marie Vogt, artistic director of the Toledo Ballet. The slim book, with whimsical illustrations by the author, offers men a crash course in dance.

Among new reference works are two dealing with the role of blacks in the arts. *Black Theater: A Resource Directory,* in addition to listing some 130 non-profit black theaters throughout the country, also includes listings of technicians, administrators, artistic directors, and playwrights. It's available from Black Theatre Alliance, 1564 Broadway, New York, New York 10036. *Afro-American Artists: A Bio-Bibliographical Directory* (Boston Public Library) is the first of its kind, a resource listing data on some 2000 black American artists from the eighteenth century to the present.

Several new periodicals on the arts appeared in recent months. *Blackstage* (Bits N' Pieces, Inc., Washington, D.C. 20009), a montly magazine, reports on the black cultural scene. *Print Review,* whose first issue appeared this spring, is a biannual magazine for print collectors and graphic arts students published jointly by Kennedy Galleries in New York and the Pratt Institute Graphics Center. New York-based organizations that have launched newsletters of national interest in 1973 include Poets & Writers, Inc., New York, whose *Coda,* available free, is published seven times a year, and the Theatre Communications Group, whose newsletter appears every six weeks.

September-October 1973

Dance is the subject of several new books including *The New York City Ballet* (Alfred A. Knopf, New York), a giant book featuring over 400 photos, with text by Lincoln Kirstein. One of the towering figures in modern dance is the subject of a biography, *Martha Graham,* by New York Times critic Don McDonagh (Praeger, New York), and Graham is the author of her own *Notebooks of Martha Graham* (Harcourt, Brace, Janovich, New York).

The Harvard Summer School Institute in Arts Administration in Cambridge, Massachusetts, has published an interesting collection of papers presented during the program's first three years by seven cultural leaders from abroad. The edited presentations, appearing in book form under the title *Cultural Policy and Arts Administration,* present backgrounds and viewpoints not generally familiar to most American administrators. The Massachusetts Council on the Arts is providing a free service to its constituents through the publication of a series of 15 cultural resource handbooks. Separate handbooks on the visual arts, performing arts, and the humanities for each of five geographical areas in the state include data on more than 1500 organizations.

A compact, highly readable, and brightly illustrated booklet at "The Place of the Arts in New Towns" has been published by Education Facilities Laboratories in New York. Available for $3.00, the report was researched and written for the American Council for the Arts in Education by its research director, Judy Murphy.

November-December 1973

New periodicals include *Cultures,* a quarterly UNESCO magazine that examines the arts role in various societies (UNIPUB, New York) and *Federal Design Matters,* a periodic National Arts Endowment newsletter focusing on architecture, graphics, industrial design, and the visual arts. Free to federal employees, it is available to others from the Superintendent of Documents, Government Printing Office, Washington, D.C. 20402). *Eddy* is a new bi-monthly on dance published by Dance Theatre Workshop in New York.

January-February 1974

The Grand Acquisitors (Houghton Mifflin Co., New York) is a devastating analysis by *New York Times* reporter John L. Hess of the Metropolitan Museum's controversial activities over the past few years under director Thomas Hoving. Margaret Croyden has written a useful and needed analysis of contemporary experimental theater in *Lunatics, Lovers, & Poets* (McGraw-Hill, New York).

The International Theatre Directory (Simon & Schuster, New York) is a worldwide reference listing information on theater, dance, and opera companies and performing facilieis in more than 100 countries.

Theatre Management in America: Principle and Practise (Drama Book Specailists/Publishers, New York) by Stephen Langley offers a comprehensive look at virtually every aspect of producing commercial, stock, resident, college, and community theater. In addition to its extensive "how-to" material, the 421-page book includes historical background and theory on each of the major areas of theater.

Cultural resource guides to two major American cities have recently been published and might serve as useful models to those interested in developing similar works for their own communities. *New York City Resources for the Arts and Artists* (New York City Cultural Council) is an easy-to-use 95-page listing of spaces, services, permits, and licenses and funding opportunities available through agencies and institutions of the city. *Culture Cracks the Blackboard* (Metropolitan Cultural Alliance, Boston) is a 96-pager that lists educational institutions and arts groups.

Materials produced by museums are the subject of several new publication services. *Museum Media* (Gale Research Co., Detroit) is a huge directory of books, catalogs, films, and monographs produced by 732 U.S. and Canadian museums. Museum Publications of America in Boston is a membership group that offers catalogs and other museum materials at reduced prices. A useful book for museum visitors is *Museum Companion,* (Hippocrene Books, New York), a dictionary of art terms and subjects. A key work for anyone involved in the visual arts has just been published in a revised second edition. *The Visual Artist and the Law* is available from Associated Councils of the Arts.

A growing number of books are examining the black heritage in the arts. Two interesting new works with self-explanatory titles are *In Search of African Theatre* (Charles Scribner's Sons, New York) and *Through Black Eyes: Journey of a Black Artist to East Africa and Russia* (Dodd, Mead, New York).

March-April 1974

Arts groups interested in the Canadian scene will benefit from a new work published by the Canadian Conference of the Arts, 49 Wellington Street East, Toronto, Ontario. *A Selective Bibliography of Canadian and International Readings in Cultural Development and Administration,* is the first major administration bibliography to focus primarily on Canada.

March-April 1974

Two new periodicals make their bow in November 1974—*The Cultural Post,* the National Endowment for the Arts' bimonthly information bulletin (Program Information Office, Arts Endowment, Washington, D.C. 20506), and *The Arts Advocate,* a quarterly newspaper published by Advocates for the Arts.

An interesting range of new directories and guides are now available. *A Guide to Community Arts Agencies* (Associated Councils of the Arts, New York) is an updated second edition of a key work with data on hundreds of arts groups, their structure, constituency, programs, and finances. *Private Foundations and Business Corporations Active in Arts/Humanities/Education, Volume Two* (Washington, D.C.) is an update from a previous work, with information on 100 private foundations and new data on the funding activities of 287 businesses. *The Bicentennial Source Book* (Taft Products, Inc., Washington, D.C.) is a 383-page directory with an update service through July 1976 to bicentennial programming and planning by government agencies, businesses, trade groups, and bicentennial organizations. *Opera Companies and Opera Workshops in the U.S. and Canada* (Central Opera Service, New York) has data on more than 1000 different performing groups. *The World Museums Guide* (McGraw-Hill, New York) is a selective rather than comprehensive guide that has brief and basic data on 200 different art museums and galleries.

Certainly one of the most expensive directories, but a useful tool for those planning new arts facilities, is the *International Association of Auditorium Managers Industry Profile Survey* (IAAM, Chicago). The 210-page report is based on an IAAM survey of more than 300 auditoriums, theaters, stadia, exhibit halls, and performing arts centers and includes comprehensive data on box office, rental rates, parking, concessions, and fiscal operations.

A dynamic administrator flies through his 1972-73 season in Stuart W. Little's incisive new book, *Enter Joseph Papp,* (Coward-McCann & Geoghegan, New York). The book chronicles Papp's activities during the momentous season when he took over two theaters at Lincoln Center and fought CBS-TV over the showing of "Sticks and Bones."

A lawyer examines laws pertaining to original art work—copyrights, sale and merchandising, taxes, and imitation as they apply to artists—and laws governing purchase, importing, lending, and donating for collectors in *What Every Artist and Collector Should Know About the Law* (E. P. Dutton & Co., New York). *Dance is a Contact Sport* (Saturday Review Press, New York) is an inside view of a single performance season of the New York City Ballet and its personalities and operations. In *Museum* (The Fiction Collection, distributed by George Braziller, New York), a novelist takes a very close look at a fictional art institution and the way in which it is managed.

September-October 1974

Philharmonic (Doubleday, New York) is a major study tracing the development of the New York Philharmonic from its founding in 1842 until now. The massive illustrated work includes pages of interesting reference materials. Another work with historical interest is John F. Wharton's *Life Among the Playwrights* (Quadrangle, New York), a fascinating excursion into the life and times of the Playwrights Producing Company.

A key reference work is *Art Works: Law, Policy, Practice* (Practising Law Institute, New York), a huge, 1200-page sourcebook dealing with virtually every legal aspect of the visual arts.

November-December 1974

Books detailing the cultural life of an arts group through a single season seem to be growing in popularity. A symphony orchestra now joins theater—*Enter Joseph Papp*—and ballet—*Dance is a Contact Sport*—in *A Season with Solti: A Year in the Life of the Chicago Symphony.* (Macmillan, New York). An intensely human document, with insights into many facets of orchestra activity, the book is important reading for administrators.

Recent fiction on arts themes includes T*he Connoisseur* (Alfred A. Knopf, New York), an unusual story of an art collector; *Number One with a Bullet* (Farrar, Straus and Giroux, New York), a far-out science fiction story of another art collector; and *Oh, Eden!* (Warner Paperback Library, New York), a frequently funny story of the making of a new nude play.

January-February 1975

With growing interest given to the rights of artists, the special January 1975 issue of the *Art Workers News* should be of interest to arts managers. Published by the Foundation for the Community of Artists, the issue includes complete examples of artists reserved rights contracts as well as a copy of the agreement reached between the city of Seattle and sculptor Tony Smith.

January-February 1975

Heading the list of new and important works is the *Foundation Directory,* Edition 5 (Columbia University Press, Irvington, N.Y.). A massive volume prepared by the Foundation Center, the directory lists significant data on each of 2533 foundations with assets of $1 million or with contributions of $500,000 or more. The 516-page book also includes useful tables as well as indices of foundation fields of interest and of donors, trustees, and administrators.

The National Directory for the Performing Arts/Educational (Baker & Taylor Companies, New York) includes basic information on over 5000 accredited schools for performing arts training including staff names, size, areas, degrees, and performing groups.

Publications of practical interest include two new theater guides available from the Foundation for the Extension and Development of the American Professional Theatre, 165 West Forty-second Street, New York, New York 10036. *Box Office Guidelines,* prepared by the Center Theatre Group of Los Angeles, is a 44-page reproduction of the actual box office system used by the Mark Taper Forum and Ahmanson Theater and includes, in addition to specific guidelines, useful samples of forms and notices. *Subscription Guidelines,* a 41-page documentation of the 1970 subscription report of the Actors Theatre of Louisville, Kentucky, also includes examples of forms and mailing pieces used by other theaters. *Marketing for Non-Profit Organizations* (Prentice-Hall, Englewood Cliffs, N.J.) is a detailed textbook that analyzes the concepts and techniques of reaching specific publics. Although not specifically oriented to the arts, the book provides a good insight into a complex area of concern.

On Understanding Art Museums (Prentice-Hall, Englewood Cliffs, N.J.), originally prepared as background for the 1974 American Assembly conference on museums, is a series of seven thoughtful essays by museum and art specialists and a psychiatrist on key areas of museum interest. *The American Music Handbook* (The Free Press, New York, 1974) is a giant directory published with narrative listings of musical organizations, performing groups, commerical firms, performers, awards, and other areas of the serious music field.

In the periodical field, the National Endowment for the Arts' newspaper, the *Cultural Post,* made its bow in March in an informal and readable format. Available free from the Endowment, Washington, D.C. 20506, the paper will be published on an irregular schedule. Introduced this April, the *Crafts Report* (Crafts Report Publishing Co., Brooklyn, N.Y.) is a monthly newsletter covering the marketing and management of crafts.

March-April 1975

Financial Management for Arts Organizations (Arts Administration Research Institute, Cambridge, Mass.) is a concise and pragmatic workbook that includes a number of easy-to-use exhibits. Also coming out of Harvard's Summer School Institute in Arts Administration is a new and revised edition of *Cases in Arts Administration.* Another arts management program, at the Center for Arts Administration at the University of Wisconsin's Graduate School of Business Administration, Madison, Wisconsin 53706, published two useful booklets. *Handbook for Tour Management,* written for the administrator rather than the technician, includes a working model and helpful charts. *Museum Sponsorship of Performing Arts* is a study based on questionnaires received from 124 museums demonstrating the growth of interest in this area since the early sixties.

Among new works of direct interest to artists is *Health Hazards for Artists* (Foundation for the Community of Artists, New York, N.Y.). This slim booklet on the hazards of several visual arts techniques is based on a series of articles that originally appeared in *Art Workers News. An Artists's Guide to Professional Security* (Iowa Arts Council, Des Moines, Iowa 50319) is a 154-page paperback based on a conference held in March 1975 at which 35 subjects relevent to artists were discussed. The book is a transcribed and edited record of the conference with reams of practical information. *Artist's Market* (Writer's Digest, Cincinnati, Ohio, 45242) is a dip-in, where-to reference listing more than 2000 different places where visual artists can see their works.

After the Fact (FACT, New York, N.Y. 10036) reports in depth on the momentous First American Congress of Theatre held last year. An alternative approach to the traditional method of evaluating arts in the classroom is presented in *Evaluating the Arts in Education: A Responsive Approach* (Charles E. Merrill Co., Columbus, Ohio). It should prove useful to professional educators and others concerned with supporting school arts programs. *The Uneasy Coalition: Design in Corporate America* (University of Pennsylvania Press, Philadelphia) is a collection of essays drawn from the Tiffany-Wharton lectures on corporate design.

Provocative new books include the *Royal American Symphonic Theater* (Macmillan, New York), which offers an interesting blueprint for the development of a fully funded professional theater that "works." Subtitled "A Radical Proposal for Subsidized Professional Theater," the book is by Herman Krawitz, former Metropolitan Opera executive, with Howard Klein of the Rockefeller Foundation. *The Straw Man* (Farrar, Straus & Giroux, New York) is a novel about a major urban museum and its opening of a grand new wing to house a $100 million art collection left it by a private collector. Dipping into varied museum controversies, it moves very close to real events in the museum world.

Cultural Directory (ACA Publications, New York) is an update to the guide to federal funds and services for the arts published in 1971. Well organized and easy to use, the directory lists basic information on a variety of resources, including several off the beaten track. New museum directories include an expanded third edition of *American Art Museums: An Introduction to Looking* (Harper & Row, New York) with narrative descriptions or major museums and *The Directory of World Museums* (Columbia University Press, New York), a mammoth volume that lists basic information on 25,000 museums and art galleries throughout the world. Organized by countries, the volume also includes an index by specialty. More specific information on museum programs, attendance, finances, and other matters of interest to administrators may be found in *Museums USA* (U.S. Government Printing Office, Washington D.C. 20402, no. 3600-00016), a report on the major survey of 700 museums undertaken by the National Research Center for the Arts for the Arts Endowment. Highlights of this study have been included in a booklet (see *AM*, no. 83) released in 1974. Art scholars will find *Performing Arts Resources* (Drama Book Specialists, New York) a helpful guide to theater library collections in America.

Summer 1975

Opulence and relatively high prices characterize some of the new works in the growing arts managers' library. *Art in Society* (The Overlook Press, Woodstock, N.Y.) is a big, handsome, and copiously illustrated work that examines art as a social activity in four main areas: work, worship, sex, and war. *The Awkward Embrace: The Creative Artist and the Institution in America* (Alfred A. Knopf, New York) is a study of nine men from such areas as legislation, business, the arts, and foundations who have influenced American Culture. *Art Talk* (Charles Scribner's Sons, New York) is a handsomely illustrated series of conversations, at times acerbic, with 12 noted women's artists.

    The Contemporary Music Performance Directory (American Music Center, New York, N.Y. 10019) is a useful compendium that defines contemporary music in a broad sense in its four areas of listings: performing facilities, performing ensembles, sponsoring groups, and festivals and series. *Awards, Honors and Prizes,* Volume One (Gale Research Co., Detroit, Mich. 48226) is a giant guide to more than 4000 different awards bestowed in the United States and Canada in virtually every field, including varied areas of the arts.

    An impressive new periodical is *American Film,* a journal of film and television arts published ten times a year by the American Film Institute, Washington, D.C. 20566. *Dance Herald* (New York, N.Y. 10023) is a new quarterly devoted to black dance. A developing trend among arts councils is the publication of newspapers rather than the traditional newsletters. Newspapers introduced in 1974 and 1975 by community arts councils include Cleveland's *Collage '75,* Durham's *The Arterie,* and Buffalo's *ADS News.*

September-October 1975

Released in time to coincide with Arts Endowment reauthorization hearings was the "National Report on the Arts." Its key recommendation called for funding of no less than 10 percent of the operating cost of arts organizations by the federal government and by each state. The 42-page report, available on request through the National Committee for Cultural Resources, 1865 Broadway, New York, New York 10023, documents both the growth of the arts industry and the increased public interest in cultural programs while pinpointing major economic concerns.

September-October 1975

Communications for the Arts Letter (New York, N.Y. 10024) is a ten-times-a-year newsletter focusing on news and developments in the gallery and visual arts world. *CODA,* the newsletter of Poets and Writers, Inc. (New York, N.Y. 10019), previously available without charge, has been expanded, and the 32-page newsletter will now be sold on a five-times-a-year subscription basis.

    Heading the list of new practical guides and research books is *About Foun-*

dations: How to Find the Facts You Need to Get a Grant, (Foundation Center, New York, N.Y. 10019). The 40-page paperback is a slim yet indispensable guide to researching information on foundations in libraries, publications, and at Foundation Center collections. Volume 2 of *Awards, Honors and Prizes* (Gale Research Co., Detroit, Mich. 48826) is a massive listing of some 3000 international awards and honors bestowed in 61 different countries. *A Course Guide in the Theatre Arts at the Secondary School Level* (American Theater Association, Washington, D.C. 20005) outlines theater concepts that may be used in the classroom.

Hands-On Museums (Educational Facilities Laboratories, New York, N.Y. 10022) is both a report on and guide to 14 museums with experience-oriented programs that permit visitors to learn through involvement with museum objects. *Museum Guide to Federal Programs* (Association of Science-Technology Centers, Washington, D.C. 20037) is a looseleaf compendium with more than 100 listings of support sources for museums from the federal government. *Art in Public Places in the United States* (Popular Press, Bowling Green, Ohio) is a large and profusely illustrated collection of articles dealing with art easily accessible to the public throughout the country.

The Art Crisis (St. Martin's Press, New York) is a readable exploration of the growing boom in art theft and smuggling. The author, Bonnie Burnham, headed a three-year project to combat the traffic in stolen art for the International Council of Museums. . .

November-December 1975

Museum Accounting Guidelines (Association of Science-Technology Centers, Washington, D.C. 20037) describes policies for preparing financial statements at museums, although the information has broader application. *Financial Management for the Arts* (ACA Publications, New York) is a welcome, easty-to-understand guide to budgeting, accounting, and other financial activities.

Beginning a Community Museum (distributed by the Publishing Center for Cultural Resources, New York) is a slim but very helpful guidebook that covers everything from funding, to getting the physical facility ready, to insurance and security.

Insights into the financial problems of cultural institutions in other countries can be gleaned from *The Arts, Economics and Politics: Four National Perspectives* (Aspen Institute Program in Pluralism and the Commonwealth, New York, N.Y. 10022), a report on an Aspen Institute seminar held in Berlin in March 1975. Another significant view of arts development outside the United States is available in the Canada Council's annual report for 1974–75, available from the council at P.O. Box 1047 in Ottawa. In addition to program description, the report lists every council grant recipient and amount during the period covered.

Still another report emanating from the collaboration between the NEA's Architecture and Environmental Arts Program and the Educational Facilities Laboratories is *The Arts in Found Places* (EFL, New York, N.Y. 10022). The study reviews some 200 recycled buildings turned into centers for arts activities and offers tips to future recyclers. An annual update is the *1976 Summer Theatre Directory* (American Theatre Association, Washington, D.C. 20005) which lists data on over 300 theaters this year.

A growing number of regional periodicals are coming on the scene, including new 1976 entries the *Michigan Art Journal,* a quarterly available through the Detroit Institute of Art and the *Performing Arts Journal,* a three-issues-a-year critical theater review published in New York. Existing periodicals not previously mentioned in *AM* include *Midwest Art,* published ten times a year in Milwaukee, the informative *Art Letter* published monthly by *Art in America* magazine in New York, and the *Feminist Art Journal,* a quarterly magazine published in Brooklyn, New York. Indicative of the economic problems of nonprofit organizations is the fact that two periodicals previously available without charge have been forced to institute subscription fees. The bimonthly *Voluntary Action News* is now $4.00 annually, and the ten-times-a-year *Art and the Law* is now $10.00 for libraries, colleges, profit-making groups, and attorneys, and a suggested $5.00 contribution for others.

January-February 1976

Arts managers seeking a change of pace from their serious activities will find it in *The Definitive Biography of P.D.Q. Bach* (Random House, New York). Written by Peter Schickele, who has made a joyous career out of presenting the works of the last and least of J.S. Bach's many children on the concert stage, the book includes "biographical" notes, a series of plates, and an annotated catalogue of P.D.Q.'s music including such works as "'Erotica' Variations for Banned Instruments," "Schleptet," and "Concerto for Piano vs. Orchestra." On the more serious side, *Our Two Lives* (Charles Scribner's Sons, New York), by the wife of the late conductor Artur Rodzinski, is a frank and sometimes revealing work about the Rodzinskis, the musical world of the thirties and forties and other key figures in it.

State Arts Agencies in Transition (Spring Hill Conference Center, Wayzata, Minn. 55391) puts together the difficult-to-follow bits and pieces of observation and conversation of state arts council leaders drawn together for a series of seminars three to four years ago. Some of the comments are interesting, even surprising, but it's difficult to read more than a few pages at a time. *Producers on Producing* (Drama Book Specialists, New York) also reproduces conversations of arts leaders, but in this instance all 24 contributors are not only identified but address themselves to specific questions. The book is based on a series of seminars held at Brooklyn College in 1973, with each session (and book chapter) limited to the observations of three participants discussing the same topic. *Cultural Re-*

source Development (Praeger Special Studies, New York) is an updated study of the several-years-old findings of the New York State Commission on Cultural Resources and will have great appeal to cultural historians. A softcover edition is available from the Publishing Center for Cultural Resources in New York.

Heading the list of resource books is *Americans and the Arts 1975* (National Committee for Cultural Resources, New York, N.Y. 10023), an update of the much-quoted 1973 study by the National Research Center of the Arts. The new survey shows even more positive attitudes to the arts as evidenced by such facts as 93 percent of Americans felt the arts were important to their community's cultural life, up from 89 percent; and 59 percent rated the arts as very important to their community's business and economic life, up from 46 percent. Between 78 and 80 percent felt that music, creative writing, and visual arts courses should be part of the core curriculum. Both the full report and a "highlights" version are available from ACA Publications, 1564 Broadway, New York, New York 10036.

Among new practical books is *The Arts Festival Planning Guide* (North Carolina Department of Cultural Resources, Raleigh, N.C. 27611), an easy-to-follow 100-page resource that includes a series of illustrations, checklists, and worksheets. *Celebration Kit for the American Revolution Bicentennial* (Publishing Center for Cultural Resources, New York, N.Y. 10019) is a very slim primer of things to consider when planning festivals. *The Art of Winning Foundation Grants* (Vanguard Press, New York) is far from comprehensive, but it has useful quick hints and is a good dip-in for the beginning grantsman. Concise and useful new pamphlets from Volunteer Lawyers for the Arts on legal and financial aspects of arts management include: *Fear of Filing; A Beginner's Handbook for Dancer and Other Artists on Record Keeping and Federal Taxes; Tax Record Keeping for Artists and Arts Organizations;* and *Exempt Organizations and the Arts.* Each is available from VLA, 36 West Forty-fourth Street, New York, New York 10036. A new *Directory of American Fiction Writers* (Poets & Writers, New York) has information on more than 800 contemporary fiction writers with work published in the United States.

New to the periodical scene are *CBAC News,* a bimonthly news roundup prepared by the Council for Business and the Arts in Canada, and *Cinema Sourcebook,* a looseleaf film information service that provides monthly sheets to subscribers, each dealing with a film released in New York the previous month. New local arts newpapers include *MPLS Review of the Arts,* a monthly published by the Minneapolis Arts Commission, and *Mid-Hudson Arts,* a bimonthly published by the Greater Middletown, New York arts council.

March-April 1976

A terse but useful brochure, *Cities, Counties and the Arts,* (ACA Publications, New York) is one of several pragmatic documents relating to local support of the arts. Published in conjunction with Associated Councils of the Arts' three-day conference in Seattle, the 44-page booklet uses several cities as examples to explore such areas as municipal arts agencies, arts programs of local government, federal and state local arts funding, and municipal policies affecting the arts.

% for Art: New Legislation Can Integrate Art and Architecture, published by the Western States Arts Foundation and available through ACA, is a hand-some, well-illustrated brochure with a helpful index which should be a handy document for arts groups attempting to work with their respective local govern-ments on percent for arts legislation. The New York State Council on the Arts' *County Funding for the Arts in New York State* (Publishing Center for Cultural Resources, New York, New York 10019) is a study that reaches several positive conclusions. During 1975, the 54 responding counties increased their funding by more than 90 percent over 1973, with only three counties, as compared to 13 earlier, failing to fund the arts. Donated services to the arts by counties also in-creased substantially.

The shaky arts economy is hitting publishers as well as arts groups. *Arts in Society,* a distinguished quarterly journal published at the University of Wisconsin for the past 18 years, will cease publication in summer 1976 unless new sponsor-ship can be found. *New Ways,* the newspaper of the Educational Arts Associa-tion, already has been discontinued, and *Catalyst,* the quarterly of Affiliate Art-ists, has temporarily suspended publication but hopes to pick up again if outside support can be found.

Practical works include *Poor Dancer's Almanac* (Association of American Dance Companies, New York, N.Y. 10019), a 100-page guide to virtually every aspect of dancing and living in New York, and *Craftsmen in Business* (American Crafts Council, New York, N.Y. 10019), a useful guide to all aspects of financial management.

Summer 1976

Several works from the Foundation Center, New York, New York 10019, should prove useful to administrators. *Foundation Annual Reports: What They Are and How to Use Them,* is a 48-page paperback that includes a cumulative listing of 1304 reports between 1970 and 1976 that are available on microfiche. The *Foun-dation Center Source Book,* in two volumes, is a guide for the sophisticated grants researcher that includes full listings of recent national and regional founda-tion grants. *The Technical Production Handbook* (Western States Arts Founda-tion, Denver, Colo. 80202) is a terse but handy paperback guide for sponsors of touring performing arts groups. For those who wish to organize arts advocacy programs at the local or state level, Advocates for the Arts, New York, New York 10036, has put together a handy packet for useful materials.

A new and beautifully written novel with an arts setting is must reading. Vance Bourjaily's *Now Playing at Canterbury* (Dial Press, New York) describes the events surrounding the premiere of a new opera in the midwest.

September-October 1976

Black Theater Alliance Touring Brochure (BTA, New York, N.Y. 10019) has information on 40 black dance and theater groups that tour, while *Theatre Directory 1976-77* (Theatre Communications Group, New York, N.Y. 10017) lists brief data on 173 professional, nonprofit theaters throughout the country. The new third edition of the *National Directory of Grants and Aid to Individuals in the Arts* (Washington International Arts Letter, Washington, D.C. 20003) gives terse descriptions of some 1500 arts funding opportunities. *Who's Who in Opera* (Arno Press, New York) is a giant compendium of data on more than 2300 active figures in opera and 100 opera companies.

A first-time directory published by Associated Councils of the Arts take a telephone book approach to the arts. *ACA Arts Yellow Pages* (ACA Publications, New York) has names, addresses, phone numbers, and key personnel listings as quick references to 1200 organizations and services across the board in the arts. Potential sellers of services will be interested in the new third edition of *Artist's and Photographer's Market '77* (Writer's Digest, Cincinnati, Ohio) which has nearly 1000 new listings among its 3500 entries. The same publisher's *Writer's Market '77* has useful information on publications.

The Directory of Management Training Programs for Nonprofit Executives (Taft Corp., Washington, D.C. 20005), while not specifically arts-oriented, describes training opportunities that could interest arts specialists in its looseleaf pages. Similarly, the *Professional's Guide to Publicity* (Richard Weiner, Inc., New York) while not zeroed in on the arts, has a gold mine of practical tips for the arts publicist.

A new periodical launched this summer, *Ocular* (Ocular Publishing, Denver, Colo. 80202), is an invaluable quarterly specifically oriented to the visual arts, Subtitled "The Directory of Information and Opportunities for the Visual Arts," the magazine goes beyond basic listings to provide data on exhibits, grants, employment opportunities, competitions, and legislative news.

A growing number of state and regional publications are appearing, with many, although locally focused, of broader interest. *Artists and the Aging: A Project Handbook* (COMPAS, St. Paul, Minn. 55102) describes the pioneer project conducted from 1974 to 1976 in St. Paul; *The Arts Trustee* (Nebraska Arts Council, Omaha) is a slim booklet summarizing a state conference on the role of trustees; *Collections of Massachusetts* is a handy, vestpocket guide to the museums and historical societies in the state available free from the state arts council; and the *Technical Assistance Directory* published by the New York Community Trust lists a variety of nonprofit assistance programs.

Several new books about artists and arts disciplines may interest administrators. *The Silent Studio* (W. W. Norton, New York) is a fascinating photo tour, deliberately uncaptioned, of Picasso's last studio home; the *Magic Mirror of M. C. Escher* (Random House, New York) is a well-illustrated portrait of an unusual artist; and *Constable and His World* (W. W. Norton, New York) is a slim but interesting work with 121 black and white photos.

Boulez: Composer, Conductor, Enigma (Schirmer Books, New York) is an excellent study of the maestro which also reveals a great deal about the composers with whom he worked. In dance, the VRI Slide Library of Dance History (Visual Resources, Inc., New York, N.Y. 10023) is an ambitious undertaking which through slides and accompanying textbook offers a survey of dance from primitive times through the nineteenth century.

November-December 1976

Presenting Performances: A Handbook for Sponsors (New England Touring Program, Cambridge, Mass. 02138) is an easy-to-read, 128-page reference offering guidelines to virtually every aspect of presentation and promotion of arts events. *The Effective Voluntary Board of Directors* (Swallow Press, Chicago) uses a large number of helpful charts, graphs, and tables as background for its exploration of the structure of a model organization and its board and staff.

Works available without charge include the National Endowment for the Arts' *Creative America: Arts and the Pursuit of Happiness* (NEA, Mail Stop 550, Washington, D.C. 20506), a slim booklet written for the general reader, and *Technical Assistance for Arts Facilities* (Educational Facilities Laboratories, New York, N.Y. 10022), a 32-page booklet listing a variety of resources. Supplement II to *The Arts and the World of Business* (GSM Publications Services, UCLA, Los Angeles, Ca. 90024) is, with its two earlier editions, a comprehensive and useful bibliography.

Books on theater include a revised third edition of what has become a standard reference on production. *From Option to Opening* (Drama Book Specialists, New York), and the sixteenth edition of the massive and comprehensive *Who's Who in the Theatre: A Biographical Record of the Contemporary Stage* (Gale Research Co., Detroit, Mich. 48226). The booming crafts industry has two new books aimed at the professional. *The Crafts Business Encyclopedia* (Harcourt Brack Jovanovich, New York) is aptly subtitled "How to Many Money, Market Your Products, and Manager Your Home Craft Business." Organized in A to Z manner, it is detailed, easy-to-use, comprehensive reference. *Career Opportunities in Crafts* (Crown Publishers, New York) offers advice on a variety of career opportunities both in crafts and in related areas.

Periodicals include a new magazine with a familiar name, *Show* (New York, N.Y. 10017), which makes its monthly bow with a June 1977 issue. Although *Show* will cover all the arts, it will be show business and people oriented and aimed at the 18 to 35 market. *What's Up in Art, the Washington Art Marketletter* (Alexandria, Va. 22307) is a monthly letter covering the visual arts in Washington, D.C.

National arts groups have recently initiated new publishing projects. Associated Councils of the Arts' free information service provides subscribers with a one-page, camera-ready *Word From Washington* bulletin ten times yearly. Including an Advocates for the Arts membership form, the bulletin can be inserted in organization programs or newsletters. The American Film Institute is introducing *Factfile,* a series of information bulletins in looseleaf format.

March-April 1977

One of the key works of recent years, the panel report *Coming to Our Senses: The Significance of the Arts for American Education* (McGraw Hill, New York), contains background and historical data, vital information on arts and education programs, and 98 recommendations. Another work on the same topic, much more limited in its scope but worth reading, *Arts in Education Partners: Schools and Their Communities* (ACA, New York) summarizes the results of a conference held in December 1976. *A Survey of Arts Administration Training in the United States and Canada* (ACA, New York), prepared by the University of Wisconsin MBA program, updates data on existing programs.

The focus is on foundation giving in several new works and updates from the Foundation Center at 888 Seventh Ave., New York, New York 10019. *The Foundation Center Source Book Profiles* is a looseleaf service that offers readers 40 to 45 foundation profiles each month, while *About Foundations: How to Find the Facts You Need to Get a Grant* is an updated edition of a practical 48-page guide. Upcoming is the new *Foundation Grants to Individuals.* Free from the Ford Foundation (New York, N.Y. 10017) is *Theater Reawakening,* a review of the foundation's 20 years of grants to theater programs.
years of grants to theater programs.

An essential new work for the individual artist is *Legal Guide for the Visual Artist* (Hawthorn Books, New York), a well organized and easy-to-read handbook. *Law and the Arts,* a slim booklet prepared by Lawyers for the Creative Arts, (Chicago), includes basic information on such topics as copyright and contracts.

ACUCAA Handbook: Presenting the Performing Arts (ACUCAA, Madison, Wisc. 53701) is a dip-in cookbook of ideas for administrators. The 150-page looseleaf includes articles by a number of authors—some previously published by ACUCCA—and samples of budgets, contracts, and other materials. An important work available for the first time in paperback is *Regional Theatre: The Revolutionary Stage* (Da Capo Press, New York).

A newly developing trend appears to be the publication of "whole catalogues" including all kinds of information and listings about the arts and artists, and less formal in appearance than the usual directories. Works in this genre now in preparation include *The Whole Culture Catalogue of California, The Whole Arts Catalogue of New Jersey,* and in New York State, *A People's Guide to the Arts in Erie County.*

Summer 1977

The long-awaited book by Danny Newman on season subscriptions and audience development is finally out. *Subscribe Now!* (Theatre Communications Group, New York, N.Y. 10017) is a more than 300-page compendium of the kinds of practical advice Newman has given to several hundred arts groups on developing subscription promotions. Pragmatic as well as entertaining, the book is a must for administrators.

Another essential tool is the new sixth edition of the *Foundation Directory* published by the Foundation Center in New York and distributed by Columbia University Press, New York. The mammoth 661-page volume updates the 1975 edition and includes full entries on 2818 foundations. Also of use to the fund seeker is *The National Directory of Arts Support by Private Foundations* (Washington International Arts Letter, Washington, D.C., 20003), a listing of 1217 private foundations including examples of the kinds of grants they have given to arts groups. *The International Who's Who in Music and Musicians' Directory* (Gale Research Co., Detroit, Mich. 48226), just published in its eighth edition, includes listings on over 10,000 musicians in its more than 1100 pages.

Financial Practice for Performing Arts Companies (Arts Administration Research Institute, Cambridge, Mass. 02138) is a work manual divided into separate financial management sections—on organization, process, and use of the system. Author Mary M. Wehle is a member of the Harvard Summer Institute in Arts Administration.

On the periodicals scene, a new monthly magazine, *New York Theatre Review,* has just published its first issue. The *Review* includes feature articles, reviews of New York productions, and reports on theater activity around the country and abroad . . .

September-October 1977

Nonprofit organizations, whatever their areas of involvement, share some common concerns such as funding, promotion, and management. Arts groups can frequently learn a great deal from reading materials prepared not only for the arts, but for the nonprofit field generally. The Public Relations Society of America at 845 Third Avenue, New York, New York 10022 has just issued a series of six booklets under the cover-all title *Managing Your Public Relations: Guidelines for Nonprofit Organizations.* The booklets cover such topics as publicity, special events, planning, and evaluation. Available free from the Edna McConnell Clark Foundation at 250 Park Avenue, New York, New York 10017 is the new *Resource Directory for Funding and Managing of Non-Profit Organizations.*

September-October 1977

One of the most beautiful new books and one of the most valuable as well is *The Art World* (Rizzoli International Publications, New York), a super collection of stories and illustrations drawn from 75 years of *ARTnews Magazine.* *Palaces for the People: A Social History of the American Art Museum* (Little,

Brown, New York) is one of the first books to explore the background and development of art museums in America and covers its broad spectrum well. *Danseur, The Male in Ballet* (McGraw Hill, New York) is a handsome book, most interesting perhaps because of its photography.

New books continue to come out of university arts administration programs. The University of Wisconsin's Center for Arts Administration (Madison, Wisc. 53706) has just published *Administration in the Arts: An Annotated Bibliography of Selected References,* an updated edition of an earlier work. Harvard's Arts Administration Research Institute (Cambridge, Mass. 02138) now has three works availabe in its series, "Conflict in the Arts: The Relocation of Authority." Each volume—*The Arts Council, The Orchestra,* and *The Museum*—consists of a series of interviews with persons involved in the respective institution or discipline designed to help readers identify the kinds of issues and tensions confronting the arts group.

A number of useful directories are now available in new updates. *Musical America 1978 International Directory* (ABC Leisure Magazines, Great Barrington, Mass.) is a massive 544-page compendium of domestic and international listings for various aspects of the music world. As less expensive and more limited directory in the same area is the *Music Journal 1978 Artists Directory* (Elemo Publishing, Southampton, N.Y.). *Dance Magazine Annual '78* (Danad Publishing, New York) includes within its listings on all aspects of dance more extensive information on dance companies than ever before. *The Directory of Artists' Organizations* (The Boston Visual Artists Union, Boston, Ma. 02108) is a new coded directory listing 1600 different organizations that are involved with visual artists. Descriptive material on over 400 of the groups is included. *Theatre Directory 1977-78* (Theatre Communications Group, New York) lists basic information about 158 nonprofit professonal theaters in the United States.

New market directories from *Writer's Digest* (Cincinnati, Ohio 45242) that interest administrators include *Arts & Crafts Market, Writer's Market, and Photographer's Market. Fine Arts Market Place,* third edition (R. R. Bowker, New York) is a 400-page directory listing varied arts resources.

Dissemination of arts literature will be facilitated because of several new development. The American Federation of Arts has launched a pilot museums publications distribution service, the American Dance Guild has started a new book club, and the Kennedy Center, in cooperation with the Library of Congress, will open a new library of the performing arts.

November-December 1977

Musical Chairs: A Life in the Arts (G. P. Putnam's, New York) is Schuyler Chapin's reflections on his career in music, especially his three years in top management at the Metropolitan Opera. While lively and gossipy, the book is more a personal rememberance than an insightful study of how our nation's largest cultural group operates. Janet Baker-Carr's *Evening at Symphony* (Houghton Mifflin

Co., New York) is an informative although somewhat brief historical excursion through the nearly 100-year history of the Boston Symphony.

Pragmatic new works include the *Facility Development Workbook,* a brief but useful checklist for the planners of cultural facilities by Brian Arnott Associates in Toronto. Planned as a working tool, the slim planning guide, available from Canada's Ministry of Culture and Recreation in Ontario on request, consists of introductory notes followed by lists of questions citizen committees should ask in each stage of a facility's development. *Corporate Fundraising: A Practical Plan of Action* (ACA, New York) is W. Grant Brownrigg's account of the successful approach used by his organization, the Greater Hartford Arts Council, to raise funds from business annually.

Somewhat off the beaten path but interesting nonetheless are *The Bibliography of Corporate Social Response: Problems and Policies* (Bank of America, San Francisco, Ca. 94137) which includes within its listings three pages on the arts and the free *Foundation Center Annual Report* (New York, N.Y. 10019), which explains the varied services and materials offered by the center.

January-February 1978

The Subsidized Muse: Public Support for the Arts in the United States (Cambridge University Press, New York) heads the list of new works. The Twentieth Century Fund Study by Professor Dick Netzer of NYU's Graduate School of Public Administration appraises government arts funding since 1965 and analyzes its effect on arts institutions. While presenting cogent arguments for public subsidy, the author concludes that thus far it has only been partially successful, and there is not necessarily a case for greatly increased public support of the arts. Some other conclusions are certain to arouse controversy, particularly those urging drastic reduction in subsidy for amateur activities and for programs in such areas as arts education and therapy.

The Performing Arts and American Society (Prentice-Hall, Englewood Cliffs, N.J.) is a compilation of background papers prepared for the American Assembly panel (see *AM,* no. 103) on the performing arts future. The papers present brief but interesting looks at developments in different disciplines.

New legal guides in the arts should be of major interest. The *Writer's Legal Guide* (Hawthorn Books, New York) is an insightful look at such areas as contracts, copyrights, and writer support by Tad Crawford, the author of a similar work for artists. *Art Law: Representing Artists, Dealers and Collectors* (Practising Law Institute, New York, N.Y. 10019) is a comprehensive examination of virtually every kind of legal problem in the visual arts and is aimed at art lawyers and arts institution heads.

The individual is the focus for two slim books with a similar focus. *Fear of Filing* (Volunteer Lawyers for the Arts, New York, N.Y. 10036) is an update of an essential work for performers, writers, and visual artists on taxation and finances with easy-to-follow guidelines. *A Guide to Taxes and Record Keeping for*

Performers, Designers, Directors (Drama Book Specialists, New York) offers sample forms along with information.

March-April 1978

Two interesting publications dealing with arts programs for the institutionalized and disadvantaged are available free to arts administrators. *The Healing Role of the Arts* is a working paper that includes discussion summaries and position papers from two symposia on the arts in social service settings. For copies write the Rockefeller Foundation, 1133 Avenue of the Americas, New York, New York 10036. *Annotated Bibliography* includes over 50 pages of references to materials for use in arts programs dealing with the handicapped. For copies write ARTS, Box 2040, Grand Central Station, New York, New York 10017.

March-April 1978

A deluge of new books and reports has flooded the arts management field. Recent bibliographies include: *A Bibliography on Arts Administration* (MBA/Arts Program, SUNY Binghamton, Binghamton, N.Y. 13901); *Arts Management: An Annotated Bibliography* published by the NEA (available from Publishing Center for Cultural Resources, New York); and *Arts Education: A Guide to Information Sources* (Gale Research Co., Detroit, Mich. 48226). Two useful bibliographies for craftspersons published by the American Crafts Council (New York, N.Y. 10019) are *Crafts Business Bookshelf* and *Bibliography: Grant References for the Craftsman.*

New directories also abound. *Theatre Profiles/3* (Theatre Communications Group, New York, N.Y. 10017) contains detailed information on 152 resident theatres in the United States, while *Community Arts Agencies: A Handbook and Guide* (ACA, New York, N.Y. 10018) has useful data on budgets, programs, and services and hundreds of community arts groups. Companion volumes published by John Wiley & Sons (New York), *National Directory of the Performing Arts and Civic Centers, 3rd edition* and *National Directory of the Performing Arts/ Educational, 3rd edition* are updates of massive works containing thousands of terse but informative listings in each area. *Directory for the Arts* (Center for Arts Information, New York, N.Y. 10036) describes programs of 145 different organizations and agencies that provide funding and services to arts groups. Although intended for a New York State audience, the work with its subject guide of 240 different services should prove generally useful. *A Guide to Federal Funding in the Arts and Humanities* (Association of American Colleges, Washington, D.C. 20009) is oriented to college and university programs seeking government funding.

Several works are specifically aimed at individuals. *Foundation Grants to Individuals* (Foundation Center, New York, N.Y. 10019) profiles over 1000 foundations who among them make grants to individuals totaling more than $56 million annually. *Law and the Writer* (Writer's Digest, Cincinnati, Ohio 45242) is a compendium of chapters, each dealing with a different area of legal concern, while *The Awards List: 100 Grants, Fellowships, and Prizes Offered in the United States to Poets & Fiction Writers* (Poets & Writers (New York) is the first guide of its kind ever developed exclusively for the creative writer.

Buildings for the Arts (McGraw-Hill, New York) surveys some of the more interesting structures built to house cultural activities from 1970 to the present. Photographs, drawings, and floor plans accompany the descriptions of 61 different buildings, including theaters and arts centers, libraries, art museums, and historic and regional museums. *The Smithsonian Experience* (W. W. Norton, New York) is a big, handsomely illustrated excursion into the incredibly varied collection and program of a giant cultural institution. *Blacks in Classical Music* (Dodd, Mead, New York) is a interesting and somewhat informal look at an area that has received scant attention in the past.

Anyone interested in arts and education will find *Arts Education 1977 in Prose and Print,* subtitled, *An Overview of Nine Significant Publications Affecting the Arts in American Education* must reading. One of the works discussed by author Junius Eddy, *Research in Arts Education, A Federal Chapter* is well worth reading on its own. Both are available free from the U.S. Office of Education, Washington, D.C. 20202. Other works available without charge include *Protection of Cultural Properties During Energy Emergencies* (Arts/Energy Study, Box 241, New York, N.Y. 10024); *Matching Gifts to the Arts* and *The Partnership of CETA and the Arts* (U.S. Department of Labor, Employment and Training Administration, Washington, D.C. 20013).

A new periodical, *Grants Magazine: The Journal of Sponsored Research and Other Programs* (Plenum Publishing, New York) is a quarterly that includes the arts as a regular area of coverage.

Summer 1978

Arts Administration: How to Set Up and Run A Successful Nonprofit Arts Organization (Chicago Review Press, Chicago) is a useful although somewhat limited work that is complete with charts, checklists, sample applications, forms, and a variety of appendices. The actual written portions, however, are quite terse and not particularly insightful or relative to current developments in the arts.

How to Open Your Own Shop or Gallery (St. Martin's Press, New York) offers some practical guidelines in easy-to-follow manner from the concept stage through planning, financing, and promotion. The 1978 *"TCG Conference Report"* (Theatre Communications Group, New York, N.Y. 10017) is a 121-page summary of an important national conference held only in June 1978 which includes copies of speeches, summaries of working sessions, and an accompanying 40-page booklet of background papers.

Of practical interest is *Planning and Cooperative Use of Resources for the*

Arts (Educational Facilities Laboratories, New York, N.Y. 10022), a slim, 24-page booklet that disucsses the planning process and offers some good examples of cooperative ventures by arts groups. *Marketing the Arts: A Selected and Annotated Bibliography* (ACUCAA, Madison, Wisc. 53701) is another useful addition to the bookshelf.

The Art Museum as Educator (University of California Press, Berkeley) is a giant 830-page compendium of reports and case studies in museum education that should prove to be an essential resource volume for administrators. In all, 105 different programs are described.

Several new works are of specific interest to artists working in a variety of fields. *Money Business: Grants and Awards for Creative Artists* (Artsist Foundation, Inc., available through ACA Publications, New York, N.Y. 10018) includes separate listings for some 300 different organizations that have grant programs for artists. *Career Guide for the Young American Singer* (Central Opera Service, New York, N.Y. 10023) includes information and listings on a range of key areas of concern, including vocal competitions, apprentice programs, grants and hiring, and audition policies of American and Canadian Opera companies. *Literary Agents: A Complete Guide* (Poets & Writers, New York) provides information on writer-agent relationships and the use of agents.

A new periodical of interest is the *Working Arts,* a bimonthly newsletter of the Bay Area Lawyers for the Arts in San Francisco. Issues, include articles on finance, management, and legal aspects of the arts.

September-October 1978

A CHECKLIST OF RELEVANT ARTICLES (1969-1978)

The Artist and the Arts Organization

Animating Disney's Dream (on the California Institute of the Arts), *Saturday Review,* January 29, 1972, p. 33.

Arena Stage: Full Speed Ahead, *Saturday Review,* March 27, 1971, p. 63.

The Artist as Teacher, *Saturday Review,* December 19, 1970, p. 51.

Artists: A Shadow Community and its Permanent Government, *Village Voice,* March 20, 1978, p. 38.

Artists Use an Industrial Palette, *Business Week,* November 8, 1969, p. 96.

The Arts Need Help, Too! *Voluntary Action News,* August 1973, p. 3.

Balanchine & Co. at 40, 20 and 10, the *New York Times Magazine,* November 11, 1973, p. 62.

BAM Grows in Brooklyn, the *New York Times Magazine,* October 24, 1976, p. 68.

A Brooklyn Dropout in the Thick of It, *Saturday Review,* April 2, 1977, p. 40.

The Business of Managing the Arts, *Harvard Business Review,* July-August 1978, p. 123.

Can a Troupe Survive Without Novelty? the *New York Times,* October 24, 1976, sec. 2, p. 12.

Can the Artist Be More 'Businesslike'? the *Wall Street Journal,* June 17, 1969, p. 22.

City Center Gets down to Business, *Fortune,* March 1974, p. 160.

The Classics, Lincoln Center and Papp, the *New York Times,* March 17, 1975, p. 36.

A Computer Aids in Picking Plays, *Business Week,* September 16, 1972, p. 84.

A Cultural Circus on Columbus Circle, the *Wall Street Journal,* July 26, 1974, p. p. 6.

Do Artists Perform True Public Services? the *Wall Street Journal,* December 15, 1975, p. 1.

Earning a Living in the Lively Arts, *Catalyst,* Fall 1975, p. 10.

Educating Museums, *RF Illustrated* (Rockefeller Foundation), September 1978, p. 10.

An Elite Still Calls Tune on Met Board, the *New York Times,* March 28, 1975, p. 21.

For Arts' Sake: Field of Modern Dance Booms but Performers Struggle to Survive, the *Wall Street Journal,* January 9, 1975, p. 1.

A Graduate Course in Managing the Arts, *Business Week,* February 23, 1974, p. 107.

Guthrie Troupe: The Cinderella Theater, Associated Press national release, October 10, 1971.

His Best Advice: Small City Arts Merger Unwise, *Variety,* January 6, 1971, p. 148.

Horowitz on the Road, *Newsweek,* December 2, 1974, p. 95.

The Hottest Show in Town is Joe Papp! *New York Magazine,* November 29, 1971, p. 33.

Houston's New Cultural Decision Makers, *Art News,* February 1977, p. 74.

Hurok and Others More than Just 10 Percenters, the *New York Times,* January 28, 1972, p. 18.

If an Artist Wants to Be Serious and Respected and Rich, Famous and Popular, He Is Suffering from Cultural Schizophrenia, the *New York Times Magazine,* September 26, 1971, p. 12.

The Inside Story of the Mellon Art Collection, the *Atlantic Monthly,* December 1972, p. 68.

The Importance of Being Fleischmann, the *New York Times Magazine,* April 11, 1976, p. 36.

The Joffrey on Its Toes Fiscally, Too, the *New York Times,* November 8, 1974, p. 22.

Joseph Papp: Play Producer for the People, *Lithopinion,* no. 35, Fall 1974, p. 73.

The Magnificent Maestro, *Time,* October 24, 1977, p. 82.

Managing Arts Programs, the *Chronical of Higher Education,* November 3, 1975, p. 6.

Managing the Culture Crunch, *MBA Magazine,* June 1974, p. 27.

Managing the Culture Explosion, *MBA Magazine,* March 1978, p. 20.

Man on the Spot (John Hightower), *Newsweek,* January 25, 1971, p. 82.

The Metropolitan Museum—It's Worse than You Think, *New York Magazine,* January 15, 1973, p. 54.

The Metropolitan Opera—The High Price of Being Best, the *New York Times,* February 12, 1978, sec. 2, p. 1.

A Met Understudy Makes it to the Top, the *New York Times Magazine,* September 23, 1973, p. 36.

Mr. Hoving's Lemonade Stand, the *New York Times,* October 15, 1972, sec. 2, p. 1.

A Modern Medici for Public Art, *Art News,* April 1977, p. 37.

Museum in Action, *Newsweek,* June 7, 1971, p. 69.

Museums Find a New Patron: The Retail Market, *Business Week,* October 24, 1977, p. 135.

Musical Chairs at the Met, *Saturday Review,* February 7, 1976, p. 39.

Musical Chairs for the Maestros, *Time,* September 11, 1978, p. 68.

New Music Man, *Life,* November 12, 1971, p. 42.

Next to Good Ryhme, Coda Proves Poet's Best Friend, the *New York Times,* January 27, 1976, p. 28.

101 Ways to Give Recognition to Volunteers, *Voluntary Action Leadership,* Winter 1977, p. 13.

On Public Art, *Saturday Review,* October 18, 1975, p. 62.

The Panovs, Airborne Again, *Saturday Review World,* September 21, 1974, p. 14.

The Philharmonic—A troubled Giant Facing Change, the *New York Times,* December 19, 1976, sec. 2, p. 1.

A Playwright's Invention Named Papp, the *New York Times Magazine,* November 9, 1975, p. 18.

Prodigious Sarah, the *New York Times Magazine,* October 5, 1975, p. 20.

The Ring's the Thing (profile of Glynn Ross) the *New Yorker,* June 26, 1978, p. 35.

Some Sour Notes, But Not a Bad Town to Work in Philharmonicsville (pop. 106), the *New York Times Magazine,* September 28, 1969, p. 26.

Special Business Supplement for Artists, *American Artist,* January 1977, p. 19-50.

The 'Straw Man' in the Rothko Case, *Art News,* December 1976, p. 32.

Stike Your MOMA? *New York Magazine,* November 19, 1973, p. 116.

This Business of the Arts, *Credit and Financial Management,* April 1973, p. 20.

Two Orchestras. Can They Live? the *New York Times,* July 15, 1973, sec. 2, p. 11.

What Sank the Dallas Symphony Orchestra—After 74th Year? the *New York Times,* June 9, 1974, sec. 2, p. 1.

Who Should Manage Museums? *Art News,* October 1977, p. 46.

Who Should Run the National Gallery? *Saturday Night* (Canada), October 1976, p. 47.

Winning Performance: At the Minnesota Orchestra, Business Blends Nicely with Art, *Barron's National Business and Financial Weekly,* October 31, 1977, p. 11.

Writers, Composers and Actors Collect Royalties—Why Not Artists? the *New York Times,* February 2, 1975, sec. 2, p. 1.

Operations and Communications

Artpark, the *New Yorker,* September 8, 1975, p. 26.

Beaubourg: A Model or a Portent, *Saturday Review,* January 22, 1977, p. 52.

Can the Transistor Save the Arts? *Forbes Magazine,* January 15, 1971, p. 18.

The Coming Impact of Technology on the Arts—Computer Violins and the Electronic Palette, the *New York Times,* February 26, 1978, sec. 2, p. 1.

Dramatic Debate: Is a Cultural Center an Appropriate Setting for Lawrence Welk? the *Wall Street Journal,* May 7, 1973, p. 1.

The Kennedy Center: Culture Comes to Washington, *Show,* August 1971, p. 32.

New Growth of Cultural Centers, *U.S. News & World Report,* October 20, 1975, p. 2.

To Read or Not to Read . . . A Look at Arts Publications, *Fund Raising Management,* November/December 1975, p. 46.

$10-Mil Artpark, Buffalo, Clocks $400,000 Deficit in 1st Season, *Variety,* October 2, 1974, p. 62.

Two Investments in Unreal Estate, *Esquire,* February 1975, p. 6.

Whatever Happened to the Kennedy Cultural Center? *U.S. News and World Report,* September 22, 1969, p. 17.

Funding the Arts

Ars Longa, Cash *Brevis* (about museums), *Forbes,* November 15, 1976, p. 44.

Art, Money and Impotence in New York, the *New York Times,* December 15, 1974, sec. 2, p. 1.

Arts Seen in Demand-Cost Squeeze, the *New York Times,* January 16, 1970, p. 28.

Bleak Picture: The Art Market Is Feeling the Financial Pinch, Too, *Barron's National Business and Financial Weekly,* July 6, 1970, p. 11.

Can the Show Go On? the *New York Times Magazine,* July 10, 1977, p. 8.

Challenge of Arts Funding: Increase Foundation Support, *Fund-Raising Management,* January-February 1973, p. 28.

First Private Foundation to Aid the Arts is Set Up, the *New York Times,* December 5, 1973, p. 1.

The 5% Law—One Company's Funding Philosophy, *Junior League Review,* September 1977, p. 10.

For Joseph Papp, Fund-Raising is an Art Surpassed Only by His Stage Skills, the *New York Times,* April 19, 1973, p. 45.

The Foundations Brace for an All-Out Attack, *Business Week,* December 7, 1974, p. 92.

*Funding the Arts: A Dollar-able Activity, *Arts Bulletin of the Canadian Conference of the Arts,* December 1977, p. 25.

Inflation, Recession and the Arts, *Foundation News,* September-October 1975, p. 8.

The Joy of Giving . . . New Ways to Support Symphony Orchestras, *Symphony News,* June 1978, p. 19.

Manhattan Arrangement of Art and Money, *New York Magazine,* December 8, 1969, p. 34.

Marathons Get Run for Their Money as Symphonies Broadcast for Funds, the *New York Times,* June 26, 1978, p. C20.

Money and Culture, *Horizon,* May 1978, p. 24.

Money for the Arts, the *New York Times,* October 6, 1975, p. 29.

Nation's Charities Feel Economic Pinch and Are Devising New Techniques to Raise Funds, the *New York Times,* October 15, 1974, p. 25.

Performing Arts, Financing the Future, the *Christian Science Monitor,* (series of five articles) December 3, 4, 7, 9, and 10, 1970).

Philharmonic, Citing a $449,000 Crisis Deficit, Inserts Plea for Donations in Program Bills, the *New York Times,* November 14, 1972, p. 52.

Radio Marathons: Symphony Smiles for Miles and Miles, *Symphony News,* December 1977, p. 13.

Recession Money, *Museum News,* September-October 1975, p. 50.

She's an Artist at Getting Money for the Arts, the *New York Times,* December 14, 1975, sec. 2, p. 1.

Since Grantsmanship Doesn't Work, Why not Roulette? *Saturday Review of the Society,* November 1972, p. 65.

Support for the Arts Has Never Been Better, the *New York Times,* July 31, 1977, sec. 2, p. 1.

Underwriting the Arts, the *Wall Street Journal,* October 2, 1974, p. 16.

Who Will Build the Financial Bridge? *Variety,* January 7, 1970, p. 133.

Yes, San Francisco, There Is Still a Ballet for You, *Fund Raising Management,* January-February 1976, p. 16.

Government and the Arts

Aiding Arts Keeps Nancy Hanks Busy, the *New York Times,* December 24, 1969, p. 12.

At Harvard Museums, Budgetary Blues, the *Wall Street Journal,* August 9, 1971, p. 8.

Citizens' Lobby for Arts Gains Power, the *New York Times,* April 14, 1972, p. 21.

Cultural Policy—A Modern Dilemma, *UNESCO Courier,* January 1971, p. 5.

Despite Budget Pinch, Federal Aid for Arts Wins Broad Support, the *Wall Street Journal,* July 24, 1970, p. 1.

Federal Aid to the Arts: Unnecessary and Unwise, the *National Observer,* October 9, 1971, p. 13.

Finding Federal Funds: ABCs of Applying for Support, *Museum News,* May-June 1976, p. 36.

Government Aid: Too Much or Little for Cultural Groups, *Fund Raising Management,* July-August 1973, p. 28.

How the South Gets Gypped (in arts money), the *Atlanta Constitution,* June 1, 1978, sec. B, p. 1.

The Humanities Endowment: 'Ballast' on the Ship of Culture? *Art News,* January 1976, p. 37.

How to Make Politics from Art, and Vice Versa, *Harper's,* August 1969, p. 21.

John Brademas, the Congressman They Call 'Mr. Arts.' the *New York Times,* September 4, 1977, sec. 2, p. 1.

The Last Picture Show at the Nassau County Museum of Fine Arts: How to Turn a Museum into a Political Plum, *Art News,* April 1978, p. 38.

The Man Who's Made 'the Most Solid Contribution to the Arts of Any President Since F.D.R.,' the *New York Times Magazine,* February 14, 1971, p. 14.

A Minor Renaissance is Turning City Hall into Center of Culture, the *Wall Street Journal,* March 15, 1976, p. 1.

Nancy Hanks, Nancy Hanks: A Melodrama Starring the Grande Dame of the National Endowment for the Arts, *Washingtonian,* March 1977, p. 102.

The National Endowment for the Arts: Will Success Spoil Our Biggest Patron? *Art News,* May 1977, p. 32.

National Endowment Puts Government into Role of Major Patron of the Arts, the *New York Times,* August 12, 1973, p. 1.

Nixon as Top Arts Patron, *Variety,* July 5, 1972, p. 1.

And Now the Arts Lobby, the *Christian Science Monitor,* November 17, 1971, p. 12.

Proposition 13's Impact on the Arts, the *Wall Street Journal,* July 14, 1978, p. 11.

Public Money and a Public Mission for American Museums, *Saturday Review,* August 12, 1972, p. 48.

The Sound of Music—Culture in the Carter White House, the *New York Times,* March 13, 1977, sec. 2, p. 1.

Survey Finds Many Would Pay $25 Tax for Culture, the *New York Times,* April 4, 1974, p. 52.

Tax Money for Arts: What It Is Buying, *U.S. News and World Report,* February 5, 1973, p. 84.

The Threat of Politicalization of the Federal Arts Program, the *New York Times,* October 16, 1977, sec. 2, p. 1.

Uncle Sam, the Angel, the *New York Times Magazine,* March 24, 1974, p. 19.

Washington Must Do More for the Arts, *Saturday Review,* April 22, 1972, p. 18.

Whither the National Arts and Humanities Endowments? the *New York Times,* December 18, 1977, sec. 2, p. 1.

Business and the Arts

The Arts and Business, *Evergreen,* July 1969, p. 63.

Arts Groups Often Perform Badly as Businesses, so Businessmen Join Them in Supporting Roles, the *Wall Street Journal,* March 9, 1978, p. 46.

The Boom in Art for Corporate Use, the *New York Times,* January 28, 1973, sec. 3, p. 3.

Business Comes to the Arts, *MBA Magazine,* March 1978, p. 11.

*Business Helps Arts Helps Business Helps Arts Helps . . . *Lively World, the Magazine of Marriott,* Spring 1975, p. 18.

Business Support for the Arts: How Corporations Win Friends and Influence People Through Cultural Investments, *Marketing Communications,* May-June 1977, p. 22.

*Business: The New Arts Patron, *Cue,* August 21, 1971, p. 7.

A Company that Marries Business and the Arts, *Museum News,* November-December 1975, p. 20.

The Corporate Medici, *Saturday Review,* July 10, 1976, p. 58.

Explosion in Corporate Patronage of the Arts, *Finance Magazine,* May 1975, p. 37.

Fueling the Arts, or, Exxon as a Medici, the *New York Times,* January 25, 1976, sec. 2, p. 1.

The Growing Corporate Involvement in the Arts, *Art News,* January 1973, p. 21.

Honor to Those Who Honor the Arts, *Esquire,* July 1969, p. 6.

I Hate Charities (on corporate donations), *Dun's Review,* September 1973, p. 58.

The Modern Medicis, *Cue,* February 29, 1976, p. 17.

The New Boom in Corporate Art, *Business Week,* December 15, 1973, p. 84.

Nonprofit Show Biz Economics: Ask Corporation Gifts as Final Stopgap, *Variety,* July 12, 1972, p. 20.

Profitable Partnership: Business and the Arts, *Saturday Review of the Arts,* April 1973, p. 26.

Rethinking Corporate Charity, *Fortune,* October 1974, p. 169.

The 7th Annual Business & Arts Awards, *Esquire,* July 1973, p. 6.

A Slowdown in Giving by Major Firms—the Reasons, *U.S. News and World Report,* January 24, 1972, p. 37.

Standard Oil of N. J. Shells Out Substantial Coin to Assist Arts, *Variety,* October, 4, 1972, p. 57.

*The Unlikely Alliance of Business and the Arts, the *American Way,* January 1973, p. 12.

Volunteer Lawyers for the Arts, *Dance Magazine,* February 1976, p. 24.

What Makes Exxon Give? *Saturday Review,* June 25, 1977, p. 34.

*When Business Aids the Arts, *Communique,* June 1974, p. 28.

Program Development

Ancient Art: Museums Merchandise More Shows and Wares to Broaden Patronage, the *Wall Street Journal,* August 14, 1975, p. 1.

*Arts as a Leisure Investment, *Mainliner,* May 1976, p. 44.

Bringing a New Show to the Broadway Stage is High Drama in Itself, the *Wall Street Journal,* February 27, 1973, p. 1.

Classical Radio Stations Find Dollars Are Harder to Come by than Fans, the *Wall Street Journal,* April 5, 1972, p. 1.

If You Gotta Have Art, *New York Magazine,* July 12, 1976, p. 68.

Management Problems Enter the Picture at Art Museums, *Fortune,* July 1974, p. 100.

*A Marketing Challenge: Finding New Audiences for the Arts, the *American Way,* February 1974, p. 24.

Marketing for Nonprofit Organizations, *Harvard Business Review,* September-October 1973, p. 123.

Marketing the Performing Arts, *Atlanta Economic Review,* November-December 1977, p. 4.

More Jobs at Nation's Museums, the *New York Times,* January 18, 1978, p. Dll.

A New Day for the Arts in Dallas? the *Wall Street Journal,* November 22, 1977, p. 22.

Orchestra Auditions: The Old Systems Are Changing, the *New York Times,* October 15, 1974, p. 45.

Special Issue on Museum Promotions, *Communication Arts Magazine,* September-October 1978.

Stifling Public TV, the *New York Times,* April 19, 1973, p. 42.

Troubled Museums—Many U. S. Exhibitors Reel under Burden of Own Popularity, the *Wall Street Journal,* November 1, 1971, p. 1.

The Arts and Education

The Artist and the University, *Harper's Magazine,* June 1969, p. 12.

*Art Education is No Longer a Coffee Break for Teacher, *Art News,* September 1973, p. 30.

The Arts in the Schools—a 200-Year Struggle, *American Education,* July 1975, p. 16.

The Battle in the Museums: Exhibition vs. Education, *New York Magazine,* February 21, 1972, p. 56.

The Community School Movement, *High-Fidelity/Musical America,* July 1977, p. MA-12.

Humanities Endowment Thrives amid Internal Strife, the *New York Times,* August 18, 1972, p. 32.

Much More Than "Eating Goober Peas" (art and education), *American Education,* October 1976, p. 27.

Teaching Schoolchildren that There Is an Art to Seeing Beauty, the *New York Times,* October 20, 1972, p. 29.

Why Children Draw: The Surprising Link Between Art and Learning, *Saturday Review,* September 3, 1977, p. 11.

The Arts and Society

Accountability in the Arts, *Symphony News,* April 1977, p. 10.

Across the Land, the Arts Are Lively, the *New York Times,* December 31, 1970, p. 10.

The American Culture 'Complex', *Bravo,* vol. 8, no. 9, p. 4.

The American Indian and the Performing Arts, the *American Way,* July 1972, p. 24.

The Arts and Quality of Life, *Saturday Evening Post,* Summer 1971, p. 72.

The Arts in Black America, *Saturday Review,* November 15, 1975, p. 12.

The Art Squad, *Saturday Review of the Arts,* December 1972, p. 33.

Bach vs. Rock, *Newsweek,* March 19, 1973, p. 83.

Black Arts for Black Youth, *Saturday Review,* July 18, 1970, p. 43.

Black Theater in America: A Round-up, *Black World,* April 1973, p. 14.

*Bringing the Arts Home. *Holiday Inn Companion,* August 1976, p. 23.

Broadway's Deceptive Glow of Health, *Business Week,* November 9, 1974, p. 53.

A Change in the Weather, *New York Magazine,* October 30, 1972, p. 71.

The Cultural Retreat of the 70s, the *New York Times,* July 23, 1978, sec. 2, p. 1.

Culture: A Miracle in Carolina, *U.S. News and World Report,* December 26, 1977, p. 84.

A Dream Grows in Harlem, *Newsweek,* September 1, 1975, p. 60.

Ethnic Nights Are a Box Office Hit, *Business Week,* October 23, 1971, p. 94.

The Future of American Museums, *Art News,* January 1975, p. 34.

A Handbook of Museum Related Resource Organizations, *Museum News* (special supplement), March 1975.

Hidden Treasure in Moscow, *Newsweek,* January 20, 1975, p. 48.

How Much is a Good Museum Worth? the *Wall Street Journal,* August 25, 1972, p. 6.

Livelier than Broadway (on regional theater), *This Week,* July 6, 1969, p. 10.

The Lively Ones: Black Theater on the Brink, *Signature,* June 1970, p. 16.

Low-Price Shows Enliven a Section of Cleveland, Raising Hopes for Awakening Other Downtowns, the *Wall Street Journal,* April 13, 1977, p. 102.

Memo to Broadway: Stage Is Alive and Well—in Suburbia, *U.S. News and World Report,* July 16, 1973, p. 80.

The Museum on Trial, the *New York Times,* September 9, 1973, p. 34.

Orchestras over Oil Wells, the *New York Times,* May 25, 1969, sec. 2, p. 29.

The Painted Word, *Harper's Magazine,* April 1975, p. 57.

The Plasterer Plays Figaro, the *Lamp,* Winter 1971, p. 16.

Theater: The Turning-Off of Off-Off Broadway, *New York Magazine,* September 1, 1975, p. 52.

The Watercolorgate Affair, *Art News,* October 1976, p. 49.

Will Our Cultural Institutions Collapse? *Los Angeles Times* syndicated article, October 26, 1971.

Artistic Development

The Arts Explosion Comes Home, *Better Homes and Gardens,* October 1978, p. 148.

The Arts Explosion Will Change Your Life (special issue on the arts), *Ms. Magazine,* December 1977.

The Arts in America: A Single Fabric, *Museum News,* November 1973, p. 42.

The Arts in America, (special issue) *Newsweek,* December 24, 1973.

Ballet Today: More Sweat and Muscle than Bouncing Tutus, *Sky,* August, 1976, p. 24.

Culture Expands into Suburbs, to Mixed Notices, the *New York Times,* January 9, 1974, p. 37.

Dance Fast Growing Art Form, the *Christian Science Monitor,* January 20, 1978, p. 2.

Dance on Mainstreet, *Saturday Review/World,* November 20, 1973, p. 50.

Dance—The Growth Industry of the Arts, *U.S. News and World Report,* January 21, 1974, p. 80.

Dance: Why Is it Booming in America? the *Wall Street Journal,* January 20, 1978, p. 11.

In English-French Canada, Dance is the Common Tongue, *Saturday Review,* October 16, 1976, p. 44.

Just Jazz—A Salute to an American Art Form, *Sundancer,* August, 1976, p. 24.

Pepsi Generation of Vipers, *New York Magazine,* September 6, 1976, p. 60.

What Makes Dance Our 'Most Vital Art Form'? the *New York Times,* June 1, 1975, sec. 2, p. 1.

Note: Articles marked by asterisks were written by Alvin H. Reiss.

Notes on Contributors

Harry J. Allen, Jr. Presently involved in operating two radio stations in a suburb of Toronto; Heywood Broun Award winner as reporter with the *Telegram* in Toronto

Norman G. Anderson Head, Molecular Anatomy Program, Biological and Medical Research, Argonne National Laboratories; formerly director of the Molecular Anatomy Program at the Oak Ridge National Laboratory

William J. Baumol Professor of Economics at Princeton and New York Universities and coauthor of *Performing Arts: The Economic Dilemma*

W. G. Bowen President, Princeton University and coauthor of *Performing Arts: The Economic Dilemma*; formerly professor of Economics at Princeton University

William A. Briggs, A.I.A. Architect and planning consultant; author of *Night and Day* and *Pre-Programming and Programming for the Live Performing Arts*

Duncan F. Cameron Director, Glenbow-Alberta Institute; formerly director, Public Relations Research, Canadian Facts, Ltd

Thomas C. Fichandler Executive Director, Arena Stage, Washington, D.C.

Kay Fliehr Coauthor of *In Search of an Audience;* community relations consultant

Carrillo Gantner Executive director, Hoopla Theatre Foundation, Ltd., Melbourne, Australia; formerly drama officer, Australian Council for the Arts

Arnold Gingrich Publisher of *Esquire* and author of *Business and the Arts: An Answer to Tomorrow* (deceased)

Sidney Green President of Sidney W. Green Associates, fund-raising consultants

Robert E. Kingsley Senior Advisor, Communications and Cultural Programs, Exxon Corporation

Harlan F. Lang Director of Development, Franklin Square Hospital, Baltimore, Maryland, formerly director of development for the American Crafts Council

Thomas Gale Moore Director, Domestic Studies Program, Hoover Institution on War, Revolution and Peace; author of *The Economics of the American Theater;* formerly member of the economics faculty at Carnegie Institute of Technology

Bradley G. Morison Senior Associate, Arts Development Associates; coauthor of *In Search of an Audience*

E. Arthur Prieve   Director, Center for Arts Administration, University of Wisconsin-Madison

William Ruder   President of Ruder and Finn, Inc.

Eleanor Oshry Shatzkin   Head of Shatzkin and Company Consultants, Inc.; formerly senior consultant in the management department of J. K. Lasser and Company

Theodore C. Sorensen   Attorney, Paul, Weiss, Rifkind, Wharton and Garrison

Gail Stockholm   Freelance writer-in-residence at Stanford University; formerly music critic of the *Cincinnati Enquirer*

Orrel Thompson   Operator of several retail stores in Minneapolis; formerly art director of the Dayton-Hudson Foundation

Alvin Toffler   Author of *Future Shock* and *The Culture Consumers.*

Richard C. Trenbeth   Development consultant in Glenview, Illinois; formerly development director for the Art Institute of Chicago

Arthur Vidich   Professor of Sociology and Anthropology, Graduate Faculty of Political and Social Science, The New School for Social Research

George C. White   President, Eugene O'Neill Theater Center

H. Lawrence Wilsey   Executive Vice Chancellor, Texas Christian University; formerly vice president of Booz, Allen and Hamilton

Joseph L. Wyatt, Jr.   Attorney, Cooper, Wyatt, Tepper and Plant

Index